T0358509

This book presents a synthesis of the most recent work on stakeholder management and opens up new fields of research. But, more deeply, it addresses the issue of corporate responsibility from the most relevant and fruitful angle: seeing responsibility as relationship management.

– Professor Hervé Dumez, École polytechnique and Centre National de la Recherche Scientifique (CNRS) en France

The book provides a treasure trove of international scholars' perspectives on stakeholder engagement. Consistent with Jerry Calton's and Stephen Payne's seminal work on multi-stakeholder dialogue and reciprocal sensemaking, the contributions address the communicative foundations of stakeholder engagement and examine its implications for organizational performance, throughout the value chain. Implicit in these important theoretical and empirical efforts is the increasing importance of relationships with individual stakeholders – rather than broad, generic stakeholder groups or collectives. Timely, context-sensitive, and comprehensive.

– Professor Marc Orlitzky, University of South Australia Business School

The editors and authors have brought together an incisive and comprehensive anthology of the role of stakeholder engagement and responsible business. The nature of the stakeholder has changed and continues to evolve. Real-time and fast moving e-communications have turned recipients of business into shapers and enablers of business, which organisations and agencies must engage with. This timely book sets out the modern landscape of responsible business and the relational strategies needed to survive and prosper in the user generated and influenced world.

– Professor Martin Hingley, University of Lincoln

A comprehensive, multi-perspective, research-based anthology, edited and written by an international group of scholars who both critically analyze stakeholder relationships and explore diverse ways to make these relationship lively and effective for the good of businesses, the good of stakeholders, and the good of society. Readers of this anthology – both business people and students – can learn much and gain some useful ideas by looking at these essays. This is a wonderfully cosmopolitan, thoughtful, and practically oriented book.

– Dr. Frederick Bird, Adjunct Professor, Political Science, University of Waterloo and Distinguished Professor Emeritus, Concordia University

This anthology provides a unique overview by leading stakeholder thinkers of recent developments and contemporary issues in managing stakeholder relationships. It's a go-to resource for scholars, students, and managers seeking to understand the frontiers of the theory and practice of stakeholder engagement.

– Professor Stephen Brammer, Executive Dean, Faculty of Business and Economics, Macquarie University

Corporate responsibility is a transactional process building ongoing alignment, across multiple parties. This book provides an excellent overview of research to date helping scholars and practitioners better understand the dynamics and learn from empirical and theoretical perspectives to activate effective solutions expected to make business a force shaping a more just and sustainable world.

– Farid Baddache, Managing Director, Business for Social Responsibility

This book is highly recommendable for anyone with an interest in stakeholder engagement. It offers novel overviews, valuable insights, and alternative approaches, as it takes the reader through some of the key practical complexities while it introduces new theoretical and empirical perspectives to explore stakeholder engagement. Congratulations!

– Professor Mette Morsing, Professor at the Copenhagen Business School and the Mistra Chair of Sustainable Markets at the Stockholm School of Economics

Engaging with Stakeholders

Engaging with Stakeholders: A Relational Perspective on Responsible Business contends that meaningful and constructive stakeholder engagement efforts should be rooted in a deep relational process of shared understanding, expectations, and viewpoints, through honest, continued dialogue between stakeholders and company management. This anthology follows and reaffirms this view, which also establishes the increasing need to explore the subtleties of how companies can respectfully engage their stakeholders in ways that reflect the corporate strategy and contribute to the ongoing development of business activities and creation of value, for themselves and stakeholders, from social, environmental, and economic perspectives.

Stakeholder engagement practices, however, remain highly complex and difficult to manage; their ability to generate value in an inclusive way requires critical consideration. Sound stakeholder engagement efforts also constitute a keystone for responsible business activities.

Drawing on a wide range of literature and studies, this book addresses key dimensions of stakeholder engagement, through a responsible business lens, and thereby contributes to identifying the opportunities, challenges, and key organizational implications associated with their unfolding. The four main topics covered are:

- Delineating the nature and multiple raisons d'être of stakeholder engagement
- Dialogical and communicational foundations of stakeholder engagement
- Engaging with diverse stakeholders throughout the value chain
- Reaping organizational returns and relational rewards of stakeholder engagement efforts

Dr. Adam Lindgreen is Professor at Copenhagen Business School where he heads the Department of Marketing. He also is Extra Ordinary Professor at University of Pretoria's Gordon Institute of Business Science. He has published in the *California Management Review*, the *Journal of Business Ethics*, the *Journal of Product Innovation Management*, the *Journal of the Academy of Marketing Science*, and the *Journal of World Business*, among others.

Dr. François Maon is Associate Professor at IESEG School of Management. He received his PhD from the Catholic University of Louvain (Louvain School of Management). Dr. Maon has published in the *California Management Review*, the *Journal of Business Ethics*, and the *International Journal of Management Reviews*, among others.

Dr. Joëlle Vanhamme is a Professor at the Edhec Business School. Dr. Vanhamme received her PhD from the Catholic University of Louvain. She has published in the *California Management Review, Industrial Marketing Management*, the *International Journal of Research in Marketing*, the *Journal of Advertising*, the *Journal of Business Ethics*, the *Journal of Retailing, Marketing Letters, Psychology & Marketing*, and *Recherche et Applications en Marketing*, among others.

Dr. Beatriz Palacios Florencio is Associate Professor at Pablo de Olavide University. Her main research focus is corporate social responsibility and tourism. She has published in the *Journal of Business Research, Total Quality Management & Business Excellence, Management Decision*, and the *Environmental Engineering and Management Journal*, among others.

Dr. Christine Vallaster is Professor at Salzburg University of Applied Sciences where she heads the Marketing & Relationship Management section. She has published in the *California Management Review, Industrial Marketing Management*, the *Journal of Business Research*, and the *Journal of World Business*, among others. She has also authored articles for the German edition of *Harvard Business Manager*.

Dr. Carolyn Strong is Senior Lecturer at Cardiff University's Business School, where she teaches postgraduate marketing and ethical issues in marketing to undergraduate students. She received her PhD from the University of Wales. She has published in the *Journal of Business Research, Marketing Letters*, the *European Journal of Marketing*, and the *Journal of Advertising*, among others. She is the editor of the *Journal of Strategic Marketing*.

Engaging with Stakeholders

A Relational Perspective on
Responsible Business

**Edited by Adam Lindgreen,
François Maon,
Joëlle Vanhamme,
Beatriz Palacios Florencio,
Christine Vallaster, and
Carolyn Strong**

Routledge
Taylor & Francis Group

LONDON AND NEW YORK

First published 2019
by Routledge
2 Park Square, Milton Park, Abingdon, Oxon OX14 4RN

and by Routledge
711 Third Avenue, New York, NY 10017

Routledge is an imprint of the Taylor & Francis Group, an informa business

British Library Cataloguing-in-Publication Data
A catalogue record for this book is available from the British Library

Library of Congress Cataloging-in-Publication Data
A catalog record for this book has been requested

ISBN: 9781138325579 (hbk)
ISBN: 9780429450341 (ebk)

Typeset in Bembo
by Apex CoVantage, LLC

For Anne Marie, who shares and supports my passion for everything Donald Duck – Adam

For Boubi and Dodu, Kiki and Flupke, Claude and Philippe who might well be the best sister and the best brother one could have – François

For my beautiful daughters, Vic and Zazou – Joëlle

For my parents Juan Miguel and Eulogia – Beatriz

For my family – Christine

For my family – Carolyn

Contents

Figures

Tables

About the editors

Adam Lindgreen

After studies in chemistry (Copenhagen University), engineering (the Engineering Academy of Denmark), and physics (Copenhagen University), Adam Lindgreen completed an MSc in food science and technology at the Technical University of Denmark. He also finished an MBA at the University of Leicester. Professor Lindgreen received his PhD in marketing from Cranfield University. His first appointments were with the Catholic University of Louvain (2000–2001) and Eindhoven University of Technology (2002–2007). Subsequently, he served as Professor of Marketing at Hull University's Business School (2007–2010); at the University of Birmingham's Business School (2010), where he also was the research director in the Department of Marketing; and at the University of Cardiff's Business School (2011–2016). Under his leadership, the Department of Marketing and Strategy at Cardiff Business School ranked first among all marketing departments in Australia, Canada, New Zealand, the United Kingdom, and the United States, based upon the hg indices of senior faculty. Since 2016, he has been Professor of Marketing at Copenhagen Business School, where he also heads the Department of Marketing. Since 2018, he also has been Extra Ordinary Professor with University of Pretoria's Gordon Institute of Business Science and, since 2018, Visiting Professor at Northumbria University's Newcastle Business School.

Professor Lindgreen has been a visiting professor with various institutions, including Georgia State University, Groupe HEC in France, and Melbourne University. His publications have appeared in *Business Horizons*, the *California Management Review*, *Entrepreneurship and Regional Development*, *Industrial Marketing Management*, the *International Journal of Management Reviews*, the *Journal of Advertising*, the *Journal of Business Ethics*, the *European Journal of Marketing*, the *Journal of Business and Industrial Marketing*, the *Journal of Marketing Management*, the *Journal of the Academy of Marketing Science*, the *Journal of Product Innovation Management*, the *Journal of World Business*, *Psychology & Marketing*, and *Supply Chain Management: An International Journal*, among others.

Professor Lindgreen's books include *A Stakeholder Approach to Corporate Social Responsibility* (with Kotler, Vanhamme, and Maon); *Managing Market Relationships, Memorable Customer Experiences* (with Vanhamme and Beverland); and *Sustainable Value Chain Management* (with Maon, Vanhamme, and Sen).

The recipient of the "Outstanding Article 2005" award from *Industrial Marketing Management* and the runner-up for the same award in 2016, Professor Lindgreen serves on the board of several scientific journals; he is co-editor-in-chief of *Industrial Marketing Management* and previously was the joint editor of the *Journal of Business Ethics'* section on corporate responsibility. His research interests include business and industrial marketing management, corporate social responsibility, and sustainability. Professor Lindgreen has been awarded the Dean's Award for Excellence in Executive Teaching. Furthermore, he has served as an examiner (for dissertations, modules, and programs) at a wide variety of institutions, including the Australian National University, Unitec, University of Amsterdam, University of Bath's Management School, University of Lethbridge, and University of Mauritius.

Professor Lindgreen is a member of the International Scientific Advisory Panel of the New Zealand Food Safety Science and Research Centre (a partnership among government, industry organizations, and research institutions), as well as of the Chartered Association of Business Schools' Academic Journal Guide (AJG) Scientific Committee in the field of marketing.

Beyond these academic contributions to marketing, Professor Lindgreen has discovered and excavated settlements from the Stone Age in Denmark, including the only major kitchen midden – Sparregård – in the south-east of Denmark; because of its importance, the kitchen midden was later excavated by the National Museum and then protected as a historical monument for future generations. He is also an avid genealogist, having traced his family back to 1390 and published widely in scientific journals (*Personalhistorisk Tidsskrift*, *The Genealogist*, and *Slægt & Data*) related to methodological issues in genealogy, accounts of population development, and particular family lineages.

François Maon

François Maon received his PhD in 2010 from the Catholic University of Louvain (Louvain School of Management). After a visiting scholarship at the University of California, Berkeley, he is now an Associate Professor at IESEG School of Management, where he teaches strategy, business ethics, and corporate social responsibility. In his research, Dr. Maon focuses on topics linked to corporate social responsibility, learning, implementation, and change-related processes; cross-sector social partnerships; and stakeholder influence strategies. He has published articles in various international journals such as the *California Management Review*, the *European Journal of Marketing*, the *European Management Review*, the *International Journal of Management Reviews*, the *Journal of Business Ethics*, and *Supply Chain Management: An International Journal*. Dr. Maon has co-edited several special issues of academic journals and books, including *A Stakeholder Approach to Corporate Social Responsibility* (with Lindgreen, Kotler and Vanhamme) and *Not All Claps and Cheers: Humor in Business and Society Relationships* (with Lindgreen, Vanhamme, Angell and Memery). He serves on the editorial boards of *Business and Society* and *M@n@gement* and is the founder of the IESEG Center for Organizational Responsibility (ICOR).

Joëlle Vanhamme

Dr. Joëlle Vanhamme is a Professor at the Edhec Business School. Dr. Vanhamme received her PhD from the Catholic University of Louvain (Louvain School of Management). She has been Assistant Professor at Rotterdam School of Management, Associate Professor at IESEG School of Management, and a visiting scholar with Delft University of Technology, Eindhoven University of Technology, Hull University's Business School, Lincoln University, and the University of Auckland's Business School. Dr. Vanhamme's research has appeared in journals including *Business Horizons*, the *California Management Review*,

Industrial Marketing Management, the *International Journal of Research in Marketing*, the *Journal of Advertising*, the *Journal of Business Ethics*, the *Journal of Consumer Satisfaction, Dissatisfaction and Complaining Behavior*, the *Journal of Customer Behaviour*, the *Journal of Economic Psychology*, the *Journal of Marketing Management*, the *Journal of Retailing*, *Marketing Letters*, *Psychology & Marketing*, *Recherche et Applications en Marketing*, and *Supply Chain Management: An International Journal*.

Beatriz Palacios Florencio

Beatriz Palacios Florencio earned her PhD in business economics from and has served as Associate Professor for the past 8 years at the University Pablo de Olavide. She also has been a visiting professor at several international schools, including the University Facsul Uniao Metropolitana-Unime and the Cardiff Business School. She is a member of the research group REINTUR (Red Hispano-Lusa de Investigadores en Turismo) and an area coordinator for social corporate responsibility for the European Academia of Firm Management and Economics (AEDEM). Her research consists of two principal lines, focused on corporate social responsibility and tourism. She has published in journals such as the *Journal of Business Research*, *Internet Research*, *Management Decisions*, *Total Quality Management & Business Excellence*, and the *Environmental Engineering and Management Journal*. She also has taken part in national projects and served as an assessor in multiple contracts with private firms.

Christine Vallaster

Christine Vallaster studied international business and management at the University of Innsbruck, where she also received her post-doctoral qualification (*habilitation*) in 2009. Her research has earned support from DFG Deutsche Forschungsgemeinschaft (Germany) and Humboldt Stiftung (Germany), among others. Throughout her academic career, she has held permanent full- or part-time jobs in Austria and Liechtenstein. In addition, she has held (or is holding) visiting professorships at University of Bolzano, University of Würzburg, and IAE Buenos Aires. She is currently Professor at the University of Applied Sciences Salzburg, where she heads the department of Marketing and Relationship Management (MRM). Her mostly qualitative research broadly pertains to strategic corporate brand management and social responsibility/sustainability in an entrepreneurial context. To contribute to these two streams of research, she largely takes an internal perspective, with the goal of finding ways to align internal processes. She has published in leading international academic journals including the *Journal of World Business*, the *Journal of Business Research*, the *California Management Review*, the *European Journal of Marketing*, *Industrial Marketing Management*, and the *Journal of Marketing Management*. She serves on the editorial board of *Corporate Social Responsibility and Environmental Management*. Her book *Connective Branding* has been endorsed by leading academics (e.g., David Aaker, Majken Schultz) and notable business people working for companies such as Patagonia and Hilti. Her latest research revolves around efforts to measure the impact of sustainability practices, for which she is acting as a research associate at the University of Armed Forces, Department of Controlling. Professor Vallaster also works as a consultant for corporate brand management and has helped companies in China, Austria, and Germany develop and implement their marketing and brand strategies. She started her consulting career with Bain & Co. in Hong Kong (China).

Carolyn Strong

Carolyn Strong, who received her PhD from the University of Wales in 2000, began lecturing at the Polytechnic of Wales while completing her part-time MBA studies at Cardiff Business School. She later joined Cardiff Business School, where she was Lecturer in marketing for more than a decade before moving to Bath University. At Bath University, she served as a member of the learning and teaching management team, MSc Marketing Director of Studies, and undergraduate admissions tutor; she also developed and taught multiple, innovative, undergraduate marketing modules. Dr. Strong returned to the Cardiff Business School in 2014, where she currently teaches ethical issues in marketing to undergraduate students and marketing to postgraduate students. Her current research focuses on small business marketing, advertising, and shopping behaviors. Recent work has been published in the *Journal of Advertising*, the *Journal of Business Research*, and *Marketing Letters*.

About the contributors

Frederick Ahen

Frederick Ahen received his PhD in international business from University of Turku, Finland. He currently serves as a research fellow at the University of Turku and a visiting fellow at the University of Tampere, Finland. His research straddles sustainable global health governance and the role of corporations in changing and being changed by institutions. Other related research areas include corporate social responsibility, ethics, and firm–stakeholder relations. His research has been published in international peer-reviewed journals such as *Critical Perspectives on International Business*; *Foresight – The Journal of Future Studies, Strategic Thinking and Policy*; the *Social Responsibility Journal*; and the *Technology and Innovation Management Review*. In addition to conference papers, he has written chapters for books published by Springer, Emerald, Palgrave MacMillan, Routledge, Edward Elgar Publishing, and Greenleaf Publishing. Dr. Ahen also is the recipient of several distinguished awards, including the 2015 Turku Finnish University Association's Best Doctoral Dissertation Award and the Emerald Literati Network Awards for Excellence's Highly Commended Paper Award in 2016. He serves on the editorial board for *Foresight*.

Ozen Asik-Dizdar

Ozen Asik-Dizdar is Assistant Professor of Management at Altinbas University, Istanbul (Turkey). She received her PhD in management and organization studies at Bogazici University, Istanbul (Turkey). During those studies, she spent a year as a visiting scholar at University of British Columbia's Sauder School of Business. Reflecting her more than 10 years of teaching experience in Turkey and Canada, her current teaching and research interests include organizational behavior, business education, positive psychology, employment relationships, and network organizations. She has participated in various academic conferences in Europe, Canada, and the United States to present her work.

Scott Banghart

Scott Banghart is Assistant Professor of Corporate Communication in the Amsterdam School of Communication Research (ASCoR) at the University of Amsterdam. His research focuses on how digital technologies reshape organizational communication practices and processes of organizing at the boundaries among private, corporate, and public life. He is particularly interested in how organizations and their members can effectively leverage technology affordances in processes such as communicating corporate social responsibility, managing internal/external stakeholder relationships, and negotiating personal/professional and private/public information boundaries in the digital age. His most recent research appears in the *Academy of Management Annals*, *Communication Quarterly*, and the *Journal of Business Ethics*.

Anne F. Barraquier

Anne F. Barraquier is Associate Professor at SKEMA Business School and a visiting scholar at the Schulich School of Business, York University, Toronto. She obtained her doctorate from the University of Nice. Her research interests include the moral behavior of managers and corporate responsibility, as well as business ethics and corporate social responsibility in China. Her research has appeared in the *British Journal of Management*, the *Journal of Business Ethics*, and *Management International*. Prior to entering academia, she worked as a strategy and international business consultant for the Chamber of Commerce of the French Riviera (1997–2006) and as an entrepreneur in Hong Kong (1991–1996).

Alexander Bassen

Alexander Bassen is Professor of Capital Markets and Management at the University of Hamburg, Faculty of Business, Economics, and Social Science. He teaches courses in finance and investment, ESG and capital markets, and reporting. He is a member of the German Council for Sustainable Development (the advisory body of the German Federal Government), the chair of the UN PRI Academic Network Advisory Committee, and a member of the Commission on Environmental, Social & Governance Issues (CESG) of the European Association of Financial Analysts Societies (EFFAS).

Ivan A. Bozhikin

Ivan A. Bozhikin holds a PhD in economics. He is Assistant Professor at the University of National and World Economy (UNWE), a research fellow at the Vrije Universiteit Brussel (VUB), and a CERGE-EI Foundation Teaching Fellow. His main research interests include environmental fiscal policy, sustainable development, corporate social responsibility, and sustainable waste management. He is the author of several research papers, as well as a reviewer for the *Journal of Cleaner Production* and the *Economic Alternatives Journal*. He served as a reviewer for the 77th Annual Meeting of the Academy of Management (United States) and 2nd International Conference on New Business Models (Austria). Dr. Bozhikin holds a bachelor's degree in business administration (University of Plovdiv); a bachelor's degree in macroeconomics (University of Plovdiv); a master's degree in business and finance (Nottingham Trent University); and a master's degree in macroeconomics (UNWE).

Peggy Simcic Brønn

Peggy Simcic Brønn is Professor of Communication and Management in the Norwegian Business School's Institute for Communication and Culture, where she also leads the Centre for Corporate Communication. She has published extensively in, for example, the

Journal of Business Ethics; *Corporate Communication: An International Journal*, the *Journal of Marketing Communication*, the *Business and Society Review*, the *International Journal of Advertising*, and the *Corporate Reputation Review*. Dr. Brønn sits on the editorial board of several international journals and is an associate editor of the *Journal of Communication Management*. Her books include (in Norwegian) *Communication for Organizations and Leaders* (Fagbokforlaget), *Transparent or Closed: Reputation Building for Organizations* (Gyldendal), and (in English) *Corporate Communication: A Strategic Approach to Building Reputation* (Gyldendal). She holds a DBA (doctorate of business administration) from Henley Management College (UK), an MBA in marketing from Georgia State University, and a bachelor of arts degree in journalism/PR from the University of Georgia.

Nelarine Cornelius

Nelarine Cornelius is Professor of Organization Studies, Associate Dean for Academic Staff Development, and a member of the Centre for Research in Equality and Diversity (CRED) at Queen Mary, University of London, as well as a visiting professor at the University of Paris (Nanterre) and Distinguished Visiting Professor at the University of Lagos. Previously, she was a visiting professor at McGill University and Visiting Scholar at École des Mines (Paris). Professor Cornelius's research interests include equality, fairness, and social justice, along with social entrepreneurship and management practices in emerging, fragile economies. She has published in many international journals, including the *Journal of Business Ethics*, the *British Journal of Management*, *Business History*, the *Human Resource Management Journal*, and the *International Journal of Human Resource Management*. She is also Council and Co-Vice Chair for the Research and Publications and Executive Committee of the British Academy of Management (BAM) and a diversity committee member for the Chartered Association of Business Schools. She co-founded the Scientific Committee of the international Paris Research Center in Norms, Management and Law (PRIMAL), hosted at Paris Sorbonne1.

Nikolay A. Dentchev

Nikolay A. Dentchev is Associate Professor of Entrepreneurship and Corporate Social Responsibility at Vrije Universiteit Brussel (VUB) and at KU Leuven, Belgium. He holds the Solvay Business School Chair of Social Entrepreneurship at VUB, which was founded through a partnership of Close the Gap, Kluwer Belgium, and Euroclear. He is passionate about supporting social and student entrepreneurs to realize their dreams. Dr. Dentchev's research has been published in various journals, such as *Business & Society*, the *Journal of Business Ethics*, and *Business Ethics: A European Review*. He has served as a guest editor for special issues in both *Business & Society* and the *Journal of Cleaner Production*. Dr. Dentchev's research interests relate to instrumental stakeholder theory, social entrepreneurship, sustainable business models, and the role of governments in corporate social responsibility.

Ayla Esen

Ayla Esen is Assistant Professor of Management at Altinbas University, Istanbul. Her professional experience includes 10 years as an expert and consultant in strategic management, organizational development, and participatory approaches, such as search conferences. She holds MBA and doctoral degrees in management and organization, along with an under-graduate degree in industrial engineering. Dr. Esen's research interests mainly focus on the relationship between business and society; she has several publications and conference papers pertaining to corporate social innovation. Dr. Esen also has studied topics related to strategic management, such as cooperative strategies, scenario planning, and participative management processes.

Cécile Ezvan

Cécile Ezvan (MBA, MA in philosophy) is a doctoral candidate and researcher at ESSEC and a consultant for private companies and government organizations. As a philosopher and economist, her research focuses on business ethics, corporate responsibility for human development, and corporate social value measures. She has presented at the HDCA, RIODD, EBEN, and EGOS international conferences, among others.

Loren Falkenberg

Dr. Loren Falkenberg is Professor in the Haskayne School of Business and Associate Dean for Strategic Initiatives. Her research interests include corporate social responsibility in resource extraction industries, as well as governance and strategy at the level of boards of directors. She has published in the *Academy of Management Review*, *Academy of Management Perspectives*, the *Journal of Management*, the *California Management Review*, and the *Journal of Business Ethics*. She is currently the case section editor for the *Journal of Business Ethics*.

Pasi Heikkurinen

Pasi Heikkurinen, D.Sc. (Economics & Business Administration), is Lecturer in business and sustainable change at the University of Leeds, Sustainability Research Institute (SRI), and Docent of sustainability and organizations at the Aalto University School of Business, Department of Management Studies. His research focuses on examining the role of busi-ness and technology for sustainability. He is the editor of the book *Sustainability and Peace-ful Coexistence for the Anthropocene* (Routledge, 2017), and his work has been published in leading scholarly periodicals, such as *Business Strategy and the Environment*, *Corporate Social Responsibility and Environmental Management*, the *Journal of Business Ethics*, and the *Journal of Cleaner Production*.

Hélène L'Huillier

Hélène L'Huillier recently received her PhD in economics from the University of Lille. She works as a consultant for social impact assessments for KiMSO and also collaborates with the CODEV research program at ESSEC. Her research mainly focuses on impact evaluations for corporate social responsibility programs. She has published in *Oxford Development Studies* and presented at international conferences, among others.

Søren Jeppesen

Søren Jeppesen is Associate Professor of Business and Development Studies, Depart-ment of Management, Society and Communication at Copenhagen Business School. He received his PhD from Copenhagen Business School. He has published in *Business & Society*, the *Journal of Business Ethics*, and *Business Strategy and the Environment*, among others. His research reports include *Corporate Social Responsibility and Competitiveness for SMEs in Developing Countries: South Africa and Vietnam* (2012, with Bas Kothuis and Angie N. Trần, AFD, Research Focales no. 16, Paris). His research interests center on developing country firms, firm-level theories, corporate social responsibility, small enterprises, upgrading, and industrial policies, with a particular focus on eastern and southern Africa, Vietnam, and India. Dr. Jeppesen also serves as a reviewer for several journals.

Trine Susanne Johansen

Trine Susanne Johansen, PhD, is Associate Professor at Aarhus University. Her main research areas include strategic communication, corporate/organizational identity, and narrativity, although she also investigates branding, marketing communication, corporate social responsibility, and stakeholder relations. She has published in multiple academic journals, including *Corporate Communication: An International Journal*, the *International Journal of Strategic Communication*, the *Journal of Marketing Communications*, and the *Journal of Communication Management*. A recent publication, "Countering the 'Natural' Organizational Self on Social Media" (2016), appeared in the edited volume *Counter-Narratives and Organization* (Frandsen, Kuhn, and Lundholt), and "Me, We and Them: Complexity in Employee and Organizational Identity Narration" (2017) was published in *Tamara: Journal for Critical Organization Inquiry*.

Liena Kano

Liena Kano is Assistant Professor of Strategy and Global Management at the Haskayne School of Business, University of Calgary. Her research interests lie at the intersection of strategic management, entrepreneurship, and international business. Dr. Kano's work has been, or is soon to be, published in the *Journal of International Business Studies*, the *Global Strategy Journal*, the *California Management Review*, *Entrepreneurship Theory and Practice*, the *Journal of World Business*, the *Business History Review*, and several other high-quality academic outlets. She serves on editorial review boards of the *Journal of International Business Studies*, the *Global Strategy Journal*, the *Journal of World Business*, the *Multinational Business Review*, and the *Management and Organization Review*. Prior to earning her PhD at the University of Calgary, Dr. Kano enjoyed a dynamic career in strategic management in various Canadian and international industry sectors.

Kaouthar Lajili

Kaouthar Lajili is Professor of Finance & Accounting at the Telfer School of Management at the University of Ottawa. She holds a PhD from the University of Illinois at Urbana-Champaign and a CPA, CGA professional designation. Her research interests are interdisciplinary and include risk management, stakeholder management and governance, financial and business reporting, and strategic human capital. She has been published in the *Journal of Management and Governance*, the *Journal of Accounting and Public Policy*, the *Journal of International Accounting Research*, the *Canadian Journal of Administrative Sciences*, *Managerial and Decision Economics*, the *Journal of Human Resource Costing and Accounting*, and the *Journal of International Accounting, Auditing and Taxation*, among others.

Laurence Lehmann-Ortega

Laurence Lehmann-Ortega is an affiliate professor in HEC Paris's Strategy and Business Policy Department. She is a graduate of HEC Paris and holds a PhD in management from the University of Aix en Provence. Her research focuses on strategic innovation, especially by incumbent firms in mature and low-tech industries. In this context, she investigates business model innovation as a response to sustainable development constraints and its consequences for multinational firms, in particular related to learning processes and mental schemes. Dr. Lehmann-Ortega co-authored *Strategor*, the leading strategic management textbook in France (translated into four languages) and has published in reviews and periodicals such as *Long Range Planning* and *M@n@gement*. She also is the co-author of "Odyssey 3.14: Reinvent Your Business Model," an original approach that combines innovation and strategy.

Xiaoyu Liu

Xiaoyu Liu is Assistant Professor at Sobey School of Business, Saint Mary's University. Her research interests lie at the intersection of strategic management, corporate social responsibility, and international business. Her research has been published in journals such as the *Journal of International Management*, *Energy Policy*, and the *Thunderbird International Business Review*. She has more than 10 years' teaching experience in China and Canada.

Ceyda Maden-Eyiusta

Ceyda Maden-Eyiusta is Associate Professor of Management at Kadir Has University, Faculty of Management. Dr. Maden-Eyiusta received her PhD from Bogazici University. She has published in the *Journal of Managerial Psychology*, the *Personnel Review*, the *International Journal of Human Resource Management*, *The Service Industries Journal*, and *Quality & Quantity*, among others. Her research interests include employee proactivity, work engagement, female entrepreneurship, and corporate social innovation.

Samantha Miles

Samantha Miles is Associate Professor at Oxford Brookes Business School. She received her PhD from the University of Reading. She has published in the *Journal of Business Ethics*, the *Journal of Management Studies*, the *British Accounting Review*, *Accounting Forum*, *Business Strategy and the Environment*, and the *Service Industries Journal*, among others. She is the co-author of *Stakeholders: Theory and Practice* (Oxford University Press) and has contributed to several texts, including *Stakeholder Management* (edited by D.M. Wasieleski and J. Weber, Emerald). Her research interests include stakeholder theory and corporate social responsibility reporting.

Bertrand Moingeon

Bertrand Moingeon is Professor of Strategic Management at HEC Paris. The author of more than 80 publications, he has served as a visiting professor at Harvard Business School and a member of HEC Paris' Executive Board for 17 years. He has published articles in international journals (e.g., the *European Journal of Marketing*, *Recherche et Applications en*

Marketing, Long Range Planning, the *European Management Journal*, the *Journal of Applied Behavioral Science*), as well as several books (notably *Corporate and Organizational Identities: Integrating Strategy, Marketing, Communication, and Organizational Perspectives* with Guillaume Soenen and *Organizational Learning and Competitive Advantage* with Amy Edmondson). His most recent projects and publications deal with organizational learning, stakeholder experience management, and strategic innovations, including articles on how innovations can contribute to alleviating poverty, as detailed in his articles co-authored with Muhammad Yunus (founder of Grameen Bank and Nobel Peace Prize winner) and Laurence Lehmann-Ortega, on social business models.

Jukka Mäkinen

Jukka Mäkinen, PhD, is Docent of Business Ethics and Corporate Social Responsibility at the Aalto University School of Business, Department of Management Studies. Dr. Mäkinen approaches the political and socio-economic roles of businesses in society from the perspective of contemporary theories of social justice and political theory. His research has appeared in journals such as the *Business Ethics Quarterly*, the *Journal of Business Ethics*, the *Journal of Global Ethics*, the *Journal of Sustainable Tourism*, the *Management and Organization Review*, and *Utilitas*. He also has co-edited and written several chapters that have appeared in books on globalization, business ethics, corporate social responsibility, social justice, and political theory.

Sarah Netter

Sarah Netter is the Centre Manager at the Centre for Corporate Social Responsibility (cbsCSR) at Copenhagen Business School (CBS) in Denmark. Prior to her appointment, Sarah was a PhD and post-doctoral fellow at the Department of Management, Society and Communication at CBS. She earned her PhD with her dissertation, "Exploring the Sharing Economy," from CBS in 2016. Her research focuses on the sharing economy, sustainable consumer behavior, business model innovation, and the fashion industry. As part of her research, Dr. Netter has conducted extensive fieldwork on the sharing economy in Europe and the United States, in an effort to explore this relatively new phenomenon and provide more nuanced understanding of the opportunities and tensions that characterize the sharing economy. She is affiliated with the MISTRA Future Fashion initiative.

Anne Ellerup Nielsen

Anne Ellerup Nielsen (PhD) is Professor of Corporate Communication at Aarhus University, Faculty of Business and Social Sciences. Her research focus involves corporate social responsibility and sustainability communication, and more specifically, stakeholder dialogue and ethics in and around organizations. Her research has been published in the *Business & Society Review, Corporate Communication: An International Journal, Business Ethics: A European Review, Corporate Social Responsibility & Environmental Management, International Studies of Management and Organization*, and the *Management Communication Quarterly*, as well as books.

Jeffrey S. Overall

Jeffrey S. Overall, Professor at Nipissing University School of Business, conducts research in three management areas: entrepreneurship, sustainability, and strategy. He previously taught at Ryerson University; Leibniz Universität Hannover; St. Petersburg Polytechnic University; and the University of Bradford School of Management. He has 20 years of experience working directly with entrepreneurs in start-ups, social enterprises, and small enterprises, across various sectors and countries. He co-founded two social enterprises that provide impoverished children in rural Nepal with educational subsidies. His work also has appeared in several journals, including *Academy of Management Perspectives, Business Ethics: A European Review*, and the *International Journal of Public Policy*.

Esben Rahbek Gjerdrum Pedersen

Esben Rahbek Gjerdrum Pedersen is Professor in Responsible Management at Copenhagen Business School. His research mainly focuses on business models for sustainability and the operationalization of corporate social responsibility/corporate sustainability in everyday organizational practices. The results of his research have been published in a wide range of academic journals, including the *Journal of Business Ethics*, the *Journal of Cleaner Production, Management Decisions*, and the *International Journal of Operations and Production Management*. This research has earned international recognition, including an Emerald Outstanding Paper Award and an Emerald Social Impact Award. Dr. Pedersen serves on the Board of Directors of the Academy of Business in Society (ABIS) and is member of the Danish Council on CSR.

Pia Popal

Pia Popal is a project officer for international cooperation in a German municipal labor and economics department. She received her PhD from the Ingolstadt School of Management at the Catholic University of Eichstätt-Ingolstadt. Her dissertation, "SME, the Civic Hidden Champions? Evidence from German Small Business Engagement in the UN Global Compact," focuses on the role of German small and medium-sized enterprises in international institutional settings. Her research interests include corporate social responsibility, business ethics, social policy, and international relations. She has served as a reviewer for the *Journal of Business Ethics* and *German International Cooperation*.

Anna Katharina Provasnek

Anna Katharina Provasnek received her doctorate in social and economic sciences at University of Natural Resources and Life Sciences, Vienna. She has published in the *Journal of Business Ethics*, the *Journal of Business Strategy and the Environment*, and *Corporate Social Responsibility and Environmental Management*, among others. Her research interests include sustainability-oriented innovation, stakeholder engagement approaches, sustainable corporate entrepreneurship, business process management, and renewable energy solutions.

Cécile Renouard

Cécile Renouard, Religious of the Assumption, is Professor at the Jesuit University of Paris (Centre Sèvres) and Director of the CODEV – Companies and Development – Research Program at ESSEC Business School. She teaches political philosophy and social ethics at the engineering school École des Mines de Paris, at Essec Business School, and Sciences-Po. She has published in the *Journal of Business Ethics, Oxford Development Studies, Corporate Governance*, and *Actes de la Recherche en Sciences Sociales*, among others. She is the author of *La Responsabilité éthique des multinationales* (PUF, 2007); *20 Propositions pour réformer le capitalisme* (coed. with Gaël Giraud, Flammarion, 2009, 2012); *Ethique et entreprise* (Ed. de l'Atelier, 2013; poche 2015); and *L'entreprise au défi du climat* (with Frédéric Baule and Xavier Becquey, Ed. de l'Atelier, 2015). She is a member of the scientific board of the Nicolas Hulot Foundation and has been a member of the board of the French Development Agency (AFD).

Jon Reast

Jon Reast joined Northumbria University as Pro Vice-Chancellor (International) in October 2015, with the primary responsibility of leading the university's international strategy. He previously was Faculty Dean of Management and Law at Bradford University. Until recently, Professor Reast served as the co-editor of the corporate social responsibility section of the *Journal of Business Ethics*. His research has been published in journals such as the *Journal of Business Research*, the *Journal of Business Ethics*, *Psychology & Marketing*, *Long Range Planning*, the *Journal of Marketing Management*, *Industrial Marketing Management*, the *Journal of Advertising Research*, and the *International Journal of Advertising*.

Kate Ringham

Kate Ringham is Principle Lecturer at the Oxford School of Hospitality Management, Oxford Brookes Business School. Dr. Ringham recently completed her PhD with a dissertation entitled "Corporate Social Responsibility Reporting in the UK Foodservice Sector: A Critical Realist Perspective," and she has continued to conduct research in the areas of corporate social responsibility reporting and stakeholder theory.

Chris Rushton

Chris Rushton is lead analyst for Germanic markets at the proxy research advisor Glass Lewis. In this role, he is responsible for governance research on and active engagement with a wide range of companies listed in the Swiss Performance Index and DAX family. Mr. Rushton completed his master's degree in international business administration at the University of Hamburg, specializing in corporate governance; he previously read management studies at the University of Nottingham.

Reiner Schaefer

Reiner Schaefer is a doctoral student at Haskayne School of Business. His received his first PhD in philosophy from the University of Guelph, where he focused on the intersection of language, mind, and knowledge. His present research applies his philosophical background to issues in business, particularly with regard to entrepreneurship in relation to knowledge. He also has a strong interest in business ethics.

Erwin Schmid

Erwin Schmid is Professor of Sustainable Landuse and Global Change at the University of Natural Resources and Life Sciences, Vienna (BOKU). He is currently head of the Department of Economics and Social Sciences at BOKU. He teaches agricultural, environmental, and resource economics. He has published in the *Journal of Business Ethics, Business Strategy and the Environment, Corporate Social Responsibility and Environmental Management, Nature Climate Change, Nature Communications, PNAS, Global Environmental Change, Environmental Research Letters, Ecological Economics, Energy Policy, Land Use Policy, Agricultural Systems*, and *Energy Economics*, among others. His research interests include developing integrated modeling frameworks to analyze the impacts of global change phenomena on production, land use/land use change, and the environment at regional to global scales. He has led more than 50 national and international research projects and supervised 18 doctoral students and more than 50 master's students.

Alan E. Singer

Alan E. Singer, PhD, is Professor in the Department of Management at Appalachian State University, North Carolina. He was the James E. Holshouser Distinguished Professor of Ethics at Appalachian State (2008–2013) and the John L. Aram Professor of Ethics at Gonzaga University (2004–2005). He has taught in the department of management at Canterbury University (New Zealand, 1985–2007); Victoria University of Wellington (1982–1985); Emile Woolf & Associates (London, 1978–1981); and the former City of London Polytechnic (now Guildhall University, 1977). Dr. Singer holds BA and MA degrees in mathematics from Queens College Oxford, a B.Sc. in psychology from Birkbeck College London, and a PhD in management from Canterbury University. He is the author of *Strategy as Rationality* (Avebury), *Integrating Ethics & Strategy* (World Scientific), and *Business Ethics in the 21st Century: Stability and Change* (Nova). He edited *Business Ethics & Strategy*, Vols. I & II (Ashgate) and was co-editor with Pat Werhane of *Business Ethics in Theory and Practice* (Kluwer). In addition to multiple articles in *Human Systems Management*, Dr. Singer has published in journals such as the *Business Ethics Quarterly, Business Ethics: A European Review*, the *Journal of Business Ethics*, the *Strategic Management Journal, OMEGA, Decision Sciences*, the *International Journal of Forecasting, Systems Practice*, the *Integral Review, Small Business Economics*, the *International Journal of Research in Marketing*, and the *International Journal of Social & Organizational Dynamics in IT*.

Cynthia Stohl

Cynthia Stohl is Professor of Communication and Director of the Center for Information Technology and Society at the University of California, Santa Barbara. She is a fellow and past president of the International Communication Association and a distinguished scholar for the National Communication Association. A leading expert in globalization, networks, and organizational processes, her most recent work addresses global organizing, collective action, and corporate social responsibility in the digital media environment. She is currently the co-primary investigator on a research grant, "Activism, technology and organizing: Transformations in collective action in Aotearoa," funded by the Marsden Fund, part of The Royal Society of New Zealand. In 2012, she received an Outstanding Book award for *Collective Action in Organizations: Interaction and Engagement in an Era of Technological Change* (with Flanagin and Bimber).

Angie Ngoc Trần

Angie Ngoc Trần is Professor of Political Economy in the School of Social and Behavioral Sciences and Global Studies at California State University, Monterey Bay. She received her PhD from the University of Southern California. She has published in *Competition and Change*, the *Journal of Business Ethics*, the *Journal of the Asia Pacific Economy*, the *International Journal of Institutions and Economies*, and the *Labor Studies Journal*, among others. Her books include *Ties That Bind: Cultural Identity, Class and Law in Flexible Labor Resistance in Vietnam* (Cornell University Press, 2013) and *Reaching for the Dream: Challenges of Sustainable Development in Vietnam* (with Beresford, NIAS Press and University of Hawaii Press, 2004). Her research interests include transnational labor migration, labor–state–management relations, labor resistance, corporate social responsibility, and trade–labor linkages.

Chiara Valentini

Dr. Chiara Valentini is Professor of Corporate Communication at Jyväskylä School of Business and Economics. Her work has appeared in international peer-reviewed journals, international handbooks and volume contributions such as *Public Relations Review, Corporate Communication: An International Journal, Corporate Social Responsibility and Environmental Management, Journal of Communication Management, Journal of Public Affairs, International Journal of Strategic Communication, International Journal of Press/Politics, The SAGE Handbook of Public Relations* and the *Wiley-Blackwell International Encyclopedia of Organizational Communication*. Her research interests include corporate communication, political public relations, stakeholder relations, crisis communication, and digital and social media communication. She serves as a reviewer of several international peer-review journals and is member of the editorial board of *Corporate Communication: An International Journal, International Journal of Strategic Communication* and *Journal of Public Interest Communication*.

James Wallace

James Wallace is Senior Lecturer in Research Methods, Enterprise, and Ethics; Director of the Business in Society Research Centre; and a former director of the PhD program at the University of Bradford. He is also Adjunct (Visiting) Professor at Varma University of Management, Head of Research Methods for PRIMAL (Paris Research in Norms, Management and Law) at the University of Paris, and a fellow of the Royal Statistical Society. Dr. Wallace's current research centers on entrepreneurship, business ethics, information, and management and the use of advanced statistical methods for business research. His work has been published in international journals in science, mathematics, engineering, and management domains; his management publications in particular have appeared in the *Journal of Management Studies, Business History*, the *European Journal of Marketing, Information and Management*, and the *Journal of Business Ethics*, as well as numerous book chapters.

Christine Zöllner

Christine Zöllner lectures at Universität Hamburg's Faculty of Business, Economics, and Social Science, in the areas of business administration and corporate finance. Her research on economics and entrepreneurship earned her a doctoral degree; currently, her research interests focus on corporate governance, and she has published several articles in this field.

Foreword and acknowledgments

Stakeholder theory has developed into a broad research tradition. As it enters maturity, it has been embraced and adopted in a wide variety of disciplines, both within and beyond strategy and management studies. In these fields, even as intense debates highlight some of its limitations (e.g., Fassin, 2009; Phillips, 1997; Sternberg, 1997), it has de facto become a foremost approach for conceptualizing and understanding business organizations. According to *stakeholder theory*, an organization exists "to bring together employees and customers, suppliers, and distributors, investors and communities and other actors in society for creating new jobs, products, and services that are needed and wanted by various stakeholders" (Freeman et al., 2017: 1). Managers seek to fulfill the needs and expectations of stakeholders, so that their interests align in the same direction (Freeman and McVea, 2001; Freeman, Wicks, and Parmar, 2004). With this basis, stakeholder theory increasingly has arisen as a central pillar for research into the relationships of business and society, because it reflects a contemporary view of business organizations as integrated within, rather than detached from, the rest of society. Pedersen (2006: 140) underlines that "some even see the company's engagement with stakeholders as the essence of corporate social responsibility." Stakeholder engagement – aimed at establishing, developing, and maintaining stakeholder relations – then can be conceived of as corporate social responsibility in action.

But even if corporate responsibilities are integral or inherent to relationships with stakeholders (Andriof and Waddock 2002; Maon, Lindgreen, and Swaen 2010), "the simplistic assumption that stakeholder engagement is directly linked to the responsible treatment of stakeholders is, just that, simplistic and an assumption" (Greenwood, 2007: 325). That is, stakeholder engagement practices can support trustful relationships between the organization and its environment, with the potential to support alignment between the business and its environment. Yet practices associated with developing more informed decision making, strengthening marketing initiatives, maintaining organizational legitimacy, and leveraging innovation and co-creation opportunities may not involve a moral dimension. They instead should be considered primarily as morally neutral. Stakeholder engagement may be used for both moral or wicked purposes, and the outcomes of these practices are not always tangible or clear. Therefore, with this research anthology, we approach stakeholder engagement as related to the practices that an organization undertakes to involve stakeholders positively in its activities, which implies "at minimum, recognition and respect of common humanity and the ways in which the actions of each may affect the other" (Noland and Phillips, 2010: 40).

Various pathways and intensities can mark engagement with stakeholders. Stakeholder engagement also can have unique meanings for different individuals or groups in various settings. Accordingly, we contend that meaningful and constructive stakeholder engagement efforts should be rooted in a deep relational process of shared understanding, expectations, and viewpoints, through honest, continued dialogue between stakeholders and company management. In this ambitious and challenging dialogue, "questions of interest and representation are constantly negotiated" (Cheney and Christensen 2001: 260).

We follow and reaffirm this view, which also establishes the increasing need to explore the subtleties of how companies can respectfully engage their stakeholders in ways that reflect the corporate strategy and also contribute to the ongoing development of business activities and creation of value, for themselves and stakeholders, from social, environmental, and economic perspectives. Early stakeholder literature sought to define and explore the key or most legitimate stakeholders, and it detailed company–stakeholder interaction processes. In recent years though, "the focus has shifted toward examining interaction with diverse stakeholders, understanding stakeholder dialogue, and learning from multi-stakeholder networks" (Freeman et al., 2017: 2). Stakeholder engagement practices remain highly complex and difficult to manage; their ability to generate value in an inclusive way requires critical consideration. Sound stakeholder engagement efforts also constitute a keystone for responsible business activities. Drawing on a wide range of literature and studies, this anthology addresses key dimensions of stakeholder engagement, through a responsible business lens, and thereby contributes to identifying the opportunities, challenges, and key organizational implications associated with their unfolding. The 22 chapters in this anthology reflect four main topics:

* Delineating the nature and multiple raisons d'être of stakeholder engagement
* Dialogical and communicational foundations of stakeholder engagement
* Engaging with diverse stakeholders throughout the value chain
* Reaping organizational returns and relational rewards of stakeholder engagement efforts

Delineating the nature and multiple raisons d'être of stakeholder engagement

In the first section of this research anthology, four chapters address the very nature of stakeholder engagement practices, as well as the strategic, political, and ethical/moral motivations and questions underlying these practices.

For example, in "Integrative Stakeholder Engagement: A Review and Synthesis of Economic, Critical, and Politico-Ethical Perspectives," Pasi Heikkurinen and Jukka Mäkinen address firms' stakeholder relationships in the politicized global economy, to answer two questions: What is stakeholder engagement, and what should guide corporations when they engage with stakeholders? The answers reflect three perspectives on stakeholder engagement: economic, critical, and politico-ethical. Because each stakeholder engagement perspective provides a different conceptualization of society, their definitions and the purpose ascribed to stakeholder engagement differ too. By analyzing the strengths and weaknesses of each perspective, these authors offer an integrative view on stakeholder engagement, with novel, more holistic implications for engaging with stakeholders.

With a structured summary of corporate moral agency, Alan E. Singer seeks to systematically inform the debate about stakeholder engagement and relationship management in "Moral Agency and Stakeholder Engagement." In guiding researchers, especially those interested in complex moral and political aspects, this article maintains that there can be no single definitive theory of stakeholder engagement and relationship management. Instead, the continuing inquiry into this domain is bound to be characterized by intense struggles, conflicting interests, and motivated viewpoints.

Arguing that the survival and growth of companies depend on their ability to deliver socially desirable ends to society and distribute benefits to political and economic entities, Anna Katharina Provasnek and Erwin Schmid consider "Stakeholder Engagement to Secure Legitimacy: The Social Licence to Operate." Social conflicts can trigger assessments and reconceptualizations of business management, by engaging stakeholder concerns. Some companies consider stakeholders' likely acceptance and approval in an effort to secure business continuity from a societal perspective. Preventive management measures aim to avoid future societal conflict; reactive management measures instead recognize stakeholders' eminent claims and their containment. These authors integrate both stakeholder engagement approaches and introduce the concept of a social license to operate, which offers one way social considerations can be included in management decision making for projects and thus avoid exposure to potentially costly social conflicts and business risks.

By "Measuring and Enhancing Relational Capabilities: In Defence of a Relational View of the Firm," Cécile Ezvan, Hélène L'Huillier, and Cécile Renouard present the Relational Capability Index (RCI), as applied through empirical surveys in Nigeria, Indonesia, Argentina, Mexico, and Brazil. The index reflects a relational vision of the firm and a capability approach framework; it measures relationship quality between the company and different stakeholders. By focusing on the relational capabilities of stakeholders and the mission of the firm, in society and toward future generations, this approach suggests ways companies can cooperate with various actors to implement sustainable business models. Thus, it expands the definition of corporate social responsibility to encourage corporations to link their business strategy with the interests of all stakeholders, including the most vulnerable ones.

Dialogical and communicational foundations of stakeholder engagement

In the second section of this research anthology, the chapters focus on the relational essence of stakeholder engagement as processes of communication, dialogue, consultation, and exchange. The wide variety of stakeholder engagement processes can fulfill different purposes in the networks in which contemporary organizations evolve. These five chapters address such relational, dialogical, and communication processes and their implications for managers, organizations, and stakeholders.

To start, Chiara Valentini notes the challenges issued by non-traditional, often unknown stakeholders that have gained importance for organizations' operations, image, and reputation. In "Communicatively Constituted Stakeholders: Advancing a Communication Perspective in Stakeholder Relations," she argues that communication can contribute to a different understanding of stakeholder identities and their relations, through a different view on how groups gain legitimacy as it relates to organizational matters. Accordingly, this chapter offers communication-based deliberation on three key points: (1) the nature of people's communicative behaviors and their empowerment as stakeholders, (2) the nature of relationships and relational dynamics, and (3) the nature of stakeholder engagement and relational expectations. In turn, a communication perspective can contribute to stakeholder relationship management.

As Peggy Simcic Brønn argues, the term "engagement" is frequently used, generally with little thought as to what it means or how to achieve it. What is clear though is that failing to engage stakeholders in issues dealing with sustainability, particularly corporate social responsibility initiatives, will raise serious doubts about an organization's motives and commitment. Mutuality and dialogue instead are key components for achieving authentic engagement. Therefore, "Stakeholder Engagement: The Importance of Mutuality and Dialogue" seeks a clearer definition and offers suggestions for what organizations should do to engage with stakeholders in an authentic manner.

In considering "How to Deal with Diverse Voices: A Framework to Support Stakeholder Engagement," Ozen Asik-Dizdar, Ceyda Maden-Eyiusta, and Ayla Esen acknowledge the diversity of stakeholder expectations, which is a common challenge to stakeholder engagement processes. The authors elaborate on three critical tools for dealing with diverse stakeholder expectations: (1) stakeholder mapping, to identify and diagnose potential areas of conflict; (2) stakeholder dialogue to engage with stakeholders that have opposing expectations and foster their participation; and (3) organizational mechanisms to support and govern stakeholder engagement. The proposed framework can help organizations cope with stakeholders' conflicting interests.

In arguing that an individual moral compass is often subordinated to group views in ethical decision-making situations for the organization, Jeffrey Overall, Nelarine Cornelius, and James Wallace explore how moral disengagement and bounded rationality theory might predict the negative effects of irrational decisions on stakeholders and stakeholder groups. With their chapter, "Enhanced Stakeholder Engagement and CSR through the UN Guiding Principles, Social Media Pressure, and Corporate Accountability," these authors propose that appeals to fundamental citizen and societal rights, especially those espoused by the UN Guiding Principles, and social media pressure, together can counter poor decision making and maintain stakeholder relationships. A proposed conceptual framework demonstrates how more robust, ethically grounded approaches to corporate accountability can lead to enhanced stakeholder engagement and corporate social responsibility. Such a "two-pronged approach" is effective, because it provides a necessary, reinforcing ethical framework that supports collective challenges to prescriptive organizational directives, while also encouraging adherence through transparency and external scrutiny.

Finally, in "Managing Corporate Social Responsibility Stakeholders in the Age of Social Media," Scott Banghart and Cynthia Stohl identify expanded contemporary notions of corporate social responsibility that have transformed the nature of stakeholder relationship management. In particular, social media blurs traditional boundaries between stakeholders and the public, making it difficult to define who counts and acts as a corporate social responsibility stakeholder. By exploring these developments and proposing a network-centered approach to strategic stakeholder relationship management, this chapter suggests that assessing stakeholder salience using network-level dynamics (i.e., relations and connections of stakeholders), rather than those at the dyadic level (i.e., attributes in a corporate social responsibility – stakeholder relationship) can help organizations identify and prioritize critical stakeholder concerns in the new media environment.

Engaging with diverse stakeholders throughout the value chain

In this third section, the chapters provide context-based examples of and reflections on engagement practices across different stakeholder groups, related to different primary and secondary activities in organizational value chains.

The first chapter addresses stakeholder relationship management in a corporate volunteering context, focusing on the complex relationships among participating stakeholder groups. As Trine Susanne Johansen and Anne Ellerup Nielsen explain, corporate volunteering involves employees who commit to donate their time and energy freely to benefit persons and communities, during work hours. Drawing on a co-creation paradigm, "Engaging Stakeholders in Corporate Volunteering: Towards a Relational Framework" seeks to establish a framework that accounts for the empowerment and engagement of all involved stakeholders. Prior studies of corporate volunteering tend to prioritize the corporation and employees, with minimal consideration of nonprofit organizations or causes. Consequently, these relationships appear asymmetrical. A more balanced, holistic consideration of all stakeholder groups instead points to relationship management that leverages their collective capacities and capabilities.

Proposing "An Efficiency-Based Relational Approach to Human Capital Governance," Kaouthar Lajili focuses on employees or human capital resources as a key, salient stakeholder group in modern organizations. This critical resource can create and sustain organizational competitive advantages, particularly in knowledge-based, intangible economies. With instrumental and normative (ethical) views of stakeholder theory, this chapter applies a transaction cost economics approach to examine relational stakeholder management; it also proposes a contingency framework to further understanding of the dynamic between relational (informal) and legal (formal) human capital resource relations. In turn, it indicates ways to balance relational and economic components in dynamic employment relationships.

The next chapter considers "The Semantic State of 'Shareholder Engagement'." Alexander Bassen, Christine Zöllner, and Chris Rushton highlight the need for research into how shareholders engage with managers of their investee companies, a topic that has been addressed by regulators in various countries and supranational bodies such as the UN and EU. Investors and managers have different perspectives on what engagement is, unique preferences for how it should be carried out, and disparate ideas of what successful engagement constitutes. This variance also marks academic publications related to these topics. Therefore, this chapter pursues a better understanding of the plurality of meanings associated with shareholder engagement terms by various parties, so that it can establish a theoretical basis for framing a broadly approved definition.

Samantha Miles and Kate Ringham note that stakeholder management literature already concurs that value increases with meaningful stakeholder relationships, in line with criticisms in marketing literature of mainstream, organization-centric, transaction-based, buyer–supplier dyad-focused thinking that fails to address complex stakeholder networks that create and destroy value. Relational co-creation associated with relationship marketing and the holistic approach embedded within stakeholder marketing address such criticisms and thus represent an exciting new frontier for marketers. This chapter on "Stakeholder Engagement in Marketing" adds to the discussion by proposing a marketing ladder of stakeholder engagement that reconfigures the ladder of stakeholder management and engagement proposed by Friedman and Miles, to reflect contemporary thought about how stakeholder management techniques can build trust and foster loyalty with the marketing function.

The next chapter, "You're Responsible, I'm Liable: Stakeholder Relations in the Face of Responsibility," investigates the relations of selected consumer goods industries (food, cosmetics) and their critical suppliers (flavors, fragrances), from suppliers' perspective. Anne F. Barraquier explores the social dynamics that emerge when they confront ethical issues related to toxicity and finds interdependence among competing supply organizations, the professional associations that represent them, and their clients, such that they negotiate responsibility among them. This discussion thus sheds light on responsibility processes and how social relations embedded in power and due to knowledge asymmetry between interdependent organizations can shape moral responsibility.

Noting that e-waste is one of the fastest growing forms of municipal waste in the world, Ivan A. Bozhikin and Nikolay A. Dentchev propose that effective e-waste management can be achieved through cooperative relations. In "Cooperative Relations for E-Waste Management," they present case studies in two distinct e-waste management environments, Belgium and Kenya. However, strong cooperation among different stakeholders leads to effective waste management, irrespective of the significant differences in the e-waste management systems described in the two cases. This illustration of effective relational stakeholder engagement contributes to a greater understanding of the inherent complexity associated with multiple constituents and their diverging stakes. If each stakeholder has a clear role and contributes to the process, the relational approach offers an advantage for resolving challenging sustainability issues.

In the chapter "Aligning Footprint Mitigation Activities with Relevant Stakeholders," Loren Falkenberg, Xiaoyu Liu, Liena Kano, and Reiner Schaefer propose a framework to manage increasingly complex corporate footprints. As assumptions underlying this framework, they propose that (1) all companies should work to optimize the mitigation of their footprints, (2) footprints cannot be fully mitigated by satisfying any one set of stakeholder expectations, (3) effective stakeholder relationships consume organizational resources, (4) appropriate relationships with different stakeholders lead to optimal footprint mitigation, and (5) both broader societal and directly affected community interests need to be satisfied. The authors discuss four types of mitigation activities and review stakeholder relationships associated with each of them.

Finally, Jon Reast, Adam Lindgreen, Joëlle Vanhamme, and François Maon study "The Manchester Super Casino: Experience and Learning in a Cross-Sector Social Partnership" as an example of a cross-sector social partnership (CSSP) among government, business, and not-for-profit entities. They identify the importance of organizational experience and learning for the successful development of CSSPs. By analyzing the Manchester Super Casino, this chapter emphasizes the significant benefits of prior experience with CSSPs that enable partners to learn and develop relationships, skills, and capabilities over time, which then have positive influences on future performance. The result is a refined learning model of the CSSP process that includes key variables for CSSP success, as well as a template for managing complex CSSPs from the perspective of different partner organizations.

Reaping organizational returns and relational rewards of stakeholder engagement efforts

Finally, the fourth section of this research anthology highlights the multifaceted challenges that organizations face in their instrumental quest for positive outcomes and returns from stakeholder engagement efforts. In addition, these chapters suggest some strategies that organizational actors can develop to reap relational rewards, while also contributing to more inclusive, stakeholder-oriented business practices.

In "On Value Destruction, Competitive Disadvantages, and Squandered Opportunities to Engage Stakeholders," Frederick Ahen combines stakeholder and consumer theories to detail the diverse value creation opportunities that get squandered when organizations act irresponsibly. Every action or inaction of a firm, responsible or irresponsible, represents a form of direct or indirect communication to stakeholders. Therefore, missing opportunities for responsible, sustainable innovations constitutes value destruction that can lead to competitive disadvantages in the long run. A proposed taxonomy of squandered opportunities when firms fail to engage productively with stakeholders includes the lost opportunity to offer value propositions, missed opportunity to co-create value, misappropriated opportunity to gain market share, stalled opportunity to attract investors and institutional support, and closed opportunity to knowledge sharing through collaboration, alliances, and new markets that facilitate new learning and disruptive innovations with, through, and for stakeholders.

The next chapter asks, "Does Relational Management Matter? The Cases of Vietnamese and South African SMEs in the Textiles, Garment, and Footwear Sector." Acknowledging the lack of insights into how corporate social responsibility practices influence manager–worker relationships in small and medium-sized enterprises, including the role of stakeholder engagement and stakeholder agency, Søren Jeppesen and Angie Ngoc Trần explore management–worker relations from a management perspective in the textile, garment, and footwear sectors. They apply Greenwood's framework to assess stakeholder engagement and stakeholder agency, based on 79 interviews with owners and managers of 41 small and medium-sized enterprises in two countries. Both management and workers value and appreciate their relationship, yet corporate social responsibility as it pertains to labor and environmental standards differ across countries. In the South African, small enterprises engage mainly in limited paternalism and market activities, but the Vietnamese enterprises embrace traditional corporate social responsibility and anti-capitalism measures.

Stakeholder theory acknowledges that each stakeholder can have multiple roles in a stakeholder network. But Sarah Netter and Esben Rahbek Gjerdrum Pedersen note a lack of research into the consequences of stakeholder blurriness. In "Blurred Lines: Stakeholder Tensions and Balancing Strategies in Partial Organizations," they use consumer service marketplaces as a contextual backdrop for discussing the potential tensions that arise from multiplicity in stakeholder roles. On the basis of emerging literature on the sharing economy and partial organizations, they analyze stakeholder tensions stemming from five organizational characteristics (membership, rules, monitoring, sanctioning, and hierarchy) and discuss balancing strategies for overcoming them in consumer service marketplaces.

Next, Pia Popal sets out to explore whether small firms' participation in macro-institutional corporate social responsibility structures can enable them to manage multiple stakeholder demands from large corporations, customers, and employees. Distinctive characteristics of small and medium-sized enterprises make their stakeholder relations paramount, and the chapter "CSR-Institutions: The Management of SME Stakeholder Relations via Institutional CSR-Practice?" sheds light on the nature and salience of these relationships. The mental models or frames that define the social identity of these small enterprises uniquely structure their perceptions of stakeholder relationships, and their national culture also can substantially affect views of corporate social responsibility. The findings suggest that institutional corporate social responsibility structures may provide a suitable frame of reference to guide small and medium-sized enterprises' stakeholder management, but using these settings to actively manage stakeholder relationships may produce different forms, reflecting the unique intentions and perceptions of institutional utility. The practical implications emerging from these findings can enhance small and medium-sized enterprises' engagement in macro-institutional settings for corporate social responsibility, such as the UN Global Compact.

In the final chapter in this text, Bertrand Moingeon and Laurence Lehmann-Ortega assert that the bottom of the pyramid offers neither fortune nor mirage. The poor may be helped, through nutritional, social, and/or employment profits, but doing so does not transform into a fortune for the multinational corporation involved. Building a social business model designed to address issues of poverty (or other sustainable development issues) requires corporate social innovation, so instead, multinational corporations can benefit from another type of return on investment. As "Neither Fortune nor Mirage at the Bottom of the Pyramid: Corporate Social Innovations as Learning Opportunities" details, by setting self-sustainability as a constraint, corporate social innovation fosters a culture that is willing to challenge the conventional wisdom. Corporate social innovations offer learning labs, in which multinational corporations experiment with new business models and learn how to develop radical innovations. The authors cite several examples of partnerships in Bangladesh between multinational corporations and the Grameen Group to demonstrate this point.

Closing remarks

The idea of stakeholder engagement has attracted progressively greater attention, in which context

> The impetus behind the use of the term 'engagement' in the stakeholder theory and corporate social responsibility literatures is the need to emphasize that, for firms merely to *interact* with stakeholders is no longer sufficient, if, in fact, it ever was.
>
> (Noland and Phillips, 2010: 40)

Scholars and practitioners alike must continue to explore and address motivations, challenges, and implications associated with the ways that organizations can design, initiate, and develop respectful, honest, proactive dialogical processes with stakeholders. The chapters included in this research anthology contribute to provide a more comprehensive account of such processes. We thus hope that this collective work stimulates and contributes to the ongoing debate about how to engage with stakeholders in a constructive, responsible fashion; it also should fill some knowledge gaps, while stimulating further thought and action pertaining to the multiple elements involved in developing a relational, stakeholder-oriented perspective on responsible business.

We extend a special thanks to Routledge and its staff, who have been most helpful. Equally, we warmly thank all of the authors who submitted their manuscripts for consideration for this book. They have exhibited the desire to share their knowledge and experience with the book's readers – and a willingness to put forward their views for possible challenge by their peers. We also thank the reviewers, who provided excellent, independent, incisive assessments of the anonymous submissions.

Adam Lindgreen, PhD
Copenhagen, Denmark and Pretoria, South Africa
François Maon, PhD
Lille, Francois
Joëlle Vanhamme, PhD
Lille, France
Beatriz Palacios Florencio, PhD
Seville, Spain
Christine Vallaster, PhD
Salzburg, Austria
Carolyn Strong, PhD
Cardiff, Wales
1 July, 2018

References

Andriof, J. & Waddock, S. (2002). Unfolding stakeholder engagement. In J. Andriof, S. Waddock, B. W. Husted & S. Rahman (Eds.), *Unfolding Stakeholder Thinking: Theory, Responsibility and Engagement* (pp. 19–42). Sheffield, UK: Greenleaf.

Cheney, G. & Christensen, L. T. (2001), Organisational communication: Linkages between internal and external communication. In F. Jablin & L. L. Putnam (Eds.), *The New Handbook of Organisational Communication: Advances in Theory, Research, and Methods* (pp. 231–269), Thousand Oaks, CA: Sage.

Fassin, Y. (2009). The stakeholder model refined. *Journal of Business Ethics*, 84(1), 113–135.

Freeman, R. E., Kujala, J., Sachs, S. & Stutz, C. (2017). Stakeholder engagement: Practicing the ideas of stakeholder theory. In R. E. Freeman, J. Kujala, & S. Sachs (Eds.), *Stakeholder Engagement: Clinical Research Cases* (pp. 1–12). New York, NY: Springer.

Freeman, R. E. & McVea. J. (2001). A stakeholder approach to strategic management. In M. Hitt, R. E. Freeman, and J. Harrison (Eds.), *Handbook of Strategic Management* (pp. 189–207). Oxford, UK: Blackwell Publishing.

Freeman, R. E., Wicks, A. C. & Parmar, B. (2004). Stakeholder theory and the corporate objective revisited. *Organization Science*, 15(3), 364–369.

Greenwood, M. (2007). Stakeholder engagement: Beyond the myth of corporate responsibility. *Journal of Business Ethics*, 74(4), 315–327.

Maon, F., Lindgreen, A. & Swaen, V. (2010). Organizational stages and cultural phases: A critical review and a consolidative model of corporate social responsibility development. *International Journal of Management Reviews*, 12(1), 20–38.

Noland, J. & Phillips, R. A. (2010). Stakeholder engagement, discourse ethics and strategic management. *International Journal of Management Reviews*, 12(1), 39–49.

Pedersen, E. R. (2006). Making corporate social responsibility (CSR) operable: How companies translate stakeholder dialogue into practice. *Business and Society Review*, 111(2), 137–163.

Phillips, R. A. (1997). Stakeholder theory and a principle of fairness. *Business Ethics Quarterly*, 7(1), 51–66.

Sternberg, E. (1997). The defects of stakeholder theory. *Corporate Governance: An International Review*, 5(1), 3–10.

Part I

Delineating the nature and multiple raisons d'être of stakeholder engagement

1.1 Integrative stakeholder engagement

A review and synthesis of economic, critical, and politico-ethical perspectives

Pasi Heikkurinen and Jukka Mäkinen

Introduction

Contemporary business organisations operate in a dynamic and an increasingly complex environment. Such dynamism and complexity that companies face can be the central after effects of the progressively global production and consumption network. While the geographical and cultural variety in the supply of goods and services adds to the complexity of the overall organisation, the fast-paced alterations on the demand side additionally signify that constant change is a rule rather than an exception in business. Moreover, the recent phenomena of the sharing economy and collaborative consumption that blur the boundaries of production and consumption (see e.g. Belk, 2014; Binninger et al., 2015) add another layer of complexity to business activity. In that context, firms, and particularly those that operate across national borders, become embedded in a multifaceted set of constantly changing relations with not only consumers and other organisations from the international private and public sectors but also within an expanding body of individuals and groups dispersed in time and place.

These so-called stakeholders of the corporation, often defined as 'any group or individual who can affect or is affected by the achievement of the firm's objectives' (Freeman, 1984, p. 46), certainly have varying interests and needs vis-à-vis the company. The expectations of shareholders, employees, and environmental activists, for instance, are often competing and even antagonistic. Hence, the modern multinational corporation is no longer a mere producer or distributor of goods and services but a nexus for stakeholder negotiation and contestation. With a legislative status and interests of its own, the corporation is also an active participant in the societal dialogue that takes place in and around the organisation. This combined with the recent upsurge of corporate power (Anderson and Cavanagh, 2000; Vitali et al., 2011) has led to a new, political role for business.

As a further consequence, large corporations that operate in the international arena are moving outside the command and control of national laws and regulations, as well as increasingly being able to exert power on policy making through lobbying practices and production decisions. Some influential scholars even argue that many companies are already to a large extent self-regulating manufacturing processes and taking over the traditional governmental responsibilities of social and environmental regulation – and hence have begun operating as the new provider of basic rights and public goods in society (Matten and Crane, 2005; Scherer et al., 2006).

This sort of voluntary political activity and responsibility of the corporation, in which stakeholder engagement plays a central part, is found to have both intended and unintended impacts on the political governance mechanisms (Frynas and Stephens, 2015) and power relations between the corporation and its stakeholders (Banerjee, 2007). According to Scherer et al. (2012, p. 473), a significant impact in this setting is 'the democratic deficit' that may arise when private firms participate in public policy, either by providing basic rights and public goods or by lobbying for their interests.

> This democratic deficit is significant, especially when multinational corporations operate in locations where national governance mechanisms are weak or even fail, where the rule of law is absent and there is a lack of democratic control. This deficit may lead to a decline in the social acceptance of the business firm and its corporate political activities and, thus, to a loss of corporate legitimacy.
>
> (Scherer et al., 2012, p. 473)

This chapter examines the corporation–stakeholder relationship in the contemporary, increasingly global and politicised business environment. This chapter aims to develop an integrative perspective on stakeholder thinking by first reviewing and then synthesising the existing perspectives on stakeholder engagement. The focus of the chapter is to answer the following questions: (a) what is stakeholder engagement about and (b) what should guide corporations when they engage with their stakeholders. The chapter provides answers to these questions from three distinct viewpoints – namely the *economic*, *critical*, and *politico-ethical perspectives* – and then synthesises the views under the *integrative perspective*.

By applying the Rawlsian idea that various conceptions of society suggest different divisions of responsibilities between institutions and societal actors (Rawls, 1996, pp. 266–267; Scheffler, 2005; Mäkinen and Kourula, 2012), this chapter maps and reviews previous literature on stakeholder engagement. The chapter finds that since each of the stakeholder engagement perspectives holds a different conception of society, their definitions of and purpose ascribed to stakeholder engagement are also distinct. The synthesis part of the chapter discusses the strengths and weaknesses of each of the three perspectives and develops an *integrative perspective* based on them. The chapter ends with a concise discussion on the managerial and policy implications on the new, more holistic perspective on stakeholder engagement.

Reviewing stakeholder engagement

The notion of the 'stakeholder' has enjoyed considerable attention in recent decades in the business and management literature. Stakeholders as a relevant concept for the business management, was first introduced in Northern Europe. Swedish scholar Eric Rhenman in his book on industrial democracy (Rhenman, [1964] 1968) and Finnish scholar Juha Näsi in his dissertation on corporate planning (Näsi, 1979) were the first people to use the notion of *stakeholder* explicitly. And then some years later, stakeholder thinking was popularised by an American scholar Edward Freeman in his seminal book *Strategic Management: A Stakeholder Approach* (Freeman, 1984). Today, the consideration of stakeholders is a widely accepted idea in both the theory and practice of organisations and comes in different forms (see e.g. Phillips et al., 2003; Jamali, 2008; Miles, 2017).

But who are these stakeholders? According to Miles (2012), the concept of 'stakeholder' classifies as an essentially contested concept, implying that a universally accepted definition will never evolve. Some scholars, however, hold that 'stakeholders are [at least] those individuals and groups which have a valid stake in the organization' (Carroll and Näsi,

1997, p. 47) or have a 'claim, ownership, rights, or interests in a corporation and its activities, past, present, or future' (Clarkson, 1995, p. 106). Freeman (1984, p. 46) again adds that a stakeholder can be 'any group or individual who can affect or is affected by the achievement of the firm's objectives'. Several authors even discuss including non-human entities among the group of stakeholders, such as trees (Starik, 1995) and Nature as a whole (Laine, 2010). An inclusive definition would thus consider a stakeholder as any entity that:

- has an interest in the organisation and/or
- can be affected by the corporation and/or
- can influence the organisation.

This extremely relational way of thinking about the management of an organisation extends the consideration of interests beyond the shareholder demands. Such an 'interest or stake might be manifested as a legal or moral right, or claim, on the organization' (Carroll and Näsi, 1997, p. 47). While the 'legal stakes are established by the accepted legal system extant in a country, . . . [m]oral claims, by contrast, are justified based upon some ethical or moral claim on the organization' (ibid, p. 47). According to the mainstream interpretation of the stakeholder approach (Freeman, 1984; Freeman et al., 2010), the task of the business management is then to manage the diversity of stakeholder claims by identifying and prioritising the different interests, and to take these interests into account in strategic – as well as operational – decision making.

In order for a corporation to know its stakeholders' needs and desires, and hence to consider their interests in its business decisions, the company must *engage* with its stakeholders. In principle, this stakeholder engagement is rather straightforward: managers ought to take into consideration any group and individual 'who can affect or is affected by the achievement of the firm's objectives' (Freeman, 1984, p. 46). Practical challenges, however, start to arise immediately as soon as one tries to compile a list of stakeholders. The realisation of the aims of multinational corporations affects millions and millions of people (as well as non-humans), both directly through their broad customer, employee, and ownership bases, and also indirectly through their suppliers and behaviour in the market place that also has a political effect. In practice, this forces corporations to select certain stakeholders from the vast mass of stakeholders. In the process of *stakeholder identification*, exclusion is unavoidable and particularly evident in the global business setting where the actions of the 100 largest multinational corporations affect almost every citizen on the planet. Unfortunately, not everyone's stake can or will be considered. Trade-offs will always be present.

Stakeholder theory certainly always includes morals and values (Phillips et al., 2003), but the kind of ethical position that emerges for the organisation depends on the stakeholders that are considered. Thus, another set of managerial challenges then appears when attempting to prioritise the interests, or stakes, of the stakeholders. To assist in identifying whose stakes matter, scholars have suggested different models and principles. For instance, the following categorisations have been employed: internal and external stakeholders (Johnson et al., 2008; Heikkurinen, 2010); salient and non-salient stakeholders (Mitchell et al., 1997); primary and secondary stakeholders (Clarkson, 1995); key and other stakeholders (Blair and Fottler, 1990; Heikkurinen, 2010); social and non-social stakeholders (Wheeler and Sillanpää, 1997); and human and non-human stakeholders (Starik, 1995). But who then are the most important stakeholders that the managerial decision making is to account for?

Table 1.1.1 Three perspectives on stakeholder engagement

Perspective	Economic	Critical	Politico-ethical
What is stakeholder engagement about?	An opportunity to increase profit and competitiveness	A means to curtail critical voices and gain power	A necessity for legitimacy and ethical conduct
What should guide stakeholder engagement?	The free market through economic instrumentalism	The democratic state through public policy and regulations	Partnerships through deliberative democracy and organisational ethics
Ideological underpinnings	Classical liberalism	Critique of classical liberalism	Republicanism and deliberative democracy
Example contributors of the perspective on stakeholder engagement	Jones (1995), Mitchell et al. (1997), Carroll and Shabana (2010)	Reed (1999), Fougère and Solitander (2009), Banerjee and Bonnefous (2011)	Scherer and Palazzo (2007), Heikkurinen and Ketola (2012), Mena and Palazzo (2012)

Building on our previous work on corporate responsibility (Heikkurinen and Mäkinen, 2016), we derive answers to these questions from three main perspectives, namely the economic, critical, and politico-ethical perspectives. As each of the perspectives on stakeholder thinking offers different descriptive explanations of what stakeholder engagement is about, they also have distinct normative suggestions on what should guide the identification and prioritisation of stakeholders (Table 1.1.1).

The economic perspective on stakeholder engagement

The economic perspective on stakeholder engagement asserts that the corporation takes, and should take, its stakeholders' interests into consideration if, or when, stakeholder engagement is economically beneficial for the company (Jones, 1995; Mitchell et al., 1997). Stakeholder engagement is used as a means to increased profits, affluence, and economic growth. Hence, the central rationale underlying the stakeholder approach is that managing stakeholder relations is key to the survival and success of a business organisation (Freeman, 1984; Freeman et al., 2007; 2010).

In conducting the economically instrumental stakeholder analysis, that is, determining whose concerns affect the success of the firm, Mitchell et al. (1997, p. 896) coined the term salience and proposed three relationship attributes, namely power, legitimacy, and urgency, to help distinguish salient stakeholders from non-salient groups and individuals. Hart and Sharma (2004) again argued that the remote groups at the fringe of a firm's operations, that is, the poor, weak, isolated, non-legitimate, and even non-human stakeholders also matter, as they might possess knowledge important to the organisation's success. Accordingly, the question of salience has remained contested within the approach, but there is still support for the notion that careful stakeholder analysis contributes to maximising shareholder value (Mitchell et al., 1997) and competitive imagination (Hart and Sharma, 2004), and support should continue.

Surprisingly, this economic perspective on stakeholder engagement is largely in line with what Milton Friedman considers to be the task of corporate leaders. Even Freeman et al. (2010) consider Friedman to be an early stakeholder theorist despite his emphasis on shareholder (not stakeholder) wealth accumulation. The primary responsibility of business managers is to increase the wealth of the organisation's shareholders, Friedman (1970) stated in his famous essay. 'Implicit in Friedman's thesis is the Smithian doctrine that the pursuit of profit is beneficial to society' (James and Rassekh, 2000, p. 650), as he connected the profit maximisation idea to the logic where responsibilities related to the consideration for others were not direct concerns of corporations. Instead, these social tasks were (mainly for reasons of economic efficiency, democracy, and individual freedom) considered to belong to the public institutions of society. Accordingly, the main task of public institutions, state officials, and citizens becomes, according to Friedman (1962; 1970), to provide the proper rules for businesses and take care of responsibility issues, such as social fairness and the efficient use of common resources.

However, it is important to note that Friedman and Adam Smith did not call for the kind of narrow self-interest to guide business action that could be referred to selfishness (James and Rassekh, 2000). As identified by James and Rassekh (2000, p. 670), '[f]or Smith the overriding principle governing his interpretation of self-interest is justice, while for Friedman the principle is freedom (i.e., absence of coercion)'. That is, these desired ends of justice and freedom are best accomplished through the market mechanism that required self-interested action in order to work effectively. In the *Wealth of Nations*, Smith coined the idea of the *invisible hand* to describe the process where individual self-interest in the market place produces greatest utility for all – as long as markets were left to operate freely without state intervention.

Although Friedman is often seen as a strong opponent of taking stakeholders' interests into account, his classical-liberal division of social responsibilities between the public and private sectors is also the dominant political assumption among many proponents of the stakeholder approach, particularly those who see stakeholder engagement as a business opportunity. This particular political position is underwritten by Jensen (2002, 2008) who, like Friedman, emphasises the moral significance of the strict separation between public and private interests in society. Jensen (2002) argued that the task of the public structures of society is to ensure that resources are used most efficiently, while the role of firms is to look beyond short-term profit maximisation and aim to maximise the long-term total value of the firm. Jensen's statement explicates Friedman's call for profit maximisation but with a longer time horizon and with the idea of the total value of the firm being a business managers' goal, 'which includes returns to debt holders as well as shareholders' (Jones and Felps, 2013, p. 209). However, what is important here is to note that both authors have emphasised corporations (surrounded by stakeholders) primarily as generators of shareholder value, albeit ones proposing slightly different means and using different terminology. In fact, stakeholder analysis is often utilised as a tool to increase shareholder wealth.

The *economic perspective* thus advances the view that firms are primarily economic actors in a society but can do well by doing good, or can perform better economically by engaging with their stakeholders. The proponents of the perspective also accept the classical-liberal idea of the economic role of private enterprises in society, as well as the normative significance of the boundaries between public and private spheres of society. The notion of voluntary stakeholder engagement thus becomes particularly suitable for the liberal political ideal, as the responsibility of corporations is focused primarily on shareholders, and any consideration for other stakeholders must be justified in fiscal terms via a business case (e.g. Scherer et al., 2006; Stefan and Lanoie, 2008; Carroll and Shabana, 2010).

The critical perspective on stakeholder engagement

The critical perspective on stakeholder engagement again reasons that a corporation takes its stakeholders' interests into consideration to depict a responsible image and to increase its power in society (Banerjee, 2007; Banerjee and Bonnefous, 2011). Stakeholder engagement is used as a means to curtail the interests of those stakeholders that are critical of the conduct of the business (Banerjee and Bonnefous, 2011), such as environmental activists. Stakeholder engagement might alternatively be used as a way to outsource a company's ethical considerations to its external stakeholders (Heikkurinen and Ketola, 2012). Furthermore, conventional stakeholder engagements are considered inadequate as they are not fully

> developed as a theory per se (i.e., they fail to address the full range of issues involved, do not provide adequate grounding for their position, etc.) . . . and because their problems may be linked not to the thoroughness of their inquiry, but rather to the adequacy of the tradition of normative theory (e.g., utilitarianism, Kantian deontology, etc.) on which they draw to develop their position.
>
> (Reed, 1999, p. 453)

Reed (1999, p. 454) claims that 'the normative theory expounded by critical theorists . . . exhibits important advantages over its rivals' and helps in overcoming the challenges of stakeholder engagement.

Within the critical perspective, scepticism that firms take stakeholder interests into consideration is rife (Banerjee, 2007; Kallio, 2007) (despite Reed (1999), who only makes this point implicitly), and there is also growing empirical evidence to support this critical argument (Ho and Welford, 2006; Guidolin and La Ferrara, 2010; Banerjee and Bonnefous, 2011). The *critical perspective* challenges that there is any such thing as genuine stakeholder engagement and perceives the interaction mainly as a managerial tool and a political discourse aimed at extending the role of markets and power of the private actors in society.

The notions of politics and power are hence important starting points for the *critical perspective* on stakeholder engagement. Walters (1977) interestingly showed how both the conservative and liberal political viewpoints employ arguments for and against corporations' engaging with their stakeholders beyond economic self-interest. The conservative side largely follows the economic perspective. On the more liberal side, Hanlon and Fleming (2009, p. 937) argue that there is a strong neo-liberal tendency in the ongoing discourse and claim that it 'is one of a suite of practices that corporations are deploying as they seek to shift the nature of social regulation away from collective to more individual solutions'. While Fougère and Solitander (2009) would certainly agree with this critique, they would probably be unsure whether the possibly harmful engagement of stakeholders is a deliberate deception or represents a false consciousness in corporations.

In terms of the division of moral labour in a society, *critical perspective* theorists tend to perceive the self-regulatory aspects of corporations to be problematic. They could claim that over time, a close corporation–stakeholder relationship leads to a reduction in the power of democratic mechanism and thus diminishes the role of democratic structures in society. In other words, corporations' increased engagement with stakeholders is assumed to change the duties in society. Through corporate self-regulation or governance, firms, and the economic elite are able to fend off social and political pressures for restrictive business laws and regulations (Paine, 2000). It is important to note here how well suited the stakeholder engagement literature and discourse is to the ideological aims of extending the political influence of the economically privileged and the business sphere in a society unhindered by normal democratic legitimation processes (see Levitt, 1958).

The politico-ethical perspective on stakeholder engagement

The *politico-ethical perspective* on stakeholder engagement suggests that a corporation takes its stakeholders' interests into consideration for moral reasons and regulatory vacuums in the business environment. This perspective also challenges the traditional idea of society being composed of distinct private and public spheres of action. As corporations have become powerful actors operating in an increasingly globalised world, questions of business and ethics (Freeman et al., 2010, see the separation fallacy); economics and politics (Scherer and Palazzo, 2007); or ecology (van Marrewijk, 2003; Ketola, 2008) are unavoidable and inseparable. Because of this amalgamation, business organisations need to develop a more comprehensive ethical identity and increase transparency in order to acquire legitimacy from their stakeholders. In this task, stakeholder engagement is a necessary process and an obligation or even a virtue of companies, as such stakeholder engagement is considered an apt way to bring together different expertise, reach consensus, and acquire legitimacy for corporate actions (cf. Fransen and Kolk, 2007; Rotter et al., 2012; Mena and Palazzo, 2012).

The *politico-ethical perspective* not only challenges the *economic* and *critical perspective* understandings of stakeholder engagement in political and ethical terms but also constructs a new approach. It notes importantly that the classical-liberal division of tasks between the political and economic spheres of society is no longer appropriate in a contemporary global economy (Scherer et al., 2006; Scherer and Palazzo, 2007; 2011; see also Matten and Crane, 2005), and thus, the regulatory powers of the state cannot be separated from private interests.

In the setting of a highly globalised economy, the advocates of the *politico-ethical* perspective suggest that corporations have a new political role and assume that the business organisation can focus on the common good in the spirit of deliberative democracy (Néron, 2016) by means of stakeholder engagement. Accordingly, to avoid economic instrumentalism of the economic perspective, which is considered to be inadequate for solving either social (Scherer et al., 2006; Gond et al., 2009) or environmental problems (Heikkurinen and Bonnedahl, 2013), the *politico-ethical perspective* advocates addressing the common societal issues in deliberative spaces where private firms along with civil society actors can play a central role as free and equal participants.

To reach beyond the economic instrumentalism and the classical-liberal division of moral labour, the major advocates of the *politico-ethical perspective* (Scherer and Palazzo, 2007; 2011; Scherer et al., 2006) turn to Habermas's political theory and the conception of deliberative democracy. Deliberative democracy is generally understood as a view 'according to which the public deliberation of free and equal citizens is the core of legitimate political decision making and self-government' (Bohman, 1998, p. 401). According to Habermas (1996, p. 107) 'just those action norms are valid to which all possibly affected persons could agree as participants in rational discourses'. According to Scherer and Palazzo (2011), Habermas's deliberative conception of democracy overcomes the traditional and old-fashioned separations between the economy and politics, as well as the division between the private-public spheres of society.

From the *politico-ethical perspective*, those corporations operating in the global setting are assumed to voluntarily self-regulate their processes, focus on the common good, and take over the traditional governmental tasks of the political and social regulation of businesses – and thus begin operating as the new provider of basic rights and public goods in society (Scherer and Palazzo, 2011; Matten and Crane, 2005; Scherer et al., 2006). It is obvious that this is not a modest responsibility. The new political role of corporations is seen to be in line with not only the deliberative democracy but also with republican conceptions of society (Scherer et al., 2006; Scherer and Palazzo, 2007, 2011). Republican political theory focuses on the issues of political freedom and understands the notion of freedom as a state of affairs characterised by the absence of domination and arbitrary power (Pettit, 1996; Hsieh, 2004). Moreover, republican philosophy is often linked with the deliberative conception of democracy, underlining the idea of democracy as public political argumentation going beyond the vote-centric and aggregative conceptions of democracy (Kymlicka, 2002). According to Scherer et al. (2006), republican political philosophy and the deliberative conception of democracy, unlike classical liberalism, are consistent with political systems lacking real boundaries between business and politics, as envisioned under the *politico-ethical* perspective.

Synthesising stakeholder engagement

Our *integrative perspective* on stakeholder engagement is based on the idea that all three existing perspectives on stakeholder engagement (economic, critical, and politico-ethical) have both some strengths and weaknesses. The *integrative perspective* aims to outline a more holistic conception of stakeholder engagement that resolves the major conflicts between the existing perspectives, while preserving their strengths. To move towards this goal, we first offer a brief critical analysis of the existing conceptions of stakeholder engagement and set out their major weaknesses. After that, we proceed to outline our solution in more detail.

Critical analysis of stakeholder engagement perspectives

As argued earlier, the *economic perspective* sees stakeholder engagement as an economic opportunity for firms to create more economic value. This dominant conception of the corporation–stakeholder relation is based on the classical-liberal idea of society, where there are clear boundaries between the public and private spheres of society and where firms are mainly economic actors operating within the private sphere of society. In this setting, the task of corporations is to manage their activities in an economically efficient way with the help of the instrumental stakeholder management techniques (e.g. Jones, 1995). The responsibility for social and environmental justice is placed on the public sector of society. Problematically, however, the classical-liberal public sector is based on the rather narrow interpretation of justice, in which the focus is on economic efficiency, the promotion of free competition, and securing private property rights, as well as the freedom of contracts (Friedman, 1962; Jensen, 2002).

The major weakness of the *economic perspective* on stakeholder engagement revolves around the inconsistencies of the classical-liberal political theory emphasising the significance of the separation between politics and business without robust institutions to back up this separation (Mäkinen and Kourula, 2012). As mentioned above, classical liberalism aligns with the notion of limited public sector institutions protecting basic capitalist rights and the promotion of economic efficiency with no real redistributive functions. In this political context, there are no robust institutions to limit the concentration of economic power over time. In the global economy, classical liberalism easily produces strong private concentrations of economic power functioning within the relatively weak and economically oriented public sectors of society (as we have witnessed in recent decades). This is exactly the setting where the private power of corporations is easily transformed into political power that leads to the separation between politics and business vanishing. Then, contrary to the classical-liberal ideal, firms become major political actors in society (Mäkinen and Kasanen, 2015, 2016) producing 'freedoms for owners of wealth while allowing non-owners the semblance of an already weak political and social democracy' (Lazzarato, 2015, p. 82).

Viewed from the *critical perspective*, extended stakeholder engagement orchestrated by firms is nothing but the part of the neo-liberal strategy that aims to justify the extension of the economic spheres of society at the expense of the public sector and democratic institutions of society (Banerjee, 2007; Banerjee and Bonnefous, 2011). From this perspective, the economically instrumental stakeholder engagement of corporations transforms the issues of social justice and democracy from matters in the public sphere of society into managerial issues addressed in corporate boardrooms, where the laws of the market and the currency of economy dominate. As a consequence, the role of democratic institutions and decision-making processes diminishes in society and the voices of the economically powerful are leveraged at the expense of the least advantaged members – be they human or non-human actors – of society and the Earth.

This *critical perspective's* deconstructive focus on the neo-liberal form of stakeholder engagement is revealing and significant. However, the *critical perspective* on stakeholder engagement does not really offer any constructive alternatives to the opposed ideological doctrine. The political theory that is implicitly favoured in the work of the critical perspective scholars builds on Marx and the critical theory. This connection, however, has been underdeveloped, and implications for contemporary policy are still missing. Furthermore, within the critical discussion, there is also an evident lack of practical management tools and techniques for business organisations that could be used when operating in the global economy characterised by various power asymmetries and injustices. Lastly, it seems that the critical perspective offers a rather cynical view on businesses and their stakeholder-related activities.

More ambitiously, the *political-ethical perspective* on stakeholder engagement aims to replace the mainstream *economic perspective* by challenging the traditional liberal idea of boundaries between politics and business and the separation between ethics and business. Perceived from this perspective, the traditional lines between different spheres of life and society are no longer so relevant in our highly interconnected and globalised world where there are no functioning public sector structures regulating and governing business practices (Scherer and Palazzo, 2007). Consequently, those scholars operating within this paradigm argue that contemporary businesses need to go beyond economic instrumentalism, focus on the common good, and take on board the traditional government responsibilities of regulating businesses and providing public goods and basic citizenship rights. Moreover, globally responsible businesses are expected to undertake new types of ethically and democratically oriented stakeholder engagement activities (that go beyond the economic rationality) in the context of different multi-stakeholder initiatives and forums (fulfilling the various governance voids in the global economy).

However, there is little empirical evidence of large-scale international business organisations operating in the ways expected or asked for by the *politico-ethical perspective* intellectuals. There seems to be a lack of empirical support for the antithesis of the *economic* and *critical perspectives* (Edward and Willmott, 2011; Moog et al., 2015). Furthermore, the empirical argumentation strategy against the political doctrine like classical liberalism and the related economic perspective on stakeholder engagement is not very strong. One might agree on the empirical issues about the amalgamated and political nature of global economy yet still argue for the stronger boundaries between business and politics from the different political perspectives, as do Mäkinen and Kasanen (2015, 2016) and Heikkurinen and Mäkinen (2016). Consequently, what is needed is a relatively convincing political argument challenging the political basis of the mainstream conception of stakeholder engagement. The problem is that, even though some influential *political-ethical perspective* scholars appeal to deliberative democracy and republican political philosophy to overcome the traditional separations between business and politics, there are some deep tensions between these philosophies and the idea of business firms being active political participants in our societies (Hussain and Moriarty, 2016; Heikkurinen and Mäkinen, 2016).

Towards a synthetic solution

To preserve the strengths of the previous perspectives on stakeholder engagement, our synthetic conception aims to reconcile the *economic, critical, and politico-ethical perspectives* with stakeholder engagement. We argue that, by making the division of moral labour in a society robust enough to ensure the public sphere can act on issues of social and environmental justice without being restricted in terms of power and legitimacy, stakeholder engagement of firms may be economically oriented (as suggested by the economic perspective). In this way, the mainly economic motive of corporations' stakeholder engagement does not jeopardise the democratic governance of society (as demanded by the critical perspective). Moreover, and importantly for the proponents of ethical conduct in business, the robust division of moral labour between the economically oriented businesses and the democratic public sector of society neither results in the absence of deliberative political spaces nor creates a barrier to any firm going beyond economic instrumentalism and focusing on the common good in the global world (as asked for by the politico-ethical perspective), if it so wishes.

Accordingly, our synthetic suggestion for the foundations of stakeholder engagement is that clear boundaries and the robust division of moral labour between the private and public sectors of society must be in place to ensure that both the economic and democratic logics can coexist in society. These different logics may in fact prove complementary. In this manner, the different point of views of the three stakeholder engagement perspectives could also coincide. The frame for stakeholder engagement would ultimately be provided by the democratic structures of the state (as suggested by the *critical perspective*), yet would enable a private sphere of society to operate with its own logic of the market (as suggested by the *economic perspective*) within the institutional structure that secures a basic level of social and environmental justice. The separation of the public from the private sphere would also allow partnerships between these two spheres (as suggested by the *politico-ethical perspective*). Nothing needs to stop actors from cooperating with one another if they are drawn to further stakeholder engagement by means of deliberative democracy and organisational ethics.

To keep the question of social and environmental justice within the public sphere is extremely important, as we have repeatedly witnessed that ethical behaviour cannot be expected from multinational companies or contemporary consumers at large. Nevertheless, the private sphere certainly must be acknowledged for its role as an efficient place for many transactions and exchanges of goods and services to take place. The market, however, must be embedded within the public sphere in order to ensure that justice reaches all stakeholders instead of only those stakeholders who can afford justice. So, for stakeholder justice to be realised, what is needed first and foremost is a strong and democratic public sector of society to design and enforce fair institutions within which the operations of private actors can be conducted. In this manner, firms can advance their ends effectively embedded within the institutional structures provided by the democratically organised and managed public sector of society (Rawls, 1996, 2001). In other words, integrating the private sector within the public sector offers room for governments to implement democratically designed regulations to ensure social and environment justice among all stakeholders. At the same time, this type of division of moral labour and clear boundaries between business and politics provides space for firms to focus effectively on their core business issues without being overwhelmed by political tasks advocated by the diversity of different stakeholder groups and individuals.

Furthermore, seen from the *integrative perspective* on stakeholder engagement, the deliberative democratic forums and initiatives suggested by the *politico-ethical perspective* are important for regulating global businesses. However, the boundaries between public and private spheres of society and the robust division of moral labour are needed for these spaces to be in line with deliberative democracy and justice (Heikkurinen and Mäkinen, 2016; Rawls, 2001; Richardson, 2002; Crocker, 2006).

Discussion

The power of the notion of 'stakeholder' is largely due to its conceptual breadth, but as noted by Phillips et al. (2003), this can also become its weakness if diverse perspectives are not grasped theoretically. When studying the corporation–stakeholder relationship, it is hence central to identify the different definitions of stakeholder engagement, and the following prescriptions for the practice of engaging stakeholders, as well as to acknowledge the underlying political ideologies (see Table 1.1.1). The awareness of the distinct theoretical positions is central to moving the field forward to incorporate more descriptive relevance and normative power for social and environmental justice. With this rationale, after reviewing the three main perspectives on stakeholder engagement and analysing their potential and weaknesses, the present chapter offers a synthesis of the three main viewpoints under the *integrative perspective*.

From the *integrative perspective*, the take on the question of who a corporate stakeholder is, is inclusive. A stakeholder is any entity that has an interest in the organisation and/ or can be affected by the corporation and/or can influence the organisation. This inclusive notion of stakeholders encompasses both salient and fringe individuals and groups, including the natural environment and other non-human actors. The consideration of stakeholders, again, can be both instrumental and intrinsic in organisations (Heikkurinen and Ketola, 2012), as demonstrated by the *economic, critical,* and *politico-ethical perspectives*. In other words, stakeholder engagement can be a means and/or an end for an organisation. But instead of trying to arrive at the all-encompassing map of stakeholders, and their priorities, that would make sense from all economic, critical, and politico-ethical points of view, the *integrative perspective* assigns this task to the actors in a specific situation. In this sense, while our perspective is motivated by, and geared towards, the universal idea of justice, it also seeks to be situationally more sensitive, as stakeholder expectations, demands, and issues vary so broadly in different cultural, geographical, and political settings. Moreover, the *integrative perspective* suggests that stakeholders' concerns are primarily addressed in the public sphere of society where the democratic logic prevails. This enables most stakeholders to partake in the engagement process on equal terms. Of course, the future generations and the non-human world are unable to even vote and participate in the deliberation outside the market, but hopefully their presence manifests through the values of the general public.

Once the issues related to stakeholders' social and environmental justice are addressed in the basic structures of society, the private sphere and corporations can address additional stakeholder concerns that are relevant for their line of business. This, however, is voluntary in the sense that the corporation may further its main economic purpose, if it wishes to do so. Although markets may emerge for initiatives going beyond the level of compliance, similar problems as are found today (related to the lack of a public voice in the business) will not arise, if the market is embedded in the private sphere. As long as the corporations are operating within society, the society can steer them with its democratic mechanisms. And once the stakeholders in need have been defined in the public sphere, the corporation may proceed to define its own key stakeholders based on whatever logic it wishes to utilise. Even economic instrumentality will not be such a huge social and environmental problem, as the state may intervene as its legitimacy is reclaimed.

The *integrative perspective*, however, does not propose the state as an overarching solution to all questions of injustice. As noted by Lazzarato (2015), there is a need for caution when assigning responsibilities to the modern state, as the contemporary state apparatus largely also operates against the vagaries of the market and is currently geared to serve the interests of the elite. However, it is worth noting that not all states are operating equally in line with global market logic. For example, the Nordic welfare state is often viewed as an example of a more balanced model that is not geared towards the elite. However, of course it is possible that the modern state might also provide the means to support the interests of the few, rather than its citizenry as a whole, as the current state-capitalist mode of governance does. It is clear that all authoritarian and high-modernist modes of governance (see Scott, 1998), be they in the public or private sphere, are something to be resisted in order to reach higher degrees of social and environmental justice. As 'any large social progress or event will inevitably be far more complex than the schemata we can devise, prospectively or retrospectively, to map it' (Scott, 1998, p. 309; see also Hayek, 1945), there is call for a radical stakeholder inclusion in both the public and private spheres, as well as the third sector. A broad spectrum of stakeholders involved in the decision making can certainly contribute important practical expertise and knowledge of the best means to improve social and environmental justice.

> Without denying the incontestable benefits either of the division of labour or of hierarchical coordination of some tasks, [there is] a case for institutions that are instead multifunctional, plastic, diverse, and adaptable – in other words, institutions that are powerfully shaped by [practical knowledge].
>
> (Scott, 1998, p. 353)

Thus, there are certainly also grounds for the deliberative democratic mechanism, in which stakeholder engagement plays a central role.

Lastly, separating the private and public spheres of society gives rise to three spheres of stakeholder engagement. The first is the public sphere, where the logic and process behind engaging is democratic (as in the case of the critical perspective). The second sphere is private, in which the private actors may use their own logics and processes to engage with their stakeholders. As said, these logics may span from economic instrumentalism (as in the case of the economic perspective) to political and ethical, even spiritual rationales (as in the case of politico-ethical perspective). And in addition to the public and public spheres where stakeholder engagement is central, the third sphere spans the common ground between the two where public and private actors can deliberate together. But what is important here is to note that the logics and processes of stakeholder engagement are all different in each sphere of society. The *integrative perspective* suggests that these spheres and their actors could coexist and even turn out to be complementary in the pursuit of just societies and organisations.

Conclusions

To answer the research questions of (a) what stakeholder engagement is about and (b) what should guide corporations when they engage with their stakeholders, this chapter divided the literature on stakeholder engagement into three major perspectives, namely the *economic, critical,* and *politico-ethical.* It can be concluded each perspective has varying ideological underpinnings, and hence, these perspectives offer different viewpoints on stakeholder engagement and distinct normative viewpoints on how to manage stakeholder relations in a global economy.

The presented perspectives on stakeholder engagement contribute to the research task set by Phillips et al. (2003, p. 135) of seeking 'a better position to see both the power and the limitations of this [stakeholder] approach'. By means of the critical analysis of the existing approaches, the chapter developed an *integrative perspective* on stakeholder engagement. According to this perspective, stakeholder engagement may continue to be primarily economic at the level of private firms but not at the expense of the democratic public sector of society. Furthermore, we have argued that establishing clear boundaries between the private and public sectors of society and by developing the robust division of moral labour between these sectors grants room for deliberative democratic spaces where the public and private interests can be mediated in the pursuit of a more just global economy.

As a limitation, it must be noted that many contemporary societies develop in a quite contrary direction. Business organisations are assigned increased responsibilities and consequently also gain the power to steering societal development. The recent blurring that takes place *within* the private sphere, such as initiatives on the sharing economy and collaborative consumption, or *within* the public sphere, such as new organisational forms and multilevel governance, however, are not considered the main sources of injustice. The problem that this chapter addressed is the current development where the boundary *between* the private and public spheres continues to disappear at the expense of democratic stakeholder engagement.

Given the theoretical focus of this chapter on the integrative conceptual work, the practical and methodological implications of this chapter are not scrutinised in the necessary detail. Consequently, we encourage further research to examine the effectiveness of the means to re-establish this boundary between the public and private spheres, as well as the research methods most suitable to study the boundaries thereof, or the lack of them.

References

Anderson, S. and Cavanagh, J. (2000). *Top 200: The Rise of Corporate Global Power.* Washington, DC: Institute for Policy Studies.

Banerjee, S. B. (2007). *Corporate Social Responsibility. The Good, the Bad and the Ugly.* Edward Elgar: Cheltenham.

Banerjee, S. B. and Bonnefous, A-M. (2011). Stakeholder management and sustainability strategies in the French nuclear industry. *Business Strategy and the Environment*, 20(2), 124–140.

Belk, R. (2014). You are what you can access: Sharing and collaborative consumption online. *Journal of Business Research*, 67(8), 1595–1600.

Binninger, A.-S., Ourahmoune, N. and Robert, I. (2015). Collaborative consumption and sustainability: A discursive analysis of consumer representations and collaborative website narratives. *Journal of Applied Business Research*, 31(3), 969–985.

Blair, J. D. and Fottler M. D. (1990). *Challenges in Health Care Management: Strategic Perspectives for Managing Key Stakeholders*. San Francisco, CA: Jossey-Bass.

Bohman, J. (1998). The coming age of deliberative democracy. *Journal of Political Philosophy*, 64(4), 400–425.

Carroll, A. B. and Näsi, J. (1997). Understanding stakeholder thinking: Themes from a Finnish conference. *Business Ethics: A European Review*, 6(1), 46–51.

Carroll, A. B. and Shabana, K. M. (2010). The business case for corporate social responsibility: A review of concepts, research and practice. *International Journal of Management Reviews*, 12(1), 85–105.

Clarkson, M. E. (1995). A stakeholder framework for analyzing and evaluating corporate social performance. *Academy of Management Review*, 20(1), 92–117.

Crocker, D. (2006). Sen and deliberative democracy. In Kaufman, A. (ed.), *Capabilities Equality: Basic Issues and Problems*. New York: Routledge.

Edward, P. and Willmott, H. (2011). Political corporate social responsibility: Between deliberation and radicalism. Available at SSRN 1904344. https://papers.ssrn.com/sol3/papers.cfm?abstract_id=1904344

Fougère, M. and Solitander, N. (2009). Against corporate responsibility: Critical reflections on thinking, practice, content and consequences. *Corporate Social Responsibility and Environmental Management*, 16(4), 217–227.

Fransen, L. W. and Kolk, A. (2007). Global rule-setting for business: A critical analysis of multi-stakeholder standards. *Organization*, 14(5), 667–684.

Freeman, R. E. (1984). *Strategic Management: A Stakeholder Approach*. Boston: Pitman.

Freeman, R. E., Harrison, J. S. and Wicks, A. C. (2007). *Managing for Stakeholders: Survival, Reputation, and Success*. New Haven: Yale University Press.

Freeman, R. E., Harrison, J. S., Wicks, A. C., Parmar, B. L. and de Colle, S. (2010). *Stakeholder Theory: The State of the Art*. Cambridge: Cambridge University Press.

Friedman, M. (1962). *Capitalism and Freedom: With the Assistance of Rose D. Friedman*. Chicago: University of Chicago Press.

Friedman, M. (1970). The social responsibility of business is to increase its profits. *The New York Times Magazine*, 13 September.

Frynas, J. G. and Stephens, S. (2015), Political corporate social responsibility: Reviewing theories and setting new agendas. *International Journal of Management Reviews*, 17, 483–509.

Gond, J. P., Palazzo, G. and Basu, K. (2009). Reconsidering instrumental corporate social responsibility through the Mafia metaphor. *Business Ethics Quarterly*, 19(1), 57–85.

Guidolin, M. and La Ferrara, E. (2010). The economic effects of violent conflict: Evidence from asset market reactions. *Journal of Peace Research*, 47(6), 671–684.

Habermas, J. (1996). *Between Facts and Norms: Contributions to a Discourse Theory of Law and Democracy* (translated by Rehg, W.). Cambridge: MIT Press.

Hanlon, G. and Fleming, P. (2009). Updating the critical perspective on corporate social responsibility. *Sociology Compass*, 3(6), 1–12.

Hart, S. L. and Sharma, S. (2004). Engaging fringe stakeholders for competitive imagination. *Academy of Management Executive*, 18(1), 7–18.

Hayek, F. A. (1945). The use of knowledge in society. *The American Economic Review*, 35(4), 519–530.

Heikkurinen, P. (2010). Image differentiation with corporate environmental responsibility. *Corporate Social Responsibility and Environmental Management*, 17(3), 142–152.

Heikkurinen, P. and Bonnedahl, K. J. (2013). Corporate responsibility for sustainable development: A review and conceptual comparison of market-and stakeholder-oriented strategies. *Journal of Cleaner Production*, 43, 191–198.

Heikkurinen, P. and Ketola, T. (2012). Corporate responsibility and identity: From a stakeholder to an awareness approach. *Business Strategy and the Environment* 21(5), 326–337.

Heikkurinen, P. and Mäkinen, J. (2016). Synthesising corporate responsibility on organisational and societal levels of analysis: An integrative perspective. *Journal of Business Ethics*, 149(3), 589–607.

Ho, M. and Welford, R. (2006). Case study: Power, protests and the police: The shootings at Shanwei. *Corporate Social Responsibility and Environmental Management*, 13(4), 233–237.

Hsieh, N. H. (2004). The obligations of transnational corporations: Rawlsian justice and the duty of assistance. *Business Ethics Quarterly*, 14(4), 643–661.

Hussain, W. and Moriarty, J. (2016). Accountable to whom? Rethinking the role of corporations in political CSR. *Journal of Business Ethics*, 1–16. Online First.

Jamali, D. (2008). A stakeholder approach to corporate social responsibility: A fresh perspective into theory and practice. *Journal of Business Ethics*, 82(1), 213–231.

James Jr, H. S. and Rassekh, F. (2000). Smith, Friedman, and self-interest in ethical society. *Business Ethics Quarterly*, 10(3), 659–674.

Jensen, M. C. (2002). Value maximization, Stakeholder theory, and the corporate objective function. *Business Ethics Quarterly*, 12(2), 235–256.

Jensen, M. C. (2008) Non-rational behavior, value conflicts, stakeholder theory, and firm behaviour. In dialogue: Toward superior stakeholder theory. *Business Ethics Quarterly*, 18(2), 153–190, 167–171.

Johnson, G., Scholes, K. and Whittington, R. (2008). *Exploring Corporate Strategy: Text & Cases*. Harlow: Prentice Hall.

Jones, T. M. (1995). Instrumental stakeholder theory: A synthesis of ethics and economics. *Academy of Management Review* 20(2), 404–437.

Jones, T. M. and Felps, W. (2013). Shareholder wealth maximization and social welfare: A utilitarian critique. *Business Ethics Quarterly*, 23(2), 207–238.

Kallio, T. J. (2007). Taboos in corporate social responsibility discourse. *Journal of Business Ethics*, 74(2), 165–175.

Ketola, T. (2008). A holistic corporate responsibility model: Integrating values, discourses and actions. *Journal of Business Ethics*, 80(3), 419–435.

Kymlicka, W. (2002). *Contemporary Political Philosophy: An Introduction* (2nd edition). New York, NY: Oxford University Press.

Laine, M. (2010). The nature of nature as a stakeholder. *Journal of Business Ethics*, 96(1), 73–78.

Lazzarato, M. (2015). Neoliberalism, the financial crisis and the end of the liberal state. *Theory, Culture & Society*, 32(7–8), 67–83.

Levitt, T. (1958). The dangers of social responsibility. *Harvard Business Review*, 36(5), 41–50.

Mäkinen, J. and Kasanen, E. (2015). In defense of regulated market economy. *Journal of Global Ethics*, 11(1), 99–109.

Mäkinen, J. and Kasanen, E. (2016). Boundaries between business and politics: A study on the division of moral labor. *Journal of Business Ethics*, 134, 103–116.

Mäkinen, J. and Kourula, A. (2012). Pluralism in political corporate social responsibility. *Business Ethics Quarterly*, 22(4), 649–678.

Matten, D. and Crane, A. (2005). Corporate citizenship: Toward an extended theoretical conceptualization. *Academy of Management Review*, 30(1), 166–179.

Mena, S. and Palazzo, G. (2012). Input and ouput legitimacy of multi-stakeholder initiatives. *Business Ethics Quarterly*, 22(3), 527–556.

Miles, S. (2012). Stakeholder: Essentially contested or just confused? *Journal of Business Ethics*, 108(3), 285–298.

Miles, S. (2017). Stakeholder theory classification: A theoretical and empirical evaluation of definitions. *Journal of Business Ethics*, 142(3), 437–459.

Mitchell, R. K., Agle, B. R. and Wood, D. J. (1997). Toward a theory of stakeholder identification and salience: Defining the principle of who and what really counts. *Academy of Management Review*, 22(4), 853–886.

Moog, S., Spicer, A. and Böhm, S. (2015). The politics of multi-stakeholder initiatives: The crisis of the Forest Stewardship Council. *Journal of Business Ethics*, 128(3), 469–493.

Näsi, J. (1979). *Yrityksen suunnittelun perusteet.* Tampere: University of Tampere, School of Business Administration, Series A1: 15.

Néron, P. Y. (2016). Rethinking the ethics of corporate political activities in a post-citizens united era: Political equality, corporate citizenship, and market failures. *Journal of Business Ethics*, 136(4), 715–728.

Paine, L. S. (2000). Does ethics pay? *Business Ethics Quarterly*, 10(1), 319–330.

Pettit, P. (1996). Freedom as antipower. *Ethics*, 106(3), 576–604.

Phillips, R., Freeman, R. E. and Wicks, A. C. (2003). What stakeholder theory is not. *Business Ethics Quarterly*, 13(4), 479–502.

Rawls, J. (1996). *Political Liberalism.* New York: Columbia University Press.

Rawls, J. (2001). *Justice as Fairness: A Restatement* (edited by Kelly, E.). Cambridge: Harvard University Press.

Reed, D. (1999). Stakeholder management theory: A critical theory perspective. *Business Ethics Quarterly*, 9(3), 453–483.

Rhenman E. ([1964] 1968). *Industrial Democracy and Industrial Management.* London: Tavistock.

Richardson, H. (2002). *Democratic Autonomy: Public Reasoning About the Ends of Policy.* Oxford: Oxford University Press.

Rotter, J. P., Özbek, N. and Mark-Herbert, C. (2012). Private-public partnerships: Corporate responsibility strategy in food retail. *International Journal of Business Excellence* 5(1–2), 5–20.

Scheffler, S. (2005). The division of moral labour: Egalitarian liberalism as moral pluralism. *Proceeding of the Aristotelian Society*, 79, 229–253.

Scherer, A. G., Baumann-Pauly, D. and Schneider, A. (2012). Democratizing corporate governance: Compensating for the democratic deficit of corporate political activity and corporate citizenship. *Business & Society*, 52(3), 473–514.

Scherer, A. G. and Palazzo, G. (2007). Toward a political conception of corporate responsibility: Business and society seen from a Habermasian perspective. *Academy of Management Review*, 32(4), 1096–1120.

Scherer, A. G. and Palazzo, G. (2011). The new political role of business in a globalized world: A review of a new perspective on CSR and its implications for the firm, governance, and democracy. *Journal of Management Studies*, 48(4), 899–931.

Scherer, A. G., Palazzo, G. and Baumann, D. (2006). Global rules and private actors: Towards a new role of the transnational corporation in global governance. *Business Ethics Quarterly*, 16(4), 505–532.

Scott, J. C. (1998). *Seeing Like a State: How Certain Schemes to Improve the Human Condition Have Failed.* New Haven: Yale University Press.

Starik, M. (1995). Should trees have managerial standing? Toward stakeholder status for non-human nature. *Journal of Business Ethics*, 14(3), 207–217.

Stefan, A. and Lanoie, P. (2008). Does it pay to be green? A systematic overview. *The Academy of Management Perspectives*, 22(4), 45–62.

van Marrewijk M. (2003). Concepts and definitions of CSR and corporate sustainability: Between agency and communication. *Journal of Business Ethics*, 44(2–3), 95–105.

Vitali, S., Glattfelder, J. B. and Battison S. (2011). The network of global corporate control. *PLoS ONE*, 6(10), e25995.

Walters, K. D. (1977). Corporate social responsibility and political ideology. *California Management Review*, 19(3), 40–51.

Wheeler, D. and Sillanpää, M. (1997). *The Stakeholder Corporation: A Blueprint for Maximizing Stakeholder Value.* London: Pitman.

1.2 Moral agency and stakeholder engagement*

Alan E. Singer

Introduction

The corporate moral agency debate is comprised of numerous arguments about the idea of collective and corporate moral agency (CMA). A critical summary of that debate can be used to systematically inform related debates involving corporate citizenship, personhood and social responsibility (e.g. Singer 2016, 2017) but also stakeholder theory and artificial moral agency (e.g. Moore 1999; Singer 2013). This approach is duly adopted here, but with an emphasis on informing debates about stakeholder engagement and relationship management (SERM; e.g. Buchholz & Rosenthal 2005; Greenwood 2007; O'Riordan & Faribrass 2014). The intention is to guide researchers in that area, especially those who are interested in its complex moral and political aspects.

The debate

The moral agency debate is comprised of at least five interrelated sub-debates, involving:

1 *Duties and responsibilities*: various assumptions and prescriptions regarding the moral-responsibility and duties of groups and for-profit corporations (as distinct from their human members);
2 *Corporate rights*: the various types of moral, political or legal rights that groups and corporations might possess;
3 *Application of moral theories*: the contested applicability of moral theories to the decisions and behaviors of group agents and for-profit corporations;
4 *Group intentionality*: the dynamics and interpretations of collective intentions and
5 *Distribution of blame*: the distribution of blame (accountability or *ex post* responsibility) amongst a corporate entity and its members, for harms caused or crimes committed.

With regard to for-profit corporations (or firms in economic theory), the first three sub-debates (duties, responsibilities and rights) are obviously part of a more general debate about capitalism and its variants (e.g. investor *vs.* stakeholder capitalism). Accordingly, there is a potential to inform the practice and ethics of stakeholder engagement and relationship management (SERM) within those contexts (Figure 1.2.1). For example, one might consider a targeted stakeholder groups' possible moral right to autonomy. The sub-debates about collective and corporate intention (and hence the distribution of blame) might seem less relevant to SERM, but they are the focus of an enduring debate in legal theory, which is in turn quite relevant to SERM.

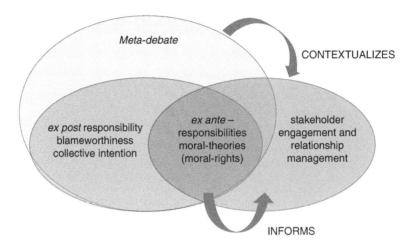

Figure 1.2.1 Corporate moral agency debates informing stakeholder engagement

There is also a *meta*-debate about whether or not CMA is an idea that is even worth discussing (arguably, it is nothing more than a metaphor, a way of speaking or a legal technicality). Arguments within this *meta*-debate are also potentially applicable to theories of SERM. For example a distraction critique has it that the CMA debate simply distracts managers from practical ethics or distracts scholars from more important tasks like moral persuasion. In similar vein, one might argue that SERM is a practical project and should be informed mainly by what works, rather than by any abstract theoretical contributions like the present chapter.

The CMA debate is highly interdisciplinary (e.g. philosophy, law, politics and economics, but also psychology and the hard sciences). Most contributions in business ethics journals combine aspects of applied philosophy with the behavioral social sciences (e.g. Manning 1984; Ewin 1991; McMahon 1995; Pruzan 2001; Gibson 2011, to mention a few). Many other contributions in the mainstream traditions of commercial-law, economics and accounting have inquired into the essential nature of the firm when it is construed as a basic unit of economic analysis. Classic contributions from Freund (1897/2000) and Berle and Means (1932) are prime examples. It seems fair to say that the ethics and economics streams have only occasionally intertwined. They contain relatively few cross-references despite their shared mission (Figure 1.2.2).

Regardless of their disciplinary origin, however, most contributions are relevant in some direct or indirect way to each of the five sub-debates. The inter-relationships between the contributions and those sub-debates are quite complex, however. At the same time, many contributions speak to the closely related notions mentioned at the outset of this chapter, such as the management of stakeholders and their interests, forms of corporate social responsibility (CSR), corporate citizenship and personhood (Figure 1.2.2). As a result, the overall CMA debate has become not only fragmented, but it is also quite confusing or "slippery" (as a reviewer of a related paper put it).

The present chapter duly indicates recent approaches to organizing and structuring the CMA debate whilst at the same time extracting some specific suggestions for the theory and practice of SERM. In the following section, a typology of SERM strategies

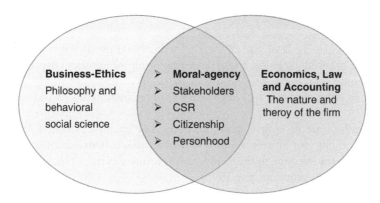

Figure 1.2.2 Moral agency in business ethics and economics

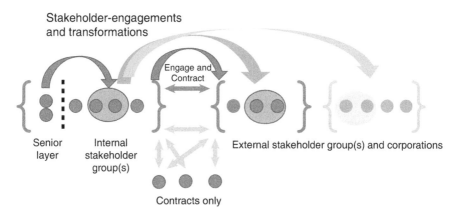

Figure 1.2.3 Types of relationship amongst group entities and individuals

is generated by considering individual and group entities in conjunction with several types of stakeholder relationship. In a later section, this is developed with reference to a dualism that pervades much of the relevant moral-philosophy and politics. The discussion then turns to claims about the behavioral limitations of group agents and for-profit corporations. Some contributions from legal philosophy that also oppose the idea of CMA are also considered before concluding with an examination of the *meta*-debate.

Typology

Much of the CMA debate focusses upon the core distinction between the corporate entity (the firm, group-agent or "it") and the individual persons who are its members, managers and external stakeholders (i.e. "them"). In some respects, this distinction resembles the distinction in mathematical logic between a set and its members or elements. The "it" *vs.* "them" classification then interacts with the standard typology of stakeholder relationship (i.e. associative, contractual, engaging, transformational or mixed). Figure 1.2.3

duly depicts some of the possibilities. As indicated in the figure, stakeholder relationships might develop, or be implanted, between:

1   a senior management layer and an internal stakeholder group or
2   an internal stakeholder group and an external group or another corporation or
3   two previously unrelated corporations or firms or
4   a corporate entity and external individuals (e.g. consultants).

Mixed relationships are of course quite common. For example, an intended behavioral transformation might also be written into formal contracts between an individual and a targeted group (as for example in the *Levi Strauss* "Business Partner Terms of Engagement" contract with its many suppliers, *circa* 1990).

Moral dualism

With regard to the ethics of SERM one has to consider not only the "it *vs.* them" distinction and the various types of relationship, but also what is meant by "moral." As in the CMA debate, the moral-political dualism serves as a useful organizing principle. On one side of that dualism one finds utilitarianism without a justice constraint (U-J), together with ethical-egoism, exchange-aspects of contractarianism and the principle of utility-maximization in (qualified) markets. Together, these constitute the moral-philosophical foundations of capitalism (MFoC) including its hyper-competitive global variant (i.e. they are associated with right-leaning political priorities). On the left (and left-leaning) side, we find utilitarianism-with-justice and the contractarian difference principles, but also the golden rule, the ethics-of-care and love (*Agapism*). These in turn (together with offshoots such as integrative social contracts theory (ISTC)) constitute the normative core of the general stakeholder model. They comprise a more-obviously-moral approach (MOMA) in that distributive justice, care and love are "obviously" amongst the primary qualities of ethics and morality as understood almost everywhere, including in much of the economic and accounting traditions (e.g. Littelton 1938).

Right vs. left engagements

Two broad classes of stakeholder engagement and transformation then correspond to these two sides or subsets of moral theories:

1   *Right-engagements* in which the initiator (actor or agent in the philosophical sense) seeks to transform, empower and assist stakeholders for instrumental purposes, in order to serve its own interests (as in the "instrumental stakeholder theory")
2   *Left-engagement* in which the actor seeks to care for stakeholders as ends-in-themselves or in order to fulfill a duty to aid (as in the "normative stakeholder theory")

The former might be described as "strategic" engagement in the game-playing sense: the ultimate goal of the engagement is to maximize the initiator's profit or theoretical utility (albeit on behalf of shareholders, often including the managers themselves). The latter, in contrast, is where the initiative is genuinely intended to serve the (initiator-perceived) interests of the target stakeholder. This indeed seems "more obviously moral" (Figure 1.2.4). However, the instrumental form of engagement is also "moral" under the

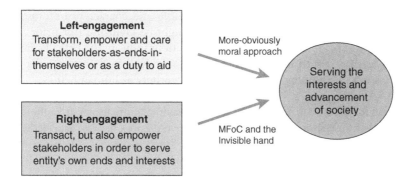

Figure 1.2.4 Left and right forms of stakeholder engagement with their moral effects

right-side forms of reasoning (egoism, etc.) that are, in turn, aligned with the invisible-hand argument or claim that self-love frequently serves the interests and advancement of society.

Returning briefly, to the *Levi-Strauss* episode, one might very well speculate about which class of engagement was operating in that case. One might further argue (at the *meta*-level) that it actually doesn't matter; all that matters is the moral effects of an engagement strategy: the extent to which various interests are served, regardless of any actual (or imputed) intentions or cognitions of the initiating entities.

Behavioral limitations

In strategic management and economic theories, the corporation is sometimes viewed as a bundle of capabilities, as distinct from a contracting party, or *nexus* of contracts or web of relationships. Many contributions to the CMA debate, however, have discussed behavioral constraints on groups and corporations that seemingly limit their moral capabilities. They have variously invoked theories of human development, rationality, emotion and cognitive processes as follows:

1   *Rationality*: Corporations display *quasi*-rationality, risky-shift (Janis & Mann 1977) and *akrasia* (a lack of resolve to follow-through on their own deliberations) all of which can cause harm. In any case, deliberations in for-profit corporations rarely sweep in concerns like care and justice. These arguments also imply that SERM initiatives are likely to be risky, to lack any enduring commitment or to be right-engagements.
2   *Emotion*: Corporate entities lack the emotional makeup that enables humans to show moral virtues (e.g. Alzola 2008). This suggests a lack of empathy in the corporate context that would be required for a more-obviously-moral approach to strategy and left-form engagements.
3   *Development:* Corporations *per se* do not (or do not appear to) engage in what psychologists have referred to as adult levels of moral reasoning (e.g. Sridhar & Camburn 1993). This also implies that SERM strategies are likely to be instrumental and transactional.

4   *Role-differentiation*: When individuals act in their capacity as a member or associate of a corporation, their personal values, intentions and characters are often distorted (e.g. Sennett 2000; Isaacs 2006). The effect might be civilizing (for prior sinners) or corrupting (for prior saints), but most contributions indicate the latter. Either way, this reminds us that SERM initiatives deal with individuals in their particular corporate role or aspect (e.g. Phillips 1995), not in their entirety as human beings.

Some contributions then claim that these behavioral limitations are inherent, whilst others argue that they should be (hence can be) overcome. One can take either of these positions regarding the qualities of SERM that are listed in Table 1.2.1 (last column). The "inherent" position then finds further support whenever the corporation (or firm) is viewed as a fiction, or artificial entity, or form of property, or metaphorical machine (refer to "Critique" section). The "can be overcome" position, on the other hand, finds support in the stakeholder model (e.g. Goodpaster & Matthews 1982; Sen 1993; Freeman 1999) but also in direct counter-arguments to each of the limitations.

With regard to rationality, for example, it has been argued that corporations and groups are indeed capable of reflective forms (e.g. May 1987; Singer 1994; Arnold 2006) just as all kinds of group intentions (whether for profit or justice) are at least "licensed as descriptions" and arguably real (French 1984; Weaver 1998; List & Pettit 2011). This in turn implies that left engagements really exist: they are a realistic strategy involving target groups as well as individuals (Table 1.2.2).

With regard to the emotion, since robots (artificial moral agents) can indeed be endowed with an emotional makeup (e.g. Wallach & Allen 2009; Gunkel 2012) it seems at least possible for corporations. The next argument about developmental stages (Table 1.2.1, row 3) is weak, because there has been considerable controversy regarding the cross-cultural and ecological-validity of the related empirical findings (e.g. Modgil & Modgil 1986). Finally, with regard to "role-differentiation" humans in their corporate aspect or role can (risk

Table 1.2.1 Behavioral limitations and stakeholder engagements

Limitation	For-profit corporations . . .	Engagement will be . . .
Rationality	display *quasi*-rationality, risky-shift, *akrasia*	unreliable, volatile, uncommitted
Emotion	lack necessary emotional makeup	un-empathic
Development	do not engage in "adult moral-reasoning"	right-engagements
Role-differentiation	induce role-differentiation and an MFoC view	

Table 1.2.2 Implications of the counter-arguments

Limitation	Elaboration	Stakeholder engagement will . . .
Rationality	Collective stable intentions do exist	Include left engagements and involve groups and members
Emotion	Artificial moral agents exist	Potentially be transformational for groups and members
Development	Lack of validity of experiments	
Role-integration	Infusion of "more obvious" morality	

attempting to) infuse their wider value-priorities into a corporate culture (Gini 1998). All of these counter-arguments, in turn, support the view that SERM strategies can be transformational and can operate at the level of stakeholder groups.

Legal philosophy

Many contributions in the legal philosophy have discussed the possible meanings of collective purpose or intention. This lies at the core of the CMA debate and it is intertwined with the economic theory of the firm. Since the relevant legal philosophy is oriented towards professional practice within a society that is historically capitalist (i.e. receptive to for-profit corporations), any arguments about intentionality tend to be declarative: they make claims about the proper (i.e. best-justified professional) understanding of collective intentionality and the practical distribution of blame (i.e. *ex post* "responsibility").

Many of these declarations carry specific implications for the ethics and practices of SERM (Table 1.2.3). For example, an assertion that the corporate "objective" should be, or was originally understood to be, profit-maximization-within-the-law implies that "right-engagements" (i.e. transactional or instrumental) are normatively justified. The metaphor of the firm as an industrial age machine (e.g. Danley 1984; Narveson 2002; Velasquez 2003) also carries this same implication. The "fiction" view of the firm, with the related "*nexus* of contracts" view, imply that a corporation lacks any kind of agency beyond its intrinsic legal-right to be party to a contract, which indicates that SERM strategies, whether left or right-form, should be contractual (because the primary quality of any firm is its role as a contracting party, not a moral agent).

On the other hand, when the corporation is regarded as property (Brown 2010) it is the shareholders (jointly and severally) who become the responsible party, but they might very well have wider social objectives implying that both left- and right-form engagements can be justified in this way. A (perhaps less well-known) view of the firm as a concession by the state to the founders of the firm, arguably implies a duty of reciprocity to the state (e.g. Avi-Yona & Sivan 2007). With regard to SERM, this serves to remind us of the political context: governments are always amongst the external stakeholders, whereupon the various forms of strategic engagement (left or right, contractual or transformational, etc.) become forms of business-government relationship.

Table 1.2.3 Arguments against forms of corporate responsibility and stakeholder engagement

Argument	Elaboration	Engagement will be . . .
Objectives	Corporate objectives are purely economic	transactional, instrumental
Machine	Corporation *is like* an industrial machine	
Fiction, *nexus*	Corporation *is* a legal fiction	contractual, left or right forms
Property (1)	Corporation *is* property	left or right forms
Concession	Granted by state, duty to compensate	with governments,
Administrator	Corporation *is* an administrator-of-duty	fulfillment of duty towards citizens
Association-mere	Lacks the substance needed for *responsibility*	between individuals only
Association-rights	Protect corporation from the state	maybe violating stakeholders' rights
Association-united	United for a special purpose	individual and collective

Another distinctive (left-leaning) type of contribution claims that corporate entities are "administrators of duty" because they can voluntarily incorporate moral principles into their decision-making processes (Dubbink & Smith 2011). This claim fits well with the earlier arguments involving deliberative or reflective rationality in strategic decision making (as in left-form engagements), but also with the idea that multi-national corporations have a moral duty to provide aid to the needy in all regions (or states) where they operate (e.g. Jackson 1993; Margolis & Walsh 2003).

A slightly more animated (right-leaning, legal) claim about the nature of the corporation is that it is "merely an association of individuals united for a special purpose" (a U.S. doctrine, originally: *Santa Clara County v. Southern Pacific Railroad* – 118 U.S. 394, 1886). There are several plausible interpretations of this each of which carries distinctive implications for SERM, as follows:

1   An emphasis upon "*merely*" seems to suggest that corporate entities lack sufficient substance to be held morally responsible or to be granted rights. It also suggests that associative relations are weak, whereupon transformative engagements operate mainly at the (individual) human level.
2   An emphasis upon "*association*" then suggests that the corporate entity should be granted the right to some protection from state power, in line with citizens' general rights-of-association. One might argue that stakeholder groups should also receive such protections; groups and their members who are targeted by a private SERM initiative might have a right to protection from unwelcome engagements (an obvious example being employees in the context of acquisitions).

Continuing with this legal claim, the term "*united*" suggests that the "special purpose" is somehow infused throughout the corporation and so collective intention really exists (in addition to intentions of the members). However, "*united*" could also be taken to mean that the special purpose or intention remains that of each member and that each individual happens to have included that common purpose amongst their other prior personal purposes. Many contributions to the CMA debate have attempted to clear up the conceptual ambiguity of notions like "common purpose" or "united for special purpose" (e.g. Freund 1897/2000; Berle & Means 1932; French 1984; May 1987; Gindis 2007; List & Pettit 2011, to mention a few) but the ambiguity must remain so long as intentionality itself retains some mystery. However, all arguments to the effect that that corporate intentions are indeed real support the view that SERM strategies operate at the level of group agents (refer to Figure 1.2.3, above).

Critique

It is by now quite apparent that arguments on either side of the CMA debate are open to quite a variety of criticisms. These include: the existence of direct counter-arguments, the political content of many ostensibly moral arguments, the disputed normative status of behavioral arguments, as well as the frequent failure to consider the underlying moral-political dualism. Each criticism has some significance for SERM, as follows (refer to Table 1.2.4):

1   *Counter-arguments:* Discussions of the ethics of SERM should recognize that such notions are all embedded within a dualistic (or dialectical) moral-political structure.

Table 1.2.4 Critique of the debate with some implications for stakeholder engagement

Critique	Summary	Implications for SERM
Counters	direct counter-arguments almost always exist	Recognize dialectical context
Re-casting	contributions often slip into politics	Make explicit references to dualism
Scope-1	ethics-shift in the debate	Identify forms of moral-reasoning
Scope-2	agent-shift in the debate (corporate, firm, layer)	Specify the related/engaged entities
Status	normative status of behavioral arguments	Relate all findings to the partitioned ethics-set

2   *Re-casting*: Discussions about CMA often slip into expressions of left *vs.* right political leanings. Discussions of SERM should avoid this temptation by making explicit reference to the political dualism.

3   *Scope-1:* Many contributions to the CMA debate fail to specify which forms of moral reasoning they are referring to (i.e. an ethics-shift). When the ethics of SERM are under discussion, the left *vs.* right forms of moral reasoning should be identified.

4   *Scope-2*: Many contributions are vulnerable to an agent-shift: that is, it is unclear whether the agent is a corporation, a layer of senior management or some other group. Accordingly, the subjects and objects (targets) of any relationship should be well defined.

Yet another general criticism of the moral-agency debate concerns the ambiguous normative status of the empirical-behavioral arguments. This is part of a wider debate in business ethics (e.g. Werhane 1994; Rosenthal & Buchholtz 2000) which in turn cautions us that any prescriptions for SERM that are derived from empirical studies or practical experiences should be carefully qualified.

The meta-debate

A different type of critique of the CMA debate is comprised of *meta*-arguments that qualify the worthwhileness of even engaging in the debate in the first place (e.g. Singer 2016). On the *anti*-debate side, for example, it has been argued that the entire moral-agency debate has taken place at the level of metaphor rather than reality. Any idea of a real moral agency (or corporate intention, soul or conscience) is simply poetic or loose talk, or woolly thinking (e.g. McMahon 1995; Narveson 2002; Moon, Crane & Matten 2005). It has also been argued (e.g., Rankin 1987) that the abstract debate distracts or diverts people from more important projects like persuading practicing managers to behave more ethically. When these arguments are applied to SERM (see Table 1.2.5), they also imply that researchers should shift away from abstractions and attend to best practices (but with "best" suitably qualified by the moral-dualism). Another argument against the CMA debate is that it is politically naïve and it downplays the intense political struggles surrounding corporate activities (Iyer 2006). Once again, abstract debate then seems far less important than concrete political action that is aimed at protecting all stakeholders and moderating corporate power.

The CMA debate has also been described as both premature and obsolete. It is premature to the extent that fundamental issues surrounding human agency remain unresolved.

Table 1.2.5 The moral agency meta-debate with implications for stakeholder engagement

Critique	Summary	Implications for SERM debate
Metaphor	"CMA" is a metaphor, loose talk, "woolly" thinking.	Focus on SERM practices
Distraction	CMA distracts from practical ethics and persuasion	
Naive	Political action more important	Protect stakeholders
Premature	Foundational ontological issues are not yet resolved	SERM should be a strategic-experiment
Obsolete	Corporate activities are increasingly mediated by AGI/AMA	SERM will involve AGI/AMA's (systems integration) with humans and *trans*-humans
Mutuality	The meanings of "moral" and "agent" can only be established jointly, as inquiry proceeds	SERM will involve new types of relationship and engagement, learning from mistakes
Attention (*pro*-CMA)	CMA directs managers' attention towards ethical concerns	The idea of SERM directs managers' attention to the possibility of transformational relationships

For example, the meanings of "individual" and "organism" continue to be contested in biology (e.g. Seabright & Kurke 1997; Bouchard & Huneman 2013). On the other hand, the debate seems obsolete to the extent that corporate activities are increasingly mediated by artificial intelligences (AIs) or artificial moral agents (e.g. Hall-Stores 2007; Wallach & Allen 2009; Singer 2013). As technology advances, one must consider the possibility that new understandings of ethics and new forms of consciousness might emerge. Traditional theories and natural-humans become less relevant. These *meta*-arguments indicate that SERM initiatives should be regarded as strategic experiments, rather than ethical missions. Indeed such projects might eventually involve technical systems integration and not much else.

Until quite recently, the CMA debate has generally failed to follow the pragmatic-philosophical approach that all of the above points seem to endorse. Classical Pragmatism has it that the very meanings of the words "moral" and "agent" are established jointly, as inquiry proceeds, so that one should not try to argue about the merits of projecting any specific or given moral categories onto any given entities (Buchholz & Rosenthal 2006; Watson, Freeman & Parmar 2008). This position is significant for SERM because it points to a mutually re-constitutive dynamic that operates amongst all humans and groups (e.g. Gindis 2007). This dynamic creates a real embodied culture (e.g. Gibson, 2011) and has real effects on human members, but also implies that any observed or intended strategy is an emergent property. SERM initiatives are then merely one possible component of this larger dynamic.

Turning to the *pro*-debate side (Table 1.2.5, last row) it has been argued that the CMA debate is "crucial" (e.g. Manning 1984) because its resolution would shape the legal and political environment. Also (and in direct counterpoint to the "distraction" critique), it has been claimed that the CMA debate serves to direct managers' attention towards ethical concerns (Freeman 1999). One might duly argue that the idea of SERM directs managers' attention to the possibility of engaging stakeholders in some new way. Finally, the distribution-of-blame aspect of the CMA debate remains obviously important in practice (e.g. Garrett 1989; Werhane 1989). Indeed, far from being obsolete, the CMA debate might become more important in the future because the entire debate can be re-deployed to systematically inform and guide the regulation of artificial moral agents and the practices of artificial-engagement (e.g. Singer 2013).

Conclusions

It is by now quite apparent that the idea of corporate moral agency remains generally useful for organizing various forms of human knowledge. The associated phenomenological and ontological problems might never be solved, but the CMA debate can be settled simply by regarding CMA as an epistemological organizing-principle. Similarly, there can be no definitive theory of SERM, only a continuing productive inquiry into this domain and arena of intense struggles, conflicting interests and motivated viewpoints.

Note

★ Parts of this chapter are adapted from "Corporate moral agency as an epistemological organizing principle" *Human Systems Management* 35 (2016): 65–77.

References

Alzola, M. (2008) Character and environment: The status of virtues in organization. *Journal of Business Ethics*, 78, pp. 343–357.

Arnold, D. (2006) Corporate moral agency. *Midwest Studies in Philosophy*, 30, pp. 279–291.

Avi-Yona, R. & Sivan, D. (2007) An historical perspective on corporate form and real entity: Implications for corporate social responsibility. In: Biondi, Y., Canziani, A. and Kirat, T. (eds.), *The Firm as an Entity: Implications for Economics, Accounting and the Law*. Routledge: Oxford, pp. 153–185.

Berle, A. & Means, G. (1932) *The Modern Corporation and Private Property*. Harcourt Brace & World: New York.

Bouchard, F. & Huneman, P. (2013) *From Groups to Individuals: Evolution and Emerging Individuality*. The Vienna Series in Theoretical Biology. Cambridge: MIT Press.

Brown, M. (2010) *Civilizing the Economy*. Cambridge University Press: Cambridge.

Buchholz, R. & Rosenthal, S. (2005) Toward a contemporary conceptual framework for stakeholder theory. *Journal of Business Ethics*, 58, pp. 137–148.

Buchholz, R. & Rosenthal, S. (2006) Integrating ethics all the way through: The issue of moral agency reconsidered. *Journal of Business Ethics*, 66, pp. 233–243.

Danley J (1984) Corporate moral agency: The case for anthropological bigotry. In: Hoffman, W. M. and Moore, J. M. (eds.), *Business Ethics: Readings and Cases in Corporate Morality*. McGraw Hill: New York, pp. 172-179.

Dubbink, W. & Smith, J. (April 2011) A political account of corporate moral responsibility. *Ethical Theory and Moral Practice*, 14(2), pp. 223–246.

Ewin, R. (1991) The moral status of the corporation. *Journal of Business Ethics*, 10, pp. 749–756.

Freeman, R. (1999) Divergent stakeholder theory. *Academy of Management Review*, 24(2), pp. 233–236.

French, P. (1984) *Collective and Corporate Responsibility*. Columbia University Press: New York.

Freund, E. (orig.1897/2000) *The Legal Nature of Corporations*. Batoche Books: Kitchener.

Garrett, J. (1989) Un-redistributable corporate moral responsibility. *Journal of Business Ethics*, 8(7), pp. 535–545.

Gibson, K. (2011) Towards an intermediate position on corporate moral personhood. *Journal of Business Ethics*, 101, pp. 71–81.

Gindis, D. (2007) some building blocks for a theory of the firm as a real entity. In: Biondi, Y., Canziani, A. and Kirat, T. (eds.), *The Firm as an Entity: Implications for Economics, Accounting and the Law*. Routledge: Oxford, pp. 266–291.

Gini A (1998) Work, identity and self; How we are formed by the work we do. *Journal of Business Ethics*, 17, pp. 707–714.

Goodpaster, K. & Matthews, J. (1982) Can a corporation have a conscience? In: Hoffman, W. M. & Moore, J. M. (eds.), *Business Ethics: Readings and Cases in Corporate Morality*. McGraw Hill: New York, pp. 150–162.

Greenwood, M. (2007) Stakeholder engagement: Beyond the myth of corporate responsibility. *Journal of Business Ethics*, 74, pp. 315–327.

Gunkel, D. (2012) *The Machine Question: Critical Perspectives on AI, Robots and Ethics*. MIT Press: Cambridge.

Hall-Stores, J. (2007) *Beyond AI: Creating the Conscience of the Machine*. Prometheus: New York.

Isaacs, T. (2006) Collective moral responsibility and collective intention. *Midwest Studies in Philosophy*, 30, pp. 59–73.

Iyer, A. (2006) The missing dynamic: Corporations individuals and contracts. *Journal of Business Ethics*, 67, pp. 433–436.

Jackson, K. (1993) Global distributive justice and the corporate duty to aid. *Journal of Business Ethics*, 12(7), pp. 547–551.

Janis, I. L. & Mann, L. (1977). *Decision Making: A Psychological Analysis of Conflict, Choice and Commitment*. Free Press: New York.

List, C. & Pettit, P. (2011) *Group Agency: The Possibility, Design and Status of Corporate Agents*. Oxford: Oxford University Press.

Littelton, A. (1938) A substitute for stated capital. *Harvard Business Review*, 17(1), pp. 75–84.

Manning, R. (1984) Corporate responsibility and corporate personhood. *Journal of Business Ethics*, 3, pp. 77–84.

May, L. (1987) *The Morality of Groups: Collective Responsibility, Group Based Harm and Corporate Rights*. Indiana: University of Notre Dame Press.

Margolis, J. & Walsh, P. (2003) Misery loves companies: Rethinking social initiatives by business. *Administrative Science Quarterly*, 48(2), pp. 268–306.

McMahon, C. (1995) The ontological and moral status of organizations. *Business Ethics Quarterly*, 5(3), pp. 543–554.

Modgil, S. & Modgil, C. (Eds.) (1986). *Lawrence Kohlberg: Consensus and Controversy*. Lewes: The Falmer Press.

Moon, J., Crane, A. & Matten, D. (2005) Can corporations be citizens? Corporate citizenship as a metaphor for business participation in society. *Business Ethics Quarterly*, 15(3), pp. 427–451.

Moore, G. (1999) Corporate moral agency: Review and implications. *Journal of Business Ethics*, 21, pp. 329–343.

Narveson, J. (2002) Collective responsibility. *Journal of Ethics*, 6, pp. 179–198.

O'Riordan, L. and Faribrass, J. (2014) Managing CSR stakeholder engagement: A new conceptual framework. *Journal of Business Ethics*, 125, pp. 121–145.

Phillips, M. (1995) Corporate moral responsibility: When it might matter. *Business Ethics Quarterly*, 5(3), pp. 555–577.

Pruzan, P. (2001) The question of organizational consciousness: Can organizations have values, virtues, visions? *Journal of Business Ethics*, 29, pp. 271–284.

Rankin, N. (1987) Corporations as persons: Objections to Goodpaster's "Principle of Moral Projection" *Journal of Business Ethics*, 6, pp. 633–643.

Rosenthal, S. and Buchholtz, R. (2000). The empirical-normative split in business ethics: A pragmatic alternative. *Business Ethics Quarterly*, 10(2), pp. 399–408.

Seabright, M. & Kurke, L. (1997) Organizational ontology and the moral status of the corporation. *Business Ethics Quarterly*, 7(4), pp. 91–108.

Sen, A. (1993). Does business ethics make economic sense? *Business Ethics Quarterly*, 3(1), pp. 45–54.

Sennett, R. (2000) *The Corrosion of Character: The Personal Consequences of Work in the New Capitalism*. Norton: London.

Singer, A. (1994) Strategy as Moral Philosophy. *Strategic Management Journal*, 15, pp. 191–213.

Singer, A. (2013) Corporate moral agency and artificial intelligence. *International Journal of Social and Organizational Dynamics in Information Technology*, 3(1), pp. 1–13.

Singer, A. (2016) Corporate moral agency as an epistemological organising principle. *Human Systems Management*, 35(1), pp. 65–77.

Singer, A. (2017) Thinking strategically about 'corporate personhood'. *Human Systems Management*, 36, pp. 129–140.

Sridhar, B. S. & Camburn, A. (1993) Stages of moral development of corporations. *Journal of Business Ethics*, 12(9), pp. 727–743.

Velasquez, M. (2003) Debunking corporate moral responsibility. *Business Ethics Quarterly*, 13(4), pp. 531–562.

Wallach, W. & Allen, C. (2009) *Moral Machines: Teaching Robots Right From Wrong*. Oxford University Press: Oxford.

Watson, G., Freeman, R. & Parmar, B. (2008) Connected moral agency in organizational ethics. *Journal of Business Ethics*, 81, pp. 323–343.

Weaver, W. (1998) Corporations as intentional systems. *Journal of Business Ethics*, 17, pp. 87–97.

Werhane, P. (1989) Corporate and individual moral responsibility: A reply to Jan Garrett. *Journal of Business Ethics*, 8, pp. 821–822.

Werhane, P. (1994) The normative/descriptive distinction in methodologies of business ethics. *Business Ethics Quarterly*, 4(2), pp. 175–179.

1.3 Stakeholder engagement to secure legitimacy – the social licence to operate

Anna Katharina Provasnek and Erwin Schmid

Introduction

This chapter focuses on preventive and reactive management approaches to secure the broader social legitimacy of a company's activities. Stakeholder engagement measures are one source of company efforts for social legitimacy and can be very challenging tasks. Questions such as *how* to integrate stakeholders into operational efforts and *which* management approaches can secure social legitimacy were considered decades ago but still require significant attention and efforts.[1] Companies operate in society based on explicit and implicit social contracts, and their legitimacy depends on the delivery of socially desirable ends to society and benefits to political and economic entities.[2] The assessment and maintenance of relationships between companies and stakeholders can secure different exchange processes. Additionally, socially oriented companies can ensure that those who bear the brunt of their operations receive appropriate benefits.[3] Efforts by a company to create social legitimacy and build relationships are doomed to fail if they are not built upon a sense of community and recognition of the importance of stakeholders.[4] Engagement activities offer stakeholders opportunities to learn about a company's activities and their potential impacts or benefits for them. Therein, stakeholders can engage with companies on diverse levels, voice their concerns, discuss potential challenges, identify new opportunities for co-operation and grant or withdraw their acceptance or approval for company activities.[5]

The concept of a social licence to operate (SLO) was coined to recognize a social component of successful, long-term company operations in light of stakeholder engagement.[6] The SLO was defined as an intangible representation of the ongoing approval or acceptance of a project by stakeholders who are affected by its progress. Distinct from a legal or regulatory licence granted by a governmental body or agency, an SLO can be withdrawn by stakeholders at any time. The withdrawal of a social licence may or may not be marked by or lead to stakeholder measures such as protests or boycotts against company activities.[7] The concept emerged from the mining industry and has now evolved to be applied to industries such as wind or paper and pulp milling. (After 20 years of research across a handful of industries, types of management approaches behind this concept remain unclear.) In this chapter, we propose a perspective on active and passive approaches. For companies vulnerable to societal conflicts, such as mining firms or wind power producers, an appropriate management process is crucial, as increasing social conflicts *can* hinder companies in accessing new markets or continuing their success in established ones.

In the following sections, we briefly introduce the reader to the main concepts on which the SLO is based: stakeholder and legitimacy theories. Then we focus on the *social licence to operate* concept in greater detail and consider its origin and development. Several frameworks have already elaborated on the key characteristics of this concept and have proposed fundamental elements that companies need to address in order to gain or secure an SLO.

Research for this chapter was conducted using an extended literature review. The integrative review of published articles was used to gain an understanding about stakeholder engagement theory, the SLO concept and its links to crisis management frameworks. Based on identified figures in the literature, we introduce our SLO framework drawing upon crisis management literature, and we illustrate a preventive and reactive management approach to gaining, retaining and repairing an SLO. Methodologically, we draw on well-established literature and connect legitimacy theory, stakeholder theory and the SLO concept for an integrated perspective. Such a perspective of an SLO management process for companies to use when stakeholder conflicts arise, as well as before and after, can be applied by practitioners and scientists interested in securing long-term operations from a societal perspective.

Legitimacy theory and stakeholder engagement

"*Legitimacy* refers to perceptions or assumptions that the actions of a company are desirable, proper or appropriate within some socially constructed system of norms, values, beliefs and definitions."[8] This is an inclusive, broad-based perspective of legitimacy that explicitly acknowledges the role of stakeholders within its dynamics. The legitimacy of companies may be resilient to rare, single events but is dependent upon factors such as the history of events or their recurrence over time, and further based on the subjective perceptions or assumptions of a collective of stakeholders as they interpret companies' operations. Divergences in regard to norms, values or beliefs between stakeholders and companies can be challenging or can go unnoticed. The latter situation does not have to affect company legitimacy, but it can become a real threat once such divergences are discovered by critical stakeholders.[9] A legitimate company can be described as one that enjoys largely unquestioned freedom to pursue its activities. Illegitimate companies are those that have lost or were never granted the right to execute operations.[10] It must be noted that no company can satisfy all audiences completely, and no manager can step completely outside of the belief system that renders the company. However, management approaches and measures can make a substantial difference in the extent to which company activities are perceived as desirable, proper and appropriate within their social environment. Herein, legitimacy rests heavily on communication between the company and its various stakeholders.[11] From a strategic perspective, companies have the four options of ignoring, maintaining, building or repairing their legitimacy in light of their societal acceptance for activities.

Societal legitimacy can be gained for an entirely new industry, for a company new to an industry or region or for a company's specific new activities. Once legitimacy *is* granted, it can also be taken *for* granted. Herein, companies must remain aware that market, financial, political or operational anomalies as well as failures or external shocks can threaten their economic and societal legitimacy. In particular, stakeholders' issues that are not addressed can have negative impacts. Once legitimacy is in need of repair, there is a reactive approach to control damage, with some form of business crisis situation. Previously successful strategies can fail, and consequently, management is requested to develop new strategies to tackle the threat to the company's societal legitimacy.[12]

Stakeholders are usually the ones who have the power to terminate a company's societal legitimacy.[13] From a historical perspective, stakeholder management emerges from an old research tradition that addresses business–society relations.[14] The nature of the relationship between companies and stakeholders is also strongly influenced by company strategies. Hence, the strategic importance of specific stakeholder groups determines the types of relationships managements choose. The positive correlation between relationship strength and the strategic importance of stakeholders is vital,[15] and these can be managed in different ways, ranging from more passive to more participatory approaches. Starting at weak relationship types, companies can observe or inform stakeholders, maintain dialogues with them, consider stakeholders in corporate decision-making processes, cooperate and network with or empower them or provide stakeholders with delegating authority and decision-making power, the highest level of stakeholder integration.[16]

Companies may respond differently to various stakeholder interests, claims or pressures.[17] Motives to act can be based on push-and-pull forces.[18] Push forces urge companies to consider certain interests. Stakeholders such as governments push companies to consider critical company activities. By contrast, pull forces attract companies to commit to specific activities; this could be the case if stakeholders such as investors or consumers were to reward firms for their activities. In that case, companies' efforts for social admission can be positively correlated to economic success.[19] Different engagement activities provide stakeholders as well as companies with opportunities to learn about each other's interests and activities, potentially negative impacts on each other and also potential benefits for one or all. Companies and stakeholders may engage on different levels to voice concerns; discuss challenges; identify new opportunities for co-operation; and grant or withdraw their acceptance or approval for the industry, the company or for specific projects.

At present, many stakeholders demand that companies align themselves more closely with principles based on sustainable development.[20] The sustainable development movement, and therefore the claims of many stakeholders, stem inter alia from the United Nations' 1987 Brundtland Report, an appeal to societies, governments and businesses to "[meet] the needs of current generations without compromising the ability of future generations to meet their needs and aspirations."[21] Generations can include present and future company stakeholders to be managed by companies in order to consider societal interests.[22] Thereby, firms can secure their legitimacy by meeting expectations of social responsibility and sustainable development through their focus on the needs, concerns and claims of their stakeholders.[23]

The bottom line for the management of relevant stakeholders' needs, concerns and claims involves different kinds of transactions between companies and affected parties. Each company has more or less deep and sophisticated relationships with its environment. Some transactions occur daily, such as customer or supplier interactions. Others occur weekly or yearly, such as paying dividends to stockholders or paying taxes. Moving away from these routine actions and comfort zones; changes in the external environment; new stakeholders; and/or newly formed stakeholder groups, shocks or catastrophes can disrupt routinized transactions and require new procedures. It is a lack of fit between company processes, stakeholder processes and new situations that causes operational turbulence as well as relational crises.[24] New stakeholder engagement activities are then practices that companies undertake to involve stakeholders in company processes for mutually beneficial outcomes at a transactional level. According to Greenwood:

> [stakeholder] engagement may be seen as a mechanism for consent, as a mechanism for control, as a mechanism for co-operation, as a mechanism for accountability, as a form of employee involvement and participation, as a method for enhancing trust, as a substitute for true trust, as a discourse to enhance fairness, as a mechanism of corporate governance.[25]

From the perspective of managerial theories, the engagement of stakeholders is a means by which companies manage risks posed by stakeholders toward their legitimacy. Engagement activities can be instruments that companies use to acquit moral duties; increase consent; enhance stakeholders' access to decision-making processes; allow stakeholders to participate; strengthen trust-based co-operation; measure and evaluate intangible assets such as social capital; learn about stakeholders' interests; deflect criticism; mitigate distrust; expand or augment managerial control; transform or reshape a company's image; and gain, maintain and repair legitimacy for an industry, a company or a company's activities.[26] Given that companies are determined to manage stakeholder engagement over time, substantive engagement must entail options for stakeholders and firms to articulate their interests and an inclusive and participatory form of relationship.[27] The legitimacy theory of company activities and stakeholder engagement processes is fundamental to the concept of the SLO.[28]

The social licence to operate

There are two sets of ways companies can adapt to the increasingly complex interests of their stakeholders: one involves acquiring beyond-compliance initiatives; the other adheres to minimum legal regulation. In contrast to the second type, the first type of company watches how closely its behaviours align with socially desirable outcomes.[29] The term *Social License to Operate* was coined by a mining executive at the World Bank in 1997,[30] and mining companies were among the first to recognize that stakeholders can determine whether their operations should continue.[31] This industry was – and still is – sensitive about social conflicts, as many mining companies have highly visible social and environmental impacts at operating sites. Past conflicts with societal groups have revealed several challenges to gaining, maintaining or repairing acceptance or approval in order to legitimize risky operations.[32] Recent decades have seen the term SLO become more pervasive, and it has been introduced in a number of industries including forestry, fossil oil and gas and paper and pulp milling. Edwards et al.[33] provide an overview of how the SLO of the Swedish forest industry developed over time. Richert et al.[34] applied the SLO to a case study of the oil and gas sector in Western Australia, where the authors evaluated the strength of the SLO the population granted to the industry.[35] Another example is the paper and pulp milling industry, where Gunningham et al. found that corporate behaviour can be explained in terms of the interplay between social pressures and economic constraints.[36]

Stakeholder theory is perhaps the most central and basic theory behind the SLO concept. The SLO focuses on the acceptance and approval of stakeholders, whereas stakeholder theory includes a broad range of internal, external and different levels of stakeholder benefits and interests.[37] In light of the SLO, stakeholders can be divided into two groups: vested and non-vested stakeholders. Vested stakeholder groups have more power than non-vested stakeholders and an active vote in the awarding of an SLO. Non-vested stakeholder groups might have an interest in a company's operation, but they have only a voice and no direct vote for company activities. However, these stakeholders can put a lot of pressure on companies via the Internet and social media, as Greenpeace or the Union of Concerned Scientists, for example, do, and they can influence vested stakeholders such as politicians to change their positions and threaten company activities.[38]

At its core, the SLO is built on relationships between stakeholders and operating firms. Companies have the option to adjust their behaviours and consider or comply with external expectations in order to reduce societal risks and the complexity of multiple stakeholder interests in regard to their operations.[39] Thereby, adjustment to local circumstances does not mean that companies simply have to adjust to local legislation; rather, firms *can* network beyond legal frameworks for local businesses and meet the needs of all kinds of local and/or global stakeholders.[40] As a result, stakeholders as well as companies can benefit from gaining an SLO. Companies can benefit from secure or even conflict-free operations, while benefits for stakeholders can be twofold: from meaningful exchanges with companies and directly from business activities via employment, training or infrastructure investments.[41] Despite potential gains for both parties, expectations regarding some business activities can differ widely, and some institutions and stakeholders will never agree upon an SLO,[42] demonstrating that the SLO concept shifts traditional assumptions about power distributions within society. Traditionally, states granted legal licences for corporate activities. Today, full legal compliance with state regulations has become an increasingly insufficient means of satisfying society's expectations with regard to numerous and shifting stakeholder interests.[43] The SLO focuses on the societal legitimacy of what the organization *does* – not what it *is*.[44]

A number of entities can be involved in granting an SLO, including societal groups, governments, larger communities, the general public, media or small local communities. Local communities can be key arbiters in the process. Herein, the proximity to projects, sensitivity to impacts and ability to influence project outcomes are critical.[45] The literature provides several recommendations for acquiring and maintaining an SLO and measures for doing so include early, ongoing communication; transparent disclosure of information; conflict resolution mechanisms; culturally appropriate decision making;[46] maintaining a positive corporate reputation; understanding local culture and history; educating local stakeholders about projects; and open communication among all stakeholders. Corruption, paying bribes or the issuance of graft, harmful activities and deceitful practices are not parts of SLO measures but sometimes are common practices that aim to gain acceptance from some stakeholder groups in some regions.[47] Even if a company has obtained an SLO, it is not guaranteed to hold it in the future. Continuous reflection on social, economic or environmental conditions; community priorities and expectations; and, therefore, stakeholders and their interests must be monitored in order to retain an SLO.[48] Companies that lose an SLO can face conflicts that may include shutdowns or slowdowns; protests, boycotts or blockades; non-issuance or retraction of government permits; harmful media campaigns; and negative government lobbying. However, some projects may never receive social support if stakeholder and company expectations are beyond reconciliation. This does not guarantee a company will go out of business, but societal forces can impede operations and limit thriving business options.[49]

Several frameworks elaborate on the main elements that constitute companies' SLOs. According to a framework from Boutilier and Thomson,[50] the social license comprises legitimacy, credibility and trust. If companies develop legitimacy and credibility with their stakeholders, acceptance and then approval of the operations can follow. Requirements for the SLO are based on economic legitimacy, socio-political legitimacy, interactional trust and institutionalized trust. Economic legitimacy is granted if companies provide a benefit to stakeholders such as employment or training. If the company does not provide basic economic benefits, stakeholders usually withdraw their acceptance and any SLO. Socio-political legitimacy focuses on companies' efforts to ensure the well-being of regions, confirmation with laws, fairness toward individuals and local culture. If any of these are lacking, the approval of business operations is unlikely. Interactional trust refers to relationships between companies and stakeholders. Listening to and responding to stakeholders, engagement and mutual dialogue are central, as the SLO will not be granted otherwise. Institutionalized trust exists if representatives of stakeholders and companies engage in enduring relationships over time. A hierarchical link exists between economic legitimacy, socio-political legitimacy, interactional trust and institutionalized trust. The lowest level is economic legitimacy, and the highest is institutionalized trust. If companies fulfill all levels, stakeholders see little or no reason to oppose company actions and an SLO. *Acceptance* of company operations reflects that stakeholders tolerate, agree with or consent to company activities. The higher level of *approval* reflects that stakeholders favour, agree to or are even pleased with company activities.[51]

Moffat et al.[52] also developed an SLO framework and found that approval and acceptance of company operations are centrally determined by trust as well. Trust is dependent upon a company's impacts on social infrastructure, contact quality and quantity with stakeholders and procedural fairness. The elements can be classified as three impact categories: operational impacts (social infrastructure, such as on the natural environment); engagement impacts (quantity and quality of contacts); and behavioural impacts (procedural fairness).[53] Prno et al.[54] provide a systems-based conceptual framework that assesses SLO determinants of companies. It describes a set of potential variables that can emerge to affect SLO outcomes, which are categorized according to whether or not an SLO was granted and whether or not operations proceeded. The variables are attributed to four main categories of a complex SLO system: system characteristics, multiscale variables, local variables and SLO outcomes. Local variables are the most tangible and influenceable by companies themselves.[55] Table 1.3.1 summarizes the main elements of the three SLO frameworks according to the stated authors.

The above frameworks present the SLO concept in close correlation to stakeholder theory and emphasize stakeholder identification and engagement measures. Company activities should be embedded in corporate strategies, as risks toward the societal legitimacy of company activities are to be managed that result from stakeholder resistance. Hence, the motivation to develop frameworks for the management of the SLO is also risk driven. Summarized key variables found in the frameworks above that can help to guide SLO management efforts are depicted in Table 1.3.2.

A high level of SLO is a societal allowance that companies earn through consistent and trustworthy behaviour and interactions with their stakeholders,[59] based on a stakeholder management process.

Table 1.3.1 SLO framework triangulation

	Moffat et al. (2014)[56]	*Prno et al. (2014)*★,[57]	*Boutilier et al. (2011)*[58]
Framework approach	Integrative model	Systems-based conceptual framework	Conceptual model
Context	Mining industry in Australia	Mining industry in the USA	Mining industry in Bolivia
Research approach & methods	— Qualitative and quantitative research — Social-psychological research in intergroup relations — Longitudinal study, online surveys, path analyses	— Qualitative research — Exploratory research case studies, interviews, literature review	— Qualitative and quantitative research — Exploratory research, original study, interviews, surveys, literature review, factor analysis
Framework objectives	Measure and model the critical elements of a SLO;	— Guide SLO analysis and management efforts — Assessing SLO determinants and outcomes	Measure the SLO quantitatively
Characteristics of framework elements	Process and integration oriented	Contextual and complexity oriented	Four factors constituting the three levels of SLO
Framework elements	— Social infrastructure — Contact quality — Contact quantity — Procedural fairness —Trust	— Mining — Community — Community relations	— Economic legitimacy — Socio-political legitimacy — Interactional trust — Institutionalized trust

Note: ★ Selected *local variable* of the framework.

Table 1.3.2 Main elements determining an SLO

Main elements	*Typical characteristics*
Social and environmental impacts	Environmental protection and risk-prevention mechanisms Social responsibility Social risk-prevention mechanisms Mitigation of operational effects
Stakeholder communication and engagement procedures on a short- and long-term basis	Transparency Ongoing exchange mechanisms Engagement culture
Company governance	Legal and voluntary agreements and policies Codes of conduct Routine and crisis behaviour and ethics Accountability structures Trust culture
Economic legitimacy	Economic benefits to legal institutions Economic benefits to stakeholders Economically beneficial long-term arrangements with stakeholders

The SLO management process

In general, management processes facilitate the structuring, analysis, decision making and communication of business activities and developments. The purposes of a management process are, further, to ensure a consistent approach to various contexts and their developments, opportunities, risks or challenges based on a logical thought process. It is a support – but not a replacement – for management judgement used as a tool to support decision making. Management activities themselves can be traced back to two main aims: to resolve problems or to prevent them. Hence, preventive management also directly influences reactive activities, as it reduces the number of incidents that require a reactive response.

Key elements central to a firm's SLO are its social and environmental impacts, company governance settings and economic legitimacy based on benefits to stakeholders and the company itself. Stakeholder engagement procedures are of particular relevance, as the SLO is tied to a process of building and maintaining stakeholder engagement.[60] To gain or maintain an SLO, preventive management measures are necessary. Reactive measures take precedence if an SLO is already lost or under severe threat. Based on our literature review, we developed Figure 1.3.1 to depict distinct preventive and reactive management approaches.

Figure 1.3.1 illustrates the management phases that can occur if the SLO has to be gained, maintained, is under threat or is lost. Activities can be attributed to preparation measures, engagement procedures, resulting events and evaluation or reaction phases. In a reactive management stance, stakeholders are considered in the engagement phase only *after* events have occurred and the SLO has been challenged. In a preventive stance, managers anticipate requirements to gain or maintain an SLO and have completed measures to address key SLO elements and stakeholders' interests. The consequences for each approach differ significantly. Companies have to weigh the investments in preventive measures to secure an SLO and anticipate stakeholders' claims against the losses that firms may incur from failing to manage variables critical to an SLO beforehand. Preventive management also directly influences reactive activities, as it reduces the number of incidents requiring a reactive response.

In order to manage the SLO based on a logical thought process and to integrate preventive and reactive approaches, we employ the crisis-process matrix from Töpfer.[61] A company's market success and existence can be significantly threatened by crisis situations, one example being lost social credibility and a weak or missing SLO. The outcomes of such cases are twofold: either firms recover and regain their operational capabilities, or they fail and disappear.[62] A gained and well-maintained SLO protects firms from social and stakeholder conflicts. Hence, socially induced crises can be mitigated. On the contrary, a threatened or lost SLO can be a socially induced crisis, as undisturbed company continuity is under threat. Figure 1.3.2 proposes a five-step management process for gaining and maintaining an SLO or reacting to a threatened or lost SLO.

Preventive management initiatives focus on (1) preventive measures and (5) revision activities to avoid disruptions based on past experiences with societal conflicts. Reactive SLO management measures can be found within (2) early recognition, (3) containment and (4a) recovery activities in the process. Herein, conflicts occur and managements react to mitigate further damage to the SLO. Figure 1.3.2 further shows the connection between preventive and reactive management approaches. Sophisticated, preventive SLO management measures decrease both the damage potential of stakeholder conflicts that require reactive responses and the likelihood of a lost SLO.

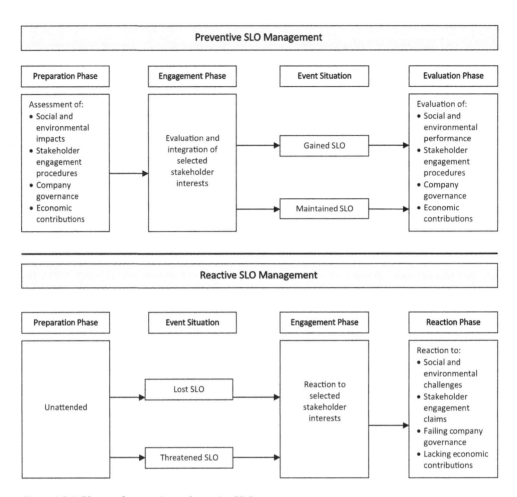

Figure 1.3.1 Phases of preventive and reactive SLO management

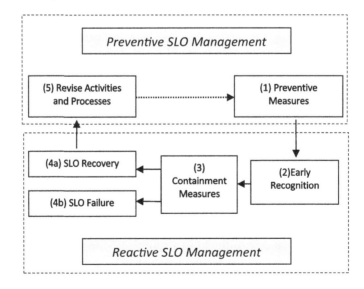

Figure 1.3.2 An SLO management process[63]

Ideally, the SLO management process starts with preventive measures to gain and maintain the SLO. These may be undertaken by management and may include environmental and social risk-prevention mechanisms; operation-effects mitigation; legal and voluntary agreements; policies, codes of conduct and ethics; accountability structures; trust-building measures; economic benefits to legal institutions and stakeholders; economically beneficial long-term arrangements with stakeholders; transparency; ongoing exchange mechanisms; and a profound stakeholder engagement culture. In the event of market, financial, political or operational anomalies; failures, external shocks, abnormalities that arrive in rapid succession; or unaddressed stakeholder claims, early recognition of the threats to the SLO is possible. The earlier threats are recognized, the more likely severe impacts to the SLO can be mitigated. If conflicts and challenges to the SLO unfold, the mitigation of damages to reputation, trust, stakeholder expectations, credibility, business success or undisturbed business continuity is central. Managements can seize containment measures, such as intensive stakeholder consultation, profound stakeholder exchange mechanisms, co-operation with stakeholders, acceptance of responsibility for misbehaviour or public remorse and reparation initiatives. If this stage is passed successfully, a company's SLO reaches an upward movement, and it can recover from a threatened or lost SLO. On the contrary, failed measures to mitigate an SLO crisis can lead to societal unrest and challenging business operations. Finally, companies that recover can revise past activities and processes within the SLO management process, review their performance, admit failures and learn from them to prevent future SLO conflicts.

Conclusions and managerial implications

Disasters in stakeholder management and engagement can lead to a lost SLO and will always be deeply regrettable. Preventive management measures can provide powerful opportunities to mitigate social conflicts, secure legitimate operations and learn from past stakeholder challenges. If companies neglect developments in their social environment and ignore stakeholders' claims toward products, services or production processes, the likelihood of an SLO crisis increases. This may unfold into a high-impact event that threatens the company's viability and is characterized by complexity, multiple interests of different entities and time pressure to make appropriate decisions, as the mining industry had to face over several decades. Then, reactive measures should prevail, and their quality will determine the societal success or failure of the affected company's future business activities.

Companies can choose between a preventive management approach and a purely reactive management approach. Ideally, managers can prevent most social incidents and are skilled at engaging with stakeholders at a preventive level, detecting vested stakeholders' fundamental interests and integrating these for successful business continuity. Engagement measures to secure the SLO may focus on activities such as providing information and seeking dialogue, including stakeholders in decision-making processes, cooperating with stakeholders and establishing a network and ultimately providing stakeholders with decision-making power in appropriate spheres of activities. The results of these transactional processes may focus on environmental protection and risk prevention mechanisms, social risk prevention, transparency and codes of conduct, accountability structures or economically beneficial long-term arrangements with stakeholders. Based on preventive and reactive SLO management capabilities, resiliencies in regard to SLO conflicts can be leveraged and anchored. An institutionalized SLO can then lead to stakeholders co-identifying with the company and actively supporting its interests. Such a strategy, if successfully implemented, shows an instrumental approach to managing the SLO that promotes extended social legitimacy for a company's activities. Implementing management processes that enable stakeholders to engage with companies could then lead to transformational effects in any regions of operation.

Limitations and recommendations for further research

The present chapter drew on literature research to develop and integrate different management approaches within a process for the development of social legitimacy and the mitigation of social conflicts on corporate activities. However, the nature of the research is based on a focus on theory rather than practical application. It has several limitations in terms of providing an in-depth understanding of real-world cases and is not applied to a specific context for further elaborations. As such, future research might usefully employ the developed management approaches to case studies in different contexts to further test and build on the findings proposed here. In addition, the necessity for understanding stakeholder engagement measures across industries may vary. The extent to which the legitimacy of companies is under threat may provide an interesting opportunity for further studies. Finally, it may also be useful to more closely examine how the management of the SLO is realized under various types of entrepreneurial settings.

Notes

1 Max E. Clarkson, "A Stakeholder Framework for Analyzing and Evaluating Corporate Social Performance," *Academy of Management Review* 20, no. 1 (January 1995): 92–117, doi:10.5465/AMR.1995.9503271994; R. Edward Freeman, *Strategic Management: A Stakeholder Approach* (Cambridge: Cambridge University Press, 1984); Michelle Greenwood, "Stakeholder Engagement: Beyond the Myth of Corporate Responsibility," *Journal of Business Ethics* 74, no. 4 (August 14, 2007): 315–327, doi:10.1007/s10551-007-9509-y; Roland K. Mitchell, Bradley R. Agle, and Donna J. Wood, "Toward a Theory of Stakeholder Identification and Salience: Defining the Principle of Who and What Really Counts," *Academy of Management. The Academy of Management Review* 22, no. 4 (October 1997): 853–886.
2 Allan D. Shocker and S. Prakash Sethi, "An Approach to Incorporating Societal Preferences in Developing Corporate Action Strategies," *California Management Review*, 15, no. 4 (1973): 97–105, doi:10.2307/41164466.
3 Juliette Syn, "The Social License: Empowering Communities and a Better Way Forward," *Social Epistemology*, 28, no. 3–4 (October 2014): 318–339, doi:10.1080/02691728.2014.922640.
4 Angela R. Dobele et al., "An Examination of Corporate Social Responsibility Implementation and Stakeholder Engagement: A Case Study in the Australian Mining Industry," *Business Strategy and the Environment*, 23, no. 3 (März 2014): 145–159, doi:10.1002/bse.1775.
5 Jason Prno and D. Scott Slocombe, "Exploring the Origins of 'Social License to Operate' in the Mining Sector: Perspectives from Governance and Sustainability Theories," *Resources Policy*, 37, no. 3 (September 2012): 346–57, doi:10.1016/j.resourpol.2012.04.002.
6 Richard Parsons and Kieren Moffat, "Constructing the Meaning of Social Licence," *Social Epistemology*, 28, no. 3–4 (October 2, 2014): 340–363, doi:10.1080/02691728.2014.922645.
7 Airong Zhang and Kieren Moffat, "A Balancing Act: The Role of Benefits, Impacts and Confidence in Governance in Predicting Acceptance of Mining in Australia," *Resources Policy*, 44 (June 2015): 25–34, doi:10.1016/j.resourpol.2015.01.001.
8 Mark C. Suchman, "Managing Legitimacy: Strategic and Institutional Approaches," *The Academy of Management Review*, 20, no. 3 (July 1995): 574, doi:10.2307/258788.
9 Suchman, "Managing Legitimacy."
10 Parsons and Moffat, "Constructing the Meaning of Social Licence."

11 Suchman, "Managing Legitimacy."

12 Ibid.

13 Dobele et al., "An Examination of Corporate Social Responsibility Implementation and Stakeholder Engagement."

14 A. B. Carroll, "Corporate Social Responsibility: Evolution of a Definitional Construct," *Business & Society*, 38, no. 3 (September 1, 1999): 268–95, doi:10.1177/000765039903800303.

15 Jeffrey Harrison and Caron H. St. John, "Managing and Partnering with External Stakeholders," *Academy of Management Executive*, 10, no. 2 (Mai 1996): 46–60, doi:10.5465/AME.1996.9606161554.

16 Stefan Schaltegger et al., "International Corporate Sustainability Barometer" (Lüneburg: Leuphana University; Centre for Sustainability Management, 2013), 31, http://www2.leuphana.de/csm/InternationalCorporateSustainabilityBarometer.pdf.

17 Reinhard Steurer et al., "Corporations, Stakeholders and Sustainable Development I: A Theoretical Exploration of Business–Society Relations," *Journal of Business Ethics*, 61, no. 3 (October 2005): 263–281, doi:10.1007/s10551–005–7054–0.

18 Indrit Troshani and Bill Doolin, "Innovation Diffusion: A Stakeholder and Social Network View," *European Journal of Innovation Management*, 10, no. 2 (May 1, 2007): 176–200, doi:10.1108/14601060710745242.

19 Steurer et al., "Corporations, Stakeholders and Sustainable Development I."

20 Prno and Slocombe, "Exploring the Origins of 'Social License to Operate' in the Mining Sector."

21 United Nations, "Our Common Future; Brundtland Report 1987 – Our_Common_Future-Brundtland_Report_1987.pdf," 1987, 15, http://conspect.nl/pdf/Our_Common_Future-Brundtland_Report_1987.pdf.

22 United Nations, "Our Common Future; Brundtland Report 1987 – Our_Common_Future-Brundtland_Report_1987.pdf."

23 Kathleen M. Wilburn and Ralph Wilburn, "Achieving Social License to Operate Using Stakeholder Theory," *Journal of International Business Ethics*, 4, no. 2 (July 2011): 3–16.

24 Freeman, *Strategic Management*.

25 Greenwood, "Stakeholder Engagement," 318.

26 Ibid.

27 Cedric E. Dawkins, "The Principle of Good Faith: Toward Substantive Stakeholder Engagement," *Journal of Business Ethics*, 121, no. 2 (May 2014): 283–295, doi:10.1007/s10551–013–1697–z.

28 Jason Prno, "An Analysis of Factors Leading to the Establishment of a Social Licence to Operate in the Mining Industry," *Resources Policy*, 38, no. 4 (December 2013): 577–590, doi:10.1016/j.resourpol.2013.09.010.

29 J. A. Howard-Grenville, "Inside the 'Black Box': How Organizational Culture and Subcultures Inform Interpretations and Actions on Environmental Issues," *Organization & Environment*, 19, no. 1 (March 1, 2006): 46–73, doi:10.1177/1086026605285739.

30 Syn, "The Social License."

31 Parsons and Moffat, "Constructing the Meaning of Social Licence."

32 Syn, "The Social License."

33 "Can't Climb the Trees Anymore: Social Licence to Operate, Bioenergy and Whole Stump Removal in Sweden, "*Social Epistemology*, 28 (July 2014): 239–257, doi: 10.1080/02691728.2014.922637.

34 Ibid.

35 "Measuring the Extent of a Social License to Operate: The Influence of Marine Biodiversity Offsets in the Oil and Gas Sector in Western Australia," *Resources Policy*, 43 (March 2015): 121–129, doi:10.1016/j.resourpol.2014.12.001.

36 Gunningham, Thornton and Kagan, "Motivating Management: Corporate Compliance in Environmental Protection," Law & Policy, 27 (April 2005): 289–316.

37 Prno and Slocombe, "Exploring the Origins of 'Social License to Operate' in the Mining Sector."

38 Wilburn and Wilburn, "Achieving Social License to Operate Using Stakeholder Theory."

39 Prno, "An Analysis of Factors Leading to the Establishment of a Social Licence to Operate in the Mining Industry."

40 Soili Nysten-Haarala, Elena Klyuchnikova, and Heidi Helenius, "Law and Self-Regulation – Substitutes or Complements in Gaining Social Acceptance?" *Resources Policy*, 45 (September 2015): 52–64, doi:10.1016/j.resourpol.2015.02.008.

41 Wilburn and Wilburn, "Achieving Social License to Operate Using Stakeholder Theory."

42 Prno and Slocombe, "Exploring the Origins of 'social License to Operate' in the Mining Sector."

43 Wilburn and Wilburn, "Achieving Social License to Operate Using Stakeholder Theory."

44 John Morrison, *The Social License* (Basingstoke: Palgrave Macmillan, 2014).

45 Prno and Slocombe, "Exploring the Origins of 'social License to Operate' in the Mining Sector."

46 Ibid.

47 Ibid.

48 Robert B. Pojasek, "Sustainability: The Three Responsibilities," *Environmental Quality Management*, 19, no. 3 (2010): 87–94, doi:10.1002/tqem.20256.

49 Prno and Slocombe, "Exploring the Origins of 'Social License to Operate' in the Mining Sector."

50 R. Boutilier and I. Thomson. "Modelling and Measuring the Social License to Operate: Fruits of a Dialogue between Theory and Practice," 2011, http://socialicense.com/publications/Modelling%20 and%20Measuring%20the%20SLO.pdf.

51 Ibid.

52 Kieren Moffat and Airong Zhang, "The Paths to Social Licence to Operate: An Integrative Model Explaining Community Acceptance of Mining," *Resources Policy*, 39 (March 2014): 61–70, doi:10.1016/j.resourpol.2013.11.003.

53 Ibid.

54 J. Prno and D. S. Slocombe, "A Systems-Based Conceptual Framework for Assessing the Determinants of a Social License to Operate in the Mining Industry," *Environmental Management,* 53, no. 3 (March 1, 2014): 672–89, doi:10.1007/s00267–013–0221–7.

55 Ibid.

56 Moffat and Zhang, "The Paths to Social Licence to Operate."

57 Prno and Slocombo, "A Systems-Based Conceptual Framework for Assessing the Determinants of a Social License to Operate in the Mining Industry."

58 Boutilier and Thomson. "Modelling and Measuring the Social License to Operate."

59 Geert Demuijnck and Björn Fasterling, "The Social License to Operate," *Journal of Business Ethics*, January 15, 2016, doi:10.1007/s10551–015–2976–7.

60 Prno and Slocombe, "Exploring the Origins of 'social License to Operate' in the Mining Sector."

61 *Plötzliche Unternehmenskrisen – Gefahr oder Chance?: Grundlagen des Krisenmanagement, Praxisfälle, Grundsätze zur Krisenvorsorge* (Luchterhand, 1999).

62 Ibid.

63 Based on *Krisenverlaufsmatrix*, Töpfer Ibid., 34.

1.4 Measuring and enhancing relational capabilities

In defence of a relational view of the firm

Cécile Ezvan, Hélène L'Huillier, and Cécile Renouard

Introduction

The purpose of this chapter is both to present the foundational principles of an index, which measures the quality of the relationships between the company and its different stakeholders, and to test this index through case studies.

The Relational Capability Index (RCI) is constructed in accordance with a relational vision of the firm and with the capability approach framework. It has been built and used for more than 10 years as an operational tool to measure companies' impacts on the quality of relationships of various stakeholders, with a focus on vulnerable groups in Southern countries. Thus, it fills the gap in the existing literature on CSR and stakeholder theory (Donaldson & Preston 1995; McWilliams & Siegel 2001; Jamali 2008), while demonstrating that companies' impacts on their stakeholders are also driven by individual and collective social capabilities. This focus on the relational capabilities of stakeholders and on the mission of the firm within society and towards future generations, as a key dimension of its corporate social responsibility (CSR), impacts the way companies can cooperate with different actors to promote sustainable business models. Thus, it opens the way for a political view of the firm, which would better link business strategy with the interests of all stakeholders, including the most vulnerable.

The literature on corporate social responsibility and stakeholder engagement to date has drawn very little on the capability approach. This is unfortunate, at least for two reasons. First, from a theoretical perspective, the capability approach (Sen 1999; Nussbaum 2000) defines the quality of relations as a key condition of individual empowerment and global human development and highlights the conditions which foster stakeholders' engagement on the long-term run. Second, from a more practical perspective, it may help organizations build long-term, mutually beneficial relationships with all their stakeholders, which includes suppliers, customers, investors, but also more vulnerable parties, such as subcontractors or the local community, whose interests are at stake. The capability approach highlights the political role of the firm, as an institution involved in society and responsible for its relations with its stakeholders. The capability approach, as such, renews the definition of CSR and its extent.

This chapter is structured as follows: first, we explain the foundations of our approach based on a relational anthropology and a political view of the firm. We then define our index, its dimensions, components, and weights. Finally, we provide examples from our empirical research carried out in Nigeria, Mexico, Brazil, Argentina, and Indonesia as evidence that the RCI is able to measure the way a company impacts relational empowerment and quality of life of groups of vulnerable stakeholders who are very often excluded from the game.

Foundations: relational capabilities as a criterion to reflect on the role of companies in societies

Why we promote a relational view of the firm

Our work is rooted in a relational anthropology that considers human as cultural and social beings, embedded in society and nature. This relational anthropology can be considered from two different perspectives, a philosophical one and a sociological one.

First, from a philosophical perspective, as shown in Renouard (2011) and Giraud and et al. (2013), a relational anthropology underpins both utilitarianism (Mill 1861) and the capability approach (Aristotle 1999, 2009; Kant 2003 (1785); Nussbaum 2007). Building on Mill (1861), we define utilitarianism as a theory that considers social utility as a final goal for each person. Mill departs from Bentham who promotes 'the greatest happiness/ utility of the greatest number' and doesn't specify what kind of happiness has to be looked for. Mill argues that the desirable utility is social: it includes, for each individual, the quest for the other's happiness. Building on Sen (1999) and Nussbaum (1999), we define the capability approach as considering individual and collective social capabilities development as final goals. The notion of capability entails three dimensions: the specific ability to do and/or to be of a person, the effective functioning (the way she can translate this capability into a concrete outcome), and the entitlement related to this capability (how the existing institutions don't impede such a choice). A relational conception of capabilities, freedoms, and rights is present in both traditions and provides adequate criteria for defining CSR towards the company's stakeholders. We therefore defend "relational capabilities" as a means of providing a common paradigm, a shared vision of a core component of human development. This perspective can play a critical role in highlighting the deadlocks of certain conceptions of CSR and business ethics, which do not consider that human and social bonds have intrinsic value. Indeed, it demonstrates the importance of quality of relations as an end in itself. Thus, it is critical of purely instrumental views of social ties, which consider the role played by social cohesion as a tool used to foster business performance. Consideration of the intrinsic importance of social cohesion implies that one cannot speak of sustainable development if the quality of the social fabric is diminished. This implies that a revision of a company's value creation assessment needs go beyond consideration of financial value. It must also integrate a measure of the social fabric improvement within the company and between the company and its main stakeholders (Renouard 2013).

Second, from a sociological perspective (Bourdieu 1980; Coleman 1988; Putnam 2000; Boltanski and Chapiello 2005; Woolcock and Narayan 2000), the analysis of the role of social capital shows the importance of networks of relations in order to enhance economic activity and social development. This raises questions on its possible ambiguous role, i.e. pretending to serve social objectives while damaging social ties. When instrumental and mainly business-oriented, social capital of a given community can lead to a deterioration of the social fabric on a larger scale. Indeed, the "structural hole" conception of social capital as theorized by Burt (1992) shows how many businesses are successful thanks to the ability of some entrepreneurs to span structural holes. The activity of these entrepreneurs is all the more fruitful when they hold a key position in a given network, as they can then provide people with access to certain goods and services that these people would not be able to obtain otherwise. This category of people corresponds to the market-makers (*faiseurs*) in Boltanski and Chapiello's (2005) typology of behaviours in connected societies. Sociologists, by contrast, show that a second category of people exist – the match-makers (*mailleurs*) – who do not try to obtain a monopoly on the ties that are created between people and groups, but act in order to enhance the quality of the social fabric. This typology helps to distinguish two ways of performing business activities. One might object that, given the current rules of the games and orientation towards competitive markets, it is quite unrealistic to imagine that businesses can be successful while paving the way to cooperation and social bonds that may endanger business objectives. However, field work on social entrepreneurs shows that they precisely develop these kinds of inclusive business models (Alkire 2005). Moreover, deterioration of the business climate is due to deterioration of the social bonds in society, which obliges classical businesses to reconsider the intrinsic importance of trust and altruistic relations (Algan and Cahuc 2013). Recent research on the societal performance of industries, such as extractive industries, which have a strong impact on their natural and human environment, has shown the importance of considering the connectors and the dividers within society (Zandvliet and Anderson 2009). The dividers often appear as those people who are focused on their own short-term and private interests and endanger the social fabric (Renouard 2015), whereas the connectors foster better relations, be they social or economic. Thus, the best interest of corporations, in the long run, should be in enhancing the quality of the social fabric.

This twofold (philosophical and sociological) perspective can lead to a set of indicators aimed at assessing corporate social performance as a maximization of the relational capabilities of people within the companies and people impacted by companies' activities, in order to ensure the sustainability of social and ecological ties within society.

Why companies should take their political responsibilities seriously

In accordance with these relational foundations, we have developed a theoretical framework for corporate responsibilities (Renouard 2007, 2013; Renouard and Ezvan 2018) – which includes economic and financial, social and cultural, societal, environmental, and political responsibilities – towards their different stakeholders. How do corporations assume each of these responsibilities? The firm, as a distributive agent, makes choices about the creation and distribution of value (economic and financial responsibility). It maintains internal and external relations with its employees and subcontractors (social responsibility). It has a profound consequence for the people of a territory by its effects on the socioeconomic and cultural fabric and on nature (social and environmental responsibility). It influences the global long-term commons (political responsibility). As a consequence, corporations can be viewed as political institutions as well as economic organizations (Capron and Quairel-Lanoizelée 2015; Renouard 2013; Renouard and Ezvan 2018; Néron 2015).

When we extend this relational view of the firm to CSR, we must reconsider responsibility not only according to a liability model, but also according to a "mission" (Ricoeur, 1991; Vallaeys 2013) or "social connection" (Young 2006) model that analyzes not only the direct consequences of a company's activities on its stakeholders, but also its emergent effects, combined with other actors, that can lead to structural harms. Thus, the company can be viewed as having a twofold responsibility as accountability/liability and cooperation/mission. As expressed by Young (2006, p. 114), taking the example of the apparel industry,

> all the persons who participate by their actions in the ongoing schemes of cooperation that constitute these structures are responsible for them, in the sense that they are

part of the process that causes them. They are not responsible, however, in the sense of having directed the process or intended its outcomes.

This shared responsibility is not only backward-looking (regarding people negatively impacted by structural harms), but also rather forward-looking, asking different stakeholders/agents participating in a harmful activity in a given value chain, for example, to take action in order to resist these unjust behaviours and actions and to change the institutional structures.

Thus, corporations can be viewed as political institutions responsible to contribute to societal changes to protect and promote global common good. In this regard, we look for the conditions of institutional transformation that will enable firms' activities to enhance social and ecological ties. The principles of eco-justice (Bernard 1999; Fraser 2009; Renouard 2013) are defined in a threefold (economic, sociocultural, and political) manner, as (i) fair value creation and fair share, (ii) recognition, and (iii) representation. They can be applied to companies in the various areas in which they operate: (i) the production and sharing-out of wealth created, (ii) the concrete attention accorded to people, and (iii) the measures implemented to allow participation or representation of all stakeholders involved (governance). For each dimension of such a relational eco-justice, justice criteria have to be determined.

The first socioeconomic dimension is centred on the enhancement of people's relational capabilities and needs to ensure that the distribution of wealth will not destroy the social fabric but, rather, will improve social cohesion at different levels. One may consider the adoption of the maximum criterion in order to give priority to people who are worse-off and try to maximize their relational capabilities first. This is related to assessment of the consequences of huge financial inequalities on the deterioration of the social fabric.

The second dimension, which focuses on the sociocultural aspect of care in society, implies a consideration for the norms and values that may endanger the social fabric. The procedures that make some people isolated, despised, or invisible in the workplace or along the value chain have to be considered as unjust and illegitimate.

The third dimension, related to political participation and representation, obliges us to reflect on governance procedures at different levels. Are the affected stakeholders involved in decision-making processes, and not only in a formal and marginal way?

The RCI index, which we will present in detail in the second part of this chapter, has been built on these three dimensions, in order to provide insight into the situation of people impacted by business activities.

In this first part, we explained the foundations of our approach based on a relational anthropology and a political definition of the firm. We will now define our index and highlight how its dimensions and components are useful in assessing business impacts on the quality of the social fabric.

Building the RCI

Inspired by Oxford Poverty and Human Development Initiative (OPHI)'s work on the missing dimensions of poverty (Alkire 2007), related to the capability approach framework, we strive to develop indices that are focused on long-term issues and that integrate sociocultural and political aspects of human life, thus complementing an increased number of economic indices related to material wellbeing and access to social services.

Two distinct approaches of index methodology can be found in the literature. One is related to the normative construction of indexes, and the other is related to data-driven indexes. Normative indexes are theoretically based and do not depend on the data considered. Data-driven indexes are computed according to the statistical significance of components. A normative computation of indexes is the most frequently used within multidimensional approaches to poverty. A large body of literature has been inspired by the Alkire-Foster method (Alkire and Foster 2011). This consists of an arithmetical aggregation of three dimensions of poverty that are theoretically defined. Each dimension is an equally weighted average of components and is also equally weighted in the index computation. As the first aim of our index is comparative, at both micro- and macro-levels, we chose to implement it normatively.

Although we define a set of possible weights and computation rules for the RCI related to different theories of justice (Giraud and Renouard 2012a), the version of the index presented here is computed using uniform weights and arithmetic means. This computational choice facilitates comparisons with the MPI from UNDP and OPHI (Alkire and Santos 2010; Alkire and Foster 2011). There are two ways of computing the RCI; each gives complementary information on the structure of social networks. The first is to average the components and dimensions values for a whole population; this gives an overview of the overall situation of the population. The second is based on decomposition between relational deprivations incidence (proportion of people who are below a relational poverty line) and intensity (average number of deprivations suffered by relationally poor persons). It gives a more comprehensive picture of the situation of the subpopulation who suffers from sociopolitical exclusion (Wolff and De-Shalit, 2007).

To assess the quality of the social fabric, we promote (advocate?) mixed methods, both qualitative and quantitative, based firstly on a qualitative understanding of the local cultures. Indeed, quantitative surveys alone cannot capture all dimensions of human development; they also tend to strengthen the propensity of instrumental rationality to quantify in order to measure the efficiency of programs. This can lead to a preference for short-term and identified action that can be contradictory with sustainable development of a company and stakeholders' long-term interest.

A qualitative approach is needed at two levels. First, it can help to interpret the results of quantitative surveys by refining the analysis of the perceptions of people and of the collective representations that constitute the frame within which individuals and groups give meaning to their action (d'Iribarne 1993, 2003, 2015). This is all the more important when we deal with surveys focused on the quality of the social fabric: knowledge and interpretation of shared norms and values is crucial in order to assess the quality of relations between stakeholders.

Second, a qualitative study (open-ended interviews, focus groups, life stories, archives, etc.) can provide useful information on the global challenges and on the institutions involved in the project.

The capability approach we build on has the advantage of integrating qualitative and quantitative approaches.

Our main quantitative tool is a composite index called the RCI (Giraud et al. 2013) and is based on three different dimensions of inclusion/exclusion: the ability to be integrated into networks, private ties, and civic commitments. These dimensions of eco-justice build on the above mentioned distinction between socioeconomic, sociocultural, and political aspects of social cohesion (Bernard 1999) and justice (Fraser 2009). Table 1.4.1 summarizes these dimensions, their components, and the weights we use in

Table 1.4.1 RCI dimensions, components, and weights

Dimension	Component	Weight	Deprived if
Integration into networks	Employment status	1/12	No stable job with regular professional relations
	Access to transport	1/12	No means of transport
	Access to telecommunications	1/12	Uses a phone, a computer or the Internet less than once a week
	Access to information	1/12	Gets news from radio, television, or newspaper less than once a week
Private relations	Household size	1/15	Lives alone
	Family ties	1/15	No trust in relatives
	Close friends, emotional support	1/15	No close friends providing psychological and emotional support
	Financial support	1/15	No financial support from relatives or acquaintances
	Trust in the community	1/15	No trust in people the individual knows
Civic commitment	Membership	1/15	No active membership in a group (religious, union, and/or business association)
	Collective action	1/15	No participation in political actions (meetings, petitions, boycotts, demonstrations)
	Vote	1/15	Does not vote
	Solidarity	1/15	No active membership in a common-interest group
	Trust in others	1/15	No trust in unknown people

the standard version of the RCI, which relies on arithmetical means with equal dimensional weights.

The first dimension of exclusion is socioeconomic and can be related to our first dimension – integration into networks. This can be illustrated by the idea of somebody who has no job and who has little access to information and to transport and is thus deprived and somehow excluded from relational material networks.

The second dimension of exclusion is cultural/social and corresponds to our second dimension – private relations. An example of this would be a person who feels that they are not loved by their family, who has no friends, or who cannot rely on others in case of trouble and is therefore socially excluded. This has to do with the lack of recognition and with the isolation they experience.

The third dimension of exclusion is political and links to our third dimension – civic commitments. A person who cannot vote and who cannot take part in community/society life is suffering from discrimination and a lack of control over their political destiny. A key issue related to civic inclusion is the ability to participate in social and public life or to be represented at different political levels.

Our index builds on Nussbaum's (1999) perspective concerning capabilities in three ways. First, our eco-justice is rooted in a relational anthropology that is close to the one defended by Nussbaum, who integrates human benevolence and strong desire for justice in her theory (Nussbaum 2007), in order to go beyond Rawls' (1971) social contract defined as cooperation for mutual advantage. Moreover, the three dimensions of our index are related to different central capabilities in Nussbaum's ten capabilities list.

The two she considers as fundamental – that is, 'affiliation' and 'practical reason' – are captured through our second (sociocultural) and third (sociopolitical) dimensions:

- Private relationships encompass friendship and love and the quality of 'affiliation'.
- Civic commitment is related to critical reasoning, one major aspect of 'practical reasoning'.
- 'Control over one's political environment' is also captured by variables related to our third dimension (political), such as membership, collective action, and vote.

Finally, by adopting cut-offs below which an individual is considered deprived, we implicitly defend the idea that a certain minimum threshold has to be looked for in each dimension of one's social life. This minimum threshold will be determined differently, depending on the dimensions, either in an absolute way or in a relativistic/cultural way: for example, as far as material wellbeing is concerned, we can consider that the minimal housing space considered as corresponding to decent living conditions differs according to the countries (on climate factors, etc.).

With the above, we combine an approach that strives to ensure entitlements in different aspects of social life with the valorization of the "complex equality" (Walzer 1983) of citizens as a key condition for personal development and social cohesion. This complex equality consists in considering the complementary skills, gifts, and abilities of different persons in different spheres of life, while avoiding a scenario in which some of the winners in one dimension become the winners – and tend to get a monopoly – in all dimensions. A fair society, according to a complex equality criterion, is one in which one person is recognized in at least one sphere of their existence and thus acquires the self-esteem that is a pre-condition for self-respect. This perspective entails a valorization of pluralism in society, as well as a concern for the quality of social bonds and bridges among citizens and groups. The complex equality is reflected in the construction of the RCI by the choice to consider that to be deprived at the index level, a person must accumulate deprivations in all three dimensions.

In this second section, we argue that quantitative index and qualitative surveys are complementary. We stress that the index alone is ill-equipped to analyze the depth and complexity of the social fabric, and needs to be complemented by qualitative interviews and studies from different fields (anthropology, sociology, geography, political science, etc.). Moreover, our RCI can and must be adapted in order to capture different kinds of relations, either within the company (e.g. among staff and between staff and top executives) or between the company and different kinds of stakeholders.

Empirical applications: the importance of RCI for two categories of stakeholders – local populations and suppliers

A company's activity can have effects on the social fabric of different categories of stakeholders: employees, clients, local populations, and suppliers along the value chain. This section focuses on the last two. Surveys led in different countries have allowed us to test the RCI and show using mixed methods how social cohesion can be affected by multinational companies' activities. We studied three companies in four countries (Nigeria, India, Indonesia, Mexico) using this perspective. Results concerning Veolia and a specific category of clients, the slums of Nagpur (India) can be found in Bommier and Renouard (2014) and Bommier et al. (2012). Future work will focus on adapting the RCI to measure companies' impacts on the other categories of stakeholders.[1]

Local populations: oil companies' area of influence in Nigeria (total)

Nigeria has the largest Growth Domestic Product (GDP) in Africa; however, it is ranked 153rd in terms of Human Development Index (HDI), with a score of 0.45, and its poverty rate is 68%.[2] Oil production dates back to 1958, and the oil sector is the greatest contributor to the national budget, accounting for 77% of revenues on average in the 2000s (2012 IMF report on Nigeria, Article 4). The Nigerian federal government has asked oil companies to invest directly in local development and dedicate up to 3% of their annual budgets to finance the Niger Delta Development Commission, created in 2000. With the implementation of the Nigerian Content Act in 2010, the Nigerian State began to organize the development and transfer of skills and expertise to local people and to promote an increase in economic benefits. Oil companies have to meet minimum levels of local employment and local contracting. They also support local programs under memoranda of understanding (MoUs) with communities in the Niger Delta.

Many of the (mainly qualitative) studies undertaken in this region point to the fact that there are clear links between oil production and social issues such as inequalities, social violence and conflicts, environmental pollution, institutional weaknesses, and state disengagement (Duruigbo 2004; Oyefusi 2007; Pérouse de Montclos 2012). As part of a research agreement with Total, our team has been studying the effects of oil activity and of the companies' CSR programs on human development in the region since 2004, using a comparative and evolutionary approach. Qualitative research (Giraud and Renouard 2010; Diongue, Giraud, and Renouard 2011; Renouard, 2011, 2015) has stressed the importance of promoting relational capability in the analysis of oil companies' contributions to local sustainable development.

In addition to the qualitative research, three waves of surveys were led in two local government areas impacted by oil production: Onelga, in Rivers State, where Total and Agip have been operating onshore since the 1960s, and Eastern Obolo, in Akwa Ibom State, where oil is produced offshore. The first two waves concerned more than 1,000 respondents in Onelga and Eastern Obolo. They provide rich information on the socioeconomic and sociopolitical situation of these areas and allow a comparative approach. The 2012 wave also allows estimations of the impact of CSR programs led by the oil companies in Onelga. The third wave was led in 2013 on a specific subsample of about 350 individuals who lived in communities of the Egi clan in Onelga, some of which suffered from a flood in 2012, the other of which formed a "control" group.

While the components of the RCI were decided from a theoretical perspective (they measure key aspects of social cohesion in its different dimensions, as explained *supra*), the specific questions and cut-offs used in Nigeria emerged from qualitative work in the field. Focus groups with village members were conducted and led us to identify what aspects of life and what dimensions of social cohesion are important for them, and how to measure those aspects in the sociocultural context in which they live. The quantitative surveys then included a set of questions that enabled us to compute the RCI in this context, at the individual level based on declarations from the respondents. The 14 components of the RCI could then be measured. Each component is equal to 1 if the person is above the cutoff – that it to say, the capability that this component measures is acquired for this person – and 0 if the person is below the cutoff – which means she is deprived of this capability. The index score was obtained from arithmetic means from the component values. We looked at the effects of oil activity and oil companies' CSR programs on each component separately and on the aggregated index.

Results on RCI and multidimensional poverty in two areas
(2008 and 2012, Onelga and Eastern Obolo)

Our 2008 and 2012 data enable us to make comparisons between the local government areas of Onelga and Eastern Obolo in terms of multidimensional poverty using the Multidimensional Poverty Index (MPI), which entails three dimensions – health, education, and living conditions (Alkire & Santos 2010; Alkire & Foster 2011) – and in terms of RCI.

Results show that Eastern Obolo suffers more from multidimensional poverty than Onelga does. Moreover, poverty declined more in Onelga than in Eastern Obolo between 2008 and 2012, as a consequence of the numerous investments in infrastructures and development projects led by oil companies in Onelga as part of the MoUs, and the much smaller scale on which they participate in local development in Obolo.

On the other hand, relational capabilities were higher in Eastern Obolo than in Onelga in 2008 and remained higher in 2012, although the RCI improved in both areas. Giraud et al. (2013) show how the families of weights chosen to compute the index can be linked to different theories of justice and apply a few examples (utilitarian, Rawlsian, etc.) to the Nigerian case. Through this application, we stress the importance of taking into account social fabric in the measure of local development, especially in vulnerable communities that are subject to inequalities and violence. Indeed, looking at the populations' situation only in terms of conventional poverty with the MPI, one would conclude that Onelga has benefited a lot from the MoUs and that the situation there is much better than in Eastern Obolo. Yet, comparisons in terms of RCI stress that Onelga's development, driven by oil money, happened at the expense of certain forms of social cohesion. Other studies we led in the area using non-experimental econometric methods support this finding.

Impact of CSR programs on MPI and RCI (2012, Onelga)

Using an instrumental variable (IV) approach[3] to the 2012 Onelga data, Giraud, L'Huillier, and Renouard (2014) study the impact of oil companies' training and job programs on the MPI and the RCI. We find that while the job and training programs improve conventional development – the impact on MPI is negative – they have paradoxical effects on RC. Deprivations in the socioeconomic dimension (integration into networks) decrease, whereas deprivations in the second dimension increase due to the programs. The impact on the third dimension, civic commitment, is insignificant and close to zero. A deeper analysis at the component level shows that the decrease in deprivations in the first RCI dimension is mainly explained by better access to transportation, information, and telecommunications. On the other hand, the increase in deprivations in the second RCI dimension is clearly explained with reference to a loss of trust in the community. This side effect of the programs on trust is the biggest in magnitude; it is more important and more significant than the positive effects we find on conventional development through MPI components. One interpretation of this could be that the (unequally spread) improvement in conventional development induced by the job and training programs happens at the expense of social bonds within local communities.

Indeed, this finding confirms some of the conclusions from the qualitative analysis. Interviews led in diverse communities in 2009, 2010, 2011, and 2012 evidenced a growing frustration expressed by community people towards those referred to as "benefit captors" – who have been able to participate in MoU negotiations with the oil companies for years and who give priority to their direct family members. Thus, although the families selected to benefit from the CSR programs are supposed to rotate every year, the same people tend to enjoy the social benefits of the MoUs. This creates rivalries and jealousies within the families themselves.

Impact of a flood on RCI (2012 and 2013, Onelga)

Focusing on a subsample of 14 communities of the Egi clan in Onelga, Giraud, L'Huillier, and Renouard (2017) study the impact of a major flood that affected the area in 2012. Indeed, seven of the surveyed communities were directly affected by the flood, whereas the other seven, located a few kilometres further from the Orashi river, only suffered it indirectly (through rising local prices or displacement of people). In reaction to the flood, the oil company present in the area provided relief materials, including rice, soap, vegetable oil, tomatoes, salt, toilet paper, and truckloads of drinking water. By conducting differences-in-differences estimations using the 2012 and 2013 data, we studied the effects of the flood, and of the relief aid provided by the oil company, on relational capability. This research contributes to the literature on social disasters and social capital, with a focus on the different types of social capital. The second RCI dimension, focused on sociocultural bonds, measures "bonding" relationships, whereas the third dimension, related to political commitment at a larger scale, measures "bridging" relations.

We find that the flood increased trust in the community – interpreted as a measure of bonding social capital – but reduced bridging social capital, measured as participation together with unknown people in common-interest projects. The aid distributed to some people, on the other hand, was associated with higher bridging social capital. The aid was not distributed according to flood damages but mostly according to social status: the "core" communities that host infrastructures of the oil company were more likely to receive aid than the "non-core" ones, and inside a given community, this was also the case for individuals with specific social status (village head, youth leader, women's representative, etc.) compared to "normal" villagers, independently of the flood damages that they suffered.

These results emphasize how a disaster can affect the repartition of bonding and bridging social capital in the short term. They show that it is important to study the impact of such events on the social fabric and not only on economic outcomes, since the reshaping of social capital can have longer-term effects and disrupt local social fabric. They also highlight the need to build social cohesion in vulnerable communities through trustworthy and impartial institutions within the studied communities in the Niger Delta of Nigeria, as our results on the distribution and impact of aid show important disparities in access to opportunities. The effort recently displayed by some oil companies to fight against clientelist relations with local communities' "benefit captors" needs to be encouraged and monitored through renewed internal procedures and mandatory regulations. Currently, there is still a discrepancy between the official new policy of the companies and its implementation, due to the presence of many old players in the field (within the companies and within local communities), who have no interest in changing their habits.

Suppliers/value chain: waste pickers in Mexico, Indonesia, Argentina, and Brazil (Danone)

The RCI was also applied in evaluations of social innovation projects led by Danone in Mexico, Indonesia, Argentina, and Brazil. In Mexico, the RCI was computed, and the impacts of the project on the beneficiaries could be studied through non-experimental quantitative methods. The other projects were evaluated from a qualitative perspective: the RCI was not computed but its main dimensions were studied throughout interviews with the stakeholders. These four programs aim to empower waste pickers who collect recycled plastic that is used in a circular economy value chain to make new water bottles. The analysis shows that the social and political aspects of empowerment (as measured by the last two dimensions of RCI: private relations and civic commitment) are critical levers of change that the company has progressively begun to take into account.

The pepenadores project (Mexico)

The RCI was applied in evaluating a project concerning *pepenadores* (waste pickers) in Northern Mexico. The *pepenadores* project, led by Danone together with a Mexican waste company and a local non-governmental organization (NG), is about the empowerment of landfill waste pickers through the construction of a waste segregation centre in which they can work with safer standards and have access to a range of social interventions (health, education, addiction recovery, money management, etc.). Mixed methods were used for the evaluation, combining survey data with 900 *pepenadores* in the project site and in other landfill sites in Mexico that serve as reference groups and in-depth qualitative interviews with project beneficiaries and stakeholders. As it was the case in Nigeria, the qualitative part of the study – which begun before the main survey – enabled to adapt the questions used to measure the RCI components and cutoff to the sociocultural context. The quantitative methodology was based on two approaches: regression analysis and difference-in-difference analysis.

Our study (L'Huillier and Renouard 2016) stresses that the initial use of the notion of empowerment by the company tends to overemphasize the economic dimension; however, the company has realized, through the project development and evaluation process, that empowerment must be understood also, and primarily, in sociocultural and sociopolitical terms. Indeed, the main levers of empowerment identified are not related to monetary or multidimensional poverty – *pepenadores* at the project site were not poor at baseline according to conventional indices – but they are linked to the waste pickers' collective organization. After 18 months, impacts are found on sociopolitical aspects of empowerment, corresponding to the third dimension of RCI. In particular, the component on collective action is positively impacted by the project. This implies a renewed reflection on the sociopolitical role of enterprises, on the limits of financial cost/benefit analysis, and on the structural and institutional conditions for their contributions to empower the most vulnerable stakeholders in relation to their core business.

Comparison with other recycling projects in Indonesia, Argentina, and Brazil

Field visits to another three waste picker empowerment projects co-funded by Danone in Indonesia, Argentina, and Brazil enable us to go beyond the results of the *pepenadores* project impact evaluation.

In the four cases, it seems essential to take into account the projects' sociocultural and sociopolitical impacts, and not only their economic impacts, in the management of change. In Indonesia, the *pemulung* project was initially centred on the objective of increasing the waste pickers' productivity through bypassing some of the intermediaries (called *bandar*). However, a deeper analysis of the recycling value chain has shown the challenges such a vision could yield, since the *bandar* play a central role in the recycling chain, and in terms of work organization, an individual-based approach is better suited to the cultural context than cooperatives would be. The project was later refocused on Danone's more direct responsibility, regarding its sourcing of recycled plastic and the work conditions of its direct suppliers; at the same time, work in cooperation with the public authorities ensures that the waste pickers reach a minimum level of wellbeing, especially through improved health programs.

The relational and economic effects of such programs can be linked: in the case of Brazil, the project is about organizing small waste-picker cooperatives into a network linked to the national waste-picker movement. This network can secure the prices at which recyclable materials are sold, because, by joining forces, the cooperatives sell higher volumes and gain bargaining power in the negotiations with their buyers. However, the network is also and above all about improving the *catadores'* (waste pickers in Brazil) collective organization, through aspects of the RCI such as facilitating communication between cooperatives of different cities, which used to be more isolated (first RCI dimension); securing the existing jobs through progressive formalization (first RCI dimension); also building trust inside the cooperatives and between different cooperatives (second RCI dimension); and improving the links between waste pickers and the society at large with new partnerships that the network brings to the cooperatives (third RCI dimension).

With respect to the *Cartoneros* project in Argentina, investment from the company happens in the context of a strong partnership between waste-picker cooperatives and the municipality of Buenos Aires: the city has a contract with these cooperatives and pays them for the collection and processing of recyclable waste. This setting facilitates the formalization and improvement of working conditions in the cooperatives. However, due to the difficult economic context of Argentina, the cooperatives explain that they have to stay strongly organized and fight for their rights (such as increases in their salaries when the price level rises). Some specific aspects of the RCI are thus key for *cartoneros'* empowerment in this project, especially in the third dimension, which focuses on civic commitment.

The Argentine and Brazilian cases indeed stress the importance of the institutional context: selective collection is in place in both cases, and the existence of regulations (a national law on waste in Brazil and a local law for the city of Buenos Aires) give a much wider scope to these projects. The contributions of private companies can then be understood as a contribution to global common goods, which take the form of a fairer share of value created through the recycling value chain. Valuing socioeconomic, sociocultural, and sociopolitical aspects of development, rather than focusing primarily on a productivity criterion, shows a transformation process in the company linked to greater consideration of the political role of the company and its shared responsibility towards the business model's contribution to social cohesion.

These field works shows how our RCI enables to analyze the socioeconomic, sociocultural, and sociopolitical dimensions of the quality of life in very different contexts. We are currently customizing our RCI index for other types of stakeholders, such as clients, employees, or investors. Indeed, it can be adapted in order to capture different kinds of relations, either within the company (e.g. among staff and between staff and top executives) or between the company and different kinds of stakeholders. In each and every context, it enables to highlight the importance of the quality of human relations, to build long-term partnerships, based on trust and fairness.

Conclusions

The nature of companies' impacts on social fabric varies according to the companies' activity and context. However, it also depends on stakeholders' decision to cooperate in promoting sustainable social ecosystems and human development versus short-term profitability and on the way in which value created is distributed among all stakeholders – including investors, executive managers, and employees – as highlighted in recent research works in philosophy and economics (Giraud and Renouard 2012a; Fleurbaey and Maniquet 2008).

The above mentioned research has focused on assessing the impact of a core business on its different stakeholders' relational empowerment in a given territory. It highlights how the capabilities approach helps to understand the true drivers of stakeholders' empowerment and development, those being local communities, customers, and employees. A key aspect to explore is the contribution of finance to relational value creation (Renouard 2013), and to the quality of the social fabric within the company and along the value chain. When dealing with investors or ethical funds, our research aims to identify certain relational criteria, which would be relevant and applicable within corporations, in order to assess the relational dimensions of socially responsible investment. These criteria could encompass earnings distribution between different groups of employees (managing directors compared to other groups of employees, for instance); operating a margin structure between a company and its subcontractors; working conditions and social dialogue with subcontractors in coherence with international working law and ILO orientations or company fiscal policy; and especially measures against tax erosion and tax havens, and taxation choices regarding transfer pricing in accordance with recent measures taken by the OECD (2013).

We argue that fair distribution of value created between investors and others stakeholders – such as subcontractors and different categories of employees – inclusive governance, and social objectives of investments can enhance relational capabilities of all stakeholders in a virtuous circle, and that, on the contrary, when equality and fairness is not sufficiently taken into account in the way created value is shared, corporations can highly damage social ecosystems. Our hypothesis is supported by the results of the projects we run in emerging countries such as Nigeria and Mexico, and consistent with international institutions (OECD 2013, BEPS action plan) and political institutions (UE 2011, Common consolidated corporate tax base) recent decisions, as well as research results in economics and social sciences that have highlighted how inequalities contribute to the pollution of the planet (Laurent 2013) and the deterioration of social bonds (Wilkinson and Pickett 2009; Stiglitz 2012). Indices such as the RCI, combined with qualitative methods, can be useful tools in helping organizations define most effective corporate responsibilities towards the creation of lasting relational value: it proposes thresholds to achieve, which are not only limits, but long-term goal corporations should promote.

Notes

1 A draft version of the index adapted to the workplace to measure employees' relational capability in France is presented in the Appendix.
2 Data from the World Bank database, using the absolute poverty line of USD 1.25 per day, for 2010.
3 The IV method is an econometric approach which can be used when the explanatory variables of a regression are correlated with the error term. IV can produce consistent causal estimates using a variable called instrument – in our case, the villages' status as defined by the companies – that affects the independent variable only through the explanatory variable of interest.

References

Algan, Y. and Cahuc, P. 2013. "Trust, institutions and economic development." *Handbook of Economic Growth*, vol. 1A–2013.

Alkire, S. 2005. *Valuing Freedoms: Sen's Capability Approach and Poverty Reduction*. Oxford: Oxford University Press.

Alkire, S. 2007. "The missing dimensions of poverty data: An introduction." OPHI Working Paper ophiwp001. Queen Elizabeth House, University of Oxford. http://ideas.repec.org/p/qeh/ophiwp/ophiwp001.html.

Alkire, S. and Foster, J. 2011. "Counting and multidimensional poverty measurement." *Journal of Public Economics* 95 (7–8): 476–487.

Alkire, S. and Santos, E. 2010. "Acute multidimensional poverty: A new index for developing countries." OPHI Working Papers, 38. OPHI, Oxford University.

Aristotle. 1999 (350 AD). *Politics*. Translated by Keyt, D. Oxford: Clarendon Press.

Aristotle. 2009 (350 AD). *Nicomachean Ethics*. Translated by Ross, D. and edited by Brown, L. Oxford: Oxford World's Classics.

Bernard, P. 1999. "La Cohésion Sociale: Critique D'un Quasi-Concept." *Lien Social et Politiques – RIAC* 41: 47–59.

Boltanski, L. and Chapiello, E. 2005. *The New Spirit of Capitalism* (Le nouvel esprit du capitalisme, Gallimard, 1999). London: Verso.

Bommier, S., Giraud, G., Renouard, C., Zerah, M. H. and Zimmer, A. 2012. "Veolia's project in Nagpur: Water supply in slums and stakeholder engagement." *ESSEC IRENE Institute Research Program "CODEV – Companies and Development" in partnership with CSH*. New Delhi: Centre de Sciences Humaines.

Bommier, S. and Renouard, C. 2014. "On equity in India's water supply public – Private partnerships." *ESSEC Working paper. Document de Recherche ESSEC/Centre de recherche de l'ESSEC*. ISSN: 1291–9616. WP 1411.

Bourdieu, P. 1980. "Le capital social." *Actes de la recherche en sciences sociales* 31 (January): 2–3.

Burt, R. 1992. *Structural Holes: The Social Structure of Competition*. Harvard, MA: Harvard University Press.

Capron, M. and Quairel-Lanoizelée, F. 2015. *L'entreprise Dans La Société. Une Question Politique*. Paris: La Découverte.

Coleman J. 1988. "Social capital in the creation of human capital." *American Journal of Sociology* 94: 95–120.

D'Iribarne, P. 1993. "La science économique et la barrière du sens." *L'Année sociologique (1940/1948)* 43: 341–356.

D'Iribarne, P. 2003. *The logic of honor: National traditions and corporate management* (La Logique de L'honneur. Paris: Le seuil, 1993).

D'Iribarne, P. 2015. "L'univers Mental et Les Attentes Des Pepenadores." Internal report for Danone. CEREBE.

Diongue, A., Giraud, G. et Renouard, C. 2011. "Measuring the contribution of extractive industries to local development: the case of oil companies in Nigeria." ESSEC Working Paper 1109.

Donaldson, T. and Preston, L. E. (1995). "The stakeholder theory of the corporation: Concepts, evidence, and implications." *Academy of management Review*, 20(1): 65–91.

Duruigbo, E. (2004). Managing oil revenues for socio-economic development in Nigeria: The case for community-based trust funds. *NCJ Int'l L. & Com. Reg.* 30: 121.

European Commission. 2011. Communication from the commission to the commission to the European Parliament, the council, the European economic and social committee of the regions, A renewed EU strategy 2011-14 for Corporate Social Responsibility. § 0681. Available on http://eur-lex.europa.eu/legal-content/EN/TXT/?uri=CELEX:52011DC0681

Fleurbaey, M. and Maniquet, F. 2008. "Fair social orderings." *Economic Theory* 34: 25–45.

Fraser, N. 2009. *Scales of Justice: Reimagining Political Space in a Globalizing World*. New York: Columbia University Press.

Giraud, G., L'Huillier, H. et Renouard, C. 2014. "Relational capability as a measure of development." Documents de travail du Centre d'Economie de la Sorbonne.

Giraud, G., L'Huillier, H. et Renouard, C. 2017. "Crisis and relief in the Niger delta (2012–2013). Assessment of the impact of a flood on relational capabilities." *Oxford Development Studies* (In press).

Giraud, G. et Renouard, C. 2010. "Mesurer la contribution des entreprises au développement local: le cas des pétroliers au Nigeria." *Revue française de gestion*, 36(208–209): 101–115.

Giraud, G. and Renouard, C. (eds). 2012a. *20 Propositions pour réformer le Capitalisme*. Paris: Champs Flammarion.

Giraud, G. and Renouard, C. 2012b. *Le Facteur 12*. Paris: Carnet Nord.

Giraud, G., Renouard, C., L'Huillier, H., de la Martiniere, R. and Sutter, C. 2013. "Relational capability: A multidimensional approach." *ESSEC Working Paper 1306*.

Jamali, D. (2008). "A stakeholder approach to corporate social responsibility: A fresh perspective into theory and practice." *Journal of Business Ethics* 82(1): 213–231.

Kant, I. 2003 (1785) *Groundwork for the Metaphysics of Morals*. Edited by Hill, E.T. and Zweig, A. Oxford: Oxford Philosophical Texts.

Laurent, E. 2013. "The social-ecological approach: Connecting the inequality and environmental crises." 16 October. Boston, MA: Tellus Institute.

L'Huillier, H. et Renouard, C. 2016. "Can social innovation drive business transformation? The case of a waste-picker empowerment project in Mexico." (Submitted article)

McWilliams, A. and Siegel, D. 2001. "Corporate social responsibility: A theory of the firm perspective." *Academy of Management Review* 26(1): 117–127.

Mill, J. S. 1861. *Utilitarianism*. Oxford: Oxford University Press.

Neron, P.Y. 2015. "Rethinking the very idea of egalitarian markets and corporations: Why relationships might matter more than distribution." *Business Ethics Quarterly*, 25: 1–32.

Nussbaum, M. C. 1999. *Women and Human Development*. Oxford: Oxford University Press.

Nussbaum, M. C. 2000. "The costs of tragedy: some moral limits of cost-benefit analysis." *The Journal of Legal Studies* 29(S2): 1005–1036.

Nussbaum, M. C. 2007. *Frontiers of Justice*. Oxford: Oxford University Press.

Oyefusi, A. 2007. *Oil And The Propensity To Armed Struggle In The Niger Delta Region Of Nigeria*. (WB Policy Research Working Paper No. 4194). The World Bank.

OECD. 2013. *Action plan on base erosion and profit shifting*. OECD Publishing. Available at: http://dx.doi.org/10.1787/9789264202719-en

Pérouse de Montclos, M. A. 2012. Boko Haram, Terrorism, and Islamism in Nigeria: A Religious Uprising, a Political Contest, or a Social Protest ? Paris: Sciences-Po working paper.

Putnam, R. 2000. *Bowling Alone: The Collapse and Revival of American Community*. New York: Simon and Schuster.

Rawls, J. 1971. *A Theory of Justice*. Cambridge: Harvard University Press.

Renouard, C. 2007. *La Responsabilité Éthique Des Multinationales*. Paris: Presses universitaires de France.

Renouard, C. 2011. "Corporate social responsibility, utilitarianism, and the capabilities approach." *Journal of Business Ethics* 98(1): 85–97.

Renouard, C. 2013. *Ethique et Entreprise*. Paris: Editions de l'Atelier, 2nd ed. 2015.

Renouard, C. 2015. "Pétrole et lien social. Pour une responsabilité politique de l'entreprise." *Revue française de socio-économie*, Hors-série 16: 89–104.

Renouard, C., er Ezvan, C. 2018. Corporate social responsibility towards human development: A capabilities framework. *Business Ethics: A European Review*, 27(2): 144–155.

Ricoeur, P. 1991. *Lectures. Autour du politique*, Tome 1, Paris: le Seuil.

Sen, A. 1999. *Development as freedom*. New York: Oxford University Press.

Stiglitz, J. 2012. *The Price of Inequality. How Today's Divided Society Endangers Our Future*. London: Norton.

Vallaeys, F. 2013. *Pour une vraie responsabilité sociale*. Paris: PUF.

Walzer, M. 1983. *Spheres of Justice*. New York: Basic Books.

Wilkinson, R. and Pickett, K. 2009. *The Spirit Level: Why More Equal Societies Almost Always Do Better.* Allen Lane, UK: Penguin

Wolff, J. and De-Shalit, A. 2007. *Disadvantage.* New York: Oxford University Press.

Woolcock, M. and Narayan, D. 2000. "Implications for development theory, research, and policy." *The World Bank Research Observer* 15(2): 225–249.

Young, I. M. 2006. "Responsibility and global justice: A social connection model." *Social Philosophy & Policy Foundation* 23(01): 102–130.

Zandvliet, L. and Anderson, M. 2009. *Getting It Right: Making Corporate-Community Relations Work.* Sheffield, UK: Greenleaf.

Appendix

Relational capabilities at the workplace: dimensions and components

Dimension	Component	Deprived if
Access to socioeconomic conditions enabling social integration	Type of contract	No stable contract
	Remuneration level	To be defined according to local and international standards
	Access to health, retirement, and unemployment insurance	No social insurance in at least one of the three dimensions (health, retirement, and unemployment insurance)
	Diversity and mutual respect	Suffers from discrimination in at least one dimension (gender, age, religion, ethnic origin, or type/level of studies)
	Access to specific support in case of vulnerability	Has no specific support when in situation of vulnerability (pregnancy, sickness, seniority, disability)
	Collective representation	Does not know or does not take part in labour unions or other collective representative organisation
Private relations within the company	Trust in management, colleagues, and subordinates	Does not trust management, colleagues or subordinates
	Trust from management, colleagues, and subordinates	Does not receive trust testimony from management, colleagues, or subordinates for more than 1 year
	Friendship	Has no close friend within the company or among the alumni network
	Mutual aid or support among colleagues	No support given or received during the previous month
Work meaning, personal, and civic commitments	Work meaning	I see meaning in my work less than 10% of the time
	Turnover	I want to quit my position as soon as possible
	Trust in companies' partners	No trust in unknown people outside the company
	Solidarity with people outside the companies	Less than one day per year spent on social activities during working time
	Time available outside work for other commitments	No time available for personal, social, or ecological commitments outside work

Part II

Dialogical and communicational foundations of stakeholder engagement

2.1 Communicatively constituted stakeholders

Advancing a communication perspective in stakeholder relations

Chiara Valentini

Introduction

Research shows that relationship management is a central tenant in stakeholder management, since organisations do not manage the stakeholders themselves but their relationships with them. Effective stakeholder relationship management is a proactive activity that influences organisational governance. Today, it is undoubtedly true that organisations of any kind cannot operate and survive without the involvement of key internal and external stakeholders, such as employees, investors, consumers and suppliers, defined as a group of individuals with specific claims or legitimacy towards an organisation's activities (Freeman, 1984), but it is also true that they cannot operate or survive without individuals who have a looser connection to the organisation, such as the general public or those considered fringe groups (Hart and Sharma, 2004). This is because a wide range of other, non-traditional individuals have become important players if not in running the organisation then in establishing its image and reputation. An individual or any social actor may at any time turn into a 'public', that is, a group of people who face a problem, recognise it and organise themselves to address it (Dewey, 1927). When a problem is caused or perceived to be caused by an organisation, publics, known or unknown, may organise themselves to influence that organisation and inevitably turn into stakeholders. As a result, when setting their corporate strategies, organisations cannot avoid listening to the demands of stakeholders and unspecified publics who may come to show some symbolic resources, for instance, through demonstrations, boycotting or verbal attacks. To effectively manage stakeholder relations, organisations first need to define and identify their key stakeholders as well as those publics who are affected by their activities.

Research on stakeholder management increased dramatically after the seminal work by Freeman in the early 1980s which defined a stakeholder as 'any group or individual who can affect or is affected by the achievement of the organisation's objectives' (Freeman, 1984, p. 46). However, research on stakeholder definition and salience is often divergent and displays a lack of agreement on who should be considered a stakeholder (Laplume et al., 2008). Early works propose loose definitions of stakeholders based on concepts such as internal versus external; primary versus secondary (Clarkson, 1995); or derivative versus normative (Phillips, 2003); and some even base their definitions on instrumental understandings, such as anyone who has a material interest in an organisation (Carroll, 1993; Donaldson and Preston, 1995) or anyone who has power and a stake in an organisation's performance (Jones, 1995). One problem with existing stakeholder identification models is that they tend to look for specific characteristics of a stake (see also Reeds, 1999) and do not necessarily help to identify those groups of individuals who may affect or are affected by an organisation but do not possess specific material stakes. Today, with the arrival of social media, any digitally active individual, whether or not considered a stakeholder, can acquire social resources and thus potentially affect an organisation's reputation. By attacking corporate image through the spreading of negative online content, any digital, organised or unorganised, entity can reach and influence key stakeholders that are digitally active on social media. It is therefore paramount to understand how organisations can identify those volatile and outspoken individuals who may possess some symbolic stakes. Can communication theories help organisations to identify and define them? And, if so, what role does communication can play in stakeholder relationship management?

A number of scholars (e.g., Carroll, 2015; Crane and Livesey, 2003; Koschmann, 2016) have suggested that the crucial element of stakeholder relations is communication. Organisational interest can be appraised through a careful observation of people's communicative behaviours, that is, what people say, talk about, share with others, what they read, watch and listen to and so on. Stakeholder communication has emerged as an important area of scholarly interest in stakeholder management literature (Andriof et al., 2003); organisational communication literature (Koschmann, 2016); and public relations and corporate communication literature (Romenti et al., 2014). Since most stakeholders are *homines narrantes* (Vasquez, 1993, 1994), that is, narrating, speaking and communicating humans, stakeholder-to-stakeholder influence is a communicative action (Mariconda and Lurati, 2015). However, the presence of communication theory in stakeholder management is still scarce, and when it is used, communication is often conceptualised as a tactical activity or as device for socially constructing ethical norms in organisational decision-making (Haas and Deetz, 2000; Meisenbach, 2006).

This conceptual chapter intends to advance early scholarly discussions on the role of communication in stakeholder relations by offering additional insights to the field of stakeholder relationship management. Specifically, the chapter will touch upon three major themes: 1) the nature of people's communicative behaviours and their empowerment to the status of a stakeholder, 2) the nature of relationships and relational dynamics and 3) the nature of stakeholder engagement and relational expectations. These three themes will be discussed by drawing insights from stakeholder management, organisational communication, public relations and corporate communication literatures. The chapter will conclude by offering reflections on the contribution of a communicative perspective in stakeholder relationship management.

Moving forward: on the need for a communication perspective in today's complex stakeholder environment

Recent societal and technological developments have challenged the suitability of existing stakeholder identification and prioritisation models in helping organisations navigate complex stakeholder relational environments. Increasing stakeholder vocality and the emergence of unknown stakeholders, that is, 'those of whom organisations are not necessarily aware of, but who have a stake in organisations and can affect positively or negatively organisations' images' (Sedereviciute and Valentini, 2011, p. 222), are two of the current manifestations of such developments. The widespread diffusion of easier and cheaper information and communication technologies coupled with growing social movement actions are another two phenomena that suggest a more central role of communication in stakeholder definition and salience (Valentini et al., 2016). The penetration of digital media in particular has provided the means through which people can make public claims and organise social actions that affect organisations. Power can be gained through the means of communication (Deetz and Mumby, 1990). When individuals use their network to talk about organisations and are able to influence the level of knowledge and thus the perception of organisational behaviours among network members, they gain legitimacy, even if they had not previously been considered key stakeholders (Sedereviciute and Valentini, 2011). Communication empowers individuals to the extent that anyone can become a stakeholder at any point of time; it only needs an individual to recognise that he/she has an issue with or a stake in an organisation and to request organisational legitimisation by using communication to influence organisations.

Today, organisational legitimacy reaches beyond performance to include social and environmental legitimacy. Individuals can indirectly affect organisations when they affect organisational image and reputation through active communicative behaviours, such as information forwarding or sharing behaviours (cf., Kim and Grunig, 2011). Non-stakeholders' active communicative behaviours can then impact key stakeholders. Studies on intra-agenda setting theory, for instance, show that contents published on social media are increasingly picked up by journalists and used to develop news media agenda in traditional media outlets (see for e.g., Messer and Distaso, 2008); they thus enjoy a spill-over effect among the general public. Individuals can also harm organisational activities directly, for instance, by creating alliances – here communication becomes an instrument for setting up such alliances – with existing key stakeholders (Rowley and Moldoveanu, 2003) through collaborative activities initiated via specific communicative actions. Studies on stakeholder mobilisation, in fact, point out that setting alliances among different stakeholder groups is a strategy used by stakeholders with limited power and legitimacy to increase these attributes with the scope of affecting organisational activities (Bliss, 2002; den Hond and de Bakker, 2008).

Despite the important role of communication in affecting stakeholders' opinions and actions, the communicative nature of stakeholders is not captured by early management definitions, which neglect to acknowledge that communication is a central element in stakeholder definition and salience. When early models on stakeholder management refer to communication, they only include it vaguely in the proposed organisational responses or see it simply as a linear process of transmitting organisational contents.[1] For instance, Freeman's (1984) generic strategies and subsequent development by Savage et al.'s (1991) and Rowley's (1997) network-based organisational responses to stakeholder pressures do not include any reference to communication theories in their strategies for the management of stakeholder relations. Harrison and St John (1996) refer to communication when discussing partnering tactics between organisations and stakeholders but do not offer insights into stakeholder communication. In management literature, communication is generally favoured as a response to stakeholders' concerns or as a device to discursively construct ethical standards in validating and acting upon stakeholders' claims (cf., Koschmann, 2016) but not as a central tenant for stakeholder definition.

Tentative attempts towards communication-based considerations can be found, but these are not systematic or established. In this context, it is important to mention the work that has addressed questions of claim validity and ethical approaches in the multiple-stakeholder model through Habermas' (1984, 1987, 1990, 1996) ideas on discourse ethics and communicative actions. Haas and Deetz (2000) and Deetz (2003) argued for the important role of communication in setting up managerial decisions regarding stakeholder claims, their legitimacy and possible managerial actions. From a Habermasian standpoint, stakeholder claims are discursively validated through communicative actions, and organisational communication should promote the standpoint of the 'generalised others' (Benhabib, 1992). Through communicative interactions that occur between organisations and stakeholders, an inter-subjective recognition of validity claims can occur. On similar grounds, Meisenbach (2006) proposed a communication-based framework for the development of an organisational ethical decision-making approach. Her model suggests that organisations follow five steps to effectively enact a discourse ethics which is essential to develop ethical standards. At the same time, discourse ethics can be used by individuals and organisations to discursively challenge organisational norms. In these efforts, communication is conceived as a device for socially constructing, validating or challenging claims and stakes (Haas and Deetz, 2000; Meisenbach, 2006; Reeds, 1999), but it is not understood as an embedded element in stakeholder definition and salience. Other scholars such as Crane and Livesey (2003), Fineman and Clark (1996) and Winn (2001) recognise that the concept of stakeholder is socially constructed; that is, stakeholder identification is per se an act of working together to construct the very essence of a stakeholder. Social constructivists acknowledge differences in understanding the same social reality and explain such differences by arguing that there are always multiple meanings for every word, symbol or event. From this standpoint, the concept of stakeholder is situational, is constructed in a social context such as the organisation and can vary from one organisation to another. To understand situational meanings and social realities, one would need to study how people communicatively express their understanding. At best, the social constructivist perspective on the stakeholder acknowledges communication as a tool to study differences in managerial understanding of the stakeholder concept, but it does not explicitly offer a communication-based definition of a stakeholder.

Crane and Livesey (2003) are among those management scholars who advance some reflections on a communication-based understanding of stakeholder relations by drawing on public relations literature. First, they build on the social constructivist view on stakeholders and acknowledge that each stakeholder group cannot be considered a homogenous group of individuals and that, consequently, the management of stakeholder relations should consider intra-stakeholder differences, which can arguably be observed by looking at stakeholders' communicative behaviours. Second, they borrow communication theories to propose organisational communication responses that are tailored to such differences and highlight that dialogue strategy is not inevitably the best approach for all stakeholder groups. However, their understanding of communication is for the most part a functionalistic view that stresses an instrumental understanding of communication as a means to reach out to, engage and create dialogue with stakeholders; it does not understand communication as central tenant that defines the very essence of a stakeholder. A recent attempt to foster a communication perspective in organisational stakeholder relations has been made by the organisational communication scholar Koschmann (2016), who offers three theoretical propositions on the communicative constitution nature of organisations' networks, stakes and relations with stakeholders. This is one of the most recent efforts that tries to systematically address the question of the contribution of communication theory to the management and, more specifically, stakeholder management field. Although Koschmann (2016) presents meaningful propositions for championing a communication perspective on stakeholder theory, further arguments can be put forward to enhance and extend the discussion. This chapter takes its point of departure in Koschmann's (2016) work and early contributions on constitutive communication in organisational settings (e.g. Arnaud and Mills, 2012; Deetz, 1992, 1995; Kuhn, 2008) to further elaborate on the contribution of a communication perspective to stakeholder theory. It presents reflections drawn from public relations and corporate communication literature that address the three themes outlined above (the nature of people's communicative behaviours, the nature of relationships and relational dynamics and the nature of stakeholder engagement and relational expectations). In the following sections, these three themes are presented and discussed.

On the nature of people's communicative behaviours

Public relations literature has paid significant attention to publics' communicative behaviours and proposed theories to identify relevant publics based on their communicative actions. Communication is recognised as an endemic characteristic of human beings (Kim and Krishna, 2014) and thus the study of people's behaviours should begin with a study of people's communicative actions. While the concept of a public is somewhat different from that of a stakeholder – publics arise on their own and select the organisation from which they will demand attention, whereas organisations can choose their markets and their stakeholders (Grunig and Repper, 1992) – the two concepts may overlap; a public is generally a stakeholder, but a stakeholder is not necessarily a public, as the latter is traditionally defined constitutively in relation to an issue. Literature on stakeholder management also includes loose definitions of stakeholders that cover groups which have interests in the corporation regardless of the corporation's interest in them (Clarkson, 1995). In this broader definition, the concept of a stakeholder is interchangeable with that of a public as it captures those loose relations with groups of individuals with societal and public demands.

Vasquez (1993, 1994) is among the few scholars who have proposed a communication-based definition of public/stakeholder. He introduces the concept of *homo narrans* to define and identify publics as a rhetorical community of individuals. A public – as a group of concerned individuals – emerges through spontaneous debates, discussions and arguments over time. It is through active communicative behaviours of sharing stories, fantasies and themes that people create and influence meanings and realities around situations, events and even organisations. The situational theory of publics (Grunig, 1997) and follow-up situational theory of problem solving (Kim and Grunig, 2011) offer a communication view on stakeholder salience by proposing to identify publics by their active versus passive communicative behaviours. According to Grunig and Hunt (1984), communicative behaviours are determined by an individual's problem recognition, constraint recognition and level of involvement with a specific issue. Depending on these three variables and the type of communicative behaviour, publics can be classified as *nonpublic, latent public, aware public* and *active public*.

The study of communicative behaviours has evolved over the years. To identify and prioritise stakeholders, other public relations scholars have proposed either to include other criteria in the situational theory of publics or to combine classical situational and socio-psychological notions with diverse public relations and communication theories. For example, Hallahan (2001) proposes that we identify publics based on their knowledge and level of involvement in the issue/event that constitutively form the basis for the formation of public groups. Rawlins (2006) offers an integrative approach that incorporates elements of organisation-public relationships, the situational theory of publics and publics' communicative behaviours. For the online environment, Sedereviciute and Valentini (2011) propose that we identify stakeholders via their communicative behaviours (posting and sharing behaviours) on social networking sites by building on notions of social network analysis and the theory of stakeholder salience put forward by Mitchell et al. (1997). These public relations theoretical underpinnings essentially provide organisations with insights on what, when and how people communicate with each other. They contribute to the understanding of stakeholder behaviours by adding important, communication-based features that can be taken into account during diverse stakeholder relationship management processes (Freeman, 1984; Preble, 2008). They offer a communication perspective on stakeholder definition and salience that is situational and contextual and in which communication plays a key role.

Given that most organisational stakeholders are human social actors, a communication perspective in stakeholder definition and salience represents a germane approach to overcome the limitations of managerial approaches that too often define stakeholders from rational, objective and often material parameters that tend to simplify the complexity of today's stakeholder environment. A communication-based definition of stakeholders that focuses on stakeholder communicative behaviours is fundamentally different from other widely accepted approaches to stakeholder definition and salience, which tend to refer to criteria such as legitimacy, power, interests, rights and type of relationship with the organisation (e.g., Ackermann and Eden, 2011; Mitchell et al., 1997; Savage et al., 1991). A communication-centred approach in stakeholder definition suggests identifying communicative actions that express people's claims and interests in organisations – what people communicate and how they communicate – as main criterion for stakeholder salience.

The communication-centred approach also addresses an important criticism of existing theories of stakeholder definition and salience. Stakeholder definition and salience is not something that is decided by managers based on their discretion (Friedman and Miles, 2006); instead, it emerges from stakeholders' communicative behaviours and their level of engagement with organisational matters. This bottom-up approach is contextual and situational, but it is beyond managerial discretion. An organisation's range of stakeholders can vary substantially from case to case. Besides primary stakeholders, such as employees, investors, customers, consumers and authorities, organisations need to address the concerns and demands of *stake-seekers* – those individuals who show organisational interest and expect to receive adequate attention – and *homo narrans stakeholders* – those individuals who may earn the status of stakeholders as a result of their communicative behaviours (either supportive or antagonist) towards organisations and their capacity to influence key stakeholders' opinions (Mariconda and Lurati, 2015).

On the nature of relationships and relational dynamics

A communication approach to stakeholder relations offers several reflections on the nature of relationships and the complex relational dynamics that organisations face. Today, successful organisations are stakeholder-oriented organisations, that is, organisations whose mission, vision, values, objectives and overall activities are driven by a desire to meet stakeholder concerns and build stakeholder relationships. Stakeholder-oriented organisations promote stakeholder engagement through communications that are two-way, dialogic and based on reciprocal respect (see Heath and Palenchar, 2008; Morsing and Schultz, 2006; Payne and Calton, 2002). Research shows that positive organisation-stakeholder relationships result in positive corporate reputation (Grunig and Hung-Baesecke, 2015); positive organisational identification; and job satisfaction and behavioural intent (Bruning and

Ledingham, 2015) and that they are essential for constructive NGO-corporate dialogues (van Huijstee and Glasbergen, 2008).

With only a few exceptions (for instance, contractual relations where a contract tangibly describes the terms and conditions of an organisation-stakeholder relation), relationships are intangible assets which, just like reputations, are sustained by communication. Communication plays a key role in informing stakeholders about corporate actions, and thus, it contributes to reputation and relationship management activities (Fombrun and van Riel, 1997). Communication is a powerful device to set relationships into action. Through specific communications, organisations try to reach existing and potential stakeholders and encourage them to engage in activities that support them. Advocacy campaigns may offer symbolic as well as material reasons for citizens and interest parties to become engaged with organisations, for example, through stakeholder initiatives such as signing petitions, donating money or attending public demonstrations. Marketing communication campaigns, for instance, can deliver product promises that may motivate consumers and potential consumers to buy a product, follow and support a brand or even engage in endorsing actions on behalf of a company. These types of stakeholder behaviours towards certain brands represent manifestations of consumer-brand relationships (Schultz and Schultz 2004). Studies concerning consumer-brand relationships point out that stakeholder engagement in marketing initiatives and product endorsement are more effective in acquiring new customers than direct advertisements (Daneshvary and Schwer, 2000; Dean and Biswas, 2001). By engaging certain key individuals who are centrally placed in a dense network, organisations can benefit from third-party endorsements that can influence a larger group of potential consumers and customers via positive communication exchanges, that is, people speaking positively and sharing positive views about an organisation/brand (see also Kozinets et al., 2010). These specific stakeholders' communicative behaviours are important relational outcomes for business objectives.

Furthermore, a communication perspective on stakeholder relations provides a different view on how relationships are formed and on relational dynamics. Stakeholder relations are formed and sustained through communications (Koschmann, 2016) which play a key role in determining with whom an individual has an interest in being connected. Communication functions as a bond to connect stakeholders with similar interests. Here the focus is on the type of content shared but also on the role of language and discourse in setting a communication context that attracts stakeholder interests. The phenomenon of social media is a perfect example, that is, Internet-based applications that allow for the creation and exchange of user-generated contents (Valentini and Kruckeberg, 2012). Social media has become so popular because of people's interest in developing social networking relations with others who share similar interests or offer contents of interest. Many organisations today have tapped into this opportunity to reach a potentially large group of customers and other relevant stakeholders, yet not all organisations have successfully leveraged the dialogic potential of social media for stakeholder engagement (Elving and Postma, 2017).

Online social networking relations result from people's online communicative behaviours (Valentini, 2015; Valentini et al., 2016). However, these relations can be volatile. Today in particular, social networking relations as well as publics can be 'formed and dissolved more quickly, depending on their [stakeholders'] interests and concerns' (Valentini et al., 2012, p. 876). Stakeholders do not need organisational communications to learn about corporate actions; they can acquire information on organisational behaviours from other sources; for instance, from network members who may not be in a specific organisation's stakeholder group. Information flows move across the network with or without an organisation as their central hub of communicative interaction (Rowley, 1997; Sedereviciute and Valentini, 2011). Hence, relationships exist beyond organisational involvement, among and between stakeholders and publics (Rittenhofer and Valentini, 2015; Valentini et al., 2012).

A communication perspective on stakeholder relations also offers insights on the role of organisations in relational networks. In general, scholars' language in management literature depicts organisations as capable of 'managing' stakeholder relations, but, in reality, organisations are not in control of stakeholder relations, as it takes the willingness of two entities to establish and maintain a relationship. Relationships are formed only if there is a mutual acknowledgement as legitimate actors and interest in being in a relationship. Hence, organisations cannot literally manage stakeholder relationships (Valentini et al., 2012), but they can manage their organisational behaviours which carry specific meanings and thus indirectly communicate something about them. They can also manage their relational communications (Finne and Grönroos, 2009), that is, communications whose scope is building relationships, in so far relationships are formed via communicative interactions. In fact, the use of different communication forms and genres plays a key role in the development of collaborative or conflictual relationships.

Organisations can carefully plan, craft and implement communications and activities that help them to cultivate and sustain stakeholder relationships. However, this does not guarantee that stakeholders receive and interpret these communications as the organisations planned. They can also establish a stakeholder relationship-based governance (Falconi et al., 2014) to facilitate organisational activities, mechanisms, processes and relations by which organisations are controlled and directed in order to sustain stakeholder relations. However, even if organisations can manage relational communications, they need to consider that relationships are not linear, dyadic interactions between organisations and their stakeholders (Rowley, 1997) and that, in a relational network, they are one of many organisations trying to connect with a myriad of current and potential *stake-holders*; *stake-watchers*; *stake-keepers* (Fassin, 2009); and *stake-seekers*. External influencers and other competing organisations that are well placed in a network can, in fact, act as moderators of organisational communications to key stakeholders in the network by filtering the information that stakeholders can obtain about an organisation or simply by providing their own interpretation of specific organisational behaviours. They can influence the stakeholder's perception of and attitude towards an organisation despite that organisation's relational communication efforts. For example, activist organisations are already using mediated communications to build relationships with publics and are thus leveraging their positions against corporations and political entities (Bliss, 2002; Taylor et al., 2001).

On the nature of stakeholder engagement and relational expectations

Perhaps the most widely used notion of communication in stakeholder relationship management is the understanding of communication as a means for stakeholder engagement through dialogue. The relevant literature is relatively rich with studies on stakeholder dialogue and engagement and definitions of these two concepts. Engagement typically presumes a 'demonstration of positive regard for stakeholders/publics' input, experiences and needs' (Taylor and Kent, 2014, p. 391) and 'interaction with stakeholders/publics for relational purposes outside of an immediate problem/issue' (Taylor and Kent, 2014, p. 391). Engagement intentions are communicatively constructed and shared, and expectations about engagement actions are unfolded through the use of specific genre and language in organisational communications. Expectations are typically defined as the beliefs of what will or should happen, affecting how stakeholders make decisions (Podnar and Golob, 2007). Expectations help stakeholders define their opportunities for being heard by, and thus their opportunities to influence, organisations.

Stakeholder engagement is a communication-constructed activity. Organisations show their interests in certain stakeholder groups and their own engagement through specific communicative and behavioural actions. There is a generalised consensus that stakeholder dialogue, as a specific type of communication, is paramount for engaging stakeholders (Taylor and Kent, 2014) and developing stakeholder relations. Dialogue is a two-way communication flow in which individuals reciprocally acknowledge the other party. It assumes that parties come to a relationship with openness and respect (Buber, 1970; Kent and Taylor, 1998). Dialogue is an indicator of organisational willingness to listen and take into consideration stakeholders' concerns, and these are indeed necessary prerequisites for stakeholder engagement as well as an indicator of a socially responsible organisation (Romenti et al., 2014). Organisations that carry out asymmetrical communications with stakeholders, that is, those communications whose goal is to achieve short-term attitude change rather than mutual understanding with stakeholders, have no genuine interest in engaging stakeholders, but rather in persuading them to accept or even adopt the organisational perspective. In other words, no stakeholder group will feel thoroughly engaged with an organisation if it does not believe it will be genuinely listened to and accounted for when organisations make decisions. Dialogue is, thus, an important component for gaining and maintaining organisational legitimacy. A positive reputation (Burchell and Cook, 2013) is often a prerequisite for developing mutual and beneficial relationships and is considered the most ethical communication strategy to keep accountability and responsibility towards stakeholders high on the corporate agenda (Johansen and Nielsen, 2011).

Implicit within the stakeholder management literature is the role of communication in the management of stakeholder relations. However, in this literature, communication is mostly reduced to a means to respond to stakeholder concerns rather than a theoretical lens to understand how stakeholders form perceptions of organisations' engagement and relational intents. From a communication standpoint, perceptions emerge as a result of organisational communications carrying specific meanings (see Figure 2.1.1).

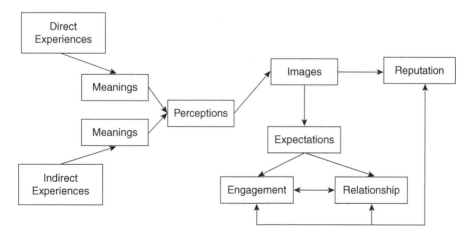

Figure 2.1.1 Role of communication in the construction of engagement and relationship expectations

Source: Own elaboration.

These are constructed out of an individual's direct and indirect experience with organisations. Grunig and Hung-Baesecke (2015) use the terms 'experiential reputation' or 'first-order reputation' to refer those perceptions that are constructed through direct experiences with organisations and use 'reputational reputations' or 'second-order reputations' to refer to those perceptions that are indirectly constructed through communications that stakeholders receive from the organisation and other non-official sources (Grunig and Hung-Baesecke, 2015). Direct and indirect experiences that are shared with others carry meanings, because people use various adjectives, expressions and idioms to talk about their or others' experiences. These meanings are reflected among stakeholders and condensed into group perceptions.

Perceptions determine stakeholders' images of an organisation. Organisational images may turn into reputation, which, in turn, can impact stakeholders' expectations on engagement and relational opportunities. These latter two factors can also impact reputation. Hence, according to the flow chart, reputation and relationship are interdependent constructs (Grunig and Hung-Baesecke, 2015). Similarly, engagement activities reinforce stakeholder relationships and solid stakeholder relationships ease stakeholder engagement.

Within this process, communication is fundamental. Metaphorically speaking, it is the fuel that keeps the engine running. Communication constructs the social reality of individuals; for instance, it enhances the direct experience with an organisation's product or service. Communication forms indirect experiences because it is through the communicative behaviours of those having the experience that others develop an understanding of organisational behaviours. Communication is the practice of sharing meanings – from Latin *comunicare* meaning to 'share in common'. It is through communication that perceptions and expectations are formed regarding what type of engagement and relationships stakeholders may assume from organisations. Organisational communications thus play a key role in the formation of perceptions and images on which stakeholder expectations are built. In short, a communication perspective offers several insights on the role of stakeholder communication in the construction of engagement expectations. Given that many stakeholders do not have direct access to organisations and cannot personally assess organisational actions, stakeholder communications represent the main approach for establishing stakeholder expectations on organisational behaviours (Olkkonen and Luoma-aho, 2015) and consequently for affecting stakeholders' interest in becoming engaged.

Communication is also a central tenant in establishing and cultivating relationships with stakeholders, and it works as device for building specific relational expectations. Relationships exist through the communicative constructions that result from at least two social actors' interactions. The manner in which people talk to each other, the way people seek 'verbal' engagement with each other, and the tone of voice people use, for example, are clear communication signs of the type of relationship these individuals have. And this is also valid when communication occurs between an organisation and stakeholders and among organisations. Relationships are configured and re-configured through communicative processes that can occur in or outside organisational settings. These processes can convergence to shared symbolic meanings of what constitutes stakeholder relationships (Koschmann, 2016).

Stakeholders build a view of their relationships with an organisation based on direct and indirect relational experiences but also on what and how organisations communicate with them (both the contents and tone of voice) and what they learn from other stakeholders and publics saying about organisations. These communications help stakeholders symbolically organise and interpret organisational actions and create a symbolic reality of a relationship. These interpreting and understanding dynamics take place at communication level. They also result in a stakeholder view of an organisation's relationship management efforts that represents the symbolic reality of stakeholder relations with that organisation. The focus on communication and its role as a process of constructing a different understanding of stakeholder relations also implies that realities can be multiple and competing, just as stakeholder claims are today.

Stakeholder claims certainly seem amplified today, mostly because stakeholders have more opportunities to express their concerns through a variety of channels and public forums. Stakeholder concerns are also more visible now, due to the increased speed of content sharing that can reach any corner of the world at any time of day. This vocalism partly comes from *homo narrans* stakeholders and partly from non-stakeholders, and it exposes stakeholders' expectations of organisations, including their relational expectations. An intra-stakeholder vocalism also influences general organisational efforts to reach out to key stakeholders, since it jams the communicative environment around an organisation. A challenge for any organisation is to separate relevant from non-relevant claims in a highly dense and clustered environment and identify supportive *homo narrans* stakeholders with whom it can work to construct relational meanings. This is essential to reinforce other, not specifically communication-based, organisational actions aimed at relationship building efforts.

Conclusions

This chapter is built on the premises that stakeholder relations today are more complex and dynamic and cannot be reduced to the management of known, key stakeholders. This is because other relevant, unknown stakeholders can affect organisational activities. This chapter advances early discussions on the role of communication in stakeholder theory and suggests additional reflections on what a communication perspective can offer to stakeholder relationship management in this complex and dynamic environment by focusing on three major points: 1) the nature of people's communicative behaviours and their empowerment to the status of a stakeholder, 2) the nature of relationships and relational dynamics and 3) the nature of stakeholder engagement and relational expectations.

A communication perspective on stakeholder relations is a recent effort undertaken to advance research and theory on stakeholder relationship management. Communication contributes to a different understanding of who a stakeholder is and what stakeholder relations are by providing a different focus, definition and explanation of how groups of individuals gain legitimacy in light of organisational matters. Given that most organisational stakeholders are social actors, adopting a communication perspective on stakeholder definition could help managers and organisations identify those groups of individuals who show an interest in organisations but do not possess specific material or symbolic resources to count as a stakeholder on traditional definitions. A communication view on stakeholder management also offers an appreciation and understanding of intra-stakeholder differences (Crane and Livesey, 2003) and the complex relations among stakeholders and organisations. This is made possible through the use of analytical tools and a specific management orientation that allows us to capture communicative behaviours of stakeholders and organisations. It also requires organisations to become active and attentive listeners of communications in and around them. As a result, organisational listening becomes an embedded activity in stakeholder relationship management. It is through listening that organisations can observe and consider who has a material interest in an organisation and who is showing to have concerns with specific organisational behaviours.

It is important to understand that a communication perspective does not reduce the complexity of stakeholder relations, nor does it offer a predefined understanding on what a relationship is and how relationships should be nourished. The potential benefits of the communication view lie in its ability to adopt a humanistic approach to stakeholder relations. A humanistic approach emphasises human needs, promotes unity and favours human virtues (Melé, 2003). A humanistic approach requires managing organisations in light of stakeholders' needs and concerns as human problems. Even when relations pertain other organisations, stakeholder relations are, for the most part, human relations, just as organisations are, after all, stable associations of people engaged in activities directed towards the attainment of specific objectives (Valentini, 2016). A humanistic approach to the whole spectrum of stakeholder relations can offer organisations a normative, ethical paradigm substantiated by interpersonal concepts such as values, trust, commitment, promises and forgiveness, which are particularly important in the development of long-lasting mutual and beneficial organisation-stakeholder relationships (Hutton, 1996). As a result, communication becomes the means through which organisations show their humanistic side and, at the same time, it allows organisations to apprehend human problems expressed through stakeholders' communicative behaviours. To unveil these mechanisms, future research should focus on understanding the role of language and discourse in constituting and shaping stakeholders' communicative behaviours and the conditions, factors and situations in which specific communicative behaviours lead to the creation and definition of diverse organisation-stakeholder relationships.

Note

1 For a more detailed review of stakeholder communication literature, see Koschmann, 2016.

References

Ackermann, F. and Eden, C. (2011). *Making strategy: Mapping out strategic success*, 2nd ed. London: Sage.

Andriof, J., Waddock, S., Husted, B. and Rahman, S. (2003). *Unfolding stakeholder thinking 2:* Relationships, communication, reporting and performance. Sheffield: Greenleaf.

Arnaud, N. and Mills, C. E. (2012). Understanding interorganizational agency: A communication perspective. *Group & Organization Management*, 37(4), 452–485.

Benhabib, S. (1992). *Situating the self: Gender, community, and postmodernism in contemporary ethics*. New York: Routledge.

Bliss, T. J. (2002). Citizen advocacy groups. Corporate friend or foe? In J. Adriof, S. Waddock, B. Husted, and S. Sutherland Rahman (Eds.), *Unfolding stakeholder thinking. Theory, responsibility and engagement.* Sheffield: Greenleaf Publishing, pp. 251–265.

Bruning, S. D. and Ledingham, J. A. (2015). Examining the influence of organization-public relationships and organizational identification with psychological group on institutional affiliation, behavioral intent, and evaluations of satisfaction. In E.-J. Ki, J.-N. Kim, and J. A. Ledingham (Eds.), *Public relations as relationship management. A relational approach to the study and practice of public relations.* New York: Routledge, pp. 130–143.

Buber, M. (1970). *I and Thou* (trans. Walter Kaufmann). New York: Charles Scribner's Sons.

Burchell, J. and Cook, J. (2013). Sleeping with the enemy? Strategic transformations in business – NGO relationships through stakeholder dialogue. *Journal of Business Ethics*, 113(3), 505–518.

Carroll, A. B. (1993). *Business and Society: Ethics and Stakeholder Management*. Cincinnati, OH: South-Western Publishing.

Carroll, C. (2015). *The handbook of communication and corporate reputation*. Malden, MA: John Wiley and Sons.

Clarkson, M. (1995). A stakeholder framework for analyzing and evaluating corporate social performance. *Academy of Management Review*, 20(1), 92–117.

Crane, A. and Livesey, S. (2003). Are you talking to me? Stakeholder communication and the risks and rewards of dialogue. In J. Andriof, S. Waddock, S. Rahman and B. Husted (Eds.), *Unfolding stakeholder thinking 2: Relationships, communication, reporting and performance*. Sheffield: Greenleaf, pp. 39–52.

Daneshvary, R. and Schwer, R. K. (2000). The association endorsement and consumers' intention to purchase. *Journal of Consumer Marketing*, 17(3), 203–213.

Dean, D. H. and Biswas, A. (2001). Third-party organization endorsement of products: An advertising cue affecting consumer prepurchase evaluation of goods and services. *Journal of Advertising*, 30(4), 41–57.

Deetz, S. A. (1992). *Democracy in an age of corporate colonization: Developments in communication and the politics of everyday life*. Albany, NY: State University of New York Press.

Deetz, S. A. (1995). *Transforming communication, transforming business: Building responsive and responsible workplaces*. Cresskill, NJ: Hampton Press.

Deetz, S. (2003). Corporate governance, communication, and getting social values into the decisional chain. *Management Communication Quarterly*, 16, 606–611.

Deetz, S. and Mumby, D. K. (1990). Power, discourse, and the workplace: Reclaiming the critical tradition. *Communication Yearbook*, 13, 18–47.

den Hond, F. and de Bakker, F. G. A. (2008). Activists' influence tactics and corporate policies. *Business Communication Quarterly*, 71(1), 107–111.

Dewey, J. (1927). *The public and its problems*. Chicago: Swallow Press.

Donaldson, T. and Preston, L. E. 1995). The stakeholder theory of the corporation: Concepts, evidence, and implications. *Academy of Management Review*, 20(1), 65–91.

Elving, W. J. L. and Postma, R. M. (2017). Social media: The dialogue myth? How organizations use social media for stakeholder dialogue and stakeholder engagement. In S. Romenti, O. Ihlen, B. van Ruler and I. Smit (Eds.) *How strategic communication shapes value and innovation in society (Advances in public relations and communication management, volume 2)*. Bingley: Emerald, pp. 123–141.

Falconi, T. M., Grunig, J. E., Zugaro, E. G. and Duarte, J. (2014). *Global stakeholder relationship governance: An infrastructure*. London: Palgrave Macmillan.

Fassin, Y. (2009). The stakeholder model redefined. *Journal of Business Ethics*, 84, 113–135.

Fineman, S. and Clark, K. (1996). Green stakeholders: Industry interpretations and response. *Journal of Management Studies*, 33(6), 715–730.

Finne, Å. and Grönroos, C. (2009). Rethinking marketing communication: From integrated marketing communication to relationship communication. *Journal of Marketing Communications*, 15(2/3), 179–195.

Fombrun, C. and Van Riel, C. B. M. (1997). The reputational landscape. *Corporate Reputation Review*, 1(1/2), 5–13.

Freeman, E. R. (1984). *Strategic management: A stakeholder approach*. Cambridge: Cambridge University Press.

Friedman, A. L. and Miles, S. (2006). *Stakeholders. Theory and practice*. Oxford: Oxford University Press.

Grunig, J. E. (1997). A situational theory of publics: Conceptual history, recent challenges, and new research. In D. Moss, T. MacManus and D. Vercic (Eds.), *Public relations research and international perspective*. London: International Thompson Business Press, pp. 3–46.

Grunig, J. E. and Hung-Baesecke, C.-J. F. (2015). The effect of relationships on reputation and reputation on relationships: A cognitive, behavioural study. In E.-J. Ki, J.-N. Kim and J. A. Ledingham (Eds.), *Public relations as relationship management. A relational approach to the study and practice of public relations*. New York: Routledge, pp. 63–113.

Grunig, J. E. and Hunt, T. (1984). *Managing public relations*. Boston, MA: Cengage Learning.

Grunig, J. E. and Repper, F. C. (1992). Strategic management, publics, and issues. In J. E. Grunig (Ed.), *Excellence in public relations and communication management*. Hillsdale, NJ: Lawrence Erlbaum Associates, pp. 117–158.

Haas, T. and Deetz, S. (2000). Between the generalized and concrete other: Approaching organizational ethics from feminist perspectives. In B-P. Buzzanell (Ed.), *Rethinking organizational and managerial communication from feminist perspectives*. Thousand Oaks, CA: Sage, pp. 24–46.

Habermas, J. (1984). *The theory of communicative action. Volume I: Reason and rationalization of society* (T. McCarthy, Trans.). Boston, MA: Beacon.

Habermas, J. (1987). *The theory of communicative action. Volume II: Lifeworld system: A critique of functionalist reason* (T. McCarthy, Trans.). Boston, MA: Beacon.

Habermas, J. (1990). *Moral consciousness and communicative action* (C. Lenhardt and S. Weber Nicholson, Trans.). Cambridge, MA: MIT Press.

Habermas, J. (1996). *Between facts and norms* (W. Rehg, Trans.) Cambridge, MA: MIT Press.

Hallahan, K. (2001). The dynamics of issues activation and response: An issues processes model. *Journal of Public Relations Research*, 13(1), 27–59.

Harrison, J. S. and St John, C. H. (1996). Managing and partnering with external stakeholders. *Academy of Management Executive*, 10(2), 46–60.

Hart, S. L. and Sharma, S. (2004). Engaging fringe stakeholders for competitive imagination. *The Academy of Management Executive*, 18(1), 7–18.

Heath, R. L. and Palenchar, M. J. (2008). *Strategic issues management*. Thousand Oaks, CA: Sage.

Hutton, J. G. (1996) Integrated relationship-marketing communications: A key opportunity for IMC, *Journal of Marketing Communications*, 2(3), 191–199.

Johansen, T. S. and Nielsen, A. E. (2011). Strategic stakeholder dialogues: A discursive perspective on relationship building. *Corporate Communications: An International Journal*, 16(3), 204–217.

Jones, T. M. (1995). Instrumental stakeholder theory: A synthesis pf ethics and economics. *Academy of Management Review*, 20(2), 404–438.

Kent, M. and Taylor, M. (1998). Building dialogic relationships through the World Wide Web. *Public Relations Review*, 24(3), 321–334.

Kim, J.-N. and Grunig, J. E. (2011). Problem solving and communicative action: A situational theory of problem solving. *Journal of Communication*, 61(1), 120–149.

Kim, J.-N. and Krishna, A. (2014) Publics and lay informatics. A review of the situational theory of problem solving. In E. Cohen (Ed.) *Communication Yearbook 38*. New York: Routledge, pp. 71–105.

Koschmann, M. A. (2016). A communication perspective on organizational stakeholder relationships: Discursivity, rationality and materiality. *Communication Research Practice*, 2(3), 407–431.

Kozinets, R.V., de Valck, K., Wojnicki, A. C. and Wilner, S. J. S. (2010). Networked narratives: Understanding word-of-mouth marketing in online communities. *Journal of Marketing*, 74(2), 71–89.

Kuhn, T. (2008). A communicative theory of the firm: Developing an alternative perspective on intra-organizational power and stakeholder relationships. *Organization Studies*, 29(8–9), 1227–1254.

Laplume, A. P., Sonpar, K. and Litz, R. A. (2008). Stakeholder theory: Reviewing a theory that moves us. *Journal of Management*, 34(6), 1152–1189.

Mariconda, S. and Lurati, F. (2015). Stakeholder cross-impact analysis: A segmentation method. *Corporate Communications: An International Journal*, 20(3), 276–290.

Melé, D. (2003). The challenge of humanistic management. *Journal of Business Ethics*, 44(1), 77–88.

Meisenbach, R. J. (2006). Ethics and principles of universalization as a moral framework for organizational communication. *Management Communication Quarterly*, 20(1), 39–62.

Messer, M. and Distaso, M. W. (2008). The source cycle: How traditional media and weblogs use each other as sources. *Journalism Studies*, 9(3), 447–463.

Mitchell, R. K., Agle, B. B. and Wood, D. J. (1997). Towards a theory of stakeholder identification and salience. *Academy of Management Review*, 22(4), 853–886.

Morsing, M. and Schultz, M. (2006). Corporate social responsibility communication: Stakeholder information, response and involvement strategies. *Business Ethics: A European Review*, 15(4), 323–338.

Olkkonen, L. and Luoma-aho, V. L. (2015). Broadening the concept of expectations in public relations. *Journal of Public Relations Research*, 27(1), 81–99.

Payne, S. L. and Calton, J. M. (2002). Towards a managerial practice of stakeholder engagement: Developing multi-stakeholder learning dialogues. *Journal of Corporate Citizenship*, 6, 37–52.

Phillips, R. (2003). Stakeholder legitimacy. *Business Ethics Quarterly*, 13(1), 25–41.

Podnar, K. and Golob, U. (2007). CSR expectations: The focus of corporate marketing. *Corporate Communications: An International Journal*, 12, 326–340.

Preble, J. F. (2008). Towards a comprehensive model of stakeholder management. *Business and Society Review*, 110(4), 407–431.

Rawlins, B. L. (2006). *Prioritizing Stakeholders for Public Relations*. Gainesville, FL: Institute for Public Relations.

Reeds, D. (1999). Stakeholder management theory: A critical theory perspective. *Business Ethics Quarterly*, 9(2), 453–483.

Rittenhofer, I. and Valentini, C. (2015). A practice turn to global public relations: An alternative approach. *Journal of Communication Management*, 19(1), 2–19.

Romenti, S., Murtarelli, G. and Valentini, C. (2014). Organizations' conversations in social media: Applying dialogue strategies in times of crises. *Corporate Communications: An International Journal*, 19(1), 10–33.

Rowley, T. J. (1997). Moving beyond dyadic ties: A network theory of stakeholder influences. *Academy of Management Review*, 22(4), 887–910.

Rowley, T. J. and Moldoveanu, M. (2003). When will stakeholder groups act? An interest- and identity-based model of stakeholder group mobilization. *Academy of Management Review*, 28(2), 204–219.

Savage, G., Nix, T., Whitehead, C. and Blair, J. (1991). Strategies for assessing and managing organizational stakeholders. *Academy of Management Executive*, 5(1), 61–75.

Schultz, D. and Schultz, H. (2004). *Brand babble: Sense and nonsense about branding*. Mason, OH: Thomson and South-Western.

Sedereviciute, K. and Valentini, C. (2011). Towards a more holistic stakeholder analysis approach. Mapping known and undiscovered stakeholders from social media. *International Journal of Strategic Communication*, 5(4), 221–239.

Taylor, M. and Kent, M. L. (2014). Dialogic engagement: Clarifying foundational concepts. *Journal of Public Relations Research*, 26(5), 384–398.

Taylor, M., Kent, M. L. and White, W. J. (2001). How activist organizations are using the Internet to build relationships. *Public Relations Review*, 27(3), 263–284.

Valentini, C. (2015). Is using social media "good" for the public relations profession? A critical reflection. *Public Relations Review*, 41(2), 170–177.

Valentini, C. (2016). Environment. In C. R. Scott and L. K. Lewis (Eds.), *International encyclopedia of organizational communication*. Malden, MA: Wiley-Blackwell, pp. 839–859.

Valentini, C. and Kruckeberg, D. (2012). New media versus social media: A conceptualization of their meanings, uses, and implications for public relations. In S. Duhé (Ed.), *New media and public relations*, 2nd ed. New York: Peter Lang, pp. 3–12.

Valentini, C., Kruckeberg, D. and Starck, K. (2012). Public relations and community: A persistent covenant. *Public Relations Review*, 38(5), 873–379.

Valentini, C., Kruckeberg, D. and Starck, K. (2016). The global society and its impact on public relations theorizing: Reflections on major macro trends. *Central European Journal of Communication*, 9(2), 229–246.

Valentini, C., Romenti, S. and Kruckeberg, D. (2016). Language and discourse in social media relational dynamics: A communicative constitution perspective. *International Journal of Communication*, 10, 1–19.

van Huijstee, M. and Glasbergen, P. (2008). The practice of stakeholder dialogue between multinationals and NGOs. *Corporate Social Responsibility & Environmental Management*, 15(5), 298–310.

Vasquez, G. M. (1993). A homo narrans perspective on public relations: Combining Bornmann's symbolic convergence theory and Grunig's situational theory of publics. *Journal of Public Relations Research*, 5(3), 201–216.

Vasquez, G. M. (1994). Testing a communication theory-method-message-behavior complex for the investigation of publics. *Journal of Public Relations Research*, 6(4), 267–291.

Winn, M. (2001). Building stakeholder theory with a decision modelling methodology. *Business and Society*, 40(2), 133–166.

2.2 Stakeholder engagement

The importance of mutuality and dialogue

Peggy Simcic Brønn

Introduction

The word "engagement" has become popularized in recent years, as organizations seek to build relationships with their stakeholders, particularly on issues associated with corporate social responsibility. A quick search on Google returns hundreds of thousands of entries discussing engagement and various stakeholders, the most prominent ones giving advice on how to do it. However, they seem to have one thing in common: they wonder what engagement is and how do we know when it is really occurring.

According to O'Riordan and Fairbrass (2014: 133), "a key feature of managing effective CSR is reliable, transparent, forward-thinking, inclusive stakeholder engagement". Morsing (2006) makes the point that one of the most important aspects of a successful sustainability program is the ability of organizational members to intelligently identify and learn about sustainability issues, concerns and expectations among stakeholders.

The discussion on engagement by stakeholders is not new as demonstrated by a technical report from the United Nations Environment Programme, Industry and Environment Programme dated from 1991 on Companies' Organization and Public Communication on Environmental Issues. The report acknowledged that providing information on environmental performance was a first step in improving communication with the public (p. 28). Communication was seen as a two-way process with a need to "listen, listen, listen" not only by organizations but also by the public. However, "listen, listen, listen" is much more difficult than merely communicating about an organization's sustainability efforts. It implies a two-way relationship that is grounded in mutuality. In that spirit, this chapter looks at engagement from the viewpoints of mutuality and from Argyris and Schön (1978), who state that the purpose of engagement is to build mutually beneficial relationships between the firm and its stakeholders.

This chapter begins with defining engagement followed by a discussion on the concepts of mutuality, a basic principle of authentic engagement. This occurs through dialogue, a very difficult construct to measure or to attain. The chapter offers some insight into how leaders can learn to engage in a dialogic process for mutually beneficial outcomes.

Defining engagement

The concept of engagement is the object of study in a broad range of fields. Applied psychology, organizational behavior and human resource management study engagement from the viewpoint of employee/work engagement and burnout. Education experts are interested in student engagement, political science in political or civil engagement and marketing and advertizing in brand and customer engagement. Haugen and Davis (2009) offer a comprehensive list of engagement from a range of perspectives with accompanying outcome variables. According to the authors' review of literature, engagement in some form leads to strategic change, organizational learning, culture change, strategy implementation, improved organizational performance and individual learning.

Their literature review furthermore supports their own research that three components "are necessary for the full meaning of engagement" (ibid, p. 398): emotion (feeling), intellect (cognition) and behavior (action). Emotion includes both positive and negative reactions such as enjoyment, fear, anger, support and belonging. The intellectual or cognitive component can be described as the willingness of individuals to exert an effort, to comprehend complex ideas or to master difficult skills. The behavior component of engagement, and the consequences of engagement, may include participation, action or involvement (Johnston, 2016).

Haugen and Davis (2009) offer what they call a "refined model of engagement", in their case for strategy implementation. In this model, what they call "social significance" provides the foundation of engagement as it acknowledges the intellectual and emotional complexity of individuals. According to Haugen and Davis, social significance "characterizes an organizational context of valuable reciprocal relationships" (p. 406) that requires trust, security/safety, respect and integrity. Trust and satisfaction are two of the most important antecedents to engagement according to Kang (2014). Kang's research findings suggest that stakeholders' level of engagement is critical for linking level of trust and satisfaction with supportive behavior intentions such as positive word of mouth or loyalty. "Engagement is an important motivator that connects the cognitive evaluations to publics' supportive actions" (p. 411). Achieving engagement thus requires:

- Freedom of expression including emotions of empathy, sympathy, hope, love
- Ownership or allowing individuals to take control
- Individual discretion to exercise important organizational choices
- Meaningfulness or significance of one's own work
- Psychological availability meaning the mental receptivity to work also associated with a sense of caring

Marcum (2000) makes the point that engagement is emerging as a replacement for motivation. According to this author, motivation relies on manipulation and control to get people to do things, while engagement stresses learning and involvement. People engage because they are, among others things, interested, enjoy what they are doing and can decide for themselves.

The following draws heavily on Johnston (2016), who describes engagement on three levels of analysis: the individual (micro) level, the organization (meso) level and the social (macro) level. At the individual level, engagement is a psychological construct defined as a "state being fully absorbed, involved, occupied, or engrossed in something" (p. 272). The individual engagement construct comprises three dimensions (see also Haugen and Davis above): cognitive, emotional and behavioral. People who are cognitively engaged are willing to immerse themselves in a topic and exert effort to comprehend ideas or master skills. Emotional engagement may include enjoyment, fear or belonging, while behavioral engagement is demonstrated through participating, acting or getting involved.

At the organizational or meso level, engagement is described as what an organization does to build relationships with stakeholders and respond to public opinion. The organization builds on individual engagement to enable, among other things, stakeholder connections, participation and involvement. An internal organizational stakeholder engagement philosophy would provide the mechanisms for identifying, understanding and responding to stakeholders' opinions; bringing these opinions in to the decision-making process and providing a way to address power imbalances. According to Johnston (ibid), this "represents a reflective practice manifesting a socially situated, relational and collective process" (p. 273).

Lastly, at the macro or social level, engagement is viewed as central for "building social capital and contributing to social outcomes" (p. 273), it is seen as a way to enhance civil society. In their research on employee volunteering, Muthuri et al. (2009) adopted Adler and Kwon's (2002, p. 23) definition of social capital as "the goodwill available to individuals or groups. Its source lies in the structure and content of the actors' relations. Its effects flow from the information, influence and solidarity it makes available to the actor". According to Spence et al. (2003),

> social capital has some important aspects for business ethics – it highlights the manner of doing business and has many points of intersection including issues such as transparency, honesty, co-operation, trust, community investment, organizational citizenship and goodwill.
>
> (p. 18)

As noted by Johnston (2016), social capital as defined here moves organizations away from solely being evaluated for financial performance but also for being evaluated for their contributions to society as a whole.

As summarized by Dhanesh (2016), engagement can be viewed as: "a cognitive, affective and behavioral state wherein stakeholders and organizations that share mutual interest in salient topics interact ethically and strategically, with an appreciation of power asymmetries between interactants, aimed at producing mutual adjustment and adaptation" (p. 31).

Engagement dependent on mutuality

Organizations face numerous stakeholders who have some interest in the organization or who are impacted by the behavior of the organization, i.e. they have some relationship with the organization. Even though Johnston (2016) refers to three levels of engagement (individual, organizational and societal), any attempt at engagement is directed at relating with another human being, both individuals and groups of people. Implicit in the stakeholder approach and the idea of engagement is the two-way nature of the relationship, i.e. there is a mutual exchange where each party is both affecting the other and being affected by the other (Jordan 1986). This implies that successful engagement requires organizations and stakeholders to not only listen, listen, listen but to feel comfortable to express themselves when discussing their respective interests. This is often referred to as mutuality.

While the concept of stakeholders is well covered in literature on sustainability, the concept of mutuality has received much less attention, and understanding this concept is key to achieving engagement. Hagerty et al. (1993) consider mutuality as one of four major processes or social competencies involved in establishing and promoting relatedness, defined as "an individual's level of involvement with persons, objects, groups or natural environments" (p. 292). Mutuality competency is then the "experience of real or symbolic shared commonalities of visions, goals, sentiments, or characteristics, including shared acceptance of differences that validate the person's world-view" (p. 294). Arnould and Rose (2016) refer to mutuality as an

> action that entails the assumption that another party would act toward the first party in a similar, mutual, fashion if circumstances were reversed, as guaranteed by their mutual inscription in a common social frame, as kin, coworker, or colleague, for example, and vice versa.
>
> (p. 88)

Mutuality assumes, among other things, that each party has perfect information, that neither party has more power than the other and that one party will not try to gain advantage of the other. According to Arnould and Rose, the model therefore needs to be seen as a system where the relationship between the stakeholders and the firm are mutually interacting.

In short, mutuality means that both parties in a relationship receive some sort of benefit. Further, the relationship is viewed as equally shared, i.e. it is two-way and no one party is of greater importance than the other. The concept of freedom of expression (emotions of empathy, sympathy, hope, love) from Haugen and Davis perhaps comes closest to describing mutuality. This is supported by Archbold et al. (1990, 1992) who defined mutuality as an enduring quality of a relationship with four components: shared values, love, shared activities and reciprocity.

Harrison and St. John (1994) characterize stakeholder management as including communicating, negotiating and contracting, managing relationships and motivating them to respond to the organization in ways that benefit it. In this interpretation, organizations enter into relationships with stakeholders for their own benefit. Based on the above discussion, it is clear that organizations that practice mutuality or have the concept of mutuality as their over-riding operating principle are more likely to relate better with their stakeholders and thus are more likely to achieve engagement by those same stakeholders.

However, as pointed out by Johnson and Wilson (2006: 3), mutuality is an ideal view, but there is an opposing skeptical view that contends that mutuality is not possible "because of inequality, especially unequal power relations". Inequalities might also include resources, both human and financial, which may enhance a power relation. In any case, one party has more of something than the other party resulting in an asymmetric relationship. For example, small environmental groups who challenge oil companies to change operating practices to be eco-friendlier (or who may even want to shut down the firm) may have less money and human resources than mega oil firms. Other examples include attempts by small investors to pressure firms to address issues such as executive pay. The asymmetry of the relationship leaves one party at a disadvantage.

In order for mutual learning to take place (for both organizations and their stakeholders), all parties need to be aware of and understand the others' knowledge, positions and preferences. The point is to avoid basing decisions and initiatives on assumptions of the other party's points of view, one of the critical barriers to achieving successful engagement. For our purposes we can identify a gap that hinders mutuality: the differences in agents' perceptions or mental models. Closing this gap is important because people relate to each better the more they think similarly about ideas or issues. Furthermore, knowing what each parties' viewpoints are, whether agreement or disagreement, can aid organizations in designing strategies for dealing with them in a way that can be beneficial for both parties.

Co-orientation

Fortunately, it is possible to measure the gap between for example an organization's perceptions and their stakeholders' by using the co-orientation model of McLeod and Chaffee (1973). The model shows the two views held by each party: their self-perception of a particular topic or issue and their perception of what the other party thinks about that particular topic or issue. There are three measures of co-orientation – agreement, accuracy and understanding. Agreement indicates the degree to which the organization's view matches a stakeholder's view, and accuracy indicates the degree to which the organization correctly *perceives* the stakeholder's viewpoint, and vice versa. Third is the degree to which the parties have a common understanding of the facts of a particular issue. Congruency is the degree to which the organization's view matches its *perception* of others' viewpoint, and vice versa, as shown in Figure 2.2.1.

Von Kutzschenbach and Brønn (2006) provide an example of the use of co-orientation model in ascertaining if there is agreement, understanding and accuracy of the concept of sustainable development by two stakeholder groups representing the end points of the value chain for the forest industry: forest owners in Norway and end consumers in the form of the printing and publishing sector in Germany. It is essential to the survival of the forest industry that end users believe that the industry is employing sustainable practices, as both the printing and publishing sectors are being pushed by their own customers to provide environmentally friendly products.

The researchers operationalized principles of sustainable development in the chain-of-custody based on a review of sustainability and certification literature resulting in three dimensions: social responsibility, environmental and the organizational. Results indicated that, when it came to social responsibility, both parties have significantly different views but they were aware of their differences. On the environmental dimension, the forest industry believed that end users viewed it the same way they did, when in fact they did

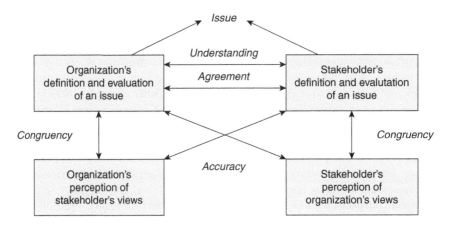

Figure 2.2.1 Co-orientation model

not. Conversely, forest owners and end consumers agreed on the organizational dimension but believed they disagreed.

The forestry industry needs to understand the basis for the end users' different views on what constitutes sustainable development. But when there is a gap in perceptions, there is no basis for achieving mutuality and thus little possibility for achieving engagement. However, the insight provided by the model can be used by managers to fine-tune their organization's communication strategy to be more sensitive to the specific requirements necessary for achieving mutuality. While the co-orientation model illustrates the conditions that need to exist for leveling the playing field if you will, it gives no guidance on how to achieve accuracy, understanding or agreement. As noted by Von Kutzschenbach and Brønn (2006), some of the recommendations to manage the communication process include assumption surfacing, organizational reflection, improved stakeholder management and dialogue. Key is dialogue.

Dialogue and the mutual learning model

In 2014, the *Journal of Public Relations Research* published a special edition dedicated to engagement and public relations. Special editor Kim Johnston (2014) refers to Heath (2014), who states, "Engagement is more than two-way communication and 'requires an understanding of, appreciation for, and commitment to dialogue with and among stakeholders and organizations as community-building discourse and power resource co-management'" (p. 382). Taylor and Kent (2014) return to this theme, explaining that dialogue "as an established theory of ethics, says that organizations should engage with stakeholders and publics to make things happen, to help make better decisions, to keep citizens informed, and to strengthen organizations and society" (p. 388).

The ISO 26000 principles for social responsibility define stakeholder engagement as all those activities that are undertaken by organizations to create opportunities for *dialogue* between an organization and one or more of its stakeholders with the aim of providing an informed basis for the organization's decisions (ISO 2010: 4, italics added). Taylor and Kent propose situating engagement within dialogue theory. According to them, a "dialogic engagement" facilitates interaction between organizations and stakeholders as it fosters understanding, goodwill and what might be described as co-orientation, a shared view of reality. The researchers propose five components of what they call the public relations conceptualization of engagement that requires organizations to:

1   Interact with stakeholders only after sufficient research is done to adequately understand an issue, key stakeholders and cultural variables
2   Demonstrate positive regard for stakeholders' input, experience and needs
3   Interact for relational purposes (long term) and not just to solve or deal with immediate problems or issues
4   Interact with stakeholders to get their advice and counsel on issues of mutual concern
5   Interact in a way that contributes to society where organizations and stakeholders are aware of their mutual dependencies and act together for the greater good

Engaging stakeholders in a dialogue that seeks to explore mental models and uncover assumptions is difficult. According to Argyris and Schön (1978), people have a tendency to engage in two models of what they call unilateral control: take control or give up. In the control model, an agent asserts their view, takes their own views for granted and does not inquire into the view of others. In the give up control model, the agent gives in because they think the other person is wrong, but it is not worth engaging further. In both cases, the outcome is that we believe we are right and the other person is wrong. This leads to, among other things, miscommunication, little commitment and minimal engagement.

Kent and Taylor make the point that achieving dialogic engagement requires training. Wiig-Berg (2005) suggests training managers in what she calls ethical communication can be done by using the mutual learning model of Argyris and Schön (1978). According to Wiig-Berg, this model represents a concept of good communication because it espouses a mindset where people are "willing to exchange information, to admit they may not understand a point, that another's view may have some merit, and that perhaps we have something to learn" (p. 173). This requires that agents (organizations and stakeholders) are ready to explain the basis of their views and inquire into the views of others and to invite challenges to their own views. Further, they need to express themselves in a way that encourages others to question them.

The mutual learning model is antithetic to the give up and take control models where engagement would be impossible. It is also extremely difficult to enact in practice. The organizational learning literature identifies skills needed to achieve mutuality (see Brønn and Brønn, 2003): reflection, inquiry and advocacy. Combining these skills requires active work with mental models. The objective is to be able to surface mental models and their underlying assumptions that are activated in a given communications situation.

Reflection

Reflection is an internally focused skill where agents are more aware of their own thinking and reasoning processes. Slowing down the thought processes and avoiding drawing quick conclusions can accomplish this. The first step in the reflection process is distinguishing between what is actual "data" (what is being said and done) and what are abstractions based on the data. As mental models build upon a set of assumptions, another important reflection activity is to formally identify these assumptions and to test them in light of the current situation. This is done by, for example, explicitly identifying the data behind a particular statement, seeking agreement on what is and what is not relevant data, clarifying lines of reasoning and confirming interpretations of others' statements.

Inquiry

Inquiry engages the two parties in a communication process in a joint learning process. Here the objective is to understand the thinking and reasoning processes of the other. This is accomplished by asking questions that seek to establish the basis for conclusions and statements – essentially, helping the other part to not jump to conclusions and to investigate the set of assumptions under which they operate. This activity implies a significant interaction with intended receivers of messages (i.e. stakeholders) and may in practice be difficult to accomplish.

Advocacy

Advocacy here is defined as the process of communicating one's own thinking and reasoning in a manner that makes them visible for others but in a way that does not shut down response. From the organizational learning perspective, the advocacy role is based

Table 2.2.1 Communication activities for stimulating dialog and learning

Activity	Description
Explaining	"Here's how the world works and why I can see it that way".
Asserting	"Here's what I say and here's why I say it".
Testing	"Here's what I say. What do you think of it?"
Skillful discussion	Balancing advocacy and inquiry, makes reasoning explicit, asks others about their assumptions but without being critical or accusing.
Dialogue	Suspending all assumptions and creating a "container" in which collective thinking can occur.
Clarifying	"What is the question we are trying to answer?"
Interviewing	Exploring others' points of view and the reasons behind them.
By standing	Making comments that pertain to group processes, but not to content.
Sensing	Watching the flow of conversation but without contributing much, nonetheless, being aware of what goes on.

on communicating parties wanting to learn from each other with each recognizing that the other party has valid interests that must be respected.

Thoughtful agents seek to find a balance between inquiry and advocacy. Too much advocacy results in one-way communication with little feedback; too much inquiry means getting bogged down. Skill in finding this balance is a function of experience, but there are guidelines available to help initiate the process. The balancing act involves four dimensions: telling, generating, asking and observing. Telling is directly associated with advocacy, and asking is related to inquiry. Generating and observing combine elements of both advocacy and inquiry. Table 2.2.1 summarizes some specific communication activities needed to develop the balance.

"Involving" communication

In 2005, the United Nations Environment Programme published a report titled *Communicating Sustainability, How to Produce Effective Public Campaigns*. The guide merely provides advice on how to create a campaign in order to get the public to change their behavior. As noted by Herremans et al. (2016), organizations primarily communicate their sustainability performance through reports. These are examples of the transmissive or transaction model of communication model, where organizations focus on communicating to the public as opposed to communicating with the public.

Morsing and Schultz (2006) recommend that companies avoid these types of one-way communication strategies about their social responsible initiatives. The danger is that companies run the risk of being blinded by their own interests and goals. Firms should rather try to create some common space for themselves and their stakeholders where hard subjects can be discussed. Morsing and Schultz refer to this strategy as "involving". However, the transformational strategy model of Bowen et al. (2010) is cited by Herremans et al. (2016) as more intense than the involving strategy and results in dialog. This is because "transformational engagement leaders to involvement and thus to an opportunity for learning from stakeholders" (p. 421).

In their study of engagement and sustainability reporting, Herremans et al. (2016) identified five characteristics associated with a firm's engagement with stakeholders: directness of communication, clarity in stakeholder identification, deliberateness of collecting feedback, broadness of stakeholder inclusiveness and utilization of stakeholder engagement for learning. Firms who had learning as an objective were more likely to use an involving engagement strategy, recognizing that the "communities in which they operate are affected by their activities and therefore communities have a right to ask companies for transparency" (p. 429). Communication style was characterized more as "with" as opposed to "to" stakeholders.

Communicating about CSR initiatives is likely to create higher expectations by stakeholders as society's expectations and perceptions are influenced by the external communications of the organization. Fulfilling the communicated promises that build expectations must be done by the entire organization. Business leaders who list building reputation and brand equity as primary motives for engaging in CSR understand this very well. The "ultimate" test for the organization is whether its behavior meets created expectations. Success depends on how well the organization listens to its stakeholders, how it interprets their desires and wishes, how well it delivers what it promises and lastly how credible its communications are (Brønn, 2012).

Building reputation is also about recognizing that organizations are dependent on others to survive and also that their behavior affects others. Black and Härtel (2004) propose that management capacity to develop CSR initiatives is dependent on their PR and CSR orientation. A PR orientation is demonstrated by value attuned public relations and dialogue. Value attuned PR is defined as the ability of PR managers to "detect and transmit information about social values to guide executive decision-making" (p. 130). Dialogue is the "conscience and respectful effort to share power in a discourse" (p. 130), where parties can feel free to co-create and challenge each other. The difference between dialog and merely informing or reporting is captured in the concepts of bridging and buffering. Organizations whose public relations or communication staff are viewed as "buffers" engage in symbolic communication with little or no substance (Grunig, 2006). Bridging on the other hand, is viewed as a more strategic communication approach comprising focused and coordinated processes and efforts designed to understand and engage key audiences in order to create, strengthen or preserve conditions favourable to advance organizational interests and objectives.

Conclusions

It is safe to say that an organization cannot manage stakeholders, but they can manage stakeholder relationships. Andriof et al. (2017) support this in their belief that the idea of "managing stakeholders" is out of date "in recognition of engagement and mutuality" (p. 9). Greenwood (2007, p. 317) makes the point that, when engagement enables co-operation that is mutually benefitting, it may be viewed as morally positive. But when used as a "deceptive control mechanism when masqueraded as corporate responsibility" (p. 320), may also be morally negative. This implies that engagement must be perceived as genuine or authentic if it is to be believable. An organization is authentic when its actions, its character and its sense of purpose are aligned with and supported by each other (Harquail, 2010), and authenticity is highly correlated with perception of CSR performance as well as with supportive behavior and reputation (Brønn, 2013).

Authentic stakeholder engagement and stakeholder dialogue is critical for sustainable CSR management. According to O'Riordan and Fairbrass (2014: 132), this is because "it enables the integration of an inclusive stakeholder perspective into strategic business planning, and it facilitates decision-makers to initially establish how their business decisions impact collective value creation for all interest groups throughout the entire value chain". As noted by Cranfield School of Management's Doughty Centre, if done poorly, engagement can potentially undermine an organization's relationships with stakeholder resulting in long-term loss of trust (Jeffery, 2009). It thus behooves organizations not only to incorporate engagement as part of their strategic planning processes but to ensure an organizational learning environment that emphasizes "involving" communication models over transmissive ones. As we have seen in this chapter, it is not easy, but it is possible.

References

Andriof, J., Waddock, S., Husted, B. and S. S. Rahman (2017). *Unfolding Stakeholder Thinking: Theory, Responsibility and Engagement*. New York, NY: Routledge.

Adler, P. S. and S. W. Kwon (2002). Social capital: Prospects for a new concept. *Academy of Management Review*, 27, 1, 17–40.

Archbold, P. G., Stewart, B. J., Greenlick, M. R. and T. A. Harvath (1990). Mutuality and preparedness as predictors of caregiver role strain. *Research in Nursing and Health*, 13, 375–384.

Archbold, P. G., Stewart, B. J., Greenlick, M. R., and T. A. Harvath (1992). The clinical assessment of mutuality and preparedness in family caregivers to frail older people. In *Key Aspects of Elder Care* (Funk, S. G., Tornquist E. M., Champagne, M. T. and L. A. Copp, eds). New York, NY: Springer, pp. 328–339.

Argyris, C. and D. A. Schön. 1978. *Organizational Learning: A Theory of Action Perspective*. Reading, MA: Addison-Wesley Publishing Company.

Arnould, E. J. and A. S. Rose (2016). Mutuality: Critique and substitute for Belk's "sharing". *Marketing Theory*, 16, 1, 55–79.

Black, L. D. and C. E. Härtel (2004). The five capabilities of socially responsible companies. *Journal of Public Affairs*, 4, 2, 125–144.

Bowen, F., Newenham-Kahindi, A. and I. Herremans (2010). When suits meet roots: The antecedents and consequences of community engagement strategy. *Journal of Business Ethics*, 95, 2, 297–318.

Brønn, P. S. (2012). Adapting the PZB service quality model to reputation risk analysis and the implications for CSR communication. *Journal of Communication Management*, 16, 1, 77–94.

Brønn, P. S. (2013). CSR and communication, in: A. Midttun (Ed.), *CSR and Beyond: A Nordic Perspective*. Oslo: Cappelen Damm.

Brønn, P. S. and C. Brønn (2003). Organizational implications of the coorientational model. *Journal of Communications Management*, 7, 4, May.

Dhanesh, G. S. (2016). Putting engagement in its proper place: State of the field, paper presented at engaging people in a disengaged world. *23rd International Public Relations Research Symposium*, BLEDCOM 2016–July 1–2, Bled, Slovenia.

Greenwood, M. (2007). Stakeholder engagement beyond the myth of corporate responsibility. *Journal of Business Ethics*, 74, 315–327.

Grunig, J. (2006): Furnishing the edifice: Ongoing research on public relations as a strategic management function. *Journal of Public Relations Research*, 18, 2, 151–176.

Hagerty, B. M. K., Lynch-Sauer, J., Patusky, K. L. and M. Bouwsema (1993). An emerging theory of human relatedness. *Journal of Nursing Scholarship*, 25, 4, 291–296.

Harrison, J. S. and C. H. St. John (1994). Managing and partnering with external stakeholders. *Academy of Management Executive*, 10, 2.

Harquail, C. V. (2010). What is an Authentic Organization?: An elevator speech. http://authenticorganizations.com/harquail/2010/11/17/what-is-an-authentic-organization-anelevator-speech/.

Haugen, L. K. and A. S. Davis (2009). The engagement process: Examining the evidence from diverse perspectives. *Journal of Behavioral and Applied Management*, 396–414.

Heath, R. L. (2014). *Public Relations' Role in Engagement: Functions, Voices, and Narratives* Paper presented at the Engagement as strategy, theory and practice: ICA preconference 2014, Seattle.

Herremans, I. M., Nazari, J. A. and F. Mahmoudian (2016). Stakeholder relationships, engagement, and sustainability reporting. *Journal of Business Ethics*, 138, 417–425.

ISO. (2010). *Guidance on Social Responsibility. International Standard ISO/DIS 26000*. Geneva: International Organisation for Standardisation.

Jeffery, N. (2009). Stakeholder engagement: A road map to meaningful engagement Doughty Centre, Cranfield School of Management. www.networkedcranfield.com/doughty/Document%20Library/How%20To%20Guides/Stakeholder%20engagement%20A%20road%20map%20to%20meaningful%20engagement.pdf.

Johnson, H. and G. Wilson (2006). North-South/South-North partnerships: Closing the "mutuality gap". *Public Administration and Development*, 26, 1, 71–80.

Johnston, K. A. (2014). Public relations and engagement: Theoretical imperatives of a multidimensional concept. *Journal of Public Relations Research*, 26, 5, 381–383, DOI: 10.1080/1062726X.2014.959863.

Johnston, K. A. (2016). Engagement, in: C. E. Carroll (Ed.), *The Sage Encyclopedia of Corporate Reputation*. Thousand Oaks, CA: Sage, pp. 272–275.

Jordan, J. V. (1986). The meaning of mutuality. Working paper 23, Jean Baker Miller Training Institute at the Wellesley Centers for Women.

Kang, M. (2014). Understand public engagement: Conceptualizing and measuring its influence on supportive behavior intentions. *Journal of Public Relations Research*, 26, 399–415.

Marcum, J. W. (2000). Out with motivation, in with engagement. *National Productivity Review*, Autumn, 57–60.

McLeod, J. M. and S. H. Chaffee (1973). Interpersonal approaches to communication research. *American Behavioral Scientist*, 16, 4, March–April, 469–499.

Morsing, M. (2006). Corporate social responsibility as strategy auto-communication: On the role of external stakeholders for member identification. *Business Ethics: A European Review*, 15, 2, 171–182.

Morsing, M. and M. Schultz (2006). Corporate social responsibility communication: Stakeholder information, response and involvement strategies. *Business Ethics: A European Review*, 15, 4, 323–338.

Muthuri, J. N., Matten, D. and J. Moon (2009). Employee volunteering and social capital: Contributions to corporate social responsibility. *British Journal of Management*, 20, 75–89.

O'Riordan, L. and J. Fairbrass (2014). Managing CSR stakeholder engagement: A new conceptual framework. *Journal of Business Ethics*, 125, 121–145, DOI: 10.1007/s10551–013–1913-x.

Spence, L. J., Schmidpeter, R. and A. Habisch (2003). Assessing social capital: Small and medium sized enterprises in Germany and the U.K. *Journal of Business Ethics*, 47, 17–29.

Taylor, M. and M. L. Kent (2014). Dialogic engagement: Clarifying foundational concepts. *Journal of Public Relations Research*, 26, 5, 384–398, DOI: 10.1080/1062726X.2014.956106.

UNEP/IEO (1991). *Companies' Organization and Public Communication on Environmental Issues*. Technical Report, series 6.

UNEP (2005). *Communicating Sustainability, How to Produce Effective Public Campaigns*. DTI/0679/PA.

Von Kutzschenbach, M. and C. Brønn (2006). Communicating sustainable development initiatives: Applying coorientation to forest management certification. *Journal of Communication Management*, 10, 3, 304–322.

Wiig-Berg, R. (2005). Mutual learning in practice: Making a different kind of sound, in: P. S. Brønn and R. Wiig-Berg (Eds.), *Corporate Communication: A Strategic Approach to Building Reputation*. Oslo: Gyldendal.

2.3 How to deal with diverse voices

A framework to support stakeholder engagement

Ozen Asik-Dizdar, Ceyda Maden-Eyiusta and Ayla Esen

Introduction

Over the last couple of decades, corporations have been increasingly facing expectations to go beyond accomplishing economic functions only and to contribute back to society through discretionary efforts to support various stakeholder groups (Carroll, 1979; Clarkson, 1995; Maignan, 2001; Wartick and Cochran, 1985). In this regard, it is more and more recognized that the utilization of various participative techniques is key to engage stakeholders with corporate decision-making, so as to ensure that all voices are heard and concerns raised. However, managing stakeholder engagement can be a rather difficult and complicated endeavour, given the fact that stakeholder expectations, in most cases, may be in conflict or entirely opposite to one another. Despite the vast amount of research on stakeholder engagement focusing on tools and methods to manage stakeholders effectively (Aaltonen and Kujala, 2010), very little attention has been given to how to address opposing stakeholder expectations. It is essential to note that it is almost impossible to meet all the diverse needs of different stakeholder groups; however, a holistic approach may help organizations to handle this challenge in a streamlined manner.

The proposed chapter will contribute to our current understanding of stakeholder engagement by focusing on the challenge of opposing stakeholder expectations. We will provide a conceptual review on the ways in which organizations can achieve effective stakeholder engagement while highlighting potential areas where opposing expectations can be addressed and managed. In the following pages, we will describe three critical tools we identified to address diverse voices from stakeholders: (1) stakeholder mapping, (2) stakeholder dialogue and (3) organizational mechanisms to support and govern stakeholder engagement. We then intend to analyze our three-stage model over illustrative examples for effectively dealing with polarized stakeholder positions and managing opposing stakeholder expectations.

Stakeholder mapping

Stakeholder engagement, a process which involves initiating and sustaining constructive relationships with stakeholders for focusing on a broader set of interests when planning and implementing corporate activities, comprises stakeholder mapping as one of the integral components (Jeffery, 2009; Lerbinger, 2006; Morris and Baddache, 2012). Through stakeholder mapping, organizations attempt to identify a key list of stakeholders across the entire stakeholder spectrum by comprehending who their stakeholders are, where they come from and what they are seeking in their relationship with the organization (Morris and Baddache, 2012).

For more than two decades, a number of mapping models are presented in the academic work, and managerial practice, all of which tend to serve to the purpose of helping managers to (1) determine who the stakeholders of a corporation are, (2) to classify and prioritize these stakeholders and (3) to decide on what actions managers should take towards each individual stakeholder (Clifton and Amran, 2010). According to Morris and Baddache (2012), mapping can be broken into four phases which involve:

(1) *Identifying*: Forming a relevant list of groups, organizations and individuals by including everyone who has an interest in organizational objectives as well as those who may have one in the future.
(2) *Analyzing*: Comprehending stakeholder perspectives and relevance based on their contribution (i.e., the extent to which a stakeholder has information or expertise on the issue that could be beneficial for the firm); legitimacy (i.e., legitimacy of the stakeholder's claim for engagement); willingness to engage; influence (i.e., the degree and target of the stakeholder's influence); and necessity of involvement (i.e., the extent to which a specific stakeholder can derail certain practices if they are not included in the engagement).
(3) *Mapping*: Visualizing where stakeholders stand compared to each other when assessed based on the same criteria. Morris and Baddache state that mapping can help companies visualize the complex interplay of issues and relationships based on the criteria defined in the analyzing phase.
(4) *Prioritizing*: Ranking the stakeholders into a prioritized list of engagement which comprises the most relevant issues and the most relevant stakeholders.

Majority of the stakeholder mapping methods described in existing research are built on the initial classification and segmentation of stakeholders by Mitchell, Agle and Wood (1997). In an attempt to identify and prioritize stakeholders, Mitchell et al. have suggested three attributes of stakeholders, namely, the power to influence the firm's practices, the urgency of the claim stakeholders place on the firm and the legitimacy of the relationship between the stakeholders and the firm (Mitchell et al., 1997). In general, for any actor identified as a stakeholder, the greater the extent to which it has any particular attribute, the more the managers should pay attention to or prioritize that stakeholder (Clifton and Amran, 2010).

Similar to Mitchell et al.'s seminal work, Newcombe (2003) introduces two methods of stakeholder mapping based on the contingencies of power: predictability and interest. Different combinations of these contingencies result in the following stakeholder management strategies:

• *Power/Predictability Matrix*: Plotting of the stakeholders in this matrix reveals that predictable stakeholders with low power present fewer problems to the firms whereas unpredictable but powerful stakeholders may represent the greatest danger if they use their power to destroy strategies. Powerful but predictable stakeholders may have a constraining impact on strategy which may not cause a problem during times of stability, however, may be dangerous when environmental pressures are present. Finally, unpredictable stakeholders with low power may not constitute a big problem for the implementation of strategies since these stakeholders are relatively manageable.
• *Power/Interest Matrix*: This matrix demonstrates that stakeholders with little interest and little power to influence management will necessitate minimal effort on the side

of the managers while the stakeholders with high level of interest and power may require specific attention when formulating strategy. Additionally, stakeholders with high level of interest but little power need to be kept informed about the major decisions in order not to experience confrontation when they get more powerful. Lastly, powerful stakeholders with low level of interest need to be kept satisfied with the policies adopted as they can easily increase their interest, and become key players, when or if they feel dissatisfied.

The power-interest matrix introduced by Newcombe was also used by Johnson, Scholes and Whittington (2005) for stakeholder analysis purposes. These authors suggest that various stakeholders may have different levels of interest in corporate actions and, together with the power attribute, different degrees of influence to draw attention to their particular interests.

Although previously discussed stakeholder mapping models help managers identify and analyze stakeholders on the basis of different attributes, they have been intensively challenged due to the conceptual difficulties they create. A major problem with the previous models is the fact they have adopted a simplistic assumption of the usual stakeholder roles. In the real world of value creation and trade, stakeholders may assume different roles challenging the borders between traditional stakeholder groups. For instance, customers may play a significant role in designing, not simply just buying, innovative products. Similarly, employees may be direct shareholders of the company and act differently than other, non-shareholder employees. McVea and Freeman (2005) state that, if managers are able to avoid generic analysis of stakeholder groups while making decisions and see stakeholders as individuals with names and faces, there may be opportunities for finding creative and entrepreneurial solutions to inherent conflicts among various stakeholders. As the boundaries between stakeholder groups are becoming blurred, stakeholder relationships are becoming even more complex and necessitate the establishment of intense and individualized/customized relationships with different stakeholders, even within same stakeholder group.

Another criticism on Mitchell et al.'s framework and other mapping models that use similar attributes is about their approach to 'who really matters' for the organization (Derry, 2012). According to Mitchell et al. (1997), stakeholders are those individuals or groups with legitimate, urgent and/or powerful claims on the firm's operations and without one or more of these core attributes, a claimant cannot be considered a stakeholder. On the other hand, when a particular individual or group holds an increasing number of these attributes, its salience to management increases. The primary rationale behind Mitchell et al.'s framework is that resources, responsiveness and responsibility are directed to those who have legitimate claims, whose demands are most urgent to the firm and who have influential power on the firm from the managerial perspective. Challenging all of these assumptions, Derry (2012) states that Mitchell et al.'s model is an inappropriately discriminant one, endorsing the contemporary structure of corporate neglect of powerless individuals and natural systems. This model permits that the claims of the people and organizations with no negotiating clout (e.g., those who do not control resources and those who are the least advantaged) can be overlooked as their voices are not considered legitimate or powerful. Similarly, Banerjee (2000) points out that assigning the final decision on stakeholder salience to managers equates social legitimacy with the interest and the power of corporate managers and weakens the voices of and the rights of marginalized groups, such as civil rights activists, outsourced labour and radical environmentalists.

These criticisms emphasize the fact that it has almost become customary (i.e., it's not the exception, but the norm) for corporate managers to ignore the claims of groups who are disadvantaged by power asymmetry and only attend to the needs and wants of groups who are capable of exerting influence.

Having reviewed different stakeholder analysis and mapping techniques together with the particular criticisms directed to them, we can argue that a thorough analysis and prioritization of stakeholders can be achieved when managers or decision makers create multiple maps with different stakeholders at the centre (Derry, 2012). Exploring the same issue/decision with workers, customers, shareholders, natural environment and government at the centre of the map would result in a comprehensive analysis of the opposing interests of the stakeholders that would help organizations develop an effective, multifaceted and sophisticated communication strategy, shaped by an effective stakeholder dialogue. As will be discussed in the next section, establishing effective platforms for stakeholder dialogue is a must for stakeholders to communicate their expectations well, see their expectations are listened to and be assured that these expectations will be given due consideration by the organization.

Stakeholder dialogue

Stakeholder dialogue is a two-way process of information-sharing and communication between an organization and its various stakeholders (Burchell and Cook, 2013). It may assume a variety of forms – from simple information dissemination about an organization's conduct to an open dialogue with multiple stakeholders on a wide range of issues (Pedersen, 2006). As such, stakeholder dialogue brings different perspectives together and enables stakeholders to jointly seek solutions without ignoring those differences. On the contrary, the differences and conflicts existing between stakeholders mean that stakeholder dialogue has the potential for identifying innovative solutions for a variety of problems (Kuenkel et al., 2011).

As a matter of fact, the term 'dialogue' is said to denote a challenging process, as it implies bringing together too many diverse voices, exploring and loosening up one's own tight assumptions and reaching an agreement by building a common ground out of confrontation of claims and ideas (Campbell and Mark, 2006). Stakeholder dialogue, therefore, transcends traditional conflictual processes and is considered to be a progressive form of stakeholder engagement and understanding (Burchell and Cook, 2008).

However, it is not easy to bring together diverse voices and then reconcile them all in one solution. For this purpose, stakeholder dialogue rests on the following ten principles (Kaptein and van Tulder, 2003; Veldhuizen, Blok and Dentoni, 2013):

(1) *To know and to be understood:* Organizations must know their dialogue partners well and have a good understanding of their own and shared areas of interest.
(2) *Trust and reliability:* Parties must act with integrity, allow themselves to be open and vulnerable so as to build a constructive dialogue platform and develop trust.
(3) *Clear rules for the dialogue:* In addition to trust, rules and procedures to follow during the dialogue (e.g., how to deal with confidential information) must be clearly defined and respected by all parties. After all, dialogue is a power game, but with the added value of learning from and influencing one another and finally reaching an agreement (Jonker and Nijhof, 2006).

(4) *A coherent vision on the dialogue:* How should the stakeholder meetings/discussions be held (e.g., frequency, manner)? What is the underlying philosophy? What is the ultimate aim? Effective dialogue is comparable to an integrative negotiation process (Campbell and Mark, 2006). The organization must find a balance between accepting invitations to stakeholder meetings and inviting stakeholders themselves.

(5) *Dialogue skills:* Parties must possess the necessary skills for taking an effective part in the dialogue (e.g., integrity, openness, vulnerability, empathy, accountability).

(6) *Expertise in the subject matter:* Parties must be prepared well and possess expert knowledge about the subject so as to make clear sense of each other's standpoint.

(7) *Clear dialogue structure:* Parties must know what to expect (possibilities and limitations) of a dialogue, which requires a clear agenda, careful recording and timely follow-up.

(8) *Valid information as basis:* Parties must present facts accurately rather than distorting them to fit their own agenda and, in doing so, must eliminate any bias or doubts. If needed, a third party may be used to verify the validity of information.

(9) *Consecutive meetings:* Successive meetings must be held, as more frequent interaction between the parties will result in better understanding of the issues and closer relationship. After all, meetings intend to build joint ownership for actions to be taken following the dialogue.

(10) *Feedback of results:* Each party must make sure that they properly represent their constituent groups and must communicate the results to their respective constituents so as to obtain their support and trust in implementation.

In short, stakeholder dialogue describes the involvement of stakeholders in the organizational decision-making processes with regard to a variety of issues that raise stakeholder concerns (Pedersen, 2006). However, the level of engagement of stakeholders and the ultimate success of a dialogue will vary based on some essential characteristics of an organization. More specifically, the more inclusive, open, tolerant, empowering and transparent an organization is willing to be, the less these diverse voices will be suppressed (Pedersen, 2006). That is, the organization will stand at equal distance to all diversity and will not let one stakeholder group get priority over another. In addition, stakeholder dialogue will benefit from diversity by means of constructive conflict (Cuppen, 2012), that is, conflict generating new solutions to old problems with the ultimate aim of 'learning'.

According to Cuppen (2012), stakeholder dialogue enhances learning through deliberation rather than consensus-building. That is, instead of focusing on consensus, stakeholder dialogue should focus on confrontation of opposing viewpoints, and hence, a quality decision will not be compromised. As such, when stakeholder dialogue is open-ended and is focused on the productive task of listening to and learning from one another (Burchell and Cook, 2006), the parties will be able to achieve a synthesis of divergent perspectives with a vigorous understanding of the problem and its solutions. This kind of stakeholder involvement strategy establishes a frequent, systematic and proactive dialogue and thus builds relationships (Morsing and Schultz, 2006).

Another perspective on this issue is offered by Freeman and Velamuri (2006) who propose to revise the concept of corporate social responsibility as 'company stakeholder responsibility', which, as suggested by the authors, rests on some principles among which intensive dialogue and negotiation with stakeholders are key elements. Furthermore, the authors emphasize that criticisms are an especially important component of stakeholder dialogue, even though not every criticism is legitimate and not each expectation or need can be met. Even so, showing each stakeholder group that their concerns, large or small, positive or negative, are taken into consideration is the first step of building better communication, hence turning stakeholder relationships into positive ones.

As mentioned earlier, with its emphasis on openness, proactivity and willingness to consider alternative perspectives, stakeholder dialogue helps parties co-define the solutions to their common problems. For different stakeholders, the dialogue may take place through different communication channels. For example, while the organization may choose to hold regular meetings and assemblies to communicate with its partners/shareholders, it may engage in meetings with labour representatives or run periodic meetings and assessments to communicate with its employees (Agudo-Valiente, Garces-Ayerbe and Salvador-Figueras, 2015). In a similar vein, customer satisfaction surveys, customer complaints and suggestions and marketing visits may be more suitable to communicate with the customer stakeholder group, whereas open meetings and forums may be the best medium of dialogue with representatives of various societal interest groups (Agudo-Valiente et al., 2015). Whichever the communication channel, the aim in stakeholder dialogue is to achieve higher levels of trust, mutual understanding and learning (Ayuso, Rodriguez and Ricart, 2006; Burchell and Cook, 2006; Burchell and Cook, 2008; Campbell and Mark, 2006). Furthermore, it may be argued that matching alternative communication channels with differing stakeholder needs and expectations may, in fact, pave the way for stakeholder dialogue to help overcome the power asymmetry surrounding some stakeholder groups.

Another important outcome of stakeholder dialogue is the variety of benefits experienced by the parties involved. On the organizational side, it can be said that organizations benefit from increased reputation and positive publicity for being open to stakeholder input and giving careful consideration to stakeholder voice in their decision-making process. On the stakeholder side (especially for external stakeholders such as NGOs, special interest groups, etc.), it can be said that stakeholders are recognized for the rightful criticisms they bring to the organizations and are held accountable for their part into the solution; that is, the partnership between the organization and its stakeholders is recognized as a constructive force (Burchell and Cook, 2013). At the end of the day, stakeholder dialogue works for the benefit of everyone, as it helps manage the power asymmetry surrounding some stakeholder groups and turns previously adversarial relationships into open and cooperative partnerships.

Organizational mechanisms for stakeholder engagement

Harrison and Freeman (1999) address stakeholder relationship as a 'multifaceted, multi-objective, complex phenomenon' (p. 483). In the case of facing expectations from diverse stakeholder groups, a comprehensive stakeholder map or effective stakeholder dialogue platforms alone will not be sufficient towards achieving success in stakeholder engagement. In dealing with this complex issue, the *hardware* of the company in stakeholder engagement is also critical (Castka et al., 2004; Zadek, 2004). Companies have to develop organizational structures (management systems, procedures etc.) to provide a backbone for managing the relationship with stakeholders.

There has been a significant amount of interest in corporate sustainability in the last two decades (Friedman and Miles, 2001; Gao and Zhang, 2006). Sustainability has been recognized as a strategic asset for organizations. Therefore, the 'triple bottom line' (Elkington, 1997) of corporate financial, ecological/environmental and social performance gained importance as more and more contemporary management practices started to revolve around the concept of sustainability. In line with this shift in managerial paradigms, many organizations, such as the Global Reporting Initiative (GRI) and the Institute of Social and Ethical Accountability (ISEA), were established to develop sustainability standards and mechanisms.

Today, there are many organizational systems and tools which are utilized by companies in supporting stakeholder management. Among these, social auditing has emerged as a system that encompasses the mechanisms to ensure corporate sustainability. Social auditing is a key example of an organizational mechanism due to the salience of corporate social responsibility (CSR). According to Vinten (1990), social auditing is

> a review to ensure that an organization gives due consideration to its wider and social responsibilities to those both directly and indirectly affected by its decisions, and that a balance is achieved in its corporate planning between these aspects and the more traditional business-related objectives.
>
> (p. 127)

Zadek (1994) defines social auditing as 'the process of defining, observing and reporting measures of the ethical behaviour and social impact of an organization in relation to its aims and those of its stakeholders' (p. 632). Social auditing is formalized within many organizations under the process known as Social and Ethical Accountability, Auditing and Reporting (SEAAR) and is considered as *sine qua non* for corporate sustainability (Gao and Zhang, 2006).

Perrini and Tencati (2006) propose a similar model for tracking and monitoring performance from a stakeholder viewpoint. The proposal, called the Sustainability Evaluation and Reporting System (SERS), is a three-module framework that has similarities with the SEAAR system. The system comprises of three main pillars: (1) the overall reporting (sustainability reporting) system (including the annual report, social report, the environmental report and a set of integrated performance indicators); (2) the integrated information system; and (3) the key performance indicators (KPIs) for corporate sustainability (Perrini and Tencati, 2006). These systems ensure the structuring of formal procedures for sustainability of relationships with stakeholders.

According to ISEA (1999), stakeholder engagement process needs to include 'a public disclosure and feedback process that offers stakeholders information that is valuable in assessing the engagement' (p. 64). However, in most cases, a formalized SEAAR process utilizes standards which are homogeneous, but these standards are applied to a heterogeneous set of stakeholders (Owen et al., 2000). Therefore, there is a need for tailor-made engagement rules to address conflicting stakeholder groups and their expectations. Organizational mechanisms that support the social auditing process have to be designed so as to provide the flexibility to understand and respond to different stakeholder needs.

However, one should also note that stakeholder engagement should be embedded in the values and philosophy of an organization to reach successful results in social auditing and sustainability reporting processes. An open culture, involvement of senior management and employees in the dialogue process, and a vision for sustainability are listed as essential organizational drivers of stakeholder dialogue (Veldhuizen et al., 2013).

A model to address diverse stakeholder expectations

Having defined three important elements in stakeholder engagement, we propose a conceptual model to cope with diverse voices raised by stakeholders that connects these three pillars (Figure 2.3.1). Organizations should first identify potential areas of conflict during the stakeholder mapping stage. This will help organizations to identify and prioritize which stakeholder groups should be invited for dialogue and be confronted within stakeholder dialogue platforms. For instance, the local community of a certain region can be listed as 'high priority' due to its ability to influence primary stakeholders, such as the government. An energy company that plans to initiate a new power plant investment in this region should assume the local community as a critical actor to be involved in dialogue. However, as mentioned previously, marginalized stakeholders who lack power, legitimacy or urgency should also be considered in the mapping phase. Utilization of multiple stakeholder maps could guide organizations to develop diverse engagement strategies for diverse voices. Through stakeholder mapping, organizations can decide how to design social auditing systems that will best answer the needs of different stakeholder groups as well. Social reports or sustainability reports should be structured to address the concerns of these groups.

Through stakeholder dialogue, organizations can build open and cooperative relationships with their stakeholders. Parties learn from each other through deliberation that leads to consensus-building. Through well-designed social auditing mechanisms, these relationships will get stronger through formalized interactions. Improving relationships and partnerships can alter the perceptions of organizations towards their stakeholders and can eventually affect the prioritization stage during stakeholder mapping. In the case of our above example, the energy company could define formal processes to ensure continuous and open communication with stakeholders. Local community and consumers could be informed through periodic reports, blogs and social media to ensure transparency on the

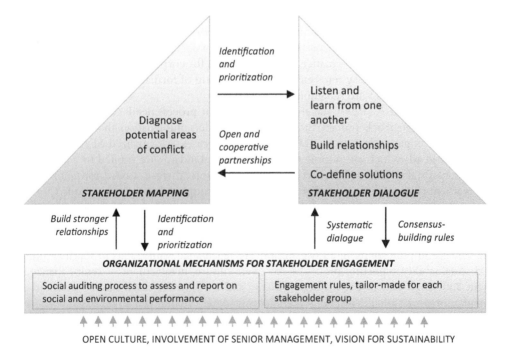

Figure 2.3.1 Proposed model for dealing with diverse stakeholder expectations

company's agenda. Annual meetings and workshops could be organized to bring stakeholder groups into a participative platform. A wide variety of communication channels should be used to ensure higher levels of trust and mutual learning. A formalized social auditing system and tailor-made engagement rules for different stakeholder groups also feed into the dialogue phase and lead to systemic dialogue between parties. Continuous dialogue will help organizations to realize the most optimal consensus-building rules. All these discussions and our suggested framework are summarized in Figure 2.3.1.

Conclusions

Coping with diverse and usually conflicting interests of stakeholders is a big challenge for organizations. In this chapter, we proposed a framework for organizations to overcome this challenge. Identification of possible areas of conflict in stakeholder mapping is an essential starting point. Effective stakeholder dialogue is the second building block that ensures confrontation of all parties where they can co-define solutions through building relationships. Finally, organizational mechanisms, specifically social auditing systems that are carefully designed to respond flexibly to different stakeholder groups, have to be adopted. The motivation and skills to initiate and manage stakeholder expectations have to be formalized for successful stakeholder engagement. The three pillars in our proposed model have to complement and mutually reinforce each other to manage opposing stakeholder expectations.

Although stakeholder mapping, dialogue and organizational mechanisms are critical for addressing diverse stakeholder expectations, our model has its limitations particularly in cases where there are high levels of power asymmetry. For example, a policy change of a government in favour of nuclear energy might leave no space for dialogue among special interest groups and the government. Another challenge is the multiple roles that stakeholders may occupy. A member of a local community may also be an employee, or similarly an investor may at the same time be a customer. Future research addressing these issues through empirical studies would be worthwhile to pursue.

Acknowledgment

Parts of this chapter have appeared in Asik-Dizdar, O., Maden-Eyiusta, C., and Esen, A. (2016), How to address opposing stakeholder expectations: Towards a conceptual framework, *Proceedings of the 12th Corporate Responsibility Research Conference*, Istanbul, 13–15 October, 2016.

References

Aaltonen, K. and Kujala, J. (2010). A project lifecycle perspective on stakeholder influence strategies in global projects. *Scandinavian Journal of Management*, 26(4), 381–397.

Agudo-Valiente, J. M., Garces-Ayerbe, C. and Salvador-Figueras, M. (2015). Corporate social performance and stakeholder dialogue management. *Corporate Social Responsibility and Environmental Management*, 22, 13–31.

Ayuso, S., Rodriguez, M. A. and Ricart, J. E. (2006). Using stakeholder dialogue as a source for new ideas: A dynamic capability underlying sustainable innovation. *IESE Business School Working Paper, WP-633*, Barcelona: University of Navarra.

Banerjee, S. B. (2000). Whose land is it anyway? National interest, indigenous stakeholders, and colonial discourses: The case of the Jabiluka uranium mine. *Organization & Environment*, 13(1), 3–38.

Burchell, J. and Cook, J. (2006). Assessing the impact of stakeholder dialogue: Changing relationships between NGOs and companies, *Journal of Public Affairs*, 6, 210–227.

Burchell, J. and Cook, J. (2008). Stakeholder dialogue and organisational learning: Changing relationships between companies and NGOs. *Business Ethics: A European Review*, 17(1), 35–46.

Burchell, J. and Cook, J. (2013). Sleeping with the enemy? Strategic transformations in business-NGO relationships through stakeholder dialogue. *Journal of Business Ethics*, 113, 505–518.

Campbell, B. and Mark, M. M. (2006). Toward more effective stakeholder dialogue: Applying theories of negotiation to policy and program evaluation. *Journal of Applied Social Psychology*, 36(12), 2834–2863.

Carroll, A. B. (1979). A three-dimensional conceptual model of corporate performance. *Academy of Management Review*, 4(4), 497–505.

Castka, P., Bamber, C. J., Bamber, D. J. and Sharp, J. M. (2004). Integrating corporate social responsibility (CSR) into ISO management systems – in search of a feasible CSR management system framework. *The TQM Magazine*, 16(3), 216–224.

Clarkson, M. B. E. (1995). A stakeholder framework for analyzing and evaluating corporate social performance. *Academy of Management Review*, 20(1), 92–117.

Clifton, D. and Amran, A. (2010). The stakeholder approach: A sustainability perspective. *Journal of Business Ethics*, 98, 121–136.

Cuppen, E. (2012). Diversity and constructive conflict in stakeholder dialogue: Considerations for design and methods. *Policy Sciences*, 45(1), 23–46.

Derry, R. (2012). Reclaiming marginalized stakeholders. *Journal of Business Ethics*, 111(2), 253–264.

Elkington, J. (1997). *Cannibals with forks, The Triple Bottom Line of 21st Century*. Oxford: Capstone.

Freeman, R. E. and Velamuri, S. R. (2006). A new approach to CSR: Company stakeholder responsibility. In A. Kakabadse and M. Morsing (eds.), *Corporate Social Responsibility: Reconciling Aspiration with Application*. New York: Palgrave MacMillan, pp. 9–23.

Friedman, A. L. and Miles, S. (2001). Socially responsible investment and corporate social and environmental reporting in the UK: An exploratory study. *The British Accounting Review*, 33(4), 523–548.

Gao, S. S. and Zhang, J. J. (2006). Stakeholder engagement, social auditing and corporate sustainability. *Business Process Management Journal*, 12(6), 722–740.

Harrison, J. S. and Freeman, R. E. (1999). Stakeholders, social responsibility, and performance: Empirical evidence and theoretical perspectives. *Academy of Management Journal*, 42(5), 479–485.

ISEA (1999). *AccountAbility 1000 (AA1000): Standard, Guidelines and Professional Qualification*. London: Institute of Social and Ethical AccountAbility.

Jeffery, N. (2009). Stakeholder engagement: A road map to meaningful engagement. *The Doughty Centre for Corporate Responsibility, Cranfield School of Management*. Retrieved from www.som.cranfield.ac.uk/som/dinamic-content/media/CR%20Stakeholder.pdf (accessed 3 May 2016).

Johnson, G., Scholes, K. and Whittington, R. (2005). *Exploring Corporate Strategy*. Essex: Pearson Education Limited.

Jonker, J. and Nijhof, A. (2006). Looking through the eyes of others: Assessing mutual expectations and experiences in order to shape dialogue and collaboration between business and NGOs with respect to CSR. *Corporate Governance*, 14(5), 456–466.

Kaptein, M. and van Tulder, R. (2003). Toward effective stakeholder dialogue. *Business and Society Review*, 108(2), 203–224.

Kuenkel, P., Gerlach, S., Frieg, V., Gorg, C., Ferguson, M., Kohler, J. and Herde, J. (2011). *Stakeholder Dialogues: Manual*. Frankfurt: Deutsche Gesellschaft fur Internationale Zusammenarbeit (GIZ) GmbH. Retrieved from www.mspguide.org/sites/default/files/resource/giz_stakeholder_dialogues_kuenkel.pdf (accessed 6 June 2016).

Lerbinger, O. (2006). *Corporate Public Affairs: Interacting with Interest Groups, Media and Government*. London: Lawrence Erlbaum Associates.

Maignan, I. (2001). Consumers' perceptions of corporate social responsibilities: A cross-cultural comparison. *Journal of Business Ethics*, 30, 57–72.

McVea, J. F. and Freeman, R. E. (2005). A names-and-faces approach to stakeholder management: How focusing on stakeholders as individuals can bring ethics and entrepreneurial strategy together. *Journal of Management Inquiry*, 14(1), 57–69.

Mitchell, R. K., Agle, B. R. and Wood, D. J. (1997). Toward a theory of stakeholder identification and salience: Defining the principle of who and what really counts. *Academy of Management Review*, 22(4), 853–887.

Morris, J. and Baddache, F. (2012). Back to basics: How to make stakeholder engagement meaningful for your company. *BSR Stakeholder Engagement Consulting Services*. Retrieved from www.bsr.org/reports/BSR_Five-Step_Guide_to_Stakeholder_Engagement.pdf (accessed 30 April 2016).

Morsing, M. and Schultz, M. (2006). Corporate social responsibility communication: Stakeholder information, response and involvement strategies. *Business Ethics: A European Review*, 15(4), 323–338.

Newcombe, R. (2003). From client to project stakeholders: A stakeholder mapping approach. *Construction Management and Economics*, 21(8), 841–848.

Owen, D. L., Swift, T. A., Humphrey, C. and Bowerman, M. (2000). The new social audits: Accountability, managerial capture of the agenda of social champions? *European Accounting Review*, 9(1), 81–98.

Pedersen, E. R. (2006). Making corporate social responsibility (CSR) operable: How companies translate stakeholder dialogue into practice. *Business and Society Review*, 111(2), 137–163.

Perrini, F. and Tencati, A. (2006). Sustainability and stakeholder management: The need for new corporate performance evaluation and reporting systems. *Business Strategy and the Environment*, 15(5), 296–308.

Veldhuizen, M., Blok, V. and Dentoni, D. (2013). Organisational drivers of capabilities for multi-stakeholder dialogue and knowledge integration. *Journal on Chain and Network Science*, 13(2), 107–117.

Vinten, G. (1990). The social auditor. *International Journal of Value-Based Management*, 3(2), 125–135.

Wartick, S. L. and Cochran, P. L. (1985). The evolution of the corporate social performance model. *Academy of Management Review*, 10(4), 758–769.

Zadek, S. (1994). Trading ethics: Auditing the market. *Journal of Economic Issues*, 28(2), 631–645.

Zadek, S. (2004). The path to corporate social responsibility. *Harvard Business Review*, 82(12), 125–132.

2.4 Enhanced stakeholder engagement and CSR through the UN Guiding Principles, social media pressure, and corporate accountability

Jeffrey S. Overall, Nelarine Cornelius, and James Wallace

Introduction

The conventional view of stakeholder engagement follows the belief that organizations that form long-term relationships with stakeholders, will stand to maximize their earnings (Freeman, 1984). This view, also echoed in the customer relationship management literature (Morgan & Hunt, 1994), has since been supported empirically (Carroll & Shabana, 2010). As a result, organizations typically take the interests of important stakeholders into consideration when making decisions that impact various partnerships and groups. However, when conflicts between stakeholder groups arise, such as shareholders and members of the community, managers are expected to default in their decision-making to ensure that the interests of the organization, and particularly those of the shareholders, are held paramount (Philips, Freeman & Wicks, 2003). When this happens, ethical issues can arise.

It has been said that managers are ethically minded, care about society, and behave in responsible ways (Collins, 2012). Nonetheless, although they do not want, for example, to unnecessarily pollute the environment, deceive members of society, or outsource the jobs of their community members, they often make decisions that run counter to their moral value systems. Such actions can be sanctioned by managers when being obliged to following prescriptive organizational policies that advantage shareholders or those of the organization, *per se*. This can also occur less overtly when decision-making within the organization is taken at a group, not individual, level. In the transition from the individual to the collective organizational entity, there appears to be a breakdown of accountability that can lead to moral disengagement (Tsang, 2002). Moral disengagement is "the cognitive restructuring of inhumane conducts into a benign or worthy one by moral justification, sanitizing language, and . . . disavowal of personal agency in the harm one causes by diffusion or displacement of responsibility" (Bandura, 2002, p. 101). By morally disengaging, business people do not feel as though they are individually accountable for the decisions of the group. Such actions can have profound negative consequences and are well documented in the academic literature, as well as the news media.

This lack of responsibility and accountability is a consequence of the collective bounded rationality of the group involving the knowledge and computational limitations of decision-makers and their inability to make perfectly rational choices (Simon, 1955). Coupled with collective bounded rationality, individuals also encounter cognitive biases (Kahneman & Frederick, 2002) that may further hinder their ability to make an ethical choice. As a result of the limitations in the decision-making process, employees can become indifferent to moral issues relating to the conduct of the firm. When this occurs, decision-makers can sacrifice the interests of others in preference for organizational ends.

In this chapter, our aim is to explore how organizations make irresponsible decisions and how this might be resolved. To address the former, we rely and build upon moral disengagement (Bandura, 1986) and bounded rationality theory (Simon, 1955). For the latter, we demonstrate that through rights, especially those proposed as Guiding Principles by the United Nations, and social media pressure, accountability and the management of stakeholder relationships should improve. Such a "two-pronged attack" will serve to counter irresponsible prescriptive directives, provide a reinforcing ethical framework for group decision-making, and encourage adherence by external scrutiny and exposure. To this end, we contribute to the extant literature by developing a conceptual framework that we use to demonstrate how more robust, explicitly ethically grounded approaches to corporate accountability can lead to enhanced stakeholder engagement and, subsequently, CSR.

Theoretical framework

Collective bounded rationality

In neoclassical economic theory, it is suggested that individuals are fully rational: they make value-maximizing decisions (Simon, 1996). *Homo economicus* is a logical, profit-maximizer, focused solely on maximizing his or her long-term (economic) self-interests. He or she is completely aware of all available alternatives to a decision and has the capacity to compute and evaluate each alternative, consistently and coherently, to assess which best maximizes utility (Carrier, 2012; Simon, 1945). Once the information is computed, the alternative that maximizes utility or produces what they perceive to be the best outcome can be selected (March, 1994).

In contrast, psychologists have shown that individuals are far from rational; they experience challenges processing information (Schwenk, 1986). They consider that the judgments made by individuals are susceptible to systematic errors, such as those associated with attention, memory, comprehension, and communication and that these limit their ability to make perfectly rational decisions (Kahneman, 2011; March, 1994). The human mind is imperfect, our attention is severely limited, and as a result, our awareness is selective, at best (Brocas & Carrillo, 2008). In this vein, the Nobel Laureate economist Herbert Simon (1955) contended that individuals are rational but argued that it is unreasonable to assume there are no limitations to their level of rationality (Holton & Naquin, 2005). Simon suggested that individuals have bounded rationality – knowledge and computational limitations of decision-makers and their inability to make perfectly rational choices (Lipman, 1995). It is believed that the complexity of the environment, coupled with the limited cognitive ability of humans, cause maximization to be elusive (Simon, 1955). Importantly, individuals attempt to make rational choices, but they do not always have the computational capabilities, knowledge, or access to complete information that may be relevant to making a fully rational choice (March, 1994; Simon, 1945). Therefore, the decisions that are made, even with the best intentions of being rational ones, cannot always be relied upon to be rational (March, 1994).

In their desire to make decisions, people "*satisfice*" whereby they make decisions perceived as satisfactory or sufficient given imperfect knowledge. A full-cost benefit analysis of all available alternatives is rarely conducted with decision-makers choosing an acceptable option that fulfills a preconceived adequacy criterion (Campitelli & Gobet, 2010). As a result, they do not consider all available alternatives as they often limit their evaluation when they encounter an alternative that addresses their basic requirements (Lindenberg, 2001). In this way, individuals "develop decision procedures that are sensible, given the constraints, even though they might not be sensible if the constraints were removed" (March, 1978, p. 590). From this, it can be seen that *homo economicus* is a "*satisficer*" that makes good enough decisions that may not be perfectly rational choices, as suggested in classical economics (Simon, 1996).

To assist us in making decisions, individuals rely on heuristics. Heuristics allow people to process a great deal of information quickly but not necessarily accurately (Forbes, 2005) or optimally. In this way, "heuristic processing is easy and adequate for most tasks heuristic processing (the intuitive process) is generally used unless there is a special need to engage in systematic processing" (Haidt, 2001, p. 820). Heuristics, therefore, lighten the mental load that is needed to make decisions (Zindel, Zindel & Quirino, 2014) since, by reducing complexity, they involve "mental short-cuts" to arrive at decisions quickly (Ajzen & Fishbein, 2000). In this way, we simplify complex problems so that we can understand them. However, because the full gamut of the problem is not necessarily addressed, individuals can fail to consider all relevant information when making a decision. Consequently, heuristics can lead to cognitive biases with a focus on certain relevant facts while ignoring others that might conflict with the alternative that they show a preference for (March, 1994).

Cognitive biases lead to thought processes that contain systematic errors or assumptions that influence the decision-making process (Fleischmann, Amirpur, Benlian & Hess, 2014; Forbes, 2005). They include planning fallacy, optimism, hindsight bias, confirmation bias, illusion of control, escalation of commitment, overconfidence, and bounded ethicality.

Planning fallacy involves a failure in understanding how long a task will take to complete (Adomdza & Astebro, 2012). Optimism involves being unrealistically positive about the future outcome of an event with hindsight bias involving perceiving past events as more predictable than they actually were (Sanchez, Carballo & Gutierrez, 2011). With confirmation bias, we retain any information that validates our decision but ignore any competing information that contradicts our choice (Baron, 2004). This can lead us to treat our opinions or assumptions as fact (Kannadhasan, Aramvalarthan & Kumar, 2014). The illusion of control involves the belief that individuals can control outcomes that they have no control over (Kannadhasan et al., 2014; Thompson, Armstrong & Thomas, 1998), namely, exogenous factors. In these situations, chance tends to have more of an impact on the outcome than our abilities (Keh, Foo & Lim, 2002). Escalation of commitment involves deciding to continue to work on a project even when we know that the chances of success are minimal. Put differently, individuals will continue to pour good money after bad. This can explain why 47% of entrepreneurs continued working on a venture when they have received credible data that it will fail. As a result, they doubled their initial losses prior to giving up (Kahneman, 2011). This behavior can be explained in part by the willingness of individuals to maintain a positive self-image as they do not want to be perceived as a failure, not only to themselves but also to others (Astebro, Jeffrey & Adomdza, 2007). In the case of overconfidence, decision-makers have excessive confidence in their competencies whereby they overestimate their abilities (Adomdza & Astebro, 2012; Kahneman, 2011) and their likelihood of success; this limits their ability to understand the full extent of their ignorance (Astebro et al., 2007) leading to poorly informed decision-making. Finally, bounded ethicality enables people to make ethically questionable decisions that conflict with their moral principles (Moore, 2008; Tenbrunsel, Diekmann, Wade-Benzoni & Bazerman, 2010). As a result of our bounded ethicality, at times, we might fail to recognize an ethical dilemma (Bazerman & Tenbrunsel, 2011). When this happens, we might frame the problem incorrectly, such as through a "business problem" lens that does not have an ethical dimension (Tenbrunsel et al., 2010). Given this lack of realization, they are able to maintain a positive self-concept by viewing themselves as an ethical person. This can explain how managers can make decisions that are inconsistent with their ethical and moral value system and that harm others.

In the dynamic marketplace, where information is uncertain and the outcomes of our decisions are contentious or poorly recognized, cognitive biases play a significant role in developing our perceptions, recognition of a problem, and perceptions of the outcomes (Keil, Depledge & Rai, 2007). Unfortunately, they can also lead to discounting relevant information that might lead to an unethical decision, potentially resulting in harm to others (Fleischmann, Amirpur, Benlian & Hess, 2014). When this happens, people typically rely on rationalization techniques, such as moral disengagement, to maintain a positive self-concept.

Moral disengagement

Freud (1900) suggested that rationalizations are ego-defense mechanisms that assist individuals to portray themselves in a positive way, despite making unethical decisions that lead to harmful actions. They, therefore, allow individuals to delude themselves and deceive others by helping to create the illusion of reasonableness associated with a harmful act (Taylor, 1923). Aligned with this, moral disengagement is a form of rationalization, with individuals providing *post-hoc* excuses, justifications, and explanations for their offensive, harmful, or immoral actions (Maruna & Mann, 2006). It evokes "cognitions which restructure one's actions to appear less harmful, minimize one's understanding of responsibility for one's actions, or attenuate the perception of the distress one causes others" (Moore, 2008, p. 129) helping to minimize the guilt associated with harmful behaviors (Maruna & Mann, 2006). By relieving guilt, they also minimize stress and anxiety whilst maintaining one's self-concept as a good person. Moral disengagement can therefore be seen as a process which enables managers feel empowered to behave in reprehensible ways (Tsang, 2002) either by refusing to accept that moral imperatives are applicable in a particular context and by euphemistic reassessments which lead to favorable appraisals of harmful actions.

Moral disengagement consists of seven variables, namely moral justification, diffusion of responsibility, advantageous comparison, displacement of responsibility, distorting harmful consequences, euphemistic labeling, and dehumanization of victims. Moral justification involves reconstructing the behavior to appear more benign than it actually is. To achieve this, individual's reframe the behavior to appear as though it is socially acceptable by addressing a moral end (Bandura, 2002) or that it serves a worthy purpose (White et al., 2009). The diffusion of responsibility involves "obscuring or minimizing the agentive role in the harm one causes" (Bandura, 2002, p. 106), "which often involves a division of labor or a chain of command" (Tsang, 2002). Through the diffusion of responsibility, in a group setting, managers will view their actions as part of the collective group where each individual performed separate parts of a particular task. Because the group is responsible for their decisions, individual accountability is minimized as they feel the group as a whole is responsible for the unethical behavior (Tsang, 2002). In this way, individual managers are not the actual agents of their behavior and, as a result, are spared from any guilt that may occur from their collective actions (Bandura, 2002).

Advantageous comparison is used by individuals that compare their behavior to another that is far more severe in nature. In this way, reprehensible acts can be used to make other, less extreme acts appear relatively benevolent (Bandura, 2002). Displacement of responsibility is often used when individuals minimize their role in wrongdoing. In this way, they often argue that they were a mere agent in the harmful act and were not actually responsible – they were simply doing what they were told, appealing to their agentic state: they were being obedient, carrying out the wishes of their superiors (Milgram, 1974; Tsang, 2002). Distorting perceptions of harmful consequences can be used by individuals when they attempt to claim that an injury did not actually occur.

Euphemistic labeling is another approach used to assuage responsibility. It involves reducing moral self-sanctions through "cloaking harmful activities in sanitized, convoluted, and innocuous language. Double-speak renders them benign and socially acceptable" (Bandura, 2007, p. 18). Euphemisms are used as "'linguistic novocain' that numbs us to unpleasant and harmful realities; and the convoluted form as 'semantic fog' that obscures and conceals detrimental practices" (p. 18).

Similarly, the dehumanization of victims is used when individuals suggest that there were no victims associated with the behavior or that the victims brought on the consequences, themselves. For example, during the financial crisis of 2008, lenders could justify pursuing subprime lending strategies by arguing that consumers sought credit and, therefore, are not victims. They could further argue that they have no control if consumers over-borrow and cannot afford their repayments.

When managing within an organizational culture that relies on group-based decision-making, accountability is perceived as shifted from the individual to the group. This lack of individual ownership can cause organizational members to become blind to their moral obligations regardless of how ethically minded they may be. By morally disengaging, decision-makers deflect responsibility onto the group, their superiors, or the organization as a whole through their attainment of corporate objectives. As a result, obedience to the group can lead to a lack of engage with stakeholders and fuel unethical acts (Tsang, 2002).

In this way, two moral disengagement dimensions, namely, the diffusion of responsibility and euphemistic labeling, are particularly relevant to explaining how organizations can make unethical decisions. Moral disengagement, through the diffusion of responsibility and euphemistic labeling, occurred during the Ford Pinto crisis (Gioia, 1992). In the 1970s, the Ford Pinto car had a design fault – the fuel tank was liable to rupture and ignite at low-impact, causing numerous disfigurements and fatalities. However, in a collective meeting, where eight recall coordinators reviewed the issue, they decided to avoid recalling the vehicle. Specifically, they diffused their responsibility for making the decision by relying on the volumes of corporate policies, developed to facilitate organizational decision-making focused more on corporate objectives than moral imperatives. Through these manuals, the organization effectively prescribed the logical reasoning. The value of a human life was set at $250,000 and, through cost-benefit analysis, managers concluded the cost to rectify the design flaw outweighed the cost of human life that would have been paid as compensation during litigation (Gioia, 1992). To assist in desensitizing their decision, euphemistic language was used whereby instead of managers stating that the fuel tanks were rupturing, which resulted in fires that caused passengers to die, they used phrases such as the Pintos were "lighting up" (Gioia, 1992, p. 358). A recall coordinator at the time stated that:

> before I went to Ford I would have argued that Ford had an ethical obligation to recall. After I left Ford I now argue and teach that Ford had an obligation to recall. But, while I was there, I perceived no strong obligation to recall and remember no strong ethical overtones to the case whatsoever.

A collective bounded rationality of the group occurred whereby they became blinded to moral reasoning. A "pack mentality" formed whereby individuals failed to question the group or seek alternative views. Morally disengaging thus allowed managers to deflect accountability and any negative psychological feelings, such as guilt, associated with their collective unethical decision onto the group and, ultimately, the organization.

A model of stakeholder engagement and CSR

In this section, we introduce a model of stakeholder engagement and CSR (see Figure 2.4.1) designed to counter possible harms associated with the cognitive limitations of managers and their propensity to morally disengage. It is based on the premise that social media pressures; the UN Guiding Principles (Human Rights Council, 2011); and government regulation of social responsibility through the management of operating licenses can help to ensure that managers fully understand their responsibilities and are held accountable, individually and collectively, for their decisions. Considering that accountability is the bedrock of stakeholder engagement, this should lead to more socially responsible behaviors.

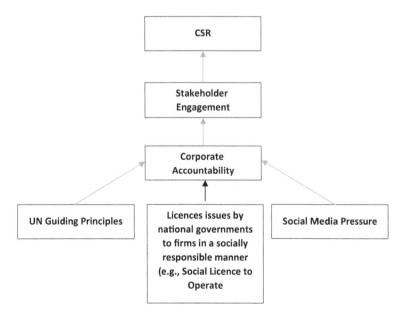

Figure 2.4.1 A model of stakeholder engagement and CSR

Social media pressure

Social media facilitates challenges to the actions of organizations and can influence relevant practice, legislation, regulations, and the opinions of influential stakeholders. Pavitt (2012) argues that through the power of word-of-mouth communications, informed consumers can communicate through various social media channels to air their concerns and share information (Kang & Hustvedt, 2014). This increased level of scrutiny and exposition due to readily available Internet access and the willingness of whistle-blowers and interested parties to exploit social media makes the risk of negative publicity too great for organizations to be reckless with their actions. Indeed, damage to corporate brands can lead to million-dollar losses in share value, consumer boycotts, and employee turnover (Boele, Fabig & Wheeler, 2001). To avoid this, organizations are consequently striving to be more transparent about their operations by disclosing important aspects of their supply chains through enhanced communications with affected stakeholders (Pavitt, 2012) to ensure social norms are followed.

In the business-to-consumer (B2C) sectors, where organizational behaviors and subsequent interactions with stakeholders through social media have a direct impact on profitability, social media can deter irresponsible behavior. However, companies in the business-to-business (B2B) industry, such as energy companies, that do not directly (or indirectly, through intermediaries) sell their products and services to the end consumer, are not as adversely impacted by social media pressure. Examples of B2B companies include automotive component manufacturers, plastic injection molding suppliers, and importantly oil exploration and extraction corporations and mining companies, the latter of which as primary industries can often have direct and highly disruptive and damaging effects on the environment and communities. As a result, social media pressure alone might be insufficient to ensure that B2B firms remain accountable to others. To attempt to engage all stakeholders in such areas and provide some recourse and protection for unethical actions, the concept of a social license to operate (SLO) has been into introduced (Warhurst, 2001; Owen & Kemp, 2013; Moffat & Zhang, 2014). We argue that this process of having a uniform and encompassing platform to set acceptable standards as benchmarks is essential, in a broader context. We further suggest that the Guiding Principles developed by the UN would fulfill this requirement.

UN Guiding Principles

According to principles of natural justice (Asiedu-Akrofi, 1989), there are basic rights that are guaranteed to individuals. These include the right to a fair hearing; procedural due process (Robertson, 1988); an unbiased tribunal (Schauer, 1976); and the right to evidence (Van Essen et al., 2004). Most of the developed economies support natural justice and attempt to protect human rights through legislation. However, in many emerging markets, jurisprudence is often relatively weakly developed or utilized. To capitalize on the often weak enforcement of regulations in many emerging markets' legal systems, multinational companies (MNCs) often move their operations abroad to, particularly, fragile and conflicted-affected states (Porter, Andrews, Turkewitz & Wescott, 2011). An increase in trade agreements between nations, such as the Trans Pacific Partnership (TPP), is perhaps making it easier for organizations to effectively delegate ethical wrongdoing by outsourcing to such off-shore intermediaries. Through a complex supply chain network of intermediaries, companies are able to conceal their irresponsible activities, disconnect from domestic legal systems of the headquarters of parent companies, and remain unaccountable to stakeholders (Zyglidopoulos & Fleming, 2011). As a result, there are numerous examples of human rights violations from apparel companies, children's toy manufacturers, and coffee retailers in Vietnam, Indonesia, and Guatemala, respectively (Klein, 2000), through to larger-scale environmental transgressions by oil companies in the Niger Delta region in Nigeria (BBC, 2013; Escritt, 2015).

To address instances of human rights violations such as these abroad, stakeholder groups have looked to CSR as a means of holding organizations accountable for their actions. These stakeholder groups have therefore suggested that CSR be embedded in legislation (Kovacs, 2006) whereby penalties for non-compliance are introduced and victims have access to restitution (Utting, 2008). Given that organizations want minimal intervention in the marketplace by governments, however, they want CSR to remain voluntary, selectively proactive, and not necessarily codified into law (Bowen, 1953; Kovacs, 2006; Taylor, 2011).

To address these conflicting preferences whilst ensuring organizational accountability, a "middle-ground" or "hybrid" approach was consequently advocated by Professor John Ruggie who developed a "protect, respect, and remedy" framework on the behalf of the United Nations. Under his direction, the Human Rights Council (2011) developed a set of "Guiding Principles" to minimize the instances of corporate malfeasance (Jägers, 2011). The Guiding Principles are founded on three pillars: first, through policies, regulations, and legislation, nation states have a duty to protect the rights of individuals from the abuses of organizations. Second, organizations must perform due diligence to ensure that all facets of their operations do not adversely impact the rights of others. Not only are organizations required to respect human rights, they are also mandated to address all facets of their supply chains where human rights abuses might exist (Human Rights Council, 2011). This includes their immediate supply chains and those of their contracted partners (Mares, 2010). The third pillar involves greater access to remedies for victims of human rights abuses (Human Rights Council, 2011).

The principles are grounded in the belief that states are responsible for ensuring that human rights are respected and protected through fundamental freedoms, within their territories. Importantly, to ensure that there is a lasting effect from aligning CSR with corporate accountability, the framework uses soft law through a self-regulatory approach whereby voluntarism and law reinforce the behavior of organizations to protect human rights (Mares, 2010; Taylor, 2011). When human rights are violated, states are obligated to ensure that the offending organizations are held accountable (Taylor, 2011). Through these pillars, organizations are being forced to "do no harm" by proactively implementing policies to protect human rights as opposed to taking reactive actions (Taylor, 2011).

Legal aspects of natural justice are embedded in the legal frameworks of society, which demand that all entities, including individuals and organizations, have a duty to act fairly. This is not voluntary, but codified in law. Natural justice has existed in statutes for centuries; however, the UN is now making the position of the firm clearer through the Guiding Principles. Importantly, transnational companies usually find loopholes to avoid local social and legal pressures, but it may be that the logic underpinning the Guiding Principles might make that increasingly difficult; the link of fairness to natural justice appears to be leading to legal accountability of firms for their socially irresponsible behavior. Indeed, the Guiding Principles appear to influence the manner in which relationships between stakeholder groups are managed to ensure that organizations behave responsibly and are held accountable.

Prior to the Guiding Principles and agreed SLO practices, there were no mechanisms to address human rights violations in regions with lax regulations. In the Niger Delta region in Nigeria, there are many instances of human rights violations by multinational oil corporations. The oil exploration and extraction industry is the largest financial contributor to the Nigerian Government with the revenues from the Niger Delta being the main source (Ako, 2012). Given the importance of oil to the Nigerian economy, the government holds legal ownership of all oil resources in Nigeria, which is upheld in both the law and the constitution (Ako, 2012). In turn, the Government secures arrangements with MNCs, charging high rent levels for the oil to be extracted (Garvey & Newell, 2005). However, these arrangements provide MNCs with preferential treatment as they are extracting oil on behalf of the Government. This can lead to conflicts of interest, which often favors the MNCs or the Nigerian government, to the detriment of community members.

Typically, MNCs in the oil industry in Nigeria receive all the monetary benefits from extraction whilst the inhabitants of the local communities are left to bear all the negative consequences, such as environmental devastation, social inequities, and economic hardships (Ako, 2012; Frynas, 2005). This has contributed to social unrest leading to several instances of violence aided and often caused by MNCs such as Shell (Agbonifo, 2011). Shell has been accused of employing mercenaries to repress social unrest amongst local communities. They have also been accused of reneging on agreed compensation for community members due to the harm caused by their extraction activities (Agbonifo, 2011). As a result of these issues, conflicts that typically involve (1) disputes between the Nigerian Government and local communities regarding ownership of the oil resources and (2) legal redress for the harms caused by oil extraction (Ako, 2012) perpetuate. According to the latter, given the close relationships between the Nigerian Government and the MNCs, it is often difficult for community members that have been harmed by the extraction activities to seek legal remedies.

For example, as a result of the pollution generated from oil producing activities, farmers and fishermen have been displaced. Although individuals have a natural right to petition the state, in many ways, they do not have the right to petition the firm. As the oil extracting companies are typically supplied with governmental contracts that provide them with the right to extract, it has been very difficult for farmers and fishermen to seek redress from these companies when their land is adversely impacted.

However, through the Guiding Principles, there is a clear duty for organizations to act fairly and reasonably with individuals having the right to natural justice from the firm. According to a recent case of a Nigerian farmer suing Shell in the Netherlands for damage to his land in the Niger Delta (BBC, 2013; Deva & Bilchitz, 2013; Reuters, 2015; Khoury & Whyte, 2016), four out of the five cases against the MNC were rejected but crucially, one was upheld. Given that most cases against the oil companies in the Niger Delta are tried in Nigeria with the oil companies usually prevailing, this outcome poses a victory for victims of human rights abuses. Given that Shell lost the case in the Netherlands (Shell is an Anglo-Dutch company incorporated in London with headquarters in The Hague), it means that, through the Guiding Principles and aided by the support of NGOs and pro bono legal provision, there appears to be a route for natural justice to be upheld, even by the poorest of communities.

Corporate accountability

Corporate accountability, defined as "the ability of those affected by a corporation to regulate the activities of that corporation" (Bendell, 2004, p. 19), is rooted in the participation and engagement between organizations and their major stakeholders (Garvey & Newell, 2005). More specifically, "Corporate accountability often refers, in a managerial sense, to issues of disclosure, auditing, and monitoring of business practices" (Garvey & Newell, 2005, p. 391). Central to corporate accountability, is (1) an obligation that organizations have to account for their decisions and (2) sanctioning of organizations for their decisions that harm others by providing stakeholders with mechanisms to seek redress (Valor, 2005), often through the legal infrastructure of a state (Garvey & Newell, 2005). According to the former, organizations are increasingly willing to interact with important stakeholders, which seem to be assisted by word-of-mouth that is exchanged between consumer groups through social media outlets.

According to the latter, as in Nigeria, the mechanisms for redress have largely been insufficient in holding organizations accountable for the harms that they cause others. However, if the legal infrastructure of a jurisdiction is sufficiently developed, it can create an environment of accountability (Garvey & Newell, 2005). To this end, in his development of the Guiding Principles, Ruggie makes reference to the importance of the pragmatic use of national laws rather than the creation of new ones. This suggests that there is a need for national governments to change their relationships with MNCs. If this does not occur or, in situations where the legal infrastructure of a state is often difficult to engage with and corporate accountability weakly addressed, there is the need for supra-national governmental agencies to facilitate holding MNCs accountable. The European Court of Human Rights (ECHR), as a supra-governmental agency, was the appropriate body for judging Shell's operations in the Niger Delta, as it held legitimate authority over Shell.

In addition to the ECHR, there are other supra-governmental agencies that can be instrumental in ensuring that organizations are held accountable for their actions. The Inter-American Court of Human Rights (IACHR) is the human rights protection system of the 35 states in the Americas (inclusive of North, South, and Central America). In this, the IACHR provides a platform to ensure that organizations are respecting human rights and being held accountable for their actions. However, in contrast to the ECHR, individual citizens cannot directly petition the court; a complaint must be first submitted to the IACHR, and if deemed a suitable case to be heard in the court, the IACHR will then formally refer the case directly to the IACHR.

In Africa, the African Court of Human Peoples' Rights provides a platform for the hearing of human rights violations. The jurisdiction of the court involves 29 African states. Similar to the IACHR, individuals may only petition their state in seven nations. In the remaining nations, an application must be brought forward from the African Commission or an inter-governmental entity. Importantly, as suggested earlier, individuals may only petition the state for violations, not other individuals or organizations. Even with these limitations, there have only been a small number of individuals successfully pursuing human rights violations to the African Charter (Amao, 2008).

At present, there are no Asia-wide or Oceania-wide organizations or supra-national entities that promote or protect human rights. However, according to the latter, the Oceania nations of Australia and New Zealand have well-established human rights legislations within their national jurisdictions. From this, it can be seen that there are supra-national organizations that operate in Europe and America that can be helpful in both ensuring that organizations are held accountable for their actions and redress and compensation, according to their injuries, to offended parties. It appears that, for universal accountability to be present, appropriate jurisdiction in Africa and Asia will need to be implemented so that no matter where MNCs operate, their actions will be held accountable.

Stakeholder engagement

At its core, stakeholder engagement involves transparency and accountability (Bowen, 1953). It requires organizations to communicate with relevant stakeholders and to take their interests into consideration when making decisions. This includes involving important stakeholders in the decision-making process, where appropriate. When organizations do this, it is argued that they will be in a better position to maximize value (Philips et al., 2003).

Without a keen focus on profitability, organizations could be compromised in their ability to provide employment, pay wages, meet consumer needs, or required returns on investment. Whilst engaging with stakeholders, it is vital that organizational members do not lose focus of their *raison d'être*, namely, maintaining the long-term sustainability of the organization. However, in striving for sustainability, problems often arise when competing claims exist between stakeholder groups. When this occurs, it can lead to one stakeholder group receiving most of the value and other stakeholders not being compensated fairly (e.g. shareholders over employees) (Philips et al., 2003). In this way, maximizing firm value could not be accomplished if employees are unmotivated, customers dissatisfied, shareholders not receiving a return on investment, and the local community is not considered. To this end, a careful balance is needed, and to achieve this, organizations have to communicate all aspects and objectives to their important stakeholders. To provide a suitable channel to all stakeholders to facilitate this communication, social media pressures and the Guiding Principles should help in stimulating CSR.

Conclusions and managerial implications

As the actions of organizations often have substantial social implications, business people have social responsibilities (Bowen, 1953; Lee, 2008) and, by extension, accountabilities. To this end, CSR is defined as "the obligations of businessmen to pursue those policies, to make those decisions, or to follow those lines of action which are desirable in terms of the objectives and values of our society" (Bowen, 1953, p. 6).

Social media pressure and a centralized framework with agreed values and mechanisms for recompense, such as the UN Guiding Principles, have been shown to facilitate corporate accountability. This is underpinned by stakeholder engagement whereby organizational members communicate and engage, regularly, with a broad spectrum of important stakeholders. Through this engagement with stakeholders, it is likely that organizations will be fully informed and in an improved position to balance the needs of business with their obligations to society enshrined in their formalized CSR procedures.

In the current organizational environment, managers often work in groups to make strategic decisions that have organization-wide implications. In these group settings, accountability is often attributed to the group, not the participating individual managers. Alternatively, the decision the individual makes, as well as that by a group, may well be essentially determined, or even mandated, by company policy. Moreover, although managers might well be inherently good and want to make good ethical choices, they possess cognitive limitations that can prevent them from doing so; bounded rationality and cognitive biases prevent managers from assessing all the relevant details associated with an ethical dilemma. As a result, they might make unethical decisions and, to maintain their self-concept, morally disengage.

To bring accountability back into an organizational context so that managers, regardless of operating within a group or otherwise, engage with important stakeholders, the UN Guiding Principles and the pressure that can be exerted through social media and SLO can help. If managers then behave unethically, they can be exposed through social media which could lead to reputational damage to both the organization and individual manager. Coupled with this, if important stakeholders are harmed through the actions of organizations, the organization could be held accountable through legal remedies present in the UN Guiding Principles. Through these Guiding Principles, social media pressures and SLO, organizational members might be deterred from making decisions that sacrifice the interests of one stakeholder group for that of another. Ultimately, this helps in ensuring that organizations remain accountable and engaged with those important members of their environment, which should foster sufficiently engaged CSR in organizations.

References

Adomdza, G. K. and Astebro, T. (2012) Cognitive biases may not be all that bad: The socio-psychological influence of cognitive bias on investments and venture performance, Unpublished manuscript, pp. 1–51.

Agbonifo, J. (2011) Corporate social responsibility: An oversocialised view of multinational corporations in Africa? *Journal of International Relations and Development*, 14(1), pp. 126–136.

Ajzen, I. and Fishbein, M. (2000) Attitudes and the attitude-behavior relation: Reasoned and automatic processes, *European Review of Social Psychology*, 11(1), pp. 1–33.

Ako, R. T. (2012) Re-defining corporate social responsibility (CSR) in Nigeria's post-amnesty oil industry, *African Journal of Economic and Management Studies*, 3(1), pp. 9–22.

Amao, O. O. (2008) Corporate social responsibility, multinational corporations and the law in Nigeria: Controlling multinationals in host states, *Journal of African Law*, 52(1), pp. 89–113.

Asiedu-Akrofi, D. (1989) Judicial recognition and adoption of customary law in Nigeria, *The American Journal of Comparative Law*, 37(3), pp. 571–593.

Astebro, T. Jeffrey, S. A. and Adomdza, G. K. (2007) Inventor perseverance after being told to quit: The role of cognitive biases, *Journal of Behavioral Decision Making*, 20, pp. 253–272.

Bandura, A. (1986). *Social foundations of thought and action: A social cognitive theory*. Englewood Cliffs, NJ: Prentice-Hall.

Bandura, A. (2002) Selective moral disengagement in the exercise of moral agency, *Journal of Moral Education*, 31(2), pp. 101–121.

Bandura, A. (2007) Impeding ecological sustainability through selective moral disengagement, *International Journal of Innovation and Sustainable Development*, 2(1), pp. 8–38.

Baron, R. A. (2004) The cognitive perspective: A valuable tool for answering entrepreneurship's basic 'why' questions, *Journal of Business Venturing*, 19, pp. 221–239.

Bazerman, M. H. and Tenbrunsel, A. E. (2011) *Blind spots. Why we fail to do what's right and what to do about it*. Oxford: Princeton University Press.

BBC (2013). Shell Nigeria case: Court acquits firm on most charges, 30 January 2013. Retrieved from www.bbc.com/news/world-africa-21258653 on 1 October 2014.

Bendell, J. (2004) Barricades and Boardrooms: A Contemporary History of the Corporate Accountability Movement. P19 UNRISD Paper PP-TBS-13, 6 June 2004, United Nations Research Institute for social Development (UNRISD), Switzerland.

Boele, R., Fabig, H. and Wheeler, D. (2001) Shell, Nigeria and the Ogoni. A study in unsustainable development: II. Corporate social responsibility and 'stakeholder management' versus a rights-based approach to sustainable development, *Sustainable Development*, 9, pp. 121–135.

Bowen, H. R. (1953) *The social responsibilities of the businessman*. New York, NY: Harper and Brothers.

Brocas, I. and Carrillo, J. D. (2008) *The psychology of economic decisions*. Oxford: Oxford University Press.

Campitelli, G. and Gobet, F. (2010) Herbert Simon's decision-making approach: Investigation of cognitive processes in experts. *Review of General Psychology*, 14(4), pp. 354–364.

Carrier, J. G. (2012) *A handbook of economic anthropology*. 2nd Edition, Cheltenham, UK: Edgar Elgar.

Carroll, A. B. and Shabana, K. M. (2010) The business case for corporate social responsibility: A review of concepts, research and practice, *International Journal of Management Reviews*, 12(1), pp. 85–105.

Collins, D. (2012) *Business ethics. How to design and manage ethical organizations*. Hoboken: John Wiley & Sons Inc.

Deva, S. and Bilchitz, B. (2013). *Human rights obligations of business. Beyond the corporate responsibility to respect*. London: Routledge.

Escritt, T. (2015). Dutch ruling on Nigeria could prompt more environmental cases. Reuters, UK, December 18 2015. Retrieved from http://uk.reuters.com/article/us-shell-nigeria-pollution/dutch-ruling-on-nigeria-could-prompt-more-environmental-cases-idUKKBN0U11C520151218 on 1 June 2018.

Fleischmann, M., Amirpur, M., Benlian, A. and Hess, T. (2014) Cognitive Biases in Information Systems Research: A Scientometric Analysis, In: Proceedings of the 22nd European Conference on Information Systems. Tel Aviv: AIS.

Forbes, D. P. (2005) Are some entrepreneurs more overconfident than others? *Journal of Business Venturing*, 20, pp. 623–640.

Freeman, R. E. (1984) *Stakeholder management: Framework and philosophy*. Mansfield, CT: Pitman.

Freud, S. (1976) *The interpretation of dreams* (J. Strachey, Trans.). New York: Norton.

Frynas, J. G. (2005) The false developmental promise of corporate social responsibility: Evidence from multinational oil companies, *International Affairs*, 81(3), pp. 581–598.

Garvey, N. and Newell, P. (2005) Corporate accountability to the poor? Assessing the effectiveness of community-based strategies, *Development in Practice*, 15(3–4), pp. 389–404.

Gioia, D. A. (1992) Pinto fires and personal ethics: A script analysis of missed opportunities, *Journal of Business Ethics*, 11(5/6), pp. 379–390.

Haidt, J. (2001) The emotional dog and its rational tail: A social intuitionist approach to moral judgment, *Psychological Review*, 108, pp. 814–834.

Holton, E. F. III. and Naquin, S. (2005) A critical analysis of HRD evaluation models from a decision-making perspective, *Human Resource Development Quarterly*, 16(2), pp. 257–282.

Human Rights Council. (2011) Promotion and protection of all human rights, civil, political, economic, social and cultural rights, including the right to development. A/HRC/17/31, 1–27.

Jägers, N. (2011) UN Guiding principles on business and human rights: making headway towards real corporate accountability? *Netherlands Quarterly of Human Rights*, 29(2), pp. 159–163.

Kahneman, D. (2011) *Thinking, fast and slow*. London: Penguin Books.

Kahneman, D. and Frederick, S. (2002) Representativeness Revisited: Attribute Substitution in Intuitive Judgment. In Gilovich, T., Griffin, D. and Kahneman, D. (Eds.), *Heuristics and Biases: The Psychology of Intuitive Judgment*. Cambridge: Cambridge University.

Kang, J. and Hustvedt, G. (2014) Building trust between consumers and corporations: The role of consumer perceptions of transparency and social responsibility, *Journal of Business Ethics*, 125(2), pp. 253–265.

Kannadhasan, M., Aramvalarthan, S. and Kumar, B. P. (2014) Relationship among cognitive biases, risk perceptions and individual's decision to start a venture, *Decision*, 41(1), pp. 87–98.

Keh, H. T., Foo, M. D. and Lim, B. C. (2002) Opportunity evaluation under risky conditions: The cognitive processes of entrepreneurs, *Entrepreneurship Theory and Practice*, 27(2), pp. 125–148.

Keil, M., Depledge, G. and Rai, A. (2007) Escalation: The role of problem recognition and cognitive bias, *Decision Sciences*, 38(3), pp. 391–424.

Khoury, S. and Whyte, D. (2016) *Corporate human rights violations: Global prospects for legal action*. London: Routledge.

Klein, N. (2000) *No logo*. New York: Picador.

Kovacs, R. (2006) An interdisciplinary bar for the public interest: What CSR and NGO frameworks contribute to the public relations of British and European activists, IPRRC – 283, pp. 1–18.

Lee, M. P. (2008). A review of the theories of corporate social responsibility: Its evolutionary path and the road ahead. *International Journal of Management Reviews*, 10(1), pp. 53–73.

Lindenberg, S. (2001) Social rationality as a unified model of man (including bounded rationality), *Journal of Management and Governance*, 5(3), pp. 239–251.

Lipman, B. L. (1995) Processing and bounded rationality: A survey, *The Canadian Journal of Economics*, 28(1), pp. 42–67.

March, J. G. (1978) Bounded rationality, ambiguity, and the engineering of choice, *The Bell Journal of Economics*, 9(2), pp. 587–608.

March, J. G. (1994) *A primer on decision making. How decisions happen.* New York, NY: The Free Press.

Mares, R. (2010) A gap in the corporate responsibility to respect human rights, *Monash University Law Review*, 36(3), pp. 33–83.

Maruna, S. and Mann, R. E. (2006) A fundamental attribution error? Rethinking cognitive distortions, *Legal and Criminological Psychology*, 11, pp. 155–177.

Milgram, S. (1974) *Obedience to authority: An experimental view.* New York, NY: Harper & Row.

Moffat, K. and Zhang, A. (2014) The paths to social licence to operate: An integrative model explaining community acceptance of mining, *Resources Policy*, 39, pp. 61–70.

Moore, C. (2008) Moral disengagement in processes of organizational corruption, *Journal of Business Ethics*, 80 (1), pp. 129–139.

Morgan, R. M. and Hunt, S. D. (1994) The commitment-trust theory of relationship marketing, *Journal of Marketing*, 58(3), pp. 20–37.

Owen, J. R. and Kemp, D. (2013) Social licence and mining: A critical perspective, *Resources Policy*, 38, pp. 29–35.

Pavitt, H. (2012) No place to hide: New technological advances in Web 2.0 and social media may force organisations to improve their corporate social responsibility, *Social Alternatives*, 31(2), pp. 22–28.

Philips, R., Freeman, R. E. and Wicks, A. C. (2003) What stakeholder theory is not, *Business Ethics Quarterly*, 13(4), pp. 479–502.

Porter, D., Andrews. M., Turkewitz, J. A. and Wescott, C. G. (2011) Managing Public Finance and Procurement in Fragile and Conflicted Settings, *International Public Management Journal*, 14(4), pp. 369–394.

Robertson, J. E. (1988) Judicial review of prison discipline in the United States and England: A comparative study of due process and natural, *American Criminal Law Review*, 26(1323), pp. 1–30.

Sanchez, J. C., Carballo, T. and Gutierrez, A. (2011) The entrepreneur from a cognitive approach, *Psicothema*, 23(3), pp. 433–438.

Schauer, F. (1976) English Natural justice and American due process: An analytical comparison, *William and Mary Law Review*, 18(1), pp. 47–92.

Schwenk, C. R. (1986) Information, cognitive biases, and commitment to a course of action, *Academy of Management Review*, 11(2), pp. 298–310.

Simon, H. A. (1945) *Administrative behavior. A study of decision-making processes in administrative organizations*, 4th edition. New York, NY: The Free Press.

Simon, H. A. (1955) A behavioural model for rational choice, *The Quarterly Journal of Economics*, 69(1), pp. 99–118.

Simon, H. A. (1996) *The sciences of the artificial.* Cambridge, MA: The MIT Press.

Taylor, M. B. (2011) The Ruggie framework: Polycentric regulation and the implications for corporate social responsibility, *Nordic Journal of Applied Ethics*, 5(1), pp. 9–30.

Taylor, W. S. (1923) Rationalization and its social significance, *The Journal of Abnormal Psychology and Social Psychology*, 17(4), pp. 410–418.

Tenbrunsel, A. E. Diekmann, K. A. Wade-Benzoni, K. A. and Bazerman, M. H. (2010) The ethical mirage: A temporal explanation as to why we aren't as ethical as we think we are, Harvard Business School Working Paper 08–012, pp. 1–65.

Thompson, S. C., Armstrong, W. and Thomas, C. (1998) Illusions of control, underestimations, and accuracy: A control heuristic explanation, psychological bulletin, *American Psychological Association*, 123(2), pp. 143–161.

Tsang, J. A. (2002) Moral rationalization and the integration of situational factors and psychological processes in immoral behavior, *Review of General Psychology*, 6(1), pp. 25–50.

Utting, P. (2008) The struggle for corporate accountability, *Development and Change*, 39(6), pp. 959–975.

Valor, C. (2005). Corporate social responsibility and corporate citizenship: Towards corporate accountability. *Business and Society Review*, 110(2), pp. 191–212.

Van Essen, G. L., Story, D. A., Poustie, S. J., Griffiths, M. M. J. and Marwood, C. L. (2004) Natural justice and human research ethics committees: An Australia-wide survey, *MJA*, 180, pp. 63–66.

Warhurst, A. (2001) Corporate citizenship and corporate social investment drivers of tri-sector partnerships, *Journal of Corporate Citizenship*, 1(Spring), pp. 57–73.

White, J., Bandura, A. and Bero, L. A. (2009) Moral disengagement in the corporate world, *Accountability in Research*, 16, pp. 41–74.

Zindel, M. L., Zindel, T. and Quirino, M. G. (2014) Cognitive bias and their implications on the financial market, *International Journal of Engineering and Technology*, 14(3), pp. 11–18.

Zyglidopoulos, S. and Fleming, P. (2011) Corporate accountability and the politics of visibility in 'late modernity', *Organization*, 18(5), pp. 691–706.

2.5 Managing corporate social responsibility stakeholders in the age of social media

Scott Banghart and Cynthia Stohl

Introduction

A signature feature of the last two decades is increasing corporate influence over our lives as citizens, private individuals, and community members, as well as our environment. From both scholarly and managerial perspectives, greater interdependence among private, corporate, and public spheres means that who counts or acts as a corporate stakeholder has become more complex, fluid, and difficult to manage (Mitchell, Van Buren, Greenwood, & Freeman, 2015; O'Riordan & Fairbrass, 2013). This complexity is amplified by the ubiquity of digital technologies, particularly public social media platforms (e.g., Facebook, Twitter, and YouTube), which provide unparalleled opportunities for interaction among corporations, stakeholders, and the general public (Castelló, Morsing, & Schultz, 2013). Against this backdrop of greater interdependence and heightened connectivity, it is not surprising that public demands for corporate social responsibility (CSR), accountability, and communicative transparency have increased (Christensen, Morsing, & Thyssen, 2011).

Today, CSR engagement and stakeholder relationship management are increasingly entwined. Corporations are expected to act responsibly – not only in their own narrow interests, but also in the interests of the public at large. At its core, CSR has become "a stakeholder oriented concept that extends beyond the organization's boundaries and is driven by an ethical understanding of the organization's responsibility for the impact of its business activities" on the broader global community and the environment (Maon, Lindgreen, & Swaen, 2009, p. 72). Consequently, corporate stakeholders have come to embody a larger and more diverse set of groups and individuals than ever before, many of whom are loosely connected and relatively detached from a corporation's primary goals, products, and profit-making motives. In other words, stakeholders who previously may have been conceived as low priority by organizations are becoming more salient (Whelan, Moon, & Grant, 2013).

In this chapter, we examine the intersections of these burgeoning developments to consider the kinds of choices organizations must make as they manage CSR stakeholder relationships in the age of social media. *CSR stakeholders* include groups and/or individuals who are engaged in some form of dialogue with a corporation for the purpose of influencing its social, economic, political, and environmental decisions (Pedersen, 2006). Historically, when corporations have treated business and profit-making as their primary responsibilities, stakeholders have included only those who can directly impact or be impacted by their financial performance or product development (e.g., employees, stockholders, customers, vendors, local community members, etc.; Freeman, 1984). However, as social media make corporations more accessible and information about their CSR-related issues more available, it is increasingly common for global citizens (i.e., members of the general public who are not and may not ever be customers, employees or shareholders but who are nonetheless affected by corporations' social and environmental activities) to interact with organizations about their issues. Thus, Freeman's (1984) original conception of interactivity as a key component of the organization–stakeholder relationship has evolved considerably from instrumental, asymmetric communication *about* CSR to an ongoing dialogue in which corporations and CSR stakeholders collectively create, debate, negotiate, and explore what it means to be a socially responsible organization (Ihlen, Bartlett, & May, 2011; Morsing & Schultz, 2006).

The proliferation and widespread adoption of social media have played a fundamental role in emerging communicative expectations and participatory norms associated with CSR and stakeholder relationship management, particularly by affording new possibilities for dialogic engagement, transparent information sharing, and negotiated responsibilities (see Stohl, Etter, Banghart, & Woo, 2017). These shifts are typically seen as positive because they encourage organizations to become more responsible by facilitating direct connection and mutual exchange with CSR stakeholders (Whelan et al., 2013). At the same time, however, these practices generate new challenges because the polyphony of voices in the online environment can generate a host of conflicting interests, contradictory expectations, and competing demands (Castelló et al., 2013). In effect, today's corporations are embedded in a global online network in which countless interested parties can raise concerns, engage in discussions, and participate in organizational decision-making processes about CSR-related issues. Thus, it is becoming more difficult – if not impossible – to either segment stakeholder groups or address the totality of their diverse needs and interests through traditional engagement strategies (Besiou, Hunter, & Van Wassenhove, 2013). In other words, organization-centered stakeholder management approaches are becoming obsolete as engagement moves from traditional modes of communication to more dynamic "issue arenas" of digital interaction and discussion facilitated by social media (Luoma-aho & Vos, 2010).

Clearly, social media uses and affordances are transforming all types of corporate–stakeholder relations. However, these dynamics are particularly relevant in the context of CSR given the increasing involvement of global citizens in CSR-related issues, activities, and conversations. For organizations, managing these new types of relationships requires novel strategies because CSR stakeholders who were not previously considered as such exhibit different characteristics than those associated with traditional stakeholders. Typically, CSR stakeholders are more issue-focused (i.e., they express concerns in terms of specific social or environmental problems), volatile (i.e., they engage with organizations on the basis of perceived wrongdoing), and transient (i.e., connectivity is often unplanned and they may not continue to engage with organizations once their concerns are addressed) than traditional stakeholders (Luoma-aho & Vos, 2010). They also have the capacity to organize collective action more quickly and efficiently through social media (Luoma-aho, Tirkkonen, & Vos, 2013). Taken together, today's CSR stakeholders are more efficient, have stronger voices, and are more emotionally bonded than ever before, presenting new challenges and opportunities for stakeholder relationship management (Freeman, Dmytriyev, & Strand, 2017).

Although scholars are beginning to grapple with the complexities of CSR communication and stakeholder engagement in the digital age (e.g., Busch & Shepherd, 2014; Lyon & Montgomery, 2013), a majority of studies to date have focused on the instrumental benefits and inherent dangers of social media (e.g., Lindgreen & Swaen, 2010; Linke & Zerfass, 2013) with minimal attention to relational dynamics among organizations and CSR stakeholders. What is missing from this literature is an analysis centered on the relational challenges facing organizations as stakeholders and global citizens alike use social media as co-creation mechanisms for CSR dialogue and engagement (Stohl et al., 2017). For example, the carmaker Porsche's ten million Facebook followers are "not necessarily customers or community members, but they are interested in following the development of Porsche models and they share their opinions on Porsche's Facebook page from time to time" (Freeman et al., 2017, p. 124). These new types of CSR stakeholders are especially prominent among digital natives (Vodanovich, Sundaram, & Myers, 2010) who are not just passive consumers of CSR information but expect to engage with organizations in real-time and exert influence over their business, social, and environmental practices, irrespective of their actual involvement with the company (Luoma-aho, 2015).

In what follows, we first explicate how the affordances of social media have expanded corporate responsibilities and transformed the nature of identifying, prioritizing, and communicating with CSR stakeholders. Next, we advance a network-centered approach for strategic stakeholder relationship management in the digital age – one that can help organizations to develop new strategies for CSR engagement based on the intensity of a stakeholder's connectivity and participation as well as the degree of relational multiplexity and issue involvement the stakeholder exhibits. To conclude, we discuss the potential for this framework to inform future research on managing CSR stakeholder relations in the age of social media.

Linking social media affordances to evolving CSR stakeholder relationships

We adopt an "affordance" perspective (Treem & Leonardi, 2013) to explore how social media technologies transform the nature of CSR stakeholder management. Traditionally, stakeholder relationships have been conceptualized through discrete categories based on simplistic boundary distinctions such as internal–external (Carroll, 1989); cooperative–competitive (Freeman, 1984); primary–secondary (Clarkson, 1995); direct–indirect (Frooman, 1999); necessary–contingent (Friedman & Miles, 2002); and core–peripheral (Su, Mitchell, & Sirgy, 2007), among others. However, such rigid boundary logics are unsustainable and unrealistic given the affordances of social media, the "physical reality of a virtual stakeholder" (Freeman et al., 2017, p. 125) and the communicative expectations of contemporary CSR (Castelló et al., 2013; Stohl et al., 2017). According to Treem and Leonardi (2013), affordances are the possibilities for action that emerge in the ongoing and reciprocal relationships among material artifacts and social actors (i.e., how organizations and stakeholders leverage the technical features of social media as co-creation mechanisms for CSR). There are four social media affordances that alter the nature of corporate–stakeholder relations: visibility, association, persistence, and editability.

Visibility

Visibility refers to the capacity for social media to make information about organizations and their CSR stakeholders as well as the communicative interactions between them readily available and publically accessible (Treem & Leonardi, 2013). Collective information sharing is the currency of public social media. Thus, corporations can easily view and broadcast information about their activities, just as CSR stakeholders can consume and share more information about corporate behaviors and their consequences. Visibility also makes meta-knowledge about both the nature of connections among organizations and CSR stakeholders (e.g., tie strength) as well as what is at stake within their relationships (e.g., material, financial or symbolic resources) more transparent. Network nodes can become more knowledgeable as the links among organizations and CSR stakeholders become more visible to the broader global audiences who engage with these platforms. The widespread availability of information and the ease and speed with which social media users can respond to organizational messages (e.g., through comments, "likes," and "retweets") makes it increasingly possible for individuals and groups who did not previously consider themselves as CSR stakeholders to become aware of problematic corporate behaviors and engage in CSR dialogue. For example, the success of Greenpeace's campaign to stop a partnership between LEGO and Shell Corporation has been attributed to the power of the 2014 YouTube video "LEGO: Everything is NOT awesome" (GreenpeaceVideo, 2014). This video made visible the link between Shell Oil's artic drilling and the LEGO Corporation. With more than 8 million views, the video began a global dialogue among a diverse set of stakeholder groups including environmental activists, parents, human rights champions, LEGO fans, and child advocates who theretofore were unconnected (Vaughan, 2014). In such a communicative environment, organizations are no longer able to control the audiences with whom they engage (i.e., who they are talking to, who is talking about them) or the CSR-related issues they address (i.e., what topics they are talking about) because dialogue is multi-vocal and multidirectional rather than dyadic (two-way) and bidirectional.

Association

The affordance of association refers directly to the capacity for social media to connect people to people (e.g., individuals concerned with similar CSR issues); people to content (e.g., access to relevant CSR issues and information); and content to content (e.g., through hyperlinks, hashtags; Treem & Leonardi, 2013). Thus, it draws attention to the complex socio-material networks and relational structures that comprise the social media environment and support the connections between organizations, traditional stakeholders, and global citizens. As Whelan et al. (2013) note, "the increased speed, the reduced costs, and the multi-directional nature of social media means that individual citizens can, along with corporations and (functional/formally organized) stakeholders, communicate and organize with other individual citizens (and corporations and stakeholders)" (p. 781) in ways that were never before possible. Specifically, when organizations and CSR stakeholders share and exchange social media content and engage in dialogue, they generate social capital and make their associations with CSR actors and issues more explicit. In turn, it becomes easier for public audiences to gather around shared interests and concerns, organize formal and informal CSR stakeholder coalitions, and participate in collective action. Association also enables organizations to gain a better sense of how particular CSR stakeholders are responding to their efforts and initiatives, as connections among network actors and CSR issues are both visible and searchable through social media. Yet, at the same time, the fluidity of CSR stakeholders and public participation makes it challenging for organizations to segment audiences and proactively manage their agendas around specific concerns because associations continuously evolve with the ongoing flow of CSR dialogue.

Persistence

Persistence concerns the temporal dimensions of social media and the stability of messages, information, and multimedia content over time (Treem & Leonardi, 2013). On the one hand, conversations on social media are ongoing and interactions are observable in real-time as they emerge. Thus, the nature of dialogue between organizations and CSR stakeholders is processual and dynamic rather than intermittent and static (Castelló et al., 2013). On the other hand, CSR communication takes on more permanence in social media because messages are recorded and stored as information that can be "searched, browsed, replayed, annotated, visualized, restructured, and recontextualized" (Erickson & Kellogg, 2000, p. 68) long after their initial transmission. Consequently, relational history becomes more salient because the persistence of information and conversations provides CSR stakeholders and public audiences with a narrative for reviewing past organizational behaviors and relations, and contextualizing present/future actions and decisions (Majchrzak, Faraj, Kane, & Azad, 2013). In other words, current CSR objectives can be compared and evaluated in terms of previous efforts, events, and circumstances; thus, it is more difficult for organizational (inter)actions to be forgotten (e.g., past problems can reemerge, corporate scandals can be revisited). For example, when social media conversations linked Nestlé corporation's use of palm oil to the destruction of rainforests and the death of orangutans (Dearing, 2010), users were also reminded of and provided archives relating to the company's infamous record of corporate irresponsibility dating back to the 1970s scandals involving infant formula and newborn health (Mattera, 2013). In sum, while the speed and ease of CSR dialogue are heightened through social media, the affordance of persistence diminishes the ephemerality and contextual integrity of CSR communication by extending its reach and permanence. In turn, companies must be mindful that conversations with CSR stakeholders are preserved over time and may potentially be taken out of context, reinterpreted, and/or used against them in the future.

Editability

Finally, editability centers on the creation, modification, and elimination of user-generated content (i.e., messages, information, photos, videos) on social media (Treem & Leonardi, 2013). The affordance of editability enables organizations to retain some level of control over their CSR messages, as managers can spend a considerable amount of time contemplating, crafting, and reviewing them before making them visible to CSR stakeholders and public audiences. Even after messages are shared through social media, it is possible for organizations to modify or remove them. However, because social media messages are public, users can easily record and save them (e.g., through screen captures) before they are revised or deleted. Although organizations may desire to alter or remove unwanted social media content, certain forms of message manipulation may be perceived as inauthentic or untrustworthy – especially in the context of CSR, where corporate messages often already evoke skepticism from CSR stakeholders and the general public (Christensen et al., 2011). Yet, even when organizations do not attempt to modify their CSR messages, the combined affordances of visibility, persistence, and editability enable external audiences to (re)appropriate them in unintended, unanticipated, and sometimes consequential ways (Albu & Etter, 2016). When social media users create mashups through combining corporate messages or images with other user-generated content, they detach pieces of information from their original contexts and potentially alter the meanings that people construct around them. In the aforementioned Nestlé case, for example, Nestlé sued Greenpeace for "copyright infringement" and had an offending video removed from YouTube and Facebook (Greenpeace had reformatted the KitKat logo to read "killer"), but Facebook users independently began to upload variations of the logo and post negative comments and criticism under different avatars on Nestlé's public page (Ionescu-Somers & Enders, 2012). Overall, then, while the affordance of editability can be beneficial in terms of strategic CSR communication, the capacity for social media users to modify and redirect content means that organizations must constantly monitor the online environment to assess how their CSR messages and activities are being represented and interpreted by CSR stakeholders and the general public.

In summary, the affordances of social media combine to make the management of CSR stakeholder relations and interests far more complex and nuanced. The next section explicates what this new communication environment means for managing CSR stakeholder relations.

Managing CSR stakeholder relationships in the digital age: a network-centered approach

Traditional approaches for managing stakeholder relations focus primarily on identifying stakeholders, segmenting them into groups with similar interests, and prioritizing engagement with each stakeholder group based on the importance of its claims. However, the classic distinction between stakeholders (i.e., those who directly affect and are affected by organizational CSR actions; see Freeman, 1984) and publics (i.e., recipients of organizational CSR messages; see Grunig & Repper, 1992) is no longer very useful in online networked environments (i.e., social media) where the boundaries between private, corporate, and public spheres are increasingly porous and fluid. Today, it is more apparent than ever that CSR stakeholders and their interests can neither be fully identified a priori nor defined at a single point in time.

Moreover, prioritization – a key process in both CSR engagement and stakeholder relationship management in general – is typically based on particular attributes and those stakeholders with a greater degree and number of those attributes are the ones that are most likely to receive managerial attention. For example, in Mitchell, Agle, and Wood's (1997) classic stakeholder salience model, stakeholders are classified and prioritized based on three central attributes – power, legitimacy, and urgency. *Power* is defined as the degree of influence a stakeholder has over managerial behaviors and/or corporate decision-making processes. Thus, CSR stakeholders have power when they can get corporations to take action that they would not have taken if the relationship was not as salient. *Legitimacy* refers to the "generalized perception or assumption that the actions of an entity are desirable, proper, or appropriate within some socially constructed system of norms, values, beliefs, and definitions" (Suchman, 1995, p. 574). In corporate–stakeholder relationships, legitimacy is granted when managers consider the concerns (i.e., needs, claims) of CSR stakeholders to be socially acceptable and deserving of attention. *Urgency* involves both the criticality of a particular stakeholder's concern and the extent to which it requires immediate managerial attention (Mitchell et al., 1997). In other words, when corporations perceive a CSR stakeholder's claim to be important and believe that a time delay in addressing it is unacceptable, interaction becomes more urgent. In the context of CSR, this model suggests that the agendas of more salient CSR stakeholders should take precedence in managerial decision-making about which issues to address because their relationships are characterized by more frequent interaction and greater interdependence (Peloza & Papania, 2008).

Yet, in an online environment where corporate responsibilities are expected to be mutually defined and continuously negotiated through deliberative public dialogue and where who counts and participates in dialogue as CSR stakeholders is constantly in flux, such an organization-centric model is no longer adequate. Rather, CSR stakeholder relations are embedded in ongoing, emergent, and increasingly interconnected communication networks that develop outside of managerial decision-making processes as corporate actions and messages are processed by individuals, groups, and other organizations across the dimensions of time and space (Luoma-aho, 2015). In particular, the ability to access and link information in more visible, robust, and dynamic ways; the potential for increased connectivity within and across stakeholder groups; the capacity to transcend spatio-temporal boundaries, making past relations and communication more salient and present interactions more interconnected; and the entrepreneurial facility to reshape, modify, decontextualize, and recontextualize corporate–stakeholder messaging all suggest that, when the attributes of power, legitimacy, and urgency are assessed at the dyadic level rather than at the network level, they provide an insufficient picture of emerging relations and concerns.

A network-centered approach offers one way to move beyond individual attributes and dyadic-level relationships to address the relational connections between and among CSR stakeholders and issues in the online environment. This approach involves news ways of understanding the well-known attributes of power, legitimacy, and urgency as well as assessing new relational dynamics at the network level.

Reconsidering CSR stakeholder attributes at the network level

According to dyadic stakeholder models (Mitchell et al., 1997), the accumulation of power, legitimacy, and urgency determines the salience of a particular stakeholder and the extent to which organizations should prioritize and manage its concerns. However, these constructs operate in fundamentally different ways at the network level, particularly when we consider the relational and communicative dynamics of the social media environment.

Power as betweenness centrality

The participatory affordances of social media make power dynamics among corporations, traditional stakeholders, and everyday citizens more balanced and decentralized in the digital age (Castells, 2009). Whereas power at the dyadic level is primarily conceived in terms of a CSR stakeholder (e.g., an activist group) having more or less influence over an organization, power at the network level is oftentimes derived from a CSR stakeholder's betweenness centrality, or the degree to which the stakeholder is connected to other network actors who are not directly linked to each other (see Freeman, 1979 for a detailed discussion of different types of centrality). When a CSR stakeholder exhibits high betweenness centrality, it holds a structural power advantage in the organization's stakeholder network because it can control the flow and timing of CSR-related information between multiple network actors who are otherwise disconnected. For example, a CSR stakeholder might serve as an information broker who fills structural holes in the network by engaging previously unlinked actors (e.g., organizations, other CSR stakeholders, civil society members) in CSR dialogue to mobilize support around a particular concern, and in turn, place pressure on a corporation to engage in more socially responsible behavior. Accordingly, a network-centered approach to managing CSR stakeholder relations moves beyond power dynamics *within* organization–stakeholder relationships to consider how power and influence are also manifested in the relations *among* stakeholders in the broader CSR network enabled by social media. Thus, we see, for example, that contemporary organizations are moving toward "virtual stakeholder dialogue" projects for managing stakeholder relations, such as Nike's GreenXchange, Intel's CSR @Intelblog, and Google's Chromium project (Driessen, Kok, & Hillebrand, 2013).

Legitimacy as betweenness centrality

Legitimacy is also conferred in different ways in the age of social media. In traditional dyadic models (Mitchell et al., 1997), legitimacy is typically assessed in terms of the influence and impact of a stakeholder's claims on an organization with minimal attention to whether actors in the broader network perceive the concern to be legitimate. However, in the social media environment, CSR stakeholders may secure their legitimacy by engaging in business, social, and political dialogue with other key network actors and institutions in the CSR domain – not necessarily with a particular organization. Thus, stakeholder legitimacy is also based on degree centrality, that is, the extent to which a CSR stakeholder is connected or hyperlinked to other CSR stakeholders and/or members of the global community. For example, when CSR stakeholders who were once considered secondary/ peripheral (i.e., those who are indirectly affected by organizational CSR efforts) become connected to primary/core stakeholder groups (i.e., those who are directly involved in organizational CSR efforts) through social media, it becomes necessary for companies to prioritize their concerns because of their potential to influence primary/core stakeholders' perceptions of what constitutes a legitimate CSR claim (Castelló et al., 2013). Hence, a network-centered approach to CSR stakeholder relations extends the scope of traditional legitimation processes to consider how the legitimacy of CSR claims is corroborated in ongoing mediated discussions between multiple organizations, stakeholders, and public citizens who may or may not fall within the company's typical sphere of influence.

Urgency as information diffusion

The attribute of urgency can also be conceived through network terms in the social media environment. Conventional understandings of urgency in organization–stakeholder relationships predominantly center on an organization's evaluation of whether a CSR stakeholder's claim is critical and requires immediate attention (Mitchell et al., 1997). However, given the affordances of visibility and association, determining the importance and time-sensitivity of a particular concern is no longer simply a function of managerial perception. Rather, the criticality of a CSR claim becomes evident in how quickly and widely information diffuses across social media networks and the degree of attention it receives from multiple stakeholder groups and the general public (e.g., through likes, retweets, comments). Social media "operate like a giant word-of-mouth machine, catalyzing and accelerating the so-called viral distribution of information" (Gallaugher & Ransbotham, 2010, p. 199). Consequently, when CSR-related concerns are propagated through social media, organizations have minimal control over the subsequent flow of information across their stakeholder networks and the extent to which their activities are implicated in the discussion.

In turn, it is vital for organizations to monitor the social media environment for emerging concerns and assess how different CSR stakeholders are responding to them in order to stay informed as issues develop, avoid potential crises, and mitigate reputational risks. For example, corporations increasingly engage in "social media listening" through various web-based monitoring platforms (e.g., Hootsuite, Reputology, Social Mention, etc.) that enable them to collect and analyze data about what's being said about their brands, products, and social and environmental impact online (Rendler-Kaplan, 2017). Overall, while companies have little choice but to accept that CSR claims (both bad and good, urgent and non-urgent) are communicated more fervently, broadly, and in less time on social media, a network-centered approach directs attention to the ongoing circulation of information among CSR stakeholders and can provide more nuanced insights around whether and how quickly a CSR claim may become urgent and require managerial attention.

Taken together, the three key attributes associated with determining stakeholder salience (i.e., power, legitimacy, and urgency) can no longer be conceived in terms of a dyadic organization–stakeholder relationships. Rather, it is necessary to consider the broader networked environment within which social norms and expectations for corporate responsibilities are continuously communicated, negotiated, and developed by corporations, stakeholders, and global citizens. We suggest, however, that a network-centered approach to relational stakeholder management goes beyond expanding the conceptual definitions of previously established constructs. As scholars and practitioners address CSR engagement in the social media environment, other network dynamics need to be considered.

New network variables for assessing CSR stakeholder salience

We propose two additional variables to consider as organizations manage CSR stakeholder relations in networked communication environments. Given the centrality of dialogue in contemporary stakeholder engagement and the capacity for social media to make associations between individual stakeholders and CSR-related issues more visible, the level of communicative *intensity* exhibited by CSR stakeholders may help organizations to assess their salience and determine the level of priority with which to address their concerns. Of course, examining intensity alone may not provide enough context for organizations to effectively prioritize CSR stakeholders (Golob & Podnar, 2011). Individual actors within and across CSR stakeholder networks will not only differ in their respective interests and expectations, but also vary in their desired and actual levels of involvement and interaction with organizations (Bimber, Flanagin, & Stohl, 2012; O'Riordan & Fairbrass, 2008). Moreover, individuals are often embedded in multiple stakeholder networks simultaneously (e.g. customers may also be employees, stockholders, and members of the broader community in which the organization operates). This type of relational *multiplexity* increases the strength of these actors' ties as well as their mutual interdependence with organizations and each other (Stohl, 1995). Moreover, multiplex relational embeddedness will strongly influence stakeholder salience and has implications for how CSR stakeholder relations need to be managed.

Intensity

We propose *intensity* as a new network variable to evaluate in managing CSR stakeholder relationships in the digital age. Intensity refers to the magnitude of participation and connectedness a CSR stakeholder group exhibits in the social media environment, which can vary in both breadth and depth. Driessen et al. (2013) described possible differences as the relative intensity and richness of the dialogue. In terms of participation, intensity encompasses how much social media content is authored by a particular stakeholder and the level of detail the stakeholder provides in the information it shares. Stakeholders who share and exchange CSR content more frequently reflect a higher degree of intensity than those who do not. Participation in the network takes a significant amount of time and effort and only when CSR-related issues have high saliency will there be high levels of engagement. However, whether a highly participative stakeholder requires prioritization and managerial attention also depends on the depth of the social media content the stakeholder contributes to the CSR network. In particular, stakeholders who share CSR information in cursory ways (e.g., posting content authored by others, links to news stories) may require less attention than those who author their own content and/or participate extensively in deliberative CSR dialogue and public debates about ongoing concerns. Whereas the former use social media as vehicles for sharing and circulating information *about* organizational CSR efforts and activities, for the more intense stakeholder, social media are *part of* CSR communication itself insofar as they enable stakeholders to become more intensely involved with corporations in co-constructing and negotiating what it means to be socially responsible (Stohl et al., 2017).

Second, in terms of connectedness, intensity can be evaluated based on the number of social ties a CSR stakeholder maintains in its social media network (i.e., degree centrality) as well as the relative strength and diversity of those ties. Examining the quantity and quality of social ties that a CSR stakeholder exhibits (e.g., Twitter followers, Facebook friends or public page "likes") can provide important insights into the CSR stakeholder's scope of influence and impact vis-à-vis its participation and information sharing practices in the social media environment. Generally, online communication networks are low in density (i.e., not every actor is connected to one another) and high in diversity (i.e., actors represent a variety of characteristics, interests, viewpoints – see Easley & Kleinberg, 2010). Thus, we would expect CSR stakeholders' social media networks to be comprised primarily of weak connections to actors who span a variety of different social groups, including both formal/functional group memberships and ascribed affiliations to demographic categories (e.g., gender, age, class). Accordingly, CSR stakeholders who have a greater number of social ties are also higher intensity stakeholders because there are more paths along which information and influence can flow between actors in their networks. Highly connected CSR stakeholders not only have greater potential to reach and influence broader and more diverse audiences with their concerns and viewpoints, but are also more likely to be exposed to and affected by new CSR information and different opinions from those audiences in return. Moreover, because interactions between connections are visible and accessible to the entirety of a stakeholder's social media network, CSR information and dialogue can spread more widely to individuals and groups who corporations may not have considered to be CSR stakeholders.

Taken together, when CSR stakeholders maintain large networks of diverse connections and participate extensively in the social media environment through collective information sharing and ongoing dialogue, they exhibit greater intensity because they have the potential to expand the scope of an organization's CSR stakeholder network through the strength of weak ties (Granovetter, 1973). Specifically, highly connected and participative stakeholders may serve an intense bridging function in an organization's CSR network by providing broad and disparate audiences with increased access to new and different kinds of information that may prompt them to engage corporations in dialogue. In effect, both the breadth of exposure to CSR-related issues and depth of public interest in corporate activities are potentially heightened. Overall, as individuals and groups who were once perceived as more or less inconsequential become increasingly interconnected with CSR stakeholders through social media, it is important to track the development of these relations at the network level. In particular, evaluating and comparing the intensity of multiple CSR stakeholder groups by mapping their networked interrelationships and the flow and direction of CSR dialogue among them (e.g., through social media monitoring) may help organizations to determine which issues and whose concerns are most critical to address in a given situation or at a particular point in time.

Multiplexity

A second network variable that is important to evaluate in the age of social media is the degree of *multiplexity* a CSR stakeholder exhibits in relation to an organization. Generally, multiplexity refers to an overlap of contents, activities, and/or functions in a relationship (Stohl, 1995). In the context of CSR, multiplexity is evident when a tie between network actors (i.e., an organization and stakeholder) encompasses multiple role relations and/or CSR-relevant issues rather than a single role or shared concern. For example, Johansen and Nielsen (2016) identify the ways in which stakeholder complexity constructs multiple identities and roles for the nonprofit organization KIVA in its stakeholder network. *Role multiplexity* captures the various roles that stakeholders represent when they engage in online CSR dialogue. Given that social media platforms collapse multiple contexts and audiences into single online environments (Marwick & boyd, 2011), individuals who participate in online discussions with organizations about CSR-related issues often represent their roles as employees, customers, activists, and/or community citizens simultaneously. For example, an individual may use his or her Facebook account to talk about work-related experiences as an employee, and as a customer and consumer of the organization's products and services. Stakeholders may also exhibit *issue multiplexity* by discussing and becoming involved in multiple CSR-relevant topics that connect them to a corporation and its CSR agenda. For instance, an employee might use Twitter as both a vehicle for promoting company-sponsored local community initiatives (e.g., volunteer efforts, charity events) and as a platform for participating in ongoing dialogue about societal issues (e.g., global human rights, environmental sustainability) that are also tied to the company's CSR repertoire.

Whether it involves overlapping roles or issue-based affiliations, multiplexity has important implications for managing CSR stakeholder relations because it increases tie strength and mutual interdependence in the organization–CSR stakeholder relationship (Ibarra, 1993; Shipilov, 2012). Multiplexity provides multiple bases for communication and dialogue (Verbrugge, 1979) and studies suggest that both the quantity and quality of interaction in these relationships are heightened (Methot, Lepine, Podsakoff, & Christian, 2016). On the one hand, multiplex ties can be more supportive, reliable, trustworthy, and collaborative than other relational ties (Bullis & Bach, 1991; Lazega & Pattison, 1999; Lee & Lee, 2015). Thus, in the online world, multiplex CSR stakeholders may be important sources of high-quality information and advice as well as active proponents of a company's CSR efforts and activities. On the other hand, multiplex ties can also be constraining because the breadth and depth of involvement in these relationships increases the costs associated with breaking them (Brass, Butterfield, & Skaggs, 1998; Shah, Parker, & Waldstrom, 2016). Multiplex CSR stakeholders not only have greater knowledge about the organization and its CSR initiatives, but also care more about its ongoing activities because they expect managers to act according to their interests (Mayer, Davis, & Schoorman, 1995). As a result, we might expect multiplex CSR stakeholders to pay more attention to what is being said about an organization online and to respond more intensely when issues arise (Besiou et al., 2013).

In sum, what all of this suggests is that CSR stakeholders who are linked to an organization through a greater number of roles and/or issues (i.e., those with higher degrees of multiplexity) are more likely to be actively involved in the organization's CSR communication network (both online and offline). By extension, CSR stakeholder relations that exhibit greater multiplexity may also require more managerial attention. In terms of prioritization, mapping CSR stakeholders' overlapping roles and connections to issues at the network level can help to identify patterns of multiplexity among different CSR stakeholders in an organization's network and determine the likelihood of their respective involvement. Pragmatically, such efforts might involve classifying networked CSR stakeholders into more abstract groups based on relational multiplexity and the nature of their engagement. For example, recent work by Luoma-aho (2015) suggests that organizations might benefit from distinguishing among digital faith-holders (i.e., positively engaged stakeholders who exhibit high levels of interdependence with the organization); hate-holders (i.e., negatively engaged stakeholders who dislike the organization and/or its social and environmental activities and thus seek to express their dissatisfaction and anger online); and fake-holders (i.e., inauthentic stakeholders, socio-bots, and artificial opinions generated by persona-creating software and algorithms to either support or oppose an issue). However, given the complex and potentially conflicting expectations associated with different CSR-related roles and issues, relations with multiplex stakeholder groups are likely to be fraught with incompatible goals, competing demands, and ethical dilemmas (Shah et al., 2016). Thus, prioritizing stakeholders a priori may be unfeasible. Rather, as managers continue to grapple with an array of multiplex CSR stakeholders in the social media environment, it will be important to attend to the inherent tradeoffs and tensions they face and the implications of their prioritization strategies.

Conclusions

The advent of digital technologies and social media has dramatically altered the communicative expectations and participatory norms associated with CSR engagement and stakeholder relationship management. In today's world, corporate responsibilities are defined, negotiated, and modified through ongoing and mutually interactive dialogue among businesses, governments, traditional stakeholders, and global citizens (Whelan et al., 2013). These CSR stakeholders are also demanding more transparency and accountability from organizations as they increasingly engage in CSR-related issues and actively participate in corporate decision-making processes (Castelló et al., 2013; Golob & Podnar, 2011). Moreover, against the backdrop of prominent scandals linking corporate activities to human rights violations, CSR stakeholders expect to have rights, respect, and greater access to effective remedy in their relationships with corporations (Ruggie & Nelson, 2015). Combining these new normative expectations for society with the affordances of social media means that contemporary CSR stakeholder relations are far more complex than previous literature suggests.

In summary, the affordances of social media not only render traditional distinctions between CSR stakeholders and publics obsolete, but also shatter the assumption that

CSR stakeholders can be identified a priori and managed based on their individual influence and impact alone. Namely, the fluidity of online role performances makes it increasingly difficult to classify stakeholders into discrete functional categories. Traditional stakeholder groups (e.g., employees, customers, stockholders, community members, etc.) have become an abstraction, as any one person can potentially represent a whole set of overlapping stakeholder groups to which he or she belongs. Furthermore, in the context of intensifying interconnectedness and widespread participation in CSR dialogue, prioritizing stakeholders based on their individual attributes (e.g., power, legitimacy, urgency; Mitchell et al., 1997) in relation to an organization (i.e., at the dyadic level) without accounting for their relationships with each other is no longer adequate. Rather, as we have argued, the new relational dynamics afforded by social media demand consideration at the network level.

A network-centered approach not only suggests alternative ways to understand CSR stakeholder relations based on the well-known attributes of power (betweenness centrality), legitimacy (degree centrality), and urgency (information diffusion), but also introduces new variables to consider, including the *intensity* of CSR stakeholders' participation and connectedness as well as the degree of *multiplexity* they exhibit. Examining CSR stakeholder relations at the network level can provide organizations a more focused account of emerging relations and help them to determine whether CSR stakeholders may require attention at particular points in time. In pragmatic terms, implementing a network-centered approach may also require organizations to invest in social media monitoring services and to develop new skillsets around managing big data networks and social media analytics (Luoma-aho, 2013, 2015).

However, even as social media monitoring services and "social listening" software open up new possibilities for identifying and prioritizing CSR stakeholders, the complexities of the social media environment should not be underestimated. Historically, communication with CSR stakeholders has been one-way/asymmetrical (i.e., sharing information about CSR); two-way/asymmetrical (i.e., responding to CSR stakeholders' concerns); or two-way/symmetrical (i.e., dyadic interaction, see Morsing & Schultz, 2006) with relatively well-defined contexts and audiences. In contrast, CSR stakeholder dialogue in the social media environment is many-to-many, multidirectional, and embedded in complex socio-material networks where contexts are collapsed, audiences are fluid, and CSR concerns are emergent.

Under these conditions, scholars and practitioners face a fundamental paradox when it comes to managing CSR stakeholder relations, namely, that the ubiquity of social media diminishes the capacity for organizations to control relations, manage contexts and issues, and forestall audiences from engagement (Luoma-aho, 2015). Given the affordances of social media, seemingly inconsequential CSR stakeholders can quickly and easily become high influence and high impact in the right circumstance (e.g., by Tweeting confidential information, exposing company secrets). Thus, while we maintain that a network-centered approach can help organizations to better understand the potential scope of influence and impact of their CSR stakeholders (i.e., based on intensity, power, legitimacy) and anticipate their potential involvement (i.e., based on multiplexity), the attribute of urgency is volatile in the online environment and requires constant attention. The latter point suggests a second paradox: the same social media affordances that offer the greatest benefits for CSR stakeholder relations (e.g., the ease/speed of dialogic engagement) are also the ones that present the greatest risks (e.g., the ease/speed of whistleblowing) and most significant burdens (e.g., monitoring the online conversation at all times to mitigate risk). Ultimately, as digitization continues to transform the nature of contemporary stakeholder relationship management, understanding the socio-technical strategies organizational practitioners employ to identify and prioritize CSR stakeholder concerns and minimize risks through monitoring will be important directions for future research. Moreover, the network variables we have suggested may wax and wane in importance, as new affordances and novel forms of digital networking emerge. An essential key, however, to understanding the complex world of digital CSR stakeholders is to move beyond a focus on the attributes of individual stakeholder groups and pay closer attention to the dynamic structures and patterns of connectivity that are generated through the transmission and ongoing exchange of messages across time and space.

References

Albu, O. B. & Etter, M. (2016). Hypertextuality and social media: A study of the constitutive and para-doxical implications of organizational Twitter use. *Management Communication Quarterly, 30*(1), 5–31.

Besiou, M., Hunter, M. L. & Van Wassenhove, L. N. (2013). A web of watchdogs: Stakeholder media networks and agenda-setting in response to corporate initiatives. *Journal of Business Ethics, 118*(4), 709–729.

Bimber, B. A., Flanagin, A. J. & Stohl, C. (2012). *Collective action in organizations: Interaction and engagement in an era of technological change.* New York, NY: Cambridge University Press.

Brass, D. J., Butterfield, K. D. & Skaggs, B. C. (1998). Relationships and unethical behavior: A social network perspective. *Academy of Management Review, 23*(1), 14–31.

Bullis, C. & Bach, B. W. (1991). An explication and test of communication network content and multiplexity as predictors of organizational identification. *Western Journal of Speech Communication, 55*(2), 180–197.

Busch, T. & Shepherd, T. (2014). Doing well by doing good? Normative tensions underlying Twitter's corporate social responsibility ethos. *Convergence-the International Journal of Research into New Media Technologies, 20*(3), 293–315.

Carroll, A. B. (1989). *Business and society: Ethics and stakeholder management.* Cincinatti, OH: South-Western.

Castelló, I., Morsing, M. & Schultz, F. (2013). Communicative dynamics and the polyphony of corporate social responsibility in the network society. *Journal of Business Ethics, 118*(4), 683–694.

Castells, M. (2009). *Communication power.* Oxford: Oxford University Press.

Christensen, L. T., Morsing, M. & Thyssen, O. (2011). The polyphony of corporate social responsibility: Deconstructing accountability and transparency in the context of identity and hypocrisy. In G. Cheney, S. May & D. Munshi (Eds.), *The handbook of communication ethics* (pp. 457–474). New York, NY: Routledge.

Clarkson, M. E. (1995). A stakeholder framework for analyzing and evaluating corporate social performance. *Academy of Management Review, 20*(1), 92–117.

Dearing, S. (2010). Greenpeace boycotts Nestle: 'Don't have a Kit Kat break today'. *Digital Journal.* Retrieved from www.digitaljournal.com/article/289481.

Driessen, P. H., Kok, R. A. W. & Hillebrand, B. (2013). Mechanisms for stakeholder integration: Bringing virtual stakeholder dialogue into organizations. *Journal of Business Research, 66*(9), 1465–1472.

Easley, D. & Kleinberg, J. (2010). *Networks, crowds, and markets.* Cambridge: Cambridge Unviersity Press.

Erickson, T. & Kellogg, W. A. (2000). Social translucence: an approach to designing systems that support social processes. *ACM Transactions on Computer-Human Interaction, 7*(1), 59–83.

Freeman, L. C. (1979). Centrality in social networks conceptual clarification. *Social Networks, 1*(3), 215–239.

Freeman, R. E. (1984). *Strategic management: A stakeholder approach.* Boston, MA: Pitman.

Freeman, R. E., Dmytriyev, S. & Strand, R. G. (2017). Managing for stakeholders in the digital age. In A. Rasche, M. Morsing & J. Moon (Eds.), *Corporate social responsibility: Strategy, communication, governance* (pp. 110–128). New York, NY: Cambridge University Press.

Friedman, A. L. & Miles, S. (2002). Developing stakeholder theory. *Journal of Management Studies, 39*(1), 1–21.

Frooman, J. (1999). Stakeholder influence strategies. *Academy of Management Review, 24*(2), 191–205.

Gallaugher, J. & Ransbotham, S. (2010). Social media and customer dialog management at Starbucks. *MIS Quarterly Executive, 9*(4), 197–212.

Golob, U. & Podnar, K. (2011). Corporate social responsibility communication and dialogue. In Ø. Ihlen, J. L. Bartlett & S. May (Eds.), *The handbook of communication and corporate social responsibility* (pp. 231–251). Malden, MA: Wiley-Blackwell.

Granovetter, M. (1973). The strength of weak ties. *American Journal of Sociology, 78*(6), 1360–1380.

Greenpeace Video. (2014). *LEGO: Everything is NOT awesome.* Retrieved from www.youtube.com/watch?v=qhbliUq0_r4.

Grunig, J. E. & Repper, F. C. (1992). Strategic management, publics, and issues. In J. E. Grunig, D. M. Dozier, W. P. Ehling, L. A. Grunig, F. C. Repper & J. White (Eds.), *Excellence in public relations and communication management* (pp. 117–158). Mahwah, NJ: Lawrence Erlbaum.

Ibarra, H. (1993). Personal networks of women and minorities in management: A conceptual framework. *Academy of Management Review, 18*(1), 56–87.

Ihlen, Ø., Bartlett, J. L. & May, S. (2011). Conclusions and take away points. In Ø. Ihlen, J. L. Bartlett & S. May (Eds.), *The handbook of communication and corporate social responsibility* (pp. 550–571). Malden, MA: Wiley-Blackwell.

Ionescu-Somers, A. & Enders, A. (2012). How Nestlé dealt with a social media campaign against it, *Financial Times*. Retrieved from www.ft.com/content/90dbff8a-3aea-11e2-b3f0-00144feabdc0.

Johansen, T. S. & Nielsen, A. E. (2016). Constructing non-profit identity in the midst of stakeholder complexity. *International Studies of Management & Organization, 46*(4), 216–227.

Lazega, E. & Pattison, P. E. (1999). Multiplexity, generalized exchange, and cooperation in organizations: A case study. *Social Networks, 21*(1), 67–90.

Lee, S. & Lee, C. (2015). Creative interaction and multiplexity in intraorganizational networks. *Management Communication Quarterly, 29*(1), 56–83.

Lindgreen, A. & Swaen, V. (2010). Corporate social responsibility (Special issue). *International Journal of Management Reviews, 12*(1), 1–105.

Linke, A. & Zerfass, A. (2013). Social media governance: Regulatory frameworks for successful online communications. *Journal of Communication Management, 17*(3), 270–286.

Luoma-aho, V. (2013). Corporate reputation and the theory of social capital. In C. E. Carroll (Ed.), *The handbook of communication and corporate reputation* (pp. 279–290). West Sussex: Blackwell Publishing Ltd.

Luoma-aho, V. (2015). Understanding stakeholder engagement: Faith-holders, hateholders, and fakeholders. *Research Journal of the Insitute for Public Relations, 2*(1), 1–27.

Luoma-aho, V., Tirkkonen, P. & Vos, M. (2013). Monitoring the issue arenas of the swine-flu discussion. *Journal of Communication Management, 17*(3), 239–251.

Luoma-aho, V. & Vos, M. (2010). Towards a more dynamic stakeholder model: Acknowledging multiple issue arenas. *Corporate Communications: An International Journal, 15*(3), 315–331.

Lyon, T. P. & Montgomery, A. W. (2013). Tweetjacked: The impact of social media on corporate greenwash. *Journal of Business Ethics, 118*(4), 747–757.

Majchrzak, A., Faraj, S., Kane, G. C. & Azad, B. (2013). The contradictory influence of social media affordances on online communal knowledge sharing. *Journal of Computer-Mediated Communication, 19*(1), 38–55.

Maon, F., Lindgreen, A. & Swaen, V. (2009). Designing and implementing corporate social responsibility: An integrative framework grounded in theory and practice. *Journal of Business Ethics, 87*, 71–89.

Marwick, A. E. & boyd, d. (2011). I tweet honestly, I tweet passionately: Twitter users, context collapse, and the imagined audience. *New Media & Society, 13*(1), 114–133.

Mattera, P. (2013). Nestlé: Corporate rap sheet, *Corporate Research Project*. Retrieved from www.corp-research.org/nestle.

Mayer, R. C., Davis, J. H. & Schoorman, F. D. (1995). An integrative model of organizational trust. *Academy of Management Review, 20*(3), 709–734.

Methot, J. R., Lepine, J. A., Podsakoff, N. P. & Christian, J. S. (2016). Are workplace friendships a mixed blessing? Exploring tradeoffs of multiplex relationships and their associations with job performance. *Personnel Psychology, 69*(2), 311–355.

Mitchell, R. K., Agle, B. R. & Wood, D. J. (1997). Toward a theory of stakeholder identification and salience: Defining the principle of who and what really counts. *Academy of Management Review, 22*(4), 853–886.

Mitchell, R. K., Van Buren, H. J., Greenwood, M. & Freeman, R. E. (2015). Stakeholder inclusion and accounting for stakeholders. *Journal of Management Studies, 52*(7), 851–877.

Morsing, M. & Schultz, M. (2006). Corporate social responsibility communication: Stakeholder information, response and involvement strategies. *Business Ethics: A European Review, 15*(4), 323–338.

O'Riordan, L. & Fairbrass, J. (2008). Corporate social responsibility (CSR): Models and theories in stakeholder dialogue. *Journal of Business Ethics, 83*(4), 745–758.

O'Riordan, L. & Fairbrass, J. (2013). Managing CSR stakeholder engagement: A new conceptual framework. *Journal of Business Ethics, 125*(1), 121–145.

Pedersen, E. R. (2006). Making corporate social responsibility (CSR) operable: How companies translate stakeholder dialogue into practice. *Business and Society Review, 111*(2), 137–163.

Peloza, J. & Papania, L. (2008). The missing link between corporate social responsibility and financial performance: Stakeholder salience and identification. *Corporate Reputation Review, 11*(S2), 169–181.

Rendler-Kaplan, L. (2017). Four benefits of effective social listening, *Social Media Today*. Retrieved from www.socialmediatoday.com/smt-influencer/4-benefits-effective-social-listening

Ruggie, J. & Nelson, T. (2015). Human rights and the OECD guidelines for multinational enterprises: Normative innovations and implementation challenges. Retrieved from http://shiftproject.org/sites/default/files/Ruggie-Nelson_OECDNCPanalysis_May2015.pdf.

Shah, N. P., Parker, A. & Waldstrom, C. (2016). Examining the overlap: Individual performance benefits of multiplex relationships. *Management Communication Quarterly*.

Shipilov, A. (2012). Strategic multiplexity. *Strategic Organization, 10*(3), 215–222.

Stohl, C. (1995). *Organizational communication: Connectedness in action.* Thousand Oaks, CA: Sage.

Stohl, C., Etter, M., Banghart, S. & D. Woo (2017). Social media policies: Implications for contemporary notions of corporate social responsibility. *Journal of Business Ethics, 142*(3), 413–436.

Su, C. T., Mitchell, R. K. & Sirgy, M. J. (2007). Enabling Guanxi management in China: A hierarchical stakeholder model of effective Guanxi. *Journal of Business Ethics, 71*(3), 301–319.

Suchman, M. C. (1995). Managing legitimacy: Strategic and institutional approaches. *Academy of Management Review, 20*(3), 571–610.

Treem, J. W. & Leonardi, P. M. (2013). Social media use in organizations: Exploring the affordances of visibility, editability, persistence, and association. *Annals of the International Communication Association, 36*(1), 143–189.

Vaughan, A. (2014). Lego ends Shell partnership following Greenpeace campaign, *The Guardian*. Retrieved from www.theguardian.com/environment/2014/oct/09/lego-ends-shell-partnership-following-greenpeace-campaign.

Verbrugge, L. M. (1979). Multiplexity in adult friendships. *Social Forces, 57*(4), 1286–1309.

Vodanovich, S., Sundaram, D. & Myers, M. (2010). Research commentary: Digital natives and ubiquitous information systems. *Information Systems Research, 21*(4), 711–723.

Whelan, G., Moon, J. & Grant, B. (2013). Corporations and citizenship arenas in the age of social media. *Journal of Business Ethics, 118*(4), 777–790.

Part III

Engaging with diverse stakeholders throughout the value chain

3.1 Engaging stakeholders in corporate volunteering

Towards a relational framework

Trine Susanne Johansen and Anne Ellerup Nielsen

Introduction

Along with the growing pressure on companies to respond to stakeholder demands and expectations in order to maintain their licence to operate, companies have become increasingly focused on the importance of engaging stakeholders in corporate social responsibility (CSR) strategies and policies (Burchell and Cook, 2006). As CSR processes and practices rely on cooperation, stakeholder relationship management and efforts to maximise stakeholder benefits are crucial elements in strategic CSR management (Bhattaharya et al., 2009). Simultaneously, developments within stakeholder literature and practice reflect a similar move towards engagement through partnerships, participation and dialogue (Aluchna, 2015). Stakeholder engagement is a popular concept with a variety of meanings and definitions. One broad definition sees it as the "process of involving individuals and groups that affect or are affected by the activities of a company" (Sloan, 2009, p. 26). Stakeholder engagement is not merely a question of managing stakeholder expectations or maximising stakeholder benefits, but rather a question of creating networks of mutual responsibility through relationships (Devin and Lane, 2014). One explicit form of responsibility which highlights engagement is corporate volunteering where corporations support and encourage employees to become involved in social issues (Plewa et al., 2015).

Corporate volunteering includes different types of global and local activities related to various social and environmental causes or responsibilities. Many multinationals have developed extensive, formalised programmes. Hewlett Packard, for instance, has implemented a "VolunteerMatch" programme, allowing employees to volunteer during work hours and to select specific social causes to support with donations. The programme's strategy is focused on creating a better life for young people by e.g. establishing an educational programme concerning online risks and building schools in third world countries. Another example is Timberland's "Path of Service™" programme (Timberland) which allows employees to engage in community service during company time for 40 hours a year (Miller, 2012). Focusing particularly on the environment, Timberland has introduced "Earth Day" events, inviting employees to work on common projects such as maintaining trails, installing or refurbishing community gardens, cleaning up parks or beaches, planting trees or building outdoor classrooms for local schools (Timberland). Corporate volunteering initiatives can also involve activities that explicitly draw on the skills or expertise of employees, such as when banks allow or encourage their employees to engage in consulting services for social groups living at the edge of society; do the bookkeeping for local NGOs (e.g. sports clubs, churches and drop-in centres); or give lessons on personal finance at public schools.

Besides the corporation and its employees, multiple stakeholders, e.g. non-profit organisations, beneficiaries and society, are engaged in and by these initiatives (Hess et al., 2002; Peloza et al., 2009; Van der Voort et al., 2009). The complexity of stakeholders involved in corporate volunteering suggests it to be a fruitful area for exploring stakeholder engagement in light of relationship management. Management of relations is a key focus area for multiple disciplines, and as a result, there are a plethora of definitions and understandings of what it is and entails. In the context of this contribution, relationship management is conceptualised from within a co-creation perspective. Albeit a multifaceted concept, born out of consumer relationship management, co-creation is initially defined as "a shift in thinking from the organisation as a definer of value to a more participative process where people and organisations together generate and develop meaning" (Ind and Coates, 2013, p. 86). As a lens for conceptualising relationship management, co-creation points to addressing all involved stakeholders as in possession of value and meaning creating capabilities.

Consequently, the purpose with this chapter is to approach stakeholder relations within corporate volunteering from within a co-creation perspective in order to create a framework that extrapolates stakeholder engagement as a complex network and takes into account the joint responsibility constructions of the corporation and other stakeholders. The main research questions that guide this chapter are: how can stakeholder engagement as co-creation be conceptualised in a corporate volunteering context? And what are the implications for stakeholder relationship management?

The contribution thus comes in the form of a framework for understanding and managing stakeholders within corporate volunteering based on insights from co-creation. The framework is envisioned from within dialogical reflexivity where theoretical conceptualisations act as a backdrop for entering into dialogue with, and reflecting on, empirical material (Alvesson and Kärreman, 2007, 2011). Presently, we seek to develop a backdrop for future studies. The approach taken entails firstly the exploration of extant literature on corporate volunteering. Secondly, focus is placed on the identification and articulation of different stakeholders and the dyadic relationships between the identified stakeholders, e.g. corporation-employee, corporation-non-profit organisation and non-profit organisation-corporate volunteer. Thirdly, these relationships are framed within a co-creation perspective leading to the construction of a framework characterised by collaboration and reciprocity between stakeholders. The framework then functions as a point of departure for addressing stakeholder engagement as a complex and multifaceted phenomenon with implications for relationship management.

Corporate volunteering

This section introduces extant corporate volunteering literature focusing on the terminology, definitions and forms of corporate volunteering that inform our understanding. Corporate volunteering, also known as "employee volunteering" and "corporate sponsored volunteering" (Pajo and Lee, 2011) is of increasing interest to both academics and managers (Plewa et al., 2015). Three main streams can be identified within corporate volunteering literature. One stream is CSR literature where corporate volunteering is seen as a CSR initiative that allows corporations and employees to join forces in helping community, society and environment (e.g. Aluchna, 2015; Muthuri et al., 2009; Pajo and Lee, 2011; Plewa et al., 2015). A second stream stems from volunteering literature where corporate volunteering is conceptualised as one particular volunteer type alongside e.g. member volunteering and involuntary volunteering (e.g. Bussell and Forbes, 2002; Wilson, 2000), and finally, partnership literature views corporate volunteering as one particular form of for-profit and not-for-profit partnership (Samuel et al., 2016). In addition to the different concepts and the different streams of literature that can be identified, different approaches seem to influence the field such as organisational behaviour, psychology, sociology, marketing, corporate governance and non-profit management (Rodell et al., 2016).

As a result of the multifaceted and plentiful scholarly interest, corporate volunteering also has multiple definitions. However, in general, it is described as "giving one's time, knowledge, or skills as part of a community service, outreach, or social responsibility activity on company time without additional compensation or direct personal remuneration" (Grant, 2012, 592–593). Corporate volunteering is anchored in volunteerism identified by groups of volunteers committing themselves to a formalised, public and proactive choice to donate their time and energy freely to benefit persons, groups or organisations (Snyder and Omoto, 2009; Wilson, 2000). It is thus suggested that volunteering is an act of charity containing a motive of altruism (Bussell and Forbes, 2002).

Different systems for classifying or typologising corporate volunteering are in use. Corporate volunteering may be classified according to the perspective that regulates the relationship established between the involved stakeholders. Hence a transactional corporate volunteering relationship articulates the creation of an arrangement between a company and a non-profit organisation for the sake of self-interest, while an integrative relationship is conceptualised as a strategic relationship facilitating cooperation between a company and a non-profit organisation with the aim of creating value for all involved stakeholders Austin, 2000; Van der Voort et al., 2009).

Corporate volunteering can also be classified according to volunteering types (Peloza et al., 2009). Extra-organisational volunteerism is the most common type of volunteering and refers to activities carried out outside the workplace where the employer has no involvement and thus no commitment towards or relationship with the non-profit organisation facilitating the volunteering activity. Consequently, it can be argued, this type has little to do with *corporate* volunteering. Inter-organisational volunteerism takes place within the workplace, but the goals and strategies of the corporation are secondary to the volunteering activity and the employer support is passive. The volunteer employee is the relationship builder and facilitator between the corporation and the non-profit organisation assuming the role as boundary-spanner Peloza et al., 2009). Finally, intra-organisational volunteerism refers to initiatives where the employer develops the volunteer opportunity (and selects the non-profit organisation) and offers it to employees. Consequently, while extra- and inter-organisational volunteerism are driven by the employee, intra-organisational volunteerism is a formally integrated corporate strategic initiative contributing to maintenance and enhancement of the work context through "organisational citizenship behaviour". The argument is that employees are inspired by the desire of their organisation to be a good corporate citizen (Peloza et al., 2009).

Stakeholders in corporate volunteering

Numerous stakeholders participate in corporate volunteering activities, e.g. corporations, employees, non-profit organisations and causes (i.e. beneficiaries). Often the relationship between these stakeholders is articulated as a win-win situation since each stakeholder is said to benefit from the partnership (Caligiuri et al., 2013). However, the different stakeholders are articulated differently in relation to their motivations, benefits and challenges when it comes to corporate volunteering.

Corporations

Corporations are often of key interest to extant corporate volunteering literature (De Gilder et al., 2005; Geroy et al., 2000; Ellen et al., 2000; Roza et al., 2011). In the literature, corporations are seen as decision makers and are, consequently, framed as having a number of strategic choices in relation to planning and implementing corporate volunteering activities and initiatives. Amongst these choices is how to design the volunteering initiatives that the corporation chooses to support. This choice involves whether to let employees decide for themselves where and how to volunteer, i.e. inter-organisational voluntarism, or to choose one specific cause or activity where employees are allowed to volunteer, i.e. intra-organisational volunteerism (Peloza and Hassay, 2006). If choosing the latter approach, the corporation in addition needs to decide which cause and activity to support. In addition, different combinations of inter- and intra-organisational volunteerism exist, e.g. having different causes and activities that the employees can choose from. Moreover, corporations can decide how to manage the volunteer programmes vis-à-vis employees, i.e. to facilitate participation, to encourage participation or to require participation, in which case "mandatory voluntarism" is implemented (Grant, 2012).

In addition to these different choices residing with corporations when it comes to planning and implementing volunteering activities, they also have to decide how corporate volunteering is to be perceived in the organisation and how it is assigned different strategic roles or purposes. In some organisations, it is seen as human resource management focused on employees, i.e. as a tool for recruitment and retention (Grant, 2012). Other corporations approach it as a reputation or brand management tool, i.e. as a way of securing positive stakeholder perceptions and competitive advantage in the marketplace (Allen, 2003; Brammer and Millington, 2005; Peterson, 2004). And yet others view it as a provider of social capital Aluchna, 2015) or as an act of citizenship (Grant, 2012; Pajo and Lee, 2011) proving societal, rather than marketplace, commitment and value (Peloza et al., 2009).

Employees

A second key stakeholder group addressed in the literature is the employees. Employees are articulated in a double role as employees and as volunteers. When articulated as an employee, focus is on the relationship between the individual and the corporation where he or she is employed. However, when engaging in corporate volunteering initiatives, the employee also becomes a volunteer placing emphasis on the relationship between the individual and the non-profit organisation and/or the cause.

For the individual employee, volunteering is said to carry a number of benefits, e.g. increased motivation (Rodell, 2013); growing identification; socialisation; and belonging with the workplace (Grant, 2012; Jones, 2010), as well as enhanced commitment and satisfaction with one's job (do Paco and Nave, 2013; Pajo and Lee, 2011; Peloza and Hassay, 2006). These benefits are associated with a human resource approach to corporate volunteering where the corporation sees volunteering initiatives as primarily or exclusively internally focused. However, although many employee benefits are acknowledged in the literature, corporate volunteering is also associated with additional expectations and pressures on the employee (Basil et al., 2009; Hall et al., 2001; Walker and Pharoah, 2002). According to Eisner et al. (2009), a loss of $38 billion worth of corporate volunteer time has been registered in the US as a result of employees stopping to volunteer after only one year due to the lack of strong leadership, missing appreciation and recognition and out burn. The authors suggest that the problem of missed recognition of work executed by employee volunteers lies in the concept of "volunteering" connoting a service free of charge and with a free will, but of high value (Eisner et al., 2009). One of the reasons employees volunteer is thus that they want to create meaning while still expressing a need of appreciation and recognition of their volunteer contribution (Rodell, 2013).

When the individual is seen as a volunteer, rather than as an employee, an additional number of themes or issues are identified as relevant. These issues relate to e.g. volunteer identity (vs. employee identity) along with related issues of identification (or even misidentification), socialisation and belonging. Issues of identity and identification stem from the dual role as employee and volunteer. As the employee internalises the volunteering role making it part of his or her identity or self-enhancement, it may lead to a potential source of conflict vis-à-vis the individual's work identity (Grant, 2012). Moreover, altruism plays an important part in connection with addressing the employee as a volunteer first and as an employee second (Pajo and Lee, 2011; Zappala, 2004). The notion of altruism fosters that volunteers should express care and compassion towards beneficiaries (Grant, 2012), i.e. give something back to society and community (Muthuri et al., 2009; Peloza and Hassay, 2006). As such, the volunteer identity may displace the employee identity transforming the employee into a concerned citizen.

Non-profit organisations

Non-profit organisations are less frequently addressed in corporate volunteering literature compared to corporations and their employees (Samuel et al., 2013). When addressed, non-profit organisations are said to view collaboration as a necessity as they are dependent on the contributions of additional human resources from corporations. Hence collaboration with corporations becomes a question of recruiting and retaining volunteers (McPherson and Rotolo, 1996). Seemingly, the employees and members of the non-profit organisations are not included as resources and are, moreover, absent from the literature. In addition, to providing additional hands, the corporate volunteers may also benefit the non-profit organisation with their unique professional skills and expertise. However, non-profit organisations are said to balance the dependency on human resources and competencies against costs (Allen, 2003), including potential reputational backlashes and identity conflicts (Samuel et al., 2013). Thus, while awareness and credibility can increase with collaboration, the non-profit organisation also risks being co-opted or exploited by business. Moreover, they are also challenged with being subject to large corporate expectations and demands diverting them from their key activities (Allen, 2003).

In relation to the partnership with for-profit organisations, non-profit organisations are cast as either passive or active actors. As passive actors, they are seen as strategically chosen because of a good corporation fit, status or respectability (Muthuri et al., 2009). Whereas as active actors, they are strategic agents in their own right that choose to collaborate with corporations in order to secure key organisational goals (Allen, 2003).

Causes

The cause refers to those who benefit from corporate volunteering initiatives, i.e. those whom the non-profit organisations aim to help or support. Although arguably an important stakeholder, the causes are often absent from corporate volunteering literature (Samuel et al., 2016). As such, the "the distant other" (Chouliaraki, 2006) is displaced by "the absent other". When actually addressed, causes are often referenced in very abstract terms, e.g. Grant's (2012) notions of beneficiaries and recipients or Muthuri et al.'s (2009) focus on mentees. One exception is Samuel et al.'s (2016) recent study on the perceptions of different beneficiaries, e.g. young adults, addicts and people with visual or mental impairments, in relation to their experiences with corporate volunteers. While enjoying the attention from the volunteers, the beneficiaries raise concerns in relation to the temporary or short-term nature of the initiatives as well as the "voyeuristic" nature of the volunteer experience due to a felt lack of reciprocity in the relationships (Samuel et al., 2016, 9). These experiences match the tendency in extant literature to view beneficiaries as passive and disempowered objects, rather than active, involved subjects. In addition, they challenge the view that all involved stakeholders automatically benefit from corporate volunteering initiatives.

Stakeholder relationships

The different key stakeholders articulated in corporate volunteering literature suggests that it is possible to construct multiple dyadic relationships between the stakeholders, e.g.:

- Corporation–non-profit organisation
- Corporation–cause
- Corporation–employee/volunteer
- Employee/volunteer–non-profit organisation
- Employee/volunteer–cause
- Cause–non-profit organisation

There are elements of asymmetry in the way these relationships are described in the extant literature. Whereas some stakeholders are given priority, most notably the corporations, the non-profit organisations are rarely addressed, and the causes or beneficiaries are almost absent. Consequently, focus is on the business aspect of volunteering activities privileging the relationships involving the corporation, and ignoring other relationships, e.g. the ones between employees and cause and between non-profit organisation and cause.

The dyadic relationships, moreover, appear as asymmetrical in the sense that corporations are inscribed in positions of strategic choice giving them an a priori power in choosing collaboration partners and in designing volunteering activities for their employees. The corporate focus is inscribed in a transactional logic framing corporate volunteering relationships as resource exchanges; often described as a win–win–win situation reciprocally benefitting the company, the non-profit organisation and the employees in different ways as described above (see also Caligiuri et al., 2013). However, the frequent framing of non-profit organisations as dependent upon corporate support and resources seemingly positions them in a submissive role. Moreover, it can be argued that the lack of reciprocity in the relations between employees and causes Samuel et al., 2016) implies that the beneficiaries are positioned as powerless in the sense that they, as a stakeholder group, are not said to possess resources, e.g. time, competences or reputation, desired by the other stakeholder groups involved in volunteering initiatives. In contrast, the employees' contact with the beneficiaries is said to help them see their own personal problems in a different perspective reducing feelings of distress or discontent (Grant, 2012). This view, combined with a number of other employee benefits already mentioned, suggests that employees are generally seen as empowered (Aluchna, 2015). However, if voluntarism is required or mandatory (as suggested by e.g. Grant, 2012), the employee has little or no choice in terms of participation and engagement and becomes a passive stakeholder. Consequently, a critical reading may suggest that non-profit organisations, cause and employees potentially are framed as mere props used by corporations to stage themselves as responsible social actors.

This understanding of stakeholders and stakeholder relationships within corporate volunteering forms the point of departure for developing a different conceptual framework. However, rather than focusing on the individual stakeholder group or the individual dyadic relationships, all the relationships between the stakeholders are included. These relationships are the point of departure for developing a holistic framework for stakeholder engagement. In constructing the framework to conceptualise stakeholder engagement within corporate volunteering, we draw on the notion of co-creation as an explicit perspective on relationship management that has emerged from consumer research. In so doing, we are inscribing our framework in a symmetrical logic where all stakeholder groups, in principle, are recognised as co-creators of meaning and value. And where the otherwise silent stakeholder voices are included.

Relationship management as co-creation

Co-creation is a concept with multiple meanings defined from within different approaches, e.g. participatory design, literary theory, collaborative innovation and psychotherapy (Ind and Coates, 2013). However, in this context, we initially approach co-creation from an interpretive point of view originally rooted in literary theory. Consequently, co-creation is defined as "a shift in thinking from the organization as a definer of value to a more participative process where people and organizations together generate and develop meaning" (Ind and Coates, 2013, 86). Similar to a text open to multiple interpretations, the actions of organisations and their interactions with stakeholders can be understood differently. Organisations, or marketers, are no longer seen as the sole definers of the symbolic understandings embedded in their brands, identities and market offerings. Instead, consumers are recognised as active interpreters who assign value to brands, organisations and identities that they perceive to be meaningful symbolic resources in constructing their individual and collective identities (Ind and Coates, 2013).

This shift in thinking suggested by co-creation originates from consumer relationship literature and the changing or converging roles of companies, or producers, and consumers. The convergence of production and consumption marks a transition from a company-centric approach to the value chain to a participatory approach characterised by dialogue between company and consumer as well joint problem definition and problem solving, e.g. in relation to product development and innovation. Thereby, the consumer is recognised as informed, connected, empowered and active in both production, consumption and value creation (Prahalad and Ramaswamy, 2004). In the production process, the consumer is involved in product design decisions, e.g. choosing the colour and pattern of a pair of sneakers. In the consumption process, the consumer has the opportunity of further customising the product through specific uses and sharing his or her experiences with other consumers in real life but also on various social media platforms, and thereby, he or she also plays an active role in the defining both the material, or use, value of the product as well as the immaterial value, i.e. the symbolic meaning of the brand. The consumer is consequently redefined or recast as a prosumer (Xie et al., 2008). In light of the co-creation perspective, as explicated here with reference to consumers, all stakeholders can be viewed as co-creators of meaning through their interpretive and communicative practices. Thus, stakeholders are not instrumentalised or considered as the means to an end within a transactional logic, as is frequently the case within traditional stakeholder literature, but seen as partners in meaning and value-creation processes (Botan and Taylor, 2004).

The co-creation of value is the locus for the co-creation paradigm as described by Ramaswamy and Ozcan. Here, co-creation is defined as the "joint creation and evolution *with stakeholding individuals*, intensified and enacted through *platforms of engagements*, virtualized and emergent from *ecosystems of capabilities*, and actualized and embodied in *domains of experiences*, expanding *wealth-welfare-wellbeing*" (Ramaswamy and Ozcan, 2014, 14). In other words, co-creation implies collaboration between organisations and individuals in order to produce shared value for mutual benefit. This conceptualisation thus expands the boundaries of co-creation beyond consumer relations to stakeholder relations, and beyond a market or business context to a societal context. In this societal context, value is not linked to brands, products and organisations, but is conceptualised as "enactment of agency through creative, intentional, integrative, and transformative engagement platforms embodied in dialogic, transparent, accessible, and reflexive domains of stakeholder experiences emerging from inclusive, generative, linkable, and evolvable ecosystems of capabilities" (Ramaswamy and Ozcan, 2014, 27).

Value, accordingly, is seen as performed in emerging acts of stakeholder engagement contextualised in the potentials of dynamic, interdependent communities. This marks a different way of conceptualising value from the traditional notion of value as a relational property to a humanisation of value as affective and subjective as well proprietorial. As pointed out by Ramaswamy and Ozcan, the co-creation paradigm "accommodates shared, mutual, and even 'symbiotic' value creation" (2014, 251). Co-creation is seen as both the means and the end within an on-going cycle of evolution producing even better outcomes. It is, moreover, suggested that

> it mandates that we do even better for ourselves by doing well for others, too. In other words, a co-creation based view of economy and society is about expanding collective self-interests for you and me, and me and you, in 'win more – win more' fashion.
> (Ramaswamy and Ozcan, 2014, 236)

Thereby, the co-creation paradigm expands and transcends the win-win idea articulated within corporate volunteering and suggests that by focusing on the collective or shared interests, rather than the isolated interests and benefits of the individual stakeholder groups, greater value can be generated.

Stakeholders are thus considered as paramount in the co-creation paradigm. Due to the democratisation of value creation, stakeholders are transformed from passive recipients of organisational defined value to active participants or co-creators: "Whether as customers, employees, managers, financiers, partners, or citizens in communities, every stakeholder brings 'capital' to the value creation process through their 'value creative capacities' and, in doing so, becomes a co-creator" (Ramaswamy and Ozcan, 2014, 222). The capacity of the individual stakeholder is linked to his or her ability to co-create based on unique capabilities. Consequently, it is suggested that the capability of a consumer is different from that of a manager or from an employee or from a beneficiary. However, it is not the value creation capability and practice of the individual that are centre stage but rather the joint capabilities of networked individuals. As pointed out above, individuals are seen as inscribed in different ecosystems consisting of social, business, civic and natural communities. Consequently, all "co-creators are part of 'entrepreneurial' assemblages of persons, artifacts, interfaces and processes, whose strategic architecture creates outcomes of value together" (Ramaswamy and Ozcan, 2014, 250).

Although the co-creation paradigm privileges the collective, it still emphasises the role of the individual stakeholder. Central to understanding stakeholders as co-creators are the notions of agency and empowerment. Agency is described as the capacity of individuals to act independently and to make their own free choice, whereas empowerment is understood as requiring power over resources, relationships, information and decision making (Ramaswamy and Ozcan, 2014). Consumers, for instance, have agency in their choice of which products to buy and are empowered by their opportunity to share consumption practices and experiences with other consumers. They can also display agency and empowerment in withholding consumption, e.g. through boycotts in response to perceived illegitimate or irresponsible business practices.

In a corporate volunteering context, as previously mentioned, corporations are given agency as they are seen as the primary initiators and decision makers in launching initiatives, choosing non-profit organisations for cooperation etc. Non-profit organisations have agency in choosing corporate partnerships; however, they are seen less empowered because they are said to rely on the resources made available by corporations. Employees have agency when choosing whether or not to participate in volunteer programmes and are empowered in the sense that they have the freedom to donate their personal resources (i.e. their time and expertise) to an activity or cause. It should be noted that such agency and empowerment are influenced by e.g. formal corporate policies or organisational culture which impose opportunities and constraints onto the employees. As suggested elsewhere, volunteering may not be voluntary, but rather a mandatory activity (Grant, 2012). In contrast to the perceived relative agency and empowerment of corporations, non-profit organisations and employees, the causes or beneficiaries of the programmes are often treated as lacking in power or as powerless in the sense that their unique resources are not recognised for their potentially value creating capabilities. As Ramaswamy and Ozcan comment, the beneficiaries or recipients end up being "on the receiving end of control rather than being engaged". Consequently, employees are seen as expects "brought in from outside to build capacity" both in relation to the causes and the non-profit organisations. Moreover, as experts, they "tend to overlook that communities might already possess capacities. They also miss opportunities to learn from the very communities in their zeal to engineer ways to address capacity shortages" (Ramaswamy and Ozcan, 2014, 268). In contrast to such asymmetrical views on value creation, mirroring the imbalance detected in extant corporate volunteering literature, the co-creation paradigm suggests that agency and empowerment are bestowed on all stakeholders, as all are recognised as being in possession of capacities and unique resources of importance for value and meaning creation.

A relational framework of corporate volunteering

Based on the conceptualisation of stakeholders as co-creators of value, we develop our relational framework of corporate volunteering (Figure 3.1.1). The framework suggests

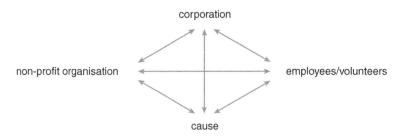

Figure 3.1.1 Relational framework

that by combining the different dyadic relationships, a complex network is formed. The double arrows indicate that there are multiple, reciprocal relationships connecting the different stakeholders. Thus, the co-creation perspective allows us to replace the corporation-centric view, found in extant corporate volunteering literature, with a stakeholder-centric view where there is symmetry between the corporation, the non-profit organisation, the employees and the cause.

In addition to offering a holistic, symmetric view on corporate volunteering, the framework also suggests new roles for und understandings of the involved stakeholders:

- The corporation goes from being seen as a strategic decision maker to being positioned as an initiator and/or facilitator of social exchange who can establish and support platforms of engagement by involving different ecosystems.
- The employee goes from being seen as someone who benefits from the social exchange to being seen as someone who contributes to the social exchange thereby replacing a focus on the individual with a focus on the collective.
- The non-profit organisation goes from being seen as a somewhat blurred actor lacking resources, professionalisation and reputation to being seen as more prominent and as an important boundary-spanner.
- The cause goes from being seen as absent or passive, disempowered victims to being seen as empowered capacities in relation to generating solutions to overcome societal problems – and as equal contributors to social exchange.

Viewing relationship management through a co-creation perspective suggests engagement to be action, performativity and collaboration. In other words, engagement is something stakeholders do together in joint action within areas such as governance, infrastructure, development and sustainability in order to build shared co-creative capacities (Ramaswamy and Ozcan, 2014). In relation to governance, it is suggested that stakeholders should be involved in issues such as accountability and policy decision making by establishing a shared agenda with common rules for collaboration, protection of property rights etc. Transferred to corporate volunteering, it implies working together to ensure common rules of engagement. In social partnership literature, joint policy decision making is addressed as a complex issue, which only makes sense provided that the implied stakeholders accept the complexity arising from the diverging interests and agendas and perceive it as desirable and manageable (Teisman and Klijn, 2002). Acknowledging this complexity, paves the way for corporate volunteering partnerships to co-establish policy systems where all stakeholder groups possess the right to control the processes. Whereas governance concerns policies, infrastructure relates to management systems and to the need for developing shared systems and structures across organisations. In a corporate volunteering context, corporations and non-profit organisations should develop coherent managerial practices for addressing corporate volunteers and volunteering activities. Detailed process models that integrate legitimacy and accountability of collaborative actions and dynamics between participating actors must be established concerning the organisational design of the corporate volunteering partnership including congruence on which joint goals to achieve and which performance indicators to adopt for joint social action (Seitanidi and Crane, 2009). Development is about social change where joint actions are to empower stakeholders and draw on community capacity. As already mentioned, corporate volunteering should involve beneficiaries as active participants and integrate, to a larger extent, their particular plans, intentions and ambitions into the design and framework. Finally, sustainability is about knowledge sharing actions and maintaining the diversity and complexity of the different ecosystems. For the stakeholders participating in corporate volunteering, this translates into balancing the need for shared policies and systems with a need for autonomy in order to sustain the relational framework.

A co-creation view on relationships focuses attention on the collective learning, skills, knowledge and creativity of all participating stakeholders in an equally valuable fashion. The shift in understandings holds implications for what becomes important in working with and managing stakeholder engagement in corporate volunteering initiatives as all relationships are considered as equally important. Compared to the existing literature where the relationships involving the corporation are given priority, additional relationships require managerial attention. In particular, those relationships that involve the beneficiaries, i.e. between non-profit organisation and cause, between volunteers and cause and between corporation and cause. Involving the cause or the beneficiaries as co-creators implies that they are actively participating in designing and planning the initiatives from which they are to benefit – something, which both corporation and non-profit organisation should acknowledge. Moreover, these initiatives should be based on mutual exchange recognising the capacities of both beneficiaries and volunteers. In addition, the relationship between volunteers and non-profit organisation suggests that attention needs be paid towards how volunteers are involved in volunteering activities, i.e. how they become part of the practices and processes of the non-profit organisation. In turn, this also implies focusing on how corporate volunteers interact with non-corporate volunteers and other members of the non-profit organisation, who potentially can be considered a stakeholder group in their own right.

Central to managing stakeholder relationships based on mutual understanding and collaboration is dialogue (Prahalad and Ramaswamy, 2004; Ramaswamy and Ozcan, 2014). Dialogue implies symmetry between the involved stakeholders as well as joint willingness to engage and participate in problem identification and solutions. Thereby, it also calls for perceived equality and recognition amongst the different stakeholders acknowledging that meaningful dialogue hinges on understanding their various agendas and stakes (Johansen and Nielsen, 2011). This also implies that all stakeholders should have access to information and knowledge. Consequently, it points, yet again, to the importance of empowering those stakeholders who currently seem to be under-prioritised in corporate volunteering literature, most notably the beneficiaries and to the need for recognising their capacities and value co-creation capabilities.

Conclusions

This chapter points to some interesting insights in relation to stakeholders within corporate volunteering. Firstly, the most prominent relationship addressed in existing literature is the relationship between the corporation and the employee. This is particularly reflected in corporate volunteering research being linked to human resource management (Muthuri et al., 2009). Secondly, the employee is articulated in a double role as both employee and volunteer. This suggests that employees may experience conflicts of identity and identification as they are suspended between their loyalty and obligations towards both corporation and non-profit organisation. Thirdly, the beneficiaries or cause are remarkably absent as a stakeholder group in the extant literature. They are almost solely engaged and represented through the non-profit organisation. Finally, the relationships are framed within a market discourse and a transactional logic privileging a company-oriented strategic approach designed to fit the corporation's competencies, strategy and values (van der Voort et al., 2009). In sum, it appears that there are certain asymmetries in how the different stakeholders are portrayed and positioned within a corporate volunteering context.

As a means to a more symmetrical stakeholder engagement and relationship management approach, these apparent imbalances, regarding how much emphasis is given to each stakeholder group, are readdressed in our conceptual framework based on the notion of co-creation. Co-creation views relationships as participatory processes that tap into the capacity and capabilities of all stakeholders and argues that value is continuously created through interaction and democratisation.

The co-creation inspired framework incorporates all key stakeholders to ensure their visibility and equal emphasis. Equal emphasis is a prerequisite for involving the different stakeholders in mutually rewarding relationships attributing voice to each stakeholder group and recognising both their unique and collective co-creative capabilities. This reflects the underlying principles of engagement as a "two-way, relational, give-and-take between organizations and stakeholders" that aims to improve understanding amongst stakeholders and to make decisions that benefit all those involved in organisational activities (Taylor and Kent, 2014, 391). The framework thus articulates corporate volunteering as a network of relationships, rather than as particular, privileged dyadic relations, e.g. the relation between corporation and employee.

The complexity of the relational framework holds implications for managing stakeholder engagement and relationships. Tentative implications are a different view on stakeholder salience that incorporates all key stakeholders, e.g. the causes or beneficiaries need to be included in the stakeholders relevant for corporate volunteering. Instead of treating the beneficiaries as silent voices, they need to be actively engaged through dialogue with all the other stakeholders in the network. Such empowerment of the disempowered is a key driver for social entrepreneurship and innovation projects, e.g. homeless people designing their future homes, giving guided city tours or selling newspapers (e.g. Hibbert et al., 2002). This suggests that corporate volunteering is not a question of choosing an appropriate cause and motivating employees to participate, rather it is a question of simultaneous nurturing and facilitating engagement across the entire network of stakeholders.

Developed with a reflexive methodology in mind – where theoretical conceptualisations act as a backdrop for entering into dialogue with, and reflecting on, empirical material – the framework calls for future studies into the complex, dynamic value co-creation in stakeholder engagement practices as embedded in concrete corporate volunteering initiatives. It suggests that studies should address how volunteering initiatives are played out in practice by observing how the different stakeholders, corporations, employees, non-profit organisations and causes interact and engage with each other to co-create meaningful, valuable experiences. In addition, it suggests that certain questions become important, in particular those pertaining to the non-profit organisations as well as the causes or beneficiaries, i.e. those stakeholders that are currently underrepresented in corporate volunteering literature. These questions include: how can non-profit organisations take on increased strategic ownership of corporate volunteer programmes? How do beneficiaries become actively involved in corporate volunteering initiatives? How can the resources and capacities of the beneficiaries be leveraged through collaboration with the employee volunteers as well as the non-profit organisations? And how can the beneficiaries be empowered through the collaborative projects?

A final point of interest is the role of the consumer in corporate volunteering initiatives. Traditionally, the consumer is not addressed as a relevant stakeholder in such activities. If mentioned, the consumer is seen as a target audience in relation to the potential such initiatives offer in terms of branding and reputation building for the corporations. However, the co-creative paradigm potentially suggests that future corporate volunteering initiatives may also seek to engage consumers as active participants, e.g. by allowing them to select causes to support. Such consumer involvement is known from other types of responsibility initiatives, e.g. the Pepsi Refresh Project where consumers submitted and voted for local projects ideas (Andersen and Johansen, 2016). Consequently, the relational framework may not only reconceptualise how stakeholders and relationships are understood but also expand the existing understanding of what stakeholders are involved and contribute to value co-creation in corporate volunteering.

References

Allen, K. (2003). The social case for corporate volunteering. *Australian Journal on Volunteering* 8(1), 57–62.

Aluchna, M. (2015). Employee volunteering as an element of corporate social responsibility: The evidence from polish listed companies, in Idowu, S. and Schmidpeter, R. (eds.), *CSR, Sustainability, Ethics & Governance*. Switzerland: Springer International Publishing.

Alvesson, M. and Kärreman, D. (2007). Constructing mystery: Empirical matters in theory development. *Academy of Management Review*, 32(4), 1265–1281.

Alvesson, M. and Kärreman, D. (2011). *Qualitative Research and Theory Development: Mystery as Method*. Thousand Oaks, CA: Sage.

Andersen, S. E. and Johansen, T. S. (2016). Cause-related marketing 2.0: Connection, collaboration and commitment. *Journal of Marketing Communications*, 22(5), 524–543.

Austin, J. (2000). *The Collaborative Challenge*. San Francisco: Jossey-Bass.

Basil, D. Z., Runte, M. S., Easwaramoorthy, M. and Barr, C. (2009). Company support for employee volunteering: A national survey of companies in Canada. *Journal of Business Ethics*, 85(3), 387–398.

Bhattaharya, C. B., Korshung, D. and Sen, S. (2009). Strengthening stakeholder – company relationships through mutually beneficial corporate social responsibility initiatives. *Journal of Business Ethics*, 2(85), 257–272.

Botan, C. H. and Taylor, M. (2004). Public relations: State of the field. *Journal of Communication*, 54(4), 645–661.

Brammer, S. and Millington, A. (2005). Corporate reputation and philanthropy: An empirical analysis. *Journal of Business Ethics*, 61(1), 29–44.

Burchell, J. and Cook, J. (2006). Assessing the impact of stakeholder dialogue: Changing relationships between NGOs and companies. *Journal of Public Affairs*, 63(3/4), 210–227.

Bussell, H. and Forbes, D. (2002). Understanding the volunteer market: The what, where, who and why of volunteering. *International Journal of Nonprofit and Voluntary Sector Marketing*, 7(3), 244–257.

Caligiuri, P., Mencin, A. and Jiang, K. (2013). Win-win-win: The influence of company-sponsored volunteerism programs on employees, NGOs, and business units. *Personnel Psychology*, 66(4), 825–860.

Chouliaraki, L. (2006). Towards an analytics of mediation. *Critical Discourse Studies*, 3(2), 153–178.

De Gilder, D., Schuyt, T. N. M. and Breedijk, M. (2005). Effects of an employee volunteering program on the work force: The ABNAMRO case. *Journal of Business Ethics*, 61(2), 143–152.

Devin, B. L. and Lane, A. B. (2014). Communicating engagement in corporate social responsibility: A meta-level construal of engagement. *Journal of Public Relations Research*, 26(5), 436–454.

do Paco, A. and Nave, A. C. (2013). Corporate volunteering: A case study centred on the motivations, satisfaction and happiness of company employees. *Employee Relations*, 35(5), 547–559.

Eisner, D., Grimm, Jr, R. T., Maynard, S. and Washburn, S. (2009). The new volunteer workforce. *Standford Social Innovation Review*, Winter, Leland Stand Jr. University, 31–37.

Ellen, P. S., Mohr, L. A. and Webb, D. J. (2000), Charitable programs and the retailer: Do they mix? *Journal of Retailing*, 76(3), 393–406.

Geroy, G. D., Wright, P. C. and Jacoby, L. (2000). Toward a conceptual framework of employee volunteerism: An aid for the human resource manager. *Management Decision*, 38 (4), 280–286.

Grant, A. M. (2012), Giving time, time after time: Work design and sustained employee participation in corporate volunteering, *Academy of Management Review*, 37 (4), 589–615.

Hall, M. H., McKeown, L. and Roberts, K. (2001). *National Survey of Giving, Volunteering and Participating*, Ottawa: Ministry of Industry.

Hess, D., Rogovsky, N. and Dunfee, T. W. (2002). The next wave of corporate community involvement: Corporate social initiatives, *California Management Review* 44(2), 110–125.

Hibbert, S. A., Hogg, G. and Quinn, T. (2002). Consumer response to social entrepreneurship: The case of the Big Issue in Scotland. *International Journal of Nonprofit and Voluntary Sector Marketing*, 7(3), 288–301.

Ind, N. and Coates, N. (2013). The meanings of co-creation. *European Business Review*, 25(1), 86–95.

Johansen, T. S. and Nielsen, A.E (2011). Strategic stakeholder dialogues: A discursive perspective on relationship building. *Corporate Communications: An International Journal*, 16(3), 204–217.

Jones, D. A. (2010). Does serving the community also serve the company? Using organizational identification and social exchange theories to understand employee responses to a volunteerism programme. *Journal of Occupational and Organizational Psychology*, 83(4), 857–878.

McPherson, J. M. and Rotolo, T. (1996). Testing a dynamic model of social composition: Diversity and change in voluntary groups. *American Sociological Review*, 61(2), 179–202.

Miller, S. (2012), Volunteerism ROI tracker case study: Timberland. www.trueimpact.com/social-impact-resources/bid/74964/Volunteerism-ROI-Tracker-Case-Study-Timberland.

Muthuri, J. N., Matten, D. and Moon, J. (2009). Employee volunteering and social capital: Contributions to corporate social responsibility. *British Journal of Management*, 20(1): 75–89.

Pajo, K. and Lee, L. (2011). Corporate-sponsored volunteering: A work design perspective. *Journal of Business Ethics*, 99(3), 467–482.

Peloza, J. and Hassay, D. N. (2006). Intra-organizational volunteerism: Good soldiers, good deeds and good politics. *Journal of Business Ethics*, 64(4), 357–379.

Peloza, J., Hudson, S. and Hassay, D. N. (2009). The marketing of employee volunteerism. *Journal of Business Ethics*, 85(2), 371–386.

Peterson, D. K. (2004). Recruitment strategies for encouraging participation in corporate volunteer programs. *Journal of Business Ethics*, 49(4), 371–386.

Plewa, C., Conduit, J., Quester, P. G. and Johnston, C. (2015). The impact of corporate volunteering on CSR image: A consumer perspective. *Journal of Business Ethics*, 127(3), 643–659.

Prahalad, C. K. and Ramaswamy, V. (2004). Co-creation experiences: The next practice in value creation. *Journal of Interactive Marketing*, 18(3), 5–14.

Ramaswamy, V. and Ozcan, K. (2014). *The Co-Creation Paradigm*. Redwood City: Standford Business Books.

Rodell, J. B. (2013). Finding meaning through volunteering: Why do employees volunteer and what does it mean for their jobs? *Academy of Management Journal*, 56(5), 1274–1294.

Rodell, J. B., Breitsol, H., Schröder, M. and Keating, D. J. (2016). Employee volunteering: A review and framework for future research. *Journal of Management*, 42(1), 55–84.

Roza, L., Becker, A, van Baren, E. A. and Meijs, L. C. P. M. (2011). The 'Why' of older volunteers: Do employment and loss of spouse influence the motivation of older volunteers? *The International Journal of Volunteer Administration*, 28(1), 292–298.

Samuel, O., Lonneke, R. and Meijs, L. (2016). Exploring partnerships from the perspective of HSO beneficiaries: The case of corporate volunteering. *Human Service Organizations: Management, Leadership & Governance*, 40(3), 220–237.

Samuel, O., Wolf, P. and Schilling, A. (2013). Corporate volunteering: Benefits and challenges for nonprofits. *Nonprofit Management and Leadership*, 24(82), 163–179.

Seitanidi, M. M. and Crane, A. (2009). Implementing CSR through partnerships: Understanding the selection, design and institutionalisation of nonprofit-business partnerships. *Journal of Business Ethics*, 85(2), 413–429.

Sloan, P. (2009). Redefining stakeholder engagement: From control to collaboration. *Journal of Corporate Citizenship*, 36, 25–40.

Snyder, M. and Omoto, A. M. (2009), Who gets involved and why? The psychology of volunteerism. In Liu, E. S. C., Holosko, M. J. and Lo, T. W. (Eds.), *Youth Empowerment and Volunteerism: Principles, Policies and Practices*, 3–26.

Taylor, M. and Kent, M. (2014). Dialogic engagement: Clarifying foundational concepts. *Journal of Public Relations*, 26(5), 384–398.

Teisman, G. R. and Klijn, E. H. (2002). Partnership arrangements: Governmental rhetoric or governance scheme? *Public Administration Review*, 62(2), 197–205.

Timberland/How we serve: www.timberland.com/responsibility/stories/how-we-serve.html.

Van der Voort, J. M., Glac, K. and Meijs, L. C. P. M. (2009). Managing corporate community involvement. *Journal of Business Ethics*, 90(3), 311–329.

Walker, C. and Pharoah, C. (2002). *A Lot of Give – Trends in Charitable Giving for the 21st Century*. London: Hodder.

Wilson, J. (2000). Volunteering. *Annual Review of Sociology*, 215–240.

Xie, C., Bagozzi, R. P. and Troye, S. V. (2008). Trying to prosume: Toward a theory of consumerss co-creaters of value. *Journal of Academic Marketing Science*, 36, 109–122.

Zappala, G. (2004). Corporate citizenship and human resource management: A new tool or a missed opportunity? *Asia Pacific Journal of Human Resources*, 42(2), 185–201.

3.2 An efficiency-based relational approach to human capital governance

Kaouthar Lajili

Introduction

This chapter focuses on the rapidly evolving and changing role of human capital resources (HCR) in modern corporations and organizations in general. Ployhart et al. (2014) define human capital resources as "individual or unit-level capacities based on individual knowledge, skills, abilities, and other characteristics (KSAOs) that are accessible for unit-relevant purposes" (p. 374). Research on strategic human capital (resource) management has intensified in the past decade and interest is growing in various management fields such as strategic management, organizational theory, human resource management, accounting, and other related fields. The extent to which human capital resource management contributes to organizational performance and sustained competitive advantage is one of the main objectives such research attempts to answer particularly in high knowledge-driven and service-oriented global economies (e.g., Agarwal et al. 2009; Campbell et al. 2012). Furthermore, there are ongoing debates in academic and regulatory circles about executive compensation packages and the increasing disparities between executive and other employees' compensation suggesting that a comprehensive human and organizational capital perspective to governance is warranted and perhaps even necessary in today's fast-paced business environment. Thus, there seems to be a "disconnect" between value creation and value distribution in the instrumental (mainstream) approach of HCR management potentially leading to unstable and unrealized gains in the employer-employee stakeholder relationships (Blair 1995; Blair and Stout 1999; Coff 1997; Williamson 1985). In this chapter, we argue that the instrumental approach of HCR management and governance needs to be complemented (or supplemented) with an ethical and normative perspective (e.g., Donaldson and Dunfee 1994; Greenwood 2002, 2013) to help achieve long-term value and growth for firms and society in general. Specifically, a normative approach to HCR management and governance is needed because people (human capital resources) have intrinsic and fundamental, non-instrumental values and could freely choose to stay or leave an organization. Thus, an ethical normative view to HCR relations is necessary to keep both parties (employers/firms and employees/HCR) committed to their relational/social and economic contract and relationship.

We posit that employees represent a salient and critical stakeholder group in modern organizations, and consequently their engagement, commitment, direct involvement, and participation in business decisions and governance could shape strategic organizational objectives and performance in the future. More specifically, we argue that a *relational-based* governance structure based on employee engagement, mutual trust, and benefits (vis-à-vis their employers) could potentially lead to a long-term sustained competitive advantage. In this chapter, we attempt to answer the following research question: what are the conditions under which implicit (or relational) employment contracting is preferred, from an economic and social efficiency points of view, to explicit (or legal) contract terms?

By proposing a framework based on the extant human capital and organizational economics research, and using a transaction cost economics (TCE)-based stakeholder theoretical lens (e.g., Jones 1995; Ketokivi and Mahoney 2016), we highlight the conditions under which relational contracting facilitates human capital resource management and governance. The choice between implicit and explicit contract terms (such as compensation contracts and other benefits) will be examined within this framework which could help organizations further understand the importance of relational contracting and better manage their strategic human capital resources.

The chapter proceeds as follows: In the first section, we briefly discuss human capital and stakeholder governance. Then, we focus on relational contracting as a governance mechanism to facilitate (or enable) HCR engagement and commitment. The subsequent section presents and discusses the proposed conceptual framework. The chapter concludes with some managerial and policy implications, limitations of the proposed framework, and suggestions for future research opportunities in this area.

Human capital and stakeholder governance

Human capital resources and capabilities are embedded in organizational structures, routines, and processes, as well as relationship-specific assets (Teece 1986; Dyer and Singh 1998); thus human capital management and governance are inherently intertwined. Both mainstream human resource management and strategic organization research recognize that human capital resources (HCR) are critical to firm performance and represent a crucial source of competitive advantage particularly in knowledge-based firms (Coff 1997; 2011; Mahoney and Kor 2015; Wright et al. 2014). However, important challenges in managing and governing this critical asset remain largely present. For example, high employee turnover, safety, dignity, and well-being of employees, as well as power inequities and potential conflicts of interests between employers and employees, are important human capital governance issues which need to be addressed in order to unlock and achieve the long-term value proposition of human capital resources.

In this vein and in response to some of the shortcomings of the mainstream instrumental approach of HCR management, Greenwood (2013) offers an alternative and complementing ethical normative perspective. Rooted in social philosophy, socio-political pluralism, and applied ethics, Greenwood (2013) positions the ethical perspective to HRM as a normative conceptual framework "to explore and promote the ethical analysis of HRM" (Greenwood 2013, p. 363). The human and moral aspects of the employer–employee relational contract are central to the ethical view of HRM within a stakeholder, pluralistic approach extending beyond the firm's limited managerial view focused on managers and organizational goals, to cover all legitimate stakeholders and society in general. Drawing on both the instrumental approach and the ethical view of HRM, this chapter contributes to the understanding of balancing relational (implicit) and financial (explicit) components in dynamic employment relationships and contracts. Using a transactions costs economics lens, it examines relational stakeholder management in the context of human capital development, and provides a contingency framework to improve understanding of the dynamic between relational (informal) and legal (formal) HCR relations. By adopting an efficiency-based dynamic perspective to HRM, and highlighting the conditions for the use of implicit (relational) and explicit (market-based and legally enforced) contract terms in the employment relationship, this work extends both the ethical and economic (instrumental) views of HCR management and governance.

In the neoclassical view, labor (or human capital) is considered to be homogenous, divisible, and measurable and operating in perfectly competitive markets. In this case, the production (or revenue) function can be used to estimate the marginal contribution of each production factor/input to firm value (as measured by revenues or total output). This framework is still useful for determining hiring and compensation levels in corporations, industries, and markets and can be potentially useful for providing a theoretical base to measure and capture human capital contributions to firm value (Friedman and Lev 1974; Lajili and Zéghal 2006). However, this "black box" approach to firm production and factor productivity fails to address the key attributes of human capital resources (i.e., "knowledge, skills, abilities, and other" or KSAOs) based on "superior" specific know-how or tacit knowledge built by individuals and facilitated by an organizational governance structure (i.e., a continuum from market-based to firm hierarchy with contract governance in the middle). This human capital heterogeneity and specificity lead strategy and organizational scholars to focus on human capital characteristics that can potentially lead to competitive advantage. Once identified, the attributes could be matched to different governance structures and mechanisms to promote, protect, and leverage the human capital competitive advantage (Campbell et al. 2012; Chadwick 2017; Coff 1997; Williamson 1985).

In management theory and practice, it is increasingly accepted that viewing shareholders as the only residual claimants is a tenuous and overly simplified description of the actual relationships among a corporation's various stakeholders (e.g., Blair 1995; Coombs and Gilley 2005; Donaldson and Preston 1995; Freeman 1984; Mahoney 2005; Mitchell et al. 1997; Post et al. 2002). The shareholder wealth perspective is increasingly unsatisfactory for effectively answering the two fundamental questions concerning the nature of the firm (Coase 1937; Williamson 1985): how is economic value created and how is this economic value distributed among the firm's key stakeholders (i.e., distributional justice). The stakeholder approach in corporate governance is particularly noteworthy of fundamental differences between some countries. For example, Donaldson and Preston (1995) quote the following from a 1993 issue of *The Economist* (p. 52):

> In America, for instance, shareholders have a comparatively big say in the running of the enterprises they own; workers . . . have much less influence. In many European countries, shareholders have less say and workers more. . . . In Japan . . . managers have been left alone to run their companies as they see fit – namely for the benefit of employees and of allied companies, as much as for shareholders.

As mentioned in the above quote, human capital governance varies across socio-political and institutional contexts consistent with the view that there may not be a "one size fits all" or "cookie cutter" approach to human capital governance. Moreover, the legal and institutional environment underlying international governance with respect to human capital resources is embedded in cultural and moral or ethical views (e.g., Aguilera and Jackson 2010; Greenwood 2013). This calls for more research in the theory and practice of HCR governance across firms, sectors, and countries to further our understanding of its antecedents and drivers. This chapter examines the nature, role, and efficiency of governance mechanisms in facilitating and supporting human capital investments for the purposes of total value creation and realization (e.g., Freeman et al. 2004; Jensen 2002; Williamson 1985). More specifically, what are the conditions under which human capital relational governance is superior *economically and socially* to explicit (or legal) governance (third-party enforcement)?

Relational contracting and human capital

The employment relationship could be approached from several conceptual and theoretical bases. (e.g., Campbell et al. 2012; Coff 1997; Mahoney 2005; Mahoney and Kor 2015; Lajili 2015). This chapter uses a transactions costs economics (TCE) theoretical lens within a stakeholder theory approach to shed more light on the conditions under which relational (implicit) and legal (explicit or formal) are needed to support HR relations in dynamic business environments.

Ouchi (1980) shows how the employment relationship is an incomplete contract. Driven by market failures due to human factors such as bounded rationality (Williamson 1985) combined with environmental uncertainty and complexity in product and factor markets, performance ambiguity and task design complexity, the employment relationship is more efficiently organized inside the firm (or hierarchy). This effect is even more significant when firm-specific human capital investments are needed to help create and sustain a competitive advantage such as a unique technology, business model, or operating systems.

Therefore, employment contracts are by definition (or design) relational and social/implicit contracts between the firms (employers) and the employees. However, the employment relationship could be more efficiently organized under various governance structures and the firm (or hierarchy) form is not the only solution to contract incompleteness. For example, large bureaucratic costs including the difficulty to assess individual performance contributions particularly in team production, and coordinating efforts of different employees who might have different goals that could diverge from the firms,' i.e., goal incongruence could lead to more efficient solutions including "clan" or relational governance (Ouchi 1980).

As will be discussed below, and to protect employees' interests, the employment contract contains both explicit and implicit terms. For instance, the explicit terms include salary and compensation scales, general job or tasks description, benefits such as pension and postretirement benefits, training, and career advancement opportunities. The implicit components may consist of promises from the firm to offer long-term employment to its employees (i.e., job security) who promise to be loyal, honest, and work hard to achieve the firm's goals and performance targets. This social/implicit contract assumes cooperation, mutual interdependence and alignment of interests and objectives between firms and their employees. Thus, the concepts of equity, fairness, mutual cooperation and trust underlie the employment relational contract as stated by Ouchi (1980, pp. 130–131):

> In a bureaucratic relationship, each party contributes labor to a corporate body which mediates the relationship by placing a value on each contribution and then compensating it fairly. . . . [T]he perception of equity in this case depends upon a social agreement that the bureaucratic hierarchy has the legitimate authority to provide this mediation.

More recently, Dyer and Singh (1998) also adopt a relational approach to firms' critical resources as drivers of competitive advantage and show that these resources span firm boundaries in the form of alliance-specific inter-firm relationships or assets, knowledge sharing routines, and complementary capabilities. Recognizing that the level of analysis for the competitive advantage and its maintenance is now the inter-firm relationship (and not the focal firm only) and given the importance of human capital resources in implementing and executing this relational advantage, this approach seems appropriate for our discussion of relational contracting in employee engagement and governance in general. Dyer and Singh (1998) note that effective governance of the inter-firm relationship is a building block of the relational approach proposed. Incentives and safeguards are needed to support this inter-firm relationship and its specific investments and provide formal and informal assurances of relational rents fair distribution, reciprocity, and equity (Williamson 1985, 1996; Mahoney 2005).

Having established the importance of relational contracting in governing human capital and the employment relationship, we now turn to discussing the human capital and firm attributes the combination of which we argue will affect the nature and extent of the use of implicit vs. explicit employment contracts.

Human capital specificity and uncertainty

Human capital specificity is one of the most important human capital attributes that has been advanced and examined both conceptually and empirically in extant organizational and strategic human capital research (Williamson 1996; Wang et al. 2009; Lajili 2015). Firm-specific human capital refers to knowledge, skills, and experience acquired and accumulated on the job (Becker 1962, 1993; Gibbons and Waldman 2004) which is specific to the firm's assets, business model, and knowledge processes and networks such as drug research and development in pharmaceutical companies. More refined definitions of specific human capital include task-specific, occupation and/or industry-specific human capital (Gibbons and Waldman 2004; Mayer et al. 2012). The degree of firm specificity in human capital accumulation depends on the transferability of knowledge and skills acquired by employees in alternative jobs and whether or not this knowledge loses value in its next best use (Williamson 1985). Human asset specificity could also be embedded in inter-firm alliances thus providing potential relational rents. Dyer and Singh (1998) define human asset specificity as "transaction-specific know-how accumulated by transactors through long-standing relationships (e.g., dedicated supplier engineers who learn the systems, procedures, and the individuals idiosyncratic to the buyer)" (p. 662).

Human capital specificity is one category of asset specificity in the transaction-cost literature where opportunism and potential rent appropriation by one party (employer or employee) is critical in designing efficient governance structures. This specificity/efficiency factor is a building block of the resource or knowledge-based view of the firm which helps create and sustain valuable competitive advantages based on valuable, rare, hard to imitate and substitute resources or assets (Barney 1991; Grant 1996; Oliver 1997).

In this chapter, we further expand the human capital specificity attribute/construct to include combinations (or bundling) of human assets with other organizational assets such as specific information operating systems, procedures, and routines as well as other tangible and intangible assets including brand and reputation capital (Dyer and Singh 1998; Lajili and Mahoney 2006; Teece 1986, 2011). When human capital is bundled with other co-specialized assets inside the firm or across firm boundaries, it can be the source of competitive advantage particularly in highly competitive and high-growth firms and industries. However, the higher the degree of asset specificity and associated bundling at the firm (or alliance) level, the higher the likelihood of "core rigidity" and inertia risk particularly in fast changing technological and environmental uncertainty such as changing consumer demands, regulatory, and competitive market conditions (Teece 2011; Dyer and Singh 1998). Furthermore, this co-specialization creates the potential for ex-post opportunism given environmental (external) and behavioral (internal) uncertainty which could lead to under-investments in these strategic bundled assets ex-ante (Williamson 1985; Hart 1995). In particular, bundling human capital with other firm assets can put human capital resources at a disadvantage vis-à-vis their employer by increasing the level of individual performance ambiguity and consequently individual output contribution assessments (i.e., positive agency costs). Property and decision rights embodied in ownership and control structures or governance mechanisms further complicate the employment relational contract. If not explicitly identified and allocated ex-ante (Hart 1995; Rajan and Zingales 1998; Oxley 1999) they may lead to the instability and ultimately failure of the employment relationship unless an efficient and effective governance structure is designed simultaneously with the co-specialized asset accumulation. The following section presents a conceptual framework which attempts to answer this employment relationship dilemma.

A relational framework for human capital resources governance

As discussed above, a contractual and relational approach to stakeholder engagement and management is appropriate for examining modern challenges in strategic human resource management where the firm/organization is viewed as a nexus of both implicit and explicit contracts (Hill and Jones 1992; Joseph 2007). We adopt a TCE-based stakeholder approach to propose a relational contingency framework where employees are explicitly viewed as a key and salient stakeholder group contributing and investing in their human capital and knowledge building inside or across firm boundaries such as in alliance relationships (e.g., Dyer and Singh 1998; He and Wang 2009; Jensen and Meckling 1976; Mitchell et al. 1997; Williamson 1996).

Mitchell et al. (1997) provides a theory of stakeholder identification and salience guided by the question or principle of "who or what really counts" and centered on managers' perceptions of stakeholder salience classification based on three main attributes and their combinations, namely: *power, legitimacy, and urgency*. According to Mitchell et al. (1997, p. 878) stakeholder salience is defined as "the degree to which managers give priority to competing stakeholder claims" arguing that stakeholder salience is dynamic and changing over time based on the levels of each attribute and the nature of their interactions or combinations. For instance, they refer to high stakeholder salience if all three stakeholder attributes (i.e., power, legitimacy, and urgency) as perceived by managers are present. Employees as holders of critical human capital resources could have different levels of stakeholder salience based on the presence of one, two or all three critical attributes. For example, during the global financial crisis of 2008, excessive risk taking and corporate greed led to an outrage in the working middle class in the US and around the world. The large disparities and excessive compensation of some executives and key employees in large financial services firms largely due to distortions in incentives and lack of regulatory oversight, led both shareholders (activist shareholders) and employees to voice their discontent and distrust. However, tensions could exist among these two groups of salient stakeholders (Hillman and Klein 2001; Jensen 2002; Liu et al. 2014).

Following a TCE stakeholder approach and building on prior literature of stakeholder salience (Mitchell et al. 1997; Jensen 2002) and the ethical view of human resource management (Jones 1995; Greenwood 2013) we propose a simple conceptual framework to help explain and predict relational and market-based human capital governance as illustrated in Table 3.2.1.

Following the seminal work of Williamson (1985, 1996) and building on more recent extensions of transactions costs and agency theoretical strands in explaining and predicting optimal organizational forms in dynamic settings (Mahoney 1992; Lajili and Mahoney 2006) we focus on two key transaction (or contract) attributes, namely asset specificity and uncertainty. As discussed earlier in this chapter, human asset specificity involves unique, valuable, and potentially non-substitutable knowledge, skills, abilities, and other assets (Barney 1991). Teamwork and learning processes and routines and how these are bundled, deployed, and adapted to changing environments (i.e., dynamic capabilities) are particularly valuable for firms striving to create and sustain human capital-based competitive advantages (Teece 2011). There is a continuum of human asset specificity where we can distinguish high from low levels at each extreme. For instance, high human asset specificity at the firm level could be illustrated by unique experience, skills, knowledge, as well as team-based procedures and routines (e.g., high technology, telecommunications, and pharmaceutical firms). Another key attribute of the employment relational contract is the degree of uncertainty to which both firms and employees are exposed to in the course of their business operations and mutual exchanges. In the current chapter, and following prior literature, we focus on environmental uncertainty (i.e., external to the firm's boundaries) such as demand and technological uncertainties as well as firm-specific (or internal) uncertainty. Internal sources of risk or uncertainty could include for example high employee turnover, the loss of key employees and/or management team members, and litigation and reputation risks due to defects in products or services. For instance, the recent United Airlines incident where one passenger was violently forced to give his seat to the airline crew member, and the BP oil spill disaster in the gulf of Mexico in 2010 are some of the examples of how reputation risks linked to internal people and processes (i.e. operational risks) could have a significant impact on firms' image, reputation and ultimately its economic value. Due to uncertainty, human bounded rationality, asset specificity and potential hold up problems, contracts are incomplete (Hart 1995) and fail

Table 3.2.1 An efficiency-based relational framework for human capital resources governance

	High human asset specificity	Low human asset specificity
High Internal/External Uncertainty	(1) Relational/social contracting (reciprocity, trust, self-enforcing safeguards, high employee engagement, "clan" governance) Implicit terms	(2) Blended explicit and relational contracting (mainly market-based compensation with frequent renegotiation and bargaining) (implicit < explicit terms)
Low Internal/External Uncertainty	(3) Blended relational and explicit contracting (financial safeguards/bonds, high economic incentives, hierarchy/ bureaucracy) (implicit > explicit terms)	(4) Arms'-length explicit contracting (market-based compensation, low economic incentives) Explicit terms

to foresee all possible contingencies in transactions including employment relationships (Masten 1988). This limitation creates the potential for relational stakeholder-based efficiently designed and implemented employment contracts. In addition to asset specificity and uncertainty main effects on efficient governance, the interaction between these two attributes in an employment contract is expected to impact its nature and main characteristics and terms (e.g., relational/implicit vs. market-based/explicit). In the current chapter, we summarize the outcomes of these interactive effects in Table 3.2.1 and give some examples of industries and firms who could be in each quadrant at any point in time or growth in their business cycle.

Quadrant (1) illustrates the situation where there is a high level of human capital specificity coupled with a high level of both internal and external uncertainties. Internal uncertainty includes firm-specific sources such as operational, process and business model-based, financing and legal risks, performance assessment ambiguity (Ouchi 1980; Lajili and Zéghal 2005). External or environmental uncertainty refers to risk sources outside the control and boundaries of the firm/organization and include for example demand and supply shocks (mainly unexpected changes), competitive pressures and conditions (industry structures), as well as regulatory changes. An example or illustration of this quadrant could be high technology and pharmaceutical firms/sectors. For example, Apple Inc. has a highly specific supply chain and alliance network which is bundled with its human capital as innovation and talent holders. Furthermore, Apple operates in a highly dynamic and competitive technology environment where innovation and consumer preferences change fast and competition is fierce in addition to regulatory changes and pressures (e.g., privacy regulations). This combination of high human capital specificity and uncertainty suggests that relational contracting is the most preferred and efficient way to govern human capital in this case. Implicit terms in such relational contracts could include commitment to employee well-being and safety, work-life balance arrangements and flexible work hours, gender equality in career advancement and development, as well as high employee engagement, high incentives for innovation, teamwork, and loyalty thus favoring an employee-friendly corporate culture (i.e., stakeholder management). For example, compensation and human-resource management could be represented as a separate committee at the board level and key employees could be appointed to the board of directors (e.g., scientists on the pharmaceutical firms' boards). Although common in two-tiered boards with a supervisory and a management board in some code law countries in Europe and Asia (e.g., Germany and Japan for example), this participatory governance choice is at odds with the independence criterion for effective governance promoted in the Anglo-Saxon institutional governance context (e.g., Sarbanes Oxley act). However, it appears to be preferred in this high human capital specificity and complexity environment to help protect and sustain the competitive advantage position of such firms/sectors.

Another example illustrating this quadrant could be the Japanese and German auto manufacturing sectors. In Japan, the corporate culture is built upon social and relational contracting where cooperation among employees, suppliers, customers, and shareholders (i.e., stakeholder governance) is fundamental and implicitly underlies the functioning, governance, and global competitiveness of Japanese firms. Ouchi (1980) refers to this form of organization as "clan" governance where goal congruence is high and environmental and internal uncertainty is also high. Similarly, the German auto sector could be another example fitting into this quadrant. For example, the Volkswagen group's recent gas emission test scandal in the fall of 2015 is a good illustration of the range and significance of both internal and external uncertainty and their interaction with specific and bundled human capital. Unethical and fraudulent behavior by some Volkswagen's engineers probably driven by the desire to expand market share and power, and increase competitiveness in North America and other big markets (such as Asia) lead this car manufacturer to cheat on the emissions test (a regulatory hurdle) with significant negative reputation and stock performance effects (the stock price dropped 40% in the few weeks following the scandal announcement). Although the implicit social contract terms have been broken in this case with multiple stakeholders (e.g., employees, customers, suppliers, shareholders, the community at large), the "clan" governance suggests that the company was able to face this major blow to its reputation by taking corrective actions such as replacing the top executive team and investigating and reprimanding the engineers involved. The violation of the implicit claims and contracts in this case and its immediate impact on firm performance and reputation suggests that stakeholder management and governance are increasingly important in today's global economies (Benson and Davidson 2010; Cornell and Shapiro 1987; Joseph 2007).

Quadrant (2) in Table 3.2.1 refers to a situation of low human capital specificity interacting with high levels of uncertainty. Examples of firms that could illustrate this quadrant include Walmart, United Airlines, and British Petroleum (BP). The governance solution in this case points to a blended explicit and implicit contract governance for the employment relationship with the explicit component outweighing the implicit one. Explicit terms in employment contracts include for example compensation and benefits and are usually market-based following competitive industry norms and benchmarks, and legally enforced. As an illustration of this quadrant in Table 3.2.1, we consider the airline sector which is known for its multiple uncertainty or risk factors ranging from macroeconomic and hard to control factors (such as the high volatility in oil prices and investment costs, terrorism threats, and other geopolitical conflicts) to more operational and firm-specific sources such as labor relations and disputes, labor costs and unionization as well as potential mechanical and process failures including human errors. This high risk environment is matched with relatively low human capital specificity as employees could move from one firm to a rival one without loss of value in their earnings potential and with little to no bundling existing in such a sector. In this case, explicit claims in employment contracts covering for example compensation, job descriptions and schedules as well as benefits and other non-financial claims will emerge as the most efficient outcome. However, frequent renegotiations and bargaining are expected to occur with this form of dynamic governance as firms and sectors adjust continuously to changing supply and demand conditions, technological innovation in the physical assets such as airplanes, and regulatory and market global conditions (e.g., environmental regulations). By engaging their employees and treating them fairly and respectfully, firms in these sectors could outperform their rivals who fail to pay attention to the implicit and relational governance positive impacts on their bottom line, survival and financial stability.

Quadrant (3) illustrates the case where human capital specificity is high and uncertainty is low. Industries and firms potentially representing this case include big commercial and investment banks in North America (such as JP Morgan and Goldman Sachs in the US), largely diversified and global luxury retail firms (such as LVMH group in France), and large telecommunications companies (such as Verizon and AT&T in the US, and Rogers and Bell in Canada). The low uncertainty level in this case could be related to a monopoly (or oligopoly) power and positioning in the industry sometimes supported by favorable regulations and strategic relationships and alliances with various stakeholders including regulatory and lobbying groups. The low risk situation could also arise from a scale and scope (size and diversification) advantage allowing the firm/sector to absorb or manage a high level of uncertainty both of the internal and external kinds. The predicted employment relationship governance structure shows a blended implicit/explicit contracting mode with the implicit component outweighing the explicit one and the firm (or hierarchy) organizational form would be efficient in this case. Financial or formal safeguards such as equity ownership and performance-based bonuses provide good incentives for both the executive team and the entire workforce to stay with the firm (low voluntary turnover). The low uncertainty in this case suggests that contingent claims contracting and explicit terms for the employment contract could be drafted and enforced with reasonable cost effectiveness. However, the co-specialized assets (e.g., high human capital specificity bundled with a proprietary internet platform) also suggests that implicit and relational rents could be significant and therefore additional non-financial and implicit safeguards and incentives may be needed to support employment relationships in this case. As an illustration of this interesting case, we compare the compensation intensity (i.e., the ratio of labor expenses to sales) for a matched sample of financial services firms in Canada and in the US during the 2005–2009 time periods. The sample matching is based on the size of assets (or sales) and on the similarity of business segments as well as profitability. Figure 3.2.1 shows the compensation ratio for this matched sample.

There is a generally higher ratio of total compensation to sales for the US sample compared to the Canadian one. This observation seems to suggest that US financial

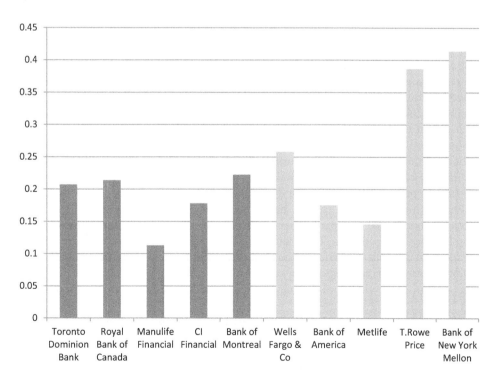

Figure 3.2.1 Average total compensation relative to total sales for a sample of US and Canadian financial services firms (2005–2009)

services employees in this sample and during this period were extracting (or appropriating) more rents from their employment contracts than their Canadian counterparts. This could be partly explained by the fact that the US financial services sector is bigger in size (has a lot more firms and competition as well as geographic diversification) than the Canadian financial services market which is more concentrated (oligopoly) and where the firms enjoy more bargaining power and control. With further examination of the characteristics and nature of the employment relationships in these two countries, detailed disclosures about human capital resources in two banks (TD bank in Canada and its matched firm Wells Fargo in the US) were collected from the annual reports and stakeholder reports including the companies' website when available. As shown in the Appendix at the end of this chapter, the Canadian bank (TD bank) discloses voluntarily more and detailed information about the extent of training and development, turnover rates, workforce diversity and career advancement, wellness, pension, and mentoring programs than its US counterpart (Wells Fargo). This additional information provided by TD bank points to an implicit and social relational contracting approach adopted by this bank. Similar disclosure reports from the other Canadian firms show similar trends and findings.

The last quadrant (4) in Table 3.2.1 illustrates the situation where relational employee contracting may not be needed because the market mechanism can be efficiently used to match general and unbundled human capital with firms or individuals seeking the good or service. The food and agricultural sector could fit into this case (e.g., fast food restaurants such as McDonald's and Dunkin Donuts) and the transportation sector (e.g., Uber, Amazon, private trucking firms, and public transportation). Market-based competitive compensation and wage structures characterize this governance mode with the explicit terms of the employment contract clearly laid out making job design and performance assessment possible particularly under a low uncertainty environment. Furthermore, and with the expansion of e-commerce and internet-based search and provision of goods and services, customers can enjoy easier and more transparent access to services such as house cleaning or construction services with more competitive prices and lower search costs (e.g., Amazon mechanical Turk internet platform, and e-Bay).

In summary, the framework presented in Table 3.2.1 shows the impact of human capital attributes as they interact with the business environment of the firm/employer in bringing about an efficient employment relationship. More specifically, it provides a conceptual base for predicting the nature and extent of implicit vs. explicit contracting in the employment relationship. Employee engagement increases with implicit and relational contracting but formal safeguards (explicit terms) are still needed to further support and strengthen the social contract. The framework is not static in the sense that firms, industries and even different countries and institutional systems could move from one quadrant to another over time and depending on the maturity, life cycle, stakeholder power and influence, and competitive positioning among other factors. For example, it seems that Uber, the share riding internet-based service company is probably better fitted to quadrant (2) rather (4) because it is still at the early stage of business growth and maturity. Moreover, the uncertainty surrounding the regulatory aspect of its business operations and disruptive nature in relation to the taxi driving service would suggest that this company and its competitors will continue to evolve and search for the optimal way to organize the employment relationship. On the other hand, Uber drivers are also trying to figure out the best way to organize and govern their employment relationship such as forming a union or a collective association, to be able to exert more power and influence on the relational rents distribution and appropriation in the future.

Conclusions and suggestions for future research

This chapter adopted an efficiency-based stakeholder approach to examine the conditions under which relational employment contracting and the associated use of implicit vs. explicit terms is preferred and warranted in today's modern organizations. Building on an integration of common elements and findings in the extant organizational and strategy research with regards to human capital and knowledge governance (e.g., Ketokivi and Mahoney 2016; Lajili and Mahoney 2006 Mahoney 1992; Williamson 1996) we highlight the role of human capital attributes and their interaction with firms' uncertainty attributes to drive the most efficient and transaction cost minimizing employment relationship. This chapter further contributes to ethical HRM (Jones 1995; Greenwood 2013) and stakeholder salience and relevance theory (Freeman 1984; Mitchell et al. 1997) by highlighting the importance of relational implicit and social contracting aspects of human capital resources management and governance in a dynamic context. In addition to the economic explicit terms of the employment contract, we argue that the long-term stability, efficiency, durability, and maintenance of human capital-based competitive advantages require that firms and organizations pay close attention to their employees' well-being, health, and safety, and ongoing development and engagement.

The current chapter proposed a simple conceptual framework based on a 2*2 matrix denoting high and low levels of human capital specificity and uncertainty at the firm level, to capture the conditions and contractual outcomes/terms for the associated employment relationship. In this framework, relational contracting emerges as an effective governance mode providing both incentives and safeguards to protect and align investments in firm-specific human and other bundled assets to help create and sustain firm competitive advantage. Given the increased complexity and globalization of business operations coupled with human capital intensive services and innovative technologies, relational contracting with employees may provide the necessary and sufficient conditions for creating and maintaining a certain level of human capital and intellectual-based competitive advantage. Indeed, most of the innovation and creativity is embodied in individual human brains that will have to be persuaded to work and keep on working for a firm or establish their own firm, i.e., entrepreneurial ventures. Furthermore, the proposed framework could provide a human capital governance map designed to guide firms in choosing and negotiating employment contracts and firms could use several quadrants or cells (from Table 3.2.1) at any point in time and depending on the nature of the task or job design as well as the types of employees. For instance, large companies such as Apple, Google, and Amazon among others could use more than one quadrant from Table 3.2.1 at any time for various aspects of their business operations (e.g., manufacturing, engineering design, management, and strategic positioning). Thus, the proposed framework allows for flexibility and dynamism by accommodating various changes within and across firms based on the nature of the employment relationship and its strategic importance. The creation, appropriation, and distribution of relational labor rents are at the heart of the human capital and knowledge governance puzzle. Relational governance based on employee engagement, fairness, and equity could prove to be efficient and superior in periods of financial distress or temporary setbacks (e.g., BP oil spill or Volkswagen emission test scandal). By focusing on collective goals and fostering cooperation and a sense of mutual interdependence, relational governance has the advantage of avoiding costly and incomplete legal safeguards writing and enforcement and will thus be more economically, socially, and environmentally effective.

Some limitations of this conceptual study include at least two potentially related issues. First, the proposed framework does not explicitly address the possible agency conflicts between management, other employees, and shareholders (or investors in general). The fact that firms have different kinds of employees as above-mentioned may require a further refinement of the proposed framework to specifically help explain and predict various governance and contractual arrangements across employee types and job/task designs. Second, the proposed framework focused on economic efficiency and optimal governance and assumed that the implicit contractual terms are fair, equitable and in the best interests and well-being of employees and all other stakeholders. In reality and as the financial crisis of 2008 confirmed it, firms or management could be focused on more short-term gains, opportunism, and excessive risk taking which could ultimately lead to financial distress or bankruptcy and puts all stakeholders at risk (Blair 1995).

Moreover, the proposed framework could be further refined by adopting a non-instrumental (or intrinsic) value of humans in organizations thus firmly embedding the relational HCR governance into the ethical aspect and approach of stakeholder engagement and management. For example, firms (such as TD bank in the Appendix to this chapter) appears to focus on caring for and promoting the well-being, health, and safety, as well as the continuous development of their employees regardless of whether the employees choose to stay with the bank or leave for a competitor or pursue other career paths. Similarly, focusing on efficiency and competitive advantage from a firm's point of view could have limitations in assessing the performance and nature of HCR management and governance from a stakeholder normative (or ethical) perspective. Future research could expand the set of organizational actions and measures to include non-instrumental and intrinsic value constructs capturing employees' gains in training and development skills, social networks participation and expansion, health, and wellness, as well as board participation and governance (e.g., two-tiered board structures).

Future research could address these limitations and empirically test the conceptual predictions of the framework proposed to help shed more light on the nature and extent of the use of both explicit and implicit contract terms in modern employment relationships across firms, industries, and countries. The impact of relational governance could be examined in both positive performance impacts and in situations of business and financial distress. Moreover, the governance mechanisms adopted by firms and industries could be further examined in light of their role in supporting or hindering human capital specific assets. The framework proposed in this chapter shows the close relationship and potential endogeneity in choosing the level and nature of contractual safeguards (implicit vs. explicit). Future research in governance could look more closely at the impact of ownership and control structures, board composition and independence, as well as executive and other employee's compensation, and link these governance mechanisms to human capital performance and advantage. Stakeholder management, reporting, and governance provide a more comprehensive and balanced approach to business success and failure in modern organizations and more research is needed to establish its merits both economically and socially in the future.

References

Agarwal, R., Barney, J. B., Foss, N. J. and Klein P. G. (2009). Heterogeneous resources and the financial crisis: Implications of strategic management theory. *Strategic Organization*, 7(4), 467–484.

Aguilera, R.V. and Jackson, G. (2010). Comparative and international corporate governance. *Academy of Management Annals*, 4, 485–556.

Barney, J. B. (1991). Firm resources and sustained competitive advantage. *Journal of Management*, 17, 99–120.

Becker, G. S. (1962). Investment in human capital: A theoretical analysis. *Journal of Political Economy*, 70, 9–49.

Becker, G. S. (1993). *Human capital: A theoretical and empirical analysis with special reference to education.* 3rd ed. Chicago: University of Chicago Press.

Benson, B.W. and Davidson,W. N. (2010).The relation between stakeholder management, firm value, and CEO compensation: A test of enlightened value maximization. *Financial Management*, 39(3), 929–964.

Blair, M. (1995). *Ownership and control: Rethinking corporate governance for the twenty-first century.* Washington, DC: Brookings Institute.

Blair, M. and Stout, L. A. (1999). A team production theory of corporate law. *Virginia Law Review*, 85, 247–328.

Campbell, B.A., Coff, R.W. and Kryscynski D. (2012). Rethinking sustained competitive advantage from human capital. *Academy of Management Review*, 37, 376–395.

Chadwick, C. (2017). Toward a more comprehensive model of firms' human capital rents. *Academy of Management Review*, 42(3), 499–519.

Coase, R. H. (1937). The nature of the firm. *Economica*, 4, 386–405.

Coff, R. W. (1997). Human assets and management dilemmas: Coping with hazards on the road to resource-based theory. *Academy of Management Review*, 22, 374–402.

Coff, R. W. (2011). Maximizing value from human capital. In *The Oxford Handbook of Human Capital.* Burton-Jones, A. and Spender, J. C. (eds). Oxford: Oxford University Press, 359–381.

Coombs, J. E. and Gilley, M. (2005). Stakeholder management as a predictor of CEO compensation: Main effects and interactions with financial performance. *Strategic Management Journal*, 26, 827–840.

Cornell, B. and Shapiro, A. C. (1987). Corporate stakeholders and corporate finance. *Financial Management*, 5–14.

Donaldson,T. and Dunfee,T.W. (1994).Toward a unified conceptualization of business ethics: Integrative social contract theory. *Academy of Management Review*, 19, 252–284.

Donaldson,T. and Preston, L. (1995).The stakeholder theory of the modern corporation: Concepts, evidence and implications. *Academy of Management Review*, 20, 65–91.

Dyer, J. H. and Singh, H. (1998).The relational view: Cooperative strategy and sources of interorganizational competitive advantage. *Academy of Management Review*, 23(4), 660–679.

Freeman, R. E. (1984). *Strategic management: A stakeholder approach.* Englewood Cliffs, NJ: Prentice-Hall.

Freeman, R. E., Wicks, A. C. and Parmar B. (2004). Stakeholder theory and "The Corporate Objective Revisisted." *Organization Science*, 15, 364–369.

Friedman, A. and Lev, B. (1974). A surrogate measure of a firm's investment in human capital. *Journal of Accounting Research*, 235–250.

Gibbons, R. and Waldman, M. (2004). Task specific human capital. American *Economic Review*, 94(2), 203–207.

Greenwood, M. (2002). Ethics and HRM: A review and conceptual analysis. *Journal of Business Ethics*, 36(3), 261–279.

Greenwood, M. (2013). Ethical analyses of HRM: A review and research agenda. *Journal of Business Ethics*, 114, 355–366.

Grant, R. M. (1996). Toward a knowledge-based theory of the firm. *Strategic Management Journal*, 17, 109–122.

Hart, O. (1995). *Firms, contracts and financial structure.* Oxford: Oxford University Press.

He, J. and Wang, H. C. (2009). Firm innovative knowledge assets and economic performance: The asymmetric roles and incentives- and monitoring based governance mechanisms. *Academy of Management Journal*, 52, 919–938.

Hill, C. W. L. and Jones, T. M. (1992). Stakeholder-agency theory. *Journal of Management Studies*, 29, 131–154.

Hillman, A. J. and Klein, G. D. (2001). Shareholder value, stakeholder engagement, and social issues: What's the bottom line? *Strategic Management Journal*, 125–139.

Jensen, M. C. (2002). Value maximization, stakeholder theory, and the corporate objective function. *Business Ethics Quarterly*, 12(2), 235–256.

Jensen, M. C. and Meckling, W. H. (1976). Theory of the firm: managerial behavior, agency costs and ownership structure. *Journal of Financial Economics*, 3, 305–360.

Jones, T. M. (1995). Instrumental stakeholder theory: A synthesis of ethics and economics. *Academy of Management Review*, 20(2), 404–437.

Joseph, G. (2007). Implications of a stakeholder view on corporate reporting. *Accounting and the Public Interest*, 50–65.

Ketokivi, M. and Mahoney, J. T. (2016). Transaction cost economics as a constructive stakeholder theory. *Academy of Management Learning & Education*, 15(1), 123–138.

Lajili, K. (2015). Embedding human capital into governance design: A conceptual framework. *Journal of Management & Governance*, 19 (4):1–22.

Lajili, K. and Mahoney, J. T. (2006). Revisiting agency and transaction costs theory predictions in vertical financial ownership and contracting: Electronic integration as an organizational form choice. *Managerial and Decision Economics*, 27, 401–423.

Lajili, K. and Zéghal, D. (2005). A content analysis of risk management disclosures in Canadian annual reports. *Canadian Journal of Administrative Sciences*, 22(2), 125–142.

Lajili, K. and Zéghal, D. (2006). Market performance impacts of human capital disclosures. *Journal of Accounting and Public Policy*, 25, 171–194.

Liu, X., van Jaarsveld, D. D., Batt, R. and Frost, A. C. (2014). The influence of capital structure on strategic human capital: Evidence from US and Canadian firms. *Journal of Management*, 40(2): 422–448.

Mahoney, J. T. (1992). The choice of organizational form: Vertical financial ownership versus other methods of vertical. *Strategic Management Journal*, 13(8), 559–584.

Mahoney, J. T. (2005). *Economic foundations of strategy*. Thousand Oaks, CA: Sage.

Mahoney, J. T. and Kor, Y. (2015). Advancing the human capital perspective on value creation by joining capabilities and governance approach. *Academy of Management Perspectives*, 29(3), 296–308.

Masten, S. E. (1988). A legal basis for the firm. *Journal of Law, Economics and Organization*, Oxford University Press, 4, 181–198.

Mayer, K., Somaya, D. and Williamson, I. O. (2012). Firm-specific, industry-specific, and occupational human capital and the sourcing of knowledge work. *Organization Science*, 23(5), 1311–1329.

Mitchell, R. K., Agle B. R. and Wood, D. J. (1997). Toward a theory of stakeholder identification and salience: Defining the principle of who and what really counts. *Academy of Management Review*, 22(4), 853–886.

Oliver, C. (1997). Sustainable competitive advantage: Combining institutional and resource-based views. *Strategic Management Journal*, 18: 697–713.

Ouchi, W. G. (1980). Markets, bureaucracies, and clans. *Administrative Science Quarterly*, 25, 129–141.

Oxley, J. E. (1999). Institutional environment and the mechanisms of governance: The impact of intellectual property protection on the structure of inter-firm alliances. *Journal of Economic Behavior and Organization*, 38(3), 283–309.

Ployhart, R. E., Nyberg A. J., Reilly, G. and Maltarich, M. A. (2014). Human capital is dead: Long live human capital resources!. *Journal of Management*, 40(2), 371–398.

Post, J. E., Preston, L. E. and Sachs, S. (2002). *Redefining the corporation: Stakeholder management and organizational wealth*. Stanford, CA: Stanford University Press.

Rajan, R. G. and Zingales, L. (1998). Power in a theory of the firm. *The Quarterly Journal of Economics*, 113, 387–432.

Teece, D. J. (1986). Profiting from technological innovation: implications for integration, collaboration, licensing and public policy. *Research Policy*, 15, 285–305.

Teece, D. J. (2011). Human capital, capabilities, and the firm: Literati, numerate, and entrepreneurs in the twenty-first century enterprise. In *The Oxford Handbook of Human Capital*. Burton-Jones, A. and Spender, J. C. (eds). Oxford: Oxford University Press, 527–561.

Wang, H. C., He, J. and Mahoney J. T. (2009). Firm-specific knowledge resources and competitive advantage: The roles of economic- and relationship-based employee governance mechanisms. *Strategic Management Journal*, 30, 1265–1285.

Williamson, O. E. (1985). *The Economics institutions of capitalism*. New York: Free Press.

Williamson, O. E. (1996). *The mechanisms of governance*. New York: Oxford University Press.

Wright, P. M., Coff, R. and Moliterno, T. P. (2014). Special issue editorial strategic human capital: Crossing the great divide. *Journal of Management*, 40, 353–370.

Appendix

TD Bank and Wells Fargo bank human capital resource disclosures based on annual reports, proxy circulars, and CSR reports

Toronto Dominion Bank	Wells Fargo & Co
Source: 2009–2005 Annual reports (AR)	Source: 2009–2005 Annual reports (AR)

$M	2009	2008	2007	2006	2005
Salaries	3671	3089	2737	2700	2544
Incentive compensation	1342	1235	1286	1207	1139
Pension and other employee benefits	826	660	583	578	535

$M	2009	2008	2007	2006	2005
Salaries	13,757	8,260	7,762	7,007	6,215
Commissions and Incentive Benefits	8,021	2,676	3,284	2,885	2,366
Employee Benefits	4,689	2,004	2,322	2,035	1,874

Toronto Dominion Bank

2009 Annual report (AR)

Awards:

– TRAINING INC. TD Bank, America's Most Convenient Bank, named one of the top 125 trainers (p. 14)

– CHARTERED INSTITUTE OF PERSONNEL AND DEVELOPMENT TD Waterhouse U.K. named winner in the Total Reward category (p. 14)

– HUMAN RIGHTS CAMPAIGN TD Bank, America's Most Convenient Bank, named one of the best places to work for LGBT equality (p. 14)

– MACLEAN'S TD Bank Financial Group named one of Canada's top 100 employers (p. 14)

– HEWITT CANADA TD Bank Financial Group named one of Canada's 50 best employers (p. 14)

– Options on common shares are periodically granted to eligible employees of the Bank under the plan for terms of 7 or 10 years and vest over a 3 or 4-year period. These options provide holders with the right to purchase common shares of the Bank at a fixed price equal to the closing market price of the shares

Wells Fargo & Co

2009 AR

– Issued 76 million shares from time to time during the period under various employee benefit (including our employee stock option plan) and director plans, as well as under our dividend reinvestment and direct stock purchase programs. (p. 74)

– We use four key variables to calculate our annual pension cost: size and characteristics of the employee population, actuarial assumptions, expected long-term rate of return on plan assets, and discount rate. (p. 79)

– Our expected rate of return for 2010 is 8.25%, a decrease from 8.75%, the expected rate of return for 2009 and 2008. The decrease reflects our decision to de-emphasize the use of the Tactical Asset Allocation model. (p. 80)

– All shares of our ESOP (Employee Stock Ownership Plan) Cumulative Convertible Preferred Stock (ESOP Preferred Stock) were issued to a trustee acting on behalf of the Wells Fargo & Company 401(k) Plan (the 401(k) Plan). Dividends on the ESOP Preferred Stock are cumulative from the date of initial issuance and are payable quarterly at annual rates ranging from 8.50% to 12.50%, depending upon the year of issuance. (More information 2009 Annual Report p. 164)

Toronto Dominion Bank	Wells Fargo & Co

Toronto Dominion Bank

on the day prior to the date the options were issued. Under this plan, 5.7 million common shares have been reserved for future issuance (2008–9.2 million; 2007–11.0 million). (p. 127)

– During the year, 4.0 million (2008–2.0 million; 2007–1.5 million) options were granted with a weighted-average fair value of $7.62 per option (2008 – $10.80 per option; 2007 – $11.46 per option). During the year, the Bank recognized compensation expense in the Consolidated Statement of Income of $30 million (2008 – $22 million; 2007 – $20 million) for the stock option awards granted. (p. 127)

– The Bank also offers deferred share unit plans to eligible employees and non-employee directors. Under these plans, a portion of the participant's annual incentive award and/or maturing share units may be deferred as share units equivalent to the Bank's common shares. The deferred share units are not redeemable by the participant until retirement, permanent disability or termination of employment or directorship and must be redeemed for cash by the end of the next calendar year. Dividend equivalents accrue to the participants in the form of additional units. As at October 31, 2009, 2.5 million deferred share units were outstanding (2008–2.3 million). (p. 127)

– Compensation expense for these plans is recorded in the year the incentive award is earned by the plan participant. Changes in the value of these plans are recorded, net of the effects of related hedges, in the Consolidated Statement of Income. For the year ended October 31, 2009, the Bank recognized compensation expense, net of the effects of hedges, for these plans of $235 million (2008 – $191 million; 2007 – $125 million). The compensation expense recognized before the effects of hedges was $309 million (2008 – $77 million; 2007 – $202 million). (p. 127)

– The Bank also operates a share purchase plan available to employees. Employees can contribute any amount of their eligible earnings (net of source deductions) to the *Employee Ownership Plan*. The Bank matches 100% of the first $250 of employee contributions each year and the remainder of employee contributions at 50% to an overall maximum of 3.5% of the employee's eligible earnings or $2,250, whichever comes first. Prior to March 1, 2007, employees could contribute up to 6% of their annual base earnings to a maximum of $4,500.

Wells Fargo & Co

– Total stock option compensation expense was $221 million in 2009, $174 million in 2008 and $129 million in 2007. (p. 165)

– Our Long-Term Incentive Compensation Plan provides for awards of incentive and nonqualified stock options, stock appreciation rights, restricted shares, RSRs, performance awards and stock awards without restrictions. (p. 165)

– In 1996, we adopted the PartnerShares® Stock Option Plan, a broad-based employee stock option plan. It covers full- and part-time employees who generally were not included in the long-term incentive compensation plan described above. (p. 166)

– Eligible employees who complete one year of service are eligible for matching company contributions, which are generally a 100% match up to 6% of an employee's qualifying compensation. Prior to January 1, 2010, matching contributions generally vested over the first 4 years of an eligible employee's service period. Effective January 1, 2010, prior and future matching contributions will be 100% vested. (p. 169)

– Expenses for defined contribution retirement plans were $862 million, $411 million and $426 million in 2009, 2008 and 2007, respectively. (p. 169)

– We provide health care and life insurance benefits for certain retired employees and reserve the right to terminate or amend any of the benefits at any time. (p. 169)

– Magazine Rankings (p. 194)

Pension Plan

– Pension Fund Returns (p. 170)

$M	2009	2008	2007	2006	2005
Accumulated Benefit Obligation (at end of period)	10,038	8,977	4,565	4,443	4,045
Plan assets at fair value at end of period	9,112	7,863	5,617	5,351	4,944
Excess (deficit) of plan assets over projected benefit obligation	(926)	(1,114)	1,052	908	899
Annual Pension Expense (Net periodic benefit cost)	324	90	108	113	99

Toronto Dominion Bank | Wells Fargo & Co

Toronto Dominion Bank

per calendar year toward the purchase of the Bank's common shares. The Bank matched 50% of the employee contribution amount The Bank's contributions vest once an employee has completed 2 years of continuous service with the Bank. For the year ended October 31, 2009, the Bank's contributions totaled $52 million(2008 – $52 million; 2007 – $49 million) and were expensed as part of salaries and employee benefits incurred. As at October 31, 2009, an aggregate of 8.7 million common shares were held under the Employee Ownership Plan (2008–7.4 million; 2007–6.5 million). (p. 127)

– The Bank also provides certain postretirement benefits and postemployment benefits (non-pension employee benefits), which are generally non-funded. Non-pension employee benefit plans, where offered, generally include health care, life insurance and dental benefits. Employees must meet certain age and service requirements to be eligible for postretirement benefits and are generally required to pay a portion of the cost of the benefits. Employees eligible for postemployment benefits are those on disability and maternity leave. (p. 129)

Pension Plan

– "Principal Pension Plans Obligations, Assets and Funded Status" Table (p. 130)

$M	2009	2008	2007	2006	2005
Accumulated Benefit Obligation (at end of period)	$1,988	$1,995	$1,852	$1,783	$1,810
Plan assets at fair value at end of period	$2,473	$2,138	$2,225	$2,015	$1,907
Excess (deficit) of plan assets over projected benefit obligation	$303	$(63)	$155	$404	$422
Annual Pension Expense	$114	$81	$59	$78	$51
Weighted-average discount rate for projected benefit obligation	6.90%	6.30%	5.60%	5.50%	5.20%
Weighted-average rate of compensation increase	3.5%	3.5%	3.5%	3.5%	3.5%
Weighted-average expected long-term rate of return on plan assets	6.75%	6.75%	6.75%	6.75%	6.75%

Wells Fargo & Co

Weighted-average discount rate for projected benefit obligation	5.75%	6.75%	5.75%	5.75%	6.00%
Weighted-average rate of compensation increase	4.00%	4.00%	4.00%	4.00%	4.00%
Weighted-average expected long-term rate of return on plan assets	8.75%	8.75%	8.75%	8.75%	9.00%

Proxy Statement Data

– Director/Executive compensation tables attached after the CSR section

Year	(A) Duality (1=Dual)	(B) # of Board Members	(C) # of Independents	(D) # of 5% or greater shareholders (when available)	(E) % of stock (all classes) held by (D)	(F) Multiple Voting Proportion	(G) Institutional Holding (%) From Compustat	(H) Auditor Code From Compustat ★
2005	1	14	13	0	0%	N/A		6
2006	1	14	12	1	5.7%	N/A		6
2007	1	16	14	1	6.5%	N/A		6
2008	0	16	14	1	9.4%	N/A		6
2009	0	19	16	2	13%	N/A		6

★ Auditor = KPMG

– Figures for column (D) and (E) reflect shareholders with 5% ownership or greater.

CSR Report – 2009 Report

– *DiversityInc:*
  – Among Top 50 Companies for Diversity (3/10)
  – Top 10 Companies for Asian Americans (3/10)
  – Top 10 Companies for Lesbian, Gay, Bisexual, and Transgender Employees (3/10)

– More than 98% of our team members are eligible for health care coverage and more than 80% choose to enroll in health plans with Wells Fargo. We provide equal benefits for our lesbian, gay, bisexual, and transgender (LGBT) team members and their families. (p. 33)

– We have many programs to help team members balance their lives at work and at home. We offer

Toronto Dominion Bank	Wells Fargo & Co

Toronto Dominion Bank

Proxy Statement Data

– Director/Executive compensation tables attached after the CSR section

Year	(A) Duality (1=Dual)	(B) # of Board Members	(C) # of Independents	(D) # of 5% or greater shareholders (when available)	(E) % of stock (all classes) held by (D)	(F) Multiple Voting Proportion	(G) Institutional Holding (%) From Compustat	(H) Auditor Code From Compustat *
2005	0	17	15	0	0%	N/A		4
2006	0	16	14	0	0%	N/A		4
2007	0	17	15	0	0%	N/A		4
2008	0	17	15	0	0%	N/A		4
2009	0	17	15	0	0%	N/A		4

★ Auditor = Ernst & Young

Note:
– No knowledge of any person or entity controlling more than 10% of the shares (which would not be permitted under the Bank Act).
– Does not provide information on shareholders holding less than 10% of the shares.

2009 CSR Report

– 33.78% of our senior management team are women. (p. 6)

– 6,000 managers trained in diversity. (p. 6)

– $ 67.7m invested in learning programs. (p. 6)

– We are committed to a promote-from-within philosophy and, in Canada, have filled 90% of our job opportunities internally. (p. 17)

– # of days of training per year: 3.88 Canada, 4.56 US. (More info p. 17)

– TD's investment in training per employee: $1241 Canada, $507 US. (More info p. 17)

– TD's investment in training: $55.6M Canada, $12.1 US. (More info p. 17)

– We offer tuition assistance for full-time and part-time who upgrade their knowledge by taking courses at eligible institutions. (p. 17)

Wells Fargo & Co

paid time off, and many of our team members work flexible work hours, telecommute, have part-time hours, and job share. We offer access to back-up child care and free access to LifeCare®, a resource for health and wellness information, and referrals to services such as child care and elder care. Our Employee Assistance Consulting team offers anytime support to team members and their families on issues such as emotional concerns, workplace relationships, or financial stress. (p. 33)
– We give our team members the opportunity to share their ideas and concerns through surveys, such as our annual engagement survey. In Community Banking – home to one of every three team members – our 2009 ratio of engaged to actively disengaged team members was nearly three times better than the national average. (p. 33)

– Approximately 16% of all team members were promoted and 10% made a lateral move to another job or department. (p. 31)

– Team members each received an average of 36 hours training in 2009. We invested 3% of total payroll dollars into training and offered classroom, online, and self-based study to everyone. (p. 31)

– 36 hours of training received by our team members, on average, each year. (p. 31)

– Wells Fargo offers tuition reimbursement for classes or degree programs that support career development up to $5,000 annually for full-time team members and $2,500 for part-time team members. (p. 31)

– Career development is a shared responsibility between team members and their managers. Team members discuss their professional goals with their managers annually and create an individual plan to support their professional development. (p. 32)

– Eligible team members also received a profit-sharing contribution to their 401(k) accounts in recognition of our outstanding business results in 2009. (p. 32)

– We offer college scholarships for children of full- and part-time team members, and in 2009, we increased that support from $1,000 to $1,500 annually per student for up to 2 years. We awarded 759 students a total of $1.43 million in such scholarships for the 2010–11 school year. (p. 32)

Toronto Dominion Bank	Wells Fargo & Co
– The Women in Leadership (WIL) network is an internal initiative that comprises 12 chapters representing over 2,000 women across Canada and the US These chapters work on creating networking opportunities for women. Formal networking events help women at TD strengthen their networks and meet with senior bank leaders. In 2009 more than 1,000 women participated in networking events. (p. 18)	– Team members receive free or discounted Wells Fargo financial products and services, including pretax savings on community expenses and child care costs. (p. 32)
– During 2009, our employee numbers remained consistent. In Canada, we retained approximately nine out of 10 employees, slightly above the industry standard. (p. 19)	– We have 9 Team Member Networks that represent the following diversity dimensions: Asian, Black/African American, disabilities, LGBT, Hispanic-Latino, Middle Eastern, Native American, veterans, and women (p. 35)
In the US we retained approximately seven out of 10 employees during 2009. The US banking industry typically has a higher turnover than in Canada. Despite all the integration activity in 2009, we're pleased that the voluntary turnover for TD Bank (17.8%) was lower than the US industry benchmark of 18.9%. (p. 19)	– 2009 team member composition (ex: % woman, men, senior managers, etc.) (p. 37)
– One of Hewitt Associates' 50 Best Employers in Canada for the second year in a row (p. 19)	
– For the third consecutive year, one of Maclean's magazine's Top 100 Employers in Canada (p. 19)	
– By the end of 2009, over 90% of all managers in Canada had completed our one-day Embracing Diversity workshop. (p. 20)	
– Since 2006, approximately 400 women and 120 members of visible minority groups have participated in an innovative group mentoring program. We paired women at critical stages in their career with senior executives to facilitate discussions about career planning and development. (p. 20)	
– Five of the 17 members of the TD Board of Directors are women. Women make up 33.78% of our vice presidents, senior vice presidents and executive vice presidents. (p. 21)	
– Visible minorities make up 8.11% of our vice presidents, senior vice presidents and executive vice presidents. (p. 21)	
– Our Employee Pride Network shapes our LGBTA strategy and allows employees to share ideas and experiences. With local networks in Toronto, Montreal, London, Edmonton, Calgary, Vancouver, Kitchener/Waterloo, Mississauga/Peel/Halton and Ottawa, more than 1,000 employees have joined the network since 2005. (p. 21)	

Toronto Dominion Bank	Wells Fargo & Co
– In 2009, we launched our Aboriginal Employee Circle, which includes representation from both Aboriginal and non-Aboriginal employees across TD in Canada, from coast to coast to coast. Membership in the circle grew to more than 50 employees in just a few months. (p. 21) Additional Information from the Website Employee Ownership Plan In this share ownership plan, you can invest in TD shares so you can participate in the long-term success of the bank. TD will match your first $250 each year, dollar for dollar, and the remainder of your contributions at 50% to an overall maximum TD contribution of 3.5% of eligible earnings or $2,250, whichever comes first. Employee Future Builder You can also use the Employee Future Builder savings program to achieve your long- and short-term financial goals. The plan has several investment options to choose from and TD pays all program administration and investment management fees. Save for something like a vacation in a non-registered account or for retirement in a registered account, and you can even contribute a portion of your incentive award directly into a registered Employee Future Builder account – no more waiting for a tax refund! TD Pension Plan (Canada) The TD Pension Plan (Canada) is the best fully bank-paid pension in the industry for salary up to the Year's Maximum Pensionable Earnings (YMPE) set by the government ($48,300 in 2011). You can also enroll in a top-up to earn a competitive pension on the portion of your salary above the YMPE. All permanent employees are eligible to enroll in this plan, and because it's a defined benefit pension plan, you'll receive a regular income during retirement, regardless of how the plan investments perform. And your pension becomes more valuable each year because it's based on your years of membership and salary toward the end of your career.	

Toronto Dominion Bank	Wells Fargo & Co
Pension Enhancement Account In addition, TD offers a Pension Enhancement Account that lets you save on a tax efficient basis while you work, allowing you to buy enhancements that can increase your pension when you retire. Wellness Programs ★ Wellness On Demand – an online video library of wellness topics presented by leading experts. ★ Employee Assistance Program – free confidential counseling and support services to help you and your immediate family with personal and professional issues. ★ Mental Health – access support information, online tools and professional resources. ★ Ergonomic Awareness Training – advice on workstation setup, along with stretching tips to reduce the risk of injury. ★ Wellness Discounts – details on partner discounts for gym memberships, equipment, and weight loss programs. ★ Personal Health Improvement Program – create a customized online program that will help you improve your well-being. ★ Specialist services – should you become seriously ill or injured, we help connect you and your physician with world-renowned specialists to confirm the right health diagnosis and treatment options.	

3.3 The semantic state of 'shareholder engagement'

Alexander Bassen, Christine Zöllner and
Chris Rushton

The historical and semantic development of shareholder engagement

Introduction

The interest in how shareholders engage with the management of their investee companies has been rekindled recently by the global financial crisis. The topic has however received little (but growing) academic attention, even though it has already been addressed by regulators in countries such as the UK and Japan[1] and is in discussion by supranational bodies such as the UN and the EU. A recent study into US corporations and shareholders conducted by corporate governance specialist ISS (ISS & IRRCI 2011) highlighted that investors and management have different understandings of what engagement actually is, different preferences of how it should be carried out and different ideas of what successful engagement constitutes. This variance in understanding of shareholder engagement can also be seen in academic publications concerning the topic. The aim of this chapter is to better understand the plurality of meanings associated with terms related to shareholder engagement by various parties and to produce a theoretical basis for framing a definition, which is broadly approved.

Voluntary and mandatory standards – from corporate governance to engagement

Shareholder engagement, loosely understood, is a phenomenon whereby shareholders participate and influence the ways in which their investee companies operate (Chow 2010, p. 22). Its premise is anchored in the legal provision of shareholder rights, which rule how, by which means and to what extent shareholders can influence the operations of companies that they own and which govern the balance of power between shareholders and management board including non-executive directors or supervisory board. Typical instruments are voting rights and direct or indirect communications.

Although the term "shareholder engagement" is a relatively new one, the explicit rights and protection afforded to shareholders by law or company statutes as well as the influence of the owners on management decisions have existed since corporations were founded. For instance, themes that are still current in corporate governance, such as equal voting rights, have been a topic of popular discussion from as early as the 18th century (Dunlavy 2006, p. 1356). Since the mid-20th century, there have been swings in interest in corporate governance and swings in the power relations between management and shareholders in different regulatory regimes. However, the spate of corporate scandals at the start of the

21st century, followed by the global financial crisis, has cost shareholders dearly. Institutional investors have also had to weather a share of the blame for not noticing corrupt business practices in their investee companies and for their focus on short-term profits over long-term sustainability. Shareholders are starting to become increasingly active as owners, and the interest of the general public, legislators and other institutions in the relationship between shareholders and the management of their investee companies has never been higher. The participation of shareholders in corporate decision-making is becoming an important measure of good corporate governance (Winter 2011b, p. 1), and shareholder rights and responsibilities related to this involvement are starting to be addressed by legislators and academics alike. The following section focuses on US, UK and EU developments.

For instance in July 2010, the United States passed the 'Dodd-Frank Wall Street Reform and Consumer Protection Act' (Dodd-Frank Act) in response to what were seen as the "systemic failures" that led to the global financial crisis (Anand 2011). Its main objectives being to limit the damage caused by the failure of large financial institutions and limit the risks in contemporary finance (Skeel 2011, p. 4). As part of this regulatory overhaul, new rights were bestowed upon shareholders, including a mandatory non-binding vote on executive pay, and more responsibilities were placed upon companies to increase disclosure, accountability and transparency. The issue of shareholder engagement was left unaddressed in the Dodd-Frank Act, and this is an area in which the SEC (US Securities and Exchange Commission) has yet to attempt to regulate. However, SEC communications affirm that this was premeditated, rather than an oversight. Mary Schapiro, the former SEC Chair, has stated that the SEC is not interested in determining individual communications strategies or appropriate levels of engagement, but in "breaking down barriers that may prevent effective engagement" (Schapiro 2010). She believes communication to be "the first pillar of effective engagement" (Schapiro 2011), which can be promoted through increased disclosure. SEC Commissioner Luis Aguilar has also stated that Dodd-Frank provisions have led to increased disclosure and that the say-on-pay requirements have been a catalyst to sparking engagement (Aguilar 2011). Aside from a recent study published by ISS and IRRCI (2011), there has been very little quantitative research into this – for instance in visible improvement of transparency – and it remains to be seen to what extent the implications of the Dodd-Frank Act will impact shareholder engagement in the United States. In February 2009, the British government commissioned Sir David Walker to conduct a review into corporate governance in UK banks as a result of the financial crisis. The terms of reference in the resulting 'Walker Review' were subsequently extended to determine whether the recommendations were applicable to other financial institutions (Walker 2009, p. 5). One of the recommendations of the Review was that the ISC's voluntary comply-or-explain Code for best practice for institutional investors that choose to engage with investee companies should be adopted as an official UK code of practice for institutional investors by the FRC (UK Financial Reporting Council). The adapted 'UK Stewardship Code' (FRC 2010) was released by the FRC in July 2010 and followed the seven principles format of its predecessor. It immediately applied to all UK-based institutional investors, and compliance with the Code requires disclosure on a comply-or-explain basis. It does not, however, constitute a need to engage or an invitation to micro-manage, but institutional shareholders should consider the extent of their engagement based on their investment approach.[2] The principles of the Code call institutional shareholders to publicly disclose how they will discharge their stewardship responsibilities, to disclose their policy on managing conflicts of interest related to stewardship, to monitor their investee companies, to establish clear guidelines on intervention activities, to be willing to act collectively with other investors, to disclose voting policies and to regularly report on stewardship and voting activities.

As the first official 'non-voluntary' code to actively approach shareholder engagement, the implementation process and outcomes related to the Code are being closely observed, with other countries such as France and the Netherlands working on similar schemes (Wong 2010, p. 406). This is despite reservations from some academics, claiming that the Code is not far-reaching enough due to the fall in UK-based institutional share owner-ship,[3] that it is unlikely to have a large effect due to deeper regulatory and cultural condi-tions in the financial industry (Wong 2010). In addition there is doubt that the question, of what adherence with the Code actually constitutes, has not been effectively dealt with (Heineman 2010). After 4 years, the UK Stewardship Code includes almost 300 signa-tories (201 asset managers, 81 asset owners and 13 service providers, status as of Janu-ary 2015). In spite of this fact, the FRC is concerned that a lot of these signatories do not follow the principles of the Code. Therefore, the FRC will start a new project to promote a culture of stewardship and its advantages (FRC 2015, p. 17).

Although it is far too early to predict the impact on engagement that the Code will have, it was certainly revolutionary and it is likely to be influential on developments in the field of shareholder engagement, both in the UK and internationally, in the coming years.

Aside from national regulators, other institutions and supranational bodies have also been active in the field of shareholder engagement, particularly since the financial crisis. The European Commission, on the basis of the de Larosière Report (de Larosière 2009), released a 2010 Green Paper (COM 2010, 284 final) dealing with corporate govern-ance in financial institutions. Based on some of the findings and feedback received, the Commission released a further green paper in 2011 (COM 2011, 164 final), in which the corporate governance framework in the EU was considered. One of the conclusions from the 2010 Green Paper was that shareholder engagement is important not only for financial institutions, but for companies in general. However, the Commission was eager to revisit this topic with the view that the envisaged solutions for financial institutions may not be suitable for all companies (COM 2011, 164 final, p. 3). The Commission Staff Working Document that accompanied the 2010 Green Paper asserted that levels of shareholder engagement have been insufficient, due to the business models of insti-tutional investors, the costs of engagement, conflicts of interest, lack of risk disclosure and obstacles in cooperating with other shareholders and exercising shareholder rights.[4] However, in the 2011 Green Paper, it was the short-termism in capital markets and the agency relationship between asset managers and institutional shareholders that were the main topics explored in relation to shareholder engagement. As such, the questions posed in the Paper only explored some of the current issues prevalent in shareholder engage-ment. As it stands, the European Commission has shown interest in the topic over the last few years, but has yet to take any definitive action. Given the background of new leg-islative amendments concerning corporate governance from the Commission in recent years,[5] but with a 'comply or explain' approach to corporate governance being favoured in the national codes of some Member States, and with the EU Principle of Subsidiarity to be taken into consideration due to the differences between the financial markets and business practices in the Member States, it is hard to predict the course of action that the Commission will follow. Based on the Green Paper and analysis in the last years, the European Commission established in 2014 a new framework to solve two main problems: lack of transparency and inadequate engagement of shareholders. With this Directive, shareholders should gain more rights for a long-term sustainability of companies in the EU (COM 2014, 213 final).

The United Nations Principles for Responsible Investment (UNPRI) is a voluntary initiative whereby signatories commit to, and report upon, applying six principles for responsible investment, with 'possible actions' as a form of best practice. It represents an alternative approach to encouraging engagement where commitment to the Principles is purely voluntary but signatories are required to disclose on a 'comply or explain' basis. As of October 2012, it lists more than 1,000 investment institutions as signatories and was listed by respondents to a recent ISS and IRRCI study (ISS & IRRCI 2011, p. 10) as a reason for increased engagement activity. Although only 44 per cent of signatories published their response to the PRI's annual Reporting and Assessment Survey online (UNPRI 2011b, p. 35), there have been questions raised about the lack of validation of responses from signatories (Richardson 2007, p. 85). The actual number of signatories amount 1,453 in total, thereof more than 300 asset owners, 955 investment managers and almost 200 professional service partner (status as of January 6th, 2016).[6] The list of signatories is growing year on year, and it appears to be a strong platform for sharing information and encouraging collaboration between investors that believe in engagement (Chow 2010, p. 63).

Although the term "shareholder engagement" was not prominent for the majority of investors or fund managers until the turn of the century, it has quickly become an important topic in the contemporary corporate governance debate and has been applied to in several different ways under various synonymously used terms. In general, shareholder engagement has been addressed by states in line with overall developments in their national corporate governance systems. For example, the SEC has focused on regulation to encourage engagement (although there is as yet no regulation that specifically deals with engagement), whereas the 'UK Stewardship Code' has used a 'soft law' approach preferring the 'comply or explain' system already in use in the UK Code of Corporate Governance. This method has so far gained more interest and support than the legislative method and, with several countries and the European Commission considering its applicability, it is likely to become a prominent approach to addressing the issue in coming years. The European Commission has been contemplating the subject and collecting information for a few years now, but it is difficult to predict how they will deal with engagement. They will most likely be following developments in the Member States very closely to help decide the level of action required. The UNPRI initiative is a successful alternative. Although it is unlikely that any international or industry-based voluntary Code or set of guidelines could be a legitimate substitute for more binding solutions for the issue of shareholder engagement in the near future at least, it is currently a welcome supplement to the still developing national codes. It is helping to raise the profile of engagement and is helping like-minded investors to connect with one another.

Different understandings of engagement

Introduction

Despite the recent surge in attention in the topic, the term 'shareholder engagement', and related terms such as 'shareholder activism' and 'stewardship' are often used in academic literature and by other bodies without a definition. When definitions are given, they are often indirect or vague, as if the terms were universally understood and equally applied.

The study by ISS and IRRCI (ISS & IRRCI 2011) is the first to comprehensively investigate understandings of the term 'shareholder engagement' by various investor groups and managements. To our knowledge, a similar semantic investigation into the understanding of the term by academics and institutions has not yet been attempted. There are further related terms, such as 'investor engagement',[7] 'activist shareholder',[8] and 'shareholder empowerment'.[9]

In a recent study, ISS & IRRCI attempt to establish the understandings of engagement by issuers, asset owners and asset managers and to paint a picture of how and with whom engagement is taking place, how its success is perceived, what engagements concern and what factors are recognised as impediments to engagement by these parties. For use in the survey, a very broad definition of engagement was used, defining it as "direct contact between a shareowner and an issuer (including a board member)" (ISS & IRRCI 2011, p. 7), to allow incongruences in understanding of the term by the respondents to be shown. Some of the results of the survey strongly suggest that issuers, asset owners and asset managers understand engagement differently. For example, more than 50 per cent of asset owners and managers reported that an engagement typically lasts more than a month, whereas 55 per cent of issuers responded that an engagement typically lasts a week or less (ISS & IRRCI 2011, p. 11). Inconsistencies are also seen in the reported methods of communication used during the engagement process. Further research into the understandings of engagement by the parties that are involved could be sensible, as it is difficult to draw clear conclusions from the results due to the sample only including large asset owners and managers. But the findings of this study highlight that the term is perceived differently – for instance asked about the time frames of engagement investors (asset owners and managers) answered in majority "more than one month", whereas issuers most commonly stated "a week or less" (ISS & IRRCI 2011, p. 11). This variety in understanding is also present in literature concerning shareholder engagement by various academics and institutions. Up until now, very little attention has been paid to this situation and, when it is dealt with, it is usually in the form of creating a reference framework for defining terms (see Winter 2011a, p. 12; Butler 2011, p. 16). Here, we will focus on the terms 'shareholder engagement', as well as 'shareholder activism' and 'stewardship', as they are closely related and there is some evidence of them being used as synonyms for engagement.

For instance, Chow (2010, p. 25) states that "[a]ll three forms of engagement are also referred to as shareholder activism" with Gifford (2009, p. 23) affirming that shareholder engagement is also known as shareholder activism or advocacy and Schäfer and Hertrich (2011, p. 1) stating that they use the terms 'activism' and 'engagement' interchangeably. Winter (2011a, pp. 11–12) writes that at a meeting of various institutional investors, the terms 'engagement' and 'stewardship' were also used synonymously. 'Engagement' and 'stewardship' are sometimes also used interchangeably in literature, predominantly by UK academics, although it is rarely explicitly stated that these terms are considered synonyms. This may be due to the fact that 'engagement' and 'activism' are used far more frequently in corporate governance literature in this context than 'stewardship', where usage has grown only since the release of the UK Stewardship Code in July 2010. In addition, 'activist investors' is also used to include hedge funds and private equity investors, which confuses the topic even more.

Definitions considered in this section are ones used by the US Securities and Exchange Commission (SEC), the UK Financial Reporting Council (FRC), the European Commission and the United Nations Principles for Responsible Investment (UNPRI), as well as a selection of definitions from various academic works. The aforementioned institutions were chosen due to their relative power and involvement in the theme of shareholder engagement and the field of corporate governance.

Shareholder engagement

The term 'shareholder engagement' (often used as just 'engagement') has been defined in a different ways, when defined at all. In the European Commission's *The EU Corporate Governance Framework* Green Paper, engagement is

> generally understood as actively monitoring companies, engaging in a dialogue with the company's board, and using shareholder rights, including voting and cooperation with other shareholders, if need be to improve the governance of the investee company in the interests of long-term value creation.
>
> (European Commission 2011; COM 2011, 164, p. 11)

However, the Commission has never attempted to attribute a strict definition to the term 'shareholder engagement', as it is seen as an "evolving concept in the EU Member States" (Tijssen 2011). In the UK Stewardship Code, it is stated that "[e]ngagement includes pursuing purposeful dialogue on strategy, performance and the management of risk, as well as on issues that are the immediate subject of votes at general meetings" (FRC 2010, p. 1). The SEC sees shareholder engagement as a "term of art that has been used in reference to shareholder activity" (Garner 2011) and has yet to be dealt with in a legislative format by the SEC. As such, the SEC has not defined engagement, although in a speech at the 2010 NACD Annual Corporate Governance Conference, the SEC chairman Mary Schapiro described engagement as "more than just disclosure" that entails "clear conversations with investors about how the company is governed – and why and how decisions are made", moving "beyond the minimum [of] required communications" (Schapiro 2010). From the institutions considered, the UNPRI is clearest with its definitions, describing engagement as "an overall description for a two-way conversation between a company and its shareholders and/or potential shareholders for the purpose of communicating views and concerns on issues that can impact the long-term performance of the company" (United Nations Global Compact & PRI 2010, p. 7) and as "non-voting contact with companies to discuss concerns regarding ESG issues" (UNPRI 2011a, p. 46). According to the PRI, "[s]uch dialogue can vary from regular correspondence to resolutions on company ballots at Annual General Meetings (AGMs), or in-depth meetings over a significant time period" (United Nations Global Compact & PRI 2010, p. 7) and usually involves "written communications, phone calls and meetings with management" (UNPRI 2011a, p. 46).

Surprisingly, academics have been even more reluctant to attribute a definition to shareholder engagement than institutions. When definitions are given, they are generally short and imprecise, without allowing for the scope of activities that could be considered as engagement. Further insight into how academics understand the term can however be gained from additional analysis of the literature that they have produced. Gifford (2009, p. 6) defines engagement as "shareholder dialogue with companies with the goal of influencing various aspects of corporate behaviour"; Chow (2010, p. 22) defines it almost synonymously as "shareholders participating and influencing the way in which their investee companies operate"; and Deakin and Hobbs (2007, p. 68) see engagement as "steps taken by shareholders to put pressure on companies to make effective use of corporate assets". To our knowledge, Winter (2011a, p. 12) is the only academic who has addressed the variance in understanding of the term 'shareholder engagement' and attempted to clearly define it. He uses the term 'shareholder engagement' as a superordinate that, in his opinion, should be applied neutrally and can vary in intensity. He shows three levels of engagement to be distinguished: 'compliance' (= minimal efforts, thoughtless, no added value); 'intervention' (= incidentally, understanding of the company, value opportunity/prevent loss); and 'stewardship' (= continuous, commitment, defines value of investment strategy).[10] Barker (2011, p. 146) similarly sees shareholder engagement as a "generic term used to describe the on-going relationship between shareholders and company boards".

Although many of the definitions attributed to the term "shareholder engagement" are fairly broad or unspecific, some differences in understanding can be noted amongst institutions or academics who attempt to further define the term. Notably, there is disagreement to the extent of actions that are considered engagement. For instance, the European Commission believe that engagement is generally understood to include the usage of voting rights (COM 2011, 164, p. 11), whereas the UNPRI uses the definition of engagement for "non-voting contact" only (UNPRI 2011a, p. 46). Related to this, there appears to be some disagreement on actions that constitute engagement. Whereas the UNPRI restrict their understanding of engagement to "an overall description for a two-way conversation between a company and its shareholders" (UNGC & PRI 2010, p. 7) involving "written communications, phone calls and meetings with management" (UNPRI 2011a, p. 46), the European Commission lists the active monitoring of companies, the use of shareholder rights and cooperation with other shareholders in its understanding of the term (European Commission 2014; COM 2011, 164, p. 11).

Gifford (2009, pp. 29, 33) is in agreement. He states that, beyond dialogue, the use of formal shareholder rights to send a message of disapproval to company management, as well as the support of other shareholders' resolutions to amplify the signal sent to management, are part of the engagement process and that monitoring is part of the cost of engagement. In addition, he points out that shareholder resolutions are often used in the US as part of the engagement process to attract the attention of management as the first step in a dialogue. It becomes obvious that national cultural differences are important in terms of the "tone" of engagements as well as its forms and styles. Barker (2011, p. 146) writes that engagement "also covers the entire range of processes employed by investors for monitoring investee companies". Chow (2010, pp. 24–25), conversely, writes that engagement is carried out predominantly in three ways: through private or public dialogue or through public critique in the media. However, she includes the submission of voting-related actions such as shareholder resolutions and counter motions as types of public dialogue.

Where the subject or intent of engagement is addressed, there seems to be agreement that engagement is concerned with a broad spectrum of issues, although this has been defined in different ways. For example, the UNPRI state the intention is to "discuss concerns regarding ESG issues" (UNPRI 2011a, p. 46), Chow (2010, pp. 175–176) considers engagement to address "environmental, social, ethical and governance issues". The FRC believe engagement to concern "purposeful dialogue on strategy, performance and the management of risk" (FRC 2010, p. 1), and Gifford (2009, p. 6) regards the intention as "influencing various aspects of corporate behaviour". In essence, there appears to be agreement that engagement can relate to almost any aspect of the business. Some of these differences are driven by different interpretations of fiduciary duties. These differ between the common law and the civil law countries.

The main differences here can be seen as the question of whether monitoring should be understood to be a part of shareholder engagement or as a prerequisite for it. Secondly, whether dialogue as part of engagement is limited to non-voting, direct contact between shareholders and the investee firm or whether the use of shareholder rights or public critique to send signals to management is also a form of dialogue and a part of the engagement process.

Shareholder activism

The term 'shareholder activism' is much more widely used in corporate governance literature and has a longer history than the term 'shareholder engagement'. According to Google Books Ngram Viewer, 'shareholder activism' can be found in English language books since as early as the 1930s, compared to 'shareholder engagement', which was not used until 1998.[11] The term 'shareholder activism' appeared approximately 15 times more often in English language books published in 2008 than 'shareholder engagement'. However, despite the prevalence and relative length of use of the term in the English language, there also seems to be no common prevalent definition (Sturm, 2008, p. 4). As previously stated, some academics have explicitly stated that they consider engagement and activism to be synonyms, yet wider usage seems to indicate semantic differences between the signifiers.

Some academics have defined shareholder activism in a very similar way to shareholder engagement, although this appears to be a more restricted definition of the term compared to its usage by others. For example, Sparkes (2002, p. 29–30) defines activism as "the use of voting rights attached to ordinary shares to assert political, financial, or other objectives . . . [and] can be classified into three types of action: publicity, dialogue and the filing of shareholder resolutions". This is strikingly similar to Chow's (2010) understanding of engagement. Kim's (2011, p. 20) definition of activism is also analogous, defining activism as "activity of an investor who tries to change the status quo through voice", commonly though activities such as shareholder proposals, direct negotiation and public targeting of a corporation. Bauer et al. (2011, p. 2) state that "in the United States, corporations are often faced with activist shareholders who strive for changes in corporate governance structures or corporate behaviour" and see voice engagement through proxy proposals as one particular form of shareholder activism. Sjöström also defines activism as

> the use of ownership position to actively influence company policy and practice through letter writing, through company dialogue with corporate management or the board, through asking questions at open sessions at annual general meetings and through the filing of formal shareholder proposals.
>
> (Sjöström 2008, p. 142)

According to this definition, Sjöström emphasises the role of shareholder activism and its instruments related to corporate social responsibility (CSR). This provides insights of the influence from institutional investors (such as NGOs) with regard to the implementation of social and environmental behavior in corporations. Respective to their conceivableness and relation to critical issues, Sjöstrom's results showed that targets of shareholder activism particularly depend on the size and publicity of a corporation. Generally, there is an increasing number of shareholders which invest in, do not invest in or divest from corporations reasoned by their social and environmental performances. This movement can be understood as "strategy of engagement", and "responsible ownership" emerges especially in form of voting or advocacy at annual shareholder meetings (O'Rourke 2003). In this context, Neubaum & Zahra showed that the more frequent activism comes up and the higher the level of activism is in a corporation, the greater the influence on future corporate social performance. In addition to this, Fulton et al. (2012, p. 22) refer to sustainable investing of responsible investors who "exhibit active ownership, which entails shareholder engagement with the corporations they invest in".

However, some academics consider a larger range of actions to also be understood under the term "shareholder activism", although this extension of the definition appears to be a relatively recent (post-1998) development. For example, Gillan and Starks (1998, p. 12) consider activism "as representing a continuum of responses to corporate performance". On one end of the extreme, buying and selling shares are forms of active participation and expresses opinions on the corporation's performance. On the other end of the extreme, shareholders involved in takeovers are also 'active' in that they are forcing fundamental changes in the corporation's structure. Gillan and Starks were among the first to consider the so-called 'Wall Street Walk'[12] as a form of, rather than an alternative to, activism. However, this idea has since been shared and developed by others. Admati and Pfleiderer (2005) tested Palmiter's (2002, p. 1437) assertion that large mutual funds find greater success in 'big stick' diplomacy, with an actual or implied threat of selling their holdings rather than through voting or making proposals. Admati and Pfleiderer (2005, p. 1) state that this threat of sale is a form of activism, but note that this isn't recognised by all. Chung and Talaulicar (2010, p. 253) also agree, differentiating between 'voice' and 'exit' activism.

While Chung and Wynn (2014) describe shareholder activism as a common occurrence, McNulty and Nordberg (2015, p. 1) used the term "active ownership" for a better understanding of institutional investor heterogeneity and related motivations, processes and effects. The term includes the definition of shareholder activism as "actions taken by shareholders with the explicit intention of influencing corporations' policies and practices" from Goranova and Ryan (2014, p. 1232), but was extended to a broader spectrum that includes institutional investor behaviour. Following this definition, it consists a difference between active ownership and passive ownership. Passive ownership means holding shares and voting, but in an unintentional way (McNulty & Nordberg 2015, p. 1).

For Denes, Karpoff and McWilliams, shareholder activism survives as a popular strategy because it yields sufficiently large expected net benefits in some situations (2015, p. 23).

Although some academics have clearly stated that they consider engagement and activism as synonymous, not everyone appears to be in agreement. It is worth noting that activism has not been defined in a similar way to which engagement is defined by ISS or UNPRI – restricting its meaning to either "direct contact" (ISS & IRRCI 2011, p. 7); "non-voting contact" (UNPRI 2011a, p. 46); or as "an overall description for a two-way conversation between a company and its shareholders" (United Nations Global Compact & PRI 2010, p. 7). Additionally, there was also no evidence of anyone considering threat of, or actual divestment, or corporate control as forms of engagement. Although there is a similar level of disagreement amongst academics of what shareholder activism constitutes, it is generally understood as including a broader range of activities.

Stewardship

'Stewardship' is another term that is becoming more popular in corporate governance literature. Its usage, in the context of shareholder engagement, is fairly recent and predominantly by academics either based in the UK or researching in the field of UK corporate governance. This is due to its usage in the FRC's 'UK Stewardship Code', which sets out best practice in shareholder engagement for UK-based institutional investors. However, it is a term that has been seldom clearly defined.

Even in the UK Stewardship Code, a clear definition of what the FRC understands 'stewardship' to be is not given, yet a general understanding can be gleaned by reading the Code's principles. The Code states that institutional investors should publicly disclose their policy on how they will discharge their stewardship responsibilities (FRC 2010, p. 5). This includes monitoring policies and intervention strategies, as well as voting policies and arrangements for how stewardship is integrated in the investment process. They must also set out circumstances in which they will intervene, with intervention ranging from initial private discussions to public statements before meetings and even the requisitioning of an Extraordinary General Meeting (EGM) – for instance proposing to change board membership. However, it is not stated whether intervention is considered a form of stewardship. On a comply-or-explain basis, investors must also publicly display their voting records (and are advised to seek to vote all shares), although voting is differentiated from stewardship in Principle 7 of the Code.

In the Walker Review (Walker 2009, p. 71), the recommendations of which led to the adoption of the ISC's Code as the UK Stewardship Code, Walker states that a stewardship obligation may on occasion lead to specific engagement. From this, it is only possible to say that monitoring policies and the preparation of intervention strategies, investment strategies and voting policies are seen as stewardship responsibilities, but that voting activities are not considered a form of stewardship. Stewardship, according to the FRC, therefore appears to be more of a forward planning and oversight function, with engagement as a possible necessary consequence. Although the FRC have not publicly defined stewardship, they were keen to share their views when contacted. They confirmed that they see stewardship as "activities aimed at assisting a company with producing better long-term returns to the providers of capital" with engagement as a "subset of stewardship activities" (Lawton 2012). Some academics see stewardship in a similar way. For example, Bruner (2011, p. 330) states that the term denotes 'oversight' with shareholders having both a right and an obligation to manage management, and Talbot (2010, p. 2) sees stewardship as requiring shareholders to take an active role in corporate governance and empowering them, both legally and morally, to do so.

However, 'stewardship' has also been defined differently. As previously stated, Winter (2011a, p. 11–12) notes that the terms 'engagement' and 'stewardship' are often used interchangeably and that he considers stewardship to be a continuous and committed form of engagement. Tomorrow's Company, a not-for-profit UK-based business-led think tank, have set out a framework for stewardship, defining five different levels: no engagement; voting practice (establishing and operating a voting policy); reactive engagement (continuous monitoring and dialogue, but only full engagement when necessary); strategic engagement (participation in the process to make engagement effective, both individually and with other investors); and stewardship engagement (direct exercise of ownership responsibilities with engagement focus on leadership, board composition, strategy and performance appraisal) (Butler 2011, p. 16). As such, they consider stewardship to be more than just engagement, but that engagement is an integral part of stewardship, with most of the levels of stewardship actually being named as a type of engagement.

In accordance with the stewardship theory, there is a further approach in investors' engagement specific to business angel engagement. The term 'business angel' describes an individual who risks capital to firms with high-potential venture growth, such as startups,

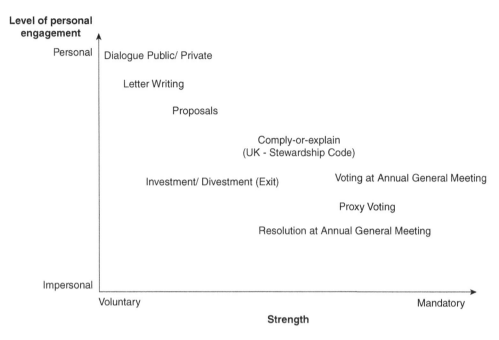

Figure 3.3.1 Reduction of complexity through engagement and strength

additionally offering their personal business experience and networks. In exchange, the individual claims a return of investment above the usual (Politis 2008). The firms in which business angels invest do not involve family connections, and these firms operate on additional capital from venture capital investing with a related decline in bank lending (Mason & Botelho 2016; Mason and Harrison 2010).

On the whole, there appears to be some agreement that 'stewardship' is a term of wider meaning than engagement. Engagement is often seen as either an integral part of stewardship or as a sometimes necessary means of fulfilling stewardship responsibilities.

Although there is evidence of the terms 'shareholder activism' and 'stewardship' being used as synonyms for 'shareholder engagement', these terms are often used with a much broader scope. On the basis of our research, we were unable to find evidence of divestment being defined as a feature of engagement as it has been by some when defining activism, and there is some consensus that stewardship is more of an oversight function, with engagement as a component or by-product of fulfilling this function. Generally, academics and institutions have been reluctant to define these terms although some have noted the disparity in understanding that is present.

Two possible criteria to reduce the complexity at least graphically are the level of personal engagement and strength – visible in Figure 3.3.1.

Conclusions

The aim of this chapter was to create a better understanding of the term 'shareholder engagement' and its related terms and therefore to better understand the plurality of meanings associated with them.

The terms 'shareholder engagement' and its related terms such as 'shareholder activism' and 'stewardship' are defined in different ways by academics and institutions. There was some evidence to suggest that these terms are often used synonymously, and there is some overlap in their definitions, but there were certain facets that allowed them to be distinguished from one another.

Shareholder engagement is the active participation of shareowners using shareholder rights to influence the company's strategy, performance and risk management. A fundamental part of this engagement is represented through the dialogue the shareholders have with management (the board). This dialogue can be distinguished between private (letter writing, management meetings, phone calls etc.) and public dialogue in the media (resolutions, countermotion etc.). Generally, activism and stewardship are terms of wider comprehension than engagement with activism involving some activities, such as divestment, that are not considered part of engagement, with engagement often seen as a level of minimum commitment or a subset of stewardship activities. Dialogue is usually deemed to be at the core of shareholder engagement, but there are dissenting views on activities that constitute engagement.

The most interesting finding is the general reluctance in defining shareholder engagement and the often vague definitions of the term that are offered. There are a number of possible reasons for this situation. Firstly, the term 'shareholder engagement' is relatively recent and 'stewardship', in its relation to engagement, is newer still. The EU and the SEC are yet to legislate in these fields and the Commission sees engagement as an "evolving concept" (Tijssen 2011). It is highly likely that the definition of engagement will evolve as it is addressed by legislators and the debate concerning it continues. It is therefore not unreasonable to think that many commentators are purposefully avoiding trying to define a term that is considered to be somewhat fluid.

Although it is likely that this is due to shareholder engagement being a relatively new topic, we are of the opinion that the term will be able to carry more weight when there is a more consensual understanding of the term, and this should be instigated by powerful institutions with an interest in engagement.

Notes

1 The Japan Stewardship Code "refers to the responsibilities of institutional investors to enhance the medium- to long-term investment return for their clients and beneficiaries" (The Council of Experts Concerning the Japanese Version of the Stewardship Code, 2014).

2 FRC, 2010, p. 1. Although some form of disclosure is required by all UK-based institutional investors, it is possible for an investor to simply disclose that it is believed that Code does not apply to him or her due to the investment strategy.

3 Cheffins, 2010, pp. 1015, 1017–1018. Cheffins notes that share ownership by UK-based pension funds, insurance companies, investment trusts and unit trusts had fallen from nearly 60 per cent of shares of publicly traded companies in 1993, to less than one-third in 2008. The FSA has no jurisdiction over foreign fund managers who invest on the London Stock Exchange on behalf of overseas clients

4 Commission Staff Working Document, accompaniment to COM (2010)284, pp. 7–8.

5 e.g. CRD IV.

6 www.unpri.org/signatories/signatories/

7 Occasionally used in place of 'shareholder engagement'. See Heineman 2010 and Martin et al. 2007 for examples.

8 Often used to refer to shareholders involved in activism or engagement.

9 e.g. Talbot (2010, p. 2) uses 'shareholder stewardship' and 'shareholder empowerment' synonymously and postulates that what UK academics refer to as 'stewardship' is usually referred to in the US as 'empowerment'.

10 Martin et al. (2007, Section 2.1) have also expressed a similar idea that the term 'investor engagement' ranges from a minimum of acquiring information about a particular company decision to active intervention in the development and implementation of corporate strategy.

11 Google Books Ngram Viewer displays the frequency of a word or phrase in the corpus of books over a determinable timescale (up to 2008), normalised by the number of books published in each year. It allows the user to gain an insight into the frequency of use of words in print over time (Google 2010).

12 Sale, or threat of sale, of shareholdings.

References

Admati, A. R. and Pfleiderer, P. C. (2005) The "Wall Street Walk" and shareholder activism: Exit as a form of voice. Stanford University, Working Paper.

Aguilar, L. A. (2011) *An Inflection Point: The SEC and the Current Financial Reform Landscape.* June 10, 2011. Available online under www.sec.gov/news/speech/2011/spch061011laa.htm, accessed May 29, 2018.

Anand, S. (2011) *Essentials of the Dodd-Frank Act.* Hoboken, NJ: Wiley.

Barker, R. (2011) Ownership structure and shareholder engagement: Reflections on the role of institutional shareholders in the financial crisis, in W. Sun, J. Stewart, & D. Pollard. eds. *Corporate Governance and the Global Financial Crisis.* Cambridge: Cambridge University Press. Ch. 8.

Bauer, R. and Moers, F. and Viehs, M. (2011) *The Determinants of Withdrawn Shareholder Proposals.* Available online under http://ssrn.com/abstract=1885392, accessed May 29, 2018.

Bruner, C. M. (2011) Corporate governance reform in a time of crisis. *Journal of Corporation Law,* 36(2), pp. 309–341.

Butler, P. (2011) Closing address: The future path of stewardship. *3rd ICSA Corporate Governance Conference.* London UK, 16th March 2011. Available online under www.governanceforowners.com/images/upload/press_80.pdf, accessed November 28, 2011.

Cheffins, B. R. (2010) The stewardship code's Achilles' heel. *The Modern Law Review,* 73(6), pp. 1004–1025.

Chow, S. (2010) Cross-country comparison of shareholder engagement for responsible investment. *The University of Melbourne, Working Paper.*

Chung, H. and Talaulicar, T. (2010) Forms and effects of shareholder activism. *Corporate Governance: An International Review,* 18(4), pp. 253–257.

Chung, H. and Wynn, J. (2014) Corporate governance, directors' and officers' insurance premiums and audit fees. *Managerial Auditing Journal,* 29(2), pp. 173–195.

Deakin, S. and Hobbs, R. (2007) False Dawn for CSR? Shifts in regulatory policy and the response of the corporate and financial sectors in Britain. *Corporate Governance: An International Review,* 15(1), pp. 68–76.

Denes, M. and Karpoff, J. and McWilliams, V. (2015) Thirty years of shareholder activism: A survey of empirical research. Available online under http://ssrn.com/abstract=2608085.

Dunlavy, C. A. (2006) Social conceptions of the corporation: Insights from the history of shareholder voting rights. *Washington and Lee Law Review,* 63, pp. 1347–1388.

Financial Reporting Council (2010) *The UK Stewardship Code.* Financial Reporting Council, July 2010. Available online under https://frc.org.uk/getattachment/e223e152-5515-4cdc-a951-da33e093eb28/UK-Stewardship-Code-July-2010.pdf, accessed May 29, 2018.

Financial Reporting Council (2015) Developments in Corporate Governance and Stewardship. Financial Reporting Council, January 2015. Available online under https://frc.org.uk/getattachment/6f0a7c78-abd2-4480-bf6f-188e02b06a9c/Developments-in-Corporate-Governance-and-Stewardship-2014.pdf, accessed May 29, 2018.

Fulton, M. and Kahn, B. M. and Sharples, C. (2012) Sustainable investing – establishing long-term value and performance. Available online under www.dbcca.com/dbcca/EN/_media/Sustainable_Investing_2012.pdf, accessed April 17, 2012.

Garner, L. M., help@sec.gov, 2011. *Shareholder Engagement.* [email] Message to C. Rushton. Sent Friday 2 December 2011, 16, p. 49. Further information available on request.

Gifford, E. J. M. (2009) *Effective Shareholder Engagement: An Analysis of the Factors that Contribute to Shareholder Salience.* University of Sydney, School of Business, Sydney.

Gillan, S. and Starks, L. (1998) A survey of shareholder activism: Motivation and empirical evidence. *Contemporary Finance Digest*, 2(3), pp. 10–34.

Goranova, M. and Ryan, L. (2014) Shareholder activism: A multidisciplinary review. *Journal of Management*, Vol. 40 No. 5, pp. 1230–1268.

Heineman Jr., B. W. (2010) *A "Stewardship Code" for Institutional Investors*. Available online under http://blogs.hbr.org/cs/2010/01/a_stewardship_code_for_institu.html, accessed May 29, 2018.

Institutional Shareholder Services & Investor Responsibility Research Center Institute (2011) *The State of Engagement Between U.S. Corporations and Shareholders*. Available online under www.irrcinstitute.org/pdf/IRRC-ISS_EngagementStudy.pdf, accessed December 9, 2011.

Kim, K. A. (2011) *Global Corporate Finance: A Focused Approach*. Singapore: World Scientific.

de Larosière (2009) *The High-Level Group on Financial Supervision in the EU*. Available online under http://ec.europa.eu/internal_market/finances/docs/de_larosiere_report_en.pdf, accessed May 29, 2018.

Lawton, C. (2012) C.Lawton@frc.org.uk, 2012. *FRC's Understanding of 'engagement' and 'stewardship'*. [email] Message to C. Rushton. Sent Monday 30 January 2012, 12:10. Further information available on request.

Martin, R. and Casson, P. D. and Nisar, T. M. (2007) *Investor Engagement: Investors and Management Practice Under Shareholder Value*. Oxford: Oxford University Press.

Mason, Collin and Botelho, T. (2016). The role of the exit in the initial screening of investment opportunities: The case of business angel syndicate gatekeepers. *International Small Business Journal*, 34(2), pp. 157–175.

Mason, Collin and Harrison, R. T. (2010). *Annual Report on the Business Angel Market in the United Kingdom: 2008/09*. London: Department of Business, Innovation and Skills.

McNulty, T. and Nordberg, D. (2015) Ownership, Activism and Engagement: Institutional Investors as Active Owners. Corporate Governance: An International Review. University of Liverpool Management School.

Neubaum, D. O. and Zahra, S. A. (2006). Institutional ownership and corporate social performance: The moderating effects of investment horizon, activism, and coordination. *Journal of Management*, 32(1), 108–131.

O'Rourke, A. (2003). A new politics of engagement: shareholder activism for corporate social responsibility. *Business Strategy and the Environment*, 12, 227–239.

Palmiter, A. R. (2002) Mutual fund voting of portfolio shares: Why not disclose? *Cardozo Law Review*, 23(4), pp. 1419–1491.

Politis, D. (2008). Business angels and value added: what do we know and where do we go? *Venture Capital*, 10(2), pp. 127–147.

Richardson, B. J. (2007) Financing sustainability: The new transnational governance of socially responsible investment. *Yearbook of International Environmental Law*, pp. 73–110.

Schapiro, M. (2010) *Speech by SEC Chairman: Remarks at the NACD Annual Corporate Governance Conference*. October 19, 2010. Available online under www.sec.gov/news/speech/2010/spch101910mls.htm, accessed December 6, 2011.

Schapiro, M. (2011) *Remarks at the Transatlantic Corporate Governance Dialogue*. December 15, 2011. Available online under www.sec.gov/news/speech/2011/spch121511mls.htm, accessed May 29, 2018.

Schäfer, H. and Hertrich, C. (2011) Shareholder Activism in Germany: Theoretical Considerations and Empirical Evidence. *University of Stuttgart, Working Paper*.

Sjöström, E. (2008) Shareholder activism for corporate social responsibility: What do we know? *Sustainable Development*, 16, pp. 141–154.

Skeel, D. (2011) *The New Financial Deal: Understanding the Dodd-Frank Act and Its (Unintended) Consequences*. Hoboken, NJ: Wiley.

Sparkes, R. (2002) *Socially Responsible Investment: A Global Revolution*. Chichester: Wiley.

Sturm, S. (2008) *The Influence of Institutional Investors on Corporate Management and Corporate Governance in Germany*. Norderstedt, Germany: Grin.

Talbot, L. (2010) *The Coming of Shareholder Stewardship*. Legal Studies Research Paper 2010–22, University of Warwick.

Tijssen, L. (2011) Elizabeth.tijssen@ec.europa.eu. *Shareholder Engagement.* [email] Message to C. Rushton. Sent Monday 12 December 2011, 10:26. Further information available on request.

United Nations Global Compact & Principles for Responsible Investment (2010) *Guidance on Responsible Business in Conflict-Affected and High-Risk Areas: A Resource for Companies and Investors.* Available online under www.unpri.org/files/Guidance_RB.pdf, accessed May 29, 2018.

United Nations Principles for Responsible Investment (2011a) *Reporting and Assessment Survey, 2011.* United Nations Principles for Responsible Investment. Available online under www.unpri.org/reporting/20110309_offline_survey_2011.pdf, last accessed May 29, 2018.

United Nations Principles for Responsible Investment (2011b) *Report on Progress, 2011.* United Nations Principles for Responsible Investment. Available online under www.unpri.org/publications/2011_report_on_progress.pdf, accessed May 29, 2018.

Walker, D. A. (2009) *A Review of Corporate Governance in UK Banks and Other Financial Industry Entities: Final Recommendations.* (Walker Review). Available online under www.hm-treasury.gov.uk/d/walker_review_261109.pdf, accessed November 12, 2011.

Winter, J. (2011a) *Shareholder Engagement and Stewardship: The Realities and Illusions of Institutional Share Ownership.* Available online under http://ssrn.com/abstract=1867564, accessed November 24, 2011.

Winter, J. (2011b) The financial crisis: Does good corporate governance matter and how to achieve it? *Duisenberg School of Finance Policy Paper Series, 2011/14.*

Wong, S. C. Y. (2010) Why stewardship is proving elusive for institutional investors. *Butterworths Journal of International Banking and Financial Law,* July/August, pp. 406–411.

Documents of the European Union

COM (2010) 284 final or June 2nd 2010 concerning Corporate governance in financial institutions and remunerations policies.

Commission Staff Working Document (2010) Corporate Governance in Financial Institutions: Lessons to be drawn from the current financial crisis, best practices. Accompanying document to the GREEN PAPER Corporate governance in financial institutions and remuneration policies COM (2010) 284.

COM (2011) 164 final of April 5th 2011 concerning the EU Corporate Governance Framework.

COM (2014) 213 final of April 9th 2014 concerning the encouragement of long-term shareholder engagement and certain elements of the corporate governance statement.

3.4 Stakeholder engagement in marketing

Samantha Miles and Kate Ringham

Introduction

It has long been recognised by proponents of stakeholder theory that value is enhanced through meaningful stakeholder relationships based on trust, commitment, loyalty and transparency (Freeman, 1984). This resonates with developments in the marketing literature whereby contributors acknowledge that a focus on a narrow set of stakeholders (customers, consumers and shareholders) is inappropriate as it fails to capture the complex stakeholder networks that create and destroy value. For Grönroos (1994, 1996), this represented a 'paradigm shift' within marketing, moving away from a managerial perspective that viewed consumers as a source of cash to be exploited, towards relationship building, relationship management and viewing customers as co-producers and co-creators.

Relationship marketing has received a lot of attention from marketing academics (e.g. Ahearne et al., 2005; Conway and Whitelock, 2007). This area of marketing adopts the same language as stakeholder theorists: both disciplines speak of collaboration, interaction, trust, empathy, reciprocity, commitment, symmetry and transparency. Nevertheless, apart from a few exceptions (see for example Ferrell and Ferrell 2008; Maignan and Ferrell, 2004; Maignan et al., 2005; Stearns et al., 1996; Whysall, 2000), stakeholder applications to the marketing context have historically been partial and restricted, simply incorporating additional stakeholders within empirical analysis or recognising multiple stakeholder interests (Hill and Martin, 2014). Stakeholder marketing emerged (Bhattacharya and Korschum, 2008) in response to this criticism.

The growing body of literature on stakeholder marketing recognises the potential benefits for marketers to recognise, map, analyse and evaluate the value adding, and detracting, activities of stakeholder networks along the marketing value chain (Hillebrand et al., 2015; Hult et al., 2011; Mena and Chabowski, 2015). Stakeholder marketing explicitly recognises that stakeholder interests are interrelated and value creation is driven by stakeholder networks. The emphasis on the value of relationships with stakeholder networks to improve customer experiences and address societal concerns and sustainability, has been described as a 'Kuhnian shift . . . [which] significantly bends the marketing worldview' (Achrol and Kotler, 2012: 35) and an opportunity for marketers to become more involved in strategic decision-making (Hillebrand et al., 2015; Webster and Lusch, 2013). This field of enquiry, yet to fully emerge (Kull et al., 2016), presents an exciting new frontier for marketers.

This chapter makes a contribution to the stakeholder marketing literature by exploring the applicability of a recognised stakeholder theory model to stakeholder marketing. The ladder of stakeholder management and engagement proposed by Friedman and Miles

(2006) is reconfigured to reflect contemporary thought in relation to how a closer consideration of stakeholder management techniques can help to build trust and foster loyalty within the marketing function. Before the proposed model is presented, we provide a brief discussion of stakeholder theory and the stakeholder marketing literature. This leads on to a discussion of the attributes of relationship quality derived from both perspectives to inform the marketing ladder. Finally, conclusions are drawn which highlight implications for future research.

Stakeholder theory

Stakeholder theory is often referred to as an amalgamation of eclectic narratives (Gilbert and Rasche, 2008) or an umbrella concept that captures a range of thinking in relation to stakeholder management, stakeholder engagement, stakeholder power, stakeholder influencing strategies and so forth. Miles (2017a, 2017b) presented a systematic overview of stakeholder concepts and ideas, demonstrating how these narratives interconnect into a coherent frame of reference that emphasise the need to attend to a wide range of stakeholders rather than prioritising shareholders and how to achieve this. We refer to this body of literature as 'stakeholder theory'.

Freeman (1984) argued that managers should consider all organisation-stakeholder relationships as part of strategic management and many authors argue that this is good for business, culminating in enhanced brand and reputation (e.g. Harrison et al., 2010; Hillman and Keim, 2001). If a relationship is to endure it requires an investment of time, active multi-way interaction, honesty and transparency to build trust and commitment (Freeman, 1984; Freeman et al., 2010; Phillips, 2003). So, a relational approach to stakeholder management is based on integrity and fairness (Bosse et al., 2009) and is more likely to contribute to social welfare than the more traditional transactional approach (Bridoux and Stoelhorst, 2016). It is therefore 'the right thing to do', regardless of cost or accruing of benefits (Donaldson and Preston, 1995).

Central to stakeholder theory is the notion of value creation. Organisations create and destroy value through trade, and this is achievable because stakeholders supply organisations with resources. Stakeholders and organisations come together, through supportive collaborative action, to create value that neither party could have created on its own (Crane et al., 2014; Freeman and Liedtka, 1997). This can be viewed from a stakeholder value chain perspective in which managers identify value-creating projects, financiers invest funds, the local community and regulators grant development permissions, employees provide human capital, suppliers provide inputs, and customers buy into the output. Competitive advantage is generated through the development of stronger relationships which drive growth and create value by enhancing yields, increasing efficiency and resource use and reducing externalities and societal harm, leading to cost reduction (e.g. reduced accident rates, pollution penalties or clean-up costs).

The networks that stakeholders form affect how stakeholders influence the firm and how the firm responds to these influences, suggesting a need to undertake coalition analysis to evaluate the commonality of behaviours and interests of stakeholder groups (Freeman, 1984). Dense ties between and within stakeholder groups facilitate communication through the transfer of norms and expectations: the greater the density of stakeholder networks the higher the potential to help or harm the organisation (Rowley, 1997). Bridoux and Stoelhorst (2016) argued that contributions to joint value creation are influenced by how individuals perceive their relationships relative to that of others, emphasising the need to explore psychological and sociological factors evident in stakeholder networks that may have adverse impacts on the stakeholder's willingness to engage in value creation. This highlights the need for stakeholder management to identify solutions that avoid situations in which stakeholders realign behaviour downwards and reduce value creation opportunities.

Stakeholder marketing

It has long been recognised that marketers could increase firm value if a wider set of stakeholders were considered beyond customers (Christopher et al., 1991; Miller and Lewis, 1991; Polonsky and Ottman, 1998; Polonsky et al., 1999) or by building lasting stakeholder relationships (Bejou, 1997; Podnar and Jancic, 2006). Payne et al. (2005) argued that the external environment should not be viewed as an uncontrollable variable but as a source of indirect value creation, through customer interaction in a number of markets (referral, employee, influencer, internal and supplier markets). Consequently, stakeholder thinking has influenced a number of strategic marketing management models (Kotler; 2003; Maignan et al., 2005; Maignan and Ferrell, 2004; Murphy et al., 2005; Polonsky, 1996; Polonsky and Scott, 2005).

A revised perspective, known as relationship marketing, emphasised building long-term relationships by developing trust so that the objectives of all parties are met and future service is improved (Ahearne et al., 2005; Berry, 1983; Conway and Whitelock, 2007), leading to enhanced profit and sales growth (Palmatier et al., 2006). The relational perspective was extended to include customers as collaborators, co-producers and co-creators (Bendapudi and Leone, 2003; Prahalad and Ramaswamy, 2004; Vargo and Lusch, 2004) with an adaptive position within the supply chain. The extent and diversity of customer experience, knowledge and skills can be used advantageously through joint problem solving to improve product or service delivery and create a competitive advantage (Payne and Frow, 2006; Payne et al., 2009). Polonsky and Ottman (1998) highlighted the advantages of customer input into the design of new products from the opportunity stage through design, testing, introduction and life-cycle management. This recognises the potential increased value in actively engaging customers in co-production as part of a customer relationship management strategy. Whilst co-creation presents a mind-set change in the way marketers view customers (Bharti et al., 2015) the focus of relationship marketing predominantly remains with buyer-supplier relationships (see Payne and Frow, 2006; Payne et al., 2009). Consequently relationship marketing has been criticised for failing to progress significantly beyond the recognition of multiple stakeholder interests or merely extending empirical analysis to include additional stakeholders (Hill and Martin, 2014; Mena and Chabowski, 2015).

This criticism has been addressed through the development of the concept of stakeholder marketing (Bhattacharya and Korschum, 2008). This is considered to be a new frontier in marketing (Mena and Chabowski, 2015) concerned with 'maintaining value through exchange relationships with multiple stakeholders' (Hult et al., 2011:57). Hillebrand et al. (2015) noted that stakeholder marketing differs substantially from a traditional marketing perspective in that proponents recognise that 1. Stakeholder interests are interrelated, not independent; 2. Value creation is driven by stakeholder networks not by the firm alone; 3. Customer primacy is inappropriate, given the above. Hillebrand et al. (2015) criticised the buyer-supplier dyad focus of mainstream marketing literature and argued that value creation can only be understood by exploring the impact of complex stakeholder networks within the marketing function. Mena and Chabowski (2015) evidenced that simply responding to stakeholders does not guarantee enhanced value creation as it is the manner in which companies respond that is important. They advocated the use of more expansive stakeholder-focused organisation learning, whereby organisations develop new stakeholder-related knowledge activities and learn from past actions to enable enhanced understanding of, and response to, stakeholders' needs. Mena and Chabowski (2015) argued that this approach more accurately reflects the complex environment in which organisations now operate, in which control over marketing activities have become dispersed and decentralised (Hillebrand et al., 2015) and where value is created through stakeholder networks (Hult et al., 2011). Stakeholder marketing is still in its infancy, with much of the extant contributions focusing on conceptual papers. In adding to this literature, we now turn our attention to the reconfiguration of a recognised stakeholder theory model, the ladder of stakeholder engagement (Friedman and Miles, 2006).

A marketing ladder of stakeholder engagement

The ladder of stakeholder engagement

There are many stakeholder models that offer practical advice on how to manage stakeholder relationships (e.g. Freeman, 1984; Savage et al., 1991); how to prioritise conflicting claims (e.g. Mitchell et al., 1997); how to predict stakeholder influencing strategies (e.g. Friedman and Miles, 2002; Frooman, 1999); or how stakeholders use networking capabilities (e.g. Rowley, 1997). Few stakeholder models have been applied to the marketing context. Given the external facing nature of marketing, we have selected the ladder of stakeholder management and engagement (see Figure 3.4.1) proposed by Friedman and Miles (2006) for reconfiguration to the marketing function. The ladder illustrates 12 levels of stakeholder engagement, ranging from reactive, non-participatory exercises associated with strategic, public relations (PR) exercises, to holistic, proactive and collaborative engagement characterised by mutual dependency, risk sharing, empowerment and trust.

At the lowest level is *non-participation* relating to one-way information releases differentiated into three levels: 'Manipulation', 'Therapy' and 'Informing'. Part of PR management, 'manipulation' is used to skilfully manoeuvre opinion to change stakeholder expectations. To align opinion companies may intensively bombard stakeholders with self-laudatory materials. Some examples, aimed at curing an ideological gap between stakeholder and corporate opinion, relate to 'therapy'. 'Informing' is positioned higher on the ladder as it encompasses activities predicated out of transparency, not manipulation, although in practice this may be difficult to distinguish.

The next category of levels is *tokenism*. Here stakeholders have a voice but lack influence. 'Explaining' activities may be used to reduce conflict, dispel misconceptions or facilitate buy-in from stakeholders, if the stakeholders perceive the relevance of the issue involved. 'Placation' may provide opportunities for stakeholder influence, through advisory panels or task forces but only to the extent that the firm decides to act upon advice solicited. Stakeholder engagement at this level may be political, for example to gain legitimacy. If stakeholders are informed of, and participate in, the decision-making process, they are more likely to agree with the outcome, leading to enhanced public perception (Darnall and Jolley, 2004). Seeking real consultation through dialogue differentiates level 6 'Consultation' from lower levels, where stakeholder interests and opinion are solicited.

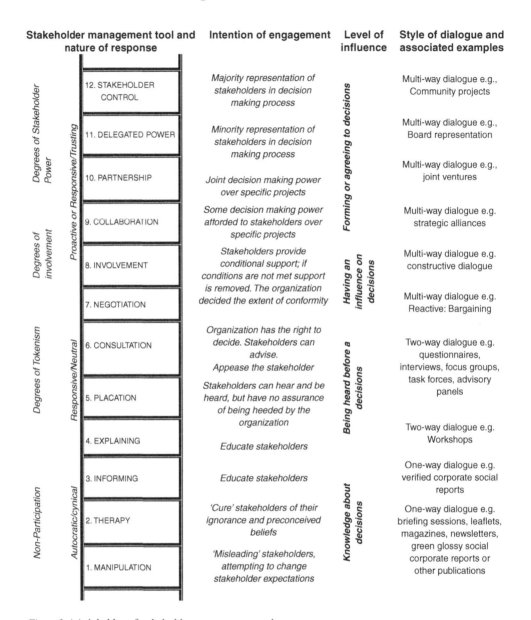

Figure 3.4.1 A ladder of stakeholder management and engagement

Stakeholders are more involved in level 7 'Negotiation' as the stakeholders invest on a conditional basis. If conditions are not met within a reasonable timeframe, stakeholder support is withdrawn e.g. employees strike, investors divest or suppliers terminate contracts to supply goods. As negotiation occurs prior to reaching a final decision stakeholders have power to influence the decision, although the extent of power is dependent on the substitutability of resources (Frooman, 1999).

Levels 8 (Involvement) and 9 (Collaboration) are *degrees of involvement*. These are resource-intensive proactive forms of engagement. Organisation-stakeholder goals are compatible, and decision-making power is afforded to stakeholders, for example roundtable participation to draft proposals. Involvement may be stakeholder initiated, for example using constructive dialogue to influence organisational behaviour, as popularised by the socially responsible investment sector (Friedman and Miles, 2001) or raising a shareholder resolution over environmental management policies. 'Collaboration' uses strategic alliances of complementary skills or resources to pursue mutually beneficial goals, which include corporate sponsorships and product endorsements.

The top levels of engagement relate to *degrees of stakeholder power*. Level 10 'Partnerships' and level 11 'Delegated Power'. This is dependent on high levels of trust and strategies need to be collaborative which build on interdependences. The final level is 'Stakeholder Control'. Examples are exceedingly rare as this requires genuine stakeholder empowerment (see Kochan and Rubinstein, 2000, for a discussion of the Saturn project at General Motors).

Despite the step-wise progression implied, it is inappropriate, and undesirable, to conduct all engagement at the highest levels, as stakeholder management is resource constrained and issue and time sensitive. Nevertheless, engagement activities at the higher levels are associated with stronger relationship building underpinned by trust and commitment. Likewise, used in isolation, non-participation is associated with treating stakeholders with neglect or contempt and would be contrary to a stakeholder management philosophy.

In analysing the applicability of the ladder to a marketing context, it is necessary to explore the antecedents of a successful stakeholder-organisation relationship from the marketing perspective and to compare this with stakeholder management thinking. This is addressed in the next section.

Dimensions of relationship quality

Stakeholder marketing is concerned with the development of successful, long-term, mutually beneficial relationships. What constitutes relationship quality may be easy to discern but it is difficult to analyse. Marketers have differentiated between dimensions, antecedents and consequences of relationship quality but there is no accepted framework for analysis, with multiple variables identified (Athanasopoulou, 2009). Table 3.4.1 summarises the main variables highlighted in this literature. Stakeholder theorists refer to aspects of relationship quality but have not analysed this concept with equal consideration. In this section, we take the notion of relationship quality from both perspectives. This provides three dominant dimensions, two which dominate the marketing literature: trust and commitment (Coote et al., 2003; Goodman and Dion, 2001) and power that, whilst recognised as a dimension of relationship quality within the marketing discipline, is central to stakeholder management (Mitchell et al., 1997).

Trust

Trust (D22) is the willingness to rely on an exchange partner in whom one has confidence (Orth and Green, 2009). It is a complex dimension, closely linked to other relationship quality variables, for example trust is central to leveraging customer lifetime value (Aurier and N'Goala, 2010; Bove and Johnson, 2006; Chaudhuri and Holbrook,

Table 3.4.1 Dimensions of relationship quality

Dimension	Definition
D1. Attractiveness of alternatives	Clients' estimate of the likely satisfaction available in an alternative relationship
D2. Bond	The psychological process through which the buyer and the provider build a relationship to the benefit of both parties
D3. Commitment	The desire for continuity manifested by the willingness to invest resources in a relationship
D4. Communication	The formal as well as informal sharing of meaningful and timely information between firms
D5. Competence	The buyer's perception of the supplier's technological and commercial competence
D6. Conflict	The overall level of disagreement in the working partnership
D7. Cooperation	Similar or complementary coordinated actions taken by firms in interdependent relationships to achieve mutual outcomes or singular outcomes with expected reciprocation over time
D8. Co-ordination	The extent to which different parties in a relationship work well together to accomplish a collective set of tasks
D9. Customisation	The extent to which a seller uses knowledge about a buyer to tailor his offerings to the buyer
D10. Dependence	The extent to which there is no equivalent of better alternatives available in the market
D11. Empathy	Seeking to understand the desires and goals of someone else
D12. Goal compatibility/ goal congruence	The degree to which partners share goals that could only be accomplished through joint action and maintenance of the relationship
D13. Opportunistic behaviour	The behaviour of a party that endangers a relationship for the purpose of taking advantage of a new opportunity
D14. Power	The ability of one individual or group to control or influence the behaviour of another
D15. Reciprocity	The component of a business relationship that causes either party to provide favours or make allowances for the other in return for similar favours or allowances at a later stage
D16. Relationship benefits	Partners that deliver superior benefits will be highly valued and firms will commit themselves to establishing, developing and maintaining relationships with such parties
D17. Relationship-specific investment.	The relational-specific commitment of resources that a partner invests in the relationship
D18. Satisfaction	An overall evaluation based on the total purchase and consumption experience with a good or service over time
D19. Service quality	A comparison between customer expectations and performance
D20. Shared values/ similarity	The extent to which partners have beliefs in common about what behaviours, goals and policies are important, appropriate or inappropriate and right or wrong
D21. Switching costs	The one-time costs that customers associate with the process of switching from one provider to another
D22. Trust	A willingness to rely on an exchange partner in whom one has confidence
D23. Uncertainty	The anticipated changes in the circumstances surrounding an exchange

Source: Adapted from Athanasopoulou (2009) and Theron and Terblanche (2010).

2001). Palmer and Huo (2013) argued that trust is positively correlated with integrity, benevolence (aligned with D15: reciprocity and D11: empathy), predictability (inverse of D23: uncertainty) and competence (D5), whilst Morgan and Hunt (1994) demonstrated a positive correlation with cooperation (D7). Trust is inversely related to the organisation's opportunistic behaviour (D13) (Morgan and Hunt, 1994) and uncertainty (D23) (Bell et al., 2005; Morgan and Hunt, 1994). A number of authors (e.g. Crosby and Stephens, 1987; Doney and Cannon, 1997; Sirdeshmukh et al., 2002) relate trust to multi-facets in consumer evaluations extending beyond trust in the organisation to include trust in the contact person and core service.

Trust is embedded as a concept within stakeholder theory (Clarkson Center for Business Ethics, 2002; Swift, 2001), in which stakeholder relations should be based on mutual trust and cooperation (Jones, 1995). Calton and Kurland (1995) recognised three forms of trust in the stakeholder engagement literature: calculus-based trust, knowledge-based trust and identification-based trust. Whilst nomenclature varies, these parallel marketing concepts of calculative-based trust, cognitive-based trust and affective-based trust. Calculus-based trust is based on economic switching costs (D21), or terminating the relationship, and the benefits associated with attractiveness of continuing the relationship (D1). Knowledge (cognitive)-based trust develops with experience: future bonding is more likely if a firm has demonstrated competence (D5) in previous transactions, for example through demonstrating high levels of service quality (D19). Identification (affective) trust is associated with the principles of reciprocity (D15) and empathy (D11) with regards to meeting stakeholder needs. This is a stronger form of 'affective trust' which is evident in examples of customers as co-producers.

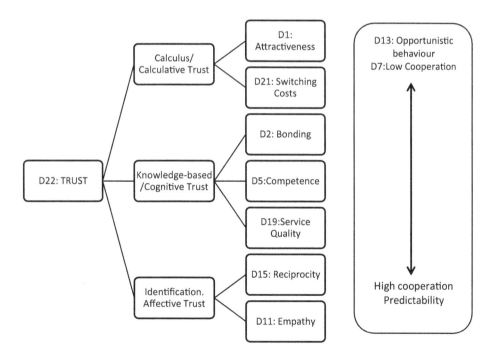

Figure 3.4.2 Trust, stakeholder engagement and dimensions of relationship quality

Given the importance of trust in both literatures, trust is explicitly included in the reconfiguration of the ladder of engagement. Calculative-based trust is associated with lower levels (1–3) of engagement, whereas cognitive trust requires stronger bonds and expectations of competence generated from reputation or experience and would span from 'Explaining' to 'Involvement'. Effective higher-level engagement ('Collaboration' upwards) has to be underpinned by good citizenship created from integrity, fairness, empathy and reciprocity which are associated with affective trust.

Commitment

Commitment (D3) relates to the strength of the relational ties between parties and the enduring desire to invest resources to maintain a relationship. The strongest form of commitment is normative commitment derived from moral obligations (Gruen et al., 2000) and empathy (D11). An instrumental investment represents the weakest form of commitment, driven by self-interest and opportunistic behaviour (D13) (Gundlach et al., 1995) from an assessment of relationship benefits (D16) and the costs incurred of exiting the relationship (D21) if attractive alternative offers exist (D1). Two forms of psychological bonds are evident between these extremes. Firstly continuance commitment, associated with the feeling of being compelled to stay in a relationship, for example dependence (D10) arising from a customisation (D9) of the offering and leading to a lack of alternatives. Affective commitment is derived from shared values (D20) and belongingness, creating a willingness to remain in the relationship. Affective commitment positively impacts relationship bonds (D2) (Verhoef, 2003) and is underpinned by reciprocity (D15) and responsibility derived from shared values (D20) and goal congruence (D12).

Stakeholder theory is relatively silent on the issue of commitment, but there are aspects of stakeholder engagement that provide interesting insights. Frooman (1999) argued that commitment is determined by concentration of suppliers and non-substitutability of the offering (D10), controllability, non-mobility of the stakeholder and essentiality (the relative magnitude of exchange and criticality). Rowley and Moldoveanu (2003) linked commitment to the psychological attachment derived from shared values (D20) and belongingness and suggested that the degree to which a stakeholder group will be mobilised into action is dependent on interest and identity overlap (D20). Commitment is also aligned with stakeholder capacity and willingness to threaten or cooperate (Freeman, 1984). If both the potential for threat and the potential for cooperation are high, collaborative strategies should be sought, requiring high levels of commitment. Conversely no commitment is required if both the potential for threat and for cooperation (D7) are low (Savage et al., 1991). This is also related to conflict management, stemming from divergent stakeholder interests (Friedman and Miles, 2002; Frooman, 1999). Carroll (1979) proposed four conflict management strategies. Firstly, reactive strategies are aligned with opportunistic behaviour (D13) to promote brand or firm image. Defensive strategies involve attempts to alter stakeholder opinion to maintain relations through informing or educating activities, for example where legitimacy has been breached. Accommodative strategies involve listening to the concerns of stakeholders and aiming to fulfil their expectations. This will require cooperation (D7) and co-ordination (D8) to accomplish outcomes with which both parties to the transaction are satisfied (D18). Finally, proactive strategies go beyond normal expectations to deliver high levels of satisfaction (D18) and enduring relationships built on the principles of goal congruence (D12), shared values (D20) and reciprocity (D15). Figure 3.4.3 illustrates how the dimensions of relationship quality are aligned to commitment and stakeholder strategies.

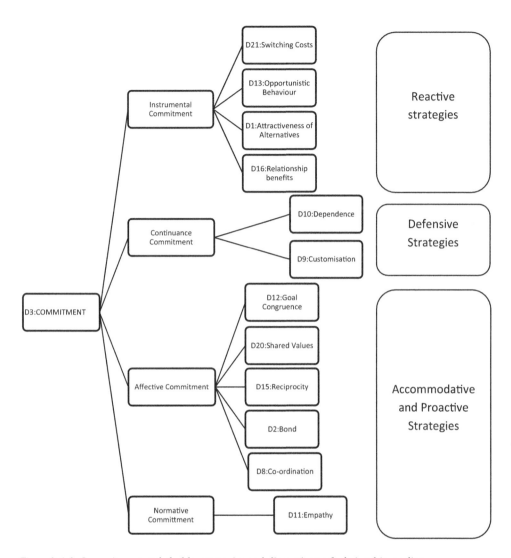

Figure 3.4.3 Commitment, stakeholder strategies and dimensions of relationship quality

Commitment has been explicitly included in the marketing ladder of engagement. Instrumental commitment is associated with levels 1–3, whereas continuance commitment requires stronger bonds (levels 4–5). Affective commitment, based on shared values and reciprocity is reflected in levels 6–9. At the very highest levels (10–13), normative commitment is evident as this has to be underpinned by empathy and facilitated through proactive stakeholder strategies.

Power

Power (D14) relates to 'the ability of one individual or group to control or influence the behaviour of another' (Theron and Terblanche, 2010: 390). Nguyen (2012) argued that asymmetric relationships emphasise power imbalances and provide scope for opportunistic behaviour (D13), whereas symmetric relationships are based on a commonality of interest (D12, D20) which promotes information sharing (D4). Consumer power increases with greater levels of mutual dependency (D10), as reflected in the extension of the role of consumers to collaborators, co-creators and co-producers of value (Bhalla, 2011). Conflict (D6) is positively correlated with power (Morgan and Hunt, 1994). Functional conflict, resulting in beneficial outcomes, and dysfunctional conflict, leading to negative outcomes, such as opportunistic behaviour (D13) are differentiated (Massey and Dawes, 2007).

Power is a recognised attribute for stakeholder recognition (Miles, 2017a; Mitchell et al., 1997) and is linked to resource dependency. Frooman (1999) indicated that stakeholders who are dependent on the firm for resources are more committed to long-term relationships. He argued that the higher the resource dependency the greater the power to influence. Power is therefore associated with commitment (D3), dependency (D10) and relationship-specific resources (D17) (Frooman, 1999). Mitchell et al. (1997) classified power as coercive power related to physical force, utilitarian power derived from relationship-specific resources (D17) and normative power associated with moral obligations (D11, D15). Normative power is closely linked to trust (D22), dependence (D10) and commitment (D3). Miles (2017a) argued that power is the dominant stakeholder attribute, as without the power to influence the level of reciprocity will be low. Stakeholder power will be highly limited if both parties act independently and there is no firm commitment (D3), whereas stakeholders will have some power to influence corporate decisions if there is mutual dependency (D10) and intention to build long lasting relationships.

Bridoux and Stoelhorst (2016) analysed four stakeholder relational models and concluded that the highest contribution to value creation was evident in 'communal sharing' situations as participants view themselves as part of a community and align the collective interest with their own (D12 goal congruence; D20 shared goals), facilitating co-ordination. This is aligned with normative power and empathy (D11). The lowest contribution was evident in 'market pricing' approaches. Power is derived from resources and behaviour is dominated by self-interest (D13). 'Authority ranking' models of behaviour rely on the hierarchal power from an asymmetric relationship, in which the firm is viewed as authoritative because of perceptions of legitimacy and competence (D5). This leads to lower levels of value creation when compared to 'equality matching', characterised by equivalent retaliation behaviour (D15 reciprocity) stemming from shared understanding and viewing network participant as equal. The model adopted is reliant on individual personality traits and the perception of the firm's accountability and intention. Stakeholder engagement approaches, as illustrated in the ladder, can act as indicators of firm's accountability and intention. Bridoux and Stoelhorst (2016) argued that, in situations where there is a mismatch between higher personal relational models and lower firm relational models, stakeholders will either realign behaviour, leading to lower levels of value creation or sever the relationship. This provides justification for not focusing all stakeholder management activity at lower levels. Figure 3.4.4 illustrates how the dimensions of relationship quality are aligned to power from a stakeholder theory perspective.

Engagement activities at the very lowest level of the ladder not only fails to incorporate the stakeholder voice but actively attempts to manipulate perception. In such situations, stakeholders are powerless and have no say. Utilitarian power, associated with resource investment relate to 'Therapy' through to 'Consultation', depending on whether a market pricing approach or authority ranking approach is adopted by stakeholders. Normative power is only evident at the higher levels of the ladder, from 'Negotiation' or conciliation levels.

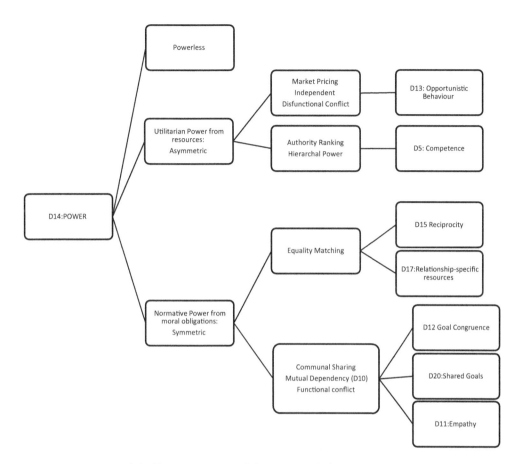

Figure 3.4.4 Power, stakeholder engagement and dimensions of relationship quality

A stakeholder marketing ladder of engagement

We present a stakeholder marketing ladder of engagement in Figure 3.4.5. One-way stakeholder communications are included at the bottom of the ladder (e.g. promotions that inform customers of available offerings). Campaigns that aim to skilfully manoeuvre stakeholder expectations would be included under 'Manipulation'. Marketers need to be wary of targeting engagement at this level as many companies have been fined or forced to remove adverts seen to be misleading. For example L'Oréal's advertisement for Olay's Definity eye cream was banned in the UK in 2009 for airbrushing wrinkles, and its advert for Lancôme Génifique and Paris Youth Code skincare products banned in the USA in 2014 for claiming unsubstantiated scientific evidence (Federal Trade Commission, 2014). 'Therapy' does not involve a direct effort to control opinion but attempts to 'cure igno-rance' or realign stakeholder expectations. Tesco (UK), for example ran the advertisement campaign 'what burgers have taught us' in 2013 following accusations that own brand beef burgers and ready meals contained horsemeat. The full page 'apology' highlighted Tesco's current CSR approach to farmers and a pledge to change the way the industry works (Wheeler, 2013) in an attempt to change opinions of the media, pressure groups

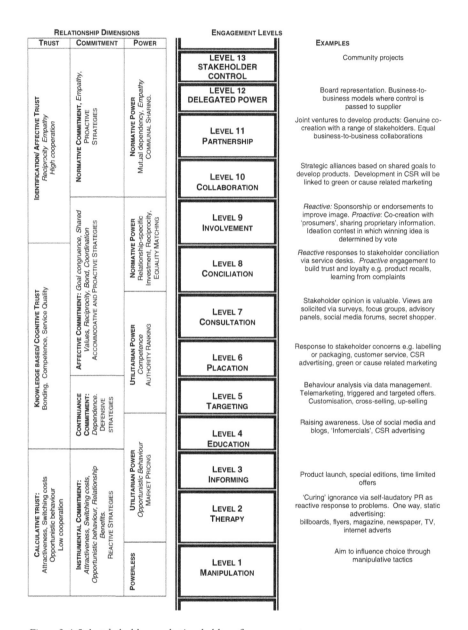

Figure 3.4.5 A stakeholder marketing ladder of engagement

and consumers. These forms of engagement do not attempt to build lasting relationships through cognitive or affective trust but tend to be based on opportunistic behaviour associated with reactive or defensive strategies. 'Informing' engagement is used effectively by companies that sell complex products in which key benefits which are not easily discernible or communicated without demonstration, such as the longevity of Duracell batteries or the functions of the latest Apple iPhone. Packaging is a key element in informing strategies, as good packaging not only enhances the attractiveness of the offering and is influential in purchasing decision, but provides opportunities to inform the public of strategic messages to reinforce brand and corporate image. Successful engagement of this type therefore necessitates close co-ordination with packaging suppliers. Focusing marketing activities at lower levels will not achieve the advantages associated with stakeholder marketing, necessitating a mixed engagement strategy.

Marketing can enhance understanding and so 'Education' replaces 'explaining' from the stakeholder engagement ladder. 'Infomercials' are used by not-for-profit organisations to inform the public on health, social or environmental issues and by politicians during election campaigns. Education campaigns are less common with corporates but have been used when responding to stakeholder pressure to rebuild reputational damage, to prevent boycotts and to minimise loss in stakeholder value. British Petroleum's rebranding campaign to Beyond Petroleum in 2000 following a spate of environmental and social misdemeanours is a clear example (Macalister and Cross, 2000).

A further marketing-specific level has been added called 'Targeting'. Marketing has responded effectively to technological advancements in consumer behaviour and as a consequence is more advanced than other business functions at developing innovative data management systems to track and store stakeholder information which facilitates targeted cross-selling, up-selling and customisation of the offering. Data gathering has been extended by online retailers, such as Amazon and eBay, to include 'wish/watch lists'. The increasing need for third-party support and increased data analysis logically extends the range of stakeholders that can impact the marketing function. For example, services such as Google AdWords pay-per-click online advertising enables adverts to be posted online in relation to frequent searches made by the user. Targeting is positioned at level 5 because it is a responsive strategy, responding to demographic/transaction data or consumer behaviour whilst remaining opportunistically driven.

'Placation' is also a responsive strategy aimed at addressing stakeholder concerns over issues such as packaging, labelling, CSR issues, quality of service and so forth. Whilst consumers may have a legitimate interest in such issues, the range of stakeholders raising these concerns can be wide. Consequently the 'marketing' response to these concerns needs to be fully informed by the relevant functional areas to ensure a consistent corporate message. For example, CSR marketing can increase customer commitment due to shared values and beliefs, but it needs to be supported by appropriate CSR investment, as with Levi's 2010 'Go forth' campaign (Taylor, 2010), to avoid reputation damage via social media if CSR credentials are found inadequate. Stakeholder engagement may be positive or negative and include completing online reviews, contacting the company directly or word-of-mouth activity.

Marketers have long realised that collecting and responding to customer feedback is an essential part of delivering outstanding customer satisfaction. There are many forms that 'Consultation' can take including surveys, 'secret shopper' and social media forums. Some organisations have taken consultation to a higher level. For example DeWALT, operates an 'insight community' of over 10,000 end users of its power tools which gathers information on user needs, ideas and concerns (Dupre, 2015). The resulting collective wisdom enables DeWALT to undertake more confident product development decisions. This complements other data sources such social media analytics. Insight communities rely on stakeholders opting in to the group, and so attention needs to focus on how stakeholders are treated to ensure long-term relationships are formed.

'Conciliation' replaces 'negotiation' on the original ladder. This differs from 'Placation' to the extent that stakeholder concerns are accommodated rather than defended. A product recall offers an opportunity to demonstrate conciliation and whilst a product recall may appear a costly strategy, brand and share price will struggle to recover if a company fails to respond expediently to problems, particularly if human life is at risk. The iconic example of Johnson & Johnson and the recall of Tylenol in 1982 resulted in increased brand value for consumers and employees and buoyant share price because of the proactive response to the isolated contamination of drugs by a disgruntled employee. This contrasts sharply with the slow response from Ford to recall vehicles fitted with faulty Firestone tyres that led to 174 deaths and 700 injuries in the USA and subsequent $590 million lawsuit bill (Greenwald, 2001).

Co-creation, such as Lego's 'Ambassador Program' in which consumers work with brands to create an improved offering informed by the consumers' needs and knowledge (Antorini et al., 2012) is classified as 'Involvement'. Mutual benefit is gained from customer input into the design of new products from the opportunity stage through design, testing, introduction and life-cycle management (Polonsky and Ottman, 1998). Co-creation can lead to low cost product development coupled with increased stakeholder loyalty and satisfaction derived from the sense of ownership in the brand that is created through stakeholder participation. There is no universal engagement approach, and some examples of engagement are more successful than others. Involvement such as co-creation is a change in mind-set in the way that marketers view stakeholders by acknowledging the value of the extent and diversity of knowledge, experience and skills held (Bharti et al., 2015). Success is facilitated by a culture of exchange and open communication, which may include the sharing of proprietary information with stakeholders. This is only possible if there is a high level of trust.

Involvement is differentiated from 'Collaboration', as in the former stakeholders are able to influence the company through ideas and feedback but the company still retains the balance of power and may decide how it uses information gathered. Collaboration may be as simple as an ideation contest in which winning idea is determined by stakeholder vote, as demonstrated by the 2017 campaign 'choose or lose' Walkers crisps brand at PepsiCo. Collaboration may involve a wider stakeholder group than consumers. For example the farmer owned company Arla Foods, developed Cravendale milk, through co-creation with farmers/owners (who wished to add value to their milk and investment), consumers (who desired longer use-by dates), technical engineers (who developed the ceramic filtration system to remove bacteria) and its packaging suppliers to provide an opaque bottle that prevented deterioration through light exposure. Collaboration may also relate to business-to-business models. For example, online market and hospitality services that work together to extend the reach of advertising for individual hotels and holiday accommodation.

Companies may engage in third-party endorsements of products or corporate sponsorship to improve the offering through 'Partnership' engagement. For example Coca-cola partnered with WWF, donating $2 million to help with the plight of polar bears (its animal mascot) and global warming. This may be a fraction of the $9.8 billion advertisement budget but it is still a substantial contribution. The 'Coca-cola Artic Home' advert was launched in 2013 on the back of this, achieving a further $3 million in donations from customers (Frazier, 2014). Genuine green or cause-related marketing may focus around such engagement, but this may be viewed cynically if manipulated for image transfer.

Examples of 'Delegated Power' and 'Stakeholder Control' in the original ladder of stakeholder engagement are rare within business (Friedman and Miles, 2006), and this also applies to the marketing function. With the onset of the sharing economy examples exist where firms engage in joint ventures to develop products in business-to-business models (Payne and Holt, 2001) or share resources.

Conclusions

The ladder of stakeholder management and engagement proposed by Friedman and Miles (2006) is reconfigured to reflect contemporary thought in relation to how a closer consideration of stakeholder management techniques can help to build trust and foster loyalty within the marketing function in the modern business environment.

This model is firstly intended as a self-evaluating tool for marketers to use to map the range of activities undertaken. Both marketing and stakeholder theorists acknowledge that long-term relationships need to be based on loyalty and trust founded on empathy, reciprocity, commitment, transparency, fairness and collaboration. This should emanate from an underlying palpable ethical objective towards stakeholders rather than as a selective by-product of opportunistic behaviour, as historically witnessed within the marketing function.

Relationship building, if sought, is promoted as a way to secure a strategic advantage through increased referrals and associated cost reductions and reduced opportunistic behaviour. These aims will not be achieved by focusing marketing activities at the lower levels of engagement as this will fail to develop long-term relationships and will miss the opportunity to unlock stakeholder knowledge and experience for product development. Organisations that adopt an ethical duty of care to their stakeholders gain in the long-term, especially if things go wrong as procedural fairness is central to retention. How organisations deal with product faults, the exercise of warranties and product recalls can be pivotal in terms of reputation management and repeat custom.

Relationship quality is dependent on procedural quality, responsiveness quality and quality of outcomes (Friedman and Miles, 2006) which extend beyond the direct sales experience to encompass after sales service provisions (Homburg and Griering, 2001). A retail organisation that refuses to accept responsibility for problems or refers complaints down the supply chain may reduce short-term costs but at the cost of lost reputation, distrust and high levels of customer attrition. In order to progress engagement to higher engagement levels marketers are advised to formalise procedures, provide facilities for stakeholders to initiate engagement and provide assurance that stakeholders are empowered to raise critical or time sensitive issues (Zadek and Raynard, 2002). This is particularly important in light of the findings from Bridoux and Stoelhorst (2016) in which value creation potential can be eroded if stakeholders perceive firm relational models to be lower than personal relational models, thereby providing further justification for not focusing all stakeholder management activity at the lower levels of the ladder.

Secondly, this model is intended to reveal the kinds of engagement activities that would be required in order to change focus, particularly where a stakeholder marketing approach is intended. Whilst a range of engagement activities are desirable, marketers are advised that, in order to build relationships of enduring quality, they should concentrate on collaboration and interaction with stakeholders using a range of engagement strategies including some evident at the higher levels of the ladder. Marketers must recognise that long-term relationship building requires personal and expert interaction and cannot be generated by systems driven data analysis.

Hillebrand et al. (2015:412) argued that 'Embracing a stakeholder marketing perspective and developing the associated capabilities may be a promising avenue to overcome the declining influence of marketing in firms'. Despite academic advances in stakeholder marketing, the stakeholder focus in marketing remains narrow and does little to acknowledge the wider range of relationships that contribute to value creation (channel members, retailers, wholesalers, agents and sales representatives, manufacturers, warranty providers, customer service staff, internet advertising agents etc.) but also the interconnectedness of stakeholders stemming from service constellations (Hillebrand et al., 2015). The sales experience is no longer a one-to-one experience with sales personnel, agent or retailer, due to online review sites, such as Trip Advisor or TrustPilot, and direct customer reviews via agent sites such as eBay or Amazon. In addition sales can be impacted by sourcing decisions, packaging and labelling and reputational issues. This is evident by the range of consumer boycotts due to poor environmental (e.g. pollution – Coca Cola, BP); social (e.g. tax avoidance – Amazon, Starbuck; human rights – Shell, Starbucks); or ethical (e.g. animal rights – Adidas, Air France) practices. This provides greater justification for marketers to adopt a stakeholder marketing approach as more effective stakeholder mapping exercises which capture the actual behaviour of all the marketing stakeholders would help to facilitate marketers to fulfil their objectives and devise appropriate engagement strategies. Stakeholder mapping techniques exist to identify resource dependency (Pfeffer and Salancik, 1978), proximity of stakeholder (Drisco and Starik, 2004) and centrality of the organisation in the stakeholder network as a power determinant (Frooman, 1999) when identifying stakeholder influencing strategies and formulating corporate stakeholder strategies but there is limited application of such models within the marketing literature. This chapter has provided such an example. Whilst this is a conceptual effort, future research could test this model empirically through the development of propositions that explore the relationship between relationship quality determinants and engagement strategies or via in-depth case analysis.

References

Achrol, R. S. and Kotler, P. (2012). Frontiers of the marketing paradigm in the third millennium. *Journal of the Academy of Marking Science*, 40(1):35–52.

Ahearne, M., Bhattacharya, C. B. and Gruen, T. (2005). Antecedents and consequences of customer-company identification: Expanding the role of relationship marketing. *Journal of Applied Psychology*, 90, 574–585.

Antorini, Y. M., Muñiz, A. M. Jr. and Askildsen, T., (2012). Collaborating with customer communities: Lessons from the Lego group. *MIT Management Review*, March 20th.

Athanasopoulou, P. (2009). Relationship quality: A critical literature review and research agenda. *European Journal of Marketing*, 43(5/6):583–610.

Aurier, P. and N'Goala, G. (2010). The differing and mediating roles of trust and relationship commitment in service relationship maintenance and development. *Journal of the Academy of Marketing Science*, 38:303–325.

Bhalla, G. (2011). *Collaboration and co-creation new platforms for marketing and innovation*. New York: Springer.

Bejou, D. (1997). Relationship marketing: Evolution, present state, and future. *Psychology & Marketing*, 14(18):727.

Bell, S. J., Auh, S. and Smalley, K. (2005). Customer relationship dynamics: Service quality and customer loyalty in the context of varying levels of customer expertise and switching costs. *Journal of the Academy of Marketing Science*, 33:169–183.

Bendapudi, N. and Leone, R. P. (2003). Psychological implications of customer participation in co-production. *Journal of Marketing*, 67(1):14–28.

Berry, L. L. (1983) Relationship marketing. In: L. L. Berry, G. L. Shostack and G. Upah (eds) *Emerging Perspectives on Services Marketing*. Chicago: American Marketing Association, pp. 25–28.

Bharti, K., Agrawal, R. and Sharma, V. (2015). Value co-creation: Literature review and proposed conceptual; Framework. *International Journal of Market Research*, 57(4):571–603.

Bhattacharya, C. B. and Korschum, D. (2008) Stakeholder marketing: Beyond the four Ps and the customer. *Journal of Public Policy & Marketing*, 27(1): 113–116.

Bosse, D. A., Phillips, R. A. and Harrison, J. S. (2009). Stakeholder reciprocity and firm performance. *Strategic Management Journal*, 30:447–456.

Bove, L. L. and Johnson, L. W. (2006). Customer loyalty to one service worker: Should it be discouraged? *International Journal of Research in Marketing*, 23(1):79–91.

Bridoux, F. and Stoelhorst, J. W. (2016). Stakeholder relationships and social welfare: A behavioral theory of contributions to joint value creation. *Academy of Management Review*, 41, 229–251.

Calton, J. M. and Kurland, N. B. (1995). A theory of stakeholder enabling: Giving voice to an emerging postmodern praxis of organisational discourse. In D. M. Boje, R. P. Gephart and T. J. Thatchenkery (eds) *Postmodern Management and Organization Theory*. London: Sage, pp. 154–177.

Carroll, A. B. (1979). A three dimensional conceptual model of corporate social performance. *Academy of Management Review*, 4:497–505.

Chaudhuri, A. and Holbrook, M. B. (2001). The chain of effects from brand trust and brand affect to brand performance: The role of brand loyalty. *Journal of Marketing*, 65(2):81–93.

Christopher, M., Payne, A. and Ballantyne, D. (1991), *Relationship Marketing: Bringing Quality, Customer Service and Marketing Together*. Oxford: Butterworth-Heinemann.

Clarkson Center for Business Ethics (The). 2002. Principles of stakeholder management. *Business Ethics Quarterly*, 12(2):257–264.

Conway, T. and Whitelock, J. (2007). Relationship marketing in the subsidised arts: The key to a strategic marketing focus? *European Journal of Marketing*, 41(1/2):199–222.

Coote, L. V., Forrest, E. J. and Tam, T. W. (2003) An investigation into commitment in non-Western industrial marketing relationships. *Industrial Marketing Management*, 32(7):595–604.

Crane, A., Palazzo, G., Spence, L. J. and Matten, D. (2014). Contesting the value of "creating shared value". *California Management Review*, 56(2):130–153.

Crosby, L. A. and Stephens, N. (1987). Effects of relationship marketing on satisfaction, retention, and prices in the life insurance industry. *Journal of Marketing Research*, 24:404–411.

Darnall, N. and Jolley, G. J. (2004). Involving the public: When are surveys and stakeholder interviews effective? *Review of Policy Research*, 21(4):581–593.

Donaldson, T. and Preston, L. E. (1995). The stakeholder theory of the corporation: Concepts evidence and implications. *Academy of Management Review*, 20:65–92.

Doney, P. M. and Cannon, J. P. (1997). An examination of the nature of trust in buyer-seller relationships. *Journal of Marketing*, 61(2):35–51.

Drisco, C. and Starik, M. (2004). The primordial stakeholder: Advancing the conceptual consideration of stakeholder status for the natural environment. *Journal of Business Ethics*, 49, 55–73.

Dupre, E. (2015). Customer insight is DeWALT's power tool. *Direct Marketing News*, November 20th.

Federal Trade Commission (2014). L'Oréal Settles FTC Charges Alleging Deceptive Advertising for Anti-Aging Cosmetics, June 30th. Accessed on April 2nd, 2016 at www.ftc.gov/news-events/press-releases/2014/06/loreal-settles-ftc-charges-alleging-deceptive-advertising-anti.

Ferrell, O. C. and Ferrell, L. (2008). A macromarketing ethics framework: Stakeholder orientation and distributive justice. *Journal of Macromarketing*, 28(1):24–32.

Frazier, M. (2014). Should the polar bear still sell Coca-Cola? *The New Yorker*, November 6th.

Freeman, R. E. (1984). *Strategic Management: A Stakeholder Approach*. Boston: Pitman Publishing.

Freeman, R. E., Harrison, J. S., Wicks, A. C., Parmar, B. and de Colle, S. (2010). *Stakeholder Theory: The State of the Art*. Cambridge: Cambridge University Press.

Freeman, R. E. and Liedtka, J. (1997). Stakeholder capitalism and the value chain. *European Management Journal*, 15:286–396.

Friedman, A. L. and Miles, S. (2001). Socially responsible investment and corporate social and environmental reporting in the UK: An exploratory study. *British Accounting Review*, 33:523–548.

Friedman, A. L. and Miles, S. (2002). Developing stakeholder theory. *Journal of Management Studies*, 39(1):1–21.

Friedman, A. L. and Miles, S. (2006). *Stakeholders: Theory and Practice*. Oxford: Oxford University Press.

Frooman, J. (1999). Stakeholder influence strategies. *Academy of Management Review* 24(2):191–205.

Gilbert, D. and Rasche, A. (2008). Opportunities and problems of standardized ethics initiatives – A stakeholder theory perspective. *Journal of Business Ethics*, 82, 755–773.

Goodman, L. E. and Dion, P. A. (2001). The determinants of commitment in the distributor – manufacturer relationship. *Industrial Marketing Management*, 30(3):287–300.

Greenwald, J. (2001). Inside the ford/firestone fight. *Time Magazine*, Tuesday, May 29th.

Grönroos, C. (1994). From marketing mix to relationship marketing: Towards a paradigm shift in marketing. *Management Decision*, 32(2):4–20.

Grönroos, C. (1996). Relationship marketing: Strategic and tactical implications. *Management Decision*, 34(3):5–14.

Gruen, T. W., Summers, J. O. and Acito, F. (2000). Relationship marketing activities, commitment and membership behavior in professional associations. *Journal of Marketing*, 64(3):34–49.

Gundlach, G. T., Achrol, R. S. and Mentzer, J. T. (1995). The structure of commitment in exchange. *Journal of Marketing*, 59(1):78–92.

Harrison, J. S., Bosse, D. A. and Phillips, R. A. (2010). Managing for stakeholders, stakeholder utility functions, and competitive advantage. *Strategic Management Journal*, 31(1):58–74.

Hill, R. P. and Martin, K. D. (2014). Broadening the paradigm of marketing as exchange: A public policy and marketing perspective. *Journal of Public Policy & Marketing*, 33:17–33.

Hillebrand, B., Driessen, P. H. and Koll, O. (2015). Stakeholder marketing: Theoretical foundations and required capabilities. *Journal of the Academy of Marketing Science*, 43:411–428.

Hillman, A. J. and Keim, G. D. (2001). Shareholder value, stakeholder management, and social issues: What's the bottom line? *Strategic Management Journal*, 22(2):125–139.

Homburg, C. and Griering, A. (2001). Personal characteristics as moderators of the relationship between customer satisfaction and loyalty – an empirical analysis. *Psychology & Marketing*, 18(l):43–66.

Hult, G. T. M., Mena, J. A., Ferrell, O. C., & Ferrell, L. (2011). Stakeholder marketing: A definition and conceptual framework. *Academy of Marketing Science Review*, 1:44–65.

Jones, T. M. (1995). Instrumental stakeholder theory: A synthesis of ethics and economics. *Academy of Management Review*, 20(2):404–438.

Kochan, T. A. and Rubinstein, S. A. (2000). Towards a stakeholder theory of the firm: The Saturn approach. *Organization Science*, 11, 367–386.

Kotler, P. (2003). *Marketing Management: Analysis, Planning, Implementation and Control*, 11th Edition. Upper Saddle River, NJ: Prentice Hall.

Kull, A. J., Mena, J. A. and Korschum, D. (2016). A resource-based view of stakeholder marketing. *Journal of Business Research*, 69, 5553–5560.

Macalister, T. and Cross, E. (2000) BP rebrands on a global scale. *The Guardian*, July 25th.

Maignan, I. and Ferrell, O. C. (2004). Corporate social responsibility and marketing: An integrative framework. *Journal of the Academy of Marketing Science*, 32(1):3–19.

Maignan, I., Ferrell, O. C. and Ferrell, L. (2005). A stakeholder model for implementing social responsibility in marketing. *European Journal of Marketing*, 39:956–977.

Massey, G. R. and Dawes, P. L. (2007). Personal characteristics, trust, conflict, and effectiveness in marketing/sales working relationships. *European Journal of Marketing*, 41(9/10):1117–1145.

Mena, J. A. and Chabowski, B. R. (2015) The role of organizational learning in stakeholder marketing. *Journal of the Academy of Marketing Science*, 43:429–452.

Miller, R. L. and Lewis, W. F. (1991). A stakeholder approach to marketing management using the value exchange models. *European Journal of Marketing*, 25(8):55–68.

Miles, S. (2017a) Stakeholder theory classification: A theoretical and empirical evaluation of definitions. *Journal of Business Ethics*, 142(3):437–459.

Miles, S. (2017b) Stakeholder theory classification, definitions and essential contestability. In: D. M. Wasieleski and J. Weber (eds) *Stakeholder Management*. Business & Society 360, Bingley: Emerald, pp. 21–47.

Mitchell, R. K., Agle, B. R. and Wood, D. J. (1997). Towards a theory of stakeholder identification and salience: Defining the principle of who and what really counts. *Academy of Management Review*, 22(4):853–886.

Morgan, R. M. and Hunt, S. D. (1994). The commitment-trust theory of relationship marketing. *Journal of Marketing*, 58(3):2–38.

Murphy, B., Maguiness, P., Pescott, C., Wislang, S., Ma, J. and Wang, R. (2005). Stakeholder perceptions presage holistic stakeholder relationship marketing performance. *European Journal of Marketing*, 39(9/10):1049–1069.

Nguyen, B. (2012). The dark side of customer relationship management: Exploring the underlying reasons for pitfalls, exploitation and unfairness. *Journal of Database Marketing & Customer Strategy Management*, 19:56–70.

Orth, U. R. and Green, M. T. (2009) Consumer loyalty to family versus non-family business: The roles of store image, trust and satisfaction. *Journal of Retailing and Consumer Services*, 16(4):248–259.

Palmatier, R. W., Dant, R. P, Grewal, D. and Evans, K. R. (2006). Factors influencing the effectiveness of relationship marketing: A meta-analysis. *Journal of Marketing*, 70:136–153.

Palmer, A. and Huo, Q. (2013). A study of trust over time within a social network mediated environment. *Journal of Marketing Management*, 29(15–16):1816–1833.

Payne A., Ballantyne D. and Christopher M. (2005). A stakeholder approach to relationship marketing strategy. *European Journal of Marketing*, 39(7/8):855–871.

Payne, A. and Frow, P (2006). Customer relationship management form strategy to implementation. *Journal of Marketing Management*, 22(1/2):135–168.

Payne, A. and Holt, S. (2001). Diagnosing customer value: Integrating the value process and relationship marketing. *British Journal of Management*, 12(2):159–182.

Payne, A., Storbacka, K. and Frow, P. (2009). Co-creating brands: Diagnosing and designing relationship experience. *Journal of Business Research*, 62(3):379–389.

Pfeffer, J. and Salancik, G. R. (1978). *The External Control of Organizations: A Resource Dependence Perspective*. New York: Harper & Row.

Phillips, R. A. (2003). *Stakeholder Theory and Organizational Ethics*. San Francisco: Berrett-Koehler.

Podnar, K. and Jancic, Z. (2006). Towards a categorization of stakeholder groups: An empirical verification of a three-level model. *Journal of Marketing Communication*, 12(4):297–308.

Polonsky, M. J. (1996). Stakeholder management and the stakeholder matrix: Potential strategic marketing tools. *Journal of Market Focused Management*, 1(3):209–229.

Polonsky, M. J. and Ottman, J. (1998). Stakeholders' contribution to the green new product development process. *Journal of Marketing Management*, 14:533–557.

Polonsky, M. J. and Scott, D. (2005). An empirical examination of the stakeholder strategy matrix. *European Journal of Marketing*, 39(9/10):1199–1215.

Polonsky, M. J., Suchard H. T. and Scott, D. R. (1999). The incorporation of interactive external environment: A stakeholder approach. *Journal of Strategic Marketing*, 7(1):41–55.

Prahalad, C. K. and Ramaswamy, V. (2004). Co-creation experiences: The next practice in value creation. *Journal of Interactive Marketing*, 18(3):5–14.

Rowley, T. J. (1997). Moving beyond dyadic ties: A network theory of stakeholder influences. *Academy of Management Review*, 22:885–910.

Rowley, T. J. and Moldoveanu, M. (2003). When will stakeholder groups act? An interest and identity based model of stakeholder group mobilization. *Academy of Management Review*, 28(2):204–219.

Savage, G. T., Nix, T. W., Whitehead, C. J. and Blair, J. D. (1991). Strategies for Assessing and Managing Organizational Stakeholders. *Academy of Management Executive*, 5(2):61–75.

Sirdeshmukh, D., Singh, J., & Sabol, B. (2002). Consumer trust, value and loyalty in relational exchanges. *Journal of Marketing*, 66(1):15–37.

Stearns, J. M., Walton, J. R., Crespy, C. T. and Bol, J. W. (1996). The role of moral obligations to stakeholders in ethical marketing decision-making. *The Journal of Marketing Management*, 6(2):34–47.

Swift, T. (2001). Trust, reputation and corporate accountability to stakeholders. *Business Ethics: A European Review*, 10:16–26.

Taylor, V. (2010). The most imaginative CSR ad campaigns. *Forbes*, September 7th.

Theron, E. and Terblanche, N. S. (2010). Dimensions of relationship marketing in business-to-business financial services. *International Journal of Market Research*, 52(3):383–402.

Vargo, S. L. and Lusch, R. F. (2004) Evolving to a new dominant logic for marketing. *Journal of Marketing*, 68(January):1–17.

Verhoef, P. C. (2003). Understanding the effect of customer relationship management efforts on customer retention and customer share development. *Journal of Marketing*, 67(4):30–45.

Webster, F. E., Jr. and Lusch, R. F. (2013). Elevating marketing: Marketing is dead! Long live marketing! *Journal of the Academy of Marketing Science*, 41:389–399.

Wheeler, B. (2013). Tesco and a strange bit of poetry. *BBC News Magazine*, March 8th.

Whysall, P. (2000). Addressing ethical issues in retailing: A stakeholder perspective. *International Review of Retail, Distribution and Consumer Research*, 10(3):305–318.

Zadek, S. and Raynard, P. (2002). Stakeholder engagement: Measuring and communicating the quality. *Accountability Quarterly*, 19:8–17.

3.5 "You're responsible, I'm liable"

Stakeholder relations in the face of responsibility

Anne F. Barraquier

Introduction

Business organizations need to be increasingly compliant to ethical and social demands. Thus far, empirical studies about the interactions that such compliance requirements produce among suppliers, competitors and clients of the same industry are scarce. Indeed, business firms reluctantly discuss regulatory and ethical issues with outsiders and, most of all, rarely provide detailed accounts of such interactions. One important issue at stake is to know to what extent the different stakeholders bear responsibility or negotiate their responsibility with the others, in particular when they face critical problems such as health and safety, related to their products and activity. There is not much research about how the actors of the same industry discuss these issues together to determine if and how much they should each be responsible.

These interactions are particularly interesting to understand how the process of responsibility between interdependent stakeholders is constructed in a particular industry. How do the different groups of stakeholders use dialogue and negotiation to create and elaborate this process? How do they share, transfer and use information to contest or claim responsibility? Strongly industrialized sectors that have incrementally become highly regulated under the pressure of activism seldom see their managers commenting on how they face such situations and design ad hoc protocols to respond. They are traditionally reluctant to discuss such contexts, dilemmas, choices and decisions.

To investigate the social dynamics of these relations, this chapter presents a case study in the flavour and fragrance industry (F&F). F&F provides flavours to clients in the food industry and fragrant compounds to clients of the cosmetics sector. The study reveals the intricacy of such relations, the involvement of other stakeholders like competitors and professional associations and the complexity of negotiated relations of power between these interdependent groups. Around the sensitive issue of product toxicity in food and personal care industries, this chapter aims to understand how the intensity of this issue and the specific social dynamics it produces shed light on the way responsibility is negotiated between interdependent stakeholder organizations. The discussion elaborates on the embeddedness of expert knowledge in responsibility processes and how it affects the dissemination of responsibility.

Responsibility, compliance and liability

Stakeholder, firm and society perspectives

Stakeholder-oriented perspectives suggest that organizations have duties toward society and should contribute to the welfare of those stakeholders affected by their activities or the achievements of their economic objectives, and to the betterment of the communities among which they operate, through a binding social contract (Donaldson and Dunfee, 1994). In that respect, corporations are entitled to not only legal, but also social responsibilities that go beyond the mere expectations of society. In exceeding their legal responsibilities, firms signal their ethical engagement and might even get involved in the voluntary funding of charitable activities entirely disconnected from their business operations (Griffin and Prakash, 2010). In this context, organizations are value-oriented, assess their responsibilities and establish their social policies in accordance with their philosophy, values and principles (Weaver and Treviño, 1999).

From a firm-centred perspective, stakeholder relations also play an important role in the firm's strategy: they are vital to maintain its activity, reputation capital and long-term capacity to create value (Porter and Kramer, 2002). In other words, corporations are keen to maintain good relations with their stakeholders because their institutional and market legitimacy could deteriorate if they failed to do so (Harrison, Bosse and Phillips, 2010). Yet, in that perspective, the necessity to comply with the needs of their stakeholders shapes managers' responsibility. Thus, the level of analysis (organizational or societal) that managers use to respond to these needs determines whether responsibility is compliant or moral and its purpose strategic or altruistic (Tashman and Raelin, 2013).

Finally, corporations are accountable to the societies they belong to and liable to the legal systems they depend on. From that angle, their responsibility is engaged to the point that, in case of failure, their agents can be prosecuted for an offence or a crime. In that case, the moral responsibility may result in criminal liability. Thus, the notion of responsibility can encompass moral, compliant, social and legal dimensions.

Stakeholder orientation

Whether they refer to moral, compliant or legal responsibility, organizations develop a variety of stakeholder orientations that range from keeping an individualistic and distant connection, to being part of a broader community (Brickson, 2005). A number of determinants can prompt organizations to develop weak or strong relations with their stakeholders: leadership, the organization's culture and history, markets, strategies, etc. Amid them, the intensity of specific ethical issues (Jones, 1991; Roberts, 2003) with social consequences (safety, public health, pollution hazards, etc.), exacerbated by public and political pressure, affects the business environment and shapes the social dynamics that exist at various levels of the supply chains of large industries. Inevitably, the question of responsibility is critical under such circumstances due to the potentiality of ensuing legal charges and criminal prosecution. Combined with the dependence of organizations upon their suppliers, clients and professional associations, high-intensity social issues introduce tension and conflict in business social relations.

High-intensity ethical issues are common in highly regulated industries such as chemicals, pharmaceuticals, nuclear energy or mining industries. In addition to those, two business activities also encounter such issues: food and cosmetics. The food industry is frequently under the scrutiny of consumer associations, NGOs and the media: drinking too much soda is a factor of obesity, aspartame can be carcinogenic and beef has deceitfully been replaced by horse meat in some of the most famous European brands of frozen foodstuffs, to name just a few among the most recent food scandals. The cosmetics industry, although more discrete, is also regularly accused of unethical practices.

Allergenic substances and animal testing are among the issues that made the headlines in recent years.

Business activities with direct interaction with consumer markets (business-to- consumers, or B2C) are particularly sensitive to ethical issues, given the high exposure of brand names and ensuing reputational damage. Conversely, business-to-business (B2B) firms suffer less from public exposure, but more from the demanding requirements from their clients. When the scandal erupts, B2C organizations urgently install a state of emergency to make urgent decisions and decide upon communication strategies and the implementation of action plans. The informants reported that preceding crises, such as the mad cow disease or BSE (bovine spongiform encephalopathy), traumatized the industry. When such crises occur, flavourists and perfumers need to reformulate a large number of products, and the whole organization strives to reconquer customers. In the aftermath of these events, managers tend to establish defence parameters in their work processes to avoid facing "tyrannical" customer demands (as one of my informants, the CEO of Beta, put it). Such circumstances necessarily affect the relationships with customers, their most critical stakeholders.

The business of flavours and fragrances

This industry is highly innovative, discreet and even secretive (Barraquier, 2013). As early as the seventeenth century, artisans located in Grasse, in Southern France began the distillation of fragrant flowers to elaborate perfume compounds made from rose, jasmine, lavender and violet. Fragrances were initially used in the leather gloves industry. Leather possesses a persistent and unpleasant smell. After World War II, the chemical industry in Germany and Switzerland became interested in the development of artificial flavour and synthetic fragrance. Large industrial firms emerged in Japan (Takasago, Hasegawa) and the United States (IFF). Nowadays, the industry produces fragrant compounds for perfumery, cosmetics and detergents, as well as sophisticated flavours for the food and pharmaceutical industries. Although distinctive in their extraction processes, flavours and fragrances are core products stemming from the same core competences.

To obtain fragrant compounds, conventional methods are steam distillation processes and solvent extractions. Flavours can be natural or artificial. Artificial flavours result from a complex chemical process reproducing natural olfaction molecules. Different processes can extract natural flavours. Maceration of raw materials with water and alcohol produces infusions, while maceration and distillation of peel, pulp, leaves or flowers produce alcoholates. Extraction of a soluble product from an essential oil, concentration from infusions, introduction of a washing phase in the concentration process that results in concentrates, depectinization followed by pressing of the pulp, centrifugation and evaporation to obtain aqueous concentrates are among the most common processes. All these operations therefore provide mixtures that vary in concentration and density. Mixtures are liquid flavourings obtained from raw materials. Natural flavours can also be extracted by solvents.

The flavours and fragrances industry is a business-to-business activity, working with high-profile customer organizations such as Nestlé, Coca-Cola, Unilever, Johnson & Johnson, LOréal, Danone, Estee Lauder, Chanel, Dior etc. As a result, F&F organizations are never in contact with final consumers, and none of its products can be found in retail stores. Informants in the study insisted that they were not the direct market providers. This is probably why the F&F industry is unknown to the public. In 2015, the total sales figure of the sector accounted for about 24 billion dollars.[1]

Methods

This chapter elaborates from previous work done with the same set of data. The first study explored how F&F organizations have come to share common attributes of identity with their competitors under the pressure of clients and regulators (Barraquier, 2013). Through an analogy drawn from anthropological studies, the analysis defined the relations of F&F organizations as clannish: "managers described their organizations as forming a family (that I call 'clan') whose members may fight, but are bound by strong ties such as values, attributes of identity, and common interests. The clan comprises the organization, and its competitors and clients". In continuity with the first study, this chapter examines further the relations among F&F organizations (competitors), and between these organizations and their clients, to look at the question of how responsibility is discursively negotiated over the critical issue of product toxicity.

The study was conducted in six organizations of the F&F industry, ranking in the top ten companies of the sector. The top ten represent 70% of the total sales worldwide.[2] They are all highly internationalized. Some are smaller (from 500 to 1,500 employees) compared to bigger competitors (> 5,000 employees). Among the top ten, ownership is public, semi-private (publicly traded with family control) or private. The two leading corporations in the field, Givaudan and Firmenich, are respectively public and private and display very different management styles. They all compete on the same markets, often for the same customers. A qualitative study conducted in different organizations of the same industry enables the researcher to have a criterion of comparability between these companies and to achieve a replication of the results (Yin, 2003). In summary, the study includes thirty-six interviews in six companies and one professional association. All companies are European, with five different national backgrounds. To preserve the anonymity of firms and informants, they have been renamed with Greek letters (Alpha, Beta, Gamma, Delta, Kappa and Sigma).

The case study consists of three units of analysis in each case (organization): strategic management, support functions managers and operation managers. Strategic management comprises top executives such as CEOs. Then, support functions encompass quality, environmental management, safety and regulatory affairs managers. Support function managers interact on a regular basis with one or more external stakeholders of the organization. Operation managers (sales, R&D, production) form the last group. They enact solutions for social issues of the company and are in direct contact with primary stakeholders such as customers, suppliers and the employees forming their teams. To do so they work with the managers of support functions. They are users of the services and recommendations provided by support functions.

All three categories of managers are very much involved with two groups of stakeholders: competitors and customers. The data collected showed their predominance over other stakeholders in the social relations of F&F managers. That is why this chapter focuses on this specific relationship.

Findings

Competitors

An "incestuous" pattern of relations

The F&F industry has a long history and ancestry, and its member organizations have known each other well for a long time. In addition, F&F organizations do not only compete against each other when final products' customers[3] shortlist them and send their commercial briefs, but they also serve as suppliers or buyers of their fellow industry members. Therefore, competitors have a dual status; one is the classical enemy, the other the opportunistic ally.

Such circumstances promote close relations that the informants of the study described as "incestuous" in several occasions. These frequent relationships create strong and weak links between individuals of competing organizations. It is the consistency and the continuity of these links that create permeability between businesses and result in leakage of skills to the competitors. The F&F industry becomes, for those entering it, a small world. This is why there is little migration outside the industry, a phenomenon amplified by the development of specific knowledge assets.

Innovation, the basis for competition

In the F&F business, various professional and technical lines of expertise coexist. Upstream is the fabrication of natural (essential oils) or synthetic raw materials, and downstream, the composition and manufacturing of fragrant compounds and flavours. Raw materials manufacturers often practice the second field of expertise, that of composition. It is the most artistic (with star perfumers and flavourists), most rewarding and most profitable one. It requires much know-how and little capital.

In the creation process, perfumers and flavourists use a large variety of substances. A perfume is comparable to a music composition, a frequently used metaphor in the industry: an incense–licorice–violet accord or raspberry–peach–vanilla–orange blossom accord are illustrations of the way perfumers define their compositions. These substances are usually available in the lab where formulas are designed, yet, perfume or flavour designers cannot always find them within their organization, even if it manufactures raw materials. Therefore, it is customary to purchase them from competitors. In particular, research units of an F&F company can discover a new molecule and patent it. Innovation lies in the discovery and the patenting of new molecules capable of delivering a new flavour or fragrance, because the patent holder can hold it captive, providing a profitable economic rent for the company. Logically, the opposite is also true: a competitor can become a client when he does not dispose of the raw material he needs to manufacture a particular flavour or fragrance for a client.

Holding a patent represents a considerable competitive advantage and provides the holder with the capacity to either disseminate or restrain the use of the molecule. Yet, the industry's self-regulation highest authority, IFRA,[4] its scientific institute the RIFM[5] and expert panel RexPan[6] all monitor the commercial use of these molecules. Indeed, odour molecules may contain substances that become allergenic at a certain quantity level. For some of these substances, regulatory agencies have imposed thresholds. In most cases, the industry has self-regulated the use of these substances to avoid unfavourable regulation, and the patent holder has a say in the decision over the limitation of use of its product.

A regulatory affairs manager (Beta) interviewed for the study could not repress his admiration for a competitor (Sigma) who had deliberately limited the use of a captive molecule to minimize sensitization effects:

> Sigma, in their great wisdom, said that this product should not be used to a concentration level higher than 0,01% in final products. I remember, when it happened 15 years ago, everybody in the profession shouted in rage, saying that they were mad, because

this product was so marvellous. They were holding the patent. Well, they demanded that an IFRA standard be created, and we can pay tribute to their determination because today this product is not on the list of potential allergens.

By making a responsible decision, Sigma increased its competitive advantage produced through costly technological innovation. It provided its competitors/customers with a unique fragrant molecule, still in use in numerous formulas and protected the whole profession from tougher regulation.

The conclusion of this story is that responsibility pays, but the vivid discussion that took place then over the use of this molecule is a reminder of the reality that short-term prospect of commercial gains can blind less responsible competitors.

> We shouted, and I was among those who shouted, I was furious, the perfumers were furious, because we were using it in massive doses resulting in 0,2% on the skin. And there, it was limited to 0,01%. . . . Well, now it is an IFRA standard . . . so the industry has nonetheless, acted responsibly.

While Beta managers initially opposed resistance to the decision, this manager in his candid statement not only recognizes his initial error, but also takes credit for a decision viewed as collective (the industry, the clan). He describes the use of this product as a common good that members have been able to use on the long-term as a community.

Regulation, the basis for cooperation

Yet, a crucial element of the development of business in this industry is the high level of state regulation. Regulatory issues prevail in the discussions and social relations between managers but also capture the attention of managers in their interactions with counterparts in rival organizations. Highly regulated organizational fields institutionalize spaces of dialogue, neutral grounds free from the hostility of market competition. For instance, all F&F organizations mandate executives in charge of regulatory affairs to attend work sessions organized by dedicated professional associations. On these grounds, cooperation between member organizations is the rule. Decisions bound to self-regulation practices and defence strategies against government regulation are popular topics in these meetings.

Cooperation is needed to avoid legal sanctions. In that respect, when asked whether he envisioned the vigilance over product toxicity as a responsibility towards society, the president of a national-level professional association responded:

> In this domain I would speak of criminal liability of the manager. Now, what about our responsibility about product safety? First, we are not consumer market providers. We manufacture industrial goods. To what level do we guarantee these intermediary goods, and how do we guarantee them? Well, for fragrances, we have an ethical conduct code, which means that our products are thoroughly tested and can be used safely if prescribed quantities are respected. This is written in the IFRA code of good conduct, an international code widely recognized by our clients". And then, later, he added that "an IFRA member who does not respect the code is ostracized, sanctioned, and can be excluded by the profession.

This particular quote reveals that a procedure defined in collaboration between competitors is creating a bond between competitors, a form of sacred commitment. This tacit agreement can turn against any member breaking the rules. In doing so, they use cooperation to share responsibilities. This results in an equal sharing of the risk, making the procedure quite egalitarian. For instance, when the profession was required to disclose the allergenic substances contained in their perfume formulas on the labels of cosmetic products, they organized meetings to discuss it. One of the leading companies argued that they preferred to set up their own labelling strategies. The others, feeling that this position was defended to secure a competitive advantage, all came together to say no to a "label competition" (story reported by the CEO of Alpha). Attacks from hostile stakeholders (consumer associations and other NGOs) against consumer goods containing fragrance (i.e. shampoo) or flavour (i.e. a yoghourt), generate a greater need for cooperation. Such attacks produce a shockwave in the industry. They target their clients, who invariably turn to their supply chains. Crises tend to enhance cooperation strategies within the industry.

Another field of cooperation can also be the use of common resources for expensive innovations. A 2006 EU regulation stipulated that, in the future, the cosmetics industry should not resort to animal testing for their in-vivo experiments. Instead, it develops tests to formulate non-toxic and non-allergenic products. Alternative solutions necessitate costly fundamental research protocols that a company alone can hardly finance. To respond efficiently and responsibly to the new regulatory dispositions, the F&F industry in Europe organized public-private partnerships to be able to fund this research programme and benefit from it on an equal footing. Does this undermine competition or a competitive mindset within the industry? As put by the CEO of Alpha, "Let's not forget that we are all competitors, and put in common not what we have, but what we don't have".

Clients

Clients are considered as dominant stakeholders in many industries, and for decades, the dominant motto of business was "The customer is king". Like elsewhere, clients are dominant stakeholders of F&F organizations, and they are particularly prevalent in the lives of F&F managers. However, top management confesses, "I tell the company's executives that the 'customer king' had turned into a 'customer tyrant'. Clients impose a ruthless logic that does not leave any free space for our companies" (Beta CEO). A product safety executive at Kappa complained that, after Greenpeace launched a campaign to boycott an ingredient, "Even though this ingredient is considered to be totally safe, clients will ask you what your policy is concerning this ingredient, and if you don't respond, they will blacklist you. This is more or less terrorism!".

As discussed in the previous section – IFRA standards to self-regulate the use of substances –, the question about what "totally safe" means, is critical to understand the dilemmas that F&F executives are facing. Molecules and other products are vital to the creation of new flavours and fragrances and if NGOs, consumer associations or regulatory agencies target a core product, it can be a tragedy for perfumers or flavourists. "Now the perfumers are disillusioned, they spend their time cutting formulas – 'customers don't want this ingredient, let's remove it'. They don't even try to see how it smells. We are heading towards a McDonald's type of perfumery" (Beta head of regulatory affairs).

Informants confirm that the pressure about social and environmental concerns has moved up the value chain. Retailers have transferred social claims to consumer goods manufacturers, who in turn ask ingredient manufacturers to deal with it. Prior literature about CSR practices in the supply chain described this shockwave phenomenon, but mostly in the context of international sourcing in emerging economies. F&F suppliers (top 10) are in Europe, the US and Japan, and so are their clients. The issue of toxicity differs from ethical and responsible practices commonly discussed in the supply chain management literature (i.e. safety and labour conditions).

Yet, the major difference lies in the level of expertise involved in the products. It produces an odd situation, an asymmetry of specialized knowledge between F&F organizations and their clients, a dependence of customers who do not have the control over expert knowledge and an increase of the knowledge codification in response to transparency demands from customers. All three dimensions affect the meaning of responsibility, its perception by organizations and their clients and provide clues to understand how it affects their engagement in responsible practices.

Knowledge asymmetry

The context of high-expertise results in a closed network of expert organizations and highly skilled individuals talking the same language and developing strong ties amid themselves. This is due to the complexity of the knowledge required to navigate the field. Clients buy this expertise because they do not possess the know-how, knowledge or technology: "market providers are increasingly inviting us to inform them and supply knowledge on what they provide to markets" (President of a national professional association).

Customers need to reduce the uncertainty created by the complex knowledge environment, and requirements to supply that information is growing: "Direct market providers are increasingly going to demand information on what they put on the market. So there, the responsibility will increase exponentially, I'm absolutely sure of that". F&F organizations therefore acknowledge the increasing level of responsibility they will have to bear, as the president of this professional association stresses:

> If we are not aware of our social responsibility and criminal liability, we cannot progress economically. We live in a world where this is just going to grow. . . . This responsibility will grow considerably, we will be responsible over an enormous amount of things in the coming years even though I do not have a crystal ball, I draw from my own experience of the past ten years.

Knowledge dependence

Clients find themselves to be information-dependent. One key account manager provides an illustration of this ambiguity:

> We all supply ingredients lacking definitive evidence of non-toxicity. . . . We could easily make false allegations to our clients. They are not in capacity to verify them, if we do not tell them that such substance is part of the product, while it should not be there. . . . So, we engage our responsibility.

Yet, in parallel, he makes clear that clients are ultimately liable: "our responsibility is not direct, it comes second, behind our clients". In 2005, consumer associations in Europe denounced the opacity over the use of allergenic ingredients in cosmetics, mostly contained in the fragrant compounds. The debate was vivid in Europe, and the cosmetics industry had to face an unprecedented wave of negative publicity conveyed by the media. The same informant reports that clients were inquiring about "the presence of benzene and formaldehyde in the formulas, etc. They imposed us not to go to the media, saying WE go; however everything we say will be based on what you told us".

Knowledge codification and transparency

In parallel to the dependence created by the asymmetry of expert knowledge, clients are increasing their demands of knowledge transparency. The need for greater accountability towards consumers, the regulator and society disperses the locus of responsibility and creates defiance between the suppliers of flavours and fragrances and their clients. Clients strive for the most complete insurance of their liability while they expect their suppliers to elaborate products with responsibility. "We must bring total evidence of the non-toxicity of the ingredients we provide" (Pres-national-association). This request may sound mundane, but in reality, it implies the disclosure of formulas in most cases.

For instance, the obligation to include the list of ingredients on personal care products labels in Europe in 2006 followed the publication of 26 allergenic substances found in perfume formulas. F&F organizations fought the EU directive that increased their vulnerability to counterfeiting. Clients retorted: "look people, whose product is it, ours or yours? Ours of course! And we agree to the labelling" (president of a national professional association). The informant then added: "I can show you a letter where the COLIPA[7] says 'we cannot conceive that your position could be different from ours'". A winning formula is the result of the qualified work of flavourists (i.e. new flavour for an ice cream) or perfumers (i.e. perfume compound in a lotion). Flavourists and perfumers receive several years of training in specialized schools to develop their ability to taste and smell and to combine scents and tastes harmoniously. At the highest level of the profession, a talented perfumer is considered an artist (a nose) and is paid a high salary. Once they have conceived a new flavour or perfume, the formula cannot be patented. Therefore, the labelling of the list of ingredients serves formulas on a platter to anyone wanting to imitate it. The formula is a codified (explicitly written) form of knowledge but is the result of an intangible, experiential form of knowledge.

The findings have implications in several ways, both ethical and strategic. These implications are discussed in the following section.

Discussion

How do personal care and food industries assume their ethical responsibilities, given the specific supply chain conditions described in the previous section? The study examined a highly regulated business activity supplying critical ingredients to their clients, where fierce competition, combined with the increasing pressure from governments, consumers and activists about the safety of consumer goods, drives organizations to innovate. In that process, the sophistication of the knowledge needed to pursue innovation programmes has steadily grown in recent years. F&F manufacturers have developed high-level technological expertise that remains largely inaccessible to non-experts. As a result, the complexity of that expertise has created a distance between them and their clients that consists of a knowledge asymmetry making clients knowledge-dependent, in particular in a social context where ethical issues concerning food or cosmetics can be raised unpredictably. In such circumstances, the moral responsibility as well as the legal liability of food or personal care products manufacturers is at stake.

Their response to the F&F industry is to reduce the knowledge gap and use their customer power to require either more transparency on the knowledge used in their final product or a modification of formula if an ingredient is the subject of mere suspicion from consumer associations. Such social dynamics are interesting to discuss responsibility, because they raise important questions. One is the legitimate concern over the potential risk of inconsistency of the moral responsibility; another is the growing increase of complexity in the development of products that consumers use daily, and a third one is about the variation in the way suppliers and customers characterize responsibility. The discussion concludes that organizations, professional associations and consumer goods manufacturers do not thrive to achieve moral responsibility but to preserve their respective legitimacies.

Customers, professional associations and suppliers share responsibilities among themselves. F&F organizations have organized standard procedures of responsibility, through the classical market mechanisms of competition and cooperation. Competition spurs innovation, while cooperation furthers self-regulation. At the heart of both mechanisms, complex expert knowledge plays an important role. To lower their financial efforts and increase the recognition of their scientific credentials, F&F organizations institutionalize their practices within professional associations that organize the self-regulation procedures and play an active role in the promotion of responsible practices among industry members.

Finally, they deliver fragrant compounds or flavours to their customers who bear the legal liability of the final products. It seems that responsibility is shared among stakeholders, but in reality, the locus of responsibility is disseminated rather than shared, generating a risk of inconsistency in the pursuit of a common ethical objective. The ethical issue at stake in food and personal care products is the safety and health of the consumer. It is likely that F&F organizations as well as their clients internally discuss that issue in ethical terms. Yet, because they are based on power and coercion, coordination mechanisms among F&F competitors, and with their clients, are not implicitly designed in the interest of the consumer and, thus, may not be able to fully deal with the ethical dimension of product toxicity. Power-based relations do not encourage a dialogue between competitors and with customers. The F&F industry knows that its reliability is at stake if an ingredient is found toxic, and its customers permanently risk legal prosecution and the ensuing loss of reputation. It is not the ethical engagement, but the fear over the loss of trust and reputation that predicts responsibility. The protection of the consumer appears in the commercial discourse, but not in business interactions.

The second issue is that the stock of codified knowledge in F&F organizations is decreasing to the benefit of their clients. Clients tend to come down with a sledgehammer when less radical measures could be negotiated. The case of the totally safe ingredient that has to be eliminated from the formula is an illustration of this sledgehammer strategy. As soon as an NGO, consumer association or press article expresses doubts about a substance, consumer goods manufacturers blacklist it even though there might be no scientific evidence to support those doubts. In large corporations, micro-level operations (such as procurement departments), are subordinate to the financial objectives of their business unit. Putting at risk the organization's brand(s) is unconceivable. Therefore, covering up with a large umbrella is viewed as the most efficient and radical way to achieve their objectives, and using their customer power is part of the game to lower the risk to zero. In the short term, it appears to be effective; yet, in the long run it can produce negative outcomes.

If codified knowledge value is lower, F&F organizations will increasingly turn to complex knowledge to survive and compete, leveraging complexity and opacity of the sector for non-experts. This trend has accelerated in the past decades with the introduction of biotechnologies and of a more complex chemistry arsenal. Flavours are developed at molecular level, and consumers would be surprised to know that an animal origin is possible at the molecular level of a fruit flavour. Soon enough, nanotechnologies will enter flavourists' labs. Consumer goods procurement managers cover up because the complexity of the products they buy increases their opacity and ambiguity. Yet, the more they will use this heavy artillery as a negotiation technique over the question of safety, the more F&F organizations will resort to complex knowledge. The question here is . . . somewhat of a chicken and egg debate.

Finally, this chapter shows that the meaning and representation of responsibility is constructed in very different ways by the F&F industry (organizations and professional associations) and by customers. The former refers to science, while the latter define it as the response and behaviour expected by the public (consumers, NGOs, media, etc.) to avoid prosecution and damage to the brand's image. F&F organizations (and associations) rely on scientific expertise to build and consolidate what they consider and perceive to be their responsibility. Even though their success is challenged by fierce competition and is dependent upon their capacity to innovate, they admit that their customers, as direct market providers, are exposed to public disgrace and legal liability, while they are not. Of course, a serious accident involving an ingredient can potentially trigger a chain reaction, but their responsibility is mostly based on their accountability to their customers and the collectively constructed scientific expertise. As a result, they are dismayed when a product considered as very safe by the profession is questioned. Evidence-based and scientifically secured processes leading to rational conclusions are, for them, the best response to irrational fears.

F&F organizations perceive their customers' approach with disbelief. Even though their accounts only reflect their perception, and not the perspective of consumer goods manufacturers themselves, the evidence emerging from a number of stories is interesting. According to them, customers' decisions to eliminate a product from a formula are guided by different motivations: the fear of public scrutiny, the desire to control risks at any cost, the avoidance of legal prosecution and finally the preservation of these firms' most precious asset, their reputation. Inevitably, these firms construct responsibility not as an engagement but as a set of precautions designed to protect themselves before anything else. The responsibility towards the consumer appears as a positive outcome of this behaviour, not as an objective.

Limitations and conclusions

As for any qualitative study, this chapter does not suggest that its conclusions are generalizable. Qualitative papers are more exploratory in nature and propose new insights testable in further studies. Nevertheless, the collection of data in the same industry lead to a saturation of results, meaning that the similarity of the data increased as more data was collected, leading to a repetition of patterns. It is likely that a similar interview protocol used in other highly regulated industries would produce very similar results. For instance, other industries like chemicals, pharmaceuticals and biotechnologies face similar health and safety issues. Furthermore, we think that some service industries like banking and insurance could very well show very similar results.

Even though there is a clear tendency of the markets to demand more transparent and responsible processes, in reality, responsibility is diluted and the sophistication of technological and industrial processes has intensified in the past decades. Instead of simplicity and transparency, the industry (clients and suppliers) provides markets with more complexity and opacity. In examining the negotiations between customers and suppliers over responsibility issues, this study sheds a new light on the power relations between them. The findings reveal the intensity of the social dynamics involved and point at the outcomes they produce.

Several trends emerge: the pressure of civil society for zero-tolerance over consumer safety increases, consumer goods manufacturers toughen up their procurement policies, and the expertise intensifies. This chapter elaborated on the dissemination of responsibility, on the divergence in perceptions of responsibility and on the transformation of the knowledge (from simple to complex) used to manufacture food and personal care products. Simultaneously, we observe a determination of organizations to be recognized as scientific experts (F&F), as regulation authorities (professional associations) and as highly regarded brand names (consumer goods manufacturers). Suppliers, professional associations and consumer goods industries seek different types of legitimacy in order to pursue their business objectives.

Do consumers really want more food technology in their plates? Are they unaware of the silent wars taking place between buyers and suppliers? Do they support the instrumental use of ethical issues to their expense? Chances are they do not.

Notes

1 *Source*: Leffingwell & Associates, www.leffingwell.com/top_10.htm
2 *Source*: Leffingwell & Associates, www.leffingwell.com/top_10.htm
3 For instance, the customer could be Nestlé (customer) buying a mint flavour for a chocolate bar (final product) or Estee Lauder (customer) buying a fragrant compound for a body lotion (final product).
4 IFRA: International Fragrance Association. It is a major professional association regrouping all F&F organizations as members at the international level. It establishes standards and provides technical and regulatory guidance to its members and is the highest self-regulation authority in the field (www.ifra.org).
5 RIFM: Research Institute on Fragrance Materials. It publishes research on the industry, either from the private research conducted by organization members or from university researchers.
6 RexPan: Research Expert Panel, a permanent committee of RIFM consisting of scientific experts from various academic institutions across the world, which RIFM describes as independent.
7 COLIPA is the former name of Cosmetics Europe, a professional association representing member companies operating in the field of cosmetics and personal care.

References

Barraquier, A. (2013). A group identity analysis of organizations and their stakeholders: Porosity of identity and mobility of attributes. *Journal of Business Ethics*, *115*(1), 45–62.

Brickson, S. (2005). Organizational identity orientation: Forging a link between organizational identity and organizations' relations with stakeholders'. *Administrative Science Quarterly*, *50*, 576–609.

Donaldson, T. and Dunfee, T. W. (1994). Toward a unified conception of business ethics: Integrative social contracts theory. *Academy of Management Review*, *19*(2), 252–284.

Griffin, J. J. and Prakash, A. (2010). Corporate responsibility: Initiatives and mechanisms. *Business & Society*, *49*(1), 179–184.

Harrison, J. S., Bosse, D. A. and Phillips, R. A. (2010). Managing for stakeholders, stakeholder utility functions, and competitive advantage. *Strategic Management Journal*, *31*(1), 58–74.

Jones, T. M. (1991). Ethical decision making by individuals in organizations: An issue-contingent model. *Academy of Management Review, 16*(2), 366–395.

Porter, M. E. and Kramer, M. R. (2002). The competitive advantage of corporate philanthropy. *Harvard Business Review, 80*(12), 56–68.

Roberts, S. (2003). Supply chain specific? Understanding the patchy success of ethical sourcing initiatives. *Journal of Business Ethics, 44*(2–3), 159–170.

Tashman, P. and Raelin, J. (2013). Who and what really matters to the firm: Moving stakeholder salience beyond managerial perceptions. *Business Ethics Quarterly, 23*(04), 591–616.

Weaver, G. R. and Treviño, L. K. (1999). Compliance and values oriented ethics programs: Influences on employees' attitudes and behavior. *Business Ethics Quarterly, 9*(02), 315–335.

Yin, R. (2003). *Case Study Research Design and Methods*, 3rd edition. Thousand Oaks, CA: Sage.

3.6 Cooperative relations for e-waste management

Ivan A. Bozhikin and Nikolay A. Dentchev

Introduction

One of the world's fastest growing municipal waste streams is the waste of electrical and electronic equipment (WEEE) (Perkins et al., 2014; Sarapuu, 2015; Baldé et al., 2015; Man, Naidu and Wong, 2013; Cucchiella et al., 2015). The fast growing character of WEEE as a waste stream is relevant to both the European Union (EU; Eurostat, 2015) and to Africa (Sarapuu, 2015; Cucchiella et al., 2015), two continents with totally different approaches to waste management. Despite the difference on both continents, WEEE requires to be processed in an effective manner (Robinson, 2009; Fu et al., 2012). To that end, this chapter focuses on the cooperative relations among the most important stakeholders in the e-waste sector: municipalities, industry organizations, NGOs, residents, private owned collectors and recyclers. The cooperative relations among these stakeholders are key for at least three reasons: 1) for improving the collection and treatment of e-waste, 2) for achieving high levels of eco-efficiency and recycling and 3) for reducing the transaction cost in the whole process (Coase, 1937; Williamson, 1981; Williamson, 2010). In other words, a relational approach to stakeholder engagement improves the effectiveness of e-waste management.

In this chapter, we argue that the cooperative relations of stakeholders are necessary in distinct contexts. In this sense, the contexts of the EU and East Africa are quite different in terms of e-waste management. In the EU, there are well-established policies and legislations for e-waste management (Widmer et al., 2005; RoHS Guide, 2015; Atasu and Wassenhove, 2012). The WEEE take-back obligation was also implemented (Leysen and Preillon, 2014; Oguchi et al., 2011; Nakajima and Vanderburg, 2005), increasing the responsibility of the producers and distributors of electronic appliances (Executive Environment Agency, 2013; Atasu and Subramanian, 2012; Sander et al., 2007). After all, well-established regulations for e-waste management provide a solid frame for the cooperative relations between various stakeholders. We note the collaboration of NGOs, public organizations and private organizations to realize the e-waste management according to the respective regulations.

However, in contrast to EU, East African countries are lacking such elaborated regulations on e-waste management (Ongondo, Williams and Cherrett, 2011; Tedre, Bangu and Nyagava, 2009). Moreover, East African countries are also lacking state-of-the-art e-waste management facilities (Ongondo, Williams and Cherrett, 2011; Oguchi, Sakanakura and Terazono, 2013; Asante et al., 2012). And there is no take-back obligation. Therefore, the collection, dismantling and recycling of e-waste is carried out by private companies. These private initiatives are supported by NGOs and public officials in order to establish effective e-waste management (Wasswa and Schluep, 2008). In other words, even without strict regulations, we note that the relational cooperation of NGOs, private organizations and public organizations is also present in East African countries. Our chapter contributes to understand the cooperative relations of stakeholders to resolve challenging e-waste management issues, despite their diverging interests (cf. Dentchev, 2009). Diverging stakeholder interests are quite straightforward in the case of e-waste management. Private companies have profit objectives. Government organizations focus typically at the enforcement of regulations and the generation of social goods, while NGOs focus at the resolution of issues close to their organizational mission. In contrast to private organizations, government organizations and NGOs have a non-profit orientation.

This chapter is organized in four sections. Firstly, we present a literature review of e-waste management. Secondly, we elaborate on the research method adopted in this study, and the quality measures taken in terms of validity and reliability. Thirdly, we present the results of the study, focusing on the cooperation as an important factor of an effective e-waste management. Fourthly, we present the conclusions of this study.

E-waste management

E-waste is defined in Oxford Dictionaries as "discarded electronic appliances such as mobile phones, computers and televisions". More detailed definition of e-waste is provided by Baldé et al. (2015, p. 11) who determine e-waste as "a term used to cover all items of electrical and electronic equipment and its parts that have been discarded by its owner as waste without the intent of re-use". The rapid growth of e-waste volume during the last few years is a result mainly of the extremely rapid development of the technological innovations and of the short lifespan of many electronic devices (Yamane et al., 2011; Polák and Drápalová, 2012). However, the increasing pile of e-waste is not the only issue associated with it. Environmental concerns related to waste management are another important consideration. In fact, e-waste contains typically dangerous materials like cadmium, lead and mercury, which form an environmental concern if not treated effectively (Leung, Cai and Wong, 2006; Wäger, Hischier and Eugster, 2011; Morf et al., 2007; Robinson, 2009; Song, Wang and Li, 2013). Therefore, e-waste management under primitive methods (e.g. open burning) could be dangerous (Gullett et al., 2007), and thus better regulated processes are recommended (Robinson, 2009; Fu et al., 2012; Sepúlveda et al., 2010; Söderström, 2003; Jain and Sareen, 2006). In other words, we consider as an effective e-waste management one that contains sound economic and environmental logic.

One of the most often used policy instruments for processing WEEE are the so-called extended producer responsibility (EPR) schemes (Widmer et al., 2005; Baldé et al., 2015; Wang and Chen, 2013). EPR schemes are associated with the adoption of specific legislation, which determines the responsibilities of producers, waste managers, government authorities and consumers (Nnorom and Osibanjo, 2008; Khetriwal, Kraeuchi and Widmer, 2009; Wang and Chen, 2013). While EPR schemes are common in Europe, to many developing countries, such legislation is simply absent (Schluep et al., 2008; Ongondo et al., 2011; Baldé et al., 2015; Widmer et al., 2005; Nnorom and Osibanjo, 2008). Hence, in many developing countries from Asia, Africa and Latin America, the informal sector plays an essential (Oteng-Ababio, Amankwaa and Chama, 2014; Chi et al., 2011). Yet, e-waste management in the informal sector is has not much concern for environmental footprint (Rochat and Laissaoui, 2008; BAN, 2005; Ongondo et al., 2011; Schluep et al.,

2008). And we need to emphasize here that developing countries lack both the infrastructure and the institutional governance necessary to guide economically and environmentally effective e-waste management.

Moreover, we need to also acknowledge the dumping of e-waste from developed countries to developing ones under the name of "second hand goods" (BAN, 2005; Widmer et al., 2005; Zhang, Schnoor and Zeng, 2012; Kahhat and Williams, 2012; Ongondo et al., 2011) despite the adoption of the Basel Convention (United Nations Environment Programme, 2011; Basel Convention, 2011; Sepúlveda et al., 2010). According to Sthiannopkao and Wong (2013, p. 1151), "more than half of the e-waste collected for recycling in developed countries is sent for processing or disposal to the developing world". Unfortunately, this practice is making the problem of e-waste management worse. More effective approaches in economic and environmental terms are thus needed in developing countries.

Overall, we note that EU countries have a regulative frame that guides the cooperation with different stakeholders in the context of e-waste management. While developing countries do not have such a regulative frame, we question how it is possible to have an effective e-waste management in those countries. How can we resolve the above mentioned issues of lacking regulations, informal economy and environment unfriendly practices and realize effective e-waste management in terms of economics and ecological footprint?

Methods

We have adopted a case study (Yin, 2003; Brewerton and Millward, 2001) to address the above mentioned issues. We have studied e-waste management in Belgium (Europe) and Kenya (Africa) and formulated three research questions that guided our study: 1) Does the cooperation between actors from different sectors (public, private and voluntary) contribute to effective e-waste management? 2) How strong is the role of NGOs in e-waste management in Belgium? 3) How can an NGO contribute to better e-waste management in Kenya?

Data collection

We have studied how e-waste management is organized in Belgium and compared it the successful attempts of WorldLoop in e-waste management in Kenya. Data was collected in the first place by means of 22 semi-structured interviews with a length of 66 minutes on average. The interviews were conducted face-to-face, in English with a single waste management expert. Two out of 22 interviews were held over Skype. The conversations with our respondents were recorded and transcribed. The interviews were conducted in a period of 4 months: from April, 2015 to July, 2015. Respondents had various background and were affiliated to eighteen different organizations. To improve data reliability, interview data (primary information) were complemented with other sources of evidence, such as articles, reports and policy documentations (secondary information).

Respondents

Twenty-one of our 22 respondents are Belgian waste management experts, and one is Kenyan waste management expert (cf. Table 3.6.1). Yet, the case of WorldLoop in Kenya

Table 3.6.1 Interviews with 22 waste experts

№	Position	Organization	Country
	Public sector		
	(including two associations representing municipalities responsible for waste management)		
1	Head of Service Policy Innovation	OVAM	Belgium
2	Belgium Expert in Waste Management	EC, DG Environment	Belgium
3	Secretary General	Municipal Waste Europe	Belgium
4	Expert 1 in Circular Economy Department	Bruxelles Environnement – IBGE	Belgium
5	Expert 2 in Circular Economy Department	Bruxelles Environnement – IBGE	Belgium
6	Coordinator and Member of Staff Waste Management	Interafval (VVSG)	Belgium
7	Inspector General	ABP/ANB (Agence Bruxelles-Proprete)	Belgium
8	Secretary of the Board of the Directors	IVM	Belgium
9	Managing Director	EcoWERF	Belgium
	Private sector and producer responsibility organizations (PROs)		
	(including two associations representing PROs and private owned companies involved in waste management)		
10	Manager Strategy and Communication	SUEZ	Belgium
11	General Director	FEBEM	Belgium
12	Manager	WEEE Centre	Kenya
13	Communications Manager	Recupel	Belgium
14	Operation Manager	Recupel	Belgium
15	Business Relations Manager	Fost Plus	Belgium
16	Regulatory and Public Affairs Manager	EXPRA	Belgium
	Voluntary sector		
17	Project Director	WorldLoop	Belgium
18	Director of External & Partner Relations	WorldLoop	Belgium
19	Secretary General	ACR+	Belgium
	Scientific		
20	PhD	KU Leuven	Belgium
21	Professor	KU Leuven	Belgium
22	PhD candidate	Hasselt University	Belgium

Source: Drawn by authors based on the information gathered.

is a Belgian initiative; about half of the Belgian waste management experts provided valuable information about it, so we gathered enough evidence for e-waste management in Kenya. The criteria for choosing waste management experts include 1) their extensive knowledge in the field of e-waste management; 2) their experience and position in the organization in which they work; and 3) the type of the organization in which they work (private, public or voluntary sector). Most of our respondents have long experience in the waste management and leading positions in the organizations in which they work.

The selected waste experts for our study were government authority representatives, NGO representatives, scientists, waste management experts from different organizations and WorldLoop representatives. This range of respondents is a good basis for understanding how the strong cooperation between different actors from various sectors (public, private or voluntary) contributes to effective e-waste management in Belgium and in Kenya. Our respondents were asked ten questions that were similar for all of them.

Quality measures

In terms of reliability, a database was created with primary information (interview transcripts) and existing documents (secondary information) (Yin, 2003; Brewerton and
Millward, 2001). We recorded all interviews as a measure of reliability. The transcriptions
of interviews were sent to the respondents, who had 10 days to react. No reaction in that
timeframe means agreement with the transcripts.

In terms of validity, we took several methodological strategies to strengthen the constructive validity of our study. First, we combined the interview data with both internal
and external documents such as journal articles, reports, speeches and presentations, plans
and case studies of waste management, reports, newspapers. Second, two experts judged
the accuracy of gathered secondary information and the transcription of interviews without to provide their conclusions at the end. In addition, we interviewed 22 respondents in
order to receive information that would help us better understand how the cooperation
between different actors from various sectors (public, private and voluntary) improve the
e-waste management (Dentchev, 2005). As to the external validity of our findings, they
cannot be guaranteed with a single case.

Results

The results of our study are presented in two separate sub-sections. The first sub-section
elaborates on the sustainable e-waste management in Belgium while the second one
discusses the sustainable e-waste management in Kenya. Both sub-sections focus on the
cooperative relations as key elements for achieving effective e-waste management in these
two countries.

E-waste management in Belgium

There are well-established policies and legislations for WEEE in the European Union.
The first WEEE Directive and Restriction of Hazardous Substances (RoHS) Directive
(restricting the use of hazardous substances in electrical and electronic equipment) were
adopted in 2003 and revised respectively 2013 and 2014 (European Commission, 2015a,
2015b; Ongondo et al., 2011; RoHS Guide, 2015). Belgium, as a member state of the
EU, had to harmonize its legislations and policies to both directives. A key aspect of this
WEEE legislation is the Extended Producer Responsibility (EPR) scheme for e-waste
in Belgium (Eygena et al., 2016; EIMPACK, 2012). As a result, a producer responsibility
organization (PRO) called Recupel was created. It organized the whole system of e-waste
management in the country: from collection, sorting and treatment of e-waste to monitoring and reporting of activities (Eygena et al., 2016).

> Recupel is a management system. . . . Our role is to organize collection, to bring
> materials to treatment operators, to focus on the activities of treatment operators that
> they do and whether they achieve the targets.
>
> (Operation manager in Recupel)

Recupel is an industry-driven non-profit organization. It is organized in seven entities that
focus on different type of WEEE, and each entity has its own financial autonomy (Recupel, 2013a, p. 24). This non-profit organization collects both household and professional

equipment and aims at covering the full scope of e-waste (excluding solar panels) (Recupel, 2010). Moreover, this PRO has legal objectives that the European directive stipulates, applied in each collection category of e-waste (Recupel, 2014).

> [*Communications manager in Recupel*]: *"We are industry driven organization because the take-back obligation is the obligation of producers and importers. They are founders of Recupel. It is a collective system. We offer a national solution. . .. We are organizing collection and recycling. Behind that organization, there are seven different sectorial organization, different entities, different non-profit organizations [. . .] and they take the most important decisions relate to the high of the fee that the consumer has to pay, which appliances fell under the scope, and etc.".*

Recupel works closely with different stakeholders from various sectors (public, private and voluntary) based on tender procedures. It cooperates closely with municipalities and intermunicipal organizations, private collectors, recyclers, re-use centres and with the citizens (Recupel, 2013c). Based on these cooperative relations, Recupel constitutes one of the best e-waste management systems in the EU, reaching rates of 84% and 96% for all kinds of WEEE (Recupel, 2013a).

> [*Operation manager in Recupel*]: *"We have objectives for each material streams (Ferrous, not-ferrous and synthetics). I think this is unique in Europe, that we are only country have these targets. And all recycling objectives are reached easily. The reason for that is that companies working with Recupel, they work in cooperation with Recupel, with some of them we work from the beginning".*

However, Recupel cannot function without cooperative relations with other organizations. The most important stakeholders involved in e-waste management system are analyzed and discussed below (cf. Figure 3.6.1).

E-waste is collected by three main actors: retailers, municipalities (intermunicipal organizations) and re-use centres (Recupel, 2013c). Municipalities and intermunicipal

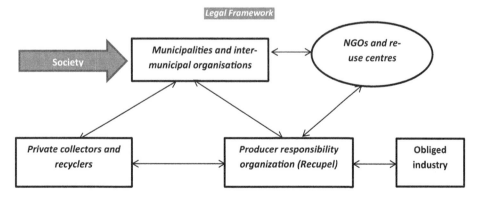

Figure 3.6.1 Important actors involved in the e-waste management system in Belgium and the cooperation between them

Source: Authors drawing based on the gathered information.

organizations have their own container parks to collect various solid wastes, including e-waste. In Belgium, there are over 540 container parks that form a very strong network for e-waste collection (EIMPACK, 2012). Moreover, municipalities keep close connection to their citizens and provide a lot of information campaigns on separate collection of e-waste. As a result, the municipalities play an essential role in the WEEE collection in Belgium. Based on tender contracts, Recupel keeps strong partnership with municipalities and intermunicipal organizations.

> *[Communications Manager in Recupel]: "There are three main collection possibilities. The most important are container parks. They are responds for 60% of total volume. Then, retailers ... [a] nd used-good centers are also responsible for certain percentage (8–10%)".*

Retailers of electronic appliances are also involved in the collection of e-waste due to their take-back obligation (Recupel, 2013a). Everyone selling electronics and electricity equipment is obliged to take back redundant material from consumers. But, retailers are not necessarily obliged to work with Recupel. They can choose another operator. But, if retailers decide to work with Recupel, they sign individual contracts with the minimum requirements of e-waste collection. Such minimum requirements are meant to increase the volume of e-waste collected from the citizens.

In addition to retailers, Recupel has also good cooperative relations with the sectors for re-used goods (Recupel, 2012). Re-used goods players have access to the volume collected by Recupel and can select re-usable appliances. But on the other hand, re-used goods players have also appliances that are redundant and hence constitute an important e-waste collection stream for Recupel. Re-used goods players are typically organized by NGOs and charitable organizations, and thus their network has a significant role in the whole process of e-waste management. They play an important role in raising the awareness of re-use and e-waste collection.

> *[Manager Strategy and Communication in SUEZ]: "NGOs can inform people to not buy a new phone every six months because there are new models on the market but to use their phone as longer as they can. They can encourage people to re-use some of the goods and second hand materials. . .. I think NGOs can play a big role here and they are definitely strongest in these fields".*
>
> *[PhD from KU Leuven]: "NGOs can collect a lot of waste materials by implementing a door-to-door collection system . . . then they can sell those materials to companies such as Recupel to collect more from these goods. Yes, NGOs have a role in waste management but it is limited".*

It is important to note here that private container parks do not have the same objectives as public container parks. The later exist because municipalities are responsible for the collection of household waste, containing both valuable and invaluable materials. In contrast, private container parks focus mainly on the collection of valuable e-waste and have profit objective. Private initiatives will also like to reduce the costs of e-waste collection and processing. The difference in objective between private and public organizations is well presented in the following two quotes:

> *[Expert 1 in Circular Economy Department at Bruxelles Environnement]: "The public sector has to give service to the population and private sector focus not only on the service but also try to make some money from this".*

[Expert 2 in Circular Economy Department at Bruxelles Environnement]: "On the one hand, the private owned companies, for example, have more knowledge and investment capacity. On the other hand, public owned companies are more responsible for environment and for achievement of environmental goals and not so focus on the profit".

We note that the divergent interests mentioned above are mitigated by the cooperation between Recupel with municipalities, intermunicipal organizations (public sector), private retailers (private sector) and re-use centres (voluntary sector). After e-waste collection, WEEE is recycled in the well-established recycling infrastructure of Belgium. According to EIMPACK (2012), there are more than 95 plants for processing of WEEE located in this country. This guarantees that almost all e-waste can be recycled in Belgium. Recupel are choosing the recyclers for their collected volume, but the Belgian waste management authorities certify whether a chosen recycler and its subcontractors fulfil the legal requirements to treat e-waste. Therefore, Recupel cooperates with the government authorities to select good recycling partners. In addition to the quality of recycling, Recupel is preoccupied with its dependency on single contractors that can treat one specific e-waste stream.

[Communications Manager in Recupel]: "We work together with a dozen recycling plants mostly in Belgium. . ... [W]e always ask for advice the authorities. . ... If they say 'for us is OK, this company fulfils all obligations' then there are not reasons for us to refuse. The treatment operator can work with that company".

[Operation manager in Recupel]: "There is also one German company to which we send at about 6% of the volume of fridges. In Belgium there is another installation for fridge recycling. The quantity is big, that is why we want to be sure that we have a back-up plan. If anything goes wrong, we can always use another installation. And that's why a small part is going to Germany, whereas the main e-waste stream is still recycled in Belgium".

Recupel follows a detailed tender procedure for e-waste recyclers (Recupel, 2013c). They typically work based on a 3-year contract. In the first phase of the recycling process, all hazardous components are removed. Then, the recyclers have to achieve the recycling targets set up by Recupel. On some occasions, Recupel financially supports recyclers in order to improve their recycling process by investing in research and development, as well as in state-of-the-art technology (Recupel, 2012).

Recupel cooperates also with producers and importers of electronic and electrical appliances. In fact, they finance the Recupel's system through the payment of visible fees for processing of WEEE (Recupel, 2013c). Manufacturers, importers and distributors declare quarterly or monthly the number of appliances that they sell and based on the sales visible fees are paid. While, visible fees are invoiced to wholesalers and to retailers, the bill is finally paid by the consumers. Because of paid visible fees, consumers have the right to dispose WEEE in all collection points in Belgium.

[Communications Manager in Recupel]: "The financing of our systems is quite simple. It is the importer/manufacturer who declares quarterly or monthly the number of appliances that they put somewhere in the market and then visible fees, through invoice, are received by our organization. But, the visible fee is then invoiced to the wholesaler, to retailer and in the fact the consumers who ends up paying the visible fee".

Yet, there is a difference between the fee paid for household appliances and professional ones. The visible fee for household appliances covers the costs for collection and recycling. In addition, the visible fee for the professional equipment is used to cover the Recupel administrative and reporting costs. European Foundation for Quality Management (EFQM) certification is used by Recupel to improve its financial efficiency and operational impact (Recupel, 2011).

> *[Communications Manager in Recupel]: "There are important distinguish to be made between household and professional appliances. Visible fee that is paid for household appliances covers all the costs. The visible fee that is paid for the professional equipment is only used to cover our administrative and reporting costs. But, the amount that is needed for collection and recycling is determined in the moment when the appliances become end of life. It is completely different systems, different collection possibilities".*

Overall, Recupel cooperates closely with different stakeholders (cf. Figure 3.6.1), and these cooperative relations result in effective e-waste management. Such cooperation is guided by various contracts but, most importantly, by the regulation of e-waste management in Belgium. Illustrative for the solid relational stakeholder perspective in this case are Recupel's long-standing relationships with many of the key players of e-waste systems from the beginning.

E-waste management in Kenya

E-waste management in Kenya is quite a different story than the one in Belgium (Mureithi and Waema, 2008). In the first place, the regulative frame in Kenya on e-waste is almost nonexistent. There is no "the polluter pays principle", nor are there "take-back" obligations for WEEE (Tedre et al., 2009; National Environmental Management, 2010). The producers and importers of electronic and electricity appliances do not pay any fees for collection, sorting, dismantling and treatment of e-waste. They were also not obliged to set up a producer organization (like Recupel in Belgium) or to develop a system for economically and ecologically effective system for sustainable e-waste management (Ongondo et al., 2011; Mbogo, 2013). Moreover, there are no financial incentives for the collection and treatment of non-valuable e-waste.

> *[Manager in WEEE Centre]: "We do not have any regulatory framework for e-waste which makes our work very difficult. If we have regulatory framework for e-waste that is responsible for sustainable e-waste management, then people would not throw their e-waste together with general waste on the dumpsites. … We want the government in Kenya to adopt a specific legislation for e-waste management".*

In the absence of regulatory framework, we note that one of the best practices of e-waste management in Kenya is coordinated by WorldLoop, a Belgium-based NGO. WorldLoop manages 15 e-waste management projects spread across various African countries, e.g. Kenya, Burundi, Central Africa, Democratic Republic of Congo, East Africa, Ghana, Morocco, Northern Africa, Rwanda, Senegal, Southern Africa, Tanzania, Togo, West Africa and Zambia (Kuhn, 2014). WorldLoop does not have any ownership in these African e-waste projects (Kuhn, 2014; WorldLoop, 2013), which suggests the relational importance of stakeholder collaboration.

> *[Director of External and Partner Relations in WorldLoop]: "It is important to know that Worldloop, as an organization, does not have any ownership in these e-waste projects in*

Africa. Worldloop is focusing on ICT waste (Information and communications technology waste) today".

The government of Kenya and local municipalities do not take any actions to facilitate the development effective e-waste management (Ongondo et al., 2011). Hence, WorldLoop puts a lot of effort in organizing e-waste management in Kenya. WorldLoop cooperates with different organizations to realize its objectives. WorldLoop works closely together with Recupel.

2014). It does also team up with many recycling companies (like Umicore and Galloo Group) and numerous other organizations (WorldLoop, 2013). In the reminder of this section, we elaborate on how the cooperation between WorldLoop and other relevant stakeholders contributes to the establishment of effective e-waste management in Kenya (cf. Figure 3.6.2).

In a first step to stimulating an effective e-waste management system in Kenya, WorldLoop provides financial support to entrepreneurs who want to start their own recycling business. This financial support has a tender maximum of 5 years. Entrepreneurs are thus facilitated with seed capital to start operating. WorldLoop readily provides this seed capital, since local entrepreneurs face high interest rates of bank loans, i.e. in the range of 15% to 30%.

> *[Project director in WorldLoop]: "We see that getting start-up capital for e-waste recycling in Africa is very difficult. Why? Because banks there do not know anything about e-waste recycling; they do not know about the value of the materials; they do not know if it has been successful in other countries. In Africa, the interest rates are very high because of the risk premium. . ... That is really one of the biggest obstacles and that's why we try to step in by providing some funds and helping them to get start it".*

In a next step, WorldLoop tries to convince e-waste management entrepreneurs to process also not valuable waste. The convincing arguments are related to the seed capital in the beginning. In the words of one of the WorldLoop's directors:

> *[Director of External and Partner Relations in WorldLoop]: "We say to entrepreneurs in Africa: 'We will support you but you have to agree to take the non-valuable waste.' And we support them to reduce the cost of treatment of these low valuable materials".*

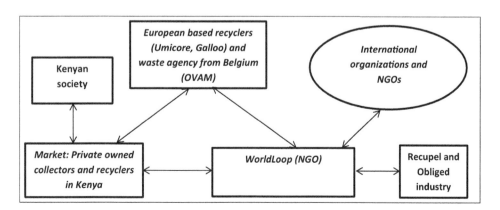

Figure 3.6.2 Important actors involved in the e-waste management system in Kenya and the cooperation between them

Furthermore, WorldLoop provides entrepreneurs in Kenya with technical assistance. To that end, seminars are organizes in support of entrepreneurs. On these seminars, local entrepreneurs can learn a lot from the e-waste experts working in European recycling companies. Therefore, this technical assistance contributes to the knowledge exchange between Belgian and Kenyan e-waste management specialist, who share best practices and sustainable solutions in the collection, dismantling and recycling of e-waste (UNIDO press, 2014).

> *[Manager in WEEE Centre]: "WorldLoop provides us with some seed capital and funding for problematic e-waste fractions. They also provide us with technical support, and training in specific areas by organizing training sessions and sending technical support from Europe and Brussels to teach us how to deal with e-waste".*

Moreover, WorldLoop makes the link between the international recycling market and small-scale recyclers in Kenya (Wang et al., 2012). E-waste materials are sometimes exported to partners in Belgium, if they cannot be recycled in Kenya due to economic, environmental or safety considerations (Vanegas et al, 2014). WorldLoop facilitates that process, since Kenyan collectors are confronted with high working capital needs.

> *[Project director in WorldLoop]: "A collector of circuit boards that pays 5 000 euros per ton on average (from 3 000 to 9 000 euros per ton) will have to pre-finance 100 000 euros for just one container of 20 tons plus transport costs. . .. EU recycling companies usually ask for a minimum quantity of 20 tons for a container. . .. And Kenyan collectors receive their revenue within 4 months".*

If WorldLoop does not provide its support, then recyclers in Kenya usually choose to sell materials to locally based traders of Chinese or Lebanese origin, since they pay cash immediately. The main issue in this scenario is that WEEE is sent to inferior-quality e-waste management partners instead of shipment to high-quality smelters in Belgium.

> *[Project director in WorldLoop]: "These traders could buy the same material from them for the price of 3 000 euros per ton but they pay cash on delivery. These traders then organize shipments but often to second best smelters".*

WorldLoop helps Kenyan e-waste entrepreneurs by working directly with international recycling companies (AWARD, 2014). They cut out the middlemen and organize shipments. WorldLoop has agreements with some of the international recycling companies (like Umicore and Galloo), which help Kenyan collectors of e-waste to overcome the obstacles they face otherwise (Umicore, 2014).

> *[Manager in a private owned company]: "We succeeded because we have been working together with WorldLoop and without their support it would be impossible for us to ship some fractions from e-waste to Europe".*
> *[Director of External and Partner Relations in WorldLoop]: "One of the roles we also play (Worldloop), for instance, is to be an intermediary between international recycling companies and the local entrepreneurs. . .. This is also a role that NGOs can play: to be a facilitator between the private sector, between governments and between different stakeholders; and to bring all these stakeholders together to achieve something together".*

In general, WorldLoop works in close cooperation with many Belgian organizations (AWARD 2014). Many European organizations support WoorldLoop in order to organize the e-waste management in Africa, among which Recupel, Umicore (international recycling company), producers of electronic and electric equipment and OVAM (the Public Waste Agency of Flanders) (Recupel, 2014). Recupel provides its expertise in the collection and processing of waste electrical appliances (Recupel, 2012; Recupel, 2014). Recupel advises WorldLoop to build recycling installations in Africa and connects it with recyclers in Belgium.

> *[Communications Manager in Recupel]: "We support Worldloop. We finance it so it can develop local projects in Africa; we help Worldloop to contact the local recyclers, here in Belgium. But the reason we have decided to support them (Worldloop and before that Close the Gap), is because we are an industry-driven organization and our brands (such as Philips, Siemens and all other big brands) are also worried whether e-waste is legally shipped to Africa or not. And in fact, they (African citizens) also use appliances of those brands that cannot be recycler locally".*

The big international recycling companies in Europe (like Umicore and Galloo) provide their international recycling infrastructures and expertise for the end-processing of complex and hazardous e-waste fractions originally from Kenya. Moreover, these international companies provide knowledge and expertise in order to improve the efficiency of their e-waste management. The Kenyan recyclers have improved their knowledge and expertise in e-waste management, whereas the international recycling companies have increased their volume of e-waste (by receiving some e-waste components from Africa.

> *[Manager in WEEE Centre]: "WorldLoop organizes training and send waste experts from Europe and Brussels that come to teach us how to deal with e-waste. And some specialists of our center had the opportunity to go to Europe (Belgium and Denmark) and watch what other recyclers in Europe doing in the field of e-waste management. We have been able to visit Umicore and Coolrec and to understand the collection strategies and also to understand the legal framework in Europe. . ... WorldLoop help us to export some of the dangers material to Europe by helping us to get green certificates for export".*

OVAM provides additional technical support to recyclers from Kenya and legal permission to ship e-waste materials from Kenya to Flanders. Producers of electronic and electricity equipment provide financial support to WorldLoop to continue its operation in Africa. All these organizations work together to address the environmental risks of e-waste in Kenya (UNIDO Press, 2014). in fact, WorldLoop builds a bridge between the private sector, between governments and between different stakeholders by bringing all these stakeholders together to achieve an efficient e-waste management in Kenya.

Discussion and conclusions

Our study has provided valuable information for e-waste management in Belgium and Kenya. The organization of the whole process of e-waste management in Belgium is conducted by Recupel. This PRO has been established due to a specific legislation for WEEE. Recupel cooperates successfully with actors from the public, private and voluntary sector in order to organize and recycle the e-waste in one of the best possible and most efficient ways in the EU. Based on this cooperation and clear designation of the role between all actors in the EPR system, one of the highest recycling results of e-waste among the EU countries has been achieved. In Kenya, the organization of e-waste management is done by the European NGO (WorldLoop) due to the lack of a specific legislation and implemented EPR schemes for e-waste. WorldLoop cooperates with actors from different sectors and different countries to organize sustainable and efficient e-waste management in Kenya. This NGO cooperates with Kenyan recyclers. It provides three basic services to facilitate the latter to build their own recycling plants and manage their e-waste in a sustainable and efficient manner. WorldLoop cooperates also with many actors from Belgium and other countries that support the NGO to continue its operation in Kenya (to organize the e-waste management there and provide services of recyclers and entrepreneurs).

These two case studies from Belgium and Kenya are also a good basis to compare the different models for e-waste management implemented in the EU (Belgium) and Africa (Kenya). The specific legislation for e-waste management and particular EPR schemes, which the processing of WEEE is organized through, is adopted in all EU countries. In contrast, many of the African countries do not implement any specific legislation for e-waste and governments and municipalities are not involved in the collection, sorting or treatment of this waste stream (Ongondo, Williams and Cherrett, 2011; Osibanjo and Nnorom, 2007). However, the sustainable e-waste management is established in Kenya and many other countries from Africa based on the efforts of WorldLoop and the strong cooperation between this NGO and its stakeholders from different sectors and countries. To keep this cooperation stable, in absence of specific legislation for WEEE and engagement of government authorities in the whole process, what is necessary to have is a win-win-win situation for all parties involved in the e-waste management in Kenya. For example, local NGOs focusing on raising awareness or collection of e-waste will probably expect some compensation from the recyclers, from producers or the government. For recyclers, partnerships with NGOs can be interesting if they lead to increase in e-waste collection. It is also important for partners to understand each other. Hence, one of the roles WorldLoop plays, for instance, is to be an intermediary between international recycling companies (with a lot of complex procedures), local entrepreneurs and other partners because they have very different expectations and different ways of operating. Based on the existence of such a strong and successful cooperation, WorldLoop facilitates the creation of environmentally sound, socially responsible, accessible and sustainable e-waste collection and recycling in Kenya. However, the volume of collection and recycling of e-waste in the country would be increased further if government authorities and municipalities participate actively in the e-waste management process.

In conclusion, e-waste management is a complex process that involves a lot of actors, and without strong cooperation between them, it would be impossible to achieve high recycling results as well as sustainable and efficient e-waste management. This is confirmed by the presented two case studies from Belgium and Kenya where strong cooperation is a key factor for sustainable and efficient e-waste management and for achieving strong recycling results.

Acknowledgements

This chapter benefited from the critical comments of Rumen Gechev, Jan Jonker, Romana Rauter, Ortrud Kamps, Sheila Killian, Bastiaan van der Linden, Jos Verstegen, Joao Carvalho, Celio Sousa, Simon De Jaeger, Alain Verbeke and Statty Stattev. We sincerely thank these colleagues for helping us to improve our chapter. We also wish to express our gratitude to all our respondents that agreed to participate in our study and for the information, time and collaboration provided. We are also indebted to Olivier Vanden Eynde, Thomas Poelmans and Barbara Toorens from WorldLoop for their helpful information about the operation of WorldLoop in Africa and useful contacts they provided. We also would like to thank the editors of this book, as well as the anonymous reviewer for the valuable comments and guidance to improve our contribution.

References

Asante, K. A., Agusa, T., Biney, C. A., Agyekum, W. A., Bello, M., Otsuka, M., et al. (2012). Multi-trace element levels and arsenic speciation in urine of e-waste recycling workers from Agbogbloshie, Accra in Ghana. *Science of The Total Environment, 424*, 63–73.

Atasu, A., & Subramanian, R. (2012). Extended producer responsibility for e-waste: Individual or collective producer responsibility? *Production and Operations Management, 21*(6), 1042–1059.

Atasu, A., & Wassenhove, L. N. (2012). An operations perspective on product take-back legislation for e-waste: Theory, practice, and research needs. *Production and Operations Management, 21*(3), 407–422.

AWARD 2014. (2014). Sustainable partnerships award 2014. Retrieved from: www.sustainablepartnerships.be/websites/suspar/assets/uploads/files/spa2014_brochure.pdf. (accessed 6 May 2017).

Baldé, C. P., Wang, F., Kuehr, R., & Huisman, J. (2015). The global e-waste monitor – 2014. United Nations University, IAS – SCYCLE, Bonn, Germany. Retrieved from: http://i.unu.edu/media/unu.edu/news/52624/UNU-1stGlobal-E-Waste-Monitor-2014-large-optimized.pdf (accessed 6 May 2017).

BAN. (2005). The digital dump: Exporting high-tech re-use and abuse to Africa. Basel Action Network (BAN). Retrieved from: www.ban.org/films/TheDigitalDump.html (accessed 16 May 2017).

Basel Convention (2011). Parties to the Basel convention. Retrieved from: www.basel.int/Countries/Statusofratifications/PartiesSignatories/tabid/1290/language/en-US/Default.aspx (accessed 6 May 2017).

Brewerton, P., & Millward, L. (2001). *Organisational Research Methods*. London: Sage.

Chi, X., Streicher-Porte, M., Wang, M.Y. L., & Reuter, M. a. (2011). Informal electronic waste recycling: A sector review with special focus on China. *Waste Management, 31*(4), 731–742.

Coase, R. H. (1937). The nature of the firm. *Economica, New Series, 4*(16), 386–405.

Cucchiella, F., D'Adamo, I., Lenny Koh, S. C., & Rosa, P. (2015). Recycling of WEEEs: An economic assessment of present and future e-waste streams. *Renewable and Sustainable Energy Reviews, 51*, 263–272.

Dentchev, N. (2005). Corporate social performance: Business rationale, competitiveness threats and management challenges. Ghent University, Faculty of Economics and Business Administration, Ghent, Belgium.

EIMPACK (2012). EIMPack – economic impact of the packaging and packaging waste directive. The European Investment Bank.

European Commission. (2014). Towards a circular economy: A zero waste programme for Europe. Retrieved from: http://eur-lex.europa.eu/resource.html?uri=cellar:50edd1fd-01ec-11e4-831f-01aa75ed71a1.0001.01/DOC_1&format=PDF (accessed 6 May 2017).

European Commission. (2015a). Circular economy strategy. Retrieved from: http://ec.europa.eu/smart-regulation/impact/planned_ia/docs/2015_env_065_env+_032_circular_economy_en.pdf.

European Commission. (2015b). Waste electrical & electronic equipment (WEEE). Retrieved from: http://ec.europa.eu/environment/waste/weee/index_en.htm (accessed 6 May 2017).

Eurostat. (2015). Waste electrical and electronic equipment (WEEE). Retrieved from: http://ec.europa.eu/eurostat/web/waste/key-waste-streams/weee (accessed 6 May 2017).

Executive Environment Agency. (2013, November 13). An ordinance on WEEE. Retrieved from: http://eea.government.bg/bg/nsmos/waste/naredba-eeo (accessed 1 May 2017).

Eygena, E., Meestera, S., Trana, H., & Dewulf, J. (2016). Resource savings by urban mining: The case of desktop and laptopcomputers in Belgium. *Resources, Conservation and Recycling, 107*, 53–64.

Fu, J., Wang, T., Wang, P., Qu, G., Wang, Y., Zhang, Q., et al. (2012). Temporal trends (2005–2009) of PCDD/Fs, PCBs, PBDEs in rice hulls from an e-waste dismantling area after stricter environmental regulations. *Chemosphere, 88*(3), 330–335.

Gullett, B. K., Linak, W. P., Touati, A., Wasson, S. J., Gatica, S., & King, C. J. (2007). Characterization of air emissions and residual ash from open burning of electronic wastes during simulated rudimentary recycling operations. *Journal of Material Cycles and Waste Management, 9*(1), 69–79.

Jain, A., & Sareen, R. (2006). E-waste assessment methodology and validation in India. *Journal of Material Cycles and Waste Management, 8*, 40–45.

Kahhat, R., & Williams, E. (2012). Materials flow analysis of e-waste: Domestic flows and exports of used computers from the United States. *Resources, Conservation and Recycling, 67*, 67–74.

Khetriwal, D. S., Kraeuchi, P., & Widmer, R. (2009). Producer responsibility for e-waste management: Key issues for consideration – Learning from the Swiss experience. *Journal of Environmental Management, 90*(1), 153–165.

Kuhn, M., (2014). Bridging the digital divide without creating a digital dump. R/ E-SCRAP.

Leung, A., Cai, Z. W., & Wong, M. H. (2006). Environmental contamination from electronic waste recycling at Guiyu, southeast China. *Journal of Material Cycles and Waste Management, 8*, 21–33.

Leysen, A., & Preillon, N. (2014). Belgian Waste & Recycling Solutions. Belgian Foreign Trade Agency. Report. Retrieved from: www.abh-ace.be/en/binaries/20140822_ace_brochure_waste_BD_tcm450-254639.pdf (accessed 6 May 2017).

Man, M., Naidu, R., & Wong, M. H. (2013). Persistent toxic substances released from uncontrolled e-waste recycling and actions for the future. *Science of The Total Environment, 463–464*, 1133–1137.

Mbogo, S. (2013). Promoting awareness and research in managing electronic waste in Kenya. The EastAfrican, Special feature, E-waste management.

Morf, L. S., Tremp, J., Gloor, R., Schuppisser, F., Stengele, M., & Taverna, R. (2007). Metals, non-metals and PCB in electrical and electronic waste – Actual levels in Switzerland. *Waste Management, 27*, 1306–1316.

Mureithi, M., & Waema, T. (2008). E-waste management in Kenya. Kenya ICT Action Network (KICTANet), Kenya. Retrieved from: http://ewasteguide.info/Waema_2008_KICTANet (accessed 6 May 2017).

Nakajima, N., & Vanderburg, W. H. (2005). A failing grade for WEEE take-back programs for information technology equipment. *Bulletin of Science, Technology & Society, 25*(6), 507–517.

National Environmental Management. (2010). Guidelines for e-waste management in Kenya, 1–57. Retrieved from: http://gesci.org/assets/files/Knowledge%20Centre/E-Waste%20Guidelines_Kenya 2011.pdf (accessed 10 May 2017).

Nnorom, I. C., & Osibanjo, O. (2008). Overview of electronic waste (e-waste) management practices and legislations, and their poor applications in the developing countries. *Resources, Conservation and Recycling, 52*, 843–858.

Oguchi, M., Murakami, S., Sakanakura, H., Kida, A., & Kameya, T. (2011). A preliminary categorization of end-of-life electrical and electronic equipment as secondary metal resources. *Waste Management, 31*(9–10), 2150–2160.

Oguchi, M., Sakanakura, H., & Terazono, A. (2013). Toxic metals in WEEE: Characterization and substance flow analysis in waste treatment processes. *Science of The Total Environment, 463–464*, 1124–1132.

Ongondo, F. O., Williams, I. D., & Cherrett, T. J. (2011). How are WEEE doing? A global review of the management of electrical and electronic wastes. *Waste Management, 31*(4), 714–730.

Osibanjo, O., & Nnorom, I. C. (2007). The challenge of electronic waste (e-waste) management in developing countries. *Waste Management & Research, 25*, 489–501.

Oteng-Ababio, M., Amankwaa, E. F., & Chama, M. A. (2014). The local contours of scavenging for e-waste and higher-valued constituent parts in Accra, Ghana. *Habitat International, 43*, 163–171.

Perkins, D. N., Brune Drisse, M.-N., Nxele, T., & Sly, P. D. (2014). E-waste: A global hazard. *Annals of Global Health, 80*(4), 286–295.

Polák, M., & Drápalová, L. (2012). Estimation of end of life mobile phones generation: The case study of the Czech Republic. *Waste Management, 32*(February 2003), 1583–1591.

Recupel. (2010). Annual report 2010. Retrieved from: www.recupel.be/the-annual-reports-recupel.html (accessed 6 May 2017).

Recupel. (2011). Sustainability report 2011. Retrieved from: www.recupel.be/the-annual-reports-recupel.html (accessed 6 May 2017).

Recupel. (2012). Sustainability report 2012. Retrieved from: www.recupel.be/the-annual-reports-recupel.html (accessed 6 May 2017).

Recupel. (2013a). Annual report 2013. Retrieved from: www.recupel.be/the-annual-reports-recupel.html (accessed 6 May 2017).

Recupel. (2013c). (W)EEE Mass balance and market structure in Belgium.

Recupel. (2014) Annual report 2014. Retrieved from: www.recupel.be/the-annual-reports-recupel.html.

Robinson, B. H. (2009). E-waste: An assessment of global production and environmental impacts. *Science of The Total Environment, 408*(2), 183–191.

Rochat, D., & Laissaoui, S. E. (2008). Technical report on the assessment of e-waste management in Morocco. EMPA – Swiss Federal laboratories for materials testing and research, Switzerland. Retrieved from: http://ewasteguide.info/ Laissaoui_2008_CMPP (accessed 16 April 2017).

RoHS Guide, (2015). RoHS Compliance FAQ Retrieved from: www.rohsguide.com/rohs-faq.htm (accessed 6 May 2017)

Sander, K., Schilling, S., Naoko, T., Rossem, C. Van, Vernon, J., & George, C. (2007). The producer responsibility principle of the WEEE directive. Retrieved from: http://ec.europa.eu/environment/waste/weee/pdf/final_rep_okopol.pdf (accessed 6 May 2017).

Sarapuu, K. (2015). Dangerous e-waste is the world's fastest growing municipal waste stream. Let's do it world. Retrieved from: www.letsdoitworld.org/news/dangerous-e-waste-worlds-fastest-growing-municipal-waste-stream. (accessed 6 May 2017).

Schluep, M., Dittke, S., Newson, G., Kane, C., & Hieronymi, K., 2008. A material recovery facility in Cape Town, South Africa, as a replicable concept for sustainable e-waste management and recycling in developing countries. In: Global Symposium on Recycling, Waste Treatment and Clean Technology, Cancun, Mexico, October 12–15. Retrieved from: http://ewasteguide.info/2008_Schluep_REWAS (accessed 6 May 2017).

Sepúlveda, A., Schluep, M., Renaud, F. G., Streicher, M., Kuehr, R., Hagelüken, C., & Gerecke, A. C. (2010). A review of the environmental fate and effects of hazardous substances released from electrical and electronic equipments during recycling: Examples from China and India. *Environmental Impact Assessment Review, 30*(1), 28–41.

Söderström, G. (2003). On the combustion and photolytic degradation products of some brominated flame retardants. University of Amsterdam, The Netherlands, Sweden. Retrieved from: http://umu.diva-portal.org/smash/get/diva2:140100/FULLTEXT01 (accessed 16 May 2017).

Song, Q., Wang, Z., & Li, J. (2013). Sustainability evaluation of e-waste treatment based on emergy analysis and the LCA method: A case study of a trial project in Macau. *Ecological Indicators, 30*, 138–147.

Sthiannopkao, S., & Wong, M. H. (2013). Handling e-waste in developed and developing countries: Initiatives, practices, and consequences. *Science of The Total Environment, 463–464*, 1147–1153.

Tedre, M., Bangu, N., & Nyagava, S. (2009). Contextualized IT education in Tanzania: Beyond standard it curricula. *Journal of Information Technology Education, 8*, 101–124. Retrieved from www.jite.org/documents/Vol8/JITEv8p101-124Tedre440.pdf (accessed 6 May 2017).

Umicore. (2014). E-waste partnership between Umicore and WorldLoop wins Belgian Entrepreneurs for Entrepreneurs Trophy. Press release. Retrieved from: www.umicore.com/en/media/press/20141017WorldloopTrophyEN/ (accessed 28 May 2018)

UNIDO Press. (2014). UNIDO and WorldLoop partner with Recupel and the Belgian recycling industry to advance sustainable e-waste solutions in Africa. Retrieved from: www.unido.org/news/press/unido-sustainable.html (accessed 6 May 2017).

United Nations Environment Programme. (2011). Basel convention on the control of transboundary movements of hazardous wastes and their disposal. Retrieved from: www.basel.int/Portals/4/Basel%20 Convention/docs/text/BaselConventionText-e.pdf

Vanegas, P., Peeters, J. R., Plessers, F., Cattrysse, D., & Duflou, J. R. (2014). Synergizing industrialized and developing countries to improve resource recovery for e-waste: Case study Belgium – Kenya. *Procedia CIRP, 15,* 283–288.

Wäger, P. A., Hischier, R., & Eugster, M. (2011). Environmental impacts of the Swiss collection and recovery systems for Waste Electrical and Electronic Equipment (WEEE): A follow-up. *Science of The Total Environment, 409*(10), 1746–1756. doi:10.1016/j.scitotenv.2011.01.050.

Wang, F., Huisman, J., Meskers, C. E. M., Schluep, M., Stevels, A., & Hagelüken, C. (2012). The best-of-2-worlds philosophy: Developing local dismantling and global infrastructure network for sustainable e-waste treatment in emerging economies. *Waste Management, 32*(11), 2134–2146.

Wang, L., & Chen, M. (2013). Policies and perspective on end-of-life vehicles in China. *Journal of Cleaner Production, 44*(2013), 168–176.

Wasswa, J., & Schluep, M. (2008). e-Waste assessment in Uganda: A situational analysis of e-waste management and generation with special emphasis on personal computers. Retrieved from: http://ewaste guide.info/system/files/Wasswa_2008_UCPC-Empa.pdf (accessed 6 May 2017).

Widmer, R., Oswald-Krapf, H., Sinha-Khetriwal, D., Schnellmann, M., & Böni, H. (2005). Global perspectives on e-waste. *Environmental Impact Assessment Review, 25,* 436–458.

Williamson, O. E. (1981). The economics of organization: The transaction cost approach. *American Journal of Sociology.* doi:10.1086/227496

Williamson, O. E. (2010). Transaction cost economics: The natural progression. *Journal of Retailing, 86*(June), 215–226.

WorldLoop. (2013). 2013 Annual report.

Yamane, L. H., de Moraes, V. T., Espinosa, D. C. R., & Tenório, J. A. S. (2011). Recycling of WEEE: Characterization of spent printed circuit boards from mobile phones and computers. *Waste Management, 31*(12), 2553–2558.

Yin, R. K. (2003). *Case Study Research: Design and Methods,* 3rd ed. Vol. 5. London: Sage.

Zhang, K., Schnoor, J. L., & Zeng, E. Y. (2012). E-waste recycling: Where does it go from here? *Environmental Science & Technology, 46,* 10861–10867.

3.7 Aligning footprint mitigation activities with relevant stakeholders

Loren Falkenberg, Xiaoyu Liu, Liena Kano and Reiner Schaefer

Introduction

The concepts of corporate social responsibility (CSR) and sustainability have drawn the attention of management scholars and practitioners for decades.[1, 2] The importance of these issues in public and academic discourse has evolved to the point that any companies ignoring their social and environmental footprints create unnecessary risks.[3–7]

In both the CSR and sustainability literature, there is an implied assumption that satisfying regulatory and normative expectations leads to full remediation of footprints.[5] Yet there are operating contexts where well-intentioned companies cannot fully remediate their footprints because of factors beyond their control (e.g., lack of technical capabilities, lack of social infrastructure and cultural norms and behaviours). Research has explored how companies satisfy standards and expectations in managing their footprints; however, minimal attention has been given to appropriate activities for managing the unmitigated portions of footprints. As footprints grow in complexity,[8, 9] and societies' expectations are communicated through a complex range of stakeholder groups, difficulties in the appropriate mitigation of footprints also increase. Often companies need to balance broader societal issues with those of directly impacted communities.

Today's ambiguous and complex geopolitical environment adds an extra layer of complexity to the way multinationals must address the needs of their diverse stakeholders. Globalization, which up until recently was regarded as a more or less indisputable feature of our political, economic and social environment, appears to be at a crossroads. Political institutions – e.g. the European Union – are being challenged, international trade agreements are being questioned, and governments are being pressured to constrain the movement of capital, labour and goods and services across borders. Part of the populist backlash against globalization is attributed to the fact that economic integration has not benefitted all stakeholders equally. Those stakeholders who feel harmed by globalization, or perceive themselves as not having equally shared in its gains, see multinationals as contributors to the growing global inequality. Against this backdrop of populist backlash, it is increasingly important for firms to balance the needs of all stakeholders affected by their actions and deal with potential unequal impacts by carefully monitoring and mitigating their global footprints.

We propose a framework that distinguishes four categories of mitigation activities for managing the impact of corporate footprints, including the unmitigated portions. These four categories arise from two types of expectations, regulatory and normative, and two processes for satisfying these expectations: compliance based and consensus based. Each type of footprint mitigation involves building relationships with different stakeholders. Five assumptions underly this framework:

a)   All companies should work to optimize the mitigation of its footprints.
b)   Footprints cannot be fully mitigated by satisfying any one set of stakeholder expectations.
c)   Effective stakeholder relationships consume organizational resources.
d)   Appropriate relationship with different stakeholders leads to optimal footprint mitigation.
e)   Both broader societal and directly impacted community interests need to be satisfied.

Carroll's[1,10] pyramid of corporate responsibilities (i.e., economic, legal, ethical and philanthropic) is one of the most cited models for describing expectations of corporate activities. The value of this pyramid is that it presents corporate responsibilities, and associated activities, in an intuitive and visible manner for both researchers and practitioners. Carroll[11] wrote "the total corporate social responsibility of business entails the simultaneous fulfilment of economic, legal, ethical and philanthropic responsibilities". Economic activities are at the base of the pyramid, followed by satisfying legal standards (i.e., the next layer in the pyramid). Ethical responsibilities are the third layer. He continued, "Although economic and legal responsibilities embody ethical norms about fairness and justice, ethical responsibilities embrace those activities and practices that are expected even though they are not codified into law".[11] Philanthropic activities, the final layer, involve promoting "good" beyond what is expected ethically. For example, it is good and laudable that a business makes charitable donations to certain community organizations, but the business would not be viewed as unethical had it not made the donations.

As helpful as Carroll's model has been, over the last 25 years normative and regulatory pressures have evolved to the point that the legal and ethical components of the pyramid provide limited guidance as to the expectations and appropriate activities for mitigating footprints. As well, it does not address the additional activities that are needed for unmitigated footprints or address the need to balance the interests of broader society against those of the directly impacted community. We propose that expectations have evolved in such a way that both codified standards and norms need to be satisfied and that the processes to satisfy them involve compliance or consensus building. In this chapter, we describe four types of mitigation activities based on compliance or consensus and then discuss the stakeholders who shape the expectations associated with them and how different combinations of these mitigation activities can balance broad societal as well as specific community interests.

The four types of mitigation activities offer a useful roadmap to assist managers in developing appropriate strategies for managing different components of their footprint, including the unmitigated portion, and developing relationships with a range of stakeholders. The categories included in the framework are not mutually exclusive and independent. In practice, managers engage in mitigation activities simultaneously across different categories; however, each category is distinct in terms of the basis of expectations, primary stakeholder(s) and major consequences for non-compliance.

And engaging in one category of activities does not necessarily satisfy responsibilities in another.

Four footprint mitigation activities

Regulated mitigation

Carroll[10] identified the need for companies to satisfy legal standards as an absolute requirement for "doing business". However, societal expectations have expanded to include the need to comply with international standards and norms. Both legal and international standards establish the boundaries or minimum levels that need to be satisfied when managing footprints.[12, 13] Rating systems such as KLD, Innovest and e-Capital Partners evaluate how well CSR and sustainability programmes align with various industry and international agency standards.[14, 15] Companies are expected to comply with these standards, in contrast to negotiating or building consensus on what standards to address (see Table 3.7.1).

The development and enforcement of regulatory standards leads to a "level playing field" in that almost all firms comply, and those that don't may pay penalties and/or lose their licence to operate. Compliance also ensures generic or isomorphic outcomes, and communities, governments and rating agencies can visibly measure the mitigation that occurred. The only time complying with regulatory standards is not a relevant first step is when governments/agencies have failed to identify an issue and/or establish standards (i.e., there is a gap in the regulation).

Given that regulatory agencies set standards for a broad range of operating conditions (i.e., they are established to reduce issues influencing multiple communities), we conclude that complying with these standards most often leads to a focus on the interests of broader society over those of the directly impacted communities.

Table 3.7.1 Footprint mitigation activities

Type of expectation	Process for responding	
	Compliance based	Consensus based
Norms	**Reactive mitigation**	**Compensatory mitigation**
Basis of expectations	Community/societal norms and expectations	Agreements with community reached through collaboration
Primary stakeholder	Mostly powerful advocacy groups, non-governmental organizations	Directly impacted communities and their most vulnerable members
Consequences for non-compliance	Loss of social licence within broader society	Loss of social licence within community.
Standards	**Regulated mitigation**	**Prescribed mitigation**
Basis of expectations	Formally established standards or metrics, requiring formal reporting	Combination of explicit standards and agreements within industry and cross-sector associations
Primary stakeholder(s)	Rating agencies, regulatory bodies	Competitors/partners in association
Consequences for non-compliance	Penalties, fines	Increased mitigation costs, loss of reputation

Prescribed mitigation

Prescribed mitigation is associated with two types of footprints, common and shared. Generally these two types of footprints occur because regulated mitigation activities did not fully eliminate the footprints or because regulated standards do not exist. Common footprints occur when a company's operations create negative outcomes that are similar to other industry members or because of common production processes. Shared footprints develop from the joint contributions of multiple companies. With both types of footprints, the most effective outcomes occur when companies coordinate expertise/ resources and work jointly with impacted communities. Industry or cross-sector associations provide platforms for companies to share technical expertise and other resources thereby increasing the capacity to mitigate footprints.[16, 17]

Another role of industry associations is to establish standards or activities that members agree to support, leading to self-regulation for the unmitigated portion of footprints.[18] Given that industry associations provide a platform for consensus building there is a greater probability companies will participate in the mitigation of shared footprints.

We have labelled these industry-based activities as "prescribed mitigation". They are similar to regulated mitigation activities as both are based on explicit standards, while they differ because they are established through a consensus-based approach and involve voluntary acceptance (see Table 3.7.1). We conclude that prescribed mitigation activities address broad community interests particularly when they reduce shared footprints, and specific community interests when they influence the reduction of common footprints. The consequences of not satisfying the prescribed standards include potential loss of reputation and increased long-term remediation costs.

Reactive mitigation

Reactive mitigation activities are initiated by individual companies, generally based on normative expectations, and are intended to address gaps in footprint mitigation that regulatory and/or prescribed mitigation activities do not. Often it is a stakeholder (i.e., NPO or advocacy group) that identifies the gap and/or expected responsibilities for this part of a footprint.[19-22] Carroll[10] defined ethical responsibility as "additional behaviours and activities that are not necessarily codified into law, but nevertheless are expected of business by society's members". In contrast, we labelled these mitigation activities as reactive because they are based on reactions to the expectations/demands of specific NPOs or advocacy groups. More specifically, NPOs and advocacy groups, through their power to influence the reputation of a company, are able to influence the priorities of what issues companies should respond to and the types of activities to reduce the footprint.

Executives have overtly recognized the need to respond to normative expectations since the writings of Adam Smith.[23] Between 1950 and 1980, management scholars discussed the need to go beyond philanthropic activities and engage in voluntary restraint and alignment of operations with societal values.[24-26] For example, the "principle of public responsibility" directs every firm to repair what it has broken, avoid future breakage and help to solve social problems[27]. Others have expanded on this definition by specifying four core obligations "avoid harm to others", "respect duty of fairness", "avoid dishonesty" and "honour agreements".[28, 29] Although there is general societal agreement that corporations should satisfy these core norms, it is external groups that interpret what is appropriate compliance.

We have classified the activities developed to respond to not-for-profit expectations as a compliance-based form of footprint mitigation because they involve responding to normative standards *as interpreted by external groups* (i.e., advocacy and NPO). We have labelled this type of footprint mitigation as reactive because it involves responses to powerful external groups who are interpreting what is needed to ensure broad normative principles are satisfied.

Compensatory mitigation

Regulatory, prescribed and reactive activities do not always lead to full mitigation of a company's footprint. Regulatory and reactive activities are based on generic standards, designed to cover a broad range of operating contexts (i.e., community, employee relations, environment, products and production). Given the broad nature of these standards, the outcomes do not always align with the operating context of a company or the needs of the community.[30, 31] It is at this point that companies need to voluntarily provide some form of compensation to communities for the remaining footprint(s). The form(s) of compensation should be based on normative principles and community interests.[24, 32, 33] An example of compensatory mitigation activities is a company collaborating with indigenous communities to ensure they have appropriate resources for the long-term sustainability of their communities. We have labelled this type of mitigation activity compensatory because it is based on a company reimbursing a community for the impact of the unmitigated footprint.

Compensation activities should stem from the ethical principles "do not harm" and "respect the duty of fairness", and the application of these principles should be based on how the community interprets its long-term interests. The most *effective* compensation offsets the long-term harm (potentially) caused by the unmitigated portion of a company's footprint. Often the affected community is the best judge of not only the extent and manner in which a company's footprint has harmed them, but also the type of compensation activities that will effectively meet their long-term needs.

Summary

Footprint mitigation activities begin with isomorphic activities to comply with regulatory standards. These isomorphic activities do not always lead to fully mitigated footprints, and companies need to combine three other types of mitigation activities to reduce the unmitigated footprint. The appropriate combination of activities is dependent on the operating context. If companies do not have the capacity to fully mitigate footprints that are common with other companies, or their operations contribute to shared footprints then they need to engage in prescribed mitigation. If external agencies (i.e., NPO or advocacy groups) identify violations of normative expectations then companies need to comply with their interpretation of appropriate mitigation activities (i.e., reactive mitigation). And, companies need to be concerned with the impact of unmitigated footprints on local communities and work through collaborative processes to identify the most appropriate types of compensatory activities. Thus, some combination of these four mitigation activities is needed to manage the unmitigated portion of footprints.

An example of the application of this framework is the mitigation activities of resource extraction companies.[34] These companies often operate in remote locations where the community is willing to accept negative impacts for the positive outcomes of economic development. According to the CSR reports of these companies, the initial focus is on meeting regulatory standards, to ensure they maintain operating permits and satisfy institutional rating agencies. They also recognize that satisfying these standards does not lead to full mitigation of the footprints and work with industry associations to improve environmental and social outcomes. As well, the combined impact of resource extraction companies can have greater harm than the operations of a single company, such as reducing water supply or increasing traffic levels in the community. Thus, companies need to coordinate their activities via industry associations to reduce the impact of these shared footprints. Many not-for-profit organizations have focused on increasing the visibility of the unmitigated portions of the footprint and companies have been attempting to respond to their expectations. The CSR reports of these companies also describe the compensatory activities that occur in these communities, such as supporting education and health care initiatives. Each of these mitigation activities is based on the expectations of a specific group of stakeholders. Reducing the unmitigated portion of a footprint requires an appropriate and effective relationship with the relevant stakeholder(s).

Optimizing relationships with stakeholders

In this section, we review how effectively reducing footprints is dependent on building relevant stakeholder relationships to identify and respond to specific expectations, through appropriate types of mitigation activities. Table 3.7.2 outlines the links between stakeholders, mitigation activities and relevant contextual factors. An additional assumption is that developing stakeholder relationships consumes resources (e.g., time, expertise), and companies need to assess the most effective allocation of resources to ensure optimal footprint mitigation.

Regulatory and rating agencies

Regulatory agencies are a primary stakeholder who set the minimum level of footprint mitigation activities through concrete external standards. These agencies include government and non-government internnational organizations who often focus on specific social and environmental issues. Companies benefit from these relationships, as they can obtain external expertise, which may be too expensive for any one organization to retain.[18]

Rating agencies monitor whether companies meet the standards and failure to satisfy these standards can negatively impact the company's reputation. Although both regulators and rating agencies are focused on compliance with specific standards, the management of these stakeholders differs. Regulatory agencies are able to withdraw operating permits and apply penalties for non-compliance, while rating agencies are dependent on institutional investor expectations. When institutional investors are visibly concerned, companies need to prioritize the expectations of these institutional investors in terms of the voluntary mitigation efforts they adopt. And, company representatives need to meet with these active investors and provide explanations for the unmitigated portions of the footprint.

Table 3.7.2 Relevant stakeholder relationships for footprint mitigation activities

Stakeholder(s)	Key contextual factors	Appropriate stakeholder relationship
Industry associations (competitors, other businesses)	• Shared footprints • Common footprints • Need to share expertise and increase capacity • Ability to identify a common voice on specific issues • Ability to monitor mitigation activities of members	• Collaborative information sharing across member organizations sharing via industry association channels • Contributing to common messages to other stakeholders (e.g., regulatory agencies, NPOs) • Complying with prescribed processes/ standards
Regulatory and rating agencies Institutional shareholders	• Relevant regulatory standards are in place • Stakeholder expectations to report on compliance	• Companies individually monitor regulatory and rating agencies • Relationships based on exchanging information as to expectations for footprint mitigation and justifications for unmitigated footprints • Companies participate in industry associations to providing expertise and establishing appropriate standards
NPOs and advocacy groups	• Differences in interpretation of satisfying relevant normative expectations • Potential to be targeted by advocacy groups	• Work through industry associations to establish effective methods for satisfying normative standards • Work with NPOs and advocacy groups to understand the ripple effect of activities on a community
Vulnerable community members	• Unmitigated footprint impacting community and/or vulnerable stakeholders	• Collaborate with community members to identify activities to improve short and long-term position of vulnerable stakeholders

Industry associations

Industry associations can be an effective mechanism for improving mitigation activities by providing a platform for collaborating across organizations and by managing stakeholder expectations by being a "visible voice" as to the level of mitigation that is achievable. Collaboration across industry members is important when solutions are needed for technically difficult and complex footprints which individual companies cannot develop on their own, and when shared footprints or externalities need to be mitigated.[35]

Consensus building in industry associations is usually dependent on a larger and more prominent organizations proposing or leading the search for solutions.[36, 37] Thus, membership in these organizations can be advantageous for smaller companies as they can minimize the resources required for finding appropriate mitigation activities. Participation in industry associations should reduce reputational and financial risks associated with a shared footprint, particularly when there is monitoring of members (i.e. self-regulation) for compliance with established practices.[9, 38–40]

An example of industry-based mitigation is "Canada's Oil Sands Innovation Alliance",[41] which involves oil sands producers who share the goal of developing responsible and sustainable growth of Canada's oil sands while improving environmental performance through collaborative action and innovation. The alliance sets environmental performance goals and to date members have shared 777 distinct technologies and innovations that have cost over $950 million to develop.

One unintended outcome of participating in an industry association's mitigating efforts is "free-riding" by non-members or smaller less visible members. Such companies might acquire the benefits resulting from being a member of the industry association (e.g. increased mitigation of shared footprint and industry reputation) without themselves having to contribute towards these efforts or abide by industry association regulations. This form of free-riding is motivated by the belief that, if only one or two small companies fail to comply with industry standards the other companies' activities will lead to a reduction in the footprint. Unfortunately, if too many companies follow this logic, it is the community that suffers (i.e., a tragedy of the commons occurs). This lack of compliance is most likely to occur lack of compliance is invisible.[24, 42]

Not-for-profits and advocacy groups

NPOs have been categorized into four types, based on whether they engage in service or advocacy work and on whether the beneficiary is self or others.[43] Advocacy groups who focus on holding corporations accountable for the "betterment of society" establish normative expectations and the steps to satisfy them. Often these are powerful NPOs, with significant self-interests and a broad-based active membership, which target specific companies through various channels of public communication. The targeted companies may be in a relatively weak position to respond because of a lack of technical capacity to remediate a footprint or respond to the NPOs' expectations. Companies are therefore left in a reactive mode and can do little to respond to the public attacks. An example of this type of advocacy is Greenpeace, which positions itself as a watchdog to expose business activities that are not environmentally friendly and refuses to build collaborative relationships with companies. In 1995, Shell (based in the United Kingdom) conducted a comprehensive analysis of the most effective approach to disposing of a North Sea oil storage and loading buoy[44] (i.e., Brent Spar) which was no longer functional. The most environmentally effective alternative was to sink the buoy in the North Sea. Greenpeace activated a campaign against Shell's plan to sink the Brent Spar (partly to increase its own visibility and membership) based on the intuitive logic "the ocean environment would be harmed with a large loading buoy at the bottom".

When NPOs adopt an adversarial approach, it becomes difficult for companies to comply with their expectations,[43] and to collaborate with them. As a result, companies may ignore their claims, creating reputational risks, or may work through industry associations to build additional capacity and lobby for more realistic solutions. Unfortunately, the lack of collaboration between NGOs and corporations often leads to a lack of understanding of the complexity of the issues within an operating context and competing expectations.[45] The impact that context can have on the perceived morality of company activities has been illustrated in published cases, where so-called "good practices" can be questionable, while alleged "bad practices" can be morally justified.[30, 46] For example, Chiquita's executives argued that their decision to make "protection payments" to militant groups in Columbia was based on a need to ensure safety of Chiquita's employees.[47]

The pressure that can be exerted by advocacy NPOs is so strong that companies have engaged in reactive mitigation and chosen options that fail to effectively compensate for the footprint, but satisfied the NPO's normative expectations. This tension is illustrated in the case of Soccer ball production in Sialkot, Pakistan, where the mitigation activities recommended by NPOs were just as harmful as (or maybe more harmful than) the original footprint. In response to public and NPO pressure, the soccer ball production industry adopted a policy requiring that soccer ball stitching in Sialkot, Pakistan, be done at designated workshops which could be carefully monitored for child labour and standardized work hours. Prior to such policies, soccer ball stitching was done by women in their homes, which also led to children stitching soccer balls; with a goal of pulling their families out of poverty.[46] The requirement for soccer ball stitching to be done at designated workshops was aimed at improving the lives of Sialkot families (by stopping child labour), but these families had no voice in any of the decision-making that led up to the creation of the new policy. Furthermore, almost all stitching families opposed the change, preferring to work at home where they had greater flexibility and could avoid publicly revealing that they were "stitchers" (something that women would be insulted for while they walked to the workshops).[46]

Simply by appealing to what is taken to be unequivocally progressive, to justify imposing a particular set of practices, may produce quick, purifying results (e.g. removal of child labour), but it may also, and indeed is likely to, generate unintended consequences that are less flattering to its champions. In Sialkot, the system of monitored workshops was introduced, not through a display of military might, but with a discourse of enlightened employment practice, legitimized by NGOs, which communicated to western consumers that the interests or "rights" ascribed to the children were guiding the change process and establishing work practices as they "ought" to be. We found that this discourse took scant account of concerns expressed to be of central importance to stitching families (e.g. living wages and the right to work in the privacy of homes).[46]

Failure to comply with the expectations of primary stakeholders (i.e., advocacy groups and NPOs) can negatively impact the "social legitimacy" of a corporation. Legitimacy is the "generalized perception or assumption that the actions of an entity are desirable, proper or appropriate within a social system".[37, 48] In contrast to regulated mitigation, companies are not ranked on their legitimacy; rather, they are perceived as legitimate (or not) based on a set of normative or cognitive factors.[49] In the end, companies may need to comply with the expectations of advocacy groups and NPOs to demonstrate recognition of the impact of their footprints and maintain their social legitimacy.

Another category of NPOs are those providing service to others (i.e., community).[43] These groups are often on the ground and have a better understanding of activities that can compensate community members for the unmitigated portions of a footprint. When these groups are focused on servicing a given community and are willing to work with company representatives, there is an opportunity to increase the effectiveness of compensatory activities. These collaborations should be based on developing a common understanding of the complexities within the directly impacted communities, as well as managing competing expectations.

In summary, the relationships between companies and NPOs cannot always be collaborative, and companies responding to the expectations of the NPOs will not necessarily lead to the most effective compensatory activities. NPOs that are service oriented and work directly in the community may provide the most effective approaches to identifying and implementing compensatory activities.

Vulnerable community members

Whereas reactive mitigation activities are responses to the expectations of NPOs, compensatory activities are based on companies directly collaborating with the communities harmed by their social and environmental footprints. In these situations, there is often a silent stakeholder – the most directly impacted and vulnerable community members. Well-intentioned companies may not initially recognize the impact of the unmitigated portions of a footprint on these vulnerable stakeholders as they do not have the appropriate voice to communicate their needs. This can lead to conflicting expectations from different stakeholders (such as from NGOs and the community members) about how and what compensation should be provided. Although communities sometimes accept the benefits of economic development knowing the costs of unmitigated footprints, the impacts of the unmitigated portions still need to monitored and assessed.

The tension between societal interests and specific community needs is illustrated in production of soccer balls in Sialkot, Pakistan. [45] For the Sialkot community, their real need was moving beyond abject poverty, for the short-term improvement of their daily lives. Although this meant extending their daily work and engaging children in sewing soccer balls, which violated normative labour principles, it provided the resources to move families beyond a point of basic daily existence to eventually focusing on long-term improvements (e.g., educating children). In these types of communities, it becomes important for companies to collaborate with community representatives in identifying what the appropriate trade-off of costs and benefits. The goal should not be to apply external conceptions of harm, fairness or effective compensation; rather, it is to give the community a self-determining role in the development of both short- and longer-term outcomes. The most effective or appropriate forms of compensation will be identified by companies and community representatives working together. Through face-to-face collaboration, managers can build relationships the reinforce the accountabilities to the directly impacted communities. In contrast to reactive mitigation, companies must make themselves accountable (in the sense of answerable) to such communities because otherwise the communities.

Summary

The first step in footprint mitigation is compliance with externally established regulatory standards; however, the relationships with stakeholders for satisfying these expectations requires the least resources. Given that the most effective response for complying with regulations and externally imposed standards is through isomorphic activites, companies can mimic best practices of other companies and reduce the costs of trial and error in finding appropriate compliance activities.

The role of an industry association in footprint mitigation cannot be understated. They provide a platform for sharing information, collaborating on improving remediation of shared and common footprints and responding to the normative expectations of NPOs and advocacy groups. Industry associations can monitor the normative expectations of NPOs and respond through a collective voice. Depending on the NPO, there may or may not be potential to develop cooperative or information sharing relationships with a particular organization.

Companies should develop individual relationships with community members (i.e., management with community representatives). These relationships need to facilitate an understanding of short and long-term interests and needs, particularly in terms of compensation for the umitigated portions of a footprint.

The relationship between the different types of footprint mitigation activities (and their associated stakeholders) can become rather complex, particulary when the activities appear to span two or more quadrants. For example, a company may initially join the UN Global Compact and take steps to support UN goals as a form of regulated mitigation, that is mimic the best practices for satisfying international standards. (The UN Global Compact is "a voluntary initiative based on CEO commitments to implement universal sustainability principles and to take steps to support UN goals"[50].) However, while exploring the activities that support the principles of the UN Global Compact, the company may find that working within an industry association increases the effectiveness of their unmitigated portions of the footprint. As well, the company experiences NGO pressures to respond to conditions within a specific community and engages in reactive mitigtion to reduce its local impact. The company also recognizes that satisfying the principles of the UN Global Compact does not fully mitigate its footprint within certain communities and identifies a need to engage in compensatory mitigation.

The overlapping responses to stakeholders across quadrants is not a failing of the framework, rather it provides "pathways" for analysis or justification of different types of activities. It can be used to clarify the rational for strategic initiatives, identify where responsibilities/initiatives overlap and direct companies to move beyond regulated or prescribed mitigation and respond to the unmitigated portions of a footprint. It also guides the setting of priorities in terms of aligning relationships with the anticipated outcomes of the mitigation activities.

Discussion

Part of the rationale for this framework is the minimal attention that has been given to the management of corporate footprints that are difficult to mitigate. The framework identifies four mitigation activities for reducing footprints and in particular the unmitigated portions after regulatory standards have been satisfied. The assumptions underlying this framework include all companies should work to optimize the mitigation of its footprints; footprints cannot be fully mitigated by satisfying any one set of stakeholder expectations; effective stakeholder relationships consume organizational resources; appropriate relationship with different stakeholders leads to optimal footprint mitigation and both broader societal and directly impacted community interests need to be satisfied.

The first assumption implies that there is an optimal combination of mitigation activities which is dependent on the capacity of a company to reduce footprints, the availability of industry associations and the tension between satisfying broad normative expectations and community needs. The second assumption is based on the need to respond to multiple stakeholders, with the appropriateness of a response being dependent on the complexity of the unmitigated portion of footprints, interpretations of how best to respond to normative expectations and the severity or complexity of a footprint's impact on community members.

Participation in industry associations may be a less visible response to footprint mitigation. That is, companies are not able to build their reputation by visibly promoting a unique response to a given situation. However, we propose it may be a more effective use of resources to work through industry associations for relevant regulatory, prescribed and reactive mitigation activities.

We do not develop specific hypotheses that can be tested empirically, nor is the framework intended to be a complete theory on footprint mitigation activities. Rather, our aim is to present a framework for managing the unmitigated portions of corporate footprints that leads to new research questions and provides guidance to managers. Some of the research questions include:

1   What are the relationships between different operating contexts and combinations of mitigation activities?
2   How can industry associations work with regulatory agencies and NPOs/advocacy groups to ensure an appropriate balance between broader societal issues and local community needs?
3   What are the best approaches to working with vulnerable community members to ensure their needs are addressed, even when it may lead to violations of broader normative principles?

References

1   Carroll, A. B., *Corporate social responsibility: Evolution of a definitional construct.* Business & Society, 1999. **38**(3): p. 268–295.
2   Sharp, Z. and N. Zaidman, *Strategization of CSR.* Journal of Business Ethics, 2010. **93**(1): p. 51–71.
3   Aguinis, H. and A. Glavas, *What we know and don't know about corporate social responsibility: A review and research agenda.* Journal of Management, 2012. **38**(4): p. 932–968.
4   Basu, K. and G. Palazzo, *Corporate social responsibility: A process model of sensemaking.* Academy of Management Review, 2008. **33**(1): p. 122–136.
5   Campbell, J. L., *Why would corporations behave in socially responsible ways? An institutional theory of corporate social responsibility.* Academy of Management Review, 2007. **32**(3): p. 946–967.
6   Lockett, A., J. Moon, and W. Visser, *Corporate social responsibility in management research: Focus, nature, salience and sources of influence.* Journal of Management Studies, 2006. **43**(1): p. 115–136.
7   Vallaster, C., A. Lindgreen, and F. Maon, *Strategically leveraging corporate social responsibility.* California Management Review, 2012. **54**(3): p. 34–60.
8   Hart, S. L. and M. B. Milstein, *Creating sustainable value.* The Academy of Management Executive, 2003. **17**(2): p. 56–67.
9   Shrivastava, P., *The role of corporations in achieving ecological sustainability.* Academy of Management Review, 1995. **20**(4): p. 936–960.
10   Carroll, A. B., *A three-dimensional conceptual model of corporate performance.* Academy of Management Review, 1979. **4**(4): p. 497–505.
11   Carroll, A. B., *The pyramid of corporate social responsibility: Toward the moral management of organizational stakeholders.* Business Horizons, 1991. **34**: p. 39–48.
12   DiMaggio, P. J. and W. W. Powell, *The iron cage revisited: Institutional isomorphism and collective rationality in organizational fields.* American Sociological Review, 1983. **48**: p. 147–160.
13   Scott, W. R. and G. F. Davis, *Organizations and organizing: Rational, natural and open systems perspectives.* 2015. London: Routledge.
14   Turban, D. B. and D. W. Greening, *Corporate social performance and organizational attractiveness to prospective employees.* The Academy of Management Journal, 1997. **40**(3): p. 658–672.
15   Crilly, D., M. Zollo, and M. T. Hansen, *Faking it or muddling through? Understanding decoupling in response to stakeholder pressures.* Academy of Management Journal, 2012. **55**(6): p. 1429–1448.
16   Bondy, K., J. Moon, and D. Matten, *An institution of corporate social responsibility (CSR) in multinational corporations (MNCs): Form and implications.* Journal of Business Ethics, 2012. **111**(2): p. 281–299.
17   Fooks, G., et al., *The limits of corporate social responsibility: Techniques of neutralization, stakeholder management and political CSR.* Journal of Business Ethics, 2013. **112**(2): p. 283–299.

18 Maitland, I., *The limits of business self-regulation.* California Management Review, 1985. **27**(3): p. 132–147.

19 Hulm, P., P. de Sousa, and N. Domeisen. *Grass-roots NGOs Develop Trade.* in *INTERNATIONAL TRADE FORUM.* 2006. INTERNATIONAL TRADE CENTRE UNCTAD/GATT.

20 Haack, P., D. Schoeneborn, and C. Wickert, *Talking the talk, moral entrapment, creeping commitment? Exploring narrative dynamics in corporate responsibility standardization.* Organization Studies, 2012. **33**(5–6): p. 815–845.

21 Kong, N., et al., *Moving business/industry towards sustainable consumption:: The role of NGOs.* European Management Journal, 2002. **20**(2): p. 109–127.

22 Van Cranenburgh, K. C., K. Liket, and N. Roome, *Management responses to social activism in an era of corporate responsibility: A case study.* Journal of Business Ethics, 2013. **118**(3): p. 497–513.

23 Smith, A., *An inquiry into the nature and causes of the wealth of nations, 1st edn 1776, vol. II of The Glasgow Edition of the Works and Correspondence of Adam Smith, edited by RH Campbell, AS Skinner and WB Todd.* AS Skinner and WB Todd, 1976.

24 Arrow, K. J., *The limits of organization.* 1974. London: Norton.

25 Bowen, H. and F. Johnson, *Social responsibility of the businessman, 1953.* New York: Harper & Row.

26 Votaw, D., *Genius becomes rare: A comment on the doctrine of social responsibility pt. II.* California Management Review, 1973. **15**(3): p. 5–19.

27 Preston, L. E. and J. E. Post, *Private management and public policy: the principles of public responsibility.* 1975. Englewood Cliffs, NJ: Prentice-Hall.

28 Quinn, D. P. and T. M. Jones, *An Agent Morality View of Business Policy.* The Academy of Management Review, 1995. **20**(1): p. 22–42.

29 Weaver, G. R., L. K. Treviño, and P. L. Cochran, *Integrated and decoupled corporate social performance: Management commitments, external pressures, and corporate ethics practices.* Academy of Management Journal, 1999. **42**(5): p. 539–552.

30 Eabrasu, M., *A moral pluralist perspective on corporate social responsibility: From good to controversial practices.* Journal of Business Ethics, 2012. **110**(4): p. 429–439.

31 Wang, T. and P. Bansal, *Social responsibility in new ventures: profiting from a long-term orientation.* Strategic Management Journal, 2012. **33**(10): p. 1135–1153.

32 Bowen, H. R., *Social responsibilities of the businessman.* 2013. Iowa City, IA: University of Iowa Press.

33 Post, J. and L. E. Preston, *Private management and public policy: The principle of public responsibility.* 2012. Stanford: Stanford University Press.

34 Rankin, S., Liu, X., & Falkenberg, L., *Institutional legitimacy to internal adaptation: The evolution of CSR reporting.* 2015, August. Divisional Paper Session, Academy of Management Annual Meeting, Atlanta, Georgia.

35 Barnett, M. L. and A. A. King, *Good fences make good neighbors: A longitudinal analysis of an industry self-regulatory institution.* Academy of Management Journal, 2008. **51**(6): p. 1150–1170.

36 Ashforth, B. E. and B. W. Gibbs, *The double-edge of organizational legitimation.* Organization Science, 1990. **1**(2): p. 177–194.

37 Deephouse, D. L. and S. M. Carter, *An examination of differences between organizational legitimacy and organizational reputation.* Journal of Management Studies, 2005. **42**(2): p. 329–360.

38 Bansal, P. and I. Clelland, *Talking trash: Legitimacy, impression management, and unsystematic risk in the context of the natural environment.* Academy of Management Journal, 2004. **47**(1): p. 93–103.

39 Child, J. and T. Tsai, *The dynamic between firms' environmental strategies and institutional constraints in emerging economies: Evidence from China and Taiwan.* Journal of Management Studies, 2005. **42**(1): p. 95–125.

40 Jones, T. M., *Instrumental Stakeholder Theory: A Synthesis of Ethics and Economics.* The Academy of Management Review, 1995. **20**(2): p. 404–437.

41 COSIA, *About COSIA.* 2015. Available from: www.cosia.ca/about-cosia.

42 Hardin, G., *Extensions of "the tragedy of the commons".* Science, 1998. **280**(5364): p. 682–683.

43 Yaziji, M. and J. Doh, *NGOs and corporations: Conflict and collaboration.* 2009. Cambridge: Cambridge University Press.

44 Winter, M., Schweinserg, M., Steger, U., & Killing, P., *The Brent Spar Platform Controversy (A, B & C).* IMD004, 2002. **27**(12).

45 Scherer, A. G. and G. Palazzo, *Toward a political conception of corporate responsibility: Business and society seen from a Habermasian perspective.* Academy of Management Review, 2007. **32**(4): p. 1096–1120.

46 Khan, F. R., *Representational approaches matter.* Journal of Business Ethics, 2007. **73**(1): p. 77–89.

47 Schotter, A. and M. Teagarden, *Blood Bananas: Chiquita in Colombia.* 2010. Thunderbird School of Global Management Arizona.

48 Suchman, M. C., *Managing legitimacy: Strategic and institutional approaches.* The Academy of Management Review, 1995. **20**(3): p. 571–610.

49 Palazzo, G. and A. G. Scherer, *Corporate legitimacy as deliberation: A communicative framework.* Journal of Business Ethics, 2006. **66**(1): p. 71–88.

50 Compact, U. N. G. Available from: www.unglobalcompact.org/about.

3.8 The Manchester Super Casino

Experience and learning in a cross-sector social partnership

Jon Reast, Adam Lindgreen, Joëlle Vanhamme, and François Maon

Introduction

The increasing concerns about social issues across business environments worldwide and the resultant emphasis on the corporate social responsibility (CSR) idea (Carroll, 2004; Gabriel, 2006; Lindgreen et al., 2009; Perrini et al., 2006), have made cross-sector social partnerships (CSSPs) or interactions[1] increasingly desirable for organizations (Austin, 2000; Kanter, 1998; Korten, 1998; Seitanidi and Lindgreen, 2008; Waddock and Smith, 2000), especially those that need to burnish their CSR credentials (Seitanidi and Crane, 2009; Seitanidi and Ryan, 2007). Cross-sector social partnerships, loosely defined as collaborations by partners from two or more sectors to tackle economic and social issues, remain highly complex and difficult to manage though (London et al., 2005; Maon et al., 2009; Muthuri et al., 2009; Selsky and Parker, 2005). The involvement of several stakeholders means an organization must take multiple concerns into account when managing its various partnerships (Muthuri et al., 2009; Oxley-Green and Hunton-Clark, 2003; Selsky and Parker, 2005).

Yet CSSPs offer great potential benefits for both business and not-for-profit organizations. The former gain easier access to resources (Barringer and Harrison, 2000); enhanced reputational or social capital (Millar et al., 2004; Steckel and Simons, 1992); and increased levels of stakeholder trust and corporate legitimacy (Heugens et al., 2002; Millar et al., 2004). The nonprofit groups also enjoy increased visibility and publicity (Elkington and Fennell, 1998), easier access to financial resources, employee volunteers and training facilities (O'Regan and Oster, 2000), and greater contributions (Muthuri et al., 2009). Furthermore, both types of organizations likely achieve organizational learning as an outcome of CSSPs (Drucker, 1989; London et al., 2005; Selsky and Parker, 2005). Partnerships offer new insights into the relevant problem, and partners learn new ways to frame problems and potential solutions (Boguslaw, 2002; Huxham and Vangen, 2000). This includes, for example, societal learning that can produce innovation and change (Waddell, 1999); "reflective skills that can modify mindsets and habits" (Selsky and Parker, 2005: 858); and social, administrative, and technical abilities (Seitanidi and Crane, 2009).

Despite the clear importance of CSSPs and significant research related to them, to the best of our knowledge, only limited and indirect references have addressed the importance of prior learning for ongoing CSSP development and interactions (Seitanidi, 2007; Waddock, 1989, 1991), though such learning should have a key role in the success of CSSPs (Seitanidi, 2007; Seitanidi and Crane, 2009; Selsky and Parker, 2005). For example, government – business CSSPs change with "more experience . . . and partnering moves into more fully developed policy partnerships" (Selsky and Parker, 2005: 860). Seitanidi and Crane (2009: 424) also note the importance of "a willingness to learn and adapt" for successful CSSPs. Yet Selsky and Parker (2005: 866) recognize too that "studies which show how partners overcome (or exploit) sectoral differences to learn about their social issue, learn from each other, or encourage stakeholder learning would be valuable contributions." They indicate that extant research has examined short-term partnerships but continues to "leave gaps in understanding long-term impacts, consequences and learning" for CSSPs (Selsky and Parker, 2005: 866). In particular, extant literature has not considered the impact of prior CSSP experience and learning on the development, management, and success of new initiatives. We address this lacuna by investigating the following questions: What is the impact of organizational experience and learning on the development and management of CSSPs, and how can models of CSSP practice better reflect organizational experience and learning?

We investigate a significant, complex, tri-sector CSSP (cf. Selsky and Parker, 2005), the Manchester Super Casino project, which includes government, business, and not-for-profit organizations, and thereby critically examine prior conceptualizations and models of CSSPs. With this study, we contribute by integrating organizational learning and CSSP literature, two well-developed streams of research that so far have not been connected satisfactorily previously. Various elements of prior CSSP literature note organizational learning in passing, but no studies have fully exploited the theoretical lenses that organizational learning offers to clarify CSSP success or support an integrated framework of the learning CSSP process.

We structure the remainder of this chapter as follows: First, we offer a literature review in which we both note some gaps and deficiencies in our current understanding of CSSPs and introduce organizational learning literature. This review informs our fieldwork. Second, we describe our methodology, and third, we present and discuss the findings of our study of the Manchester City Council's proposal for a regional super casino and entertainment destination, which emphasizes the importance of prior CSSP experience and organizational learning, as well as the adoption of a long-term orientation. We thus propose a new model of the learning CSSP process. Fourth, we identify some theoretical contributions and managerial implications, including a template for managing complex CSSPs from the perspective of different partner organizations. Fifth, we discuss some limitations to our study and suggest avenues for further research.

Theoretical framework

Definitions of cross-sector social partnerships

Since the 1980s (Gray, 1989), literature on CSSPs has drawn on diverse disciplines, including collaborative strategy (Astley and Fombrun, 1983; Huxham and Vangen, 1996); CSR (Waddock and Smith, 2000); management (Austin, 2000; Gray, 1989; Seitanidi and Crane, 2009); and organization studies (Bryson and Crosby, 2006). The use of CSSPs is increasing (Berger et al., 2004; Boehm, 2005; Crane, 2000), and academic study of CSSPs has increased in parallel (Selsky and Parker 2005). Cross-sector social partnerships represent a "poorly understood phenomenon" (Googins and Rochlin, 2000: 133) and have been defined in various, and sometimes competing, ways (Kooiman, 1999; Nelson and Zadeck, 2000; Selsky and Parker, 2005; Waddock, 1991), as Table 3.8.1 shows. Most of

Table 3.8.1 Cross-sector social partnerships definitions

Author(s)	Definition	Key aspects
Kooiman (1999)	All interactive arrangements in which public and private actors participate to solve societal problems or create societal opportunities and attend to the institutions within which these activities take place.	Public and private actors; solutions to societal problems; social opportunities; governing institutions.
Muthuri et al. (2009)	Business involvement in social initiatives by contributing financial, in-kind, or human resources to meet the social and economic needs of the communities in which they operate.	Business contributions; social initiatives; community needs.
Roberts and Bradley (1991)	A temporary social arrangement in which two or more social actors work together toward a single common end, which requires the transmutation of materials, ideas, and/or social relations to achieve.	Temporary; social actors; work together; single common end.
Selsky and Parker (2005)	Cross-sector projects formed explicitly to address social issues that actively engage the partners on an ongoing basis.	Cross-sectoral; addressing social issues; ongoing.
Waddock (1991)	The voluntary collaborative efforts of actors from organizations in two or more economic sectors in a forum in which they cooperatively attempt to solve a problem or issue of mutual concern that is in some way identified with a public policy agenda item.	Cross-sectoral; voluntary; solving societal problems; mutual concern.

these definitions include notions of cross-sector societal issues and/or benefits, with some stressing mutuality and continuity as well. For the purposes of this chapter, faced with no single unified definition of CSSPs, we define them as the deliberate and ongoing collaboration of partners from two or more societal sectors working to tackle mutually important social and economic issues.

CSSP CONTINUUM OF ENGAGEMENT

Most literature on CSSPs implies a continuum of engagement. Some authors describe two levels (Selsky and Parker, 2005), though the majority support three levels, labeled in various ways, as we show in Table 3.8.2. To simplify this array of competing labels, we note that the continuum tends to range from an introductory level to an intermediate and then an advanced level. The introductory level usually involves one-way communication and power (Grunig and Grunig, 1992), associated with a short-term, narrowly defined, self-interested orientation (Selsky and Parker, 2005). The intermediate level extends to include two-way, asymmetric communication and power balances, as well as a medium-term orientation and increased levels of mutuality. Finally, the advanced level achieves two-way, symmetric communication and power balances, is associated with the longer-term, is broadly defined, and emphasizes mutuality. More CSSPs appear in introductory rather than intermediate and advanced levels (Muthuri et al., 2009; Selsky and Parker, 2005).

We are particularly interested in whether these levels on the CSSP continuum constitute a pathway, which tends to be navigated step-by-step and thus demands time and experience. Although no research has adopted a time- and experience-based view of the

Table 3.8.2 CSSP continua

Authors	Introductory	Intermediate	Advanced
Two-stage models			
Selsky and Parker (2005)	Transactional	_____	Integrative
Alberic and van Lierop (2006)	Inside-out	_____	Outside-in
Three-stage models			
Austin (2000)	Philanthropic	Transactional	Integrative
Muthuri et al. (2009)	Traditional	Developmental	Relational
Morsing and Shultz (2006)	Informing	Responding	Involving
Oxley-Green and Hunton-Clark (2003)	Informative	Consultative	Decisional

levels on the continuum, it has suggested in a limited sense that CSSP partnerships might result in organizational learning, which then affects future interactions (Waddock, 1989, 1991). Moreover, understanding, trust, and commitment might develop over time in such relationships, which then help resolve issues of power asymmetry (Seitanidi, 2007).

MODELING CSSPS

A significant research stream reflects ongoing attempts to model CSSPs. Some models define process stages in the formation and implementation of CSSPs (Chapple and Moon, 2005; Seitanidi and Crane, 2009), whereas others adopt a more strategic level. For example, Muthuri and colleagues (2009) design a framework of corporate interactive governance, in which they include a structural level that reflects the external environmental factors that influence the development, implementation, and outcome of CSSPs, as well as an action level that reflects the interactions of the partners. This framework thus acknowledges the different preferences, intentions, and expectations of various stakeholders (Muthuri et al., 2009), but as do many other models, it only relates to CSSPs involving two sectors and assumes that each sector can be represented easily as a single unit. More process-based models draw on collaborative strategies literature, such as Waddell and Brown's (1997) five-phase model (identifying preconditions for partnership; convening partners and defining problems; setting shared directions; implementing action strategies; and institutionalizing or expanding successful intersectoral collaborations) or Seitanidi and Crane's (2009) simplified three-stage process model (partnership selection, design, and institutionalization).

Prior models also tend to be static in orientation and regard CSSP efforts as individual, *ad hoc* initiatives that do not reflect relational or continuous interactions over time and different projects. Nor do the models contain learning loops that might capture the knowledge and adaptation that can result from current and prior CSSP interactions (Crossan et al., 1999). Overall then, existing efforts fail to capture the messiness of partnership practices with complex models (Selsky and Parker, 2005).

Organizational learning

For the past 40 years, organizational learning has been a key focus within management and organization research (Cangelosi and Dill, 1965; Crossan et al., 1999; Simon, 1969; Vera and Crossan, 2004). (For reviews of organizational learning, see for example Dodgson, 1993; Easterby-Smith et al., 2000; Fiol and Lyles, 1985; Levitt and March, 1988.) Simon (1969: 236) defines it as "the growing insights and successful restructurings of organizational problems by individuals reflected in the structural elements and outcomes of the organization itself." Such impacts on strategic management outcomes have been widely researched and reported (e.g., Crossan and Berdrow, 2003; Fiol and Lyles, 1985; Slater and Narver, 1995), and some observers even claim organizational learning is a critical source of competitive advantage, because "the ability to learn faster than your competitors may be the only sustainable competitive advantage" (DeGeus, 1988: 71). Organizational learning thus relates positively to organizational performance (Bontis et al., 2002).

CONCEPTUALIZATION OF ORGANIZATIONAL LEARNING

Organizational learning takes two forms (Polanyi, 1967): Tacit knowledge or learning, which is relatively intangible, often relates to habits or culture and is difficult to capture and share (Nelson and Winter, 1982), and explicit knowledge or learning, which can be more precisely defined, documented, and communicated. These two forms support each other and influence how and what organizations learn (Polanyi, 1967). Organizational learning also encompasses a tension between new learning, or exploration, and using what already has been learned, or exploitation (March, 1991). Exploratory learning refers to discovery and experimentation with new alternatives and opportunities, whereas exploitative learning pertains to the execution, refinement, or deepening of existing competences (Brady and Davies, 2004; Dodgson, 1993; March, 1991). Organizations must balance these exploratory and exploitative elements to leverage their prior knowledge while also remaining open to new knowledge (March, 1991; Schildt et al., 2005).

MODELING ORGANIZATIONAL LEARNING

Among the various models and frameworks of organizational learning (Daft and Weick, 1984; March and Olsen, 1975; Nonaka and Takeuchi, 1995), the multilevel framework by Crossan and colleagues (1999) is generally well accepted. The framework, known as 4i, reflects several key premises. In particular, it conceptualizes organizational learning as involving multiple levels within organizations, from individual to the group and then to the overall organizational level, as we depict in Figure 3.8.1.

These three levels of organizational learning are linked by four social and psychological processes, intuiting, interpreting, integrating, and institutionalizing (i.e., the four i's), that allow for "feed-forward" from the individual to the organizational level and feedback from the organizational to the individual level.

Intuiting, which refers to "the preconscious recognition of the pattern and/or possibilities inherent in a personal stream of experience" (Crossan et al., 1999: 525), is possessed by individual members who develop novel insights based on their experience, ascertain underlying or potential patterns in that experience, and then translate their insights into metaphors that can be communicated (Lawrence et al., 2005). The second process, interpreting, relates to "the explaining, through words and/or actions of an insight or idea to one's self and to others" (Crossan et al., 1999: 525). Thus interpreting begins at the individual level and extends to include others through conversation and dialog. Through interpreting, ideas become explicit, named, and incorporated into cognitive maps that relate the new idea to other ideas or external contexts (Lawrence

Level	Process	Inputs/Outcomes		
Individual	*Intuiting*	Experiences, images, metaphors		
	Interpreting	Language, cognitive map, conversation/dialogue	*Feedback*	*Feedforward*
Group	*Integrating*	Shared understandings, mutual adjustment, interactive systems		
Organization	*Institutionalizing*	Routines, diagnostic systems, rules and procedures		

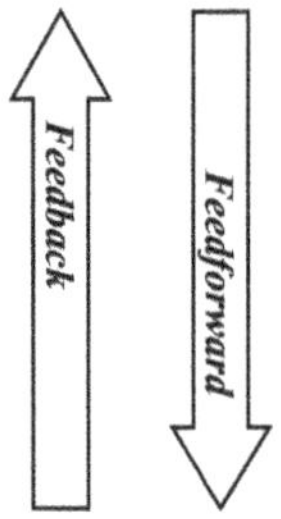

Figure 3.8.1 Learning in organizations: four processes through three levels

Source: Adapted from Crossan et al. (1999: 525).

et al., 2005). The third process of integrating occurs at the group level. As the "process of developing shared understanding among individuals and of taking coordinated action through mutual adjustment" (Crossan et al., 1999: 525), integrating aims to achieve coherent collective action. Finally, institutionalization implies that learning among individuals and groups gets embedded into organizations through "systems, structures, procedures, and strategy" (Crossan et al., 1999: 525). This process makes organizational learning distinct from individual or group learning; through institutionalizing, ideas transform into organizational institutions that are available to all members on an ongoing basis, at least somewhat independent of their individual or group origins. Together, the four processes form a learning loop.

General acceptance of this multilevel, process-based nature of organizational learning appears in prior literature (Easterby-Smith et al., 2000), and many studies in the past 10 years have either applied or refined this basic framework (Lawrence et al., 2005; Vera and Crossan, 2004). Notwithstanding such general acceptance, some authors also stress the importance of leadership styles (Beverland and Lindgreen, 2007; Slater and Narver, 1995; Vera and Crossan, 2004) and of colleagues' "approachability, credibility and trustworthiness" with regard to sharing knowledge (Andrews and Delahaye, 2000: 797), as well as the impact of the power and political status of key individuals within organizations (Lawrence et al., 2005). Additional research emphasizes the view that organizational learning depends on its history, such that organizations learn from direct experience and the indirect experience of other organizations, then develop conceptual frameworks or paradigms to interpret that experience (Levitt and March, 1988).

Research focus

Although research efforts aimed at conceptualizing and modeling CSSPs and underlying processes have offered key insights, various gaps remain. In particular, CSSPs are still a relatively poorly understood phenomenon, and though many authors cite a continuum from introductory to advanced levels, it is not clear whether this progression constitutes a pathway to be navigated. The static models of CSSP ignore any prior experiential learning or resource benefits (tangible or intangible) by partners in prior interactions.

On the basis of our literature review, we derive two focused research questions to guide our study and enhance our knowledge about CSSPs. We investigate these questions in the context of a government sector-led regeneration CSSP, which enables us to contribute further to extant literature. First, what is the impact of organizational experience and learning on the development and management of CSSPs? Second, how can models of CSSP practice better reflect organizational experience and learning? To answer these questions, we focus on a complex, tri-sector CSSP, in which each sector of the partnership has different interests. By determining if the partners' prior experience and learning enable the CSSP to operate at a more advanced or integrative level on the engagement continuum, we offer ideas for managing complex tri-sector CSSPs.

Methodology

The use of qualitative methods is appropriate for studying complex processes (Eisenhardt, 1989; Lindgreen, 2008; Yin, 2003). Using secondary data and multiple interviews also helps develop rich insights and provide the basis for greater transferability of the findings to other contexts (Eisenhardt, 1989). We therefore adopt these methods and employ a case approach.

Case selection and description

We select the tri-sector Manchester Super Casino CSSP for this research. This CSSP commenced in 2003, when the U.K. government announced the likely reclassification of gambling legislation to allow more and larger casinos. The CSSP progressed through various stages during a 5-year period and culminated in 2007, when Manchester was awarded a license (in a competitive bidding process with other U.K. locations) to run the "largest casino in Europe" (Tobin Prior, CEO, Kerzner Consortium). The Manchester City Council, as the local government body responsible for the regeneration of East Manchester and the owner of the proposed site, was the focal organization.

The complex Manchester Super Casino CSSP includes various stakeholder groups that represent governmental/public interests (e.g., Manchester City Council, New East Manchester Ltd., Greater Manchester Police, Joint Health Unit, regional planning bodies); business (private sector casino complex provider, local developer, local businesses); and not-for-profit groups (religious groups, residents, community). This case represents good practice (Casino Advisory Panel, 2007), and the focal partner, as well as other partners on the project, has had significant direct experience with CSSPs over the past 20 years. Therefore, this rich, long-term case study provides sufficient, high-quality data to investigate the research questions in this study.

Data collection

We develop a rich case history for the Manchester Super Casino CSSP and also gather data about prior CSSP projects in which all the partners were involved. The first author conducted interviews with ten key representatives from nine partner organizations across the governmental, business, and not-for-profit sectors. As we show in Table 3.8.3, most of these participants were CEOs, managers, or leading representatives from the partners, many of whom were involved in the same interactions with regard to the CSSP. Together these participants were responsible for the development and

Table 3.8.3 Organizations and respondents

Organization; respondent	Stakeholder group (public, private, nonprofit)	Mission (general)	Role in proposed regional super casino	Reason(s) for inclusion in study
Manchester City Council; Sir Howard Bernstein, chief executive	Public	To develop innovative and sustainable regeneration approaches that become recognized as best practices; to establish a CSSP engagement infrastructure and long-term relationships with partners.	The developer of the proposal.	Manchester City Council is the focal organization driving the project. It chaired the panel proposing the project to the national government.
New East Manchester Ltd.; Tom Russell, former chief executive; Ian McCormack, project executive	Public/nonprofit	To develop innovative and sustainable regeneration approaches that become recognized as best practices.	A hybrid governance, nonprofit organization developed in 1999 to manage to the development of East Manchester. A lead organization together with the City Council.	Implementation arm of the Manchester City Council, though still partner governed. Involved in many interactions with partners.
Manchester Joint Health Unit (City Council and NHS Manchester); Ged Devereux, manager	Public	To develop initiatives to improve the health of residents in the Manchester area and reduce deprivation and inequality.	Public sector organization with a stake in some potential social costs of a casino: increased crime, gambling addiction, and associated problems.	Key advisor regarding social responsibility unit developed to support casino development.
Kerzner Consortium; Tobin Pryor, CEO	Private consortium investors (casino operator and local developer, Ask Developments)	To provide innovative, attractive gambling services that profit the organization and benefit others in the process.	Private sector casino resort operator. The profit-based element of the project. Key investor of £260m for the project.	Sat on the panel proposing the project, attended many meetings.
Responsibility in Gambling Trust; Paul Bellringer, CBE	Nonprofit charity	To ensure that the gambling industry develops with due regard to issues of social responsibility and that vulnerable populations are protected and helped.	Expert advisor on social responsibility issues associated with gambling.	A nonprofit organization involved in funding research and providing support for people with gambling problems. Attended many meetings and sat on the panel proposing the project.

Stakeholder	Type	Objectives	Position	Role
Greater Manchester Faith and Community Group; Reverend Stephen Williams	Nonprofit community group	To ensure that the interests of faith groups are represented; to protect the vulnerable from the development of gambling.	Critical voice toward the proposal. Opposed to casinos, but working to minimize any damage resulting from the development.	A nonprofit stakeholder. Attended many key meetings and helped develop the social responsibility framework for the project.
East Manchester Residents' Forum; Steve Green, chair, and representative on NEM board.	Nonprofit community group	To develop and enhance the East Manchester area for the benefit of its residents; to provide sustainable jobs and enhance infrastructure and services.	People living around the development site would be impacted by the construction and the running of a major casino resort.	A nonprofit stakeholder, directly representing the views of the community in which the project would be located. Attended many meetings representing community and sat on the panel representing project.
Professor Peter Collins, director, Centre for the Study of Gambling and Commercial Gaming, University of Salford	Public, academic	To undertake research relating to the gambling industry	Expert advisor regarding gambling legislation and the social impacts of gambling.	An academic and expert assessor involved in project meetings regarding social responsibility.
Greater Manchester Police; Commander Justine Curran (now Chief Constable, Tayside Police)	Public	To ensure the development of East Manchester and minimize any issues related to crime and disorder.	Supporter of regeneration of Manchester while providing guidance regarding law and order issues.	Attended many meetings regarding the project and sat on the panel representing the project.

implementation of the CSSP, and they participated in ongoing partnership structures in the focal geographic area.

We stopped our interviews when we achieved saturation – that is, when extra interviews begin to yield few new insights (Strauss and Corbin, 1998). Each digitally recorded interview averaged 90 minutes in length (range: 45–120 minutes) and was transcribed, resulting in 240 single-spaced A4 pages. Our approach involved a constant comparative analysis. After each interview, we wrote theoretical memos as part of our theory-building process (Strauss and Corbin, 1998) to refine the research questions and provide a theoretical focus for the subsequent interviews. During the interviews, informants described their role in the super casino CSSP, responding to a mix of grand tour questions and floating prompts that aimed to reduce interviewer bias and allow for rich insights (McCracken, 1986). As the interviews progressed, it became clear that the informants agreed about the advanced, tri-sectoral nature of the project, so the interviews increasingly focused on understanding the nature of the interactions and management of the CSSP, as well as any prior CSSP experiences and learning by partner organizations and their impact on the super casino project. We also asked the informants about the factors they felt contributed to the success of the CSSP. During these phases, we undertook constant comparisons among emerging theory, new data, and prior literature, and this dialectical tacking drove our subsequent approaches. Then in subsequent interviews, we asked informants about the role of key individuals or other key internal or external influences during the CSSP process. Prior to each interview, the interviewer reviewed any publicly available secondary material to increase familiarity with the case. In all, we collected and reviewed 120 documents for this study (e.g., Final Report of the Casino Advisory Panel from 2007, Manchester Bid Proposal from 2006). These multiple sources improved the quality of our final interpretation and helped ensure triangulation (Beverland et al., 2010; Strauss and Corbin, 1998; Yin, 2003).

Data analysis

Our analysis employed QSR: NUD★IST to keep track of the data, facilitate coding, and check for relationships. During the case analysis, we elaborated on the theoretical categories through open and axial coding procedures (Strauss and Corbin, 1998). Throughout, we also tacked back and forward between literature on CSSPs and organizational learning and the data, which led us to develop multiple theoretical categories and subcategories (Spiggle, 1994). We analyzed each interview transcript to gain a richer understanding of the interactions within the CSSP, prior partner experience, and learning about CSSPs, as well as the impact of such experience on the super casino CSSP.

During open coding, we read and examined discrete parts of the interview transcripts to identify similarities and differences. Each author undertook this analysis independently and classified each interview portion according to an initial coding scheme: CSSP, tri-sector, interactions, and influences on CSSP outcomes. The authors then met to discuss and reach agreement on any parts of the analysis subject to disagreement.

We applied axial coding to reassemble the data into categories and subcategories and thereby understand the role of the core components and capabilities. For example, with their unique and often particular characteristics, different partner groups tended to focus on the specific issues they believed were most appropriate and relevant for CSSP programs. Finally, we applied selective coding by integrating and refining the theory emerging from our data.

We also adopted several methods to improve the quality of our research (Beverland and Lindgreen, 2010; Lincoln and Guba, 1985; Strauss and Corbin, 1998). In particular, the four researchers each provided independent interpretations of the findings; we conducted multiple interviews; and the respondents had the opportunity to provide feedback on initial findings, all of which reinforced the reliability of our outcomes. In addition, only one researcher conducted all the interviews, which reduced the potential for bias.

Findings

Our findings are presented as follows. First, we consider the learning processes partners achieve through their prior experience. Second, we note the impact of experience and learning on the development and management of the Manchester Super Casino CSSP. Third, we apply these findings to derive an updated model of CSSPs.

Learning processes based on prior experience

The partners in this CSSP had developed several key learning exploration areas (March, 1991) from their experience over the previous 20 years. The ongoing relationships among partners in Manchester (governmental, business, and not-for-profit), which had worked effectively in the past, helped participants perceive the long-term benefits of such approaches. Some learning gained from prior CSSPs and exploited for the super casino CSSP appeared explicit (e.g., published strategy documents), whereas other forms clearly were tacit (e.g., CSSP philosophy). Partners noted the importance of seven exploratory learning areas in particular for the success of this CSSP: visionary leadership and a clear strategy, development of a CSSP philosophy, understanding partners' needs and priorities, developing long-term deep and trusting relationships, constructing a highly developed communication infrastructure, ensuring early engagement on any new projects, and ensuring high-quality personnel to support the CSSPs.

LEARNING AREA 1: VISIONARY LEADERSHIP AND A CLEAR CSSP STRATEGY

Many of the interviewed partners noted the importance of the chief executive of the council, Sir Howard Bernstein, with the support of the leader of the council, Sir Richard Lease, who provided visionary leadership. Sir Howard was frequently described as the driving force behind the council's CSSP strategy and the regeneration of Manchester:

> Sir Howard has been really instrumental in bringing it all together. He was very instrumental in making sure the package was right for the local community, for the city as a whole, to secure something positive for the benefit of Manchester residents.
>
> (Steve, residents' forum participant)

Generally regarded as a highly visible, charismatic, transformational leader, Sir Howard was very clear about the importance of the cross-sectoral partnerships as a means to achieve regeneration of East Manchester. The critical influence of this charismatic leader, in his position of significant power, is consistent with organizational change literature (Lawrence et al., 2005), which also notes the importance of leadership styles (Slater and Narver, 1995; Vera and Crossan, 2004). The CEO's open management style enabled "feed-forward" from individual members through to their group and the organizational level as part of the CSSP process. However, this CEO also was prepared to use his powerful position to institutionalize learning and drive organizational behavior through feedback mechanisms. This approach suggests the CEO wanted to ensure that the organization and its partners exploited exploratory learning from prior projects (March, 1991).

The evidence of individual to group learning processes included the CEO's attendance at many partner meetings and involvement in shaping projects. Through his team, he also remained aware of new project opportunities and the benefits of building long-term relationships with partners, which the other participants recognized: "It was driven from the top by Sir Howard. I have to say I was incredibly impressed by that man; he made things happen" (Paul, gambling CSR expert). Through his direct involvement in previous CSSPs, Sir Howard had explored directly the mechanics of such projects and some of their success factors. He was also very aware of the experiences of some of his "competitor" councils as they developed strategies for bidding on the casino project:

> I think Howard had such an influence partly because of his personal qualities but also his experience, particularly with Manchester Millennium meant that he had very strong working relationships across a very wide range of interests in Manchester.
>
> (Tom, CEO of New East Manchester Ltd.)

In turn, the council developed a very clear strategy for the regeneration of East Manchester and reviewed all possible projects in light of this long-term strategy. The casino project represented essentially a "regeneration vehicle" to the council that could bring investments into a deprived area. The city council already had learned that capital investments needed to regenerate East Manchester would have to come from the business sector and that any investment project needed the support of local businesses, as well as other not-for-profit community partners. The casino CSSP project was thus one more regeneration project, among a wealth of such projects, and thus part of a wider CSSP philosophy:

> So you know we were very clear about what were the outcomes we were looking to deliver here . . . how this fits with the well-established aspirations of the community, where this fits with some of the key stakeholders.
>
> (Sir Howard)

LEARNING AREA 2: DEVELOPMENT OF A CSSP PHILOSOPHY

The partners chose to adopt a CSSP philosophy because of their direct experience and exploratory learning with urban regeneration CSSP projects, since the early 1990s, because "Yes, we got established in the early days in the 1990s, developed a good understanding from council officers right the way up to Sir Howard" (Steve, residents' forum member). Public–private partnerships had long been a structural component of CSSPs, but over time, these partners also had explored the importance of non-contractual factors that could influence CSSP success. These soft elements were not detailed or documented, but their importance nevertheless was well understood by the partners.

For example, the gradual development of deep and trusting relationships among key partners meant that the super casino CSSP project could be likened to a conversation among partners, in which an ongoing dialog and understanding already has been established:

> A long history really, a long tradition of doing things in this way in Manchester, and consequently it was very much easier to have those kinds of dialogs across the sectors here. I think that did help the casino project.
>
> (Tom, CEO, New East Manchester Ltd.)

Such mutual agreement about the desired outcomes (e.g., investment and regeneration, employment, and training, reduced deprivation, profits) also underpinned the success of various CSSP projects. By developing a philosophy, the council and its partners already had built an environment that supported success at the individual CSSP project level.

It is also notable that Manchester City Council, a public sector entity anchored to the Manchester area, has clear, long-term interest in this geographic location and tends to adopt a long-term perspective, with "what are known as strategic regeneration frameworks that have been the subject of extensive consultation with residents, with business, with the voluntary sector over a considerable period of time" (Sir Howard). This statement reinforces the long-term structural ties among the partners, as well as reflecting the ongoing partnership philosophy and clear long-term strategy for the region. Such a structuring of relationship interactions suggests a policy of exploiting former exploratory learning, in this case about high-quality interaction mechanisms.

LEARNING AREA 3: UNDERSTANDING PARTNERS' NEEDS AND PRIORITIES

The ongoing CSSP engagement gave the council a good understanding of the general positions and needs of the various partners – a type of feed-forward from the individual, group, and partner organization level to the CSSP organization, in the form of the lead partner. Various groups received encouragement to engage and ensure their legitimate representation, which also helped the partners develop mutual understanding. That is,

> People were encouraged to form groups to take part in community engagement, and even now to have a voice. The way forward is to actually listen to the local people who it's going to affect most.
>
> (Steve, residents' forum member)

Such encouragement can be categorized as a call for feed-forward that provides insights, views, and learning from the bottom up. This feed-forward then shaped policy proposals by the council (feedback), which in turn were reviewed by all the partners in detail (feed-forward). The council perceived its purpose was to improve the lives and livelihoods of the people of East Manchester; the other partners regarded its responsibility as serving various partners' needs. These respective roles were well understood and accepted. In this learning cycle then (Crossan et al., 1999), knowledge and understanding flowed up and down, both within and between partners.

The good level of understanding of partner needs and priorities developed through prior CSSP experiences and ongoing interactions; thus, the city council tended to propose investment projects that were more likely to be well received by partners, which facilitated cross-sector project development. In particular, the response to the idea of a super casino as a means to regenerate East Manchester, though it certainly raised some concerns, was enthusiastically welcomed:

> The casino was key to regenerating the area of providing jobs, providing training and also would bring in a host of other leisure facilities, bars, restaurants, hotels and they were going to build a training centre on the site to bring people with a lower skilled base within the hotel sector up to an NVQ standard.
>
> (Steve, residents' forum member)

Local partners understood the business partners needed a profit incentive to justify the investments required to regenerate East Manchester. Thus, the provision of a casino and other facilities in a major complex represented an acceptable trade-off to them. Partners seemed highly aware of the other partners' priorities and objectives, many of which were documented in published cross-sector material (e.g., Local Strategic Partnership, New East Manchester Ltd.). Such learning suggests movement along the CSSP continuum.

LEARNING AREA 4: DEVELOPING LONG-TERM, DEEP, TRUSTING RELATIONSHIPS

The Manchester City Council and other partners recognized the importance of establishing long-term, trusting relationships with key partners. The partners in the super-casino project thus agreed on the nature and importance of trusting relationships:

> I think that historical relationships were fairly critical to be honest. Otherwise, I think people would have been very suspicious, they would have thought 'they are only wanting to talk to us because they have already decided what they want to do and they just want us to rubber stamp it' but that wasn't the case.
>
> (Tom, CEO, New East Manchester Ltd.)

These long-term relationships reflected the nature of the dealings partners had previously experienced. Although relationship development was widely encouraged (feedback), the precise approach was difficult to formalize. Yet their importance was so widely acknowledged that relationships were developed and maintained (and exploited) even when there were disagreements and opposing views about specific element or strategies. Thus, the city council consistently was described by the CSSP partners as honest, credible, and straightforward: "Manchester City Council were genuine, were definitely listening and did take things on board and listened to the sorts of things that the faith groups were saying" (Rev. Stephen, faith group member). Of course, not all partners agreed with the use of a casino complex to regenerate East Manchester, because casinos and gambling are controversial activities. The faith groups in particular opposed the casino developments:

> We didn't want a casino. We would never want a casino because we feel that it is wrong and in a sense it was against our beliefs, but we acknowledged the likelihood of it happening and therefore that's why we engaged in the process, if you like, as a critical voice, in order to challenge assertions over benefits and raise the profile of any sort of concerns over weaknesses.
>
> (Rev. Stephen, faith group member)

Thus, partly on the basis of prior relationships and partially because these partners wanted to minimize societal risks associated with a major casino development, the faith groups agreed to play a significant role in the development of the social responsibility framework attached to the casino bid. Despite their opposition to casino development in general, the groups believed they had been genuinely consulted by the council and that their views had been acknowledged with regard to social responsibility concerns. The spirit of mutual respect for differing opinions helped build trust, in a clear example of how feed-forward from individuals and groups shaped policy and the direction. In this case, even views that did not align with the other partners' agendas were sought. Therefore, trusting relationships, which organizational learning literature deems influential in learning processes (Andrews and Delahaye, 2000), clearly encouraged the flow of knowledge throughout the super casino CSSP and therefore organizational learning among partners.

LEARNING AREA 5: CONSTRUCTING A COMMUNICATION INFRASTRUCTURE

Exposure to previous CSSPs gave the partners experience with the best ways to communicate, which they exploited for the super casino CSSP. Generally, the partners had learned the importance of good communications, both long-term and project-specific, for trusting relationships and had developed a sophisticated communications infrastructure over the years. The regular schedule included residents' meetings, business forum meetings, and a local strategic partnership of more than 30 groups from the public, private, and not-for-profit sectors:

> We had at that point been operating for probably four or five years and been operating a model, which had a high level of engagement anyway with local communities that again made it easier. There was an infrastructure for example of tenants and residents' associations which had been built up over a period.
>
> (Sir Howard)

The communications infrastructure comprised ongoing, multilevel engagements with many complementary and integrated contact points, as well as casino project-specific communications, which helped the council listen to its partner groups but also communicate its proposed development strategy. Thus, "Anything that was happening in New East Manchester came to the residents' forum for consultation. . . . To make sure residents were being protected and also listened to" (Steve, residents' forum member).

The longer-term partnership entities also communicated to support the CSSP philosophy, enable broader participation, and foster good understanding. For example, as early as 1999, a partnership-based, nonprofit organization, the New East Manchester Ltd., had been established by the council to support the regeneration of East Manchester:

> New East Manchester was a not for profit organization, a semi public body. I reported to a board of Directors which had a mix of private sector, public sector and community organizations represented on it, so although I was employed by the City Council I was effectively seconded to this partnership body.
>
> (Tom, CEO)

This semi–public, hybrid governance body featured a membership board drawn from the public, private, and nonprofit sectors. It thus represented a formalized, ongoing, cross-sector partnership entity, and all proposed developments and initiatives for the area passed through this cross-sector board for debate.

Prior experience and ongoing discussions through the well-established communications infrastructure revealed that the city council could support trusting relationships by being open, honest, and timely about possible new projects. Partners' engagement in the super casino project therefore took place at the earliest opportunity:

> We had attended meetings of that [faith] group and we went and talked to the Bishop and said 'Look, we are thinking about this, we know your views but we need to talk about it, can we come along and do a presentation to your group and can we open up that dialogue?'
>
> (Tom, CEO)

Such early engagement represented a commitment, developed from the CSSP philosophy, as well as a desire for feed-forward from individuals and groups about possible projects. The council had learned and accepted that any East Manchester development strategy needed the involvement and support of various partner groups, such that "We recognized we needed to engage and talk to local people, local interests first and foremost" (Tom, CEO).

Furthermore, as the lead partner, the council recognized that early dialog supported a mutual approach to problem identification and resolution, as well as led to improved CSSP project performance. Without feed-forward from individuals, groups, and partners, the council would have lacked the information necessary to make sound decisions. Therefore, early dialog-based learning exemplifies how the partners exploited knowledge they had gained in past CSSP interactions.

In turn, the early engagement was facilitated by the established communications infrastructure, which the partners had developed and supported over the years, such that "I think as soon as they thought it might be sort of viable that they came to us" (Justine, Police Commander). The local area Police Commander therefore was involved at an early stage and accepted her perceived role to raise any significant law and order concerns and work to provide solutions where necessary. The Police Commander also participated in the Local Strategic Partnership, such that she regarded herself as part of a "team effort" to regenerate the area. The policy of early, ongoing dialog to share information also provided evidence of the respect among partners. Even though the council had a powerful position, as the bridge across many other partner groups, it acknowledged the need for mutuality and transparency (Lawrence et al., 2005). It had learned explicitly about the need for early partner engagement and dialog about potential projects. Such lessons created an expectation among partners that it would take place; this early discussion then was facilitated by frequent interactions over the highly developed communications infrastructure.

Many of the partners commented on the quality of the CSSP team, which included representatives from the Manchester City Council, New East Manchester Ltd. (NEM),

Manchester's Experience of CSSP's - 'Milestones' (Jed Devereux, Joint Health Trust)

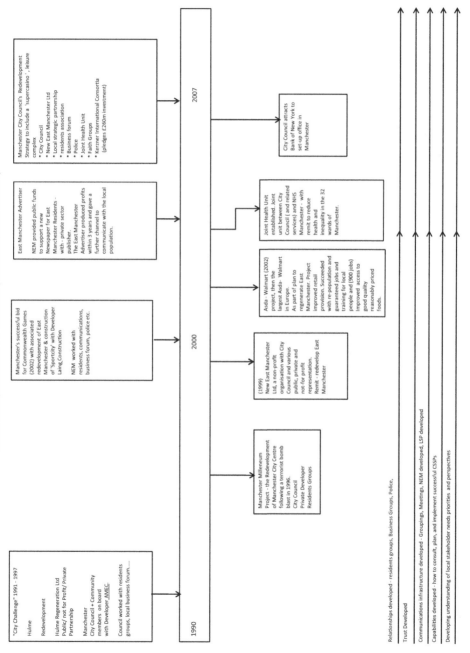

"City Challenge" 1991 - 1997

Hulme

Redevelopment

Hulme Regeneration Ltd
Public/ not for Profit/ Private
Partnership

Manchester
City Council + Community
members on board
with Developer AMEC

Council worked with residents
groups, local business forum.....

Manchester Millenuem
Project - the Redevelopment
of Manchester City Centre
following a terrorist bomb
blast in 1996.
City Council
Private Developer
Residents Groups

(1999)
New East Manchester
Ltd, a non-profit
organisation with City
Council and various
public, private and
not-for profit
representation.
Remit - redevelop East
Manchester

Manchester's successful bid
for Commonwealth Games
(2002) with associated
redevelopment of East
Manchester & construction
of 'Sportcity' with Developer
Laing Construction

NEM worked with
residents, communications,
business forum, police etc.

Asda - Walmart (2002)
project, then the
largest Asda- Walmart
in Europe
As part of plan to
regenerate East
Manchester Project
improved retail
provision. Succeeded
with re-population and
guaranteed jobs and
training for local
people and (900 jobs)
improved access to
good quality
reasonably priced
foods.

East Manchester Advertiser

NEM provided public funds
to support a new
Newspaper for East
Manchester Residents -
with - private sector
publisher.
The East Manchester
Advertiser produced profits
within 3 years and gave a
further channel to
communicate with the local
population.

Joint Health Unit
established. Joint
unit between City
Council (and related
services) and NHS
Manchester - with
remit to reduce
health and
inequality in the 32
wards of
Manchester.

Manchester City Council's Redevelopment
Strategy to include a 'supercasino', leisure
complex
* City Council
* New East Manchester Ltd
* Local strategic partnership
* residents association
* Business forum
* Police
* Joint Health Unit
* Faith Groups
* Kerzner International Consortia
(pledges £260m investment)

City Council attracts
Bank of New York to
set-up office in
Manchester

1990

2000

2007

Relationships developed - residents groups, Business Groups, Police,

Trust Developed

Communications infrastructure developed - Groupings, Meetings, NEM developed, LSP developed

Capabilities developed - how to consult, plan, and implement successful CSSPs

Developing understanding of local stakeholder needs priorities and perspectives

---

Figure 3.8.2 The history of Manchester City Council's CSSP experience

residents' groups, the casino provider Kerzner, and special advisors. These personnel, through years of experience, had become skilled at managing ongoing communication, as well as individual CSSP projects. Many projects in which the council and partners had been involved required competitive bidding or tendering for projects. Furthermore, the staff members understood the needs of partners within Manchester, as well as the expectations of external funding providers. This knowledge was not "a sort of systematic formula that you can apply, pick up and drop off somewhere else, a lot of it is about the individuals and personalities and the dynamic between that leadership group" (Ged, manager, Joint Health Unit).

If the council lacked the capabilities or knowledge in a specific area to make a credible case, it brought in specialists. For example, gambling corporate social responsibility was a specialized topic, so the council solicited the founder of Gamcare: "Paul Bellringer is a fantastic person. He was involved a lot with the responsible gambling unit and he has a wealth of knowledge and experience in that area" (Ian, project executive, NEM). By inviting specialist members from outside the organization, the Manchester CSSP benefitted indirectly from experience and learning gained through other CSSPs and in other contexts (Levitt and March, 1988). The city council ensured that the knowledge and experience of these specialists was captured (feed-forward).

The CSSP also benefited from the quality of representatives from the other partners, notably, the residents' groups, faith groups, gambling experts, the casino operator, the local developer (Ask Developments), and the local Police Commander. In our interviews, participants not only commented on the overall quality of personnel involved in the CSSP but also mentioned key individuals as influential for the CSSP success.

Beyond involvement and leadership skills of senior members of the partner organizations, they were responsible for developing a culture that supported credible teams. The manager of the Joint Health Unit (JHU), with years of experience with CSSPs in Manchester, thus suggested that, in addition to high-quality personnel, the culture of the organization influenced success. Teams were responsible for setting and maintaining ongoing engagements with partners and maintaining relationships over the long-term. The NEM teams in particular were portrayed as the delivery arm of the city council for regeneration projects. Moreover, the city council continually encouraged and motivated individual partners to represent the needs and interests of various groups. Exploiting the learning from prior CSSPs would not have been possible without high-quality people representing each of the partner organizations. For example, the CEOs of the council and NEM Ltd. clearly established the CSSP philosophy and served as figureheads for the project, but the team of personnel within the various partner organizations made the project a reality.

Impact of experience and learning on the development of the super casino CSSP

Many of the partners had prior partnering experience, whether in the governmental sector (city council, NEM, police, JHU); nonprofit sector (residents' associations, faith groups, Local Strategic Partnership, specialist advisors); or the business sector (business forum, casino venue operator, local property developers). This experience had a significant impact on the Manchester Super Casino CSSP by determining the partners' ability to plan and manage this project (Drucker, 1989; Waddock, 1991), as several partners indicated expressly. This overall finding reinforces Selsky and Parker's (2005: 858) observation that "learning is an important outcome of CSSPs," as succinctly summarized by a NEM executive:

> Some of the people involved and some of the stakeholders have been equally involved in the successful bid for the commonwealth games, you could see that they had learned from that successful experience and were now turning it to this.
>
> (Ian, project executive, NEM)

The Manchester partners had gained significant CSSP experience (Figure 3.8.2) and developed expertise, capabilities, and skills from project to project, which reflects the importance of a "willingness to learn and adapt" for successful CSSPs (Seitanidi and Crane, 2009: 424). A strong sense of organizational learning and organizational memory (Crossan

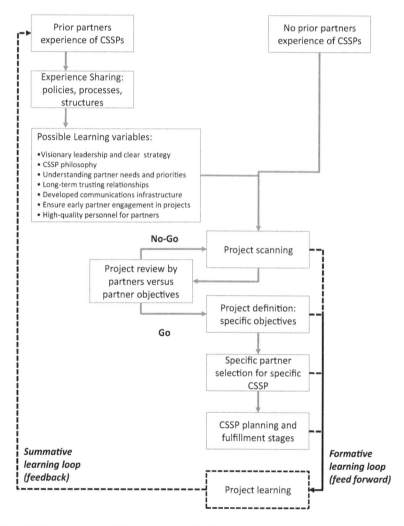

Figure 3.8.3 CSSP planning model (Reast et al., 2010)

et al., 1999) derived from past projects. The partners especially gained early exposure to CSSPs in the 1990s related to community engagement and understanding:

> Right from the early days we have always known that community buy-in to change in neighbourhoods is fundamental and giving the community the opportunity to influence what we mean by change and to get them to understand the components of change is also a fundamental part as well.
>
> (Sir Howard)

The history of the Manchester City Council's CSSP experience (Figure 3.8.2) began with the redevelopment of the Hulme housing estate, a project managed by a nonprofit partnership. Next, the Manchester Millennium partnership project aimed to renew the city centre after a terrorist bomb decimated it. In 1999, NEM Ltd., a tri-sector partnership tasked with regenerating East Manchester, was established. A few years later, the opportunity for Manchester to bid to host the Commonwealth Games (2002) catalyzed more engagement with local communities and built skill and expertise related to competitive bidding. Manchester's success in this effort meant sport stadiums and facilities were built in East Manchester, as were relationships, skills, and capabilities. This project enabled the City Council to deepen its relationships with residents, local developers, and local business operators, which it did by exploiting its learning from earlier CSSPs. For example, "we would have probably set up some kind of process similar to the Commonwealth Games to award different supply contracts" (Ian, project executive, NEM). Other notable projects included attracting ASDA/Walmart to build its largest European store in East Manchester and guarantee local residents jobs at the store:

> ASDA/Walmart was seen as a bit innovative, a lot of the employees were almost guaranteed to be local so the benefits of that store were kept within the neighborhood quite well, and that model of kind of local training and labor retention was definitely something they were going to use in the regional casino.
>
> (Ian, project executive, NEM)

Partners thus looked back at the specific prior CSSP(s) that they had directly experienced to discern what had been successful and exploit these insights for future projects. One of those lessons taught the Manchester City Council to develop strong engagement infrastructures with local community groups, local developers, and private sector partners, so for the super casino, "We had the confidence of the private sector. The private sector was universally in support of what we were doing frankly, there was never any opposition to our proposals" (Sir Howard).

The partners themselves thus supported the notion of movement along a CSSP continuum of engagement and expertise, such that each successive CSSP provided learning and strengthened understanding and bonds among the partners, which then enabled longer-term, broadly oriented relationships (Selsky and Parker, 2005). In particular, successful innovations in one CSSP entered into the planning for the next (e.g., the ASDA/Walmart CSSP's recruitment policies, Commonwealth Games CSSP supplier contract awards). The partners explicitly recognized,

> We were probably wet behind the ears when we did Hulme and probably we had to learn and improve as we did central Manchester, we had to get a lot better in terms of being in the city centre; the experience builds and the culture builds as well.
>
> (Ged, manager, JHU)

Each project successfully navigated strengthened the partner bonds, trust, and relationships, as well as formalized the long-term partnership organizational entities and introduced an engagement infrastructure (e.g., Local Strategic Partnership, NEM Ltd.) that could support a long-term CSSP strategy and philosophy. These developments then pushed the search for other CSSP opportunities, including the Manchester Super Casino. The search for future projects relied on the use of local strategic regeneration frameworks, established with the cooperation of various partners. That is, the partners in East Manchester developed seven key learning areas over many years, all of which contributed to the success of the Manchester Super Casino CSSP. The impact of these learning areas appeared closely linked and multiplicative, such that the communication infrastructure furthered good relations, which supported a mutuality-based CSSP philosophy.

Such behavioral patterns reflect Waddock and Smith's (2000) argument that experience influences future interactions. The findings also reinforce an organizational learning perspective: Partner experience and learning over time allow for the exploration of different approaches, and then the exploitation of successful approaches or innovations later (March, 1991; see also Boguslaw, 2002; Huxham and Vangen, 2000).

Furthermore, though the learning relevant to the Manchester Super Casino CSSP was not formally managed, it was achieved through several key routes. The key personnel remained largely consistent over time, which reinforced organizational experience, memory, and learning. Even new personnel learned, through colleague and partner interactions and documentation, about prior CSSPs such as Hulme, ASDA/Walmart, and the Commonwealth Games. Key figures often talked about past projects, which ensured the knowledge and learning was commonly understood. These various paths support theorizing about the routes to organizational learning (Crossan et al., 1999).

We also can consider the impact of historical experiences on the success of the Manchester Super Casino within the context of the early definition of organizational learning by Simon (1969: 236). The participants, through their interactions and prior CSSPs, clearly have learned how to frame their joint problems and manage their collaborations, which led to the development of communication structures and partnership entities. Furthermore, the findings confirm the importance of CEO leadership style (Slater and Narver, 1995; Vera and Crossan, 2004); approachability, trust, and credibility in relationships (Andrews and Delahaye, 2000); and the impact of power and political status for organizational learning (Lawrence et al., 2005).

Overall then, our findings support the notion of a continuum in CSSPs. The wealth of experience the partners gained from prior CSSPs allowed for their learning and improvement, deepened the relationships among partners, and increased levels of mutuality. Thus, whereas the Hulme CSSP was a singular, narrowly defined, short-term project, it encouraged the development of a CSSP strategy and increased levels of interaction, which started Manchester moving along the CSSP continuum. Even with our single case perspective, this study offers a strong argument that organizations, by learning from their prior direct and indirect experiences (Levitt and March, 1988), can move to more advanced levels on the CSSP continuum.

Learning model of CSSP development and implementation

In line with the accusation that simple models of CSSPs (e.g., Seitanidi and Crane, 2009; Waddell and Brown, 1997) fail to capture the "messiness" of partnerships in practice (Selsky and Parker, 2005), our findings from the Manchester Super Casino CSSP suggest that prior models could be developed further. We also show that such modeling could be enhanced by the introduction of learning loops (Crossan et al., 1999), which represent a review process during the management and implementation of CSSPs and at the start or end of any single CSSP. Learning loops can take into account the partners' prior direct and indirect experience. Furthermore, such a model can depict the flow of CSSPs for organizations with a long-term philosophy to summarize lessons for future CSSPs. If organizations engage in multiple CSSPs simultaneously, they can draw experience and learning in both the short and long term. Finally, models should be more prescriptive and capture some best practice evidence from successful CSSPs. Therefore, our proposed model includes learning loops, as well as the seven learning areas for successful CSSP performance exploited by the Manchester Super Casino CSSP.

Furthermore, our analysis of prior literature on CSSP and organizational learning, together with our case study, implies that the model of organizational learning offered by Crossan and colleagues (1999), despite its general support in existing studies, requires the addition of a "supra-organizational" level to reflect the experiences of CSSP projects. That is, CSSPs go beyond individual organizations and introduce great complexity. Therefore, they demand coordination and management of several organizational partners. Individual and group organizational learning processes may be taking place within organizations (intra-organization) or between organizations (interorganization), such that the feedback and feed-forward loops described by Crossan and colleagues (1999) entail further complications.

Conclusions

Conceptual contributions

This research emphasizes the need to consider organizational experience and learning within the context of CSSPs. Organizational learning in our revised model takes the form of a formative learning loop (feed-forward) during a specific project, as well as a summative learning loop (feedback) at the end of the project to inform various partners about the successful and unsuccessful components of that CSSP (exploratory learning). Such learning can be exploited through institutionalization in new systems, procedures, and approaches for future CSSPs (feedback). Models of CSSPs must acknowledge the long-term orientation and experience of some CSSP partners as input variables for future CSSPs.

Empirical contributions

Our rich case material draws on CSSPs in Manchester over a 20-year period and confirms the development of capabilities, skills, systems, and relationships over the course of several large- and small-scale CSSPs (Figure 3.8.2). The case findings strongly suggest that experience and learning enables progress along the CSSP continuum, from introductory to intermediate to advanced levels. We do not claim that a lack of prior experience of CSSPs prevents access to the intermediate or advanced levels, but that access is less likely. Organizations without prior experience can learn from others with CSSP experience, but the higher levels often require strong underlying relationships and mutuality between partners. Therefore, access to others' learning may not be enough to ensure success in demanding, complex CSSPs.

Managerial contributions

Direct and indirect experience with CSSPs shapes the skills and capabilities of partners. In particular, we identify seven key success lessons derived from the Manchester Super Casino CSSP. However, experience does not guarantee learning (Crossan et al., 1999), so managers must recognize that they need to ensure a balance between new learning or exploration and exploitation to capitalize on what they have learned (March, 1991). Organizations should carefully manage and enable feed-forward (from individual to group to organizational levels), such that they translate insights, innovations, and ideas for use by the whole organization. Feedback (organization to group to individual) regarding adapted policies, rules, processes, and strategies simultaneously should be passed down the organization. Organizational learning is a dynamic flow (Crossan et al., 1999) that moves up and down the organization, so its handling must ensure learning is never blocked or interrupted en route.

The influence of the CEO and senior management team (Slater and Narver, 1995; Vera and Crossan, 2004) and internal politics and power games (Lawrence et al., 2005) can either enhance or interrupt this flow. The organization therefore should work to encourage the flow of information and learning, from individuals to groups and on to the organizational level. It also must continue to explore new learning, perhaps through experimentation with different approaches, rather than simply exploiting old knowledge that has been successful in the past. Finally, overly institutionalized, top-down organizations can drive out individual intuitions, which prevents them from learning in the future (Crossan et al., 1999).

Limitations and further research

This case study, though in-depth and extensive, including contributions from all key partners, relates specifically to a local governmental organization. In one sense, this focus represents a contribution to prior literature, which usually identifies a business organization as the central player (Bryson and Crosby, 2006). However, it also limits the applicability of our findings. Local governmental organizations are necessarily geographically specific, and their investments in long-term infrastructure, relationships, and CSSP orientation may be more easily understood and justified than they would be for a private sector, profit-based firm.

Furthermore, we have aimed primarily to extend CSSP literature by integrating literature from organizational learning. This integration prompts us to call for further research within the organizational learning field that investigates supra-organizational entities and thus offers clearer guidance about the learning process in these more complex organizational forms.

Finally, the prominent impact of prior CSSP experience and learning in the Manchester Super Casino case, as well as the strong CSSP orientation of key partners, implies that further research should consider whether CSSP philosophies are common in organizations. Historical research could be undertaken at the organizational level, rather than with regard to an individual CSSP case. This research would enhance our understanding of the organizational learning benefits for CSSP management success.

Acknowledgments

This chapter was first published in Reast et al. (2010). The Manchester Super Casino: Experience and learning in a cross-sector social partnership. *Journal of Business Ethics*, 94 (Supplement 1): 197–218.

Note

1 We use the term "cross-sector social partnerships" to refer to both partnerships and interactions throughout.

References

Alberic, P. and van Lierop, K. (2006), 'Sense and Sensitivity: The Roles of Organization and Stakeholders in Managing Corporate Social responsibility', *Business Ethics: A European Review*, 15(4), 339–351.

Andrews, K. M. and Delahaye, B. L. (2000), 'Influences on Knowledge Processes in Organizational Learning: The Psychological Filter', *Journal of Management Studies*, 37(6), 797–810.

Astley, G. and Fombrun, C. (1983), 'Collective Strategy: Social Ecology of Organizational Environments', *Academy of Management Review*, 8(4), 576–587.

Austin, J. (2000), *The Collaborative Challenge*, San Francisco, CA: Jossey Bass.

Barringer, B. and Harrison, J. (2000), 'Walking a Tightrope: Creating Value Through Interorganizational Relationships', *Journal of Management*, 26(3), 367–403.

Berger, L., Cunningham, P. and Drumwright, M. (2004), 'Social Alliances: Company/Non-Profit Collaboration', *California Management Review*, 47(1), 58–90.

Beverland, M. B., Kates, S. M., Lindgreen, A. and Chung, E. (2010), 'Exploring Consumer Conflict Management in Service Encounters', *Journal of the Academy of Marketing Science*, 38(5), 617–633.

Beverland, M. B. and Lindgreen, A. (2007), 'Implementing Market Orientation in Industrial Firms: A Multiple Case Study', *Industrial Marketing Management*, 36(4), 430–442.

Beverland, M.B and Lindgreen, A. (2010), 'What Makes a Good Case Study? A Positivist Review of Qualitative Case Research Published in Industrial Marketing Management, 1971–2006', *Industrial Marketing Management*, 39(1), 56–63.

Boehm, A. (2005), 'The Participation of Businesses in Community Decision-Making', *Business and Society*, 44(2), 144–178.

Boguslaw, J. E. (2002), *Social Partnerships and Social Relations*, London: Routledge.

Bontis, N., Crossan, M. M. and Hulland, J. (2002), 'Managing an Organizational Learning System by Aligning Stocks and Flows', *Journal of Management Studies*, 39(4), 437–469.

Brady, T. and Davies, A. (2004), 'Building Project Capabilities: From Exploratory to Exploitative Learning', *Organization Studies*, 25(9), 1601–1621.

Bryson, J. M. and Crosby, B. C. (2006), 'The Design and Implementation of Cross-Sector Collaboration: Propositions from the Literature', *Public Administration Review*, 66(Special Issue S1), 44–55.

Cangelosi, V. E. and Dill, W. R. (1965), 'Organizational Learning Observations: Toward a Theory', *Administrative Science Quarterly*, 10(2), 175–203.

Carroll, A. (2004), 'Managing Ethically with Global Stakeholders: A Present and Future Challenge', *Academy of Management Executive*, 18(2), 114–120.

Casino Advisory Panel. (2007), Final Report of the Casino Advisory Panel, UK Government Department for Culture Media and Sport, at www.culture.gov.uk/cap/.

Chapple, W. and Moon, J. (2005), 'Corporate Social Responsibility (CSR) in Asia: A Seven Country Study of CSR Web Site Reporting', *Business and Society*, 44(4), 415–441.

Crane, A. (2000), 'Culture Clash and Mediation', In J. Bendell (Ed.), *Terms for Endearment*. Sheffield: Greenleaf, pp. 163–177.

Crossan, M. M. and Berdrow, I. (2003), 'Organizational Learning and Strategic Renewal', *Strategic Management Journal*, 24(11), 1087–1105.

Crossan, M. M., Lane, H. W. and White, R. E. (1999), 'An Organizational Learning Framework: From Intuition to Institution', *Academy of Management Review*, 24(3), 522–537.

Daft, R. L. and Weick, K. E. (1984), 'Towards a Model of Organizations as Interpretation Systems', *Academy of Management Review*, 9(2), 284–295.

DeGeus, A. P. (1988), 'Planning as Learning', *Harvard Business Review*, (March–April), 70–74.

Dodgson, M. (1993), 'Organizational Learning: A Review of Some Literatures', *Organization Studies*, 14(3), 375–394.

Drucker, P. E. (1989), 'What Can Businesses Learn from Nonprofits?', *Harvard Business Review*, (July–August), 88–93.

Easterby-Smith, M., Crossan, M. M. and Nicolini, D. (2000), 'Organizational Learning: Debates Past, Present and Future', *Journal of Management Studies*, 37(6), 783–796.

Eisenhardt, K. M. (1989), 'Building Theories from Case Study Research', *Academy of Management Review*, 14(4), 532–550.

Elkington, J. and Fennell, S. (1998), 'Partners for Sustainability', *Greener Management International*, 24(Winter), 48–60.

Fiol, C. M. and Lyles, M. A. (1985), 'Organizational Learning', *Academy of Management Review*, 10(4), 803–813.

Gabriel, E. (2006), 'The Role of MNEs in Community Development Initiatives in Developing Countries: Corporate Social Responsibility at Work in Nigeria and South Africa', *Business and Society*, 45(2), 93–129.

Googins, B. and Rochlin, S. (2000), 'Creating the Partnership Society: Understanding the Rhetoric and Reality of Cross-Sectoral Partnerships', *Business and Society Review*, 105(1), 127–144.

Gray, B. (1989), *Collaborating: Finding Common Ground for Multi-Party Problems*, San Francisco, CA: Jossey-Bass.

Grunig, J. E. and Grunig, L. A. (1992), 'Models of Public Relations and Communication', In J. E. Grunig (Ed.), *Excellence in Public Relations and Communications Management*. Hillsdale, NJ: Lawrence Erlbaum Associates, pp. 285–325.

Heugens, P., Van Den Bosch, F. A. J. and Van Riel, C. B. M. (2002), 'Stakeholder Integration', *Business and Society*, 41(1), 36–60.

Huxham, C. and Vangen, S. (1996), 'Working Together: Key Themes in the Management of Relationships Between Public and Non-Profit Organizations', *International Journal of Public Sector Management*, 9(7), 5–17.

Huxham, C. and Vangen, S. (2000), 'Leadership in the Shaping and Implementation of Collaboration Agendas: How Things Happened in a (Not Quite) Joined Up World', *Academy of Management Journal*, 43(6), 1159–1175.

Kanter, R. M. (1998), 'Six Strategic Challenges', *World Link*, 11(1), 28–34.

Kooiman, J. (1999), 'Social-Political Governance: Overview, Reflections and Design', *Public Management*, 1(1), 67–91.

Korten, D. (1998), *Globalizing Civil Society: Reclaiming our Right to Power*, New York: Seven Stories Press.

Lawrence, T. B., Mauws, M. K., Dyck, B. and Kleysen, R. F. (2005), 'The Politics of Organizational Learning: Integrating Power into the 4i Framework', *Academy of Management Review*, 30(1), 180–191.

Levitt, B. and March, J. G. (1988), 'Organizational Learning', *Annual Review of Sociology*, 14(1), 319–340.

Lincoln, Y. S. and Guba, E. (1985). *Naturalistic Inquiry*, Beverly Hills, CA: Sage.

Lindgreen, A. (2008), *Managing Market Relationships*. Farnham: Gower Publishing.

Lindgreen, A., Swaen, V. and Campbell, T. T. (2009), 'Corporate Social Responsibility Practices in Developing and Transitional Countries: Botswana and Malawi', *Journal of Business Ethics*, 90(3), 429–440.

London, T., Rondinelli, D. A. and O'Neill, H. (2005), 'Strange Bedfellows: Alliances Between Corporations and Nonprofits', In O. Shenkar and J. Reuer (Eds.), *Handbook of Strategic Alliances*. Thousand Oaks, CA: Sage, pp. 353–366.

Maon, F., Lindgreen, A. and Vanhamme, J. (2009), 'Developing Supply Chains in Disaster Relief Operations through Cross-Sector Socially Oriented Collaborations: A Theoretical Model', *Supply Chain Management: An International Journal*, 14(2), 149–164.

March, J. G. (1991), 'Exploration and Exploitation in Organizational Learning', *Organization Science*, 2(1), 71–87.

March, J. G. and Olsen, J. P. (1975), 'Organizational Learning Under Ambiguity', *European Journal of Policy Review*, 3(2), 147–171.

McCracken, G. (1986). *The Long Interview*, Newbury Park, CA: Sage.

Millar, C. C. J. M., Choi, C. J. and Chen, S. (2004), 'Global Strategic Partnerships Between MNEs and NGOs: Drivers of Change and Ethical Issues', *Business and Society Review*, 109(4), 395–414.

Morsing, M. and Shultz, M. (2006), 'Corporate Social Responsibility Communication: Stakeholder Information, Response and Involvement Strategies', *Business Ethics: A European Review*, 15(4), 323–338.

Muthuri, J. N., Chapple, W. and Moon, J. (2009), 'An Integrated Approach to Implementing "Community Participation" in Corporate Community Involvement: Lessons from Magadi Soda Company in Kenya', *Journal of Business Ethics*, 85(2), 431–444.

Nelson, J. and Zadeck, S. (2000), *Partnership Alchemy: New Social Partnerships in Europe*, Copenhagen, Denmark: The Copenhagen Centre.

Nelson, R. R. and Winter, S. G. (1982), *An Evolutionary Theory of Economic Change*. Cambridge, MA: Harvard University Press.

Nonaka, I. and Takeuchi, H. (1995), *The Knowledge Creating Company*, Oxford: Oxford University Press.

O'Regan, K. M. and Oster, S. M. (2000), 'Non-Profit and for-Profit Partnership: Rationales and Challenges of Cross-Sector Contracting', *Nonprofit and Voluntary Sector Quarterly*, 20(1), 120–140.

Oxley-Green, A, and Hunton-Clark, L. (2003), 'A Typology of Stakeholder Participation for Company Environmental Decision-Making', *Business Strategy and Environment*, 12(5), 292–299.

Perrini, F., Pogutz, S. and Tencati, A. (2006). *Developing Corporate Social Responsibility: A European Perspective*, Cheltenham: Edward Elgar Publishing.

Polanyi, M. (1967), *The Tacit Dimension*, New York: Anchor Books.

Reast, J., Lindgreen, A., Vanhamme, J. and Maon, F. (2010). 'The Manchester Super Casino: Experience and Learning in a Cross-sector Social Partnerships', *Journal of Business Ethics*, 94(1), 197–218.

Roberts, N. C. and Bradley, R. T. (1991), 'Stakeholder Collaboration and Innovation: A Study of Public Policy Initiation at the State Level', *Journal of Applied Behavioral Science*, 27(2): 209–227.

Schildt, H. A., Maula, M. V. J. and Keil, T. (2005), 'Explorative and Exploitative Learning from External Corporate Ventures', *Entrepreneurship Theory and Practice*, 29(4), 493–515.

Seitanidi, M. M. (2007), 'Intangible Economy: How Can Investors Deliver Change in Businesses? Lessons from Nonprofit-Business Partnerships', *Management Decision*, 45(5), 853–865.

Seitanidi, M. M. and Crane, A. (2009), 'Implementing CSR Through Partnerships: Understanding the Selection, Design and Institutionalization of Nonprofit-Business Partnerships', *Journal of Business Ethics*, 85(2), 413–429.

Seitanidi, M. M. and Lindgreen, A. (2008), 'Cross Sector Social Interactions', *Journal of Business Ethics*, 82(3), 525–526.

Seitanidi, M. M. and Ryan, A. (2007), 'A Critical Review of Forms of Corporate Involvement: From Philanthropy to Partnerships', *International Journal of Non-Profit and Voluntary Sector Marketing*, 12(3), 247–266.

Selsky, J. W. and Parker, B. (2005), 'Cross-Sector Partnerships to Address Social Issues: Challenges to Theory and Practice', *Journal of Management*, 31(6), 849–873.

Simon, H. A., (1969), *Sciences of the Artificial*, Cambridge, MA: MIT Press.

Slater, S. and Narver, J. (1995), 'Market Orientation and the Learning Organization', *Journal of Marketing*, 59(3), 63–74.

Spiggle, S. (1994). 'Analysis and Interpretation of Qualitative Data in Consumer Research', *Journal of Consumer Research*, 21(3), 491–503.

Strauss, A. and Corbin, J. (1998), *Basics of Qualitative Research: Techniques and Procedures for Developing Grounded Theory*, Newbury Park, CA: Sage.

Steckel, R. and Simons, R. (1992). *Doing Best by Doing Good: How to Use Public Purpose Partnerships to Boost Corporate Profits and Benefit Your Community*, New York: E.P. Dutton.

Vera, D. and Crossan, M. M. (2004), 'Strategic Leadership and Organizational Learning', *Academy of Management Review*, 29(2), 222–240.

Waddell, S. (1999), Business-Government-Nonprofit Collaborations as Agents for Social Innovation and Learning. Paper presented at the Academy of Management, Chicago, August.

Waddell, S. and Brown, L. D. (1997), *Fostering Intersectoral Partnering: A Guide to Promoting Cooperation among Government, Business and Civil Society Actors*, IDR Reports, Boston, MA: Institute for Development Research.

Waddock, S. (1989), 'Understanding Social Partnerships. An Evolutionary Model of Partnership Organisations', *Administration & Society*, 21(1), 78–100.

Waddock, S. (1991), 'A Typology of Social Partnership Organizations', *Administration & Society*, 22(4), 480–516.

Waddock, S. A. and Smith, N. (2000), 'Relationships: The Real Challenge of Corporate Global Citizenship', *Business and Society Review*, 105(1), 47–62.

Yin, R. (2003), *Case Study Research*, 3rd ed., Thousand Oaks, CA: Sage.

Part IV

Reaping organizational returns and relational rewards of stakeholder engagement efforts

4.1 On value destruction, competitive disadvantage and squandered opportunities to engage stakeholders

Frederick Ahen

Introduction

By their broader definition, stakeholders are those individuals and groups who affect and are affected by the practices of the organisation or have a claim, ownership or rights or socio-economic, environmental or moral interests to protect in their relationship with an organisation (Freeman, 1984). Additionally, stakeholders are both beneficiaries and risk-bearers of organisations (Donaldson and Preston, 1995; Freeman, 1984; Post et al., 2002). Put simply, the firm's dealings with these entities and natural persons in the quest to create value through proactive strategies in responding to environmental dynamics and stakeholder demands over time is what has broadly been termed 'stakeholder engagement' (Freeman, 1984; Freeman et al., 2010; Pajunen, 2006; Rhenman, 1968; Strand et al., 2015). Capital owners (stockholders, entrepreneurs and shareholders) and managers (stewards/agents) ensure that investments are put to productive use. However, it is the consumers, suppliers, competitors, employees, financiers, the local communities and the ecology of firms (Boons, 2004) who are the means and end of the organisation's raison d'être – thus, no consumers or other stakeholders, no markets. And where there is no market, there is no need for a firm to exist in the first place (Drucker, 1973). However, there is a recognisable disconnect between the communication apparatus of modern organisations and the fundamental understanding of the importance of long-term relationship (engagement and dialogue) with stakeholders (Grönroos, 2008) in the quest to create value for the firm and the society in which it is embedded (Freeman, 1984). This value is what Porter and Kramer (2006) and Ahen and Zettinig (2015a) refer to as 'shared value'.

In essence, the end goal of stakeholder engagement is to create mutually beneficial value for all parties. In this process, however, communication is misconstrued as mainly and necessarily verbal and written interaction and deceptive imagery using mass media whilst leaving action (strategy implementation), both implicit and explicit for the stakeholders to make sense of. For this reason, stakeholders remain a market (a set of preferences) to be ignored, defended against or exploited in simple exchanges for profits by any means possible, including irresponsible marketing techniques. Therefore, the purpose of the present conceptual contribution is three-fold: (i) to explore extant literature on how manipulations via creative design wrapped in gimmickry (O'Shaughnessy and O'Shaughnessy, 2003) in integrated marketing communications are used to outwit different consumer segments of different products in varieties of markets (Rotfeld, 2005; Wagner et al., 2009); (ii) to argue that authentic brand reputation (Barnett et al., 2006; Bertels and Peloza, 2008; Carmeli and Tishler, 2005; Mahon and Wartick, 2003) is not a talk but a walk (Wickert et al., 2016), which occurs only when corporate social responsibility (CSR) is fully integrated into all day-to-day operations of the firm to strategically respond to external dynamics through specific innovations that are within the limits of the firm's dynamic capabilities (Augier and Teece, 2008; Eisenhardt and Martin, 2000; Teece and Pisano, 1994) and entrepreneurial orientation (Covin and Miles, 1999); (iii) to explain why authentic brand reputation consists of socially desirable but profitable activities with a relational learning approach (March 1991) for value co-creation (with innovative offerings) (Grönroos, 2008; Ravald and Grönroos, 1996) aimed at creating a sustained competitive advantage (Porter, 1990, 1996). All these must be without emotional manipulation in marketing campaigns. Implied here is that "the company actually means what it says" as Morsing and Schultz (2006) put it.

The relevance and motivation of this chapter is that of a renewed challenge of assumptions that underpin some corporate social responsibility (CSR) practices and conceptualisations which unbeknownst to many organisations are fundamentally false logics about what represents CSR and how such actions are communicated across the board to stakeholders with varying claims. Additionally, this chapter aims to inform sustainable managerial practices that are institutionalised as an organisational culture that is oriented towards social good in real terms and communicated as the brand. This is not only ethically responsible but can also be productively reinterpreted as a profitable opportunity for creating and sustaining a competitive advantage. The above reasoning is aimed at ensuring successful, strategic brand positioning, encouraging new knowledge creation and leading the way within an industry in no ambiguous terms in the communications with stakeholders.

This chapter answers the following inter-related questions:

1   *How do strategies, operational routines and marketing communication practices in brand-building become perceived as socio-psychologically undesirable and*
2   *how does that constitute a missed opportunity to engage stakeholders and destroy value in international marketing contexts?*

Following the above, four important themes run through the present chapter: (i) a review of extant literature on manipulative forms of marketing and how they affect consumer/stakeholder choice; it is followed by (ii) discussions about strategic corporate responsibility (SCR) communications, (iii) explanation of disintegrated marketing communications as missed opportunities that lead to value destruction; and (iv) social marketing as a brand-building strategy in response to the current and future sustainability demands. Conclusions, policy recommendations and suggestions for future research are offered in the end.

Theoretical and conceptual foundations

Stakeholder engagement: weak links and lacklustre approaches

This is the problem: globalisation has created space for multinational corporations to employ private voluntary initiatives in the form of industry and corporate codes of conduct, 'green labels' certification standards as well as many multi-stakeholder initiatives as a way of communicating their green strategies or CSR initiatives (Bartley, 2007; Levy and Kaplan, 2008; Nadvi and Wältring, 2002; Rasche, 2010; Rasche et al., 2013). Nevertheless, contemporary consumers in particular and stakeholders in general, are neither passive nor unaware of the ways in which firms communicate authentic and deceptive brands – especially the firm's impact on health and environment (Ahen and Zettinig, 2015b). Stakeholders' near ubiquitous influence and display of power for all intents and purposes can hardly be denied. This increasing stakeholder awareness, which does not necessarily translate into power per se, is due to three major emergent and crucial issues, at least theoretically: (i an unprecedented global environmental crisis (global warming, climate change, air and water pollution, deforestation and desertification) leading to global health crisis and (ii) the ever-increasing power of corporations in global governance and therefore the ever-decreasing power of stakeholders to press home their demands, especially in weaker institutions, leading to bribery, corruption and all forms of corporate exploitation of employees and resources of disadvantaged communities (Banerjee, 2011; Clegg, 2006; Curtis and Jones, 2017). This situation has now led to global inequality where wealth is concentrated in the hands of a few capitalists at the expense of the rest of stakeholders – global inequality (Piketty, 2014). (iii) All the above have now led to an increasing interconnectedness of international and national non-governmental organisations (NGOs) speaking for the voiceless and bringing the core issues to the stakeholders to express their dissatisfaction using the information technologies available to them in ways never seen before. Thus, stakeholder engagement is no longer a choice but a corporate imperative. This intuitive notion is analytically obvious and holds a ring of logical plausibility towards an enlightened recognition of the necessity to embrace demand-side arguments – stakeholder engagement.

In spite of the corporate manipulations, there are, of course frivolous, hedonistic and conspicuous consumers who willingly display their wealth, power and importance or status in society (Wherry, 2008). In the latter case, their ownership of demonstrative assets (not real needs) and invidious consumption seeks to provoke others' jealousy, comparison and emulation in their quest for personal satisfaction of self-importance (Campbell, 1995; Veblen, 1899/2009). For example, economists Charles et al. (2009) have demonstrated that, in spite of racial gap in income, still, more blacks and Hispanics spend disproportionately on visible goods or demonstrative assets (clothing, jewellery and cars) than their white counterparts. Such irresponsible consumption patterns, they argue, are mainly based on the status-seeking preferences of those who pursue them and are not the fault of firms. However, there is an overwhelming desire for change among consumers and other stakeholders given the current global economic and environmental dynamics.

Notwithstanding the emerging enthusiasm in sustainability, conservatism issues and stakeholder engagement, in practice, even the savviest consumer or stakeholder can hardly deny that astute marketing managers employ more powerful marketing communications mechanisms to circumvent the delivery of promises especially in day-to-day corporate practices such as R&D, production, distribution, supply chain management, advertising and all forms of corporate activities which explicitly and implicitly communicate to the consumer with deception and subliminal manipulations (Bornstein, 1989; Moore, 1992). This ingenious, and sometimes sinister, managerial practice of deceiving stakeholders whilst dominating and shaping the discourse of CSR to meet corporate goals at the expense of stakeholders is what I conceptualise as disintegrated marketing communication. The discourse gathers more momentum and intensifies in its complexity when considering the fact that there are millions of disempowered stakeholders, mostly in developing economies, who lack the means, technology and exit possibilities. They are often voiceless, marginalised and without freedom to democratically participate in issues affecting them (especially when there are negative externalities produced by the firm) and are therefore constantly exploited by firms. Such exploitation also includes child labour (Kolk and Van Tulder, 2004) and management by dispossession (Banerjee, 2011), as well as bribery, corruption and lobbying of government officials to bend rules in favour of the firm at the expense of local communities (Dearden, 2017; Durepos et al., 2016). Popular examples of such actions that invariably communicate the insidious nature of some firms include the exploitation of employees in the fast fashion (textile) and extractive industries where people work under deplorable conditions and earn only a pittance. Additionally, human rights abuses and slavery as a management practice in weak institutions abound globally (Crane, 2013; Wettstein, 2012).

Even for those in advanced economies, having access to modern communication technologies does not in itself constitute a fair chance of serious stakeholder engagement. The empowered stakeholder knows what they desire (what their stakes are) and when and how to defend them through legal means, boycotting of some sort or public shaming and other forms of pressure. They are knowledgeable enough about issues because they possess critical thinking skills as a result of good level of education. They are also able to form alliances in order to present a common voice or belong to a constellation of stakeholders with the power to change or affect the direction of the firm's CR orientation (Campbell, 2007). Here, stakeholder theory becomes a useful explanatory concept for analysing firm–stakeholder relationships and the end goal of value creation through SCR orientation (Ahen, 2015; Freeman and Velamuri, 2006). The erosion of trust in firms is clearly the results of irresponsible and unethical behaviours with far-reaching consequences on communities (Ahen and Zettinig, 2015b; Banerjee, 2007, 2011). A stakeholder engagement through dialogue and authentic SCR communications is therefore an urgency.

SCR for stakeholder engagement is conceptualised as a proactive relationship based on decisions and actions for creating shared value. In contrast to public relations (PR) and other media manipulations for reputation management, this approach through social marketing serves as one example of numerous mechanisms for stakeholder engagement. SCR is not ad-hoc by nature but integrated into corporate strategy, not reactive, firm-oriented or inward looking but proactive, outward looking and inclusive of stakeholders who may or may not be influential or necessarily wield any political power and whose needs the firm may not consider as urgent as in arguments of Agle et al. (1999). Mitchell et al.'s (1997) most salient attributes of stakeholders (power, legitimacy and urgency) cannot be deemed satisfactory criteria for pinpointing which stakeholders deserve proper engagement. Rather, stakeholders must be respectfully engaged for their own sake (intrinsic value) as partners in value creation.

Stakeholder engagement under the grand rubric of CSR for shared value creation

Armstrong (1977) defines *socially irresponsible corporate behaviour* as "a decision to accept an alternative that is thought by the decision makers to be inferior to another alternative when the effects upon all parties are considered" (p. 185). There are countless activities that take place in organisations which are at variance with their portrayed image and above all pluralistically in sharp contrast with the interests they serve (Wagner et al., 2009). Schumpeter (cited in McCraw, 2007, p. 72) recognises this and states that "it is the producer who as a rule initiates economic change, and consumers are educated by him if necessary; they are (the consumers), as it were, taught to want new things". To assume that consumers and by extension stakeholders, despite advancements in information technology, are able to bend corporations to their will, is not only naïve but misleading. Some corporations invest a great deal in forms of communications for market responsiveness as the main tactic (Ahen and Zettinig, 2015b; Goldacre, 2012). The apparatus of emotional manipulation and other forms of persuasions is a core element of a marketing strategy (Bagozzi et al., 1999). Take the pharmaceutical industry for example: consumers are made to believe that every medicine is the result of flawless evidence-based science, whilst in fact, most information on adverse effects is hidden from the general public (Goldacre, 2012). Some corporations invent diseases with the sole aim of creating cures for profits (ibid.). But it gets even worse as articles in medical journals are nowadays fraught with cooked-up data purporting to offer new evidence (Gupta, 2013). Such behaviours fundamentally affect trust between stakeholders and organisations.

In essence, a stakeholder relationship perspective (Freeman, 1984; Grönroos, 2008; Gummesson, 1994) is proposed here as the quintessential brand-building modus operandi, reflective of ethically responsible strategic configuration of resources and intentional attitudinal change aimed at engaging (stakeholders) society. I follow Porter and Kramer (2006) to argue in no uncertain terms that actions (strategic CSR) speak louder than words. The urgent need for CSR is a self-evident truth. However, much to our chagrin some firms respond to this in almost bizarre ways. "In fact the most common corporate response has been neither strategic nor operational but cosmetic: public relations and media campaigns, the centrepieces of which are often glossy CSR reports that showcase companies' social and environmental good deeds" (Porter and Kramer, 2006, pp. 80–81), and they are scarcely coherent. And there is an "existing cacophony of self-appointed score keepers [and CSR reports which] does little more than add to the confusion" (ibid., p. 81). Even the EU Commission laments about this form of communication: "the proliferation of different CSR instruments (such as management standards, labeling and certification schemes, reporting, etc.) that are difficult to compare, is confusing for business, consumers, investors, other stakeholders and the public, and this, in turn, can be a source of market distortion" (EUCOM, 2002, p. 5).

These views underscore the importance of SCR communications and social marketing as two fundamental instruments to correct corporate deviance and green washing (Banerjee, 2011; Wagner et al., 2009) on one hand and anti-branding as well as the high cost of reactionary corporate activities for reputation recuperation on the other. Lazer and Kelley (1973, p. ix) define *social marketing* as being "concerned with the application of marketing knowledge, concepts and techniques to enhance social as well as economic ends. It is also [particularly] concerned with the analysis of the social consequences of marketing policies, decisions and activities". With additional sophistication, Andreasen (1995, p. 7) refers to social marketing as "the application of commercial marketing technologies to the analysis, planning, execution, and evaluation of programs designed to influence the voluntary behavior of target audiences in order to improve their personal welfare and that of their society". This definition is closer to stakeholder engagement through relationship marketing where dialogue plays a central role (Grönroos, 2008; Gummesson, 1994).

Method

In the present contribution, I use critical marketing theory (Burton, 2001) at the interface of strategic CSR literature (Zadek, 2004) and stakeholder theory (Freeman, 1984). The aim is to offer theoretical propositions and a framework for further analysis of disintegrated marketing communications and missed opportunities that lead to competitive disadvantage and value destruction for both the firm and society. In 1998, Saren and Brownlie in their call for papers for the critical marketing stream of the first International Critical Management Conference organized in 1999 defined critical marketing theory as "any approach drawing inspiration from the substantive critical traditions of, for example, feminism, Marxism, ethnography and symbolism, post structuralism, hermeneutics, postmodernism and environmentalism" (Burton, 2001, p. 727). Employing theories on consumer behaviour (especially emotional theories), I critique corporate practices in marketing in the light of emerging socio-economic and environmental dynamics of the 21st century. This redirects attention from traditional positivist and empiricist foundation of marketing and allows for reflection on the 'market for virtue' (Vogel, 2005). Here, I make the case for SCR through social marketing in contrast to traditional CSR that has simply been reduced to a marketing gimmick. A major distinction between branding and reputation building is necessary. Whereas a brand is *consumer-centric*, reputation is *firm-centric* (Ettenson and Knowles, 2008), and both are necessary for the success of marketing communications when stakeholder engagement becomes a centrepiece of management strategies.

Results

Disintegrated marketing communications

The hope of a just, sustainable and prosperous world has never been stronger among consumers, academics, governments and economic actors than it is now. Such future aspirations for a sustainable world now forces stakeholders to regard corporate irresponsibility as a crucial topical issue in the strategic management discourse. Disintegrated marketing communications is hence a trajectory of actions that is neither in congruence with strategy nor consistent with stakeholder expectations and yet deceptively manoeuvres its way through emotional manipulation and other communication tactics to persuade consumers and other stakeholders. Examples of such behaviours include deceptive packaging and quality misspecifications of pharmaceutical products, questionable emotional manipulations in ads, misrepresentation of products, misleading advertisements, price discrimination and escalating rhetoric in sustainability reports about environmental impacts (Smith, 1995). This does not create value but constitutes deviance and green washing which then degenerates into reputational loss and erosion (or free fall) of legitimacy. Such propagandist and press 'agentry' approaches which "spread the faith of the organizations involved, often through incomplete, distorted, or half-true information" (Grunig and Hunt, 1984, p. 21) are part of the misleading understanding of what CSR stands for. In fact, it is even argued that "if a company focuses too intently on communicating CSR associations, is it possible that consumers may believe that the company is trying to hide something?" (Brown and Dacin, 1997, p. 81).

SCR communications via authentic branding

Porter and Kramer (2006) refer to balancing strategy and specific social issues as 'corporate social integration' where social problems are viewed as business opportunities that are solved innovatively and sustainably. This is achieved by offering beyond what stakeholders expect for themselves and their environment. In this way, firms are able to position themselves in the crowd of brands in a strategically differentiated manner given their unique capabilities to offer value propositions, either through low-cost innovative products or services that appeal to a globe of eco-friendly, social-justice-minded stakeholders. This goes beyond labels and long laundry list of CSR reports which are mainly about PR with a public that perhaps seems to have an overall view of the corporate irresponsibility. Corporate identity and internally institutionalised overall routines integrated at all levels of corporate functions become SCR communications. This is the description of the identity of the firm which consumers perceptually relate to. The perceived value in the firm's offerings that are in agreement with the firm's actions and overall value creation orientation leads to loyalty and long-term relationship with the service or product (Ahen and Zettinig, 2015a; Grönroos, 2008). This symbolises an authentic brand since the firm orients its capabilities towards where it senses opportunity (Foley and Fahy, 2009).

Pointing to the crux of issues, authentic branding is operationalised as the point of equilibrium between meeting corporate goals (of sustained competitive advantage and long-term success) and stakeholder expectations, framed by the institutional and market-specific demands instead of green washing and emotional manipulations. Here, cynical strategies meant only for the firm's bottom line are not welcome. Rather stakeholder engagement and the search for organisational reputation born out of meeting institutional expectations are seen as essential and mutually beneficial intangible assets (Barnett et al., 2006; Bertels and Peloza, 2008; Carmeli and Tishler, 2005). These assets must be protected via consistent, sustainable (social, ethical and environmental) actions and communications reflective of the core beliefs, identity and sets of corporate day-to-day practices – the exact opposite of disintegrated marketing communications. Hence, reputation as a resource affects firm performance in terms of stakeholders' perception and customer loyalty (Barnett et al., 2006; Fombrun and Van Riel, 1997; Mahon and Wartick, 2003). All the above should also embody the socially desirable use of corporate power especially in international markets where firms operate in weaker institutions (Brammer et al., 2012) which characteristically lack influential stakeholder constellations (Campbell, 2007; Fransen and Kolk, 2007). This means they may lack the voice and the power to demand accountability but that does not render such stakeholders illegitimate or less urgent (Banerjee, 2011). Here, 'putting the last first' must become the goal of the firm (Murtaza, 2012).

Misleading identity representation vs authentic brand reputation

Responsible and ethical innovations, in essence, represent an opportunity to proactively engage with emerging stakeholder demands as well as institutional and environmental changes. It is argued that every action or inaction of the firm, be it responsible or irresponsible, implicit or explicit, is viewed by stakeholders as a form of direct or indirect communication. Behind firms' scramble to portray themselves as socially sensitive with unmarred reputation lies not only the concept of sustainable brand-building but also the struggle for survival. These lead firms to two very different trajectories and outcomes: (i) deceptive identity representation aligned with sporadic and tactical social programmes; both destroy value for stakeholders and create a competitive disadvantage for the firm in the long-term and (ii) the authentic identity communication that is a reflection of core values, dynamic capabilities and innovativeness in the offerings of the firm judged by the stakeholders. The latter is integrated into the operational and relational connection between firm's business essence and social good. This leads to mutual value creation for the firm and its stakeholders. Such brand-building approaches are not theatrics but socio-psychological constructs (perceptions of brand personality) which stem from systematic daily practices that resonate with stakeholders within and beyond the firms' operational milieu. In essence, this represents the strategic behaviour aimed at balancing the success of the firm with social good. Clearly, this description of most firms is not at odds with the image they claim to possess in numerous CSR reports and in consumers' minds (EUCOM, 2002; Morsing and Schultz, 2006; Porter and Kramer, 2006).

Figure 4.1.1 demonstrates the value destruction trajectory that leads to competitive disadvantage and the value creation trajectory that leads to sustained competitive advantage. Authentic identity communications are simply SCR communications and social marketing combined. This leads to legitimacy and institutional acceptance. Consumer-oriented value propositions capture consumer premium and customer loyalty in value creation, which leads to competitive advantage. On the other hand, deceptive corporate identity entails green washing and deviance, illegal and unethical practices, as well as breach of social contract (Clarkson, 1995; Donaldson and Preston, 1995). These lead to institutional rejection and loss of reputation – anti-branding. Inconsistent messages, ambiguous

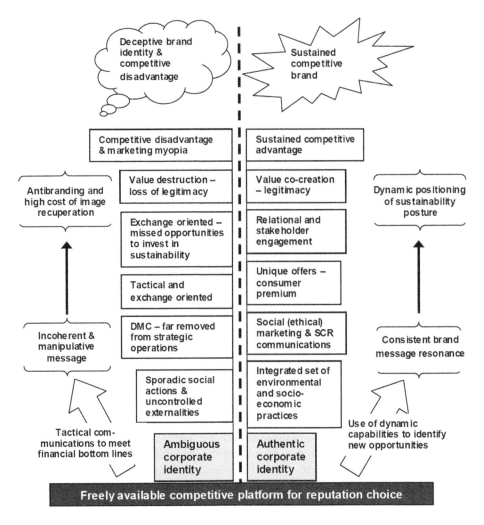

Figure 4.1.1 Value creation and value destruction trajectories

Note: DMC – disintegrated marketing communications; SCR – strategic corporate responsibility.

articulation and representation of brand personality (corporate hypocrisy) lead to value destruction (Wagner et al., 2009). Further, stakeholders' negative perceptions shape the firm's reputation in real financial terms. The consequence is a high cost of recuperating reputation. That in turn leads to competitive disadvantage.

The SCR communications as a branded posture is not once-in-a-while 'display' but rather a continuous monitoring and controlling of both internal and external challenges and opportunities, with the aim of ensuring firm–environment co-evolution. Factors that lead to competitive disadvantage emanate from both structural deficiencies and psychological lapses in terms of (i) corporate cultural-cognitive bias; (ii) power imbalance in the organisation, leading to status quo bias; and (iii) inefficient and unsound judgements with little or no checks on the competitive, dynamic environment. All this translates into managerial failure to optimise existing capabilities via strong stakeholder alliances and inability to keep abreast of the emergent technological and sociological changes that affect stakeholder demands. Implied here is that firms are unable to benefit from knowledge exchange as a valuable source of advancement in order to expand to new markets with new environmentally sustainable products and services. Such uncreative firms only concentrate on their industry and existing markets with a 'myopic marketing' tactics (Levitt, 1960). Managerial failure to capture emerging opportunities from social problems with innovation represents unpreparedness to respond to technological, market and institutional vagaries (Augier and Teece, 2008). Failure to learn from changes in the business environment and to evolve accordingly can also be attributed to myopic managerial vision and difficulties to adapt to emergent dynamics. The constant reliance on reactionary managerial tactics instead of a proactive and strategic renewal explains among others why firms perform differently in their communications. Such errors of commission and omission, lapses in judgement and failure to sense and capture valuable and crucial opportunities are what Powell and Arregle (2007) refer to as axis of errors. These are typical behavioural issues in management.

The foregoing analyses are not only based on structural conjuncturess but also point to the erroneous managerial or agency choices at the micro level. This manner of theorising is certainly interesting because it recognises basic behavioural aspects of marketing communications and strategy implementation as social efforts with values and bounded rationality. Hence, the internal drivers of corporate communications are mainly managerial belief, entrepreneurial orientation and other cognitive predispositions to innovate and capture value while satisfying stakeholders. Nevertheless, regulatory, technological and industry dynamics play a major role. Sophisticated stakeholder activism and non-governmental organisations together form a formidable force against which individual firms and industries need to contend, not content with because they are able to put into dispute "the propriety of their [firms'] continued existence and operation" (Mahon and McGowan, 1996, p. 63). This implies that reputation management is of critical importance (Fombrun and Van Riel, 1997), not least because it is desirable for all firms but because it represents a resource and defines the very survival of the firm in a competitive environment.

How is value destroyed via disintegrated marketing communications?

Schultz and Kitchen (2000) outline four stages of Integrated Marketing Communications IMC. They are: (i) tactical coordination of promotional elements, (ii) redefinition of the scope of marketing communications, (iii) the application of information technology to financial goals and (iv) the ultimate communication goal of strategic integration. Many firms hardly arrive at this level of strategic integration Schultz and Kitchen maintain. This value is what Holm (2006) defines as the ratio between benefits and costs and between what the customer obtains and what she or he offers in return.

Consumers and by extension stakeholders) are the only value creators (Grönroos, 2008) through their use of products and services, and firms, big or small get opportunities to co-create value with consumers via relationships. If emotional spins in marketing communications (O'Shaughnessy and O'Shaughnessy, 2003) lead to loss in legitimacy, then the lost opportunity to make an offer in the first place due to lack of credibility constitutes value destruction. Second, the missed opportunity to create and maintain loyal customers through a relationship for repeated buying negatively affects a firm's performance (in the form of bad reputation, low brand value, profits, market share and growth). This may reflect a reputational/legitimacy loss, leading to negative return-on-investment for shareholders. Implied here is that this can allow competitors to siphon customers. For example, the 2016 Volkswagen emission scandal (Lane, 2016) cost the firm millions of Euros (in recalls, fines and reputational damage) but so were millions of stakeholders affected, not counting the enormous environmental impact. What's more, management spent hundreds of hours in boardroom meetings doing damage control and on responding to investigators while dealing with unwelcome media attention. These lost resources could have rather been spent on searching for new innovations and dialoguing properly with stakeholders. These forms of value destruction, in fact, go beyond the firm and its stakeholders and rather set new precedents for others to follow. The next dimension of value destruction is the loss of customers to rivals (either existing customers switching or potential customers being deterred) due to reputational deficit vis-à-vis rivals. That deficiency leads to a competitive disadvantage. Consequently, since investors logically prefer profitable firms, (the fourth) stalled opportunity ushers in when firms are not opportunity seeking. Lack of investor interest means declining resources for R&D and the inability to capture new innovation frontiers; the exact opposite also holds. If the above reasoning holds, then on the operational level it represents closed opportunities for knowledge creation and sharing through partnerships and collaborations with other players as well as dialogue with stakeholders. This translates into operational inefficiency (Porter, 1996). Value is not only effectively and materially destroyed, but the missed opportunities to create value in the first place constitute value destruction – that is, when non-entrepreneurially minded managers take erroneous decisions leading to commission of resources into actions that are strategically irrelevant (e.g. short-termist behaviours) or ignore emerging and profitable opportunities (Augier and Teece, 2008). For an explanation and synthesis on the typologies of competitive disadvantage created by disintegrated marketing communications and missed opportunities that lead to value destruction, see Figure 4.1.2.

The concept of *opportunity* in all its forms and under varieties of contexts has been well explored and there is a critical mass of works which eloquently testify of its importance (see e.g. Short et al., 2010) for a comprehensive review. From extant literature, they describe how opportunities are perceived, how they come about and how they are exploited. They maintain that "without an opportunity, there is no entrepreneurship" (p. 40). Further, they define an opportunity as "an idea or dream that is discovered or created by an entrepreneurial [manager] entity and that is revealed through analysis over time to be potentially lucrative" (p. 55). They however focus mainly on certain aspects of the concept of opportunity, namely discovery, creation, temporal dynamics and the evolution of the opportunity, with little else as to how opportunities are squandered ex or post ante. All the above typologies of competitive disadvantage in the form of squandered opportunities can be

Typology of competitive disadvantage	Lost opportunity to offer value propositions	Missed opportunity to co-create value	Misappropriated opportunity to retain market share	Stalled opportunity to attract investors and institutional support	Closed opportunity to knowledge sharing via collaboration, alliances and new markets
Explanation of impact on firms' reputation and brand	Emotional spin, disintegrated and incoherent communication alienates consumers, restrains stakeholder dialogue	Lost legitimacy leads to lost loyalty and brand weakness – competitive disadvantage leads to lower performance	Lost trust and reputation gets potential and existing customers siphoned by rivals	Investors opt for profitable and opportunity seeking firms and not opportunistic firms – leads to financial handicap	Self-created barriers to collaborations with institutions and markets → non-refreshed static capabilities and operational ineffectiveness → stagnant growth
Theoretical and practical examples	Freeman (1984) - Lost opportunity to freely acquire knowledge from stakeholders	Grönroos (2008) - Relationship marketing - Built on service logic and demand side strategies	Porter and Kramer (2006) – Non-competitive firms invest in media rather than in substantive sustainability, e.g., cost-cutting technologies	March (1991) - Real action and change is impossible without attitudinal and dynamic technological resources	- Dynamic capabilities (Eisenhardt and Martin, 2000; Penrose, 1959; Teece and Pisano, 1994) - Diversification into e.g. drugs for neglected diseases, eco-friendly activities at the BOP.

Figure 4.1.2 A conceptual framework of value destruction and competitive disadvantage. Note: BOP – bottom of the pyramid.

redeemed when corporate managers effect actual changes in strategies to reflect the needs of stakeholders. Further, sustainability-oriented institutional reforms or stakeholder resistance to corporate malpractices may influence how authentic communication becomes reintegrated into the firm's actions and managerial decisions towards strategic renewal. The main argument here is that all the five forms of destroyed opportunities in their positive forms are freely available to all firms and managers as initial competitive platforms. Nevertheless, their loss is the direct consequence of managerial lapses and inability to (i) identify and capture new strategic opportunities, (ii) orchestrate important organisational assets and (iii) invent new business models and new organisational forms as the authentic communication modes (Augier and Teece, 2008, p. 1187).

The above leads to the following propositions:

1   erroneous managerial judgement and biases in decisions lead to disintegrated marketing communications. This in turn leads to missed and lost opportunities. The greater the missed or lost opportunities the lower the competitive advantage and hence lower firm performance. Clearly, lower performance reflects greater stakeholder dissatisfaction.
2   Misappropriated opportunity to gain market share either marks the mid-point of crisis or renewal. The more severe the misappropriation is, the greater the chance of renewal and change in brand communication. Also, the less severe it is, the greater the chances that the managerial attitude will remain the same.
3   Stalled opportunity to attract investors and institutional support translates into legitimacy at its lowest point, and this barrier automatically leads to a closed opportunity to alliances and support. Hence, the greater the hostility to corporate communication, the less collaborative efforts firms can gain from stakeholders and the least likely they are to optimise capabilities to create a competitive advantage.
4   Therefore, communication that is not responsibly and fully integrated into strategy at all levels is the source of competitive disadvantage. This in turn destroys value for stakeholders.

Discussion

How might firms mitigate value destruction through SCR communications and social marketing?

Hastings and Saren (2003) contend that marketing, as it is, has always been concerned with influence and certainly the (emotional and behavioural) manipulations of the consumer. This much is even truer for particular industries: mining and resource-seeking companies in developing economies destroy the environment of local people; repatriate billions to home countries; avoid taxes (Christensen, 2011); meddle in internal politics; and offer football parks, sports equipment and philanthropy in a public display of responsibility (Dearden, 2017) while some among their pharmaceutical counterparts, with the help of irresponsible doctors, sell needless and sometimes life-threatening drugs by creating false needs where they can get away with it (Angell, 2004; Goldacre, 2012). SCR communications implies that the firm anticipates stakeholder expectations and emerging opportunities, proactively articulating its communication apparatus in ways that are consistent with how it seeks to be known and perceived by stakeholders. This is achieved through authentic and transparent information about the firm's innovative brand integration into business operations – via consistent stakeholder dialogue in the social, environmental and ethical terms.

Social marketing targets consumers as the primary audience. The process is also geared towards influencing defined social and market policies to tackle broader social and environmental questions with consequences on human health (Donovan and Henley, 2003; Thackeray and McCormack Brown, 2005). For Andreasen (2003), social marketing represents an innovative corporate apparatus for influencing social change, thus, beyond the traditional quasi stereotypical notion of techniques for manipulating consumers and selling goods; Wiebe (1951), Hastings and Saren (2003) and Kotler and Levy (1969) agree. Originating with the inspiration of Kotler and Zaltman (1971), social marketing has for the past four decades seen significant contributions although it requires integration with other theoretical perspectives to underpin its importance towards both social change and to reflect the challenges and opportunities of market dynamism and consumer behaviour. The purpose of marketing is principally to inform, persuade and affect consumer choices about products and services via mechanisms that appeal to the targeted consumer segments. This appears operationally justifiable. Nonetheless, modern marketing techniques, to a large extent, involve deception, gimmickry and forms of deviance with negative social and economic consequences (Hastings and Saren, 2003). In the light of the aforementioned problems, the role of social marketing becomes one of a reconciliatory communication apparatus aimed at bringing sanity into the polarised world caused by exploitation and manipulation for economic ends; thus, to reach economic outcomes while promoting social good via practical social responsibility communication (ibid.). This mode of marketing has several implications for the firm as well as the society it serves and on which it depends for survival. Social marketing is nothing more than integrating social needs as an opportunity and an incentive into innovative corporate practices both for the firm's economic gains and social good. This is because CSR is "a concept [defined as a process] whereby companies integrate social and environmental concerns in their business operations and in their interaction with their stakeholders on a voluntary basis" (EUCOM, 2002, p. 2). SCR communications characteristically involve what goes beyond legal requirements (even if institutionally constrained). Here, social and environmental concerns are fully integrated into firm's operations and linked to sustainability. "CSR is not an additional 'add-on' to a business' core activities, rather, (this concept) concerns the way in which businesses are managed" (EUCOM, 2002, p. 5). This way of reasoning by the EU Commission supports the logic of SCR.

Branding, anti-branding and the criticality of corporate reputation building

Unquestionably closely associated with the notion of product positioning in the minds of stakeholders is the issue of branding. Branding establishes what a product actually stands for, especially in international markets, and creates higher awareness and easy identification due to differentiation from competing offers, and above all, the single most important and universal purpose is to induce customer loyalty (Hollensen, 1998). This process may involve at least four different branding decisions: (i) generic or no brand with severe identity deficiency, (ii) private label familiar with most start-ups, (iii) co-branding and (iv) manufacturer's own label (Onkvisit and Shaw, 1989). Of practical managerial relevance here is the fact that communicating a brand cannot be short-sightedly viewed as an afterthought PR issue. All these processes shape the perception of consumers and other stakeholders in terms of the overall social and environmental impact, e.g. the treatment of employees, natural resource input, as well as the total effect on the ecosystems (Hollensen, 1998).

Empowered consumers use sophisticated media tools to engage in anti-branding activities to discredit certain brand images (Kucuk, 2009; Kucuk and Krishnamurthy, 2007). The advent of the internet has given these stakeholders freedom, voice and exit possibilities in their relationship with the firm. In essence, the power dominance of the firm is being challenged by the new medium of the consumer, and this relationship needs to be managed responsibly. This however does not explain the extent to which such ways of theorising become applicable in international contexts, especially developing economies where in the absence of strong institutions and stakeholder advocacy groups (e.g. strong workers' unions, environmentally oriented organisations and consumer protection organisations) firms will continue to wield power and act as they desire (Kolk and Van Tulder, 2004; Wettstein, 2012; Wickert et al., 2016). Value is destroyed when what is communicated deviates from the optimal outcomes expected from firm-stakeholder engagement or in some cases as with weaker institutions, when there is no engagement at all. This means stakeholders are not even welcomed into any form of constructive dialogue where they can press home their demands. In other words, they are relegated to the margins and disempowered (Ahen, 2017; Durepos et al., 2016), in that they have no exit possibilities when they are dissatisfied; they are voiceless because they are not even partakers of a dialogue in any form of engagement. This leads us to the major question of power asymmetry between firms and disempowered stakeholders. Firm-stakeholder engagement then, is about overcoming the myriad systemic constraints and realigning stakeholder demands with that of the firm in ways that are consistent with the firm's mission, vision and values. These must be locally defined to respond to contextual needs but must also be treated as inalienable universal rights in the quest to create shared value. The conditions of empowered and disempowered stakeholders and prerequisites for ensuring productive stakeholder engagement are demonstrated in Table 4.1.1.

Table 4.1.1 Conditions for facilitating stakeholder engagement

Prerequisites for stakeholder engagement	Empowered stakeholders	Disempowered stakeholders
Knowledge of the stake: the right to refuse participation in unethical/illegal activities, dialogue with civil society and democratic representation of employees	Educated with critical thinking skills, not easily outmanoeuvred, understand the nature of corporate externalities on health and environment	Less educated, easily outmanoeuvred, accept philanthropy as a perfect substitute for degraded environment. Social marketing and locally situated dialogue through relationship building for value creation.
Mechanisms for holding stakes: e.g. allowing voice and formation of dissenting groups.	Ability to organise into formidable groups to use modern communication technologies to advance their cause.	Unorganised into strong and formidable constellations. Lack access and use of social media and other communication technologies to press home needs.
Enabling institutional environment. Proactive attention to stakeholder concerns and creation of communication channels for engagement	Legal and regulatory environment entails strong enforcement mechanism and clear direction for firm-stakeholder engagement either voluntarily or by law.	Such enforcement mechanisms are lacking whether in urban poor areas or developing economies because stakeholders lack bargaining power and are therefore marginalised (Derry, 2012).

The value that is lost then does not only consist of missed potential opportunities but also consumer switching, boycotting, anti-branding and shaky brand position in the market. To add up to the odds, a firm will perform badly in the long term because such factors represent a competitive disadvantage vis-à-vis rivals who adopt a proactive stakeholder dialogue and authentic brand image with a consistent message. This is in fact the criticality of the corporate reputation and how it affects the perception of stakeholders. None of these will however happen if stakeholders lack the power to effect a change or challenge the firm's status quo.

Conclusions

'No firm is an island' (Håkansson and Snehota, 2006), and even if they were, the 21st century announces a new imperative: to build bridges and create innovative ways for productive dialogue and engagement among stakeholders. The reasons outlined mainly concentrate on socio-economic and environmental demands, emerging stakeholder needs and the ultimate quest for survival through authentic value creation in a hyper-competitive world. We have argued that firms miss, lose, stall, misappropriate or close opportunities when they do not consciously seek to create value that meets stakeholders' demands. This chapter seeks to reshape managerial thinking about the intertwined nature of corporate strategic communications and its direct effect on stakeholder response. The approaches in theorising SCR communication have often been more stylistic than substantive and practice-oriented. Clearly, the global socio-economic and institutional pendulum seems to have swung towards a trajectory of the well-received wisdom of sustainability and responsible communications defined by a firm's integrity and unambiguous firm identity, and so must managerial vision adapt to shape and be shaped by such dynamics. The product of the analysis thus far aims at the fruitfulness of firm's optimisation of dynamic capabilities and entrepreneurial orientation towards the basic mission of creating and not destroying value in order to maintain its competitiveness. The test of corporate integrity that resonates among stakeholders is the managerial communication that reflects actions that are authentic and socially acceptable.

Limitations and suggestions for future research

As with all research, there are both glaring limitations and not so obvious limitations. While this conceptual work problematises the nature of stakeholder engagement or the lack of it and how that leads to varieties of value destruction, the taxonomy identified here is not an exhaustive list. A more extensive empirical study that seeks to identify how, why and what type of value is destroyed in different industries will bring much clearer managerial guidelines as to how to strategise to avoid such forms of value destruction. This is because every form of value destruction undermines a firm's competitive advantage and affects stakeholders negatively. Future research that broadens the scope of the present study by studying how new forms of innovative stakeholder engagement are positively affecting society and the firms embedded in them will certainly extend our knowledge frontier. Further, this study has focused mainly on for-profit firms. However, there are social enterprises and public-private partnerships. How stakeholder engagement works within these business and hybrid organisations is different and so are these organisations' long-term effects on society and brand and reputation building. A future study in this direction will provide a new evidence-based understanding of organisation-stakeholder engagement for value creation and competitive advantage. The socio-psychological context of managerial inter-temporal choice is necessary and needs to be studied in terms of how managers avoid certain errors and spot opportunities freely available to all firms (Powell and Arregle, 2007). Further, the motivational circumstances under which firms are likely to miss, lose, stall, misappropriate or close opportunities should also be studied.

References

Agle, B.R., Mitchell, R.K. and Sonnenfeld, J.A. (1999). 'Who matters to CEOs? An investigation of stakeholder attributes and salience, corporate performance, and CEO values', *Academy of Management Journal*, **42** (5), pp. 507–525.

Ahen, F. (2015). *Strategic corporate responsibility orientation for sustainable global health governance: Pharmaceutical value co-protection in transitioning economies* (PhD Doctoral thesis), University of Turku, Turku, Finland.

Ahen, F. (2017). 'Reforming the delinquent organization: Academia's impactful tribute to society', in J. A. Arevalo and S. F. Mitchell (eds), *Handbook of sustainability in management education: In search of a multidisciplinary, innovative and integrated approach*, Cheltenham, UK and Northampton, MA: Edward Elgar Publishing, pp. (in print).

Ahen, F. and Zettinig, P. (2015a). 'Critical perspectives on strategic CSR: What is sustainable value co-creation orientation?', *Critical Perspectives on International Business*, **11** (1), pp. 92–109.

Ahen, F. and Zettinig, P. (2015b). 'What is the biggest question in CSR research?', *Foresight*, **17** (3), pp. 274–290.

Andreasen, A.R. (1995). *Marketing social change: Changing behavior to promote health, social development, and the environment*, San Francisco, CA: Jossey-Bass Publishers.

Andreasen, A.R. (2003). 'The life trajectory of social marketing: Some implications', *Marketing Theory*, **3** (3), pp. 293–303.

Angell, M. (2004). *The truth about the drug companies: How they deceive us and what to do about it*, New York: Random House.

Armstrong, J.S. (1977). 'Social irresponsibility in management', *Journal of Business Research*, **5** (3), pp. 185–213.

Augier, M. and Teece, D.J. (2008). 'Strategy as evolution with design: The foundations of dynamic capabilities and the role of managers in the economic system', *Organization Studies*, **29** (8–9), pp. 1187–1208.

Bagozzi, R.P., Gopinath, M. and Nyer, P.U. (1999). 'The role of emotions in marketing', *Journal of the Academy of Marketing Science*, **27** (2), pp. 184–206.

Banerjee, S.B. (2007). *Corporate social responsibility: The good, the bad and the ugly*, Cheltenham: Edward Elgar Publishing.

Banerjee, S.B. (2011). 'Voices of the Governed: Towards a theory of the translocal', *Organization*, **18** (3), pp. 323–344.

Barnett, M.L., Jermier, J.M. and Lafferty, B.A. (2006). 'Corporate reputation: The definitional landscape', *Corporate Reputation Review*, **9** (1), pp. 26–38.

Bartley, T. (2007). 'Institutional emergence in an era of globalization: The rise of transnational private regulation of labor and environmental conditions 1', *American Journal of Sociology*, **113** (2), pp. 297–351.

Bertels, S. and Peloza, J. (2008). 'Running just to stand still? Managing CSR reputation in an era of ratcheting expectations', *Corporate Reputation Review*, **11** (1), pp. 56–72.

Boons, F. (2004). 'Connecting levels: A systems view on stakeholder dialogue for sustainability', *Progress in Industrial Ecology, An International Journal*, **1** (4), pp. 385–396.

Bornstein, R.F. (1989). 'Subliminal techniques as propaganda tools: Review and critique', *The Journal of Mind and Behavior*, **10** (3), pp. 231–262.

Brammer, S., Jackson, G. and Matten, D. (2012). 'Corporate social responsibility and institutional theory: New perspectives on private governance', *Socio-economic Review*, **10** (1), pp. 3–28.

Brown, T.J. and Dacin, P.A. (1997). 'The company and the product: Corporate associations and consumer product responses', *The Journal of Marketing*, pp. 68–84.

Burton, D. (2001). 'Critical marketing theory: The blueprint?', *European Journal of Marketing*, **35** (5/6), pp. 722–743.

Campbell, C. (1995). 'Conspicuous confusion? A critique of Veblen's theory of conspicuous consumption', *Sociological Theory*, **13** (1), pp. 37–47.

Campbell, J.L. (2007). 'Why would corporations behave in socially responsible ways? An institutional theory of corporate social responsibility', *Academy of Management Review*, **32** (3), pp. 946–967.

Carmeli, A. and Tishler, A. (2005). 'Perceived organizational reputation and organizational performance: An empirical investigation of industrial enterprises', *Corporate Reputation Review*, **8** (1), pp. 13–30.

Charles, K.K., Hurst, E. and Roussanov, N. (2009). 'Conspicuous consumption and race', *The Quarterly Journal of Economics*, **124** (2), pp. 425–467.

Christensen, J. (2011). 'The looting continues: Tax havens and corruption', *Critical Perspectives on International Business*, **7** (2), pp. 177–196.

Clarkson, M.B.E. (1995). 'A stakeholder framework for analyzing and evaluating corporate social performance', *Academy of Management Review*, **20** (1), pp. 92–117.

Clegg, S.R. (2006). 'Why is organization theory so ignorant? The neglect of total institutions', *Journal of Management Inquiry*, **15** (4), pp. 426–430.

Covin, J.G. and Miles, M.P. (1999). 'Corporate entrepreneurship and the pursuit of competitive advantage', *Entrepreneurship: Theory and Practice*, **23** (3), pp. 47–47.

Crane, A. (2013). 'Modern slavery as a management practice: Exploring the conditions and capabilities for human exploitation', *Academy of Management Review*, **38** (1), pp. 49–69.

Curtis, M. and Jones, T. (2017). 'Honest accounts 2017: How the world profits from Africa's wealth', available at: www.globaljustice.org.uk/sites/default/files/files/resources/honest_accounts_2017_web_final_updated.pdf (accessed 22 September 2017).

Dearden, N. (2017). 'Africa is not poor, we are stealing its wealth: It's time to change the way we talk and think about Africa', *AlJazeera.com*, available at: www.aljazeera.com/indepth/opinion/2017/05/africa-poor-stealing-wealth-170524063731884.html (accessed 25 May 2017).

Derry, R. (2012). 'Reclaiming marginalized stakeholders', *Journal of Business Ethics*, **111** (2), pp. 253–264.

Donaldson, T. and Preston, L.E. (1995). 'The stakeholder theory of the corporation: Concepts, evidence, and implications', *Academy of Management Review*, **20** (1), pp. 65–91.

Donovan, R.J. and Henley, N. (2003). *Social marketing: Principles and practice*, Melbourne: IP communications.

Drucker, P.F. (1973). *Management: Tasks, responsibilities, practices*, New York: Harper & Row.

Durepos, G., Prasad, A. and Villanueva, C.E. (2016). 'How might we study international business to account for marginalized subjects? Turning to practice and situating knowledges', *Critical Perspectives on International Business*, **12** (3), pp. 306–314.

Eisenhardt, K.M. and Martin, J.A. (2000). 'Dynamic capabilities: What are they?', *Strategic Management Journal*, **21** (10–11), pp. 1105–1121.

Ettenson, R. and Knowles, J. (2008). 'Don't confuse reputation with brand', *MIT Sloan Management Review*, **49** (2), pp. 19–21.

EUCOM (2002). *Communication from the Commission concerning corporate social responsibility: A business contribution to sustainable development*. Brussels: Commission of the European Communities.

Foley, A. and Fahy, J. (2009). 'Seeing market orientation through a capabilities lens', *European Journal of Marketing*, **43** (1/2), pp. 13–20.

Fombrun, C. and Van Riel, C. (1997). 'The reputational landscape', *Corporate Reputation Review*, **1** (1/2), pp. 5–13.

Fransen, L.W. and Kolk, A. (2007). 'Global rule-setting for business: A critical analysis of multi-stakeholder standards', *Organization*, **14** (5), pp. 667–684.

Freeman, R.E. (1984). *Strategic management: A stakeholder approach*, Boston, MA: Pitman.

Freeman, R.E., Harrison, J.S., Wicks, A.C., Parmar, B.L. and De Colle, S. (2010). *Stakeholder theory: The state of the art*. Cambridge: Cambridge University Press.

Freeman, R.E. and Velamuri, S.R. (2006). 'A new approach to CSR: Company stakeholder responsibility', in A. Kakabadse and M. Morsing (eds), *Corporate social responsibility: Reconciling aspiration with application*, New York: Palgrave MacMillan, pp. 9–23.

Goldacre, B. (2012). *Bad pharma: How drug companies mislead doctors and harm patients*, London: Fourth Estate.

Grönroos, C. (2008). 'Service logic revisited: Who creates value? And who co-creates?', *European Business Review*, **20** (4), pp. 298–314.

Grunig, J.E. and Hunt, T. (1984). *Managing public relations* (Vol. 343), New York: Holt, Rinehart and Winston.

Gummesson, E. (1994). 'Making relationship marketing operational', *International Journal of Service Industry Management*, **5** (5), pp. 5–20.

Gupta, A. (2013). 'Fraud and misconduct in clinical research: A concern', *Perspectives in Clinical Research*, **4** (2), pp. 144.

Håkansson, H. and Snehota, I. (2006). '"No business is an island" 17 years later', *Scandinavian Journal of Management*, **22** (3), pp. 271–274.

Hastings, G. and Saren, M. (2003). 'The critical contribution of social marketing: Theory and application', *Marketing Theory*, **3** (3), pp. 305–322.

Hollensen, S. (1998). *Global marketing: A market-responsive approach*. London: Prentice Hall.

Holm, O. (2006). 'Integrated marketing communication: From tactics to strategy', *Corporate Communications: An International Journal*, **11** (1), pp. 23–33.

Kolk, A. and Van Tulder, R. (2004). 'Ethics in international business: Multinational approaches to child labor', *Journal of World Business*, **39** (1), pp. 49–60.

Kotler, P. and Levy, S.J. (1969). 'Broadening the concept of marketing', *The Journal of Marketing*, pp. 10–15.

Kotler, P. and Zaltman, G. (1971). 'Social marketing: An approach to planned social change', *The Journal of Marketing*, pp. 3–12.

Kucuk, S.U. (2009). 'Consumer empowerment model: From unspeakable to undeniable', *Direct Marketing: An International Journal*, **3** (4), pp. 327–342.

Kucuk, S.U. and Krishnamurthy, S. (2007). 'An analysis of consumer power on the Internet', *Technovation*, **27** (1), pp. 47–56.

Lane, E.L. (2016). 'Volkswagen and the high-tech greenwash', *European Journal of Risk Regulation*, **7** (1), pp. 32–34.

Lazer, W. and Kelley, E.J. (1973). *Social marketing: Perspectives and viewpoints*, Irwin: McGraw-Hill.

Levitt, T. (1960). 'Marketing myopia', *Harvard Business Review*, **38** (4), pp. 24–47.

Levy, D. and Kaplan, R. (2008). 'CSR and theories of global governance: Strategic contestation in global issue arenas', in A. Crane, A. McWilliams, D. Matten, J. Moon and D. S. Siegel (eds), *The Oxford handbook of corporate social responsibility*, Oxford: Oxford University Press, pp. 432–451.

Mahon, J.F. and McGowan, R. (1996). *Industry as a player in the political and social arena: Defining the competitive environment*, Westport, CT: Quorum Books.

Mahon, J.F. and Wartick, S.L. (2003). 'Dealing with stakeholders: How reputation, credibility and framing influence the game', *Corporate reputation review*, **6** (1), pp. 19–35.

March, J.G. (1991). 'Exploration and exploitation in organizational learning', *Organization science*, **2** (1), pp. 71–87.

McCraw, T.K. (2007). *Prophet of innovation*, Cambridge, MA; London, England: The Belknap Press of Harvard University Press.

Mitchell, R.K., Agle, B.R. and Wood, D.J. (1997). 'Toward a theory of stakeholder identification and salience: Defining the principle of who and what really counts', *Academy of Management Review*, **22** (4), pp. 853–886.

Moore, T.E. (1992). 'Subliminal perception: Facts and fallacies', *Skeptical Inquirer*, **16** (3), pp. 273–281.

Morsing, M. and Schultz, M. (2006). 'Corporate social responsibility communication: Stakeholder information, response and involvement strategies', *Business Ethics: A European Review*, **15** (4), pp. 323–338.

Murtaza, N. (2012). 'Putting the lasts first: The case for community-focused and peer-managed NGO accountability mechanisms', *VOLUNTAS: International Journal of Voluntary and Nonprofit Organizations*, **23** (1), pp. 109–125.

Nadvi, K. and Wältring, F. (2002). *Making sense of global standards*, Duisburg: INEF.

Onkvisit, S. and Shaw, J.J. (1989). 'The international dimension of branding: Strategic considerations and decisions', *International Marketing Review*, **6** (3), pp. 22–34.

O'Shaughnessy, J. and O'Shaughnessy, N.J. (2003). *The marketing power of emotion*, New York: Oxford University Press.

Pajunen, K. (2006). 'Stakeholder influences in organizational survival', *Journal of Management Studies*, **43** (6), pp. 1261–1288.

Piketty, T. (2014). *Capital in the 21st century* (A. Goldhammer, trans.), Cambridge, MA: Belknap Press.

Porter, M.E. (1990). *The competitive advantage of nations*, New York: Free Press.

Porter, M.E. (1996). 'What is strategy?', *Harvard Business Review*, **74** (6), pp. 61–78.

Porter, M.E. and Kramer, M.R. (2006). 'Strategy and society: The link between competitive advantage and corporate social responsibility', *Harvard Business Review*, **84** (12), pp. 78–92.

Post, J.E., Preston, L.E. and Sachs, S. (2002). 'Managing the extended enterprise: The new stakeholder view', *California Management Review*, **45** (1), pp. 6–28.

Powell, T.C. and Arregle, J.-L. (2007). 'Firm performance and the axis of errors', *Journal of Management Research*, **7** (2), pp. 59.

Rasche, A. (2010). 'The limits of corporate responsibility standards', *Business Ethics: A European Review*, **19** (3), pp. 280–291.

Rasche, A., De Bakker, F.G. and Moon, J. (2013). 'Complete and partial organizing for corporate social responsibility', *Journal of Business Ethics*, **115** (4), pp. 651–663.

Ravald, A. and Grönroos, C. (1996). 'The value concept and relationship marketing', *European Journal of Marketing*, **30** (2), pp. 19–30.

Rhenman, E. (1968). *Industrial democracy and industrial management*. London: Tavistock.

Rotfeld, H.J. (2005). 'The cynical use of marketing to the unwitting consumer', *Journal of Consumer Marketing*, **22** (2), pp. 60–61.

Schultz, D.E. and Kitchen, P.J. (2000). 'A response to "Theoretical concept or management fashion"', *Journal of Advertising Research*, **40** (5), pp. 17–21.

Short, J.C., Ketchen Jr, D.J., Shook, C.L. and Ireland, R.D. (2010). 'The concept of "opportunity" in entrepreneurship research: Past accomplishments and future challenges', *Journal of Management*, **36** (1), pp. 40–65.

Smith, N.C. (1995). 'Marketing strategies for the ethics era', *Sloan Management Review*, **36** (4), pp. 85.

Strand, R., Freeman, R.E. and Hockerts, K. (2015). 'Corporate social responsibility and sustainability in Scandinavia: An overview', *Journal of Business Ethics*, **127** (1), pp. 1–15.

Teece, D. and Pisano, G. (1994). 'The dynamic capabilities of firms: An introduction', *Industrial and Corporate Change*, **3** (3), pp. 537–556.

Thackeray, R. and McCormack Brown, K. (2005). 'Social marketing's unique contributions to health promotion practice', *Health Promotion Practice*, **6** (4), pp. 365–368.

Veblen, T. (1899/2009). *The theory of the leisure class*, New York: Oxford University Press.

Vogel, D.J. (2005). 'Is there a market for virtue? The business case for corporate social responsibility', *California Management Review*, **47** (4), pp. 19–45.

Wagner, T., Lutz, R.J. and Weitz, B.A. (2009). 'Corporate hypocrisy: Overcoming the threat of inconsistent corporate social responsibility perceptions', *Journal of Marketing*, **73** (6), pp. 77–91.

Wettstein, F. (2012). 'CSR and the debate on business and human rights: Bridging the great divide', *Business Ethics Quarterly*, **22** (04), pp. 739–770.

Wherry, F.F. (2008). 'The social characterizations of price: The fool, the faithful, the frivolous, and the frugal', *Sociological Theory*, **26** (4), pp. 363–379.

Wickert, C., Scherer, A.G. and Spence, L.J. (2016). 'Walking and talking corporate social responsibility: Implications of firm size and organizational cost', *Journal of Management Studies*, **53** (7), pp. 1169–1196.

Wiebe, G.D. (1951). 'Merchandising commodities and citizenship on television', *Public Opinion Quarterly*, **15** (4), pp. 679–691.

Zadek, S. (2004). 'The path to corporate responsibility', *Harvard Business Review*, **82** (12), pp. 125–132.

4.2 Does relational management matter?

The cases of Vietnamese and South African SMEs in the textiles, garment and footwear sector

Søren Jeppesen and Angie Ngọc Trần

Introduction[1]

The areas of stakeholder engagement and 'relationship management' are under-researched not least when it comes to studying small and medium-sized enterprises (SMEs). In SMEs, relationships between management and workers are dynamic due to direct and continuous interactions between the two. Relationship management, defined as "forming long-term, collaborative, mutually beneficial relationships . . . as a means of navigating complex, turbulent environment',[2] is particularly important to SMEs because of increasing pressures to undertake corporate social responsibility (CSR) activities. Our understanding of CSR practices includes four dimensions namely: i) the physical environment (PE); ii) the working environment (WE); iii) labour standards and working conditions (LS&WC); and iv) 'other' (informal, culture-related) practices.[3] The more level playing field and mutually respectful relations, in which workers have a voice at the table, the easier it is to spread and embed CSR as intended by management. In contrast, when there is a large power distance and imbalance between the two groups, it is difficult to spread CSR. It is less clear why the relationship between management and workers in SMEs unfolds as it does, including why 'positive' and why negative relations are created as part of CSR practices.

In spite of a growing emphasis on the importance of SMEs and CSR in developing countries,[4] only few studies have focused on management-worker relations to CSR in these countries. These studies employing a management perspective have mostly been quantitative, focused on the public sector and the service industry and been limited to single country case studies. Recent studies[5] have highlighted the important role that the management-worker relationship has on how SMEs deal with CSR particularly within the textile, garment and footwear industry (TGF) which this chapter considers. As in the broader stakeholder management literature (see the section on 'Concptualizing relationship management through stakeholder engagement and stakeholder agency'), these studies have not explicitly addressed stakeholder engagement from a theoretical and conceptual position but have assumed that it is important for management to engage workers (key stakeholders) in order to have a 'positive' relation with them when dealing with CSR issues.

Here, we contribute to the field by providing a qualitative investigation of management-worker relations in the TGF sector in two countries, Vietnam (VN) and South Africa (SA) with different political, cultural and economic systems. While both were former colonies, their different historical and industrial contexts allow for an insightful assessment of management-worker relations. There are similarities and differences. First, at the global level, the countries are both emerging economies, both have experienced authoritarian regimes, and both have been integrating into the global market systems for some decades though over different periods. Second, at the national level, the countries showcase two different political, cultural and economic systems: democratic in SA and 'market economy with socialist orientation' in VN. Third, at the industry level, in SA, the TGF industry is mostly focused on the domestic market, while it is driven by exports in VN. The particular configuration of the industry in SA is due to the Apartheid sanctions which restricted the export possibilities of the South African firms and prevented foreign firms from establishing in the country. VN has integrated into the world trade market at an amazing speed, especially after the lifting of the 20-year US trade embargo in 1994, the VN–USA Textile Agreement in 2003 and VN's accession to membership in the World Trade Organization (WTO) in 2007. Most FDI was concentrated in labour-intensive industries such as the VN TGF industry, leading VN to become a major exporter of textiles and garments.[6] Fourth, and related to the third, CSR has developed as a kind of 'homegrown' concept in SA (termed CSI – corporate social investment) compared to a foreign concept being implemented top-down in VN by international organizations such as the World Bank, the International Monetary Foundation (IMF) and the International Labour Organisation (ILO).[7]

We contrast the two country studies based on insights from SMEs as an empirical contribution to the relationship management literature through a critical examination of the field of stakeholder engagement and stakeholder agency using Greenwood's framework[8] and her broad understanding of stakeholders as shareholders and non-shareholders, including workers.

Conceptualizing relationship management through stakeholder engagement and stakeholder agency

Stakeholder theory as formulated by Freeman (1984)[9] has made an important contribution to management studies and to the exploration and understanding of the field of CSR. Topics related to relationship management have been addressed in two ways. One approach has concerned the ontological considerations of studying stakeholder engagement, and the other has been a more practical approach to the importance of engaging stakeholders.

A minor body of literature has addressed the ontological considerations of relationship management through the concept of 'stakeholder engagement'.[10] The main conceptual distinction relates to the view on stakeholder engagement (SE). Mathur et al. argue that the strategic management perspective on stakeholder engagement mainly focuses on 'identifying which claims or persons, or groups or organizations are important for a company and to whom management must pay attention'.[11] They view the 'ethical' perspective on SE as being based on considerations of 'stakeholders as citizens having to determine (or at least influence) the services and valuing the process of participation for democratic reasons'.[12] This is understood as including, for example, workers.

Noland and Philips suggest that perceptions of SE can be viewed in a moral versus an ethical dimension. The 'moral' contributions are aligned with a so-called Habermasian position, which argues that SE should be based on a 'value free communication' in which all stakeholders are equal.[13] This basically means that strategic concerns should be subsumed under the moral rationale.[14] The 'ethical' contributions suggest that ethical and strategic concerns for SE should be integrated into management considerations, hence representing a dimension of fairness in decision making.[15] However, further conceptualization of these two concepts has not taken place so far.

The contributions from the second practical approach to the field, a more 'common sense' understanding of 'engaging stakeholders' as something for the good of company, have employed concepts like 'involvement of stakeholders'[16] and 'participation of stakeholders".[17] In light of the (modest) theoretical and conceptual grounding, we found few studies that address the connection between management-worker relations and CSR in practice. Thus far, while one study focuses on CSR practices and employee engagement in large public organizations in India,[18] two other studies investigated this relationship in the service industry in Korea[19] and Thailand.[20] We also note that these few contributions make limited usage of theoretical or conceptual frameworks. The few studies identified support the observation that a close relationship between management and workers tends to improve CSR practices and is appreciated by both parties. Still, these studies do not address the types of relationship between management and workers that result from CSR practices. None of the studies highlight the size of the firms investigated. The contributions share a common ground in arguing that SE is desirable for stakeholder management and relationship management, also when it comes to CSR, but do not go beyond 'involvement', 'participation', 'dialogue' and similar terms.

Limited attempts have been made to develop the basis for the SE concept. One such attempt is Greenwood's conceptual understanding of stakeholder engagement and stakeholder agency. These are defined as follows: 'Stakeholder engagement is understood as practices that the organization undertakes to involve stakeholders in a positive manner',[21] while 'stakeholder agency is the proxy for responsible treatment of stakeholders'.[22] Greenwood suggests that the relationship between various stakeholders can be expressed as the interplay between i) stakeholder engagement (high to low) and ii) stakeholder agency (high to low). In her view, this creates four quadrants. From the four quadrants a variance from 'high' to 'low' is added, with an optimum for each, and eventually eight sub-categories are developed (see Figure 4.2.1).[23] It is this framework we employ here.

In quadrant 1, 'Responsibility' denotes situations where stakeholder engagement and stakeholder agency both are high. As Greenwood stipulates a kind of 'optimum' for this relationship, she argues that the first sub-category (or type of relationship) can be termed 'traditional CSR (A)' where a company has a comprehensive engagement of stakeholders and 'acts in the interest of legitimate stakeholders'.[24] If the company moves beyond this optimum, characterized by 'excessive engagement with stakeholders' and 'acts in the interest of all stakeholders including the illegitimate', she labels the situation 'anti-capitalism (B)'.[25]

Similarly, quadrant 2 'Paternalism' is where stakeholder engagement is low and stakeholder agency is high. In this situation, the optimum is 'where little stakeholder engagement takes place as determined by the company' and the company 'acts in the interests of legitimate stakeholders as defined by the company'. This sub-sub-category is termed 'Limited paternalism (C)'. If there is no stakeholder engagement defined by the company, Greenwood describes the situation as 'Strong paternalism (D)'.[26]

Quadrant 3 'Neoclassic' denotes both low engagement and agency. Here, the company has limited 'stakeholder engagement according to the market demand', and it 'does not act in the interest of any legitimate stakeholder'. Hence, the 'optimum' is where the relationship reflects expectations in the industry, which is termed 'Market (E)'. If the company moves 'beyond this' (and hence beyond the expectations in the market), then the situation can be described as 'Illegal (F)'.[27]

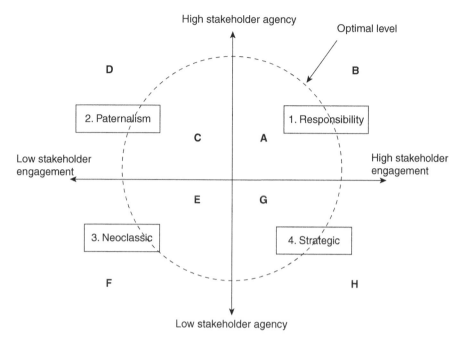

Figure 4.2.1 Stakeholder agency & stakeholder engagement model

Source: Greenwood, 2007: 322.

Finally, quadrant 4 'Strategic' is where stakeholder engagement is high and stakeholder agency is low. Here the company 'engages with legitimate stakeholders to further their shareholder interests'. This sub-category is termed 'reputation/legitimacy (G)'. If the company moves beyond the optimum and undertakes 'excessive engagement without accountability or responsibility towards the stakeholder', and 'appears to act in the interest of only one influential stakeholder', this is termed 'Irresponsibility (H)'.[28]

We offer a two-country study in the manufacturing industry, where management-labour communication is crucial among SMEs in developing countries. We assess the VN and SA cases in terms of how the engagement and agency between the two groups of stakeholders can be described and hence how they relate to the four sets of CSR practices within Greenwood's framework.

Key question and approach

We address the following key questions: How and why relations matter in small and medium-sized companies in the labour-intensive industries such as in the TGF industry in SA and VN?

First, we outline the similarities and differences of the general relationship between the two groups (management and workers) in SA and VN. Drawing on Greenwood's framework we then highlight which CSR practices the relationship mainly addressed before discussing the management-labour relationship in these two countries and why it was of the present nature.

Our approach includes comparative elements of the two countries, focusing on the TGF sector since this is the most labour-intensive SME sector in VN and SA. We undertook 79 interviews with managers. The interviews covered 41 SMEs, evenly split between VN (20) and SA (21) in the sector.[29] The interviews were carried out late 2011 and early 2012 including two rounds of interviews with interviewees on both quantitative and qualitative dimensions.[30] Mixed methods can confirm management narratives and identify discrepancies between statements and actions. We posed questions on how the managers viewed the stakeholders of the company (government, customers, NGOs, researchers, unions, workers and others) and the importance of each stakeholder for CSR practices. This chapter also draws on interviews with workers; however, given incompatible worker interview data were obtained from SA and VN (due to different fieldwork methodologies), we will include worker voices only when we have comparable data from both countries.[31]

The analysis of the data was conducted in several rounds through SPSS and thematic analysis of the data. The first rounds focused on descriptive data analysis; the next round included cross-tabulations of particular parts of the data set, while the additional rounds have included further in-depth analysis of qualitative data focused on particular empirical and theoretical elements. Empirically, the in-depth analysis has shed light on how management assessed the dynamics of CSR practices as part of the relationship with workers.

Empirical findings and analysis

Importantly, in both countries, managers and the workers in the interviewed SMEs valued and emphasized the relations between the two. Managers and workers had similar perceptions of what constitutes 'social responsibilities of business'.[32] In all areas (physical environment, working environment, labour standards and 'other'), management (and workers) nearly unanimously agreed that these areas were social responsibilities of the SMEs. Secondly, management in both countries ranked workers as the 1st to 2nd most important stakeholder for their firms. Thirdly, management – and again workers – assessed the relationship between the two as positive 'good to very good'. Management on the general level showed similar understandings of 'social responsibilities' and stakeholder ranking indicating a combination of 'high stakeholder agency' and 'high stakeholder engagement'. However, differences were present, which we turn to now.

First, the knowledge of 'CSR' differed between the managers with more SA managers knowing the concept compared to VN managers.[33] Second, regarding private (industry) standards managers in VN expressed concerns about the lack of multinational corporations' (MNC) contribution to the costs of implementing CSR in the global supply chains. A concern that managers in SA did not express, maybe due to being part of more domesticated supply chains where the customers are SA retailers. Thirdly, relating to state regulation, the VN managers in some cases expressed concern that governmental regulation was inadequate on labour standards while it was more adequate on environmental standards. In contrast, the managers in SA said that government regulations regarding environmental and labour standards were of similar importance to relations to workers.

Relationship between management and workers regarding CSR practices

Based on our examination of the four CSR practices, we found that in SA management displayed some level of engagement and agency on the four areas of CSR, however, seemingly not to the extent that they expressed in general (see the section on 'Empirical findings and analysis'). Only a (small) majority of the managers stated to engage in CSR practices in the areas of physical environment (PE), working environment (WE) and labour standards/working conditions (LS/WC). The influence of engaging external stakeholders shown as formal CSR practices, such as having Certified Management Systems and doing CSR reporting, was only found among 12–15% of the SMEs. Regarding codes of conduct, the picture was different, as nearly 60% had implemented such codes mostly due to industry pressures. This shows a relationship characterized by either 'limited paternalism (C)', 'strong paternalism (D)' or 'market (E)'.

In terms of 'other' CSR practices management claimed to have a high level of engagement and agency. This was expressed, for example, in terms of providing the workers with leave and assisting with loans (e.g. for school fees). Here, management knew and recognized the importance of the workers as a key stakeholder by supporting them on important areas. Firms also assisted the local communities (sometimes where the workers stayed) with donations to e.g. churches, sport clubs, youth clubs and similar. The 'other CSR practices' showed a relationship which resembles 'responsibility', in particular 'Traditional CSR (A)' in Greenwood's terms.

All interviewed VN managers expressed responsibilities to workers on labour standards, working conditions and physical and working environments (e.g. 90% felt responsible for physical environment). Still, most of the medium-sized garment factories (65% of the sample) are subcontractors as part of global supply chains (Tier 3). They assemble clothes and shoes for East Asian middlemen suppliers (Tier 2) who take orders from the US/European brands/MNCs (Tier 1). The US/European MNCs negotiate the low subcontracting price with the East Asian middlemen who then put the downward pressure on wages to the VN SME managers, resulting in non-livable wages to the workers who end up having to work excessive overtime to make ends meet.[34] Only 35% of these subcontractors were certified in codes of conduct. Hence, in the VN case, we found relationship characterized by 'Traditional CSR (A)', 'Limited paternalism (C)' and 'Market (E)'.

In terms of 'other' CSR practices, managers in many VN SMEs showed concern for the workers and provided e.g. 13th-month bonuses as well as work schedule flexibility in small factories so workers could go home to visit their families (or time off for family emergencies). This showed a relationship resembling 'Anti-capitalism (B)'.

Discussion

Now, we discuss why the relationship in general as well as specifically related to the four types of CSR practices can be characterized by certain dimensions and not by others of the Greenwood framework as we relate the findings to the historical, cultural and industry context of the two countries.

Drawing on Greenwood's framework, we view the three identified similarities among the SMEs in the TGF industry in the two countries: a) company social responsibilities; b) management assessment of workers as key stakeholder; and c) management's assessment of the (positive nature) of the relationship between the two, as expressions of stakeholder engagement and agency as similar to 'traditional CSR (A)' and 'anti-capitalism (B)' as they indicated the importance of the relationship, including the intense relationship between the two. Both management and workers were engaged in the relationship showing various levels of agency.

Applying the framework to the stated differences in the CSR practices between the SMEs in the TGF industry in the two countries showed a complex picture of relationships (see Table 4.2.1).

In relation to (a), a majority of the SA SMEs had implemented codes of conduct as a response to demands by domestic retailers (see below), and the responsibility clearly rested with management. However, this was without much consultation of the workers, so, in SA the relationship resembles 'Limited paternalism (C)'. In VN, fewer SMEs had implemented codes compared to those in SA, as only a limited number of the East Asian suppliers and MNCs had such requirements. In addition few provided support for the implementation of codes and did little to enforce the codes. Hence, management only enforced codes in few incidences and without engaging workers leading some migrant workers to misunderstand codes as 'company regulations' for them to follow. The relationship can be characterized as 'Market (E)'.

Regarding point (b), we found that the SA SME management viewed the buyers' demand for codes as a part of 'the business relation' which management then had to implement (see below) similar to demands being raised by government (see next point below) as well as union through the so-called bargaining council. Through the implementation of proper working conditions in terms of a healthy working environment and appropriate labour standards was in the interest of the workers, management did little to engage workers on these issues. This can be characterized as 'Limited paternalism (C)' and in some cases even 'Market (E)' as a 'necessary' response to buyers' demand, but with limited engagement and consultation of the workers.

In the case of VN, where most SMEs are subcontractors for East Asian suppliers to complete the orders for export to Western MNCs, VN managers were concerned about the lack of support (and funding) from the buyers. The supply chain pressure on the VN SMEs

Table 4.2.1 Differences in CSR practices between the SMEs in the TGF industry in SA and VN and categorization based on Greenwood's framework

Practices and segment no.	CSR practices in SA	Segments for SA	CSR practices in VN	Segments for VN
a)	Codes as a responsibility for management, including enforcement	C/Limited paternalism	Codes not enforced due to lack of financial support from Tier 1 and Tier 2	E/Market
b)	No expressed concern for buyers' responsibilities for CSR	C/Limited paternalism, E/Market★	Concern for lack of MNC responsibilities for CSR practices	E/Market, D/Strong paternalism★
c)	Government showing similar efforts to regulate environmental and labour standards	E/Market	Government showing more effort to regulate environmental standards than labour standards	G/Reputational/ Legitimacy

Source: Authors.

Note: ★ Also found to a limited extent

mentioned above forced management to balance use of funds to implement codes against not further diminishing the low wages. We found that the medium-sized enterprises, who received support from the East Asian suppliers to be certified in and compliant with codes of conduct, demonstrated some level of agency and engagement resembling 'Market (E)'. All small companies were not recognized by the East Asian suppliers and thus received NO support from them and hence the VN managers of these companies did not engage much in these CSR issues resembling 'Market (E)'.

On point (c), the SA government exercised considerable amounts of effort in regulating environmental and labour standards according to the SA SME managers. Environmental concerns had been high on the agenda of the SA government coming into power in 1994, and the alignment of unions to the government meant an emphasis on labour standards and working conditions; however, the enforcement of the regulations was somewhat limited. Inspections only took place with some interval and it was seldom that fines were given. Still, the level of enforcement was sufficient to ensure awareness among the managers and to some extent influenced the practices of the companies resembling 'Market (E)'. The situation in VN was different on two accounts. Firstly, the VN government put more emphasis on the enforcement of the environmental standards compared to the labour standards, because the Ministry of Labor, Invalids and Social Affairs are seriously under-resourced and short-staffed in terms of labour investigators. So, the VN owners/managers were on their own, informed by their own conscience towards upholding labour standards, resembling limited 'Reputation/legitimacy (G)'. Secondly, the enforcement of the environmental standards was much more stringent than in SA with more frequent inspections and a much wider use of fees and fines to be paid.

Finally, we assess the similarities and differences regarding the four types of CSR practices according to Greenwoods framework (see Table 4.2.2).

The practices among the SA SMEs concerning working environment and labour standards/working conditions are categorized as 'limited paternalism (C)' as management indicated some engagement and agency with workers and on management terms. When it comes to practices relating to PE, which mostly are due to the implementation of codes of conduct, where management responded to demands from retailers, but with hardly any engagement of workers, the practices resemble 'Market (E)'. We lean towards mainly labelling this type of engagement and agency 'limited paternalism (C)' as the CSR practices might have been undertaken in the interest of the workers, but through limited consultation. Also as management initiated these practices in a top-down manner.

Table 4.2.2 Level of stakeholder engagement and stakeholder agency related to types of CSR practices among SMEs in TGF industry in SA and VN

Spread of CSR practices in SA and VN	*Segments for SA*	*Segments for VN*
Physical environment (PE); working environment (WE); labour standards//working conditions (LS/WC)	C/Limited paternalism (or E/Market)	E/Market, C/Limited paternalism (or D/Strong paternalism)
'Other'	A/Traditional CSR, G/ Reputation-legitimacy	A/Traditional CSR, B/ Anti-capitalism, E/Market

For SA SMEs, the 'other' practices are categorized as 'traditional CSR (A)' – indicating high level of engagement and agency on both side and maybe even in some incidences as 'reputation/legitimacy (G)' as the SA SME managers are viewed to gain legitimacy by undertaking responsibilities to enhance the general conditions of the workers. These practices need to be viewed as a response to the socio-economic situation in SA, including widespread poverty, poor health system and limited social benefits as the SA state has abstained from ensuring such conditions for the workers. In some cases these practices indicated even 'irresponsibility (H)' as we see engagement as a kind of 'conscious business' move. When providing (very) modest contributions to sport clubs, management seemed to be more 'pretending' or 'acting as if the aim is to meet stakeholders' interest' (H).

In the case of VN, we also that the relationship could be characterized as 'limited paternalism (C)', 'market (E)' or even 'strong paternalism (D)' in some of the small companies that we interviewed. On the physical environment, given the need to cut costs to produce for the global supply chain, VN managers/owners have an incentive to be resource efficient and they reported using less energy and less water and producing less waste over time. Still, management undertook these initiative without consultation with workers, also in response to the VN environmental regulation showing either 'market (E)' or 'limited paternalism (C)'. In terms of the working environment, we found an interesting contradiction. VN managers tended to pay more attention to improving labour standards (such as wages and overtime work) than the working environment because most workers needed to earn livable wage. We found that many workers complained about poor working conditions including widespread lint, dust, heat, humidity, lack of ventilation and pollution in factories using real or synthetic leather assembling shoes and bags for export. Still, management responded only to extent that demands by buyers and government were met showing 'market (E)' relationship.

In terms of 'other' CSR practices we also found signs of 'traditional CSR (A)' as defined by socialist norms and values which existed before the introduction of CSR to VN. Moreover, we found signs of 'Anti-capitalism (B)' when management was forced to listen to workers' complaints and accommodated their negotiations, e.g. when workers requested time flexibility (to attend to childcare and other family needs) in return for low wages (due to low subcontracting prices). The medium-sized enterprises who received support from the East-Asian suppliers to implement codes of conduct exhibited both 'traditional CSR (A)' and 'market (E)' (see above). For those who did not receive any support from the East Asian suppliers and western MNCs, the relationship could be categorized as 'anti-capitalism (B)' where management acted in the interest of migrant workers who are more vulnerable than local workers because of the migrants do not always have household registration, a system that privileges local workers.[35] Many VN SME owners treated workers well by giving them flexible work schedules and a friendly work environment where everyone treats each other decently. Most migrant workers have obligations to their families (in far-flung rural districts and provinces) in both financial and non-monetary forms. Pregnant women or those with small children have received paid breaks, as stipulated in the progressive Vietnamese Labour Code. So, VN management-worker relations seemed to be more democratic and less top-down than in the SA case.

One important reason for the difference in CSR practices is the history of this industry in SA and VN. The 'domestic nature of the supply chain' in SA (in contrast to the 'global nature of the supply chain' in VN) meant that SA retailers had a closer and direct relation to the SA SMEs and thus a more direct influence on the management than the distant influence of the US/European brands/retailers MNCs on third-tier VN SMEs. Though codes of conduct were advocated by the SA retailers, they mainly emphasized price and quality and not necessarily CSR issues when dealing with the SA SME managers. Accordingly, the SA managers had stronger incentives to address non-CSR issues (e.g. quality of products and speed of work) compared to CSR issues when relating to the workers.[36] In contrast, the particular nature of the export orientation of the VN TGF industry forced the VN managers to balance supply chain demands and workers' needs. Most managers/owners placed high value on stable employment because they had to deliver their finished garments for on-time transport to other countries. So, they needed to maintain a reliable workforce. Finally, though few VN SMEs formally practiced any particular codes of conduct, management still treated migrant workers with compassion and understanding of their family responsibilities back home. These decent management-worker relations seem to fulfill both purposes: ensuring on-time delivery when workers are content and upholding cultural practices which are significant in SMEs.

The second part of the explanation of the differences is related to the lack of independent unions in VN which made it harder for workers to demand democratic communications and to be at the negotiating table with management. In SA, the unions have traditionally had a strong position in the industry, among others due to their alignment with the ANC-led government in the post-Apartheid period. Still, the representation in the SA SMEs was lower than for the large firms in the industry diminishing the influence of the unions as the labour regulations stipulate a certain level of unionization in order to provide unions a mandate to meet with management.

A third part of the explanation for the differences is related to the role of state regulation. SA has a history of implementation and enforcement of WE regulation and of regulation on LS/WC as the labour standards have been backed by strong unions. Environmental regulation is more recent, but received more attention and resources in the beginning of the post-Apartheid period compared to enforcement of labour standards. Nevertheless, both the responsible government entities have lately been downsized, while both have a presence and do some enforcement, it was limited compared to earlier. And SA government entities enforced the environmental and labour-related regulations to a similar extent.[37] In VN, we found a difference between the two areas, leading to stronger emphasis on environmental regulation compared to labour regulation with ineffective union representation in many medium-sized enterprises and mostly absence in small enterprises; however, enforcement of environmental regulation incurred costs that were born by the SMEs, thus putting even more downward pressures on the wage level.

In addition, political and culture factors played different roles in the two countries. In SA, the legacy of Apartheid influenced the relationship between management and workers in a negative way due to strong tensions among the different ethnic groups in particularly so-called 'White Africans' versus 'Black Africans' with limited cultural practices being brought forward. Unlike the case of SA, relations between labour and management in Vietnam are relatively smoother since most employers and workers are from the same ethnicity (Vietnamese) and share the same historical socialist legacy. On the other hand, being a democracy has led to an open process of introducing CSR practices and 'business social responsibilities' to all SA businesses, including SMEs. This was coined by influential businesses as Corporate Social Investment (CSI) as an attempt to avoid 'Responsibility' as associated with the crimes of the Apartheid period. SA businesses, including SMEs, had to advocate their share of responsibilities for the 'new democratic SA'. This meant that emphasis was directed on involvement and engagement for HIV/AIDS (including assisting workers with leave in order to attend funerals and attend to family members being hospitalized), ensuring educational quality and addressing a range of community issues, hence promoting such CSR practices.

In VN the legacy of socialism on worker rights continues to exist yet faces serious challenges in a market-based system. Here, CSR was imposed from the outside through different international institutions with a range of what were now viewed as CSR practices. Actually, these practices were the outcome of management-labour relations which had been informed by social and cultural practices, existing centuries prior to the arrival of CSR by foreign institutions. This shows that, in socialist Vietnam, cultural practices that relate to labour standards and working conditions have been passed on from one generation to the next. The decent treatment of workers was for the shared goals of a) having a stable and reliable workforce in order to stay competitive in the global supply chains and b) at the same time meeting workers' expectations in light of cultural and historical practices.

Conclusions

We found that managers and the workers had similar views on their relationship, both in terms of value, perception of 'social responsibilities of the SMEs' and assessing the relationship as positive. Management in both countries ranked workers as the 1st to 2nd most important stakeholder for their firms and showed similar understandings of 'social responsibilities' and stakeholder ranking indicating a combination of 'high stakeholder agency' and 'high stakeholder engagement'.

The more detailed assessment of the characteristics of the relationship based on Greenwoods framework, nevertheless, brought out a picture of differences, not only between countries, but also within each country as Tables 4.2.1 and 4.2.2 show. SA managers indicated 'limited paternalism' when dealing with workers regarding working environment and labour standards/working conditions but 'market' in the area of physical environment. On these practices, the VN SMEs managers indicated a relationship characterized by 'market', with managers of small firms expressed a relationship of 'limited' or even 'strong paternalism'. Regarding 'other CSR practices', SA SME managers expressed 'traditional CSR' and to some extent 'reputation-legitimacy', while VN SME managers expressed a mixture of relationship characterized by several Greenwood segments such as 'traditional CSR', 'anti-capitalism' and 'market'.

We argue that the differences are mostly due to the industry differences (a domestic focus in SA compared to an export focus in VN), government regulation and unions as well as political, historical and cultural factors. This underscores the complexity of the relationship which cannot be confined solely to management and worker relations, but also need to include a range of other actors such as customers (retailers, buyers) and unions.

We have found the application of Greenwood's framework useful for our assessment of the management perspective on similarities and differences among SMEs in the TGF industry in SA and VN. Though Greenwood is among the few contributions which conceptualize stakeholder engagement and stakeholder agency from a perspective of strategic management or 'Ethical strategic' as termed by Noland and Philips (2010), nevertheless, the basic neo-classical assumptions of optimization produces a set of terms (when it comes to the segments or sub-categories), which are more normative than practically applicable. While Greenwood suggests eight segments, we found five segments (A, B, C, E and G) to be more relevant to the SA and VN cases here than the other segments.

However, we found some shortcomings in Greenwood's framework. First of all, her framework takes the point of the departure in the concept of 'shareholders', which is difficult to transfer to SMEs. At least, most SMEs in VN do not have 'shareholders' while some SA SMEs have shareholders. Hence, the segments 'illegal' (F) and 'illegitimate (H)' make limited sense to relationship management in SMEs. Secondly, Greenwood does not explain who the 'illegitimate stakeholders' are,[38] giving rise to ambiguity on how to understand this term. Theoretically, this highlights a need for further work both with the framework and not the least concerning stakeholder engagement and relational management.

Thirdly, a key weakness of this framework is the lack of power analysis. As power rests with management and not workers, the relationship is not just one among 'equal' stakeholders. We note the absence of an analysis of power differential between labour and management and agree with the argument made by Mitchell et al. (1997)[39] that such critical discussion is needed. In spite of labour regulations stating that workers should have 'a voice at the table', this means nothing if government and unions are not capable of enforcing this. Given the lopsided management-worker power relations, workers most often cannot really engage in collective bargaining which is key to improving their labour standards and working conditions.

In addition to our contribution to the literature on stakeholders and relationship management, further work is needed. Though the perspective ensures a contribution to CSR debates, in particular the ones on SMEs in developing countries, issues of power, gender and race relations are neglected, which could have enabled a more comprehensive comparison between the two countries. Bringing in the workers' perspective, addressing more countries, different industries and making a critical assessment of the terminology are future research areas.

The practical implications of the study are that managers and workers do engage and are active in relating to CSR issues and practices, but our study suggests that more resources are needed to ensure more responsible social practices, including improved wages. The roles of buyers (whether domestic or global), governments and unions need to be included if the stated intentions of CSR are to be achieved. SME management and workers can only do so much.

Notes

1 We would like to acknowledge the French Development Agency AFD (Agence Française du Developpement) for financing the study from which we draw data for this chapter. We are also indebted to the South African and Vietnamese teams that supported us throughout this whole process, including endless hours in the collection and processing of field data as well as follow-up questions. The SA team included Bas Kothuis, Olga Fadeeva, Marianne Kohler and Ince Maree. The VN team included Huynh Thi Ngoc Tuyet, Nguyen Minh Chau, Tran Bao Ha, Nguyen Cuc Tram and Nguyen Vu from the Sustainable Development Research Institute in the Southern Region, Ho Chi Minh City, and Doan Thi Kim Khanh, ESL and Citizenship Teacher from Boat People SOS Organization. Laura Jakobeit assisted with data analysis as the then research assistant at the Centre for Business and Development Studies, Department of Intercultural Communication and Management, Copenhagen Business School. We are grateful to Joe Lubow who provided copy-editing assistance during the writing process. Finally, we are grateful to the reviewers, who provided valuable and insightful comments, which enabled us to bring the chapter to its present stage.
2 Lindgreen, A. and Florencio, B. P. 2015. *A Relational Approach to Stakeholder Engagement* (Call for Chapters), p. 1.
3 Jeppesen, S., Kothuis, B. and Tran, A. N. 2012. *Corporate Social Responsibility, Competitiveness and SMEs in Developing Countries: South Africa and Vietnam*. Research Report (Focales no 16). Paris, France: French Development Agency (AFD).

4 Historical and cultural factors play a significant role in studying stakeholder engagement and CSR compared to factors like codes of conduct and pressures from stakeholders external to the SMEs. See e.g. Prieto-Carron, M., Lund-Thomsen, P., Chan, A., Muro, A. and Bushan, C. 2006. "Critical Perspectives on CSR: What We Know, What We Don't Know and Need to Know", *International Affairs*, vol. 82, no. 5, pp. 977–988, and Tran, A.N. and Jeppesen, S. 2015. "SMEs in their Own Right: The Views of Managers and Workers in Vietnamese Textiles, Garment, and Footwear Companies", *Journal of Business Ethics*, vol. 137, no. 3, pp. 589–608. DOI: 10.1007/s10551–015–2572-x. Springer.

5 Jeppesen et al., 2012, op.cit., and Tran and Jeppesen 2015, op.cit.

6 Tran, A.N. and Nørlund, I. 2015. "Globalization, Industrialization, and Labor Markets in Vietnam", *Journal of the Asia Pacific Economy*, vol. 20, no. 1, Special Issue: Globalization, Industrialization and Labour Markets in East and South Asia: Essays in Honour of Melanie Beresford, pp. 143–163. In VN, the TGF continues to account for the largest share of the wage-earning labor force since Vietnam joined the WTO in 2007, representing over 15% of the country's total GDP and aiming for about 30 billion USD in export earnings in 2017. See; Vietnam News Summary, "Vietnam Expects Growth of Textile – Garment Exports Without TPP", 21 March 2017, www.itasean.org/en/vietnam-expects-growth-of-textile-garment-exports-without-tpp-2/ and www.bizvibe.com/blog/vietnams-textile-and-apparel-exports-continue-to-grow/.

7 See Jeppesen et al., 2012, op.cit., and Tran, A.N. 2011. "Corporate Social Responsibility in Socialist Vietnam: Implementation, Challenges and Local Solutions", in: Chan, A. (ed.) *Labour in Vietnam*. Institute of Southeast Asian Studies, Singapore, for more information.

8 Greenwood, M. 2007. "Stakeholder Engagement: Beyond the Myth of Corporate Responsibility", *Journal of Business Ethics*, vol. 74, pp. 315–327. DOI 10.1007/s10551–007–9509-y

9 Freemann, R. 1984. *Strategic Management: A Stakeholder Approach*. Marshall, MA: Pitman.

10 See Noland and Philips, 2010 for a review of the debate. Noland, J. and Philips, R. 2010. 'Stakeholder Engagement, Discourse Ethics and Strategic Management', *International Journal of Management Review*, DOI: 10.1111/j.1468–2370.2009.00279.x

11 Mathur, V.N., Price, A.D.F, and Austin, S. 2008. 'Conceptualizing Stakeholder Engagement in the Context of Sustainability and its Assessment', *Construction Management and Economics*, vol. 26, June, pp. 601–609.

12 Op.cit., p. 609–610.

13 Noland and Philips, op.cit., p. 40–41.

14 Op.cit., p. 42–45.

15 Op.cit., pp. 45–47.

16 Like Morsing, M. and Schultz, M. 2006. "Corporate social responsibility communications: stakeholder information, response and involvement strategies".

17 Mathur et al., op.cit.

18 Dhanesh, G. S. 2014. "CSR as Organization-Employee Relationship Management Strategy: A Case Study of Socially Responsible Information Technology Companies", *Management Communication Quarterly*, vol. 28, no. 1, pp. 130–149. Dhanesh states to find a clear relationship between CSR practices and employee engagement in terms of trust, control mutuality, commitment and satisfaction (p. 140).

19 Shin, I., Hur, W.-M. and Kang, S. 2016. "Employees' Perception of Corporate Social Responsibility and Job Performance: A Sequential Mediation Model", *Sustainability*, vol. 8, 493, doi:10.3390/su8050493. Shin et al. focus on employees in the hotel industry in Korea based on a survey questionnaire among four hotels (p. 5). They argue that employees' affiliation with the firm increases when CSR practices are implemented and positively assessed. However, they also conclude that the impact of the CSR practices is indirect (p. 8).

20 Supanti, D., Butcher, K. and Fredline, L. 2015. "Enhancing the Employer-employee Relationship through Corporate Social Responsibility (CSR) Engagement", *International Journal of Contemporary Hospitality Management*, vol. 27, no. 7, pp. 1479–1498. Supanti et al. focus on the hotel industry in Thailand, where they draw on management perceptions based on 23 interviews with managers. The authors argue that previous studies have shown that employees are satisfied with CSR initiatives, though few contributions exist (p. 1482). They conclude that the managers report a positive correlation between the CSR initiatives, staff responses and 'benefits to the hotels', including the relationship between management and employees (p. 1491).

21 Greenwood, op.cit., p. 316.

22 Op.cit., p. 322.

23 Op.cit., p. 322–324.
24 Op.cit., p. 323, table II.
25 ibid.
26 ibid.
27 ibid.
28 Greenwood argues that "It could be surmised that many of the stakeholder engagement practices that pass under the label of corporate social responsibility are in fact forms of strategic management" (2007, p. 323).
29 The comparative data, relevant to both VN and SA used for this chapter have not been published to date.
30 Two of the SA SMEs only took part in one interview each.
31 The study included 179 interviews with workers, individually and in groups, in the two countries. For information on the workers' views, see Jeppesen et al., 2012, op.cit.
32 Jeppesen et al., 2012, op.cit.
33 An even bigger difference existed between the management and the workers in VN as the workers had very limited knowledge of the concept. The same situation was identified in SA.
34 See Tran, A.N. 2013. *Ties that Bind: Cultural Identity, Class and Law in Flexible Labor Resistance in Vietnam*. Ithaca, NY: Southeast Asia Program (SEAP), Cornell University Press, p. 159.
35 See Tran, 2013, op.cit.
36 See Tran, 2013, p. 159.
37 Though, this might be a positive situation in the SMEs, a serious caveat is that state regulation is limited to the formally registered companies, while the nonregistered companies are not inspected at all and these companies constitute the majority of the small companies.
38 Op.cit., p. 323.
39 Mitchell, R.K., Agle, B.R. and Wood, D. 1997. 'Towards a Theory of Stakeholder Identification and Salience: Defining the Principle of Who and What Really Counts', *Academy of Management Review*, vol. 22, no. 4, pp. 853–886.

4.3 Blurred lines

Stakeholder tensions and balancing strategies in partial organizations

Sarah Netter and Esben Rahbek Gjerdrum Pedersen

Introduction: stakeholder relations in the sharing economy

Stakeholder theory has long recognized that stakeholders can have multiple roles and identities (e.g. employees as customers, owners or community members). For instance, in a comprehensive analysis of the stakeholder model's graphical representation, Fassin (2008) notes that individuals often belong to different stakeholder groups and occupy different roles at different times. Actually, acknowledging the multiple roles of stakeholders is well in line with the theory's emphasis on avoiding simplistic stakeholder categories (shareholders vs. stakeholders) and inspiring a new way of thinking about business (McVea and Freeman, 2005). As an example, Post et al. (2002) argue that acknowledging the simultaneous roles of stakeholders can inspire a more holistic view of business:

> Particular individuals and groups may simultaneously occupy several roles – employee, customer, shareowner, neighbor, and the like. Recognition of these overlaps should lead both managers and constituents to acknowledge the varied impacts of corporate activity, and to think of corporate performance in multidimensional and comprehensive terms, rather than from the perspective of any single interest.
>
> (Post et al., 2002, p. 23)

The blurriness of stakeholder roles is further accentuated by the emergence of new organizational forms which diverge from conventional business archetypes. In the last decades, scholars and practitioners have described this organizational phenomenon by emphasizing issues like pluralism, hybridity, partiality, temporality and virtuality. For instance, the rapidly growing literature on hybrid organizations highlights the fact that companies with a social mission have to serve multiple masters, which complicates the management of stakeholder expectations and comes with a risk of mission drift (Haigh and Hoffman, 2012; Hoffman et al., 2012). Moreover, the sharing economy, as part of the wider circular economy movement, is based on the premise that customers are also actively engaged in providing input for new recycled or remade products (EMF, 2013a, 2013b; Murray et al., 2015; WEF, 2014). This type of business logic differs significantly from the linear 'take-make-dispose' paradigm and set new demands for stakeholder relationships. The business model of these new forms of organization is based on stakeholder multiplicity, which blurs the boundaries of functions, roles and structures. For instance, a clear-cut distinction between logistics and marketing can be difficult in a sharing platform, where customers may also be involved in supplies, transportation, quality control and service.

The aim of this chapter is to examine the tensions in situations of blurred stakeholder relationships and organizational boundaries. It is argued that sharing initiatives face a number of oppositional demands rooted in the existence of multiple stakeholder identities characterizing these organizations. While rethinking stakeholder relationships and organizations may pave the way a more realistic and holistic view of business, as proposed by stakeholder advocates, this new perspective can also give rise to a number of challenges and dilemmas. Moreover, the chapter will outline a number of balancing strategies which can help companies in addressing these tensions in everyday organizational practices. Some tensions are built into the fabric of organizations, which means that companies should find ways to cope with them in day-to-day practices rather than looking for quick fixes to eliminate them. The chapter is in line with more recent efforts to break with the prevalent win-win logic dominating the corporate sustainability literature and giving more emphasis to the built-in conflicts, dilemmas and paradoxes (Hahn et al., 2014, 2015; Allen et al., 2015).

The analysis and discussion of the blurred lines between stakeholders and organizations will be illustrated with examples from consumer service marketplaces and the key constituents taking part in these new sharing systems. Consumer service marketplaces are part of the fast-growing sharing economy phenomenon, which is an umbrella term for a variety of business models that provides the opportunity to share underutilized assets and skills (e.g., Belk, 2010; Botsman and Rogers, 2010). With the concept making its way out of the niche into the mainstream (Grimm and Kunze, 2011; Seidl and Zahrnt, 2012), the sharing economy is said to possess disruptive potentials, which can bring about transformations in established industries (Botsman and Rogers, 2010; Walsh, 2011). While the sharing economy has already developed a rather firm grip on certain industries and sectors, such as accommodation and mobility, the phenomenon is still to establish itself in the mainstream for consumer goods, such as fashion (e.g. Birtwistle and Moore, 2007).

The remainder of the chapter is structured as follows: First, the chapter begins with a short introduction to the sharing economy and the implications of these new business models on stakeholder relationships and organizations. The introduction is followed by the analysis of tensions in consumer marketplaces arising between buyers, sellers and organizations facilitating the transactions ('host organizations'). To structure the analysis, the chapter will draw on the nascent literature on partial organizations (Ahrne and Brunsson, 2010). More specifically, the five pillars of organizing (membership, rules, monitoring, sanctions and hierarchy) are used for structuring the analysis of the tensions emerging from the blurred lines between stakeholders and organizations. The chapter will end with a reflection on balancing strategies which can be used to address stakeholder tensions in the sharing economy.

The sharing economy introduced

There is a variety of different consumer service marketplaces enabled by sharing initiatives. Among other things, business models can be distinguished based on their profit orientation (non-profit to for-profit approaches; membership-based, transaction-based or free-of-charge services) and temporality (e.g. temporary leases vs. permanent swaps, temporary pop-up stores vs. permanent setups). Some of the best known examples include *Uber*, offering transportation; *Airbnb*, allowing the rental of private homes and apartments; and *eBay* and *Poshmark*, providing consumers with means of reselling and swapping unwanted consumer goods, such as clothing, by means of information and communication technology. Most commonly, sharing platforms are smartphone enabled. These marketplaces vary not only in form – i.e. physical (offline) or non-physical (online and mobile), as well as hybrid marketplaces (offline activities coupled to online and mobile platforms or vice versa) – but also with regards to the different types of services, ownerships and userships being traded. While some marketplaces are rather free, unregulated and of an informal nature, such as temporary clothing swaps, others are more formalized with fees, regulations and sanctions in place, such as the mobile-enabled marketplaces *eBay* and *Poshmark*, to mention a few examples from the fashion context.

Sharing taxonomy

So far, there is no extensive integrated framework or typology of different sharing economy business models available, with the rather limited range of alternative frameworks offering dichotomous scales at best, frequently oversimplifying the complexity of these marketplaces or remaining at a normative level, discussing the semiotics and appropriate labels of sharing initiatives (Netter et al., forthcoming). However, Cohen's (2014) distinction between four sharing economy archetypes provides a useful starting point for giving an overview of the sharing business models, which are still emergent and part of a wider developing phenomenon. Cohen (2014) distinguishes between ownership motivation (pecuniary/non-pecuniary) and ownership structure (individual/conjoint), which can be considered two essential features of sharing initiatives. Stakeholder relationships can also be expected to differ depending on the type of sharing, as for instance flea markets are closer to conventional business models compared to fashion libraries.

While *archetype one* and *two* typify what Botsman and Rogers (2010) call collaborative lifestyle, which is mainly non-profit community based, *archetype three* and *four* constitute commercialized sharing formats, more specifically product-service systems and redistribution markets. In *archetype one*, goods are owned by a single person, eventually allowing temporary non-commercial lending to family members and friends. *Archetype two* comprises of cases enabling collective ownership and usership, such as car sharing clubs, non-commercial hospitality exchange or free-of-charge fashion libraries (e.g. *Klädoteket*). Cases belonging to *archetype three* range from short-term rentals, such as in the case of car sharing schemes (e.g. *Car2Go, DriveNow*) and fee-based clothing and accessories rental (e.g. *Kleiderei*), to subscription-based product service systems (e.g. *Mud Jeans, Le Tote*). In *archetype four*, goods or assets are owned by a single person, with a clear commercial sharing motivation. Micro-entrepreneurship cases in this *archetype four* span from classical flea markets and swap meets to Internet (e.g. *eBay, Yerdle*) or smartphone-enabled redistribution platforms (e.g. *Poshmark, Vinted*) to private commercial hospitality exchanges (e.g. *Airbnb*). This overview of examples of sharing economy archetypes is by no means exhaustive but comprises some of the most renowned sharing economy cases (see Figure 4.3.1). For a more comprehensive discussion of similarities and differences between sharing economy archetypes, see Netter (2016a).

Stakeholder relationships in the sharing economy

Instead of conceiving markets and organizations as two completely different sets of social order, Ahrne et al. (2014) suggest that both are rather similar, in the sense that they are both based on decision and decided order. Depending on the degree of organization in

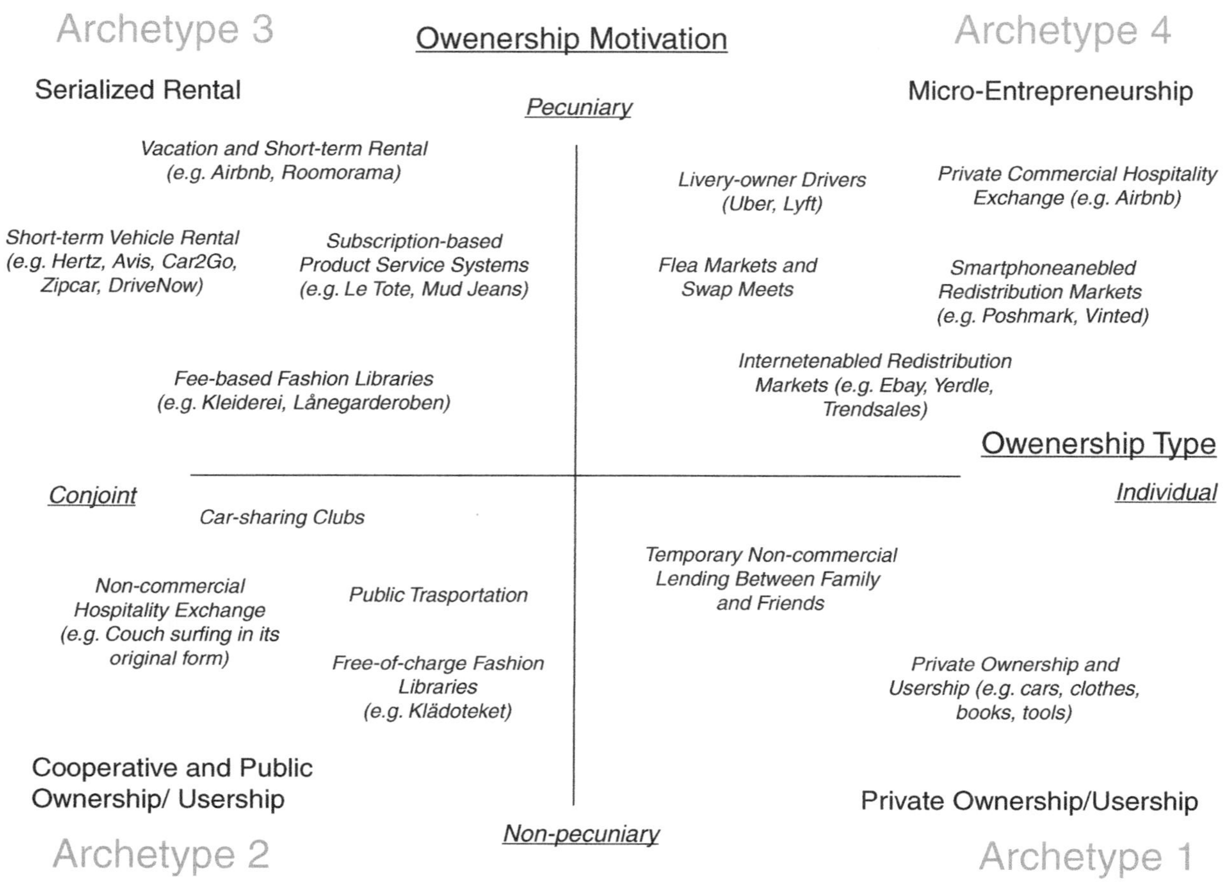

Archetype 3

Owenership Motivation

Archetype 4

Serialized Rental

Micro-Entrepreneurship

Pecuniary

Vacation and Short-term Rental
(e.g. Airbnb, Roomorama)

Subscription-based
Product Service Systems
(e.g. Le Tote, Mud Jeans)

Short-term Vehicle Rental
(e.g. Hertz, Avis, Car2Go,
Zipcar, DriveNow)

Private Commercial Hospitality
Exchange (e.g. Airbnb)

Smartphoneanebled
Redistribution Markets
(e.g. Poshmark, Vinted)

Livery-owner Drivers
(Uber, Lyft)

Flea Markets and
Swap Meets

Internetenabled Redistribution
Markets (e.g. Ebay, Yerdle,
Trendsales)

Owenership Type

Individual

Fee-based Fashion Libraries
(e.g. Kleiderei, Lånegarderoben)

Temporary Non-commercial
Lending Between Family
and Friends

Private Ownership and
Usership (e.g. cars, clothes,
books, tools)

Conjoint

Car-sharing Clubs

Public Trasportation

Non-commercial
Hospitality Exchange
(e.g. Couch surfing in its
original form)

Free-of-charge Fashion
Libraries
(e.g. Klädoteket)

Non-pecuniary

Private Ownership/Usership

Cooperative and Public
Ownership/ Usership

Archetype 1

Archetype 2

Figure 4.3.1 Sharing taxonomy

terms of *membership, hierarchy, rules, monitoring* and *sanctions*, it can be distinguished between complete and partial organization (Ahrne and Brunsson, 2010). While formal organizations have access to all five elements, identifying them as complete organizations (ibid.), markets can be conceptualized as partial organization, if one or few of these organizing elements are present (Ahrne et al. 2014). Partial organization of markets, i.e. market organizations, is accomplished by a number of stakeholders, or as Ahrne et al. (2014) would call them *market organizers*, namely *profiteers*, '*others*', *sellers* and *buyers*. This chapter suggests adjusting this simplified stakeholder definition offered by Ahrne et al. (ibid) in the context of the sharing economy. The label *profiteers* appears misleading, considering that '*others*', *sellers and buyers*, are all interested in furthering their economic interest by means of organizing. Instead of conceptualizing the organizations facilitating the transactions as *profiteers*, the authors of this chapter deem it more appropriate to refer to them as *facilitators*. In a similar vein, the label *sellers and buyers* can be considered misleading, implying that all sharing transactions are based on monetary transactions. The label *users and providers* is considered more suitable, encompassing a wider range of examples of one consumer providing a service, which is embraced by another. Lastly, this chapter suggests to broaden and adjust the definition of '*others*', originally defined as

> persons and organizations that try to influence the organization of markets, claiming that they act not in their own interest, but in the interest of specific other persons or organizations, or even in the interests of everyone. They have little or no interest in making profit, and they try to help seller, buyers or whoever is affected by what sellers or buyers do.
>
> (ibid., p. 9–10)

Instead, this chapter suggests encompassing all those stakeholders, who are or consider themselves to be affected by the actions on sharing markets and consequently try to shape the phenomenon.

Facilitators and *users/providers* constitute the two primary stakeholders of the sharing economy in terms of facilitating, initiating and maintaining the consumer service marketplaces of the sharing economy. Depending on the marketplace, different '*others*' (e.g. sharing lobby organizations, investors, media, governments, trade unions, established competing industries and their employees) exert direct or indirect influence at different life stages, such as in the case of funding and providing locations, providing financial resources or shaping the wider environment by means of protests, calls for more regulation or introduction of legislation. What makes the sharing marketplaces an interesting case is that boundaries between different stakeholder groups are not so clear and stable, but frequently being blurred and broken up, none the least as most business models are still in flux. While so called *switch-role markets* are not so uncommon (e.g., Aspers, 2009), such as in the case of the stock market with buyers and sellers switching roles within their group of market organizers (e.g. Ahrne et al., 2014), this chapter suggests conceptualizing sharing marketplaces as *blurred-role markets*, in which stakeholders might not only switch roles within their group of market organizers as in the case of the stock market. Instead, *users* might not only switch with *providers*, but take on both roles and identities simultaneously. Similarly, they might also switch roles, with the formal *facilitators*, and become formally involved in the running and maintaining of the marketplace (e.g. online forum moderators of swapping platforms, voluntary staff in fashion libraries), while formal *facilitators* also embrace their identities as *users/providers*, offering or making use of the services of their very own marketplace. Simultaneously holding multiple identities and roles, with different obligations and degrees of influence might give rise to a number of tensions and conflicts. Hence, while the power in the sharing economy is formally in the hand of the *facilitators* in regards to shaping the format of the sharing organizations and the facilitated consumer service marketplace, the high number of struggling and failed sharing initiatives indicates that these setups are rather vulnerable, with a lot of power being held by *users/providers* and '*others*' having multiple identities and roles in these marketplaces. This creates a setup with many tensions and conflicting interests, in which sharing organizations are highly dependent on their consumers and vulnerable to changes in consumer trends. In order to understand the working mechanisms, dynamics and organization of markets, it is crucial to understand the opposing interests of the acting stakeholders and the way in which their interests are distributed (Aspers, 2009).

Stakeholder tensions in the sharing economy unfolded

While it is argued that the emerging literature on partiality adopts a simplified view of stakeholders which requires adaptation to capture the nature of sharing organizations, the perspective nonetheless provides a useful typology of core organizational criteria, which serves as a useful starting point for understanding of the various sharing tensions highlighted in theory and practice. In the following sections, organizational tensions emerging in the sharing economy will therefore be identified along the lines of the five organizational criteria outlined by Ahrne et al. (2014), i.e. *membership, rules, monitoring, sanctions* and *hierarchy*. The description will be supplemented with examples from the four *archetypes*.

Membership

Membership pertains to the decisions about who can become a member and who cannot (Ahrne et al. 2014). In the context of markets, this means primarily who may act as *users/providers* in the market, as the *facilitators* are for the most part initiating a formalized framework for the market. While in some cases there might be formal rules for who can obtain member status, in other cases, this is more informally regulated (Ahrne and Brunsson, 2010). There is a wide variety of different memberships in the sharing economy. In the case of free-of-charge fashion libraries (*archetype two*) for instance, there is no decision mechanism for who can become a member (Pedersen and Netter, 2015). With users and providers in this context basically constructing and using a common wardrobe, the organization is open to everyone who decides to register as a member and wishes to contribute. Tensions might arise between *users* and *providers*, with some fearing the risk of trading down, if there is no control or entry barrier for who is joining and in terms of the level of quality and brands constituting the inventory. In the case of Internet or smartphone-enabled redistribution markets (*archetype four*), such as *eBay* or *Poshmark*, membership is only possible for those having access to the necessary information and communication technology and sometimes living in the country of origin of the platform. Furthermore, most platforms require a credit card and a permanent address. Where conventional sharing practices were mainly found between family, friends and community members, new types of sharing transactions take place between strangers, which comes with challenges in terms of identifying their 'true type' (i.e. trustworthiness). Stakeholders may not always be who they are appear to be; something which call for an element of screening before

Table 4.3.1 Overview of organizational elements and examples of tensions

Criteria	Membership	Rules	Monitoring	Sanctions	Hierarchy
Definition	The 'who is involved in the interaction'.	The 'common notions about what they are doing and how to do it'.	The 'observing each other to know how to continue'.	The 'taking measures in order to make others do what they expect them to do'.	The 'understanding of who has the initiative and power'.
Examples of tensions	– Risk of trading down (fashion libraries/ no control membership, inventory) – Entry barriers vs. community narrative. – Labels of members & legal consequences.	– Operating in legal grey areas lead to accusations of unfair completion and violation of regulation, workers' rights, etc. – Unclear standards and procedures.	– Lack of control with transactions between users and providers – Wrong accusations, transactions gone wrong, no reaction from customer service.	– Diverging stakeholder views of sharing initiatives (e.g. taxi drivers calling for more regulation) – Uneven power relationships between stakeholders.	– Tension between facilitator and users, providers and others. – Competition between sharing initiatives.
Examples of responses	– Product quality control. – Membership screening and monitoring. – Attempts to redefine business model and stakeholder roles.	– Confrontation with conventional players in the market. – Stakeholder collaboration -Formalization of standards, systems and guidelines.	– Product/ membership screening and control. – Reputation-based scoring of users and providers. – Online reviews.	– Privileges for frequent and reliable users/ providers. – Blocking of users and providers. – Hiding of listing, temporary/ permanent blocking- – Personal/app-store reviews.	– Rules of conduct. – Strengthening stakeholder relationships. – Attempts to generate more likes and positive reviews.

access to shared resources can be provided. Possible tensions might also arise from these rather high entry barriers, which are largely at odds with the common narrative, praising the sharing economy as an empowering, democratizing and inclusive force (e.g., Netter, 2016a). Furthermore, potential membership might be biased by ethnic, aesthetic, as well as socio-demographic discrimination, as found by Edelman and Luca (2014) in the case of *Airbnb* (*archetype four*). Moreover, the issue of membership and official labels of stakeholder groups is also linked to wider legal discussions, as can be seen in the case of livery-owner drivers for providers such as *Uber* (*archetype four*) (e.g., Orsi, 2013; Sørensen, 2016), raising questions whether *Uber* drivers should be considered employees of a transportation service or independent contractors of an electronic intermediary service. The legal label of stakeholders hence gives rise to issues such as public law violations (e.g. taxes, sector specific permits, unfair competition) and contractual challenges, forcing *Uber* drivers to insure themselves against accidents, illness, unemployment and retirement (e.g., Sørensen, 2016; Eichhorst and Spermann, 2015). Closely linked to the issue of rules, membership status clarification might thus cause tensions for *facilitators* and *user/providers* alike (Brown, 2016). As an attempt to circumvent legal requirements for certain categories of services and stakeholders, sharing initiatives have tried to redefine their business model and the roles of stakeholders. For instance, legal constraints have inspired some car sharing organizations to strategically redefine themselves, from being about driving persons to become about driving goods (and the persons possessing them).

Rules

Rules can concern any aspect of the market, such as product design or prices, as well as any kind of behaviour or action, i.e. user/provider behaviour, and guides for the conduct of how to handle the transactions and exchanges (Ahrne et al., 2014). Besides formal rules of participation, there can also be more informal rules or recommendations, such as standards, for which compliance is voluntary (Ahrne and Brunsson, 2010). While so far, most of the sharing economy has operated in legal grey areas (e.g., Orsi, 2013), we have recently started to witness more and more regulation, deregulation and self-regulation (e.g., Hartl et al., 2015), concerning such issues as consumer safety and protection, protection of workers' rights and the protection of established players and their employees, with different stakeholders taking different stances (e.g., Chang, 2015; Eichhorst and Spermann, 2015; Sørensen, 2016). As highlighted with regards to membership in the case of *Uber*, *Uber* has adopted a rather confrontational approach in tackling the tensions with its *users/providers* and *'others'*, such as competing established taxi operations and governing bodies. *Airbnb* on the other hand, which has also faced quite a deal of opposition from competing industries, local communities and governments on the state and local level, has chosen a rather collaborative path, in its attempts to resolve the conflicts and secure the survival of the marketplace. In the case of online and mobile redistribution marketplaces, rules, which are usually established by the *facilitator*, primarily pertain to transaction guidelines, inventory, community etiquette, logistics, return and complaint policies, as well as guidelines for setting up one's personal page. Tensions arise due to unclear standards, procedures and fees and lack of customer protection as well as uncommunicated sanctions (Netter, 2017). In contrast to these rather commercialized formats, there are fewer rules in free-of-charge fashion libraries. Rules established by the *facilitators* primarily concern the amount and duration of rental, condition of returned goods and fees for delay or damages. While *facilitators* cannot further their economic interest in these non-profit environments, they can guide the stylistic orientation and inventory of this collective wardrobe, which is interesting for them in their additional identity as *user/providers*. Possible tensions might arise from this double agenda and style-dictate, issued by the profiteers.

Monitoring

Just as in the case of rules, monitoring pertains to all aspects of the market. More specifically, it concerns how to monitor what members do, feel and think (Ahrne et al., 2014). An element of monitoring is a prerequisite of sharing and other types of business models as a system based solely on trust would eventually become vulnerable to the acts of less trustworthy stakeholders. Besides more top-down monitoring strategies, where one stakeholder group holding the power monitors another stakeholder group in the market, mutual monitoring enables the deliberation of experiences and evaluation of all members' action. Most online and mobile business models in the sharing economy are relying on reputation-based systems in terms of monitoring and sanctioning individual actors on sharing markets (Cohen and Sundararajan, 2015). In terms of monitoring and sanctioning entire stakeholder groups or stakeholders, it can be hypothesized that narratives, constructed by *'others'* are more powerful for inducing change and increasing self-regulation, as a means to circumvent foreseeable calls for more regulation by governing bodies. In the case of *Airbnb* for instance, media horror stories of people returning to find trashed apartments, rentals turned into brothels and their identities and valuables stolen (e.g., Coldwell, 2016) have caused *Airbnb* to adjust its terms and conditions. Mutual monitoring procedures are also in place in the case of most online and mobile redistribution markets. In most cases, *facilitators* have the opportunity to follow up on the individual transactions and shipping, by means of special payment systems and shipping labels. *User/providers* can give feedback to the *facilitator*, whether everything went smoothly or in case there are any concerns or complaints. Additionally, in many markets, *users and providers* have the opportunity to rate each other. Probably the most important feedback system is the overall feedback system in the app store, in which current or previous members provide feedback, not only to the *facilitator* but also to potential future members, which thus has a powerful gatekeeping mechanism. Tensions might arise in case members feel wrongfully accused, transactions go wrong and the customer service of the *facilitator* does not respond to reports or take action (e.g., Netter, 2017). In contrast, monitoring in free-of-charge fashion libraries occurs mostly in a top-down fashion, without formalized mutual evaluation mechanisms, monitoring the satisfaction or dissatisfaction of the members (e.g., Pedersen and Netter, 2015). *Facilitators* check whether deadlines are met and remind members of their delay. Tensions might arise as members are only able to express their feeling about their experiences in this market via voluntary feedback, either in person or via the fashion library's Facebook page, which might not reach other members to create a critical mass in order to bring about change and, hence, might go unheard or get deleted.

Sanctions

Sanctions can both be positive or negative approaches to enforcing members to do what they are expected to do (Ahrne et al., 2014). While positive sanctions provide incentives and rewards, such as prices, awards and diplomas, to reinforce preferable behaviour, negative sanctions, such as penalties, certificates and boycotts, deny or impede access and further membership and participation in the market (e.g., Ahrne and Brunsson, 2010). Both types of sanctions have consequences for the status, identity and resources of the recipient. In the sharing economy, different forms of sanctioning can be identified. In the case of *Uber* for instance, public protests by taxi drivers, calling for governments to intervene in the constant growth of *Uber* and other transportation providers, constitute one form of negative sanctions (Stallibrass and Fingleton, 2016). In online and mobile-enabled redistribution markets, both *facilitators* and *user/providers* make use of both positive and negative sanctioning mechanisms. Positive sanctions range from providing certain members with a special status, e.g. forum managers, which allows acting as an extension of the *facilitator*, to directing extra attention to certain profiles, generating more traffic to those featured shops or profiles, which most likely results in a higher number of transactions and revenues. *Facilitators* negative sanctioning mechanisms range from the hiding of listings, to temporary or permanent blocking of profiles. *User/providers* can sanction fellow *user/providers* with positive or negative reviews on their profiles, which will increase or decrease their chances of future transactions due to this trust building mechanism and provide an incentive to follow the guidelines. They can also sanction the entire community, i.e. both *facilitators* and other *user/providers*, in their app store reviews, by either praising the service and community or highlighting its flaws and weaknesses. Tensions might arise for *user/providers* when expectations and evaluations do not match, perceived unfair ratings, if listings are hidden, profiles get blocked for no apparent reasons, and only certain profiles receive positive attention and get featured. *Facilitators* have to handle the consequences of negative app reviews. As consumers perceive the reviews provided by other consumers on companies, services or products as more trustworthy than vendor testimonials (e.g. Walther and Parks, 2002), these reviews – which are for the most part outside of the control of the *facilitator* – are a powerful resources to tap into, in order to judge the reputation of a market, form an attitude and potentially convince future members to shy away from choosing one product or service in favour of another altogether (e.g. Hong and Park, 2012). There is no real sanctioning mechanism in free-of-charge fashion libraries, as there is no mechanism for who can become a member. Membership lasts usually until someone actively revokes their membership. In most cases, however, members rather switch from being active users to passive users, in the sense that they stop making use of the library, boycotting its services. Membership status can also be revoked by the facilitator, for instance as punishment for disregarding the rules of conduct.

Hierarchy

Hierarchy in market organizations pertains to who has the initiative and power, i.e. whose decisions are binding for current and future members. These decisions are usually binding as long as members wish to continue as members (Ahrne et al., 2014). While it could be argued that the formal initiative and decision-making power is held by the *facilitator*, social order is in most cases rather emergent and negotiated as a response to pressure, than simply decided. *User/providers* are in most cases the sole providers of inventory for these markets. This supply and demand side can exert pressure internally on the *facilitator* in terms of shaping the format of the marketplace. In a similar vein, *'others'*, such as communities, trade and labour unions, competing established industries and others, exert external pressure. In free-of-charge fashion libraries, the formal initiative and power is in the hands of the *facilitators*, as they develop the rules of conduct, which are binding, as long as one remains a member of the wardrobe. This power is frequently supported by a lack of competition in the case of these physical setups. Nonetheless, the survival of the library is highly dependent on the benevolence of *'others'*, who are facilitating the space of the market. In the case of *Klädoteket* for instance, a fashion library in Malmö, Sweden, the commune is providing the building in which the fashion library is located. Without the support of this *'other'*, fashion library profiteers would have to find another benefactor or adjust the business model, in order to be able to afford the running of the library. The facilitators are thus incentivized to uphold a system, which benefits and pleases their members, in order to secure the support from *'others'*. In a similar vein, facilitators are dependent on members supplying the library with inventory. Albeit the fact that the they have the final say in which items are allowed to enter the wardrobe, they have to be careful to balance their selective behaviour with the constant need to attract new and interesting inventory, which will please their members need for renewal and variety (Pedersen and

Netter, 2015). Similarly, the formal initiative and decision-making power is in the hands of the *facilitators* in online and mobile redistribution markets, as they develop the rules of conduct, which are binding, as long as user/providers in these markets wish to keep their membership status. These markets can be somewhat considered *facilitators'* markets, where the information asymmetry and its aftereffects are in the first place to the benefit of the *facilitator* (Netter, 2017). Tensions might arise between *user/providers* and *facilitators* in this regard. However, with the constant emergence of new online and mobile marketplaces, competition is growing and switching costs are getting lower. Considering the impact of the various reputation systems, app store reviews tip the scale in favour of *user/providers*, who have the opportunity and power to influence current and future possible members in their decision for or against any given platform. Reviews, which are crucial for the maintenance and retention of the current membership base as well as attraction and adoption of potential new members, can thus be considered an avenue of tension. As *facilitators* attempt to steer reviews in a certain direction by purchasing likes and reviews, they become a double-edged sword. *Facilitators* have to be careful how to respond to negative critique and promote positive feedback, in order to remain trustworthy and uphold their license to operate.

Discussion: the temporality of partiality

Over the past decade, there has been a massively increasing interest in the sharing economy and related/overlapping concepts, including participative economy, collaborative economy, access-based consumption, product-service systems, collaborative consumption and the mesh (Bardhi and Eckhardt, 2012; Botsman and Rogers, 2010; Gansky, 2010; Stokes et al., 2014). Until recently, the phenomenon was wrapped in lofty rhetoric about trust, community and sustainability. Increasingly, however, critics are beginning to question the sharing business models and their benefits for society and the wider environment (Awad, 2016; Netter, 2016b). After all, sharing can be an alternative marketplace for a community of sustainability-minded people as well as a conscious attempt to circumvent regulation and avoid head-to-head competition with established players.

Based on stakeholder thinking and the emerging literature on partial organizations, this chapter described the tensions emerging among stakeholders taking part in sharing business models. More specifically, the chapter demonstrated how tensions are manifested in sharing organizations when it comes to memberships, rules, monitoring, sanctions and hierarchy. In many ways, sharing represents a more fluid organizational form where stakeholders can occupy multiple roles and functions. However, the blurred lines between stakeholders also create a number of challenges, e.g. regarding what rules to apply and where to place responsibilities. The blurriness creates a vacuum and gives rise to a number of business practices which critics believe run contrary to the original ideas of sharing.

Sharing no longer exists on the fringe of the marketplace; it has become a billion-dollar industry which increasingly challenges conventional businesses operating in regulated markets. The growing popularity of sharing implies that these organizations are increasingly under fire to meet the same standards, rules and regulations as those governing more complete organizations in the market. Moreover, critics are increasingly challenging the roles and motives of the stakeholders taking part in sharing (Awad, 2016). Therefore, the question arises if these partial organizations ultimately represent a temporal phenomenon, which will eventually give way for complete organizations that are more *in sync* with the existing institutional infrastructure? Ironically, the current upsurge of the sharing economy may also mark the beginning of its demise as we have come to know it because the growing popularity will intensify stakeholder pressures to align the sharing practices with conventional market transactions orchestrated by complete organizations.

The future of sharing will thus depend much on the ability of sharing organizations to navigate between oppositional stakeholder expectations and institutional demands. On the one hand, they will have to conform with existing norms and rules to avoid negative stakeholder sanctions. On the other hand, they have to push existing business practices in order to provide alternative marketplaces. Here, inspiration may be found in the organization literature, which demonstrates how organizations actually have access to a broad repertoire of strategic responses to stakeholder pressures – from actively resisting demands to actively go beyond expectations (Oliver, 1991; Pedersen and Gwozdz, 2014). For instance, Pache and Santos (2013) elegantly describe how decoupling, compromise and especially selective coupling play out in the context of hybrid organizations which are born with competing institutional logics. Likewise, the future success of sharing businesses may well depend on their ability to cope with tensions by carefully choosing between resistance, compliance and opportunity-seeking in decision-making processes and day-to day practices.

Conclusions

Stakeholder theory describes an organization as coalitions of groups and individuals, which affect and/or is affected by its goals and activities. Stakeholder thinking has evolved rapidly since the 1980s and is today an integrated part of mainstream management vocabulary (Parmar et al., 2010). Over the years, there has been a lively debate about the constitution of a stakeholder and its relationship to other groups and networks. Moreover, the theory has explored the tensions which can emerge between stakeholders, who may have different views about contributions to, and rewards from, the coalition. However, overall the theory is characterized by a belief in harmony, i.e. that stakeholder interests will go together over time.

This chapter adds layer of complexity to the current discussions about stakeholder status and tensions. Based on the emerging literature on partial organizations, it explores some of the tensions emerging from blurred lines between stakeholders in the sharing economy, which has become a fast-growing alternative to more conventional marketplaces between complete organizations. The blurriness of stakeholder status in sharing economy businesses comes with risks of tensions which can also have implications for the organization's identity. For instance, a sharing platform means different things depending on whether it is viewed as a provider of peer-to-peer exchange of excess resources or a distribution channel of stolen goods or counterfeit products. Likewise, car sharing has different connotations to different people: some see it as a way to make better use of underused assets whereas others consider it as an unfriendly attempt to undermine a long-regulated transportation industry.

Fueled by new technology, the sharing economy has quickly established itself as one of the most interesting phenomena in business today. Some even argue that sharing economy will be bigger than the internet (Wenzel, 2013). However, as sharing economy initiatives are becoming more visible in the market landscape, we are also seeing that the discussions are moving beyond lofty rhetoric about collaboration, trust, community and sustainability. Critics are increasingly challenging the popular narratives surrounding the sharing economy and the motives of the actors engaging in these transactions. While the concept of sharing has existed at all times and in all cultures, the new sharing economy is likely to spark significant debate in the years to come, either as an increasingly consolidated player in the global economy or as a controversial actor operating in 'grey' unregulated markets.

References

Ahrne, G., Aspers, P., and Brunsson, N. (2014). The organization of markets. *Organization Studies,* 0170840614544557.

Ahrne, G., and Brunsson, N. (2010). Organization outside organizations: The significance of partial organization. *Organization,* September, 1–22.

Allen, S., Marshall, J., and Easterby-Smith, M. (20150. Living with contradictions: The dynamics of senior managers' identity tensions in relation to sustainability. *Organization & Environment,* 28(3): 328–348.

Aspers, P. (2009). Knowledge and valuation in markets. *Theory and Society,* 38(2), 111–131.

Awad, A. (2016). Uber and Airbnb underminerer demokratiet. *Djøfbladet,* Number 10, 27 May 2016, p. 40–41.

Bardhi, F. and Eckhardt, G. W. (2012). Access-based consumption: The case of car sharing. *Journal of Consumer Research,* 39(4): 881–898.

Belk, R. (2010). Sharing. *Journal of Consumer Research,* 36 (February), 715–734.

Birtwistle, G., and Moore, C.M. (2007). Fashion clothing – Where does it all end up? *International Journal of Retail & Distribution Management,* 35(3), 210–216.

Botsman, R., and Rogers, R. (2010). *What's Mine Is Yours: The rise of collaborative consumption.* New York: Harper Business.

Brown, G. E. (2016). An Uberdilemma: Employees and independent contractors in the sharing economy. University of Maryland Francis King Carey School of Law. DigitalCommons@UM Carey Law.

Chang, W. (2015). Growing pains: The role of regulation in the collaborative economy. *Intersect: The Stanford Journal of Science, Technology and Society,* 9(1).

Cohen, M. (2014). The sharing economy redux. Available at: http://ssppjournal. blogspot.dk/2014 /05/ the-sharing-economy-redux.html (accessed on May 15, 2014).

Cohen, M., and Sundararajan, A. (2015). Self-regulation and innovation in the peer-to-peer sharing economy. *The University of Chicago Law Review,* Dialogue, 82, 116.

Coldwell, W. (2016). Airbnb: New Year's Eve disaster stories around the world. *The Guardian.* Available at: www.theguardian.com/travel/2016/jan/07/airbnb-new-years-eve-disaster-stories-around-the-world (accessed on March 12, 2016)

Edelman, B., and Luca, M. (2014). Digital discrimination: The case of Airbnb.com. *Harvard Business School Working Paper,* 14–054.

Eichhorst, W., and Spermann, A. (2015). Report No. 69: Sharing Economy – Chancen, Risiken und Gestaltungsoptionen für den Arbeitsmarkt (No. 69). Institute for the Study of Labor (IZA).

EMF (2013a). Towards the Circular Economy 1: Economic and Business Rationale for an Accelerated Transition. Ellen MacArthur Foundation.

EMF (2013b). Towards the Circular Economy 2: Opportunities for the Consumer Goods Sector. Ellen MacArthur Foundation.

Fassin, Y. (2008). Imperfections and shortcomings of the stakeholder model's graphical representation. *Journal of Business Ethics,* 80(4): 879–888.

Gansky, L. (2010). *The Mesh.* New York: Penguin Group.

Grimm, F., and Kunze, A. (2011). Meins ist Deins [What's mine is yours] 3.0. Available at: www.enorm-magazin.de/leseprobe/Leseprobe_2_2011.pdf (accessed on October 26, 2013).

Hahn, T., Pinkse, J., Preuss, L., and Figge, F. (2015). Tensions in corporate sustainability: Towards an integrative framework. *Journal of Business Ethics,* 127: 297–316.

Hahn, T., Preuss, L., Pinkse, J., and Figge, F. (2014). Cognitive frames in corporate sustainability: Managerial sensemaking with paradoxical and business case frames. *Academy of Management Review,* 39(4): 463–487.

Haigh, N. and Hoffman, A. J. (2012). Hybrid organizations: The next chapter of sustainable business. *Organizational Dynamics*, 41: 126–134.

Hartl, B., Hofmann, E., and Kirchler, E. (2015). Do we need rules for "what's mine is yours"? Governance in collaborative consumption communities. *Journal of Business Research*, 69(8): 2756–2763.

Hoffman, A. J., Badiane, K. K., and Haigh, N. 2012. Hybrid organizations as agents of positive social change: Bridging the for-profit and non-profit divide. In K. Golden-Biddle and J. E. Dutton (Eds.), *Using a Positive Lens to Explore Social Change in Organizations*, 131–153. New York, NY: Taylor & Francis Group.

Hong, S., and Park, H. S. (2012). Computer-mediated persuasion in online reviews: Statistical versus narrative evidence. *Computers in Human Behavior*, 28(3), 906–919.

McVea, J. F. and Freeman, R. E. (2005). A Names-and-Faces Approach to Stakeholder Management. *Journal of Management Inquiry*, 14(1): 57–69.

Murray, A., Skene, K., and Haynes, K. (2015). The circular economy: An interdisciplinary exploration of the concept and application in a global context. Forthcoming in *Journal of Business Ethics*.

Netter, S. (2016a). Availability cascades and the sharing economy: A critique of sharing economy narratives. In Audley Genus (Ed.). *Sustainable Consumption: Design, Innovation and Practice. SpringerBriefs in Environment, Security, Development and Peace*, vol. 29 (Cham – Heidelberg – New York – Dordrecht – London: Springer-Springer International Publishing, 2016).

Netter, S. (2016b). Exploring the Sharing Economy. PhD School in Organisation and Management Studies. PhD Series 52.2016.

Netter, S. (2017). User satisfaction & dissatisfaction in the app sharing economy: An investigation into two-sided mobile fashion reselling & swapping markets. In C.E. Henninger, P.J. Alevizou, H. Goworek, and D. Ryding (Eds.), *Sustainability in Fashion: A Cradle to Upcycle Approach*. London: Springer.

Netter, S., Rahbek Gjerdrum Pedersen, E., and Lüdeke-Freund, F. (forthcoming). Sharing economy revisited: A new framework for understanding sharing models. work in progress.

Oliver, C. (1991). Strategic responses to institutional processes. *Academy of Management Review*, 16(1): 145–179.

Orsi, J. (2013). The sharing economy just got real. Shareable. net. Available at: www.mayorsinnovation.org/images/uploads/pdf/3.The_Sharing_Economy_Just_Got_Real.pdf (accessed on June 11, 2014)

Pache, A.-C. and Santos, F. (2013). Inside the hybrid organization: Selective coupling as a response to competing institutional logics. *Academy of Management Journal*, 56(4): 972–1001.

Parmar, B. L., Freeman, R. E., Harrison, J. S., Wicks, A. C., Purnell, L., and De Colle, S. (2010). Stakeholder theory: The state of the art. *The Academy of Management Annals*, 4(1): 403–445.

Pedersen, E. R. G., and Gwozdz, W. (2014). From resistance to opportunity-seeking: Strategic responses to institutional pressures for corporate social responsibility in the Nordic fashion industry. *Journal of Business Ethics*, 119(2): 245–264.

Pedersen, E. R. G., and Netter, S. (2015). Collaborative consumption: Business model opportunities and barriers for fashion libraries. *Journal of Fashion Marketing and Management*, 19(3): 258–273.

Post, J. E., Preston, L. E., and Sachs, S. (2002). *Redefining the Corporation: Stakeholder Management and Organizational Wealth*. California: Stanford University Press.

Seidl, I., and Zahrnt, A. (2012). Postwachstumsgesellschaft: Verortung Innerhalb Aktueller Wachstumskritischer Diskussionen [Post-growth society: Localization within current growth critical discussions] (own translation). *Ethik und Gesellschaft*, 1: 1–22.

Sørensen, M. J. (2016). Uber – A business model in search of a new contractual legal frame. *Journal of European Consumer and Market Law*, (1): 15–18.

Stallibrass, D., and Fingleton, J. (2016). Regulation, innovation, and growth: Why peer-to-peer businesses should be supported. *Journal of European Competition Law & Practice*, lpw021.

Stokes, K., Clarence, E., Anderson, L., and Rinne, A. (2014). *Making Sense of the UK Collaborative Economy*. London: NESTA.

Walsh, B. (2011). 10 ideas that will change the world. *Time*, March, 2011. Available at: www.time.com/time/specials/packages/article/0,28804,2059521_2059717_2059710,00.html (accessed on October 26, 2013).

Walther, J. B., and Parks, M. R. (2002). Cues filtered out, cues filtered in. *Handbook of Interpersonal Communication*, 529–563.

WEF (2014). *Towards the Circular Economy: Accelerating the Scale-Up across Global Supply Chains*. Geneva, Switzerland: World Economic Forum.

Wenzel, E. (2013). VERGE SF 2013 day one: 'Bigger than the Internet'. Available at: www.greenbiz. com/blog/2013/10/16/verge-day-one-2013-paul-hawken-sharing-economy

4.4 CSR-institutions

The management of SME stakeholder relations via institutional CSR-practice?

Pia Popal

Introduction

The engagement of multinational enterprises (MNE) beyond nation-states (Zürn, 2000) is a significant feature of globalisation. Along with the increasing business mobilisation, MNE are recently requested by their stakeholders to address governance challenges in the international setting, i.e. by engaging in activities of corporate social responsibility (CSR). Companies have contributed to determine this 'new global public domain' (Ruggie, 2004) by playing a regulatory role in deliberative and democratic decision-making processes across national boundaries (Matten and Crane, 2005; Risse, 2006; Scherer and Palazzo, 2007, 2011; Wolf, 2006).

Institutionalised forms of civic engagement by private actors have become a popular form of channelling this engagement (Bondy et al., 2012; Muthuri and Gilbert, 2011), especially in the form of multi-stakeholder initiatives (MSI). The UN Global Compact (UNGC) is by far the largest and most prominent MSI for sustainable business action on the international level (Cetindamar, 2007; Rasche and Kell, 2010). It aims at fostering dialogue with a broad set of different stakeholders from the public as well as the private sector by institutionalising learning in the form of a 'value based platform' (Kell and Levin, 2003: 152). The initiative intends to 'reach broader, consensus-based definitions of what constitutes good practices than any of the parties could achieve alone' (Ruggie, 2001: 373). Primarily, the UNGC is addressing larger corporations to undertake sustainable action.

In past years, the participation of small and medium-sized enterprises (SME) in those institutionalised forms of civic engagement has continuously increased. Bearing in mind that SME are not the primary addressees, their enthusiasm for sustainable multi-stakeholder initiatives such as the UNGC seems surprising. While the motives for sustainable civic engagement in institutionalised settings has been explored elsewhere (Hößle, 2013, 2014; 8), it has not been sufficiently analysed as to how stakeholder relationships drive small firm business engagement in institutionalised forms of CSR i.e. in MSI. Although it is acknowledged within this chapter that SME involvement in sustainable multi-stakeholder initiatives is not exclusively contingent to stakeholder relationships, it seems worthwhile to explore the practical implications that deal with the potential of CSR-institutions to strengthen existing relationships of smaller firms with their larger counterparts and legitimise their (social) action.

This chapter therefore sets out to shed light on the relationships of smaller firms with different stakeholders and, more importantly, the potential use of macro-institutional CSR-structures in order to manage those multiple stakeholder demands.[1]

The chapter will be structured as follows: First, I briefly describe the distinctiveness of SME and give reasons why they cannot simply be considered 'little big firms'(Tilley, 2000). Second, I will explain the central role of large corporations and their potential to exert coercive pressure on small firms into undertaking (institutional) CSR-practices. Third, I will provide information on other stakeholders and their salience to SME. Fourth, I will also outline research on cognition and CSR to show that the perception of sustainability has substantial impact on how stakeholder relations are interpreted. In doing so, I will also elaborate on the central role of the national context for the particular CSR-perception. Ultimately, I will elaborate on practical implications for MSI in order to attract SME. In conclusion, I contend that CSR-institutions such as the UN Global Compact may especially serve smaller firms (that do not possess resource slack) as a valuable tool in order to enhance multiple stakeholder relations. In order to make the management support of institutional structures available to SME, those MSI will have to stress more vigorously their potential to assist small firms in this endeavour. With regard to cognitive scripts and mental frames that are at the basis of sustainable business action, this inevitably includes the willingness of those MSI to approximate the particular yet heterogeneous CSR-perception prevalent in small firm logics.

SME distinctive characteristics and CSR

Because outlining the entire range of small firm characteristics is beyond the scope of this chapter, I will focus on certain stakeholder groups that coin the distinctiveness of SME. More importantly, the features outlined in the following are strong indicators as to why stakeholder relations are so paramount to smaller firms.

(Owner-)managers

Most SME are family-owned (Spence, 2007: 538) and are, in the majority of cases, also managed by the owner (Preuss and Perschke, 2010; Russo and Tencati, 2009). Family involvement demonstrates personal commitment of the owner which can be helpful in enhancing the employees' willingness to identify with the firm objectives (Spence, 1999: 165). The many forms of 'silent CSR' (Jenkins, 2004: 52) signify a high level of informality in the way sustainable matters are managed in small firms. In fact, distinct communication processes are not professionalised and are accordingly structured only rudimentarily (Preuss and Perschke, 2010; Spence, 1999).

The high level of personalisation with regard to the way things are managed in the small firm can result in substantial challenges, particularly in managing stakeholder relations:

> [F]amily businesses face a unique set of challenges in prioritizing which stake-holder groups matter most. The intimate involvement of family members often results in different goals and behaviors than what is typically found to exist in non-family firms and these differences can alter the bases of stakeholder power, legitimacy, and urgency.
>
> (Mitchell et al., 2011: 235–236)

The low administrative complexity (MacMillan, 1975) common to small enterprises is conducive for mental models, values and perceptions of (owner-)managers to trickle more easily through the organisational entity.

In accordance with the informal, sometimes described as myopic (Mazzarol, 2004), management style prevalent in small firms, the understanding of sustainability is more eclectic and intuitive (Murillo and Lozano, 2006; Russo and Tencati, 2009; Sen and Cowley, 2013; Spence and Rutherford, 2004). There is no systematic anchorage of sustainability within, for instance a particular CSR-department institutionalised in most MNE. 'The lower reliance of SME on formalised incentive structures leads to less publicity and visibility of CSR-related initiatives' than in MNE (Hermes et al., 2004, p. 21).

Existing and prospective employees

Because of the informality, employees in smaller companies are more likely to incorporate sustainable logics of the management, especially in case of long job tenure. In terms of CSR-practice, this means that SME often already have 'significant positive economic and social impacts in their local area, which are not often recognised in CR terms' (Roberts 2006: 280). In SME, apprentices normally remain in the company where they served their apprenticeship. Employee loyalty and years spent in smaller firms supersede staff affiliation in larger firms.

Customers

Accordingly, the personal character of these relational ties can be pertinent to prospective new employees, but also to potential customers.

Relationships with customers have usually been established over long time periods, demonstrating large investments of SME in (local) social capital. Trust in existing relationships also buttresses long-lasting commitments of small firms. Therefore, maintenance of customer relations, either with few or many customers, is very central to smaller firms.

Yet, customer expectations may differ substantially either among different customers or within different national contexts. This may pose severe challenges to the way CSR is pursued by SME. The customers of SME in developing countries may have different priorities than those of a global (Western) customer (Hermes et al., 2004). As Muthuri/ Gilbert have analysed for the Kenyan context for example,

> companies are increasingly aware that a healthy business depends on a healthy society and are responding to local needs arising from governance deficits in a strategic manner. . . . The provision of basic social welfare is often a struggle, and companies have to step in to fill the void. These responses enhance companies' reputation and social standing 'as citizens' in the local community and the nationstate.
>
> (2011: 748)

For smaller companies, bridging the gap between global business engagement and social capital mainly invested at the local or regional level, concomitantly becomes another challenge to implement sustainability.

National context

On the national level, smaller firms have, in many instances, demonstrated a long tradition of deeply rooted sustainable behaviour. In Germany for instance, the principle of the Honourable Merchant is rooted in the beginnings of industrialisation. In Italy, the

European country considered the most typical SME economy (Berghoff, 2006), SME are an embedded part of their local community and success is often linked to their legitimacy with local networks (Perrini, 2006: 310). Internationalisation challenges these relationships on yet another level: Because governance structures beyond national borders are weak, global governance concerns are increasingly carried to the doorstep of private actors (Fuchs, 2005: 146). The concerns about social issues across business environments worldwide and a resulting emphasis on corporate social responsibility have made stakeholder engagement increasingly desirable for smaller firms. In light of these developments, multi-stakeholder initiatives may provide a new frame of reference to structure this engagement.

But before I elaborate on this potential, let us look more closely at the particular relationship of small companies with large corporations.

SME relationships with large corporations

The active role of larger corporations in transnational decision-making processes for sustainability is extensive and has been thoroughly documented (Baumann, 2009; Baumann-Pauly and Scherer, 2013; Chandler and Mazlish, 2005; Detomasi, 2007; Fligstein, 1990; Mühle, 2010; Scherer and Palazzo, 2008; Zyglidopoulos, 2002). The motives for sustainable action by smaller firms (Moore and Spence, 2006), especially in the context of institutional CSR-engagement, went largely unnoticed by the research community. Concurrently, the relationship of SME with large corporations seems to be another blind spot of research and 'the debate over the relationship between both large corporations and SME and CSR is still far from concluded' (Perrini, 2006: 313).

In general terms, stakeholder relationships to larger firms are a dominant factor for institutionalised CSR practice, not least because participation can be seen as an investment in those societal ties. In fact, small firms supply a few large customers that are their exclusive business partners (Sen and Cowley, 2013), creating job dependencies that may also effect sustainable practices. Oftentimes, small firms supply global production chains of large companies.

Legitimisation is a central aspect of institutionalised business engagement. Whereas large corporations are increasingly admonished by society to behave in a sustainable fashion and thus seek social legitimisation, SME are mostly invisible to national and even more so to international societal expectations. That is why the legitimisation of business activities within a broader societal environment to enhance reputation cannot, at least not directly, be assumed as a prime motivator for institutionalised CSR practice of SME on the international level. For one, legitimacy of smaller firms is fundamentally granted through the establishment and maintenance of relational ties with their larger counterparts.

Thus, smaller firms are subject to the market dynamics determined by large enterprises they supply (Murillo and Lozano, 2006: 228). Because these large firms are more and more obliged to demonstrate transparent and sustainable ways of production along those supply chains, the societal pressure on MNE is 'handed on along the line'. Large corporations have the potential to determine the way for their small suppliers:

> [I]n the developing world, the adoption of good practices by major firms may exert an upward pull on the performance of local enterprises in the same sector, especially if the major firms extend those practices down their supply chains; and in the industrialized countries, the gradual diffusion of good practices by major companies' social

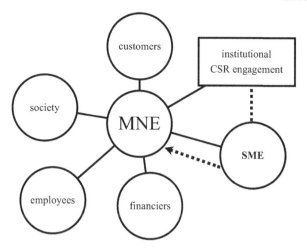

Figure 4.4.1 SME institutional CSR-engagement as determined by stakeholder relationships with MNE
Source: Partly adapted from Spence (2016).

and environmental performance abroad may lessen the fear that a global 'race to the bottom' will undermine their own policy frameworks for achieving social inclusion and economic security at home.

(Ruggie, 2004: 516)

In sum, it can be argued that stakeholder relations with large corporations are very central to SME in general, but also paramount to the motives for civic engagement in institutional settings. As illustrated in Figure 4.4.1, participation in MSIs can be centrally determined by the relationships with MNE, for instance, in case this large firm is the main customer of the SME.

Yet, as I will try to stress in the next sub-section, it cannot be argued that those relationships are the sole source for engagement. Inversely, it would be short-sighted to advance the understanding that such institutional structures are only helpful in better managing those relationships with large customers. In sum, the management of relationships with large customers (i.e. MNE) is only *one* reason for smaller firms to join institutional arrangements. Instead, I contend that stakeholder relations of smaller firms are more complex and their salience to SME is contingent upon different actors.

Relationships with other salient stakeholders

Whereas the relational character with large counterparts is predominantly characterised by coercive pressure, relationships with suppliers and sub-contractors as well as with employees are generally based on trust. In terms of relational quality, however, I can find no empirical evidence to support the claim that either internal or external stakeholders are more valuable than the other. In fact, the way in which stakeholders are prioritised is contingent upon each single SME and its very specific practical experience. In other words, the salience of stakeholders may differ substantially from one small firm to another. Hence, before we delve into the potential of institutions to manage stakeholder ties, let us be reminded that the individual firm characteristic has decisive effects on the respective stakeholder prioritisation and the variety thereof.

Nonetheless, a group of key stakeholders for small firms are identifiable. Apart from stakeholder relations with large corporations elaborated in the previous sub-section, suppliers and employees can be equally salient for small firms, in contrast to society at large, at least in terms of reputational threats put forward by the social community.

As has been stressed earlier, business interactions of SME are based on long-term relationships with customers that were shaped over long time periods. They are one of the fundamental social capitals of smaller firms and thus extremely valuable. For German SME for instance, who do not engage in economies of scale but are often hidden champions in highly specialised niche markets (Simon, 2009), customer and supplier networks are rarely diversified. The heavy investment in social ties becomes even more relevant for small companies against the background that they do not possess time or resource slack (Jenkins, 2006).

But long-term ties also characterise the relationships with employees. As I have demonstrated in earlier research, the motives for institutional CSR-practice were also contingent upon the perception of potential and prospective employees, stressing the salience of this stakeholder group for SME (Popal, 2018). Concurrently, as Dhanesh has shown in a study on the linkages between employee perceptions of their organisations' CSR practices and organisation–employee relationship dimensions of trust, commitment, satisfaction and control has revealed a strong, significant and positive association between CSR and organisation–employee relationships (2014). Especially in countries that experience a chronic shortage of qualified workforce, the relationship with existing and prospective employees becomes an increasingly relevant denominator for CSR practices as a source for employee satisfaction (Bauman and Skitka, 2012). It reveals that CSR, and in furtherance of this argument CSR-institutions, are apt to serve as a management relationship strategy. This is best illustrated in Figure 4.4.2.

What is decisive here is not so much the stakeholder's stake in the business but rather the social capital these connections create for the small firm (Sen and Cowley, 2013). The social environment the small firm is embedded in is significantly determined by

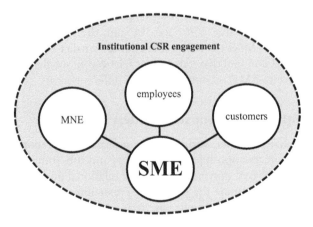

Figure 4.4.2 Salient stakeholders for institutional CSR-engagement of SME

Source: Authors' own analysis.

those stakeholders described above. Ultimately, how salient a particular stakeholder is to a respective firm is also contingent upon this role in the SME's *social environment*.

So in sum, because SME adhere to a variety of salient stakeholders, 'the SME has to make a considerably greater effort in managing its stakeholder relations' (Frank and Roessl, 2015: 230).

In contrast to constructing motives for institutional civic engagement of smaller firms as the outcome of coercive pressure exerted by large corporations on their small counterparts, viewing institutional engagement as a suitable form of relationship management in the sustainable context implies an active agency of SME. More specifically, it requires SME to interpret the potential utility of institutional structures as a means to manage salient stakeholder relations, mostly managing different claims simultaneously.

Empirical research literature supports an approach to stakeholder salience in which stakeholder attribute influence the managers' perceptions of stakeholder salience (Agle et al., 1999). In furtherance of this point of reasoning, it can be ascertained that, in order to understand the potentials of sustainable MSI for SME, one has to delve into a cognitive approach to CSR.

Cognition and CSR

Having in mind that SME are more defined by their multiple stakeholder relations and have to adhere to a plethora of very different, sometimes competing, stakeholder demands, it seems necessary to explore in what way CSR, and its institutional practice in particular, can be regarded as a potential relationship management strategy that could strengthen relationships with employees, customers in general and large corporations in particular, suppliers and contractors as well as society at large.

However, I argue that this change in practice has to be preceded by understanding the cognitive processes that underlie sustainable practices of smaller firms to date. I believe that only if we understand the way in which those relational ties are presently explored in the sustainable context can we formulate implications for business practice.

In this sub-section, I therefore argue that understanding the psychology and mental logics of owner-managers in smaller firms is paramount in reconstructing the deeper meaning and, hence, the complexity of stakeholder relations of those SME. I thus accord with earlier research that there is need to link CSR and cognition (Lee, 2008; Secchi, 2009).

In my opinion, this includes a multi-level understanding of how macro-institutional structures can assist meso- (organisational dimension) and micro-level (within the organisation itself) processes. Multi-level research includes different approaches, inter alia the analysis of how higher levels affect lower levels (downward cross-level effects), such as the influence of the companies' characteristics on employees' reactions to their firm's CSR-activities (Aguinis and Glavas, 2012) or how lower-level factors affect higher level aspects (upward cross-level effect) such as the influence of CEO values on their firm's strategic priorities (Aguinis and Glavas, 2012).

But what I aim at is best summarised in the following quote: 'Organisations acquire a social identity from the industry to which they belong, the organisational form they use, and through membership in accrediting bodies' (Rao et al., 2000: 270). In furtherance of the latter aspect, institutional arrangements may serve as one form of sustainable accreditation, something that is not (or not in that intensity) attainable by private actors that act in isolation.

At the basis, the identity of the organisation consists of the participants' shared perceptions about what their organisation is (that is the *central* attributes of the organisation); what makes the organisation *distinctive*, thus unique in contrast to other organisations; and what is perceived as *enduring* (Stuart and Whetten, 1985; Whetten, 2006).[2]

Especially for SME it seems necessary to highlight that, although CSR takes place at the organisational level of analysis, it may be important to look into the organisational black-box (Jain and Jamali, 2016) in order to reconstruct the multi-level complexity of CSR-perception and its effect on sustainable stakeholder management. Against this backdrop, it seems reasonable to look at the 'cognitive antecedents of individuals' socially responsible behaviour, which may affect their decision-making in organisational settings' (Fassin et al., 2015: 435).

More specifically, this approach helps to demonstrate how both managerial attributes such as values, beliefs, attitudes, etc. (Mitchell et al., 2011: 237) as well as institutional contexts influence managers' perceptions and prioritisation processes with regard to stakeholders. In consequence, it can be agreed that 'multiple logics create a unique perceptual setting for managers in general' (Mitchell et al., 2011: 238) that have direct repercussions on the way SME perceive and interpret their different stakeholder relations.

Certainly, a lot can be gained 'from studying internal institutional determinants, such as the mental frames and sensemaking processes within which CSR is embedded (i.e. by studying how an organisation makes sense of its world)' (Basu and Palazzo, 2008: 123). At the same time, macro-institutional parameters such as the UNGC guidelines may guide the cognitive processes of organisations.

As has been stressed by Basu/Palazzo, 'the mental models or frames that underlie organisational sensemaking, then, influence the way the world is perceived within the organisation, as well as critical decisions with respect to perceived external and internal demands'(2008: 123). Of course, this has repercussions for the assessment of stakeholder relations: As Brickson (2007) has outlined, these processes of sensemaking within an organisation lead the organisation to view its relationships with stakeholders in particular ways, which, in turn, influences its engagement with them.

Having in mind that 'cognitive complexity increases . . . depending upon the number of parties within relationships' (Mitchell et al., 2011: 239), it can be postulated that smaller firms may have more incentive than larger firms to utilise institutions in order to manage different stakeholder claims. In fact, multi-stakeholder initiatives on sustainability (e.g. the UNGC) can be even more attractive for smaller firms *because* they need to adhere to different stakeholders simultaneously. Sustainable multi-stakeholder institutions can be considered the blueprints of small firm characteristics, in that they are able to offer a large portfolio of CSR-activities that are inversely conducive to the highly individual structure and self-concept of SME in general, but also to their specific interpretation of CSR in particular. Concomitantly, they have the potential to act as a suitable tool for multi-stakeholder management (Popal, 2018).

Nonetheless, the way in which institutional arrangements can be considered an assistance in managing this relational complexity postulates that these institutional structures are sensitive to the heterogeneous and highly individual character of smaller firms.[3] This inevitably requires us to look more closely at the central role of the national culture on SME sustainable behaviour.

The central role of the national culture of SME

Drawing on previous research that has stressed the crucial impact of the particular national context of SME on CSR-perception and interpretation (Fassin et al., 2011), I find it important to make this point more explicit with reference to utilising macro-institutional CSR-structures to manage multiple stakeholder claims. For reasons I have elaborated earlier, I will do so with a focus on small companies from Germany.

In terms of innovation, Germany is generally known for optimising existing processes that eventually lead to incremental innovative ideas, instead of discovering disruptive innovative products. Interestingly, the way the use of institutional structures to manage stakeholder by German small business actors is a footprint of how innovative ideas form within the corporate context.

Transferring these insights from the impact of national culture on the utilisation of sustainable institutions, it should be borne in mind that, in case of Germany, these structures are perceived as ways to strengthen *existing* relationships, i.e. managing relations in place, instead of creating new business opportunities in the field of CSR. This means that because of national historical circumstances, German SME may be more risk aversive than, for instance, SME from the US. In consequence, investing in existing contacts may be more important to small firms than developing new contacts (Drakopoulou Dodd et al., 2002). Social capital is not newly created but strengthened through trust in existing ties and, in doing so, favouring incremental CSR-performances instead of disruptive ones. In light of these revelations, institutional CSR-structures, at least for German SME, are potentially better equipped to foster existing stakeholder relations, instead of assisting in the creation of new ones.

In general, the central role of the national culture displays that the social context has a crucial impact on the way institutional structures are perceived and deployed in order to manage stakeholder relationships.

But before I indulge into the potential utilisation of institutional structures to manage stakeholder relations, it seems important to explore the purpose of accession to CSR-institutions and, ultimately, the reason for exchange with stakeholders via such networks. This inevitably includes the delineation of the nature of communication within those structures. For instance, Swiss SME participants of the UNGC network displayed a high level of awareness in relation to their social connection to global governance issues along their supply chains (Wickert, 2010: 21).

Regarding the UNGC merely as a loose 'frame of reference' that provides guidance in sustainable issues to a large stakeholder community, it does not come as a surprise that its exploitation for actively managing existing stakeholder relationships takes on very different forms: So far, obliging with coercive pressure from large counterparts remains a central motive to join such supra-national structures, but without doubt, employees (potential and existing), become increasingly relevant to SME that are, at least in Germany, heavily affected by a serious lack of qualified personnel. The relationship with peers, for instance from the same industry, can be regarded as another driver for engagement, yet with much less significance than the previous stakeholder groups (Popal, 2018).[4]

Even though SME are not exposed to reputational threats as large MNE, the involvement in transnational contexts as well as the high impact of the regional community on the organisations' identity formation (Brickson, 2007) and the societal relevance for relational management of SME in the CSR context cannot be negated. Earlier findings have shown that the embeddedness of SME within their societal context can have a substantial impact on how socially responsible behaviour is formed (Fuller and Tian, 2006: 295; Spence, 2007: 537). In fact, 'the 'embeddedness' of SME in their wider environments may make a distinct impact SME owner-managers' cognition regarding CSR compared to managers in large organisations' (Fassin et al., 2015: 436). In the end, legitimacy also leans on social relationships (Secchi, 2009: 568).

Conclusion and implications for practice

As I have outlined in this chapter, stakeholder relations of smaller firms, and more particularly their impact on CSR-perception and performance, cannot be reduced to coercive pressure by large organisations that SME supply. Instead, I was able to show that stakeholder relations of SME are more complex and often develop over long time periods.

I conclude that institutional CSR-structures are a suitable way to manage multiple stakeholder relationships that are acting simultaneously, not least because they provide a frame of reference that can either be followed by the firm itself that acts upon coercive pressure of MNE, assist employees in the sustainable implementation of sustainable measures within the firm as well as signal trust towards other stakeholders of SME i.e. to comply with social and labour standards, but also to guide sub-contractors and suppliers to 'play by the rules of the sustainable game' the respective SME decided to follow.

In consequence, I call for a change in the way SME have been previously approached by CSR-institutions. In fact, I argue that, when the attraction of more SME is a self-proclaimed objective of those institutions that have attracted by now almost the entire range of relevant *multinational* companies and attempts to expand its attraction to small firm players, it will be necessary to change the way in which smaller enterprises have previously been approached.

For this reason, I will, in the following, advance three implications for the practice of macro-institutional arrangements that build on one another. However, I do not make any claim to completeness.

First, institutions will have to make an effort in order to regard smaller firms as organisations that fundamentally differ from MNE. This is crucial in so far as not only are SME different in nature, but as has been established in this chapter, they also adhere to much more complex stakeholder relations that represent different levels of social capital investment by SME (Fuller and Tian, 2006; Russo and Perrini, 2010; Spence and Schmidpeter, 2003; Werner and Spence, 2004). Against the backdrop that small enterprises have multiple motives to engage in institutional forms of civic engagement, institutional propositions to SME have to attend more specifically to the different needs formulated by those actors.

Second, having established that the cognition of CSR in smaller enterprises is usually based on personal values, mental models and individual sensemaking, macro-institutional structures face the challenge of addressing SME more appropriately at the micro-level. Because of the chronic resource deficiencies in small companies (Jenkins, 2004; McWilliams and Siegel, 2001; Tilley, 2000), this will have to include the effort to promote more vigorously the potential of those macro-institutional arrangements in assisting SME to manage multiple stakeholder demands. Inevitably, institutional arrangements will have to incorporate this multidimensionality of small firm stakeholder relations in order to address SME in a more appropriate manner.

Third, in order to do so, institutions will have to pay more attention and delve into the idiosyncrasies of the national cultural contexts SME are embedded in. As I have tried to exemplify, this societal context may also have repercussions for the ways in which CSR is perceived in general, but also more particularly, how institutional arrangements are intended to be used in order to manage stakeholder relations. In case of Germany for instance, the tendency to avert risks in the realisation of business opportunities rather leads to incremental processes instead of disruptive ones. In furtherance of this argument, the use of CSR-institutions such as the UNGC may only be directed at managing existing

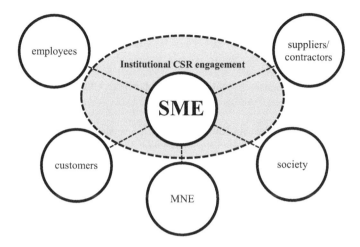

Figure 4.4.3 Institutional CSR-engagement as a way to manage multiple stakeholder relations

Source: Authors' own analysis.

stakeholder relations (that can be subsumed under the institutional frame of reference in place), instead of identifying and establishing new stakeholder paths.

In sum, the successful adaption and implementation of the aspects outlined above may determine if and in what way SME make use of institutional structures in order to manage their relations with the large plethora of stakeholders they engage with.

Limitations and further research

Inferring general conclusions from these findings has to stay at a modest level. So far, the elaborations concerning the relevance of the national culture and information on the German context can be considered a starting point for research. Further studies will have to explore different national contexts both in the developed and developing countries and, ultimately, result in cross-national comparisons on the utility of institutional CSR-structures for SME in order to manage multiple stakeholder relations. This might also reveal more information on the fact that previous experience, for instance, with intermediary, meso-institutional structures such as the German Chamber of Commerce, may either hamper or enhance the use of those macro-institutional structures to improve multiple stakeholder management of smaller companies.

Notes

1   I will repeatedly refer to SME from Germany because they usually show a long tradition of sustainable engagement (Beyer and Höpner 2003; Hiß 2009; Kinderman 2008; Wieland 2012) but also because of my previous research focus on the German context.
2   These three definitions have been advanced by Stuart/Whetten in their monumental work from 1985.
3   In contrast to classical Institutional Theory (DiMaggio and Powell 1983, 1991, Powell 1991), I focus on the enabling potential of institutions with reference to small organisations. In consequence, I contend

that looking more closely at the influence of institutions on mental models or behaviours of private actors is beyond the scope but also the aim of this chapter.

4 For more detail on the motives for institutional small business practice, see Popal (2018).

References

Agle BR, Mitchell RK and Sonnenfeld JA (1999) Who Matters to CEOs? An Investigation of Stakeholder Attributes and Salience, Corporate Performance, and CEO Values. *The Academy of Management Journal* 42(5): 507–525.

Aguinis H and Glavas A (2012) What We Know and Don't Know About Corporate Social Responsibility: A Review and Research Agenda. *Journal of Management* 38(4): 932–968.

Basu K and Palazzo G (2008) Corporate Social Responsibility: A Process Model of Sensemaking. *The Academy of Management Review* 33(1): 122–136.

Bauman CW and Skitka LJ (2012) Corporate Social Responsibility as a Source of Employee Satisfaction. *Research in Organizational Behavior* 32: 63–86.

Baumann D (2009) *Global Rules – Private Actors: The Role of the Multinational Corporation in Global Governance.* Zürich: Hochschulschrift.

Baumann-Pauly D and Scherer AG (2013) The Organizational Implementation of Corporate Citizenship: An Assessment Tool and its Application at UN Global Compact Participants. *Journal of Business Ethics* 117(1): 1–17.

Berghoff H (2006) The End of Family Business? The Mittelstand and German Capitalism in Transition, 1949–2000. *The Business History Review* 80(2): 263–295.

Beyer J and Höpner M (2003) The Disintegration of Organised Capitalism: German Corporate Governance in the 1990s. *West European Politics* 26(4): 179–198.

Bondy K, Moon J and Matten D (2012) An Institution of Corporate Social Responsibility (CSR) in Multi-National Corporations (MNCs): Form and Implications. *Journal of Business Ethics* 111(2): 281–299.

Brickson SL (2007) Organizational Identity Orientation: The Genesis of the Role of the Firm and Distinct Forms of Social Value. *The Academy of Management Review* 32(3): 864–888.

Cetindamar D (2007) Corporate Social Responsibility Practices and Environmentally Responsible Behavior: The Case of the United Nations Global Compact. *Journal of Business Ethics* 76(2): 163–176.

Chandler AD and Mazlish B (2005) *Leviathans: Multinational Corporations and the New Global History.* Cambridge: Cambridge University Press.

Detomasi DA (2007) The Multinational Corporation and Global Governance: Modelling Global Public Policy Networks. *Journal of Business Ethics* 71(3): 321–334.

Dhanesh GS (2014) CSR as Organization-Employee Relationship Management Strategy: A Case Study of Socially Responsible Information Technology Companies in India. *Management Communication Quarterly* 28(1): 130–149.

DiMaggio PJ and Powell WW (1983) The Iron Cage Revisited: Institutional Isomorphism and Collective Rationality in Organizational Fields. *American Sociological Review* 48(2): 147–160.

DiMaggio PJ and Powell WW (1991) *The New Institutionalism in Organizational Analysis.* Chicago: University of Chicago Press.

Drakopoulou Dodd SD, Jack S and Anderson AR (2002) Scottish Entrepreneurial Networks in the International Context. *International Small Business Journal* 20(2): 213–219.

Fassin Y, van Rossem A and Buelens M (2011) Small-Business Owner-Managers' Perceptions of Business Ethics and CSR-Related Concepts. *Journal of Business Ethics* 98(3): 425–453.

Fassin Y, Werner A, van Rossem A, Signori S, Garriga E, Weltzien Hoivik H von, et al. (2015) CSR and Related Terms in SME Owner – Managers' Mental Models in Six European Countries: National Context Matters. *Journal of Business Ethics* 128(2): 433–456.

Fligstein N (1990) *The Transformation of Corporate Control.* Cambridge, MA: Harvard University Press.

Frank H and Roessl D (2015) Problematization and Conceptualization of "Entrepreneurial SME Management" as a Field of Research. Overcoming the Size-Based Approach. *Review of Managerial Science* 9(2): 225–240.

Fuchs D (2005) *Understanding Business Power in Global Governance*. Baden-Baden: Nomos.

Fuller T and Tian Y (2006) Social and Symbolic Capital and Responsible Entrepreneurship: An Empirical Investigation of SME Narratives. *Journal of Business Ethics* 67(3): 287–304.

Hermes S, Jarvis M, Atacik MC, Schwittay A and El-Sharkawy A (2004) *Can Small Be Responsible? The Possibilities and Challenges of Corporate Social Responsibility among Small and Medium Enteprises*. WBI Series on Corporate Responsibility, Accountability, and Sustainable Competitiveness. World Bank Institute: Washington.

Hiß S (2009) From Implicit to Explicit Corporate Social Responsibility: Institutional Change as a Fight for Myths. *Business Ethics Quarterly* 19(3): 433–451.

Hößle U (2013) *Der Beitrag des UN Global Compact zur Compliance internationaler Regime: Ein Vergleich von Unternehmen aus den USA, Mosambik, den Vereinigten Arabischen Emiraten und Deutschland*. Baden-Baden: Nomos.

Hößle U (2014) The Contribution of the UN Global Compact towards the Compliance of International Regimes: A Comparative Study of Businesses from the USA, Mozambique, United Arab Emirates and Germany. *Journal of Corporate Citizenship* 2014(53): 27–60.

Jain T and Jamali D (2016) Looking Inside the Black Box: The Effect of Corporate Governance on Corporate Social Responsibility. *Corporate Governance: An International Review* 24(3): 253–273.

Jenkins H (2004) A Critique of Conventional CSR Theory: an SME Perspective. *Journal of General Management* 29(4): 37–57.

Jenkins H (2006) Small Business Champions for Corporate Social Responsibility. *Journal of Business Ethics* 67(3): 241–256.

Kell G and Levin D (2003) The Global Compact Network: An Historic Experiment in Learning and Action. *Business and Society Review* 108(2): 151–181.

Kinderman D (2008) *The Political Economy of Corporate Responsibility in Germany, 1995–2008*. Part Five of the Germany in Global Economic Governance Series. Working Paper Series No. 5-08. Center for International Studies: New York.

Lee MP (2008) A Review of the Theories of Corporate Social Responsibility: Its Evolutionary Path and the Road Ahead. *International Journal of Management Reviews* 10(1): 53–73.

MacMillan IC (1975) Strategy and Flexibility in the Smaller Business. *Long Range Planning* 8(3): 62–63.

Matten D and Crane A (2005) Corporate Citizenship. Toward an Extended Theoretical Conceptualization. *The Academy of Management Review* 30(1): 166–179.

Mazzarol T (2004) Strategic Management of Small Firms: A Proposed Framework for Entrepreneurial Ventures. In *Proceedings of the 17th Annual SEAANZ Conference—Entrepreneurship as a Way of the Future*, Brisbane, Queensland, Australia.

McWilliams A and Siegel D (2001) Corporate Social Responsibility: A Theory of the Firm Perspective. *The Academy of Management Review* 26(1): 117–127.

Mitchell RK, Agle BR, Chrisman JJ, Spence LJ and Arnold DG (2011) Toward a Theory of Stakeholder Salience in Family Firms. *Business Ethics Quarterly* 21(2): 235–255.

Moore G and Spence L (2006) Editorial: Responsibility and Small Business. *Journal of Business Ethics* 67(3): 219–236.

Mühle U (2010) *The Politics of Corporate Social Responsibility. The Rise of a Global Business Norm*. Frankfurt, M. [u.a.]: Campus-Verlag.

Murillo D and Lozano J (2006) SMEs and CSR: An Approach to CSR in their Own Words. *Journal of Business Ethics* 67(3): 227–240.

Muthuri JN and Gilbert V (2011) An Institutional Analysis of Corporate Social Responsibility in Kenya. *Journal of Business Ethics* 98(3): 467–483.

Perrini F (2006) SMEs and CSR Theory: Evidence and Implications from an Italian Perspective. *Journal of Business Ethics* 67(3): 305–316.

Popal P (2018) *SME – the Civic Hidden Champions in Global Governance? Evidence from German Small Business Engagement in the UN Global Compact*. Ingolstadt, Germany: in press.

Powell WW (1991) Expanding the Scope of Institutional Analysis. In: DiMaggio PJ and Powell WW (eds) *The New Institutionalism in Organizational Analysis*. Chicago: University of Chicago Press, pp. 183–203.

Preuss L and Perschke J (2010) Slipstreaming the Larger Boats: Social Responsibility in Medium-Sized Businesses. *Journal of Business Ethics* 92(4): 531–551.

Rao H, Davis GF and Ward A (2000) Embeddedness, Social Identity and Mobility. Why Firms Leave the NASDAQ and Join the New York Stock Exchange. *Administrative Science Quarterly* 45(2): 268.

Rasche A and Kell G (2010) Introduction: The United Nations Global Compact – Retrospect and Prospect. In: Rasche A and Kell G (eds) *The United Nations Global Compact. Achievements, Trends and Challenges.* Cambridge: Cambridge University Press, pp. 1–20.

Risse T (2006) Transnational Governance and Legitimacy. In: Benz A and Papadopoulos Yannis (eds) *Governance and Democracy. Comparing National, European and International Experiences.* London: Routledge, pp. 179–199.

Roberts S, Lawson R and Nicholls J (2006) Generating Regional-Scale Improvements in SME Corporate Responsibility Performance: Lessons from Responsibility Northwest. *Journal of Business Ethics* 67(3): 275–286.

Ruggie JG (2001) Global Insights: The Global Compact as Learning Network. *Global Governance* 7: 371–378.

Ruggie JG (2004) Reconstituting the Global Public Domain – Issues, Actors, and Practices. *European Journal of International Relations* 10(4): 499–531.

Russo A and Perrini F (2010) Investigating Stakeholder Theory and Social Capital: CSR in Large Firms and SMEs. *Journal of Business Ethics* 91(2): 207–221.

Russo A and Tencati A (2009) Formal vs. Informal CSR Strategies: Evidence from Italian Micro, Small, Medium-Sized, and Large Firms. *Journal of Business Ethics* 85(2): 339–353.

Scherer AG and Palazzo G (2007) Toward a Political Conception of Corporate Social Responsibility: Business and Society Seen from a Habermasian Perspective. *Academy of Management Review* 32(4): 1096–1120.

Scherer AG and Palazzo G (2008) Globalization and Corporate Social Responsibility – Anything New? Chapter 18. In: Crane A (ed.) *The Oxford Handbook of Corporate Social Responsibility.* Oxford [u.a.]: Oxford University Press, pp. 413–431.

Scherer AG and Palazzo G (2011) The New Political Role of Business in a Globalized World: A Review of a New Perspective on CSR and its Implications for the Firm, Governance, and Democracy. *Journal of Management Studies* 48(4): 899–931.

Secchi D (2009) The Cognitive Side of Social Responsibility. *Journal of Business Ethics* 88(3): 565–581.

Sen S and Cowley J (2013) The Relevance of Stakeholder Theory and Social Capital Theory in the Context of CSR in SMEs: An Australian Perspective. *Journal of Business Ethics* 118(2): 413–427.

Simon H (2009) *Hidden Champions of the Twenty-First Century: The Success Strategies of Unknown World Market Leaders.* New York, London: Springer.

Spence LJ (1999) Does Size Matter? The State of the Art in Small Business Ethics. *Business Ethics: A European Review* 8(3): 163–174.

Spence LJ (2007) CSR and Small Business in a European Policy Context: The Five "C"s of CSR and Small Business Research Agenda 2007. *Business and Society Review* 112(4): 533–552.

Spence LJ (2016) Small Business Social Responsibility. Expanding Core CSR Theory. *Business & Society* 55(1): 23–55.

Spence LJ and Rutherford R (2004) Social Responsibility, Profit-Maximisation and the Small Firm Owner-Manager. In: Spence LJ, Habisch A and Schmidpeter R (eds) *Responsibility and Social Capital: The World of Small and Medium Sized Enterprises.* Houndmills, Basingstoke, Hampshire, New York: Palgrave Macmillan, pp. 35–58.

Spence LJ and Schmidpeter R (2003) SMEs, Social Capital and the Common Good. *Journal of Business Ethics* 45(1): 93–108.

Stuart A and Whetten DA (1985) Organizational Identity. In: Cummings LL and Staw BM (eds) *Research in Organizational Behavior. An Annual Series of Analytical Essays and Critical Reviews.* Greenwich: JAI Press, pp. 263–295.

Tilley F (2000) Small Firm Environmental Ethics: How Deep Do They Go? *Business Ethics: A European Review* 9(1): 31–41.

Werner A and Spence LJ (2004) Literature Review: Social Capital and SMEs. In: Spence LJ, Habisch A and Schmidpeter R (eds) *Responsibility and Social Capital. The World of Small and Medium Sized Enterprises.* Houndmills, Basingstoke, Hampshire, New York: Palgrave Macmillan, pp. 7–24.

Whetten DA (2006) Albert and Whetten Revisited: Strengthening the Concept of Organizational Identity. *Journal of Management Inquiry* 15(3): 219–234.

Wickert C (2010) *Small- and Medium-Sized Enterprises as Political Actors in Global Governance – Evidence from the Textile Industry.* Institute of Organization and Administrative Science – University of Zurich. IOU Working Paper Series No. 121. Zurich.

Wieland J (2012) CSR in Germany – Tradition, Topicality and Challenges. In: BMAS (ed.) *CSR – Made in Germany.* Paderborn: Bonifatius, pp. 14–19.

Wolf KD (2006) Private Actors and the Legitimacy of Governance Beyond the State: Conceptional Outlines and Empirical Explorations. In: Benz A and Papadopoulos Yannis (eds) *Governance and Democracy: Comparing National, European and International Experiences.* London: Routledge, pp. 200–227.

Zürn M (2000) Democratic Governance Beyond the Nation-State: The EU and Other International Institutions. *European Journal of International Relations* 6(2): 183–221.

Zyglidopoulos SC (2002) The Social and Environmental Responsibilities of Multinationals: Evidence from the Brent Spar Case. *Journal of Business Ethics* 36(1): 141–151.

4.5 Neither fortune nor mirage at the bottom of the pyramid

Corporate social innovations as learning opportunities

Bertrand Moingeon and Laurence Lehmann-Ortega

Introduction

Corporate social responsibility (CSR) is how firms address the challenges of sustainable development, which include environmental, social, and fairness issues (Lockett *et al.*, 2006; McWilliams *et al.*, 2006).

It has become a platitude to state that CSR is a concern for contemporary business managers around the world. Many of them have adopted a defensive behavior consisting in reacting to external pressures through ill-assorted and poorly coordinated actions, and abundant communications, sometimes referred to derogatorily as "*greenwashing*" (Davis, 1992; Mahoney *et al.*, 2013). Other firms, however, are conscious of the gravity of the stakes and of their role and wish to elaborate a strategy going beyond regulatory requirements. Thus, firms consider the underlying opportunities in CSR and try to turn them into a business opportunity, doing well by doing good (Burke *et al.*, 1996; Husted *et al.*, 2006; Margolis *et al.*, 2003; Porter *et al.*, 2002; Waddock *et al.*, 1997).

Prahalad's (2004) work builds on this idea: he encourages companies to seek *Fortune at the Bottom of the Pyramid* whereby they can contribute to eradicating poverty while making a profit. Prahalad claims that multinational companies (MNCs) should address a so far untapped market: the poor, living with the equivalent of less than $2,000 a year, who are at the bottom of the economic pyramid. He builds upon examples such as Cemex Pratimonio Hoy, a program launched in Mexico by Cemex, a major international cement firm, providing credit to poor customers who want to build a house; Jaipur Foot, which managed to provide low cost prosthetic feet; and Aravind Eye Care System, an Indian clinic offering eye care and surgery at a very low price.

However, vigorous criticism about Prahalad's ideas has emerged, disparaged as naïve and fallacious. The most virulent has been Karnani's (2007), who argues that these ideas are a mirage: there are no profits possible for MNCs, and the poor are more assisted than helped. Karnani assesses the case studies used by Prahalad and shows that virtually none of them have actually made a profit by selling to the poor. Either they are selling at a target above the bottom of the pyramid (BOP), or they are not profitable, or they are not-for-profit organizations. As Karnani states: "the BOP proposition is indeed too good to be true. It is seductively appealing, but it is riddled with fallacies" (p. 91).

So how does one step out of this controversy? Can the poor be helped at all through CSR? If there is no fortune at the BOP, are there any benefits beyond financial profit of this type of CSR initiatives for firms? If they exist, can they provide grounds for competitive advantage?

The goal of this chapter is to introduce another way of looking at this controversy and to suggest what the real benefits of CSR are: the mirage can indeed be turned into real social profit for the poor, but those benefits don't directly turn into a fortune for MNCs. Simply put, there is a return to the CSR investment, but conventional[1] financial profit is not a direct part of it. To make our argument, we draw from several examples of partnerships in Bangladesh between MNCs and the Grameen Group – the microcredit pioneer founded by 2006 Nobel Peace Prize winner Muhammad Yunus.[2] Data have been collected before he resigned as CEO of Grameen Bank in 2010 due to pressure from the Bangladeshi government (see the interview of Muhammad Yunus by Allison Beard, published in 2012 in the *Harvard Business Review*). We will then show that building such businesses is similar to business model innovation, before describing the benefits of those experiments for the MNCs.

New social business models

Over the years, Grameen Group has indeed developed partnerships with MNCs to build "social businesses" (Yunus and Weber, 2007). The story behind each of these ventures is of the gradual emergence of the concept of "social business": "a self-sustaining company that sells goods or services and repays its owners' investments, but whose primary purpose is to serve society and improve the lot of the poor" (Yunus *et al.*, 2010, p. 309).

It is a hybrid form between a not-for-profit organization and a profit-maximizing organization. As the former, it will be cause-driven rather than profit-driven, but it will have the same organizational structure as the latter. Social businesses are not charity organizations but true businesses: they seek to be self-sustaining through full recovery of costs since there is the belief that only profitability can ensure sustainability. Thus, a social business is designed and operated like a business enterprise, with products, services, customers, markets, expenses, and revenues. It is a no-loss, no-dividend, self-sustaining company that sells goods or services and repays investments to its owners, but whose primary purpose is make social profit. Here it differs from NGOs, most of which do not recover their total costs from their operations and, therefore, are forced to devote part of their time and energy to raising money. As it seeks self-sustainability, a social business only relies on its investors at the beginning of a development project.

Social businesses may not be built through a simple replication in Bangladesh of the MNC's conventional (i.e., used in the developed world) business model. Although the concept of business model has been increasingly important in academic research as well as for practitioners, there is no consensus about its definition (Massa *et al.*, 2017). Business model can be seen as formal conceptual representations of a mean to compete, whether in existing markets of in emerging ones. The business model is a new unit of analysis, offering a systemic view on organizations. In a previous publication (Moingeon and Lehmann-Ortega, 2010), we proposed a framework to operationally define the different components of a business model. In this chapter, we build on our definition of a "social business model" (Yunus *et al.*, 2010) to illustrate how it is similar and how it differs from a traditional business model. We make it explicit that, in many cases, building a social business model whose main purpose it to address issues of poverty (or other sustainable development issues) requires corporate social innovation (CSI). This implies for MNCs practicing such innovations to include "learning why" capability as part of the profit equation.

What is a business model? We suggest (Moingeon and Lehmann–Ortega, 2010) that a business model has two major components:

- A value proposition, that is, the answer to the question: who are our customers and what do we offer to them that they value?
- A value architecture (or value constellation[3]) that is, the answer to the question: how do we deliver this offer to our customers? This involves the company's own value chain but also the value network with the suppliers and partners.

Those two components need to fit together as pieces of a puzzle to generate a positive profit equation.

This profit equation is the financial translation of the two preceding components: it describes the sales generated due to the value proposition and the cost structure and capital engaged resulting from the value architecture.

Hence, the business model concept offers a consistent and integrated picture of a company and the way it generates revenues and profit.

The use of the term "business model" has grown exponentially over the past years, and are particularly helpful to depict new ventures. Therefore, we use this concept to describe three of Grameen's partnerships: with Telenor in mobile phones, with Veolia in drinkable water, and with Danone in dairies.

Case 1: Grameen Phone

In 1996, in partnership with three outside companies,[4] the Grameen Bank created a mobile phone company, Grameen Phone, to extend telephone service all across Bangladesh. Twelve years later, ownership of Grameen Phone resides with just two companies: Telenor (62%), the Norwegian incumbent telecommunications company, and Grameen Telecom (38%), a non-profit company created specifically for this purpose.

Back in 1996, Grameen Phone was one of four companies licensed by the government to provide mobile phone services in Bangladesh. A UK-based consultant estimated the market in 2005 would be 250,000 mobile phones. In fact, the number of mobile phone users by 2005 turned out to be about 8 million! In 2008, it increased to 40 million subscribers. With no land-line service in most of the 80,000 villages in Bangladesh, mobile phone technology was essential to bring the country into the age of electronic communication. The success of Grameen Phone relied on both a non-conventional value proposition and value architecture (i.e., different from those used in developed countries). In developed countries, individuals buy a monthly package including the handset and the air time and are engaged for several months. This engagement enables in turn the operator to build the infrastructure.

However, this type of engagement ensuring the profitability of the operator would be too burdensome for poor people, who simply cannot afford it. Thus, Grameen Phone set up another business model. People who need to make connections with a friend, family member, or business associate can borrow a phone and buy just a couple of minutes from the now famous 300,000 "telephone ladies" who provide phone service to their villages. Grameen Bank provided them loans to buy mobile phones and bulk air time.

In 2007, Grameen Phone, run by experienced Telenor managers, had become the largest tax-generating company in Bangladesh, with over 20 million subscribers.

Case 2: Grameen Veolia

Veolia Water, a subsidiary of Veolia Environment, is the world's leading provider of water services with a turnover of €24 billion in 2016. In March 2008, Veolia Water created a joint venture with the Grameen Bank. The objective was to provide rural populations in Bangladesh with affordable access to drinking water. Previously, many people had been compelled to buy bottled water or drink polluted surface water or even water tainted with arsenic. Over the past several years, Veolia Water had been developing solutions to allow access to drinking water for vulnerable people living in urban areas, but it had not yet reached isolated rural areas. Veolia Water's conventional business model, as for other water service operators in developed countries, consisted in recycling and purifying unclean water and billing individuals or families who had water points in their homes for their water consumption. But the rural people of Bangladesh cannot afford to pay for a water point at home.

Veolia and Grameen therefore decided to build a factory and a whole network of water supply in Goalmari, a rather densely populated rural area, by the end of 2008. The value proposition was to provide drinking water at an affordable price to the inhabitants. The value architecture challenged Veolia's conventional business model in several ways. First, the cost of water treatment was to be reduced as much as possible in order to offer the cheapest price. Thus the factory needed to be kept simple. It was decided to recycle surface water as this was less costly. The drinking water produced would not meet current norms in the US or Europe, but would nonetheless meet World Health Organization standards. Second, three different water access modes needed to be implemented: inside people's homes, at the village's public drinking fountain, or by distributing water cans. The latter were dispatched to the most isolated villages by rickshaws driven by Grameen-financed entrepreneurs. This distribution mode was a first for Veolia. Finally, new payment facilities needed to be implemented and a system of prepaid cards is currently being established.

Case 3: Grameen Danone

Created in 2006, Grameen Danone is a 50–50 joint venture between the Grameen Group and the French Groupe Danone, one of the world's leading healthy food companies with a revenue of €21.9 billion in 2016. Over the past 40 years, Danone has been involved in a dual commitment to business success and social responsibility. In the context of this approach, Danone's mission evolved at the beginning of 2000 from: "bringing health through food" to "bringing health through food to a maximum number of people."

The goal of Grameen Danone is to "help the children of Bangladesh to be healthy" by offering them "a nutritious and healthy product which they may consume on a daily basis." Concerning the value proposition, the product had to be affordable for poor families on a daily basis if it was to be effective. "Shoktidoi" (literally, yogurt which makes one strong) was created with this goal. Thanks to its price – 6 BDT per container, or approximately €6 cents – it could be purchased regularly even by the poorest Bangladeshi families; a radically different target market from Danone's conventional high-end consumers. Made from cow's milk and date molasses enriched with micronutrients, Shoktidoi contains calcium and proteins essential for children's growth and bone strength.

As far as the value architecture was concerned, the cold chain system again had to be questioned. The three main processes of the value architecture – supply, production, and distribution – needed to be radically revisited. Grameen Danone favored the use of ingredients available locally for several reasons: to reduce costs in terms of raw materials (no import fees, simplified logistics); to minimize fossil energy consumption (reduced transportation); and to promote local community development and fight against rural exodus. To avoid coming into competition with other milk purchasers, and so as to limit any increases in already high milk prices, Grameen Danone had to structure the upstream market. It chose to develop micro-farms to form part of its own supply network. Micro-credits were offered by the Grameen Bank to potential owners of dairy cattle, who received a guaranteed annual fixed price and veterinary advice which helped to improve quality and output. As far as production was concerned, the Grameen Danone factory at Bogra, a town in northern Bangladesh, is small (500 square meters in surface area) and has a capacity which is approximately one-thirtieth of Danone's typical European factory. The process was simplified to the extreme and slightly automated. Concerning distribution, door-to-door sales were ensured by the "Grameen Ladies." Although illiterate, these women were trained to deliver a nutritional message and receive a commission for each yogurt they sold; they were not employees of Grameen Danone, and their unsold items were not taken back. They could reach 200 households per day and benefit from additional credit from Grameen to buy materials and sufficient product stock. As well as door-to-door distribution, Shoktidoi was also sold in existing stores which offered an array of products, mostly food products.

Due to the lack of conventional media, the standard advertising model (press and television-based ad campaigns) had to be questioned. Grameen Danone was fortunate to get the support of Zinedine Zidane, the internationally famous French soccer player, who visited the factory and contributed to a spectacular brand launch.[5]

Social business models as business model innovation

Thus, for Telenor, Veolia, and Danone, creating social businesses with Grameen could not be fulfilled through a simple replication in Bangladesh of their conventional business models. Due to the lack of infrastructure and retail outlets, Grameen partners willing to address the poor while breaking even need to revisit dramatically their business model, to come up with both new value propositions and new value architectures. Table 4.5.1 contrasts the conventional business model in use in developed countries and the new social business models of the three cases. This resembles business model innovation, which is about generating new sources of profit by finding a novel combination of value proposition and/or value architecture (Moingeon and Lehmann-Ortega, 2010).

We call this type of new business model that addresses issues of poverty, or other sustainable development issues, corporate social innovation. We see CSI as a specific form of business model innovation. The research on this type of innovation, considering business models rather than products, processes, or technologies as the locus of innovation, has led to a growing body of academic literature (Foss and Saebi, 2015; Hamel, 1998; Kim *et al.*, 2005; Markides, 2008; Schlegelmilch *et al.*, 2003). Most of this research underlines the radicalism of this type of innovation, defined as the capacity to create new strategies which modify the rules of the competitive game in an industry. Unlike conventional business models, the CSI's objective is not to maximize financial profit, but to seek full recovery of costs. Potential profits must be reinvested in the replication of the business model. Thus,

Table 4.5.1 Conventional social business model vs. social business model for Telenor, Veolia, and Danone

Grameen Partner	Conventional business model (developed countries)		Social business model	
	Value proposition	Value architecture	Value proposition	Value architecture
Telenor, the Norwegian incumbent telecommunications company	• Sale of a monthly package (phone + air time) to individual consumers	• Construction of a wireless network • Sale of package through retail	• Borrow a phone when needed and pay per minute of consumption	• Construction of a wireless network • Grameen Ladies own the phone, buy discounted air time in bulk and sell minutes on their own phone to users when needed
Veolia, one of the global leaders in water services	• Maximum water quality • Distributing water through taps located inside people's homes	• Water treatment factories with a high level of technology, recycling and purifying water	• Water quality that meets World Health Organization standards (and not US or European standards) • Village water fountains • Prepaid card payment system	• Construction of a simplified water plant, recycling surface water. • Construction of the water supply network towards the fountains • New distribution channel for isolated locations: rickshaws driven by "Grameen boys"
Danone, number 1 worldwide in fresh dairy products and number 2 worldwide in bottled water	• High end products • Emphasis on lifestyle • Strong brand name through advertisement	• Centralized purchasing and production (economies of scale) • Logistics towards distribution platforms • Sales through food retailers • Storage by end consumers	• Low price • Fulfillment of basic nutritional needs • Grameen brand image	• Local supply of raw products • Local production • Direct door-to-door sales by Grameen Ladies • Limited storage by end consumers

financial profit is not the key output of such business models. So what are the benefits of this type of innovations?

The real benefits of CSI

The literature on CSR argues that this type of strategies fosters both types of benefits: social and corporate. But we consider that, besides those "conventional" benefits, the sponsoring company is granted with yet another type of benefit.

Conventional benefits

The social business models described in Table 4.5.1 provide several major social profits and, therefore, are no mirage. All three new Grameen businesses have provided local employment, in the distribution channel, the factories and the micro-farms. In addition, Telenor offers poor people the opportunity to be connected to their families or to develop new business opportunities. The Veolia Grameen social business provides people in rural areas with drinkable water, enabling them to escape from deadly threats. The Grameen Danone partnership provides a nutritional profit – the yogurt should have a strong nutritional impact on children aged 3 to 15 who eat it on a regular basis. Thus, there is no "mirage" in those cases: there is a social profit for the poor.

The revenue generated by the Grameen ventures is a drop in the ocean for the sponsoring companies. However, those businesses have a prominent role to play, although this impact cannot be called "fortune." Many studies have tried to measure the impact of CSR on financial performance, but despite the ever growing number of such studies, researchers still argue about the existence of a positive, negative or neutral link (Barnett, 2007; McWilliams *et al.*, 2000). More generally, several studies have explored the link between CSR and firm reputation and found a positive relationship (Brammer *et al.*, 2005). Research has also shown consistent results as to the effect of CSR initiatives on employees and prospective employees (Bayle-Cordier *et al.*, 2015; Bhattacharya *et al.*, 2008; Mirvis, 2011; Sen *et al.*, 2006; Turban *et al.*, 1997). The idea is that the best employees are attracted to companies who demonstrate a commitment to CSR, thus allowing a firm to win the "war for talent." Just as companies have turned towards the external market to seek legitimacy for their CSR actions, they are now turning inside. This could be called the "people case for CSR" (Berger *et al.*, 2007): successful CSR has a positive impact on employee morale, productivity, loyalty, and retention. However, we consider there are still other benefits to earn from CSI.

Learning benefits

We believe CSI can be seen as a learning lab. In such a lab, companies experiment new business models and learn how to develop radical innovations. Indeed, CSI can be defined as a specific form of business model innovation. It consists in revisiting a number of governing conditions or values and resembles what Argyris and Schön (1978) have qualified as double-loop learning. Learning occurs when an error is identified and corrected. An error corresponds to a divergence between the consequences of the actions undertaken and the objectives sought. Single-loop learning occurs when the error is corrected by adopting a new action strategy chosen from a list of available strategies. But at times this method proves inadequate. In that case, it is necessary to intervene before the action strategy stage by questioning and changing underlying governing conditions or values. Thanks to this double-loop learning process, it becomes possible to produce innovative action strategies In the three cases, companies would not have succeeded if they had not challenged the governing values underlying their conventional business models. Furthermore, business model innovation, up to now seen as a circumstantial event, is increasingly taken as an on-going necessity, some authors (Hamel *et al.*, 2003) introducing the idea of the life cycle of business models where one learns how to replicate these innovations, turning them into a continuous, quasi-ordinary process. It is however difficult to reach a systematic approach to this type of strategic innovation since this innovation distinguishes itself precisely by its originality and singularity (Grant, 2002). Thus, the main challenge for leaders is to leverage CSIs as learning labs. They represent opportunities to train their managers in double-loop learning by developing a "learning why capability" (Edmondson and Moingeon, 1996), a capability to diagnose complex situations, test new ideas, experiment, and innovate on an on-going basis.

CSI fosters a culture of challenge to conventional wisdom and traditional mental schemes. As an example, Guy Gavelle, the Industrial Director of Danone's Asia Pacific operations, first rejected the idea of building a small plant in Bangladesh. He now considers that designing and building the Bogra plant has been one of the richest learning experiences of his decade-long career. He learned that small could be just as efficient as big, despite his years of assuming the opposite. Thus, CSI forces managers engaged in the project to double-loop learn. And this double-loop learning process is exactly what is required in the current business environment: managers constantly need to reinvent their business and question their existing frameworks and industry recipes so as to achieve business model innovation (Moingeon and Lehmann-Ortega, 2010). Thus, we believe that this type of CSR initiatives become laboratories for practice and for breeding a new culture, which will benefit the entire firm (Kanter, 1999; Mirvis *et al.*, 2006; Sharma *et al.*, 1998). As stated by Hart and Sharma (Hart *et al.*, 2004), engaging with what they call "fringe stakeholders" that is, those who lie at the periphery of a firm's established stakeholder network (shareholders, employees, suppliers, communities, etc.), fosters creativity and imagination by confronting managers with radically different settings. Moreover, we think that by setting sustainability as a constraint to CSI, companies bind their managers to radically revisit existing business models. This trains them to think out of the box and to challenge conventional wisdom, leading to double-loop learning, the most needed talent for managers in today's competitive environment. This is precisely what Muhammad Yunus explained in an interview published in the *Harvard Business Review* (Beard, 2012):

> [I]n the Danone case, they first showed me a plastic container for yogurt. I said, "In social business, plastic is not allowed. We want biodegradable material." The Danone guys said, "We use plastic all over the world." And I said, "All over the world you're a profit maker. Here you're a social business." They were unhappy, but they started looking for a solution. After four months, they came back with a new container made of cornstarch. "Can I eat it?" I asked. "Because why should poor people spend money on something they have to throw away? Why can't you put nutrition in the cup?" So they worked very hard to make an edible cup. These big companies have enormous creative power. But unless you ask, you'll never get an answer.
>
> (p. 137)

There is yet another reason why we call CSIs learning labs: such business models often start as small experiments which are then fine-tuned before being rolled out. Danone and Grameen intend to learn from the first site in Bogra and then scale up the concept all over Bangladesh and other poor countries around the world, just as Veolia does in its Goalmari site. This is another recommendation stemming from the business model innovation literature. In effect, the implementation of this type of innovation by an existing firm forces it to imagine and learn a new way of doing, and since the change needs to be radical, also learn to undo its old way of doing. Strategic experimentation appears in the literature as a specific type of knowledge acquisition. In the "classical" strategic approach, learning occurs in the preliminary phase of the diagnosis: the analysis and studies undertaken during this preliminary phase lead to strategic choices formalized in a business plan. However, the fundamentally innovative nature of business model innovation makes simple market studies or client surveys in the context of statistical studies inefficient and not very useful. People surveyed are not able to project themselves into this radical newness (Kim *et al.*, 1999). Learning must therefore come from another route, which may be, for instance, strategic experimentation (Govindarajan *et al.*, 2004; Slocum *et al.*, 1994). Learning from experimentation is fundamental to solve problems for which solutions are uncertain or when critical information sources are inexistent or unavailable. Hamel (1998) recommends that firms launch a series of small experimentations, thereby minimizing risk and maximizing a firm's rate of learning, so as to identify the success potential of a strategy. Thus, as for business model innovation, CSI can start small, be refined, and then be rolled out. This is another important feature of conventional business model innovation that managers can understand and learn from CSI.

In short, CSI may be considered not only as an end in itself, but also as a trigger for business model innovation.

Conclusions

In his 2004 best seller, Prahalad urges multinationals to seek "Fortune at the Bottom of the Pyramid": turning the poor into valuable customers can both alleviate poverty and create profit for the MNC. However, vigorous criticism has emerged. For example, Karnani (2007) argues that these ideas are a mirage: there are no profits possible for MNCs, and the poor are more assisted than helped.

The three proposed case studies show that there is neither fortune nor mirage at the bottom of the pyramid: the poor are helped, both through nutritional, social, and/or employment profits, but this doesn't turn into a fortune for the MNC involved. However, we believe MNCs engaged in such initiatives benefit from yet another type of return: by setting self-sustainability as a constraint, this type of experiment trains managers in double-loop learning (Argyris and Schön, 1978). Developing a "learning why" capability provides grounds for competitive advantage (Edmondson and Moingeon, 1996; Moingeon and Lehmann-Ortega, 2010) which may turn into financial profit in the years to come. CSI can be seen as a form of organizational learning that generates the financial return of CSR (see Table 4.5.2). We think this could be the missing link between CSI, CSR, and financial performance.[6]

Obviously, several limits to our research can be underlined. First, we have been able to show that business model innovation is taking place (as shown in Table 4.5.1); however, our research has not gone far enough yet to show the effect of the double-loop learning process on conventional business of parent companies in developed countries and how those experiments benefit the parent company. For example, how does Danone apply its

Table 4.5.2 From social business innovation to corporate social innovation

Defining a business model	Conventional business model innovation	Specificities of social business models	Specificities of corporate social innovations
Defining a value proposition (who are our customers and what do we offer to them that they value?)	Challenging conventional wisdom and basic assumptions	Favoring social profit-oriented shareholders	Developing learning labs (provide opportunities for managers at MNCs to develop a "learning why" capability, a capability to diagnose complex situations, test new ideas, experiment, and innovate on an on-going basis)
Defining a value architecture (how do we deliver this offer to our customers?)	Finding complementary partners	Clearly specifying the social profit objective	
Generating a positive profit equation (sales generated due to the value proposition minus the cost structure and capital engaged)	Undertaking a continuous experimentation process		

Source: Adapted from Yunus et al. (2010).

lessons about the local distribution system to other markets? This will be important to actually demonstrate how innovation mediates the relationship between CSR and organizational performance. In addition, we have only chosen cases related to the Grameen Group and its setting. This research could be extended to other examples of social businesses. Moreover, we have built our findings on successes: we are aware that adding some cases that failed could deeply enhance our insight in the process. All those limits provide sources for our on-going research program.

However, demonstrating that CSI resembles business model innovation already makes an important contribution. In addition, we think that highlighting the potential benefits of CSI sends a strong message to firms, since it underlines the possibility of combining the normative and the business case. This message is optimistic for managers who find it difficult to justify CSR policies in an uncertain world. Moreover, our topic here was limited to the social impact of CSI; however, it is important to stress that CSI can also apply to the other components of sustainable development, that is, environmental or ethical issues. This alternative type of CSI would also contribute to building, under the profitability constraint, learning labs.

For all those reasons, this chapter consists of a first step in a long, unchartered, and exciting journey.

Appendix

Research method

The authors' research was first focused on business model innovation, in particular in low-tech industries and established firms. This led them to an in-depth study of about 30 cases, through interviews with leaders involved, which highlighted the importance of double-loop learning in this process.

While looking for new case studies, they encountered the Grameen examples. They collected data from secondary as well as primary sources (interviews with managers and executives). All the interviews and field notes were transcribed. Narrative material can be analyzed along several dimensions such as content, structure, styles of speech, and so on (Lieblich *et al.*, 1998). We chose to focus on the content of the narrative material and our main unit of analysis were subject themes. Using the grounded theory method of moving between data and interpretation (Miles and Huberman, 1994), we identified one critical dimension. As in the previous cases, challenging conventional wisdom appeared as prominent. But in addition, the interviews highlighted the individual learning experience of the participants in the project. Thus, the idea of an organizational learning process emerged inductively based on these cases. This idea has then been confronted with the literature on business model innovation and corporate social responsibility.

Notes

1 "Conventional" refers to what is usual and regular for the MNC in the developed world.
2 For a more detailed presentation, see Yunus et al., 2010.
3 The notion of value constellation stems from Normann and Ramirez's (1993).
4 Telenor of Norway, Marubeni of Japan, and New York-based Gonofone Development Company.
5 In their framework based on four factors (affordability, acceptability, availability, and awareness), Anderson and Markides (2007) have focused on how to increase the awareness for a product launch at the bottom of the pyramid.
6 Hillman and Keim (2001) have shown that if simple social issue participation (i.e., not linked to the core business of the firm) is negatively related to firm performance as measured by shareholder value; this link is positive for CSR projects involving stakeholders.

References

Anderson J and Markides C. (2007). Strategic Innovation at the Base of the Pyramid. *MIT Sloan Management Review.* **49**(1): 83–88.

Argyris C and Schön DA. (1978). *Organizational Learning: A Theory of Action Perspective.* Reading, MA: Addison Wesley.

Barnett ML. (2007). Stakeholder Influence Capacity and the Variability of Financial Returns to Corporate Social Responsibility. *Academy of Management Review.* **32**(3): 794–816.

Bayle-Cordier J, Mirvis P and Moingeon B. (2015). Projecting Different Identities: A Longitudinal Study of the "Whipsaw" Effects of Changing Leadership Discourse About the Triple Bottom Line. *The Journal of Applied Behavioral Science*. **51**(3): 336–374.

Beard A. (2012). Life's Work. *Harvard Business Review*. **90**(12): 136.

Berger IE, Cunningham P and Drumwright ME. (2007). Mainstreaming Corporate Social Responsibility: Developing Markets for Virtue. *California Management Review*. **49**(4): 132–157.

Bhattacharya CB, Sen S and Korschun D. (2008). Using Corporate Social Responsibility to Win the War for Talent. *MIT Sloan Management Review*. **49**(2): 37–44.

Brammer S and Pavelin S. (2005). Corporate Reputation and an Insurance Motivation for Corporate Social Investment. *Journal of Corporate Citizenship*. **20**: 39–51.

Burke L and Logsdon JM. (1996). How Corporate Social Responsibility Pays Off. *Long Range Planning*. **29**(4): 495–502.

Davis J. (1992). Ethics and Environmental Marketing. *Journal of Business Ethics*. **11**(2): 81–87.

Edmondson A and Moingeon B. (1996). When to Learn How and When to Learn Why: Appropriate Organizational Learning Processes as a Source of Competitive Advantage. In Moingeon B and Edmondson A. (eds.) *Organizational Learning and Competitive Advantage*. London: Sage, 17–37.

Foss NJ and Saebi T (eds.). (2015). *Business Model Innovation: The Organizational Dimension*. Oxford: Oxford University Press.

Govindarajan V and Trimble C. (2004). Strategic Innovation and the Science of Learning. *MIT Sloan Management Review*. **45**(2): 67–75.

Grant RM. (2002). *Contemporary Strategy Analysis. Concepts, Techniques, Applications* (4th ed.). Oxford: Blackwell Publishing.

Hamel G. (1998). Strategy Innovation and the Quest for Value. *Sloan Management Review*. **39**(78): 7–14.

Hamel G and Valikangas L. (2003). The Quest for Resilience. *Harvard Business Review*. **81**(9): 52–63.

Hart SL and Sharma S. (2004). Engaging Fringe Stakeholders for Competitive Imagination. *Academy of Management Executive*. **18**(1): 7–18.

Hillman AJ and Keim GD. (2001). Shareholder Value, Stakeholder Management, and Social Issues: What's the Bottom Line?. *Strategic Management Journal*. **22**(2): 125–139.

Husted BW and De Jesus Salazar J. (2006). Taking Friedman Seriously: Maximizing Profits and Social Performance. *Journal of Management Studies*. **43**(1): 75–91.

Kanter RM. (1999). From Spare Change to Real Change. *Harvard Business Review*. **77**(3): 122–132.

Karnani A. (2007). The Mirage of Marketing to the Bottom of the Pyramid: How the Private Sector Can Help Alleviate Poverty. *California Management Review*. **49**(4): 90–111.

Kim C and Mauborgne R. (1999). Creating New Market Space. *Harvard Business Review*. **77**(1): 83.

Kim C and Mauborgne R. (2005). *Blue Ocean Strategy*. Boston: Harvard Business Press.

Lieblich, A, Tuval-Mashiach, R. and Zilber, T. (1998). *Narrative Research: Reading, Analysis, and Interpretation*. Vol. 47. Thousand Oaks, CA: Sage Publications.

Lockett A, Moon J and Visser W. (2006). Corporate Social Responsibility in Management Research: Focus, Nature, Salience and Sources of Influence. *Journal of Management Studies*. **43**(1): 115–136.

Mahoney LS, Thorne L, Cecil L and LaGore W. (2013). A Research Note on Standalone Corporate Social Responsibility Reports: Signaling or Greenwashing?, *Critical Perspectives on Accounting*. **24**(4/5): 350–359.

Markides C. (2008). *Game-Changing Strategies: How to Create New Market Space in Established Industries by Breaking the Rules*. New-York: John Wiley & Sons.

Margolis JD and Walsh JP. (2003). Misery loves companies: Rethinking social initiatives by business. *Administrative Science Quarterly*. **48**: 268–305.

Massa L, Tucci C and Affuah, A. (2017). A Critical Assessment of Business Model Research. *Academy of Management Annals*. **11**(1): 74–104.

McWilliams A and Siegel D. (2000). Corporate Social Responsibility and Financial Performance: Correlation or Misspecification? *Strategic Management Journal*. **21**(5): 603.

McWilliams A, Siegel DS and Wright PM. (2006). Corporate Social Responsibility: Strategic Implications. *Journal of Management Studies*. **43**(1): 1–18.

Miles MB and Huberman AM. (1994). *Qualitative Analysis*. Thousand Oaks, CA: Sage.

Mirvis P. (2011). Unilever's Drive for Sustainability and CSR-Changing the Game. In Mohrman S and Shani R. (eds.) *Organizing for Sustainability*. New York: Emerald.

Mirvis P and Googins B. (2006). Stages of Corporate Citizenship. *California Management Review.* **48**(2): 104–126.

Moingeon B and Lehmann-Ortega L. (2010). Creation and Implementation of a New Business Model: A Disarming Case Study. *M@n@gement.* **13**(4): 266–297.

Normann R and Ramirez R. (1993). From Value Chain to Value Constellation: Designing Interactive Strategy. *Harvard Business Review.* **71**(4): 65–77.

Porter ME and Kramer MR. (2002). The Competitive Advantage of Corporate Philanthropy. *Harvard Business Review.* **80**(12): 56–69.

Prahalad CK. (2004). *The Fortune at the Bottom of the Pyramid: Eradicating Poverty through Profits*. Upper Saddle River: Wharton School Publishing.

Schlegelmilch BB, Diamantopoulos A, and Kreuz P. (2003). Strategic Innovation: The Construct, its Drivers and its Strategic Outcomes. *Journal of Strategic Marketing.* **11**(2): 117–133.

Sen S, Bhattacharya CB and Korschun D. (2006). The Role of Corporate Social Responsibility in Strengthening Multiple Stakeholder Relationships: A Field Experiment. *Journal of the Academy of Marketing Science.* **34**(2): 158–166.

Sharma S and Vredenburg H. (1998). Proactive Corporate Environmental Strategy and the Development of Competitively Valuable Organizational Capabilities. *Strategic Management Journal.* **19**(8): 729–754.

Slocum JW, McGill M and Lei DT. (1994). The New Learning Strategy: Anytime, Anything, Anywhere. *Organizational Dynamics.* **23**(2): 33–47.

Turban DB and Greening DW. (1997). Corporate Social Performance and Organizational Attractiveness to Prospective Employees. *Academy of Management Journal.* **40**(3): 658–672.

Waddock SA and Graves SB. (1997). The Corporate Social Performance-Financial Performance Link. *Strategic Management Journal.* **18**(4): 303–319.

Yunus M, Moingeon B and Lehmann-Ortega L. (2010). Building Social Business Models: Lessons from the Grameen Experience. *Long Range Planning.* **43**(2–3): 308–325.

Yunus M and Weber K. (2007). *Creating a World Without Poverty. Social Business and the Future of Capitalism*, New York: PublicAffairs.

Index

Note: Page numbers in *italic* indicate a figure and page numbers in **bold** indicate a table on the corresponding page

For Product Safety Concerns and Information please contact our EU representative GPSR@taylorandfrancis.com Taylor & Francis Verlag GmbH, Kaufingerstraße 24, 80331 München, Germany

Printed and bound by CPI Group (UK) Ltd, Croydon, CR0 4YY

08/05/2025

01864508-0001